The
Victory Garden
Cookbook

In collaboration with
Jane Doerfer

Principal photography by
Bill Schwob

Additional photography by
James Scherer

The Victory Garden Cookbook

by Marian Morash

Alfred A. Knopf   New York, 1982

This is a Borzoi book
Published by Alfred A.Knopf, Inc.
Copyright © 1982 by Marian Morash and
WGBH Educational Foundation.

Library of Congress Cataloging in Publication Data

Morash, Marian.
    The victory garden cookbook.

    Includes index.
    1. Cookery (Vegetables)   2. Vegetable gardening.
I. Title.
TX801.M67   641.6′5   81-48132
ISBN 0-394-50897-1   AACR2
ISBN 0-394-70780-X (pbk.)

Manufactured in the United States of America

Published July 9, 1982
Reprinted Nine Times
Eleventh Printing, December 1993

Introduction

Americans have always gardened. For hundreds of years farm life was the backbone of this country; ingredients for most family meals were right in the backyard. Gradually, however, the farm family gave way to our urbanized society and packaged produce became a way of life for most households. It took a time of national emergency, World War II, to bring citizens back to the earth: "victory gardens" shot up across the nation. At the end of the war, as the country rejoiced and looked ahead to more affluent times, many of these gardens went to seed. Once again it took a traumatic event, the energy crisis of the 1970s, to get people to rethink priorities. The need for self-sufficiency became apparent. This, and economic necessity, may have triggered a renewed interest in home gardening, but it has been a combination of the emotional and physical satisfactions of gardening and a new passion for freshness that have sustained the "back-to-basics" movement. Such a climate gave birth to "Crockett's Victory Garden."

My husband, Russell Morash, had been a television producer for over twenty years and a weekend gardener for ten. It was inevitable that he would leap to the bait when a television gardening show was suggested. In his search for a host he found Jim Crockett, whose talent and

spirit would soon make millions of television friends for gardening.

In the course of working together Russ and Jim became good friends, and under Jim's tutelage Russ became a vastly improved gardener. What had once been a

hobby now became a compulsion and even caused us to move from one home to another in search of more acreage to plow under. My eventual participation and qualifications as a cook on the gardening series grew from another show Russ had produced. Way back in 1961 he had begun a television show with a new cookbook author by the name of Julia Child. Her skill and enthusiasm for good cooking radiated from the "tube" and began a revolution in the American kitchen, and I was one of her fans. While I had two talented cooks as parents I never spent much time over the stove; no need to, really, with them around. Under Julia's spell I became immersed in home cookery, as did many of our friends. The "hobby" of cooking turned professional years later when I joined Laine and Jock Gifford and Susan Mayer in a restaurant venture, the Straight Wharf Restaurant on Nantucket Island. Soon thereafter I joined Julia as executive chef on her "Julia Child and More Company" television series.

As our home garden grew, the harvest doubled, tripled, and quadrupled. Russ would bring in a loaded harvest basket at 6:30 p.m. and with great pride and delight ask me to prepare a simple supper using everything! Surely as it takes love, time, and energy to grow vegetables, it takes the same to prepare and cook them. My pleasure at having absolutely fresh ingredients to work with outweighed my alarm at the amount and variety arriving in my kitchen each day. Surrounded by garden overabundance, I fought back by cooking, cooking, cooking.

We were not alone with our burgeoning garden. Television viewers wrote in and pleaded, "I've grown wonderful big leeks but now what do I do with them?" or "What on earth can I do with all my zucchini?" It was an easy task for me to supply some recipes. I remember the first one Jim Crockett recited—he couldn't have been more charming, but since he wasn't a cook he inadvertently twisted the directions just enough to cause havoc! Nevertheless we were flooded with requests for more recipes.

Jim's health began to fail but he was determined to continue the show. It was clear that he needed an assistant and Russ suggested Bob Thompson, a well-known radio gardener. Jim agreed immediately, admitting that he had never heard Bob say anything on his radio program that he did not agree with, and Bob—another

super human being—generously came to the aid of our stricken master gardener. Jim's untimely death was a tragic loss for all who admired this wise and gentle man.

Bob replaced Jim as host of "The Victory Garden." He has contributed from his own years of experience and expertise an enlargement of what Jim Crockett had begun. The format of the show changed, allowing for many more guests and features. Since there were so many questions about vegetable preparation we thought a recipe segment within the show might work, although Russ was worried about his gardeners—would they stand for a part of the show sacrificed to the kitchen? Our first attempt was with our favorite Leek and Potato Soup. Not only did the gardeners stand for it, they wrote for the recipe and asked for more like it.

A Victory Garden cookbook then seemed to be a logical extension of the television gardening series—a book in which we would give gardeners all the tips they need to know about preparing, cooking, storing, freezing, and some ways of preserving their vegetables. I wrote a book proposal in collaboration with WGBH and it was submitted to a number of publishers. We were all thrilled when we heard that Judith Jones of Alfred A. Knopf was interested. She was Julia's editor, and distinguished in her field. Her interest suggested that the idea was right.

What I had thought of as a rather simple book grew in Judith's vision to something that would be almost a vegetable encyclopedia for gardeners who cook and cooks who wish to garden. The first objective was to share the pure pleasure, immense satisfaction, and good eating we have had by growing and cooking our own fresh vegetables. Further, I hoped to entice those who had never gardened to garden; and persuade those cooks who could not have a garden to shop at their greengrocer and at farmer's markets, which have been springing up all over the country, instead of settling for plastic-smothered, canned, or frozen goods.

This book has been laid out alphabetically, starting with asparagus and including all the vegetables we grow in our victory garden. There are some vegetables that are not included because we do not grow them or because they are not commonly grown by the home gardener. In these pages the reader will find basic planting, growing, and harvesting information. Included are guidelines for storage; yields (it's hard to follow a recipe that asks for cups when you have an armload of fresh vegetables); and marketing advice for those without a garden. The recipes begin with the most simple preparations described in general terms and always marked ◇, then there are all kinds of recipes my family has enjoyed for years, along with new creations and others contributed by friends—a broad selection that will, I trust, give variety to the gardener-cook's menu.

These recipes are designed for optimum flavor; in many cases that means butter, cream, sugar, salt, or flour. Our culinary sensibilities are ever changing and the advent of *nouvelle cuisine* has made us all more conscious of "lightness" in our food preparation. We know, as well, that too many fats and sugars in our diet not only add weight but may be hazardous to our health over a long period of time. I appreciate that, and while my own family has gradually cut its intake of these ingredients, we have a weakness for things like butter-braised leeks or broccoli mornay. We reckon we can enjoy delicious steamed, blanched, or bouillon-braised vegetables six nights of the week and splurge on a buttery concoction on the seventh. You will also see that the use of naturally sweet vegetables in desserts cuts way down on the amount of sugar required. These recipes are meant to be a jumping-off point. Use your own dietary guidelines and adapt them for your lifestyle.

A few hints on using this book. Regardless of how you prepare your vegetables, do remember that freshly harvested vegetables cook faster than storage vegetables, whether they be from your root cellar or from the local supermarket. I use "large" graded eggs in all the recipes; using another size will affect the recipe. If you are not sure what grade you have, keep in mind that a "large" egg equals three tablespoons; two are for the white and one for the yolk. I use sweet unsalted butter whenever I can, because I find its quality is better than salted butter. It seems to have a lower "water" content and is more reliable when making sauces (there is less chance of the sauce liquidizing), and this same firmness makes it an asset for all dessert and pastry recipes. In general, however, salted and unsalted butter are interchangeable in the recipes. An easy-to-prepare and practical culinary aid is *Clarified Butter* (see *Appendix*). Clarification rids butter of its "water" (it boils off) and you can remove the "milky" residue which causes butter to burn. Clarified butter is invaluable for sautéing without browning. Please use freshly ground pepper; the aroma and flavor are best. I do use vermouth and wine in some recipes, but it is optional, and you may substitute with other liquids. If you use wines, however, don't make do with cheap ones that you wouldn't drink with pleasure. They will spoil a dish just as they will leave a bad taste in your mouth. A good dry vermouth will give you a consistent quality.

When I took on this book project I could see that I would need a writer to assist me. Jane Doerfer signed aboard and promptly proved herself a calm and skilled organizer of my poorly typed dangling clauses. Her diligent research filled out the gaps in my knowledge and her

Lynn Wilson (l.), Jane Doerfer (r.)

encouraging attitude, especially when I had failures in the development stages of the recipes, has been supportive beyond belief. It has been a rewarding writing collaboration, as much for the pleasure of her friendship as for her conscientious dedication to the book.

Tom Sumida of the WGBH Design Department was in charge of the final "look" of the book. The changes that took place in the course of three years could easily drive a designer to a desert island. Thank you, Tom, for not running off to the Galápagos, and for bringing it together so beautifully. Tom was most ably assisted by Abby Gladstone, who prepared the final manuscript and photo layout and patiently went over all of it with me.

Jim Scherer, a noted food photographer, joined us and took some outstanding garden and location photographs. My good friend Sara Moulton, an excellent professional chef, prepared the food that he photographed. Jim was not able to complete the job and Bill Schwob came on to take Jim's place for the greater part of the photography. He was known as a talented photographer who got the job done, done well, on time, with no complaints, and with beautiful results. All this was so, and despite all the cooks giving photography suggestions, Bill never lost his composure. No question about it, he was a dream to work with.

My friend Lynn Wilson has been my secret weapon. She has aided me throughout, contributed her recipes without hesitation, become one of our photography cooks, and juggled her busy life to coincide with our crazy schedule. She is the perfect example of the old-fashioned neighbor who goes out of her way all the time for just about everybody. I will always be grateful for her unfailing help.

Lynn's husband, Alan, has been equally supportive. He owns the best market-garden produce center in our area. Wilson Farm has spoiled us, for even in the dead of winter we know we can find the very finest of fresh vegetables. Al has been a great help on this book, always

tracking down produce if I needed something special. And thanks to those far-flung friends: Evelyn Olsen for her recipe for *Lamb with Cauliflower* and for her mother's *Imam Bayildi;* Charlotte Layman, who allowed me to adapt her grandmother Thurber's family recipe for *Red Beans and Rice;* Sheryl Julian, who contributed *Russian Beet and Potato Salad* from her food column in the *Boston Phoenix;* and to all my other friends whose names appear in their shared recipes.

A special thanks to my family, who have lived through almost three years of testing new recipes. I think the near month spent on sweet potatoes almost undid Russ. (Thanks to him also for contributing some of his own photographs when we asked.) Our daughters, Vicki and Kate, heard a lot of "I can't do it right now, I'm working on the book" and managed to accept my distraction with grace.

I would like to insert a few very personal thank-you's. First to a most special friend whom I have watched cook for many years, Joe Hyde, author of the superb cookbook *Love, Time and Butter.* Joe has taught me much, and gave me the courage to turn to cooking as a profession. He is a culinary genius—inventive, demanding, and of most generous heart. Second—to Julia and Paul Child, whose energetic involvement and joy in cookery, in life, and in each other, has been a constant shining example. Finally I would like to dedicate this book to my parents, Erich and Kâthé Fichtner, who never lived to see me become a cookaholic; how surprised they would be! Our home was always open to friends, even to strangers, and their hospitality centered around a long oak table that my mother would load with platters of homemade food. While my father was a professional chef he never cooked at home, but brought the best of fresh ingredients for her to fix. Even so, I swear she could make a banquet out of lawn dandelions, field mushrooms, and a few kohlrabi stems. My parents knew the secret of good cooking—if you are dealing with good fresh ingredients you can turn the simplest meal into a dinner fit for a king and his court—or, more important, for your family and friends. Victory with fresh vegetables!

Marian Morash
May 1982

Contents

The Victory Garden Cookbook

Asparagus

It took me years to realize how rare and precious a flourishing asparagus bed can be. We were particularly attracted to the old farmhouse we purchased just because it had such a bed. As it turned out, the bed was less healthy than we thought, so Russ had to start from scratch.

Any long-lasting asparagus bed must begin with thorough soil preparation. Russ dug a trench 12 inches deep and 18 inches wide, setting the topsoil aside. Then, using a spading fork, he loosened the soil in the trench bottom an additional 10 inches and worked 10-10-10 fertilizer into this layer. (Our soil didn't need it, but acidic soil should be limed, for asparagus grows best in neutral soil.) Next, he spread a 4-inch layer of rich compost in the trench and pressed it down. He took locally grown two-year root divisions, spaced them 2 feet apart, fanned them out, and covered them over with 2 inches of the reserved soil. As the roots grew throughout the first summer, he filled in the trench with the remaining soil.

Growing asparagus requires patience and restraint. Two years went by before we had spears thick enough to harvest, and they provided a minimal harvest at best. The third year the harvest improved, but we held off until the fourth year before harvesting a full crop. During the second and third years, the growing spears and foliage store nourishment for the roots. (Even though I couldn't eat the asparagus during this period, I enjoyed watching it grow: surely the sight of those beautifully formed spears breaking through the soil is one of nature's wonders.) By year four, I picked freely for six weeks, then let the bed rest until the following year. Now our bed produces at top capacity and will continue to do so for decades, as long as it's well maintained.

I harvest asparagus spears once they're 5 inches tall, selecting those with tightly closed top buds. I prefer stalks at least ½ inch thick—if smaller, they are less tender with very little inner flesh. Our bed yields stalks 12 inches long and ¾ inch in diameter that grow green and completely tender. I cut off the spears at ground level, practically reaching right into the earth.

Once picked, asparagus loses quality rapidly. I try to harvest just before eating, but if that's impossible—or if I have store-bought asparagus—I take special storage precautions. I think of the spears as flowers, and treat them exactly the same way, removing the very end of the stalks and storing them upright in an inch of water. This way they absorb moisture up through their stems and stay fresh.

Then I immediately refrigerate the spears. Were they to be left standing in water at room temperature, the asparagus would continue to grow: the top buds would open, and the stalks would lose sugar. For example, asparagus stored at 32° holds two weeks before losing half its sugar; stored at 50°, one week; at 68°, two days; and at 86°, half the sugar is gone after only half a day. So you

see, leaving the asparagus on the counter in warm weather can totally destroy its quality.

Even refrigerated asparagus needs to be kept in water. If you're pressed for space, wrap the cut ends in a wet cloth or paper towels, cover with a plastic bag, and refrigerate.

When I was growing up, we ate just the portions that snapped off easily and threw the rest of the asparagus away. It wasn't until I started using Julia Child's peeling technique that I realized how wasteful we had been. Peeling asparagus doubles your harvest, actually providing up to 50 percent additional edible flesh: you'll marvel at the quantity of tender flesh hidden underneath a tough exterior.

A small, sharp paring knife works better than a vegetable peeler, because it allows maximum control gradating the cut. Insert the knife under the thicker skin at the base, and work it up toward the tip, making the cut shallower as the skin becomes thinner. About 2–3 inches from the tip, the peel tapers off completely.

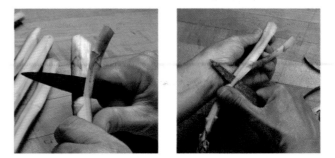

My technique is to quickly blanch asparagus in a big pot of boiling salted water so as to preserve its brilliant color. The asparagus doesn't need tying into bunches as it cooks more quickly moving freely; boiling gently, the spears don't get bruised. (You could also use a wide skillet filled with boiling water, but the water takes longer to return to the boil than in a larger pot.) See *Blanched or Boiled Asparagus.*

An asparagus steamer, fashioned so that the thicker ends boil in water while the tips cook in steam, is unnecessary because once asparagus is peeled it cooks evenly tip to tip. And I find that steaming peeled asparagus reduces much of the handsome green color.

The season for asparagus is so short and it's such a delicacy that I give it preferential treatment, serving it as a separate course, or as the highlight of a dinner party. With several other items on the menu, count on a minimum of ½ pound asparagus per person: however, as people tend to be greedy about asparagus, I usually allow ¾ pound. Uncouth as it sounds, the most enjoyable way to eat asparagus is with your fingers (the way the English *always* eat it, incidentally).

Freshly picked asparagus, cooked tender, yet crisp,

and topped with a pat of sweet butter, could be the only recipe in this section, for I consider it to be the ultimate asparagus preparation. I have included several other recipes I enjoy, but I think asparagus is best cooked simply.

One technique you should master for a fast sauté or Chinese stir-fry is a roll-cut. This attractive and practical cut, which exposes a greater cut surface area to the pan heat, allows the vegetable to absorb additional flavor from the other ingredients. Start at the end of a peeled spear, make a diagonal cut, roll the asparagus a quarter turn, make another diagonal cut, and continue rolling and cutting down the spear until you have several triangular pieces. Cut them as short or as long as you like.

European White Asparagus

We Americans look forward to each green asparagus crop as a special treat, but in Europe equal enthusiasm is awarded white asparagus. European white asparagus is a thicker variety blanched until it's completely white. I find the whole process fascinating.

The asparagus is planted in a deep trench, and, as the stalks grow, they're blanketed with earth, never seeing the light of day. Harvesting is done with a special long-handled tool lowered through the ground after some of the soil has been pushed away. The best-quality white asparagus is absolutely white. Should there be a touch of purple, the asparagus is considered of lesser value.

Frankly, I don't know what all the fuss is about. Granted, white asparagus has a delicate flavor and tender texture, but I think peeled green asparagus is equally tender and has a more interesting flavor.

Marketing

Find a supplier who stores asparagus upright in water and keeps it refrigerated. (A farm stand without refrigeration should store asparagus in water: ideally, the turnover would be so rapid that any sugar loss would be negligible.)

Look for tight-budded spears with smooth, tender skin. Fresh asparagus should not be withered, brown, or flabby. Try to find even-size spears at least ½ inch in diameter. Smaller spears are wonderful in the garden, where they're completely tender and fun to snack on, but once they've been in transit or storage for a while, the skins toughen and provide little else but waste.

Avoid any spears with large, woody, hard, white bases, which will be nothing but waste. The spears should be *at least* two-thirds green.

Special Information

Yields and Conversions

- 14 asparagus spears 9–10 inches long and ½–¾ inch thick = 1 pound
- Count on ½ pound (6–8 spears) per person
- 1 pound trimmed and peeled asparagus spears = approximately 3 cups cut up

Storage and Preserving

- Refrigerate asparagus, upright, standing in water.
- Peel just before using. If it's peeled earlier, wrap in damp paper towels, place in plastic bag, and refrigerate, because the flesh browns upon exposure to air.

Hints

- Flavor sauces with asparagus peelings.
- Make a main dish tart (see *Leek Tart*): replace leeks with cooked asparagus spears. Arrange in crust and fill with egg mixture; bake.
- Blanch spears, coat with batter, and deep-fry.
- Make individual timbales, as in *Spinach Timbale* (see *Spinach*), or a custard mold. Use 2–3 cups asparagus pieces.

Microwave

- 1 pound peeled asparagus placed in a covered dish with ¼ cup water takes 8 minutes to cook tender.

Leftovers

- Make a soufflé with ¾ cup puréed or finely diced cooked asparagus.
- Use in omelets.
- Purée; add some heavy cream and butter and use to garnish eggs or chicken.
- Sauté 2 cups cooked asparagus and use in place of celery in a *Celery Sauce* (see *Celery*).
- Chop or finely slice for fritters; see *Corn Fritters* under *Corn*.
- Diagonally slice leftover asparagus, toss in a vinaigrette sauce and add to tossed green salads, or composed vegetable salads.

◇ *Blanched or Boiled Asparagus*

This method works equally well with whole spears or asparagus pieces. Peel asparagus (see page 3). Take a large rectangular roaster or oval stove-top casserole long enough to hold asparagus spears lengthwise, fill three-fourths full of water, add 1 teaspoon salt per quart of water, and bring to a boil. Plunge the spears into the boiling water and partially cover until the water boils again, then uncover so that the asparagus stays green. Once the water boils rapidly, reduce heat and cook for 4 minutes. Then, start testing for tenderness by piercing a spear with a sharp knife point. The asparagus is done as soon as the knife first easily pierces the spear. Do not overcook! The asparagus should retain its crunch and texture.

To serve hot, using two slotted spatulas or spoons, lift asparagus to a clean towel placed on a cake rack. (The towel absorbs any excess moisture.) Then arrange on a warm serving platter.

To serve cold, place the pot in the sink and run cold water into it. The cold water immediately stops the asparagus from cooking further, keeping it green and crisp. When the water is completely cold, using two slotted spatulas or spoons, lift the asparagus to a clean towel placed on a rack and pat dry. Lift from the towel to a plate, cover, and refrigerate if not using immediately.

Finishing Touches for Warm Asparagus

- *With Butter*: After the asparagus is cooked and drained, top with pats of unsalted butter. Serve with salt and pepper.
- *With Black Butter*: Brown butter until browned but not burned; pour over warm asparagus.
- *With Butter and Cheese*: Top warm asparagus with freshly grated Parmesan cheese, melted butter, and lemon juice to taste. Place under the broiler to slightly melt the cheese.
- *With Lemon Butter*: Make *Lemon Butter Sauce* (see *Appendix*) and pour over warm asparagus. Count on ⅓ cup sauce per pound of trimmed asparagus.
- *Flemish*: For each pound asparagus, mash 2 hard-boiled egg yolks and mix into ½ cup melted butter along with 2 teaspoons lemon juice; season with salt

and freshly ground pepper. Pour over warm asparagus and top with finely chopped egg whites.
- *Hollandaise*: See *Appendix* for recipe. Spoon over asparagus.
- *Mousseline*: See *Appendix* for recipe. Spoon over asparagus.
- *Maltaise*: Substitute orange juice for water and lemon juice in the basic *Hollandaise Sauce* recipe (see *Appendix*). Add a squeeze of lemon and finely grated orange peel for maximum flavor.
- *Polonaise*: For each pound asparagus, chop 2 hard-boiled eggs, combine with 2 tablespoons chopped parsley, and sprinkle over asparagus. Melt 6 tablespoons butter and sauté ¼ cup bread crumbs until browned. Pour over warm asparagus.
- *Au Gratin*: Arrange asparagus in a buttered baking dish, and top with *Mornay Sauce* or *Béchamel Sauce* (see *Appendix*). Use 1 recipe sauce for 1–2 pounds asparagus. Sprinkle with grated cheese and buttered bread crumbs. Bake in preheated 425° oven for 15–20 minutes or until sauce is brown and bubbly.
- *With Oil and Lemon*: Extra easy and good. Serve warm with best-quality olive oil and lemon juice (or wine vinegar), coarse salt, freshly ground pepper.
- *With Vinaigrette*: Use as a delicious first course. For 2 pounds asparagus, combine ¼ teaspoon salt, ⅛ teaspoon Dijon mustard, and 2 tablespoons lemon juice. Gradually beat in 9 tablespoons olive oil or a combination of olive and vegetable oils; stir in 2 tablespoons chopped shallots. Season with salt and pepper. To thicken sauce and evenly coat the warm asparagus, add 1 beaten egg white to vinaigrette.

Finishing Touches for Cold Asparagus

I prefer to eat asparagus warm or at room temperature, but cooked chilled asparagus is an appetizing addition to cold salads and composed dishes. Follow the instructions for *Blanched or Boiled Asparagus*.
- *With Vinaigrette*: See *Finishing Touches for Warm Asparagus*. For a colorful platter, I frame asparagus vinaigrette on both sides with finely julienned carrots tossed in vinaigrette sauce.

- *With Cream Vinaigrette*: Beat together 1 egg yolk and 1/2 cup heavy or sour cream. Gradually whisk in vinaigrette sauce. Season with salt, freshly ground pepper, and your favorite herbs.
- *Mimosa*: The coarsely chopped egg resembles the mimosa flower, hence the name. Grate hard-boiled eggs; mix with 2–3 tablespoons minced fresh herbs (such as lovage, chervil, parsley, or chives). Make a *Vinaigrette Sauce* (see *Appendix*) flavored with a little extra Dijon mustard, and pour over the asparagus. Top with the mimosa mixture. Use at least 1/4 cup of sauce per pound of trimmed asparagus.
- *Oriental*: For each 2 pounds asparagus, crush together 1 clove garlic, 1 quarter-size piece of fresh ginger, and 1/2 teaspoon salt. Combine with 1 teaspoon sugar, 4 tablespoons soy sauce, 1 teaspoon sesame oil, 2 tablespoons white wine vinegar, freshly ground pepper, and 2 tablespoons chopped scallions. (This is also good over warm asparagus.)
- *With Horseradish Cream*: Whip heavy cream into soft mounds and fold in finely grated fresh horseradish. Season with lemon juice, a pinch of sugar, salt, and pepper to taste.

Sautéed Asparagus

This quick stir-fry seals in asparagus' bright green color and the quick steaming tenderizes it in seconds. I like the appearance of roll-cut asparagus (see page 4), and I even have the fantasy it tastes better this way.

    2 lb asparagus
    2 Tb peanut or corn oil or a combination of oil and
        butter
    Salt
    1/2 tsp sugar
    1/2 cup water or stock
    2 Tb butter (optional)
    Freshly ground pepper

Wash, peel, and roll-cut asparagus. (The roll-cut size is not important; anywhere from 3/4 inch to 2 inches is fine.) Heat the oil in a large sauté pan or wok. When the oil is hot, turn heat down to medium-high and toss in asparagus, stirring rapidly to coat with oil. Sprinkle with 1/2 teaspoon salt and the sugar, pour in the water or stock, cover, and steam-cook for 4–5 minutes or until asparagus is just tender. Uncover, turn up the heat, and cook for 1 minute longer, stirring to evaporate any liquid. Stir in butter, if you like, and season to taste. (*Serves 4*)

- Omit butter and swirl in soy sauce, sesame oil, or, for an extra special taste, some walnut or hazelnut oil.
- During the last few minutes, add sliced water chestnuts or toasted sliced almonds for texture contrast.

Asparagus Soup

The asparagus liquid and trimmings give a fresh-from-the-garden taste.

    2 lb asparagus
    4–6 Tb butter
    1 1/2 cups sliced leeks or 1 cup chopped onions
    3 Tb flour
    6 cups chicken broth, water, or a combination of
        both
    1 egg yolk (optional)
    3/4 cup light cream
    Salt and freshly ground pepper

Cut off the top 3 inches of the asparagus, trim, and blanch these tips for 4–5 minutes. Cool, chop, and set aside. Trim the ends of the remaining asparagus and chop the stalks into 1/2-inch pieces. Melt 4 tablespoons of the butter in a 3–4-quart saucepan. Add the leeks or onions and cook slowly until wilted but not browned, about 8 minutes. Stir in the raw asparagus and cook, covered, for 5–10 minutes. Uncover, stir in the flour, and cook for 2–3 minutes. Add the broth, bring to a boil, reduce the heat, and simmer, partially covered, for 30 minutes.

When the soup has cooked, purée the mixture and sieve to remove fibers—or put through a food mill. The texture should be very fine. Take half the reserved asparagus, add to the soup, and roughly purée. Beat the egg yolk (if you wish to use it) and cream in a bowl and slowly whisk into it 1/2 cup of the hot soup. Whisk mixture back into the hot soup. Add a garnish of the remaining chopped asparagus and reheat without boiling. If desired, add 2 tablespoons butter as a final enrichment. Season to taste. (*Serves 4–6*)

- To serve chilled, purée finely and omit the enrichment butter.
- Add 2 or more tablespoons chopped lovage to cook along with the soup.

Stir-Fried Asparagus and Beef

    1 1/2 lb asparagus
    4–5 scallions
    1 lb skirt steak or flank steak
    2 1/2 Tb cornstarch
    3 Tb soy sauce
    1 Tb sherry or rice wine
    1 Tb oil
    Sugar
    2/3 cup beef stock
    1 Tb sesame oil
    1 Tb oyster sauce (optional)
    1 cup peanut oil
    2 slices peeled ginger
    1 clove peeled crushed garlic
    Salt
    1/2 cup sliced canned water chestnuts

Wash, peel, and roll-cut the asparagus (see page 4) into 1 1/2-inch pieces. Slice scallions into 1-inch pieces. Diag-

onally cut the beef into ¼-inch slices. Make marinade: combine 1 tablespoon of the cornstarch dissolved in 2 tablespoons water, 1 tablespoon of the soy sauce, the sherry or rice wine, 1 tablespoon oil, and a pinch of sugar. Add meat and marinate for 30 minutes.

Meanwhile, mix sauce: combine remaining 1½ tablespoons cornstarch dissolved in ⅓ cup beef stock or water, 2 tablespoons soy sauce, the sesame oil, and oyster sauce (if you wish). Set aside. When meat has marinated, heat 1 cup peanut oil to 375° in a large sauté pan or wok. Toss in meat and cook, stirring, until meat is opaque, about 1 minute, and remove meat from pan. Drain oil, reserving 2 tablespoons, then reheat. Toss in ginger and garlic, and cook for 10 seconds. Add asparagus and scallions; stir in ½ teaspoon sugar and a dash of salt. Cook, stirring, for 1–2 minutes (the asparagus will turn bright green). Add remaining stock, cover, and steam for 2 minutes. Uncover, add beef and water chestnuts, and toss together. Stir in sauce and cook until lightly thickened. *(Serves 4)*

- Use chicken or pork instead of beef.

Pasta with Asparagus

Try pasta with asparagus—either cold or hot. Add whatever additional ingredients, such as tomatoes or nuts, you fancy. Here are two variations to start you thinking.

Cold Main Salad
1 lb asparagus
6 Tb olive oil
1 clove garlic, minced
1 lb pasta (such as fettucini or linguini)
1 cup tuna chunks
½ cup finely sliced ham
8 black olives, pitted and sliced
2 Tb lemon juice or wine vinegar
Salt and freshly ground pepper

Peel and blanch asparagus. Cool, drain, and roll-cut (see page 4) into 1-inch pieces. Heat olive oil, cook garlic for 1 minute, then pour into a large heatproof bowl. Cook pasta in boiling salted water for 8–10 minutes or until *al dente*; drain. Combine pasta with oil. Add asparagus, tuna, ham, olives, and lemon juice or vinegar; season with salt and pepper to taste. Either serve at room temperature, or refrigerate, and serve cool. *(Serves 4–6)*

Hot Main Course
1 lb asparagus
6 Tb butter
½ cup finely sliced ham
1 cup finely sliced mushrooms
1 lb pasta (fettucini or linguini)
2 Tb olive oil
1 clove garlic, minced
2 cups light cream
¾ cup freshly grated Parmesan cheese
2 egg yolks, beaten (optional)
Salt and freshly ground pepper
Chopped chives

Peel and roll-cut asparagus (see page 4) into 1–1½-inch pieces. Melt 2 tablespoons butter in a sauté pan and lightly sauté the ham and mushrooms; set aside. Boil a large pot of salted water and blanch the asparagus until just cooked through, 4–5 minutes or less. Scoop out the asparagus and save the water. Add more water, if necessary, and cook the pasta until *al dente*; drain.

In a large sauté pan, heat 4 tablespoons butter and the olive oil. Add garlic, cook for 1 minute, and add the pasta; toss to coat with butter and oil. Stir in the cream and cheese, and cook for 1–2 minutes until slightly thickened. If you like, lower heat, stir in the eggs, and toss together for 1 minute to set egg and thicken the sauce. Add asparagus, ham, and mushrooms; cook for a moment to heat through. Season to taste with salt and pepper; garnish with chives. *(Serves 4–6)*

Oven Asparagus Puff

Here's an easy luncheon or light supper dish. The mild Muenster cheese will accent, not overpower, the delicate asparagus flavor.

¾–1 lb asparagus
4 Tb butter
2 Tb chopped onions
½ tsp sugar
Salt
6 eggs
⅓ cup heavy cream
Freshly ground pepper
1½ cups grated Muenster cheese

Peel and roll-cut asparagus (see page 4) into 1-inch

pieces. You should have 2 cups. Melt 2 tablespoons butter in a sauté pan; sauté onion until soft and golden. Add asparagus, sprinkle with sugar, and ½ teaspoon salt, and toss for 1 minute. Add 2 tablespoons water, cover, and, shaking pan, steam-cook for 1–2 minutes. Remove cover, and cook until liquid is evaporated. Cool slightly.

Beat together eggs, cream, and ½ teaspoon salt and pepper to taste. Melt 2 tablespoons butter in an oven-proof 10 x 10-inch baking dish. Pour in egg mixture and cook over medium heat until the bottom is set (about 3 minutes). Arrange asparagus and onions in a single layer on top of the eggs. Bake in a preheated 425° oven for 5 minutes. Remove from oven, cover asparagus with grated cheese, then bake an additional 10 minutes. When the eggs have puffed and the cheese has lightly browned, the dish is finished. *(Serves 4)*

- Use leftover cooked asparagus.
- Use less cheese and top with sour cream.

Asparagus and Chicken on Toast

Asparagus is best complemented by sauces that don't overpower its delicate taste. Try this chicken combination or one of the other assembly ideas at end of recipe.

24 asparagus spears
6 chicken breasts
4–6 pieces firm-textured white bread
4 Tb melted butter
Hollandaise Sauce (page 348)
6 Tb butter
1 tsp lemon juice
Salt and freshly ground pepper

Wash and peel asparagus. Remove tendons from chicken breasts, then lightly flatten each breast. Trim crusts from bread, brush each side with melted butter, and cut each piece diagonally. Toast under the broiler until lightly browned, turning once. Keep warm. Make hollandaise sauce, and hold over warm water.

Melt 6 tablespoons butter in baking dish. Sprinkle chicken with lemon juice and salt and pepper. Turn chicken in hot butter, place in a single layer in the dish, cover with waxed paper, and bake in a preheated 400° oven until springy to the touch, 7–8 minutes. Remove from oven and keep warm.

In the meantime, bring a large pot of salted water to the boil, and blanch the asparagus until crisp, yet tender. Drain and keep warm. For each serving, arrange 2–3 slices of toasted bread, top with 6 spears of asparagus—3 tips pointing in each direction—then put on 1½ chicken breasts and dress with hollandaise. *(Serves 4)*

Other Cooked Asparagus Combinations

Asparagus with Crêpes:
Make crêpes (see *Spinach Crêpes* in *Spinach*). Line each crêpe with a thin slice of ham; spread a spoonful of *Mornay Sauce* (see *Appendix*) on the ham; and place 4–5 asparagus spears in the center of the crêpe. Roll the crêpe around the asparagus. Set in a buttered baking dish. Partially cover with Mornay sauce, sprinkle with grated cheese, and dot with butter. Bake in a preheated 400° oven until heated through.

Asparagus with Flounder Fillets:
For each serving, score the dark side (skin side) of a flounder fillet. Place the scored side up and center 4–5 buttered asparagus spears on it. Sprinkle with salt, pepper, and lemon juice. Wrap the fillet around the asparagus. Place in a buttered baking dish, drizzle on ¼ cup white wine, dot with butter, and sprinkle with fresh herbs to taste. Cover with waxed paper and bake in a preheated 400° oven for 15 minutes or until fish is flaky. Top with *Lemon Butter Sauce* or *White Butter Sauce* (see *Appendix*).

Asparagus with Eggs:
Prepare buttered toasted bread. Top with lightly buttered asparagus spears, poached eggs, and your favorite sauce. (A fresh tomato sauce is a nice change, or use eggs scrambled with a touch of Dijon mustard and lemon juice.)

Beans

I like to prepare snap beans simply. Before the beans reach pencil-thin size, I harvest them and drop into boiling water, drain and coat them with butter. Or, I might blanch the beans and serve them at room temperature tossed in a vinaigrette sauce. Those are my ultimate snap bean preparations: everything else is gilding the lily. (Some people continue to call green snap beans string beans, but that's a misnomer, for most of the beans we plant simply do not need stringing. They are also often known simply as green beans.)

But snap beans constitute only a small percentage of the hundreds of bean varieties. Shell beans (and their corollary, dried beans) can be a more versatile cooking choice and for centuries have been a protein staple for much of the world.

Snap, shell, and dried beans represent different phases in the bean's development. Snap beans are the immature pods of the bean; shell beans, the mature fresh seed, and dried beans, seed which has dried in the pod and must be reconstituted in liquid. Any bean allowed to grow long enough will give you all three stages (but not necessarily the same good flavor at each stage).

At the Victory Garden we grow mostly fresh bean varieties, and although I enjoy eating dried beans, the store-bought ones work fine for me. Often when I'm in the mood for dried beans, I'll substitute fresh shell beans and adjust the recipe accordingly. The one thing to remember is that fresh shell beans keep the same bulk whether they're raw or cooked, while dried beans swell up when cooked. For example, I'd substitute 5 cups of fresh shell beans for every 2 cups of dried beans called for in a recipe.

If you find fresh shell or dried beans hard to digest, you may wonder why fresh snap beans never bother you. The answer lies in the capacity of the bean seeds to store sugars. When the beans are immature and the seeds have barely formed (the stage at which we eat snap beans), sugars are present in low concentrations. As the seeds continue to mature to the fresh shell and dried bean stages, the sugar content increases dramatically. The types of sugars and their concentration vary depending upon the bean variety and its age. Fresh shell beans, and dried beans, contain several kinds of sugars, some of which cannot be broken down by the acids and the enzymes in the stomach. Whether or not they end up being digested by the bacteria in the large intestine completely depends upon the makeup of each person's intestinal bacteria. If the bacteria *can* utilize the sugars, flatulence occurs as a by-product of the metabolism of the sugars

by the bacteria. Some people have no reaction at all. Should you find that fresh shell beans bother you, try recipes that call for long, slow cooking. It's thought that the slower and longer the cooking period, the easier the beans are to digest.

With such a bewildering choice of beans, the varieties you decide to grow are largely a matter of flavor and regional considerations. There are as many opinions about the flavor of beans as there are varieties of beans. Some people swear that Kentucky Wonder pole beans have the best flavor of all (I consider it a meatier or mealier flavor, but not the best). Go into any grocery store in Maine and you'll probably find Jacob's Cattle, a delicious fresh or dried shell bean that Maine gardeners wouldn't be without. Southern gardeners often select Mississippi Skip beans, a fine snap or shell bean. And, who could not appreciate the subtly flavored French flageolet shell bean?

We enjoy sampling these different beans, but certain varieties remain our favorites year after year. Russ particularly likes Tendercrop, a fine-flavored green snap bean resistant to some of the bean diseases; Blue Crop, a high-yielding, tender-podded snap bean that holds well on the vine; the novelty Royalty Burgundy, a meaty purple bean that turns green when cooked and can be sown when the ground is cold; and the Italian Romano wide-podded bush bean. Kentucky Wonder, a standard pole bean; Fordhook 242, a lima bean; a yellow wax bean such as Golden Wax; the Long Pod fava bean, and Dwarf Horticultural shell beans round out his plantings.

Beans grow well in ordinary garden soil. As they're legumes they fix nitrogen from the air and need no further fertilizing.

Fava or broad beans are the first beans to be planted. These beans, popular in England and the Middle East, are planted the moment the ground can be worked, spaced 6 inches apart. Other beans will not germinate until the soil temperature reaches 55°. About June 1, Russ starts planting the remaining beans, spacing the seeds every 3–5 inches. He keeps the rows short, successively sowing seeds every two weeks until midsummer to ensure a season-long crop. The lima beans (or butter beans as they're sometimes called) go in the ground in June. Pole beans, which need planting only once because they yield over a long period of time, go in on the other side of the sugar snap pea fence, taking over once the pea crop is pulled.

The home gardener can harvest beans at a much younger stage than the commercial grower. I insist upon harvesting snap beans when they are barely mature, before the swelling of the seeds is visible through the pods. Daily picking allows us to pick young and keeps the plants producing. Bush beans usually have one big "flush" and then a series of smaller harvests for a few weeks, and then we pull up the plants and toss them in the compost pile.

It can be tricky to tell when shell beans are ready. You really have to go by the seed size and the color and texture of the pod. As shell beans vary so in size, check your seed packet, and take the size they list as the optimum. I usually harvest shell beans at a smaller size than recommended. Fava beans, for example, are often marketed when they're the size of a thumbnail. In England—where fava beans are more common—you're likely to find them harvested no larger than the nail of your first finger. The pods of shell beans frequently change color when the beans are mature (Dwarf Horticultural pods turn from green to a variegated maroon and white) and become soft like glove leather, indicating it's time to harvest.

All beans, regardless of whether they're snap or shell, should be harvested the same way: break off the stem immediately above the cap. For easiest cooking, I harvest equal-size snap beans and pick only as needed, for beans dry out somewhat during storage.

Plant breeders have just about eliminated the "string" that used to run down the bean's side. But if you've planted an old-fashioned variety or one of the French imports now available in this country, just break off the top of the bean at the stem and pull down the side to remove the string. I find the fine point at the bean tip quite attractive and see no reason to remove it.

All fresh shell beans must be shelled. The easiest technique is to pull down the string, and squeeze the pod at the end or in between the seeds, almost "popping" the pod. Then split open the seam (a long fingernail is helpful), exposing the shell beans inside. Unless they are overaged, there's no need to remove the beans' skin. Large fava beans are the only beans with a skin tough enough to require peeling. Some people also skin large lima beans, but I've never found that necessary.

I almost always prepare snap beans whole because I pick them so young. I cut larger or older beans, such as

Kentucky Wonder, diagonally into 1–2-inch pieces. I never "french" beans unless they are to garnish a clear soup because "frenching" cuts them up so badly that they lose flavor when cooked. Actually, in France, a "French cut" for beans is unknown. The French get a skinny effect by planting exceptionally long thin green snap beans such as Fin de Bagnols (available through import seedsmen, see list following *Appendix*).

Both blanching and steaming techniques work equally well for fresh snap beans, while I use a blanch-boil method for shell beans, since I often like to flavor the broth. For a plain treatment, steaming works fine.

The size of the pod or seeds determines the cooking times for all beans. Baby beans should blanch barely 1 minute. When the beans are larger, I increase the cooking times slightly: 5-inch-long snap beans will take around 5 minutes to cook to the tender crunch stage.

Marketing

Snap Beans: Shop at a market that allows you to select the size beans you want and choose beans the same size for easiest cooking. Buy crisp, fresh-looking pods that snap easily and are blemish-free. The pods should be immature with barely visible seeds. Avoid limp, tired-looking beans, or beans that are clearly too old (thick pods, huge seeds, etc.).

Fresh Shell Beans: Shell beans are difficult to find in the market. When you do locate them, select beans with well-filled-out, fresh-looking pods that are not streaked with brown (a sign of age). Feel a pod to determine the seed size. Brown limp pods are a sign of poor storage, and huge seeds indicate overaged beans.

Fresh Snap Beans

I both steam and blanch fresh snap beans. When I have a large number of beans to cook, I usually blanch them in a big kettle of boiling water, adding the beans gradually to keep the water boiling. I steam small amounts of beans. Steaming keeps them a bit drier, but, frankly, both methods retain the bright color, texture, and bean flavor that overcooking destroys. Cooking time is determined by the vegetables' size and freshness. I believe the thickness or the diameter of the bean to be the key to cooking time. For example, the flatter Romano beans take less time to cook than thick-podded beans. The best way to gauge is the taste test: it never fails.

◇ *Steamed Beans*

Bring ¾–1 inch of water to a boil in a steamer and place the beans in a basket or colander over the boiling water. Cover and steam until crisp yet tender. For example, 5-inch-long beans, ¼–⅜ inch thick, will cook in approximately 5 minutes. Smaller beans take less time; larger beans, more.

◇ *Blanched Beans*

Boil a large kettle of water. The more water you use, the faster it returns to a boil once you have added the beans: count on at least 4 quarts of water per pound of beans, and 1½ teaspoons salt per quart of water. Gradually drop in the beans so as to retain the boil as much as possible. Then, cover for a moment so that the water returns to the boil quickly. Remove cover, and boil over moderate heat until beans are tender but retain some of their crunch. A 5-inch-long bean, ¼–⅜ inch thick, will cook in approximately 4–5 minutes after the water has returned to the boil. Smaller beans (under ¼ inch thick) will cook in less than 3 minutes.

Drain beans immediately and proceed with *Finishing Touches*. For chilled beans or if you want to reheat them later on, plunge them into cold water to set the color and to stop the cooking process. Drain, pat thoroughly dry, and refrigerate.

Finishing Touches for Hot Snap Beans

Before combining with other ingredients, toss in a moderately hot frying pan to evaporate moisture, then proceed. If you're heating beans with butter, after evaporating the moisture, add the butter to the beans and toss together, but do not sauté or the beans may turn an unappetizing brown and become bitter-tasting.

- *With Butter*: Toss beans with melted butter in a hot sauté pan. (Use 2 tablespoons butter per pound of beans.) Turn over or toss beans so that beans and butter do not burn. Season with salt and pepper.

- *With Butter and Lemon Juice*: Toss beans with butter in a hot frying pan. Sprinkle with lemon juice, and season with salt and pepper.
- *With Butter and Cream*: Toss cooked beans with butter, then pour in approximately ½ cup heavy cream per pound of beans. Heat cream just long enough to coat the beans.
- *With Onions*: Lightly brown chopped onions in butter, add beans, and toss until thoroughly coated with butter and onions.
- *With Almonds*: Lightly brown slivered almonds in butter. Toss with cooked beans and season to taste.
- *With Cheese*: Toss beans with butter, and sprinkle with grated Parmesan cheese or a grated Parmesan and Swiss cheese combination. Season to taste.
- *With Oil and Garlic*: Heat 2 tablespoons oil per pound of beans, add 1 clove finely chopped or puréed garlic, cook 30 seconds, add beans; toss until heated through. Season with salt and pepper to taste.
- *With Ham*: Take ¼ pound ham per pound of beans and cut into thin strips. Sauté ham in butter for 2–3 minutes. Toss in beans, and fresh herbs such as savory or rosemary if desired. Sauté for just 1–2 minutes until beans are heated through. Season to taste and serve. Or use the oil and garlic treatment above.
- *With Bacon*: Toss beans with butter and lemon juice. Season to taste with salt and pepper, then sprinkle with crumbled cooked bacon bits.
- *With Mornay Sauce*: Make a *Mornay Sauce* (see *Appendix*). Layer beans and Mornay Sauce in a buttered

baking dish. Sprinkle with grated cheese and dot with butter. Bake in preheated 375° oven for 20–30 minutes.

- *With Mushrooms*: Sauté ¼ pound sliced mushrooms per pound of beans in butter until lightly browned. Add green beans and heat through.
- *With Shell Beans*: Toss equal parts of cut snap beans and cooked shell beans with butter, salt and pepper, and chopped parsley, savory, or basil. I particularly like snap beans tossed with white cannellini beans.
- *Warm Bean Salad*: Thoroughly drain beans, and serve with the finest quality olive oil, lemon wedges, coarse salt, and freshly ground pepper.
- *With Warm Salad Dressing*: For each pound of beans, use the following preparations: Cook 4 slices bacon. Drain and crumble. In ¼ cup bacon fat, cook ¼ cup finely chopped onion. Add ¼ cup vinegar and 1 tablespoon sugar; heat until boiling. Pour over cooked, drained, warm beans, toss, and season to taste with salt and pepper. Garnish with crumbled bacon.

Finishing Touches for Cold Snap Beans

- *Bean Salad or Beans Vinaigrette*: There are few foods more delicious than blanched young beans, dressed while still warm with olive oil, lemon juice, and salt and pepper (best served at room temperature). If you need to prepare them ahead, refresh in cold water, pat dry, and toss with *Vinaigrette Sauce* (see *Appendix*) just before serving. It is impossible to give definite proportions per person, for this salad is so good that everyone eats more than expected. Beans Vinaigrette are the base for the famous *Salade Niçoise* (see page 17). You can replace the tuna with cooked fish and mix celeriac or other exotic vegetables into the potato salad, but you must always have the beans as a base. Vary bean salad with any of the following:
- Sprinkle top of salad with finely chopped shallots.
- Garnish with red onion rounds.
- Surround with ripe tomato wedges seasoned with the bean dressing.
- Toss julienned blanched carrots with baby green beans.
- Garnish with thinly sliced raw mushrooms which have been tossed with some of the bean dressing.

Fresh Shell Beans

I prefer an old-fashioned gentle boiling technique to cook fresh shell beans. I'm amazed at how well these beans stand up to gentle cooking, regardless of the length of time. When you boil beans in water or a flavored broth, you can add herbs to perk up their taste. I have also steamed shell beans, which works fine for a plain treatment. I often like to flavor the beans, however, so I tend to use the blanch/boil method. A light butter-braise is delicious for tiny beans.

Special Information

Yields and Conversions

Fresh shell bean amounts are difficult to calculate because the number of beans per pod varies. Count on 50–60 percent waste.

- 1 pound fresh snap beans = approximately 4 cups = 4 servings
- 1 pound medium-size fresh podded shell beans (i.e., horticultural) = approximately 1½ cups = 2 servings
- 1 pound large fresh podded shell beans (i.e., large limas) = approximately 2 cups shelled = 2 servings

Storage and Preserving

Store fresh snap and shell beans unwashed in a perforated plastic bag in the refrigerator. They will keep 3–5 days. Shell beans should be left in their pods and shelled just before cooking.

Freezing

- *Snap Beans*: Blanch beans in boiling water for 3 minutes per pound of beans. Chill in ice water for 3 minutes; drain. Store in freezer bags. Beans will keep 6–12 months at 0°.
- *Shell Beans*: Blanch beans by size. Medium beans will blanch in 2 minutes in boiling water. Larger beans will take 3 minutes. Immediately chill in ice water for an equal length of time. Drain and loosely pack in freezer boxes or bags. Beans will keep for 6–12 months at 0°.

Canning

I prefer the texture and color of frozen beans so I never can them. If you can beans, use a good preserving book such as Jean Anderson's *The Green Thumb Preserving Guide*.

Pickling

See *Pickled Dilly Beans*.

Drying Shell Beans

Let beans dry in pods; when dry, remove and shell. Dry beans in a slow oven (200°) for 6–8 hours to kill weevil eggs. Store, covered, in a dry place.

Hints

- Add snap beans to stews and soups toward the end of cooking for a crunchy fresh green vegetable.
- Nibble on raw beans for snacks.
- Italians treat raw young fava beans like peanuts; shell, and eat with salt.
- Substitute fresh shell beans for cooked dried beans in dried bean recipes.
- Add fresh shell beans to soups and stews. Mash the tender beans against the pot to thicken the dish.

◇ *Blanched Shell Beans*

Shell beans, and cover with water. Add flavoring herbs such as savory, a traditional seasoning for fava beans, and/or blanched salt pork or bacon to impart a smoky flavor. Bring water to a boil, lower heat, cover, and cook gently until just tender. The cooking time depends on the size of the beans. The smallest beans will cook in approximately 5–10 minutes, while larger beans will take closer to 20 minutes. (Some shell beans can cook for hours without losing their shape; see *Boston Baked Fresh Horticultural Beans*.) Large fava beans need to be skinned before serving. Either skin them before cooking by removing the skin carefully with a paring knife or run them under cold water once they are cooked and the skins will slip right off.

◇ *Braised Small Shell Beans*

Melt butter in a saucepan and cook some shallots or finely minced onions until wilted. Add beans, cover, and stew gently for 5–10 minutes or until the beans are tender. Add a bit of water if necessary.

◇ *Steamed Shell Beans*

Bring 3/4–1 inch of water to boil in a steamer. Add the shelled beans and cook for approximately the same length of time as when blanched. (Often the skins on larger beans, such as limas, will shrivel and wrinkle more than if blanched.)

- Toss fresh cooked shell beans with pasta, olive oil, and grated cheese.
- Salt in the cooking water of fresh shell beans hardens the beans' texture. Use this to your advantage if you want firm-textured beans such as in *Boston Baked Fresh Horticultural Beans*.
- Use raw wide flat beans for dips.
- Roast a leg of lamb with 5 to 6 cups parboiled flageolets or shell beans mixed with 2 cups sautéed onions. Add 1 cup beef broth and herbs to taste, and place seasoned lamb on top. Roast in 350° oven for 1 to 1 1/2 hours.

Microwave
- One-half pound whole fresh snap beans, covered, will cook done in 4–7 minutes, depending upon size.
- 2 cups fresh shell beans with 2 tablespoons water, covered, will cook done in 4–8 minutes, depending upon size.

Leftovers
- Add leftover beans to mixed vegetable salads or stews and soups.
- Purée leftover podded beans for purées and soups.
- Toss in leftover snap beans to stir-fries at the end.

Finishing Touches for Hot Shell Beans

- *With Butter*: Toss drained beans with fresh butter, salt, pepper, and lemon juice, if desired.
- *With Butter and Cream*: After the beans are cooked and tossed or stewed in butter, add a bit of heavy cream and cook until the cream is reduced and just coats the beans. Season with salt, pepper, and lemon juice.
- *With Velouté*: Make a velouté (see *Béchamel Sauce* variation) using cooking liquids and milk. Fold cooked beans into the velouté, top with grated cheese, and bake until bubbly.
- *With Oil and Herbs*: Add 2–3 tablespoons olive oil to the cooking water, along with 2 teaspoons minced garlic and 1 teaspoon dried savory or sage. When tender, drain and toss with 1/2 cup olive oil that has been mixed with 1 teaspoon salt mashed with 1 clove of garlic. Sprinkle in chopped fresh parsley and fresh herbs, if available. Season to taste with salt and pepper.
- *With Herbs*: Stir into Braised Beans chopped herbs such as chives, dill, or savory when just tender. Let sit covered for 5 minutes for the herbs to steep with the beans.
- *With Vegetables*: Heat 2–3 tablespoons of olive oil and sauté 1 cup chopped onions and 2 chopped seeded chilies. Add 2–3 cups chopped, peeled, and seeded tomatoes and cubed winter squash. Add 2–3 cups cooked beans and enough of their cooking liquid to gently stew all the vegetables. Cover and simmer until vegetables are tender. Season to taste with salt and pepper.
- *With Snap Beans*: Combine equal amounts of cooked shell beans and cooked green bean pieces. Toss together with butter or combine in a light cream-sauce.
- *Purée*: Purée 3 cups of cooked beans in a food processor or blender with butter (4 tablespoons) and salt and pepper to taste. Thin with 2–3 tablespoons cream or cooking liquid. Reheat over high heat, stirring well.
- *With Greens*: Combine blanched broccoli de rabe (or other greens) and cooked fresh shell beans in sauté pan with olive oil and chopped minced garlic. Add 1/2 cup cooking liquid and heat together for 5 minutes. Season with salt and pepper and sprinkle with grated cheese if desired.

Finishing Touches for Cold Shell Beans

When you're cooking shell beans for a salad, flavor the cooking water with an onion stuck with 2–3 cloves, a bay leaf, or a few cloves of garlic. Use dried herbs that you may be using fresh in the salad. Toss the beans with a touch of oil after they're drained and they won't stick together.

- *With Vinaigrette Sauce*: Toss the shell beans with a good *Vinaigrette Sauce* (see *Appendix*) and some minced fresh herbs. Refrigerate, and bring to room temperature before serving. Then toss again with some more vinaigrette and fresh chopped parsley. Decorate with thinly sliced red onion rounds. You'll need 2/3 cup vinaigrette for each 4 cups beans.

- *With Tuna*: Toss 4 cups shell beans with a vinaigrette sauce as above. Top with 14 ounces tuna chunks and chopped onions. Sprinkle tuna with additional vinaigrette and fresh basil. Surround with freshly cooked green beans. For a more elaborate salad, add wedges of tomatoes, olives, eggs, etc.
- *With Meat or Chicken*: Add 1–2 cups cold sliced meat or poultry with chopped onion and/or celery. Toss with vinaigrette and season with salt, pepper, and chopped herbs.
- *With Anchovies*: Add mashed anchovy fillets to a vinaigrette sauce. Toss with beans and chopped onion.
- *In Tomato Shells*: Toss cooked shell beans with herbs and chopped onions and use to fill scooped-out tomato shells. Garnish with cold sliced sausages.

Boston Baked
Fresh Horticultural Beans

The amazing fact about substituting these shell beans for dried beans is how well they keep their shape after 4 hours of cooking. A long, slow cooking gives them the rich brown color and consistency of traditional baked beans. If need be, the beans can also be cooked half as long (or longer).

    4 cups shelled horticultural beans
    2 slices bacon or 1/2 cup blanched sliced salt pork
    1 cup chopped onions
    1/4 cup molasses
    1 Tb Dijon mustard
    1 bay leaf
    2 tsp salt
    1 Tb tomato purée (optional)

Cover beans with 4 cups water. Bring water to a boil, skim the surface, and stir in remaining ingredients. Reduce heat, cover pan, and simmer for 4 hours. When beans are done, liquid will coat the beans. *(Serves 6–8)*

New Style "Red Beans and Rice"

In early Creole homes, Red Beans and Rice was served on Mondays, the traditional wash days. The cook simmered a big pot of beans and ham while she washed and ironed clothes for the week. With fresh beans, you can simmer all day if you want, or eat them as soon as they are cooked through—in less than 30 minutes.

    4–5 cups fresh horticultural or kidney beans
    1 cup chopped onions
    1 1/2 lb ham steak or pork butt, cut into large pieces
    2 Tb vegetable oil
    2 Tb flour
    1 cup tomato sauce
    Salt and freshly ground pepper
    3 cups cooked rice
    Chopped scallions

Shell beans. Barely cover with water, bring to a boil, skim, and add onions and ham or pork. Reduce heat, partially cover, and cook gently for 30 minutes or until the beans are tender. (The longer the beans cook, the more the meat flavor permeates them.)

After the beans are cooked, make a roux: heat the oil and stir in the flour; cook slowly until just lightly browned. Stir in the tomato sauce and a few spoonfuls of the bean juice. Stir the roux into the bean mixture until well blended. Simmer for 15 minutes. Season to taste. Ladle over hot, cooked white rice, and garnish with chopped scallions. *(Serves 6)*

- For a dried bean version, substitute 2 cups dried beans for fresh. Wash and clean beans. Soak in cold water overnight, or cover with water, boil for 2 minutes, remove from heat, and let the water cool completely. Bring the beans back to a boil and continue with the recipe.

Shell Bean Succotash

    2 cups shell beans (such as a combination of limas
        and horticultural)
    1 strip bacon
    1 tsp salt
    2 Tb chopped onions
    1 cup peeled, seeded, and chopped tomatoes
    2 cups corn kernels
    2 Tb butter
    Salt and freshly ground pepper

Put beans, bacon, salt, and onions in a saucepan; add 1 cup of water. Bring water to a boil, cover, and simmer for 20 minutes. Stir in tomatoes and corn. Simmer for 10 minutes longer. Remove bacon, stir in butter, and season with salt and pepper. *(Serves 4–6)*

- Add fresh herbs to taste.
- Make a *Succotash* (see *Corn*).

Snap Beans and Tomatoes

This is a good choice for larger beans.

    1 lb green snap beans
    1 clove garlic
    2 Tb butter
    1 Tb oil
    3/4 cup chopped onions

2 cups peeled, seeded, and chopped tomatoes
1/2 tsp oregano
1 tsp salt
Freshly ground pepper

Blanch or steam the beans, and cut into 1 1/2-inch pieces. Mince the garlic. Heat the butter and oil in a large saucepan and sauté the onions until wilted, 5–10 minutes. Add garlic and cook for 1 minute. Add tomatoes, oregano, salt, and pepper, and simmer 5 minutes. Mix in beans, and cook 2 minutes longer to heat through. *(Serves 4–6)*

- Add raw small young beans along with tomatoes, and gently stew them until barely tender.
- Serve with grated Parmesan cheese.
- Add sautéed sliced mushrooms along with beans.
- Add cooked white shell beans with snap beans.
- Stir in halved cooked new potatoes.

Snap Bean Purée

I purée only large, older beans: young beans are best whole. The shell beans thicken the purée and make it easier for the machine to work.

1/2 lb green snap beans
1 Tb cooked white shell beans
2 Tb butter
1/4 tsp salt
Freshly ground pepper
2–4 Tb heavy cream (optional)

Blanch or steam snap beans, cooking until soft, approximately 20 minutes. Place in a food processor or blender along with shell beans and purée thoroughly. Heat beans in a small saucepan with butter, add salt and pepper, and cream (if you wish). *(Makes 2 cups)*

Stampfenbohnen

This old family recipe is the solution for older beans. The *stampfen* means pounding or stamping, and *bohnen*, beans.

1 lb potatoes
1 1/2 lb snap beans
6–8 Tb butter
1 cup chopped onions
Salt and freshly ground pepper

Peel and roughly chop the potatoes. Wash and cut up the beans into approximately 1-inch pieces. Cover the potatoes with salted water and bring to a boil, cooking gently for about 15 minutes. Add beans and cook for another 10 minutes or until both vegetables are tender.

Meanwhile, melt 6 tablespoons butter and sauté onions until lightly browned. Drain the potatoes and beans, setting aside some of the cooking liquid. Mash the potatoes and beans together (stamping and pounding) until the potatoes are mashed and the beans are broken up. Add some cooking liquid as needed. Beat in the butter and onions, adding the remaining 2 tablespoons butter if desired. Season with salt and pepper. *(Serves 4)*

- Substitute parsnips for potatoes.

Shell Bean "Hummus"

Hummus is a delicious Mideastern appetizer, traditionally made with cooked dried chickpeas and sesame paste. With loads of garden horticultural beans, I came up with this version, which I think is as good as the real thing. If you can't find sesame paste, omit it and step up the seasonings. (You could also use the cooking liquids rather than oil.) Serve with raw flat green snap beans and dip into the hummus with the bean, or use toasted Syrian bread and sweet onion wedges for a garnish.

2 cups shelled horticultural beans
1/3 cup plus 1 Tb lemon juice
Salt
2 cloves garlic
1/2 cup sesame paste (tahini)
1/4–1/2 cup olive oil
Freshly ground pepper

Cover beans with water; add 1 tablespoon lemon juice and 1 teaspoon salt. Bring to a boil and cook until tender, about 20 minutes. Drain, and place beans in a food processor or blender. Mince garlic. Add 1/3 cup lemon juice, garlic, sesame paste, salt to taste, and 1–2 tablespoons oil. Purée, adding additional oil until hummus is consistency desired. Season with salt and pepper. *(Makes about 3 cups)*

Bean Soup with Pistou

Here's a meal full of the natural protein of both fresh shell beans and snap beans. Pistou is the French equivalent of the Italian basil-garlic pesto sauce. Stir in to this minestrone-style soup for a Mediterranean flavor.

¼ lb spinach
½ lb zucchini
2 Tb butter
1 Tb oil
1 ½ cups chopped carrots
1 cup chopped leeks
½ cup chopped onions
1 cup diced potatoes
2 cups fresh shell beans
2 ½ qt water
Salt
3 cloves garlic
½ cup finely chopped fresh basil
1 medium tomato
½ cup grated Parmesan cheese
½ cup olive oil
½ lb tiny green snap beans, or larger beans cut into 1-inch pieces
½ cup small pasta such as ditalini
Freshly ground pepper

Wash and finely slice spinach; set aside. Wash and grate zucchini; set aside. Heat the butter and 1 tablespoon oil in a large saucepan. Add carrots, leeks, and onions and sauté for 5–10 minutes or until wilted. Add potatoes, shell beans, water, and 1 ½ tablespoons salt. Bring the water to a boil, reduce heat, and cook gently, uncovered, for 30 minutes.

Meanwhile, make the pistou. In a mortar, or with a knife, mash the garlic with 1 teaspoon salt until puréed. Add the basil and mash together. Peel, seed, and chop the tomato and add to the mixture, alternating with the cheese until the basil mixture is totally puréed. Gradually beat in the olive oil. You will end up with 1 cup of a smooth mayonnaiselike pistou. Cover and set aside.

When the soup base is ready, add the spinach, snap beans, zucchini, and pasta. Bring soup to a boil, reduce heat, and cook gently until the vegetables and pasta are tender. Season with salt and pepper. Either stir the pistou into the soup or serve it on the side and let people add to taste. *(Serves 6–8)*

- If fresh shell beans are unavailable, use canned beans, such as flageolets. Rinse, drain, and add them to the soup along with the snap beans.
- Make the soup base and pistou ahead of time and add fresh vegetables just before serving.

Puréed Snap Bean Soup

½ cup finely chopped celery
½ cup finely chopped leeks
2 Tb butter
4 cups chicken stock
1 cup cooked shell beans
1 lb green snap beans
¼ tsp savory
Salt and freshly ground pepper
½ cup light cream (optional)

Sauté the celery and leeks in butter until wilted, 5–10 minutes. Add the chicken stock and shell beans, bring to a boil, and stir in the snap beans and savory. Return to the boil, reduce heat, and simmer for 25 minutes or until the beans are soft. Purée the vegetables in a food processor or a food mill. Season to taste with salt and pepper. Add cream, if desired. *(Serves 4–6)*

- Omit the white beans. Substitute either French small green flageolet beans (found dried and canned in import stores) or canned white Italian kidney beans.
- Serve chilled. You may need to thin slightly with additional broth or light cream.

Hearty Bean Soup

For variety, combine different shell bean types.

2 Tb butter
1 Tb oil
1 cup chopped celery
1 cup chopped onions
4–5 cups fresh shell beans
2 oz blanched salt pork
1 bay leaf
1 tsp thyme
1 cup sliced carrots
2 qt chicken or beef broth
2 cups finely sliced cabbage
Salt and freshly ground pepper
Parsley
Dill

Heat butter and oil, sauté celery and onion for 5–10 minutes until wilted. Add beans, salt pork, bay leaf, thyme, carrots, and broth. Bring to a boil, skim, and simmer, partially covered, for 20 minutes, or until beans are tender. To thicken, mash some of the beans against the side of the pot. Add the cabbage; simmer 10 minutes longer or until the cabbage is tender. Remove salt pork if desired. Taste and season with salt and pepper. Chop parsley and dill and sprinkle on soup. *(Makes 2 quarts)*

- Add pasta or rice. Vary the quantities of vegetables.
- Add leftover meats or poultry.

Salade Niçoise

1 large head loose-leaf or Boston lettuce
1 cup *Vinaigrette Sauce* (page 352)
3 cups *Kâthe's Potato Salad,* omitting mayonnaise
   (page 223)
1 lb blanched and chilled snap beans
1½ cups good-quality tuna fish packed in oil
4 large ripe tomatoes
6 hard-boiled eggs
1–2-oz tin of flat anchovies packed in oil
2 Tb chopped shallots
½ cup black small Niçoise olives

Assemble salad just before serving. Wash and dry the lettuce. Toss with a few tablespoons of the vinaigrette. Line a serving bowl or individual plates with the lettuce. Mix a bit of the vinaigrette with the potato salad, and season to taste. Place the potato salad on one side of the serving platter or plates. Toss beans with ¼ cup of the vinaigrette and place on the opposite side of the platter. Break up the tuna fish, and mound in the center. Quarter the tomatoes and eggs and arrange around the tuna, beans, and potatoes; drizzle with vinaigrette. Garnish the tuna fish with anchovy fillets, sprinkle shallots over the beans, and place olives on the potato salad. Spoon the remaining dressing over the potato salad, beans, and tuna, if necessary. *(Serves 6)*

- Substitute leftover cooked fish tossed in a Vinaigrette Sauce for the tuna fish.

Salmagundi

The English salad Salmagundi dates back to the 16th century, when it contained poultry, vegetables, flower buds, and fresh and dried fruits. The recipe is very much the same today. Salmagundi is a good "do-ahead" dish, as everything can be prepared in advance and assembled at the last minute. Baby green beans are vital to this dish.

1 cup water
¼ cup dry sherry
¾ cup golden raisins
1 lb tiny green snap beans
12 tiny white onions
4 hard-boiled eggs
2 crisp Granny Smith apples
2 oranges
¼ lb green seedless grapes
1 3–3½-lb poached or roasted chicken
1 cup *Vinaigrette Sauce* (page 352) made with lemon
   juice
1 head loose-leaf lettuce
½ cup black olives
1 pimento

Boil water and sherry and pour over raisins. Let steep 10 minutes; drain. Blanch or steam beans, cool, and pat dry. Cook onions and cool. Slice eggs and apples into wedges; peel and slice oranges; halve grapes, and set aside. Remove meat from chicken, cutting the dark meat into small pieces and the white meat into small strips. Toss each with a few tablespoons of vinaigrette. Toss beans with ¼ cup vinaigrette. Wash and dry lettuce, combine with a few tablespoons of vinaigrette, and arrange on a serving platter. Heap the dark chicken meat in the center of the platter and arrange the julienned white meat strips over and around it. Surround with the eggs and the olives. Arrange the beans to one side, and surround with baby onions. On the other side of the chicken, arrange the apples, oranges, grapes, and raisins. Spoon the remaining vinaigrette over the fruits, beans, and chicken. Julienne the pimento and garnish the chicken. *(Serves 6)*

- Replace the chicken with julienned strips of cooked meat.
- Since Salmagundi is by definition a mélange or mishmash, use your imagination for varying the ingredients.

Three-Bean Salad

Three-bean salad is an all-time favorite American dish too often made with canned beans. The fresh beans in this version give it a new crispness and flavor.

1 ½ cups green snap beans
1 ½ cups yellow snap (wax) beans
1 ½ cups fresh shell beans
1 cup slivered green peppers
¾ cup thinly sliced red onions
1 clove garlic
⅔ cup wine vinegar
⅓ cup sugar
¼ cup olive oil
¼ cup vegetable oil
½ tsp Worcestershire sauce
1 tsp salt
⅛ tsp pepper

Trim and blanch green and yellow beans; cook shell beans; cool. Combine with green peppers and onions. Halve the garlic and place it in a jar along with the vinegar, sugar, oils, Worcestershire sauce, salt, and pepper. Shake well. Let stand for 5 minutes and shake again. Discard garlic; toss dressing with vegetables until thoroughly combined. *(Serves 4)*

- Substitute rinsed and drained canned kidney beans for shell beans.
- Make a two-bean salad: toss whole green and yellow beans together with chopped basil and olive oil–lemon juice vinaigrette sauce.

Easy Shell Bean Casserole

6 cups fresh shell beans
3 Tb butter
1 Tb oil
1 ½ cups finely sliced onions
1 ½ cups finely sliced green peppers
1 clove garlic
2 lb pork sausages or patties
1 cup beef broth
1 cup red wine
1 bay leaf
4 Tb tomato paste
Salt and freshly ground pepper

Blanch or steam the shell beans; set aside. Melt butter and oil and cook the onions and peppers until wilted, 5–10 minutes. Mince the garlic, stir it in, and sauté for 1 minute. Add to beans. Cook the sausage. Heat the broth, wine, bay leaf, and tomato paste. In a 3–4-quart ovenproof casserole, make three layers of the beans and pork, ending with pork, seasoning each layer with salt and pepper to taste. Pour on the broth mixture and bake for 1 hour in a preheated 350° oven. *(Serves 6–8)*

Cassoulet

Cassoulet is as famous in southern France as paella in Spain, chili in Texas, and clam chowder in New England. Although ingredients vary, depending upon what's available, dried beans and pork form the basis for this country dish. Rather than dried beans, I like fresh shell beans which don't need to be cooked as long. In some regions, sausage, preserved goose, and mutton are added as well. My version follows the same principle of available fare: I use fresh shell beans when we have them on hand, limit the pork to sausage, and include both lamb and chicken. If you wish to include the unparalleled taste of preserved goose, see *Julia Child & More Company*.

2 lb lamb
4 Tb oil
2 Tb butter
1 ½ cups chopped onions
2 cloves garlic
½ cup tomato purée
1 bay leaf
½ tsp thyme
2 tsp salt
½ cup white vermouth
2–2 ½ cups beef broth
6 cups fresh shell beans
1 small onion
1 strip bacon
Herb Bouquet:
   3 sprigs parsley
   1 clove garlic
   1 bay leaf
   ¼ tsp savory
4 chicken legs and thighs
¾ lb smoked or garlic sausage
2 Tb parsley
1 packed cup fresh bread crumbs

Cut the lamb into 1 ½-inch chunks and brown in 2 tablespoons of the oil and 1 tablespoon of the butter; remove from pan. In the same fat, sauté the onions until lightly browned. Chop the garlic and add to pan along with lamb, tomato purée, bay leaf, thyme, 1 teaspoon of the salt, vermouth, and enough beef broth to barely cover the meat. Bring the broth to a boil, reduce heat, cover, and simmer for 1–1 ½ hours or until the lamb is tender.

Meanwhile, cover the shell beans with water, bring to a boil, and skim. Halve the onion, and add along with the bacon, herb bouquet, and 1 teaspoon salt. Reduce heat and cook gently for 15–20 minutes until the beans are tender, but not soft. Cool in the cooking liquid.

In a large sauté pan, heat the remaining oil and butter. Cut up the chicken pieces so you have 4 leg pieces and 4 thigh pieces. Brown, and set aside. Thickly slice the sausage and, in the same pan, lightly brown. Set aside. Assemble the cassoulet in a deep, ovenproof 4-quart casserole. Line the bottom of the dish with one-third of the beans, one-third of the lamb, chicken, and sausage, and cover with one-half of the remaining beans.

Stir-Fried Snap Beans and Beef

3 Tb cornstarch
3 Tb soy sauce
1 ½ tsp sugar
5 Tb peanut oil
½ lb flank steak
1 tsp sesame oil
1 Tb sherry
1 clove garlic
1 slice fresh ginger
1 lb snap beans
¼ cup broth or water
1 scallion

Dissolve 1 tablespoon of the cornstarch in 1 tablespoon water. Combine with 1 tablespoon of the soy sauce, ½ teaspoon of the sugar, and 1 tablespoon of the peanut oil. Slice meat into ⅛-inch-thick strips and add to marinade. Let stand for at least 15 minutes. Drain before cooking.

Meanwhile, combine 2 tablespoons soy sauce, 2 tablespoons cornstarch dissolved in ⅓ cup water, 1 teaspoon sugar, sesame oil, and sherry; set aside. Heat 2 tablespoons peanut oil in a wok or sauté pan. When hot, add meat and toss until seared on all sides. Remove, drain, and set aside. Heat the remaining 2 tablespoons peanut oil in a wok. Crush garlic and toss with ginger for 1 minute without burning. Add whole tiny beans or larger beans cut into 1 ½-inch pieces, and toss with oil. Add the broth or water, and cover the pan. Steam-cook for 3–4 minutes, checking to make sure the liquid doesn't evaporate completely and the beans don't burn. Remove cover and boil off any remaining liquid. Chop scallion and add along with beef; toss together. Pour on the reserved soy sauce mixture and cook until vegetables and meat are coated with sauce. Season to taste. (*Serves 3–4*)

Pickled Dilly Beans

Uniformly sized straight beans are the most attractive choice for this nutritious snack. Let mellow for a few weeks before serving.

2 lb fresh green snap beans
4 small garlic cloves
4 heads of dill or 4 tsp dill seeds
½ tsp red pepper flakes
2 ½ cups white vinegar
2 ½ cups water
4 Tb kosher salt

Wash beans and break off the stem ends. Peel garlic. In each of 4 sterilized pint jars, put 1 garlic clove, 1 head or 1 teaspoon of dill seeds, and a pinch of red pepper. Fit beans in jars, allowing ½-inch head room at the top of each jar. (Trim beans if necessary.) Bring vinegar, water, and salt to a boil. Pour over beans, filling to within ¼ inch of the rim. Fasten jar tops according to manufacturer's directions and place in a boiling water bath, covering lids with 2 inches of water. Process at a hard boil for 5 minutes. Remove, and cool. (*Makes 4 pints*)

Add remaining meats, then cover with remaining beans. Pour in the braising liquid; it should cover the top layer of beans. (Add some of the bean cooking liquid if you need more liquid.) Chop parsley, mix with bread crumbs, and cover beans. Place in a preheated 400° oven and bake for 30 minutes. The bread crumbs will have formed a crust, which you should break into the casserole. Reduce the heat to 350° and bake for another 30 minutes, or until the dish is heated through and bubbly. (*Serves 8*)

Note: If you have refrigerated the assembled dish, add a bit more liquid and simmer it on top of the stove to warm before baking.

- For a boneless version, substitute boned chicken breasts for the legs and thighs.
- *Dietetic No-Fat Cassoulet*: Poach a chicken, cool, skin, and remove the meat from the bones. Slice and blanch assorted fresh vegetables such as green snap beans, carrots or zucchini, and peel, seed, and chop tomatoes. Prepare 1–2 cups of each vegetable. Cook shell beans as in the recipe above, and layer with the assorted vegetables and the chicken. Cover with the degreased stock in which you poached the chicken, layer with bread crumbs, and bake as in *Cassoulet*.

Beets

Have you ever enjoyed the sweet pungent flavor of a baked fresh beet? Or experienced the subtle but earthy aftertaste and delicious crunch of raw beets grated into a salad? These are but two of the lesser-known ways of preparing fresh beets, which don't enjoy the popularity they deserve. We become so accustomed to the convenience of canned beets that many of us never try fresh beets at all. Canned beets are quite acceptable, but fresh beets are infinitely better, with a distinctive deep flavor and a crisp texture that's lost in the canning process.

I often rely upon beets as a color accent: the rich red tones are always beautiful on a plate with other food. The distinctive flavor of beets is best as an accompaniment to simple dishes such as a roast or a baked fish. They're also nice served alone as a relish, appetizer, or salad.

Table beets constitute a small part of the beet family, which also includes foliage beets, Swiss chard, and the agricultural mainstays—mangel-wurzels and sugar beets. As foliage beets and Swiss chard are raised for their leaves, I'll discuss them later on under *Greens* and *Swiss Chard*. In Europe, the huge mangels, sometimes growing as large as 60 pounds, are a source of cattle and poultry fodder, but they have never been extensively cultivated in the United States. Sugar beets are another matter. Almost every American has eaten sugar processed from sucrose found in sugar beets. They're brownish white, rather than red, and too cloyingly sweet and fibrous for cooking, although they're cross-bred with table beets to give extra sweetness. (The new beet Pacemaker II, developed by the University of Wisconsin, has sugar beets in its background.)

As a gardener, you can try beets rarely found at the market: tiny spherical beets developed in Europe for

hors d'oeuvre; mild golden beets, with a bonus of fine-tasting greens that cook up like spinach; skinny, tubular beets, for uniform slices; and longstanding storage beets. In the Victory Garden, we've grown Detroit Dark Red, Pacemaker II, and Burpee's Golden Beet, along with foliage beets for greens. We plant beets right through the summer, sowing seeds five or six times for a supply of tiny beets and beet greens all season long. More seedlings will come up than you might anticipate, for beet seeds are really seed clusters, containing anywhere from three to five seeds. (Some of the newer beet introductions, such as Pacemaker II, have been bred to a single seed, making thinning easier.) Crowded seedlings result in stringy beets, so we thin at two weeks and again four weeks later, when the baby beets and greens are perfect to eat. (Occasionally, leaf miners devastate the greens, but when this happens, Russ clips off the tops and the greens grow again good as new.) About six to eight weeks after seed sowing, the plants are ready to harvest. For most cooking I prefer 1½-inch-diameter beets—at that point they're a decent cooking size yet still quite tender.

Remember that beets have a high water content and need lots of moisture while growing. Many gardeners don't realize this and are puzzled and disappointed when their beets end up dry and woody. Unlike many other vegetables, beets aren't rigorous in their demands. They're easy to grow and don't have to be harvested immediately, but stay in perfectly good condition for weeks. Of course, left in the ground for months, they'll deteriorate and become hard and wrinkled, with leathery crowns.

I harvest large beets with a spading fork, digging 6 inches away from the roots, loosening the soil so I can lift them out easily. Small beets can easily be pulled by hand. Late-season leaves are too coarse and bitter for cooking, so I cut them off 2–3 inches from the crown and throw them on the compost pile. These inches of stem are necessary because beets bleed when the tops are trimmed too closely or when their skin is torn or punctured in any fashion. Often gardeners carefully harvest beets, then meticulously trim the root tips, negating all they did before. Leave 2 inches of the tips on the beets and be gentle. The water content of beets makes them more delicate than they appear: bruising will shorten their storage life. I shake the roots free of soil and store them without washing, for wet beets tend to rot.

Before cooking beets, trim the stems to within 1 inch of the crowns and wash, making sure you don't scrub so vigorously you tear the skins. If beets are cooked in their skins, they bleed less, although they'll always bleed no matter how careful you are. (Their red pigmentation soon may be commercially important: researchers are experimenting with methods to make beets the major source of red food coloring, now that some other dyes have been taken off the market.)

Baking beets is the best way to retain their flavor and juices, but requires the longest cooking time. Steaming is a very satisfactory method, for there's only a slight loss of flavor and the cooking time is shorter. Baking a 1½-inch beet takes an hour at 300° while the same beet steamed takes 40 minutes. Boiling beets is the least satisfactory method of all, because so much color and flavor is lost in the water. So, try baking and steaming beets—you'll be amazed at the difference.

Beets are done when pressure upon their skins causes them to move. To be sure they are tender you can test with a sharp pointed knife or a fork but remember some color and juice will run out. I think beets are easiest to peel when they've cooled a little; just run them under cold water, as you would with hard-boiled eggs, and their skins should slip right off with the slightest pressure. If the skins are hard to remove, the beets probably need to cook longer. An exception is freshly harvested tiny beets, which can be almost impossible to peel, as I found out to my chagrin one summer at the restaurant. Our local farm stand supplied us with a bushel of baby beets. We cooked them and started to peel: the skins stayed tight as a drum. The entire kitchen staff spent the afternoon patiently skinning the beets with knives. (Of course, had I been cooking for my family, I would have just left the skins on, for they're barely noticeable on such tender beets.)

Marketing

Beets sold at the market should have fresh-looking leaves and at least 2 inches of stems. If you're planning to eat the greens, select those with small leaves; by the time the leaves are 6–8 inches long, they're inedible. Pass by any with dented or bruised flesh or a pale color. Look for a bunch of equal-size medium beets so they'll cook evenly: larger beets take longer to cook and could be tough.

◇ Baked Beets

Trim and wash whole beets, leaving skins on. Put beets into an ovenproof pan, cover, and bake at 300° until tender. Count on 1 hour for a 1½-inch beets. Beets cook best at a low temperature, but when you're baking other dishes at a higher temperature, such as 350° or 375°, add approximately ¼ inch water and check occasionally to make sure the water doesn't evaporate.
Note: High-temperature roasting of beets without water results in a richer, almost charred flavor.

◇ Steamed Beets

Wash beets, taking care not to puncture the skin. Put 1 inch of water in steamer and bring to a boil. Place beets on a rack or in a colander, cover tightly, and steam until

Special Information

Yields
- 5 2–2½-inch trimmed whole beets = 1 lb = 2½ cups cooked
- Baby beets = 1 inch and under
  Small beets = 1–1½ inches
  Medium beets = 1½–2½ inches
  Large beets = 2½ inches and over

Storage and Preserving
- Left in the refrigerator vegetable bin, beets stay in good condition for 2–3 weeks. For longer storage, layer in sand in a cool, moist cellar with a temperature below 45°. I find that higher temperatures cause beets to lose moisture and shrivel up.
- Canning is a good way to preserve beets. To can, cook beets, remove skin, and pack immediately in hot sterilized jars, leaving ½ inch headroom. Cover with boiling water and 1 tablespoon vinegar to preserve color. Adjust lids and process in a pressure canner at 10 pounds pressure for 30–35 minutes. Check seals when removed from canner and tighten if necessary.
- Frozen beets lose texture.

Hints
- Grate raw beets into a salad.

- Hard water may cause beet color to fade, but you can correct this by adding a little vinegar to the boiling water.
- Steam or boil beets with cloves in the water. The beets will pick up a slight clove fragrance.
- Always mix beets with other ingredients just before serving so the color doesn't bleed over other ingredients.
- Bake in aluminum foil: you'll have no pots to clean.

Microwave
- 1 pound whole beets (5 beets 2–2½ inches across) placed in a covered dish with ¼ cup liquid will cook tender in 10–11 minutes. A fast and easy way to cook beets.

Leftovers
- Pickle leftover cooked beets (see *Pickled Beets*).
- Use in composed salads (see *Beets Vinaigrette*). They go particularly well with endive and potatoes. For a German touch, toss with caraway seeds, onions, ground cloves, sugar, and vinegar.
- Any leftover whole beets can be hollowed out and filled with egg or ham salad and served as an appetizer or luncheon dish. Or make *Red Flannel Hash*.
- Turn into a purée.

tender. Count on 40 minutes for a 1½-inch beet fresh from the garden.

- Flavor the steaming liquid by adding the juice and peel of an orange, along with a pinch of mace or nutmeg, or try apple skin, grated lemon rind, and a cinnamon stick. After the beets are cooked, reduce the liquid to a syrup, strain, and coat the beets.

◇ *Boiled Beets*

Cover trimmed and washed beets with warm water. Bring to a boil, reduce heat, and simmer gently, partially covered, until tender. Count on 25–30 minutes for a 1½-inch beet.

Finishing Touches for Cooked Beets

- *With Butter:* Reheat in melted butter. Two and one-half cups beets would take approximately 2–3 tablespoons butter. Season with salt, pepper, and fresh lemon juice.
- *With Cream:* Coat 2½ cups beets with ¼ cup heavy cream mixed with ¼ cup sour cream and warm together without boiling. Garnish with chopped parsley or dill.
- *With Vinaigrette:* Peel, slice, and serve warm dressed to taste with *Vinaigrette Sauce* (see *Appendix*).

Beets with Cream Sauce

Try this rich combination of beets and cream when you have a simple main dish such as ham or pot roast.

    2 cups sliced cooked beets
    2 Tb butter
    2 Tb flour
    ⅔ cup beet juices or chicken stock (or combination
        of both)
    ⅓ cup heavy cream
    Salt and freshly ground pepper
    Nutmeg

Place beets in a small buttered casserole. Melt butter in saucepan, add flour, stirring, and cook for 3 minutes without coloring. Remove from heat and beat in beet juices or stock, then cook until smooth and thick. Add cream, heat, and season with salt, pepper, and a pinch of nutmeg. Pour over beets and heat in a 350° oven until the sauce is bubbly and beets are heated through. (Or gently simmer on top of the stove until beets are heated through.) *(Serves 4)*

- Sprinkle beets with ½ cup grated Swiss or Parmesan cheese, or combination of both, and brown under broiler.
- Mix beets with other vegetables such as sliced cooked potatoes, carrots, turnips—or whatever you have on

hand—and prepare half again as much sauce as vegetables.
- Add 2–3 tablespoons chopped fresh dill before serving.

Baby Beets and Beet Greens

This, my favorite beet recipe, uses both the tender greens and the baby beets. We look forward to it with each new planting.

    12–16 baby beets, ½–1 inch in diameter
    Greens from these beets
    2 Tb shallots (optional)
    5 Tb butter
    2 Tb olive oil
    Salt and freshly ground pepper

Cut stems and leaves 1 inch above beet crowns, and put leaves aside. Wash beets, steam for approximately 15 minutes or just until tender, peel if desired, and set aside.

Meanwhile, wash beet leaves, discarding any that are dried out or have thick stalks. Drain, and spin or pat dry. Cut the leaves and small stalks diagonally into ½-inch slices, or, if very small, leave whole. Chop shallots (if you wish to use them) and add to 2 tablespoons butter and the olive oil in a frying pan or wok; cook for 2 minutes, or until slightly colored. Add the beet greens and sauté for 2–3 minutes, stirring, until they wilt and become tender. Season with salt and pepper and set aside. While greens are cooking, reheat beets in 3 tablespoons butter. Serve them next to a bed of sautéed greens. *(Serves 4)*

- Prepare this dish with horticultural beet greens (see *Greens*) and standard-size beets that have been sliced or diced.
- Serve vinegar in a cruet to pour over this combination beet dish.

Grated Sautéed Beets

This recipe is simplicity itself: grate peeled or small, unpeeled raw beets and you're all set to cook. The beets retain a slight crunch and all of their basic flavor.

>4 medium beets
>4 Tb butter
>Fresh lemon juice
>Salt and freshly ground pepper
>Chopped fresh dill or parsley

Wash, peel, and coarsely grate beets. In a covered frying pan, melt butter, add beets, and stir to coat with butter, then sprinkle with lemon juice to taste. Cover and cook over medium to low heat for approximately 10 minutes, checking occasionally to see that the beets don't burn. (You could add a few spoonfuls of stock or water to prevent sticking.) Cook just until tender, then season with salt, pepper, and additional lemon juice if needed. Sprinkle with dill or parsley. *(Serves 4)*

* You can also cook beets before grating, or use leftover cooked beets.
* Grate other vegetables, such as cabbage, carrots, and parsnips, cook separately, and arrange in mounds on a vegetable platter.

One-Step Baked Beets

These beets go directly from sink to oven. Wait until just before baking to cut them up, as they dry out easily.

>4 large or 6 medium beets
>1 medium onion
>1/3 cup stock or hot water
>3 Tb butter
>Salt and freshly ground pepper

Thinly slice raw peeled or small unpeeled beets, and chop onion. Layer beets and onions in a small buttered casserole. Pour in hot stock or water, dot beets with butter, and season with salt and pepper. Cover and bake in a preheated 350° oven for 30–60 minutes, depending upon the age of the beets. *(Serves 4)*

* *Sliced Baked Beets with Orange:* Omit onions and add the grated rind and juice from 1 orange, layering throughout. Pour the juice over and bake.
* Or, layer thinly sliced orange or apple in moderate amounts so you don't overpower the beets.

Pickled Beets

Pickled beets are a favorite at our house; my daughter, Vicki, even asks me to put them up for her when she heads back to college. They're tasty on an appetizer tray, as an accompaniment to cold meat, or as a diet snack.

>4 cups cooked beets
>1 medium onion (optional)
>1 cup cider or wine vinegar
>1 cup beet juice or water, or combination of both
>1/4 cup sugar

Peel and slice cooked beets; chop onion, if you like, and mix with beets. Heat vinegar, beet juice or water, and sugar just long enough to dissolve the sugar, and pour over beets. Cool at room temperature, then refrigerate for 4–6 hours before serving. They'll keep a week or even longer, but the beets will gradually soften. *(Makes 1 quart)*

Beet Tartar

If you're fond of steak Tartar, I think you'll like this version with the surprise of pickled beets. It's lovely arranged on individual wooden dinner planks with ingredients encircling the meat. Or mix together and serve on lettuce with black bread on the side.

>1 large egg
>1 lb ground steak or extra-lean beef
>1 1/2 cups finely chopped pickled beets
>3 Tb finely chopped onions
>3 Tb finely chopped capers
>1/4 cup heavy cream
>1 tsp salt
>Freshly ground pepper

Beat egg, add ground meat, and mix well with fork. Add finely chopped beets, onions, and capers to meat along with cream, salt, and pepper. Let sit for 15 minutes to meld flavors if desired. *(Serves 3)*

Beets Vinaigrette

With beets vinaigrette on hand you can concoct a variety of salads. Recently we traveled to Holland, France, and England. Almost everywhere we went our luncheon salad plates featured beets vinaigrette. In France we had beets that were baked, then chunked and marinated before serving. Other times the beets were julienned, grated, or sliced, but each presentation exploited to the utmost the lovely look of beets.

>2 cups cooked beets
>1/4 cup chopped scallions (optional)
>1/2 cup *Vinaigrette Sauce* (page 352)

Grate, slice, julienne, or chunk the beets. Add scallions if you wish. Mix together with vinaigrette sauce. *(Serves 4)*

* *Beet and Endive Salad:* Surround *Beets Vinaigrette* with endive spears in vinaigrette.
* *Beet and Watercress Salad:* Mix watercress with vinaigrette and arrange with *Beets Vinaigrette* on top.
* *Beet and Turnip Salad:* Prepare *Beets Vinaigrette* and *Tart Turnip and Rutabaga Salad* (see *Turnips*). Arrange side by side and decorate with watercress.
* *Beet Luncheon Plate:* Use *Beets Vinaigrette*, potato salad, cabbage slaw, and pickled carrot sticks.
* *Beet and Celeriac Salad:* Place *Beets Vinaigrette* in the center of a platter, surround with *Celeriac* in a *Mustard–Sour Cream Dressing* (see page 71), and decorate with carrot curls. Serve with toast triangles.

- *Beet Appetizer Plate:* Arrange *Beets Vinaigrette,* hard-boiled eggs, chopped onions, capers, and smoked salmon, and serve with thinly sliced black bread and butter.

Russian Beet and Potato Salad

Sheryl Julian, food writer for the *Boston Phoenix,* is not only a fine journalist and cook but also shares her recipes. Thanks to her for this unusual salad.

> *Vinaigrette Sauce* (page 352)
> 4–5 medium beets
> 2 medium potatoes
> 1/4 cup chopped parsley
> 1/3 cup chopped scallions
> 1 cucumber
> 1 dill or half-sour pickle
> Salt and freshly ground pepper

Make vinaigrette sauce without garlic and put in a large bowl. Cook beets until tender, drain, rinse in cold water, and slip off skins. Dice into 1/2-inch cubes and set aside. Cook potatoes until just tender. Peel as soon as they can be handled and while still warm cut them into 1/2-inch cubes. Mix with vinaigrette along with parsley and scallions. Peel cucumber, score flesh with fork, cut in half, and remove seeds with spoon. Chop into 1/2-inch dice. Chop pickle into 1/2-inch dice. Add cucumber and pickle to potatoes and mix gently. Just before serving mix beets with potato mixture and season to taste. *(Serves 4)*

Scandinavian Beet Salad

No Scandinavian smorgasbord would be complete without a mixed beet salad. This version makes an excellent light luncheon or supper dish as well. Dice all the vegetables the same size for best appearance.

> 1–1 1/2 cups diced cooked potatoes
> 1 cup diced cooked carrots

> 1 onion, diced
> 1 large tart apple, diced
> 2 cups diced cooked beets
> *Cream Salad Dressing* (page 347)
> Salt and freshly ground pepper
> 1/2–3/4 cup marinated herring (optional)

Combine potatoes, carrots, onion, and apple. Add beets just before serving and fold in cream dressing. Season with salt and pepper. Top with well-drained sliced herring if you like. *(Serves 6–8)*

- Scandinavians use this salad as a jumping-off point for dozens of variations. Try it with peas, beans, corn, and meat.

Chilled Beet and Cucumber Soup

Fix this soup early in the morning on a hot summer's day. It's light, yet filling, and easy to prepare.

> 2 cups coarsely grated raw beets
> 1/2 cup coarsely grated onions
> 2 cups beef stock
> 2 cups chicken stock
> 3 cups finely chopped cooked beets
> 2 cups finely chopped peeled, seeded cucumber
> 2 Tb wine vinegar
> 1/4 tsp grated horseradish
> Salt and freshly ground pepper
> Sour cream
> Thin cucumber slices
> Fresh chives

Add raw beets and onions to beef and chicken stock, bring to boil in a saucepan, and simmer for 40 minutes. Strain through a sieve or colander, pressing down to extract all the juices. Combine beets and cucumber with strained broth, vinegar, and horseradish. Season to taste. Chill. Just before serving, garnish each portion with a spoonful of sour cream, a thin cucumber slice, and a touch of minced chives. *(Serves 6–8)*

- You can substitute equal parts beet juice and chicken stock to make 1 quart broth instead of simmering the beets and onions in stock.
- Vegetables can be minced in food processor.

Beet Borscht

In Eastern Europe, where borscht is king, you could eat a different borscht every week of the year, and each would be authentic. Although borscht is thought of as a beet dish, the word means any soup made with a variety of vegetables.

My version is easy to fix, yet retains the qualities found in a more time-consuming preparation. I flavor with kvas, a traditional fermented beet liquid, but it's not necessary; substitute lemon juice if you wish. Notice that the vegetables are simmered to preserve the red color of the beets; boiling turns them sienna brown. Borscht ages well; in fact, my family prefers it the next day or even later in the week. Served with sour cream, black bread, and sweet butter, you'll have a hearty and satisfying meal.

2 thick slices bacon
1 large onion
2 stalks celery
1 large beet
2 cloves garlic
2 cups fresh tomato pulp or canned plum tomatoes
1 cup peeled and chopped potatoes
1 qt beef stock
1 qt water
3 peppercorns
6 sprigs parsley
1 tsp salt
2 cups julienned or coarsely grated beets
1 cup julienned or coarsely grated carrots
4 Tb butter
3 cups shredded cabbage
Freshly ground pepper
Kvas (see recipe below) or fresh lemon juice
Fresh dill (optional)
Sour cream

Chop bacon, blanch for 5 minutes in boiling water, drain, and dry thoroughly. Lightly brown bacon in a frying pan. Remove bacon and reserve the fat. Chop onion and celery and sauté in bacon fat until barely wilted and lightly colored. Wash and grate beet, and halve garlic.

Place the bacon, onion, celery, beet, garlic, tomatoes, potatoes, stock, water, peppercorns, parsley, and salt into a large soup pot. Bring to a boil, then turn heat down and simmer uncovered for 45 minutes. Remove vegetables and put through the finest disk of a food mill, sieve, or food processor, discarding the pulp and seeds. Add the purée to the broth.

Sauté julienned beets and carrots in 2 tablespoons butter for 5 minutes. Add to the soup base and simmer for 15 minutes. While the vegetables are cooking, braise cabbage in remaining 2 tablespoons butter in a large frying pan, stirring occasionally, for 5 minutes or until wilted and slightly colored. Add to soup and simmer 15 minutes longer. Taste for seasoning, add pepper and salt if necessary; add sufficient kvas or lemon juice to give a slightly tart, but not sour, taste. Just before serving, heat to boiling and add dill if you like. Dish up with a spoonful of sour cream on each serving. (The dill can also be passed as a garnish.) *(Makes 2 quarts)*

- For a heartier meal, simmer 1 pound brisket, 1 pound meaty shinbone, and 1 teaspoon salt in 2 quarts water or combination water and beef stock for 1 hour. Then simmer vegetables in this meat stock for 45 minutes, as above. When straining, reserve meat to add to finished soup.

- Combine other vegetables such as parsnips, celeriac, beans, and turnips with the basic vegetable mixture, and proceed as above.
- To further thicken soup, mash a cooked potato into broth.
- For a light, clear broth, cook all the vegetables at one time and strain them out: the resulting clear soup is good hot or cold. Let the soup sit unstrained for a few hours to intensify the flavor.

Note: If your soup boiled and the beet red has turned to brown, grate a raw beet into a saucepan, cover it with boiling water and 2 tablespoons vinegar, bring to a boil, and remove from heat. Leave it for 30 minutes and then strain into the soup. The borscht will become red again.

Kvas
8–10 beets, peeled
½ cup milk
2 slices bread (preferably rye or whole wheat)

Chop beets, place in a crock or glass container, cover with lukewarm water, add milk, and top with bread. Cover and keep in a warm place until fermented. It will take anywhere from 24 hours to 3 days to ferment, although you can speed up the fermentation by placing near the pilot light on a stove. Strain and store in a glass container in the refrigerator until ready to use. Kvas will keep refrigerated for a week or two.

Kvas can be used to flavor and color other dishes as well. Substitute for lemon juice or vinegar in dishes such as *Russian-Style Hearty Cabbage Soup* or *Marinated Red Cabbage Relish*.

Red Flannel Hash

New England red flannel hash takes leftover corned beef, potatoes, and beets and gives them a new life. I serve it topped with poached eggs and pass the ketchup. The ratio of corned beef to potatoes and beets is optional: use whatever you have on hand.

2 thickly sliced pieces of bacon
1 large onion
4 Tb butter
2 cups (1 lb) coarsely chopped corned beef
2–3 cups coarsely chopped cooked potatoes
2 cups coarsely chopped cooked beets
4 Tb heavy cream
2–3 Tb chopped parsley
Salt and freshly ground pepper

Fry bacon in a large frying pan; crumble into small pieces, and save the bacon fat. Chop onion and sauté in 2 tablespoons butter until golden and tender. Mix corned beef, potatoes, and beets with sautéed onion, cream, and parsley; season with salt and pepper. Heat the bacon fat and add 2 tablespoons butter, or enough butter for 6 tablespoons combined. Add the hash mixture, press down in pan, and cook at a medium-low temperature until the bottom forms a crust. Turn over and cook another 20–30 minutes to blend flavors. Serve immediately. *(Serves 4–6)*

• Don't be inhibited by New England tradition. Add other leftover vegetables such as cooked cabbage and carrots.

Same-Day Beet Relish

This simple relish can be eaten on the same day it's prepared.

1 lb cooked beets
1 oz grated horseradish, or more to taste
1/2 tsp Dijon mustard
1 Tb sugar
Salt and freshly ground pepper
3 Tb red wine vinegar
1 cup yogurt or sour cream

Coarsely grate beets and mix with horseradish. Beat together the mustard, sugar, salt, pepper, and vinegar and mix with the beets. Fold in the yogurt or sour cream. Serve cold. *(Makes about 2 cups)*

Beet Chutney

Chutney, from the Hindi word *chatni*, refers to a condiment or pickle of Indian origin. Although this chutney is spicy, the beet flavor is not overpowered. Change the recipe, with nuts, currants, or other spices to suit your fancy.

2–3 lb cooked beets
2–3 medium onions
1/2 lb seedless raisins
1 tsp salt
1 cup brown sugar
1 1/2 cups cider vinegar
6 cloves
1 tsp allspice
1/2 tsp mace or nutmeg
6 peppercorns

Peel and dice beets; set aside. Chop onions and raisins and place into a saucepan along with salt, sugar, and vinegar. Tie spices in cheesecloth, add to mixture, bring to a boil, cover, and simmer until onions are tender, about 20 minutes. Add the diced beets and continue cooking until mixture has softened but the beets retain some texture. Remove spice bag and pour chutney into hot sterilized jars; cover and seal. If you're using within a week or two, there's no need to sterilize—just cool to room temperature, cover, and refrigerate. Serve chilled. *(Makes about 1 quart)*

Broccoli

Sixty years ago in America, virtually no one outside the Italian community ate broccoli. Then one day some enterprising Italian market gardeners in California shipped crates of broccoli packed in ice express to Boston, sparking an interest in broccoli as a commercial crop. Even then—long before modern refrigerated cars—broccoli shipped well enough to be an excellent out-of-season fresh vegetable.

Although I'm the first person to insist that every vegetable tastes best eaten directly from the garden, I must admit that the fresh broccoli I buy during the winter is almost as good as our home-grown kind. I consider fresh broccoli far superior to frozen broccoli because inevitably frozen broccoli is overblanched and has lost its crisp texture. Also, cooking with fresh broccoli allows separate preparation of the flowerets and stalks: one night I'll serve the blanched flowerets in a lemon butter sauce, and a day later will julienne equal amounts of broccoli stems, carrots, and turnips, which I'll then sauté in butter for a brilliantly colored vegetable trio.

The rest of the year we eat broccoli fresh from our garden. In March, Russ sows seeds of Premium Crop broccoli indoors in a 4-inch pot. When the seedlings reach 1 inch high, he transplants them to individual six-packs, burying them half their length in the packs to make the seedlings more vigorous. After three weeks, he hardens off the seedlings in a cold frame, where they stay until April when he transplants them into the garden.

Because broccoli is a heavy feeder, Russ enriches the soil with compost, rotted cow manure, and 10-10-10 fertilizer, and adds limestone to counteract clubroot disease. He spaces the plants 18 inches apart and interplants with lettuce seedlings which will be long gone by the time the broccoli needs the room. If it looks as though cabbageworm caterpillars will be a problem, Russ sprays the crop with *Bacillus thüringiensis*, a pesticide which is nontoxic to humans but fatal to chewing insects. He uses this at 7–10-day intervals until the final harvest, and keeps a close watch for root maggots.

In June he sows seeds directly in the garden for a second broccoli crop, preparing the ground as before. By mid-June the April planting is ready to be harvested. Broccoli should be harvested while the buds are blue-green in color and the buds are tightly compressed. Any light yellow flowers among the buds are a tip-off that the flowerets are too mature.

We harvest the broccoli with a sharp knife, cutting it just below the bud clusters and severing the head from the main stem. The plants continue to produce smaller shoots from the main stem to be harvested later on in the summer. When this broccoli crop is finished, the May planting will be ready and carries us through until frost.

When I'm preparing broccoli, I first rinse it and, if necessary, soak in warm salted water to flush out any aphids. Although I usually prepare the stems and flowerets separately, I sometimes cook them together too. I'll leave the peeled stalks whole with the flowerets still attached, which makes a particularly attractive presentation with hollandaise sauce.

Regardless of how the broccoli is prepared, peeling the stems is the secret of even cooking; it completely changes the cooking time. As with asparagus, once peeled, the stems cook in approximately the same time as the flowerets.

Unless I am using the broccoli whole, I cut it about 2½ inches below the top of the flowerets, or where the stalk branches into small stems. These stems should be peeled by inserting a paring knife blade under the skin at the stem base and pulling up. The skin pulls off easily, breaking off at the base of the buds. I use a knife to peel and trim the stalks by cutting away the skin and the coarse upper layer of flesh. This leaves me with pale, tender-fleshed inner stalks.

Wait to peel the broccoli until you're going to use it, because peeled broccoli skin dries up and toughens. If you must prepare the broccoli ahead of time, keep it in a perforated plastic bag in the refrigerator.

Cut the peeled broccoli into any size you fancy, depending upon the recipe. I halve or quarter the stems lengthwise, julienne them for a mixed vegetable sauté, or chop them into larger or small pieces as the recipes dictate.

For stir-fries, I'll slice the whole peeled stalk across into ¼-inch slices. As you can tell, the cutting techniques are numerous—just remember to peel!

Generally, I blanch rather than steam broccoli, because blanching takes only a few minutes and it's easier to test for doneness. (Steaming takes twice as long, and I am forever peering into a steamy pot to test it.) You can blanch broccoli in advance, cool, dry, and refrigerate it—but don't hold it too long or it will develop a mushy texture.

Sometimes, you'll read suggestions to braise raw broccoli in wine or butter in a covered pan until tender. I have tried it that way, but, although the flavor is good, the broccoli loses its beautiful green color. I would rather blanch the broccoli, then reheat it in butter or a light olive oil.

Marketing

Shop at a market which keeps broccoli cool either in refrigerated cases or on ice. Properly stored broccoli will have closely bunched blue-green flowerets and firm and resilient stalks. Any woody stalks with noticeable open cores at the base will be tough and hollow. A sign of age is yellow flower buds and loosely bunched heads. This broccoli most likely will be strongly flavored and odoriferous. Reject as well limp, tired-looking heads—they have lost all texture and it can never be revived.

◇ *Blanched Broccoli*

Wash, cut, and peel broccoli as illustrated. Bring a pot of salted water to a boil, adding 1½ teaspoons salt per quart of water. Quarter the large flowerets lengthwise; slice the larger stalks ½ inch thick, then cut into 1½–2-inch pieces. When I cook whole stalks I peel them and cut them lengthwise into even-size pieces if they are very large. Add the broccoli (if the stalk pieces are considerably larger than the flowerets, add them 1–2 minutes earlier). Return water to a boil, covering the pan so that the water returns to the boil rapidly. Boil, uncovered, for 3–5 minutes, depending on the size of the broccoli pieces. Trimmed whole, peeled broccoli with stalks ½ inch thick cooks in 4–5 minutes. Test for doneness by piercing the stalks with a knife point. The knife will pierce easily, but the broccoli will still remain crunchy. Taste to make sure: tender but textured broccoli is your aim. Remove from water with a mesh strainer, or cook in a vegetable basket for easier removal. Work gently, because the flowerets bruise easily. Then place the broccoli in a large strainer for a moment to remove any extra moisture. If you plan to use it later, cool by plunging immediately into cold water; drain, and pat dry. Reheat broccoli by immersing in boiling water until heated through.

◇ *Steamed Broccoli*

Wash, cut, and peel broccoli, see above.

Bring ¾–1 inch of water to a boil in a steamer. Fill the steamer basket with broccoli, placing the larger stalk pieces on the bottom, and set over water. Cover, and steam until tender. Steaming usually takes twice as long as blanching. Depending upon its size and age, broccoli will cook in 8–15 minutes.

Finishing Touches for Blanched or Steamed Broccoli

- *With Butter:* Arrange hot broccoli on a warm serving plate, dot with butter, sprinkle with salt and pepper, and garnish with lemon wedges. (Or omit the butter, and dress with lemon juice or vinegar.)
- *With Black Butter:* Melt 6 tablespoons butter until foamy, then cook until nutty brown. Pour over 4 cups hot broccoli.
- *With Crumbs:* Heat 8 tablespoons butter, add ½ cup fresh bread crumbs, and sauté until crumbs are lightly browned. Spoon over 4 cups broccoli, and season to taste.
- *With Garlic:* Cook 6 tablespoons butter until foamy, then cook until nutty brown. Toss in 2 teaspoons finely chopped garlic, and swirl together. Do not let garlic brown; pour over 4 cups broccoli. Replace some of the butter with oil if you prefer.
- *With Pine Nuts:* Melt 6 ounces of butter in a sauté pan until lightly browned; stir in ½ cup of toasted pine nuts. Pour over 4 cups broccoli.
- *In Butter Sauces:* Make ¾ cup *Lemon Butter Sauce* or *White Butter Sauce* (see *Appendix*) for each 4 cups broccoli.
- *With Hollandaise Sauce:* For each 4 cups broccoli, make 1 cup *Hollandaise Sauce* (see *Appendix*). Lighten sauce, if desired, by folding in whipped heavy cream or yogurt.

- *With Vinaigrette Sauce:* Try warm broccoli dressed with well-flavored *Vinaigrette Sauce* (see *Appendix*). To serve cool, place broccoli in cold water, drain, and lay on toweling to absorb water. Dress with vinaigrette. Also, toss crispy broccoli with cooked shell beans, red onion, and a vinaigrette sauce.
- *With Bacon:* Fry 2–3 slices of bacon until crisp; drain. Brown ½ cup fresh bread crumbs in 6 tablespoons bacon fat or butter, and combine with crumbled bacon. Toss with 4 cups buttered broccoli.
- *With Cheese:* Toss buttered broccoli with grated Parmesan or Romano cheese. Then, layer broccoli in baking dish with butter and additional cheese. Cover, and cook in a preheated 350° oven until bubbly. Remove cover, and lightly brown under the broiler.
- *With Anchovies:* Blanch broccoli; layer a baking dish with olive oil (¼ cup per 4 cups cooked broccoli), salt and pepper, mozzarella or Provolone cheese to taste, and anchovies. Drizzle with oil. Cover and heat through in a preheated 350° oven. If desired, add wine for flavoring.
- *With Wine:* Heat ¼ cup olive oil in a sauté pan, add 1 teaspoon chopped garlic, and cook for 30 seconds. Heat 4 cups broccoli in oil and garlic. Remove, and keep warm. Pour in 1–1½ cups dry white wine, and reduce to ½ cup by boiling rapidly. Pour over the broccoli.

Special Information

Yields
- A ½-pound bunch of broccoli = approximately 6 cups raw trimmed pieces
- A 1½-pound bunch of broccoli = 4 cups cooked = 4–5 servings

Storage and Preserving
- Keep unwashed from the garden or market, trimming only the large leaves. Store in a perforated plastic bag in the refrigerator, where it will keep 2–3 days. Blanched broccoli may be refrigerated, covered, but it quickly loses texture.

Freezing
- Wash, trim, peel, and cut lengthwise into ¾-inch-thick pieces. Blanch for 3 minutes, and plunge into cold water for 3 minutes. Drain and pack into freezer bags. It will keep 6–12 months at 0°.

Hints
- Peel, peel, peel . . .
- Serve raw in a crudités platter or as a diet snack.

- Add the peeled stalks, thinly sliced diagonally, to stir-fries.
- Use both the sliced, peeled stalks and the flowerets in *Vegetable Tempura* (see *Mixed Vegetables*).
- Use raw, peeled stems cut in quarter-size pieces in many Chinese recipes as a substitute for water chestnuts.
- Substitute broccoli in cauliflower recipes.
- Look at cauliflower *Finishing Touches*. Practically all will work for broccoli.
- Treat purple cauliflower like broccoli (see *Cauliflower*) and use in any of these recipes.
- Use julienned blanched broccoli stalks as a clear soup garnish.

Microwave
- A 1½-pound bunch of broccoli, washed, peeled, and divided into stem pieces and flowerets, placed in a covered dish with ½ cup liquid cooks done in 5–7 minutes. Cooking more than 5 minutes causes loss of color.

◇ *Sautéed Chopped Broccoli*

This is the preliminary step for almost all recipes for broccoli combined with sauces and other ingredients.

Wash, peel, and blanch a 1½-pound bunch of broccoli, undercooking by 1 minute. Drain, and chop into small pieces, approximately ¼ inch in size. (If you are making ahead, cool the broccoli, drain on a towel, then chop and store it in the refrigerator.) Heat 4–6 tablespoons butter in a sauté pan, add chopped broccoli, and toss until entirely coated with butter and heated through. Season with salt and pepper. Serve, or use one of the treatments below.

Finishing Touches for Sautéed Chopped Broccoli

- *With Cream:* Reduce 1 cup heavy cream until it coats the broccoli. For a thicker consistency, sprinkle on 1 tablespoon flour before adding the cream, and simmer for 3–4 minutes.
- *With Mornay Sauce:* This is our never-fail Thanksgiving vegetable. Make a *Mornay Sauce* (see *Appendix*). Butter a 6-cup baking dish and drizzle ¼ cup sauce on the pan bottom. Layer broccoli and sauce twice, ending with sauce. Sprinkle with grated cheese and dot with butter. Bake in a preheated 375° oven for 30 minutes.
- *With Sour Cream:* Combine sour cream, horseradish, vinegar, salt, and pepper. Serve with hot broccoli.
- *With Poached Eggs:* Use broccoli as a base for poached eggs, and top with *Hollandaise Sauce* (see *Appendix*). See also *Leftovers*, below.

Leftovers
- Broccoli is wonderful with eggs: add to omelets and quiches.
- Here's our favorite breakfast: butter small ramekins or 6-ounce Pyrex dishes. Put a layer of leftover *Sautéed Chopped Broccoli* (above) in each container; pour in 1 tablespoon heavy cream. Break in 1–2 eggs, top with 1 tablespoon cream, and sprinkle with grated Swiss cheese. Dot with butter, place in a pan, and pour boiling water halfway up the sides. Bake in a preheated 375° oven for 10–12 minutes (less if you prefer your eggs runny).
- Add to mixed dishes, such as a pasta, sausage, cream, and cheese casserole.
- Mix *Sautéed Chopped Broccoli* (above) with mashed potatoes, and make croquettes or patties.
- Use in soufflés: see *Spinach Soufflé* under *Spinach*.
- Make *Broccoli Morsels* (above).

◇ *Julienned Broccoli Stalks*

Peel stalks down to pale, tender flesh, then julienne into equal-size ¼-inch sticks. Blanch for 1–2 minutes, drain, and reheat in butter. Season with salt, pepper, and lemon juice.
- Combine blanched julienned broccoli with equal parts blanched julienned carrot, turnip, or rutabaga. Sauté in butter.
- Add to a mixed vegetable soup.
- Blanch, cool, toss with *Vinaigrette Sauce* (see *Appendix*), and mound on a composed salad plate.

Broccoli Morsels

This unusual vegetable accompaniment is also good nestled into a plate of spaghetti. Make smaller for cocktail tidbits, or serve as a cold snack.

> 2 large eggs
> 2 cups blanched broccoli chopped into ¼-inch pieces
> 1½ cups fresh bread crumbs
> ½–1 cup freshly grated cheese (such as Swiss, mozzarella, Parmesan, or a combination)
> Salt and freshly ground pepper
> 1 tsp finely minced garlic (optional)
> ⅓ cup vegetable oil

Beat eggs and combine with all the ingredients except oil. Form into 1½-inch balls. Heat oil in a sauté pan, cook broccoli until browned on all sides, approximately 5 minutes, and drain. (*Makes sixteen 1½-inch balls*)
- *Cauliflower Morsels.* Substitute cauliflower for broccoli.

Individual Broccoli Mousses

> 1 lb broccoli
> 2–3 Tb butter
> ½ cup heavy cream
> Salt and freshly ground pepper
> 1 Tb lemon juice
> 4 eggs
> *Tomato Cream Sauce* (page 317) or *Lemon Butter Sauce* (page 346)

Wash, trim, and peel broccoli (page 29). Blanch half as long as usual, 2–3 minutes, so that it is slightly underdone. Drain broccoli and chop into ¼-inch pieces. In a frying pan, heat butter and sauté broccoli until moisture evaporates and broccoli is lightly coated with butter. Add cream, salt, pepper, and lemon juice; then reduce cream until it just coats the broccoli, about 5–6 minutes. Put broccoli in a food processor or blender, and purée, adding the eggs one at a time. Season to taste. Butter six 6-ounce Pyrex baking molds or ramekins and pour in the broccoli mixture. Set in baking pan and pour boiling water halfway up the sides of the molds. Bake in a preheated 375° oven for 20–25 minutes or until a toothpick inserted in the center tests clean. Unmold, and serve with choice of sauces. (*Serves 6*)

Broccoli Custard

You can make a smooth-textured custard using puréed broccoli as in the *Cauliflower Mold with Carrots* recipe (page 66), but sautéed broccoli pieces give a rougher texture I like.

    1 cup chopped onions
    2 Tb butter
    1 tsp finely minced garlic (optional)
    2–3 cups *Sautéed Chopped Broccoli* (page 31)
    1 cup grated mozzarella and Parmesan cheeses
    1 cup medium cream
    8 large eggs
    Salt and freshly ground pepper

Sauté onions in the butter until golden. Add garlic if you wish; cook for 30 seconds. Combine with the broccoli, cheeses, and cream. Beat the eggs and stir into the broccoli mixture. Season to taste. Pour into a deep, buttered 6–8-cup ovenproof dish. Set in a larger baking pan and pour boiling water halfway up the sides of the dish. Bake in a preheated 375° oven for 10 minutes, reduce temperature to 350°, and bake 40–50 minutes longer or until a skewer inserted into the center comes out almost clean and the center is firm. Remove from oven; let stand for 15 minutes before unmolding. *(Serves 6–8)*

• Combine chopped broccoli and cauliflower.

Broccoli Soup

Broccoli thickens this garlic and oil laced soup, as well as adding two glorious shades of green.

    1 1/2 lb broccoli
    1/4 cup olive oil
    1 1/2 tsp chopped garlic
    1/4 cup rice
    4 cups chicken broth
    Salt and freshly ground pepper
    1/2 cup grated Parmesan cheese (optional)

Separate broccoli flowerets from stems, cut into small buds, and blanch for 3 minutes or until barely tender. Plunge into cold water, drain, and set aside. Peel remaining broccoli and chop into 1/2-inch chunks. Heat oil in a saucepan, add garlic, and cook for 30 seconds, without browning. Stir in chunked broccoli; add rice. Stir for 2 minutes, add broth, and bring to a boil. Reduce heat and simmer for 15 minutes or until the broccoli and rice are tender. Lift out the broccoli and some of the cooked rice, and purée in a processor or blender. (Add some broth if you're using the blender.) Return the purée to the soup base and mix well. When ready to serve, add flowerets, and cook long enough to heat through. Season to taste. Serve with grated Parmesan cheese if you wish *(Makes 1 quart)*

• For a rich, creamy broccoli soup, substitute broccoli for cauliflower in *Copenhagen-Style Cauliflower Soup* (see *Cauliflower*).
• Add hot pepper flakes along with garlic.

Pasta with Broccoli

Here's a fast, inexpensive, meatless meal.

    1 1/2–2 lb broccoli
    1/2 lb spaghetti, linguini, or other thin pasta
    1/4–1/2 cup olive oil
    4–6 anchovy fillets
    2 tsp chopped garlic
    Hot pepper flakes (optional)
    Salt and freshly ground pepper
    3 Tb butter

Wash and cut up broccoli, removing flowerets about 2 1/2 inches down the stem. Trim and peel the floweret stems and stalks; cut into 1 1/2–2-inch pieces. Blanch, drain, and dry broccoli. Boil water; add 1 teaspoon salt per quart and toss in the spaghetti. Cook until spaghetti is cooked through but still slightly chewy (*al dente*).

Meanwhile, heat 1/4 cup of the olive oil in a large sauté pan. Chop the anchovies and mash them into the oil until almost puréed. Add the garlic and hot pepper (if you wish). Stir in the broccoli and cook, tossing—for no more than a minute or two—until moisture evaporates and the broccoli is coated with oil. Season with salt and pepper.

Thoroughly drain spaghetti and toss with the butter. Scrape in the broccoli and flavored oil. Toss together, adding additional oil if desired. Season to taste. *(Serves 3–4)*

• For a "wetter" sauce, add 1/2 cup dry white wine or chicken broth along with the broccoli. Cook down a bit. Red wine is also delicious, but will discolor the broccoli and pasta.
• Before adding the broccoli, add 2–3 cups peeled, seeded, and chopped tomatoes; cook for 15–20 minutes to lightly thicken, then add broccoli and just heat through.
• Add diced prosciutto, smoked sausage, or black olives.
• After lightly sautéing the broccoli in oil, add 1 cup heavy cream. (You can omit the anchovies.) Reduce cream until broccoli is coated, and toss with pasta. Use extra cream for more sauce.

Broccoli and Crabmeat Crêpes

Here's an economical way to entertain, because only a small amount of crabmeat creates an elegant dinner.

1/2 recipe *Crêpe Batter* (page 266)
8 Tb butter
2 Tb chopped shallots
1 1/2 cups crabmeat
1/2 cup dry white wine
4 cups *Sautéed Chopped Broccoli* (page 31)
1/2 cup ricotta cheese
1/4 cup light cream
4 Tb flour
3 cups milk
Salt and freshly ground pepper
1/2 cup grated Swiss cheese

Make crêpes: you need only 12; set aside. (Freeze any remaining crêpes for another meal.) Heat 2 tablespoons of the butter and sauté the shallots until wilted, add the crabmeat, and toss in butter for a moment. Add wine, and cook until it evaporates. Combine with the sautéed broccoli; set aside. Purée the ricotta cheese and cream together. In a saucepan, melt 4 tablespoons of the butter, stir in the flour, and cook for 2–3 minutes to slightly cook flour. Add milk, whisking until smooth, and stir until thick. Combine with ricotta cheese mixture and season to taste. Mix 1 cup of the sauce into the broccoli and crab mixture.

Place equal portions of the mixture into the center of each crêpe. Then, roll the crêpes and set them into a buttered 9 x 12-inch ovenproof pan. Cover with the remaining sauce. Sprinkle with Swiss cheese, and dot with remaining butter. Bake in a preheated 400° oven for 20 minutes or until bubbly. Run under the broiler if desired. *(Serves 6)*

- Substitute any shellfish for the crabmeat.

Chicken and Broccoli Mornay

Here's a recipe that you used to find at every church supper. It's delicious—but only if the broccoli is drained thoroughly and not overcooked, so it stays crunchy.

1 1/2 lb broccoli
3 whole chicken breasts
7 Tb butter
Salt and freshly ground pepper
2 cups sliced mushrooms
Mornay Sauce (page 350)
1–2 tsp lemon juice
1/4 cup grated Swiss and Parmesan cheeses

Wash and peel the broccoli, dividing the flowerets and stems. Blanch until barely tender. Drain, roughly chop (cool if not using immediately), and set aside.

Bone the chicken breasts (removing tendons and skin) so that you end up with 6 fillets. Melt 3 tablespoons of the butter in a sauté pan until foamy, and put in the chicken breasts. Sprinkle with salt and pepper and cover with waxed paper or aluminum foil. Turn the heat to low, poach the breasts in butter for 3 minutes, turn over, and poach for 3–4 minutes longer. Remove from the pan. Turn heat to high; add mushrooms. Cook until the moisture is evaporated and the mushrooms are lightly browned; remove from pan. Heat 3 tablespoons of the butter until foamy. Add the broccoli and toss over medium heat to evaporate the moisture and coat with butter. Season with salt and pepper; set aside. Make the Mornay sauce, using 1 cup of chicken stock and 1 cup milk, and add lemon juice to taste. Season well with salt and pepper.

Butter an 8 x 8-inch baking dish. Put in the broccoli, cover with mushrooms, and spoon over about half the Mornay sauce. Top with chicken and cover with the remaining sauce. Sprinkle with the cheese and dot with the remaining butter. Bake in a preheated 350° oven for 30 minutes. At the last minute place under the broiler to brown if desired. *(Serves 4)*

- Substitute turkey slices lightly sautéed on each side for 1–2 minutes.
- Use leftover chicken along with pieces of ham or prosciutto to accent the flavor.

Broccoli Deep-Dish Pizza

Chicago-style deep-dish pizza has swept the country. Why not, since one slice fills a hungry diner?

1 package active dry yeast
1 cup warm water (110°–115°)
1 tsp sugar
3 1/2 cups unbleached flour
1 cup cake flour
1 1/2 tsp salt
1 cup plus 2 Tb olive oil
3 tsp minced garlic
6 cups peeled, seeded, and chopped tomatoes
1 tsp oregano
1 tsp basil
2 cups sliced mushrooms
Salt and freshly ground pepper
1 lb Italian sweet sausage
1/2 tsp crushed fennel seeds
2 Tb butter
8 cups blanched roughly chopped broccoli
1 Tb shortening
3 1/2 cups grated mozzarella cheese
1/2 cup grated Parmesan cheese

Dissolve yeast in warm water; stir in sugar. Combine flours and salt, and gradually add the dissolved yeast and 1/4 cup of the oil. Knead until the texture is smooth. Put in a large bowl, cover with plastic wrap, and let rise until triple in bulk, 2–3 hours.

Meanwhile, prepare the fillings. Heat 1/4 cup of the oil in a sauté pan, add 2 teaspoons of the garlic, and cook for 30 seconds, without browning. Add tomatoes; simmer gently until thickened and almost all moisture is evaporated, approximately 45 minutes. Stir in the oregano and basil, then set aside to cool. In the same pan, heat 2 tablespoons of the oil and sauté the mushrooms

1

2

3

until lightly browned and the liquid is evaporated. Season to taste, and set aside to cool. Remove casings from sausage, crumble, and add to pan along with fennel. Cook thoroughly. Remove, and cool. Heat 2 tablespoons of the oil and the butter; add 1 teaspoon garlic, and stir for 30 seconds. Stir in the broccoli until coated well and any liquid is evaporated. Season to taste; set aside.

When the dough has risen, punch down. Cut off a third and set aside. Grease a 14 x 1½-inch deep-dish pizza pan with shortening. On a floured board, roll out two-thirds of the dough to a 20-inch circle. Fit to the pan, letting the excess dough hang over the side. Brush the dough with 1 tablespoon of the oil; sprinkle with salt. Sprinkle 1 cup of the mozzarella cheese over the dough. Spread the tomatoes across the cheese. Spread the mushrooms over the tomatoes, and cover with 1 cup of mozzarella cheese. Roll out the remaining dough to approximately a 14-inch circle. Brush the sides of the dough inside the pan with water. (1) Fit the 14-inch round into the pan. (2) Press edges—pull if necessary—against the moistened dough to seal it. Trim the overhanging dough to ½ inch and wet it again. Fold inward and crimp to form a raised rim around the pan edge. Cut a steam vent in the top layer of the dough, and brush with 1 tablespoon of the oil. (3) Spread the sausage across the dough and cover with the broccoli. Combine the remaining cheeses and sprinkle across the broccoli; drizzle with ¼ cup of the oil. Bake in a preheated 425° oven for 30–40 minutes. *(Serves 8–10)*

- Put the broccoli and sausage on the lower layer, and the tomatoes and cheeses on the top layer. This way the broccoli stays moist, if you prefer it that way.
- For a vegetarian pizza, replace the sausage with 4 cups sliced onions lightly browned in 2 tablespoons oil.

Brussels Sprouts

The cabbage family includes a number of distinctive members such as kale, kohlrabi, and cauliflower; but none comes close to the miniature perfection of Brussels sprouts. Cut open a Brussels sprout and examine it closely. See how the tiny leaves curl against each other and the way the color shades from cream to bright green. Its compact shape, coupled with a delicate flavor, are the overriding reasons to grow sprouts.

Maybe many sprout eaters don't know how unusual Brussels sprouts look growing in the garden. The tiny "cabbages" develop along a thick 20–22-inch-high stalk that grows straight up from the ground. The sprouts start at the bottom and circle around the stalk, interrupted occasionally by great fanning leaves which top off the plant as an umbrella of protection for the rosettes be-

low. I never tire of marveling at Brussels sprouts: both on and off those sturdy columns.

Last year in the Victory Garden we tested thirteen different Brussels sprout varieties, and there were major differences in how well they grew. It's a good idea to get a variety recommendation from your regional seedsman or county agent. Here, we've had good luck with Peer Gynt and Jade Cross.

Around the end of June, Russ puts a pinch of seeds in the garden every 18 inches, and later thins to the strongest plant. He keeps a close eye on the seedlings, as they dehydrate quickly. If there is any sign of cabbageworm infestation, he'll apply *Bacillus thüringiensis*. In mid-October he removes the tip of the plants, which has the effect of stopping more fruit from setting, thus driv-

ing the vigor into the remaining sprouts so that they achieve maximum size.

Sprouts can be picked as early as late September, but we think they are sweeter after they've gone through a frost, so we wait until late October or November for harvesting. As the sprouts form from the bottom up, I pick the lower ones first and wait for the others to develop. Markets rarely stock the ³/₄-inch sprouts I prefer (usually they're twice that size). I'm frequently tempted to pick them even smaller, but know that after trimming almost nothing would be left.

Brussels sprouts "ripen," picking up a strong flavor during storage, so it's best to use them as soon as possible after harvesting to guarantee a delicate flavor. Sprouts mature over a long period of time; therefore it's not necessary to pick and store them all at once.

Because of the way they grow, Brussels sprouts are usually clean and free from garden soil. To prepare, take a sharp paring knife, remove any damaged outer leaves, then trim the base. Cut a crosshatch in the core to allow

for even cooking, drop the sprouts into a bowl of tepid water, and swirl them around. If it's likely that aphids are hiding in the inner leaves, soak the sprouts in salted tepid water for 15 minutes.

Brussels sprouts are at their very best when both their unique shape and their gentle flavor are preserved: leave this vegetable as close to its natural state as possible! To use sprouts in mousses, purées, timbales, or soufflés is unnecessary unless you have a batch of leftover sprouts. I've included a soup that's useful for supersized sprouts or those that didn't head up at the end of the gardening season. But otherwise, leave Brussels sprouts as they are.

Overcooking creates a mushy, strongly flavored mess rather than the crisp, green, delicately flavored vegetable Brussels sprouts should be. Just like other cabbage relatives (such as cauliflower), once sprouts are overcooked or hang around too long in the garden or market, they develop a strong, unpleasant flavor. As long as you take care to use sprouts when they're at their peak of freshness and cook them only until tender, you will always have a delightful experience.

There's no one fail-safe method for cooking sprouts. Blanching and steaming both work well, but each has drawbacks. Blanching in a large amount of boiling, salted water sets and keeps their color a truly luscious green, but the sprouts tend to absorb water and lose texture, which doesn't happen when they're steamed. On the other hand, steaming them, covered, causes sprouts to turn slightly gray: the longer they steam, the grayer they get. On balance, I think I prefer steaming sprouts, especially when they're to be eaten immediately. When I

Special Information

Yields
I divide Brussels sprouts into three categories: the small (³/₄–1 inch) garden size; the medium (1¼–1½ inch) size from the garden and market; and large (2–2½ inch) Brussels sprouts.

- ½ pound small sprouts = 28–30 sprouts
- ½ pound medium sprouts = 12–14 sprouts
- ½ pound large sprouts = 7–8 sprouts
- Trimming causes a slight weight loss, ranging from 1½ ounces for a ½ pound of small sprouts to 2 ounces in the larger sprouts. One-half pound trimmed sprouts = 2 cups = 2–3 servings.

Storage and Preserving
- Unwashed Brussels sprouts will keep 1–2 days in the refrigerator in a perforated plastic bag, but I really don't recommend it because their taste gets stronger. This holds true for cooked sprouts as well. In addition, they soften and lose texture.
- To freeze, blanch trimmed heads in boiling water (small heads for 3 minutes, medium heads for 4

minutes, and large heads for 5 minutes). Chill in ice water for 6–8 minutes. Drain, and place in freezing containers.

Hints
- Halved raw sprouts are a beautiful, delicious addition to a crudités platter.
- Crosshatch the bottom for even cooking.
- To avoid giving a cabbage taste to stews, add Brussels sprouts during the last minutes of cooking.
- Add cooked sprouts sliced lengthwise to mixed vegetable soups and clear consommés.
- Surround a poached egg on a triangle of toast with overlapping slices of cooked Brussels sprouts cut lengthwise. Dot with sweet butter. These slices are also a beautiful garnish for many dishes.
- Add steamed leaves to clear soups. (They almost look like lily pads!)
- Brussels sprouts' glorious green perks up mixed root vegetable dishes. Toss with cooked baby carrots or turnip, parsnip, or rutabaga "olives."
- If you have strongly flavored sprouts, add parsley

blanch them, it's usually because I plan to finish cooking them later, and during the wait some of the moisture trapped in the leaves drains off. I plunge the sprouts into cold water to stop the cooking process, drain them well, and put them on a towel to absorb moisture. Then, I refrigerate until the final cooking treatment (but not too long, as they'll wilt a little, and lose texture and freshness).

One of my favorite ways to serve sprouts is raw, and sliced in half lengthwise, so you can both taste their crisp freshness and see that glorious centerfold. I use them in a crudités platter or alone with homemade mayonnaise or an herb-laced yogurt.

sprigs to the blanching water to mellow their taste and diminish cooking odors.
- Cook sprouts to barely tender, cool, and thoroughly drain. Remove the top quarter of the sprouts so that you can look down into their interiors, which almost look like miniature artichokes. Use to garnish a composed salad platter.

Microwave
- Brussels sprouts stay bright green when they are cooked in a microwave. One-half pound sprouts, placed in a covered dish with ¼ cup water, cook done as follows: small sprouts, 2 minutes; medium sprouts, 4 minutes; large sprouts, 8 minutes.

Leftovers
- Leftover Brussels sprouts reheat well.
- Use in stir-fry dishes.
- Slice and use in omelets.
- Cut into halves or quarters and add to salads.
- Purée with butter and heavy cream. Reheat slowly; season with salt, pepper, and lemon juice.

Marketing
Look for firm, bright green sprouts. Yellowed outer leaves and a wilted appearance are signs of age. Purchase small sprouts, for larger ones are older and can be stronger in flavor. Also look for sprouts approximately the same size: otherwise, your cooking time will be off. The heads should be tightly closed and the leaves should be furled.

◇ *Steamed Brussels Sprouts*

Prepare Brussels sprouts (page 36).
Boil ¾ inch water in a steamer. Put washed and trimmed sprouts in basket; steam until tender. Small Brussels sprouts will cook in approximately 6–8 minutes; medium sprouts, 8–10 minutes; large sprouts, 10–12 minutes. Cooking times depend upon the freshness of the vegetables. Test with the point of a sharp knife or by eating a sprout. They should be tender but retain a slight crunch. If you are not eating them right away, cool them off immediately to preserve their color and texture.

◇ *Blanched Brussels Sprouts*

Boil Brussels sprouts in a large pan of salted water until just tender. Drain, place in cold water to set color, and drain well. Small Brussels sprouts will cook in 4–5 minutes; medium sprouts, 5–8 minutes; large sprouts, 8–12 minutes.

Finishing Touches for Steamed or Blanched Sprouts

- *With Butter:* Before serving, roll the Brussels sprouts in butter; cook until heated through. Or, top with browned butter. Season with salt and freshly ground pepper.
- *With Sauces:* Top with a favorite sauce such as *Lemon Butter Sauce*, *Béchamel* or *Mornay Sauce* (see *Appendix*).
- *With Cream:* Coat with heavy cream for a moment until the sprouts absorb some of the cream. The longer the sprouts cook, the less appealing they become.

◇ *Steamed Brussels Sprout Leaves*

This is an excellent way to cook oversized sprouts or sprouts that didn't head up. Small sprouts can be prepared the same way, but you need a bit more patience.
Carefully trim and wash sprouts. Remove the base of the outer leaves and gently peel them off. Cut out the core of each sprout, removing its central conical shape. Peel off leaf layers, and steam over boiling water for 3–4 minutes. The leaves will maintain their texture yet be incredibly delicate, needing nothing but a sprinkling of salt and freshly ground pepper. Mound these leaves on a plate or float them across a clear soup.

Brussels Sprout Halves Tossed in Butter

A simple and elegant way with sprouts: my favorite.

1 lb Brussels sprouts
4–6 Tb butter
Juice of ¹/₂ lemon
Salt and freshly ground pepper

Trim and wash sprouts; steam until barely tender. Halve each sprout lengthwise. Melt butter in a large sauté pan, toss in sprouts, and cook until heated through. Add lemon juice, salt, and pepper to taste. Toss again before serving. (*Serves 4–6*)

• Toss in toasted pine nuts or almonds.
• Coat sprouts with butter and heat through. Brown additional butter; add lemon juice. Pour over sprouts.

Brussels Sprouts with Bacon

1 lb Brussels sprouts
¹/₄ lb bacon
¹/₂ cup finely chopped onions
2–3 Tb butter
Salt and freshly ground pepper

Trim and wash sprouts. Steam or blanch until barely tender. Cook bacon until crisp. Drain bacon bits, discard all but 2 tablespoons fat; add onions. Cook until wilted and lightly browned. Add Brussels sprouts and reheat, adding 2–3 tablespoons butter if desired. Add cooked bacon, toss together, and season to taste. (*Serves 4–6*)

Brussels Sprouts Polonaise

1 lb Brussels sprouts
¹/₂ cup cold crumbled hard-boiled egg
2 Tb chopped parsley
6 Tb butter

Salt and freshly ground pepper
Juice of ¹/₂ lemon
3 Tb fresh bread crumbs

Trim and wash Brussels sprouts, and steam or blanch until barely tender. Combine egg and parsley. When ready to serve, heat 2 tablespoons of the butter in a large sauté pan and roll sprouts in it until heated through. Season with salt, pepper, and lemon juice. Remove sprouts to a hot serving dish. Cook the remaining 4 tablespoons butter until nutty brown. Toss the crumbs in the butter. Sprinkle the egg mixture over the sprouts, then pour the browned crumbs on top. (*Serves 4–6*)

Brussels Sprouts with Chestnuts

This traditional Thanksgiving or Christmas dish is very rich and filling.

1 lb Brussels sprouts
4 Tb butter
2 cups *Braised Chestnuts* (page 346)
Salt and freshly ground pepper

Trim and wash Brussels sprouts, and steam or blanch until tender. Melt butter in a large saucepan, add sprouts and chestnuts, and heat through. Season with salt and freshly ground pepper. (*Serves 6–8*)

• If chestnuts are unavailable, use other vegetables, such as baby carrots, turnip "olives," or rutabaga that's been braised in butter or broth.

Marinated Brussels Sprouts and Mushrooms

This is an attractive cocktail snack, as well as a nice addition to a salad buffet. It will hold well in the refrigerator for 2 days.

³/₄ lb small Brussels sprouts
1 lb small mushrooms
¹/₄ cup olive oil
¹/₂ cup lemon juice
1 cup water
1 tsp salt
¹/₄ tsp freshly ground pepper
2 cloves garlic
1 bay leaf
¹/₂ tsp oregano
¹/₂ tsp basil
¹/₂ tsp thyme
1 Tb chopped parsley

Trim and wash Brussels sprouts and steam or blanch until just barely tender. Cool slightly, then cut off the tip of each sprout so that the marinade will penetrate down into the innermost part of the sprouts. Place them in a bowl. Wipe mushrooms clean, stem (saving stems for another use), and place caps in bowl with Brussels sprouts. Bring remaining ingredients to a boil in a saucepan. Pour over sprouts and mushrooms. Once the marinade has slightly cooled, refrigerate for at least 2 hours. Remove from the refrigerator 30 minutes before serving to take off the chill. *(Makes 5–6 cups)*

- If you prefer, tie the herbs and garlic in a bouquet garni and remove when serving.
- Use larger sprouts, but cut them in half.
- Substitute cauliflower flowerets for the Brussels sprouts.

Brussels Sprouts and Chestnut Soup

The sweet chestnuts mellow the strongly flavored larger, older sprouts I use for soup. The tan color of the soup is flecked with the green sprouts. Without the cream, the soup tastes like fall to me; cream mellows the flavor. It's a rich soup—a little will go a long way.

4 slices bacon
1 Tb butter
1/2 cup chopped onions
1/2 cup chopped celeriac or celery
1 cup peeled chestnuts (page 346)
4 cups chicken or beef stock
1/2–3/4 lb halved Brussels sprouts
Salt and freshly ground pepper
1/2 cup heavy cream (optional)

Cook bacon in a large saucepan until crisp, drain, crumble, and set aside. Remove all but 1 tablespoon of the bacon fat; add butter. Stir in onions and celeriac or celery and cook until wilted, 5–10 minutes. Add the chestnuts and stock. Bring stock to a boil, reduce heat, cover pan, and simmer for 15 minutes. Add Brussels sprouts, return to the boil, and cook gently, uncovered, for 15 minutes or until the sprouts are quite tender. Process in a food processor or put through a sieve. Do not purée completely—you want some chestnut and sprout flecks. Season to taste, adding cream if desired. Reheat, and serve sprinkled with bacon. *(Makes 1 quart)*

- If you can't find chestnuts, substitute potatoes. The soup won't be the same, but it will be good.

Brussels Sprouts and Shrimp

Brussels sprouts are deliciously green and crunchy in a stir-fry or any fast sauté.

3/4 lb small Brussels sprouts
1 lb raw shrimp
4 Tb butter
1 Tb oil
2 Tb chopped shallots
1/2 cup sliced Jerusalem artichokes or water chestnuts
Juice of 1/2 lemon
Salt and freshly ground pepper
1/2 cup dry vermouth

Wash and trim Brussels sprouts and steam or blanch to barely tender. Drain; pat dry. Peel and devein shrimp. Melt butter and oil and, when foamy, add shallots; stir

for 1 minute. Add shrimp and cook until lightly browned on both sides, 3–4 minutes. Stir in Brussels sprouts and Jerusalem artichokes or water chestnuts, sprinkle with lemon juice, and season with salt and pepper. Toss until heated through. Remove to a warm dish. Add vermouth, and deglaze the pan. Reduce sauce slightly; pour over shrimp and Brussels sprouts. *(Serves 4)*

Cornish Hens
Stuffed with Brussels Sprouts

Brussels sprouts add taste and color to these tiny birds. You can stuff unboned Cornish hens but I think boning them is a minor amount of work for a lot of extra ease at the table. I serve the birds with a well-flavored rice and our sweet fall carrots. This is a good company dish because the birds can be stuffed ahead of time and roasted just before serving. This stuffing also complements small game birds such as pheasant, quail, and duck.

4 Cornish hens (or other small birds)
3/4 lb Brussels sprouts
5 Tb butter
1/2 cup chopped onions
1 egg
1 cup cottage or ricotta cheese
1 cup grated Provolone or Swiss cheese
Salt and freshly ground pepper
1/4 lb chopped Genoa salami or cooked sausage
3 Tb melted butter
1/2 cup white wine or dry vermouth
1 cup chicken stock or stock made with bones

Bone hens, as in following recipe, and set aside. Wash, trim, blanch, and cool Brussels sprouts. Cut lengthwise into quarters and set aside. In 3 tablespoons of the butter, sauté onion until wilted, 5–10 minutes. Add Brussels sprouts, sauté for 3 minutes, and set aside. Beat the egg and combine with cottage or ricotta cheese and 2/3 cup of the grated cheese; season with salt and pepper. Combine with Brussels sprouts and salami or sausage. Spread out hens, skin side down; season with salt and pepper. Evenly divide stuffing among the 4 birds. Fold the sides of the birds up around the stuffing. Either sew together or mold a piece of aluminum foil across the overlapping sides of the bird. Tie legs together. Place in a roasting pan, breast sides up. Brush with melted butter and sprinkle with salt and pepper. Roast in a preheated 350° oven for 25 minutes. Raise the oven temperature to 425° and roast 5 minutes. Sprinkle birds with the remaining grated cheese; roast 5 minutes longer. The birds should be lightly browned and just cooked through. Set the birds on a warm plate. Deglaze the pan with wine, add the broth, and boil until it is reduced by half. Beat in remaining butter and serve. *(Serves 4)*

- Replace some of the Brussels sprouts with braised chestnuts.
- Substitute a creamy goat cheese for some of the cottage cheese.

Boning Small Birds

Everyone hates picking little bones out of birds. Boning them first, which may seem complicated, eliminates all that bother, and is relatively simple and quick. After you've tried it once or twice, you'll always bone small birds.

Cut off the wings at the second joint, and save them for stock. Turn the bird so that its backbone is facing you. With a sharp knife, slit the flesh along one side of the backbone. Working down one side of the rib cage, gently scrape the meat off the bones. With a knife or kitchen scissors, cut through the leg and shoulder joints. Continue scraping flesh off the bones until you reach the end of the chestbone. Start again at the top of the back and repeat the procedure down the second side, ending at the bottom of the breastbone, being careful not to cut through the breast skin. Remove the entire rib cage, including the breastbone, and save for stock. Cut out thigh bone if desired, removing it at knee joint. That's it.

Now you're ready to stuff the bird: then either sew it up or overlap the sides around the stuffing and mold aluminum foil over the cut to keep it in place.

Cabbage

Most Americans are familiar with the green, solid-cored storage cabbage found at the supermarket, but that's only one choice. Seed companies now stock cabbage varieties found around the world. You could choose the delicate loose-leaf Savoy of France and Belgium; the long, skinny celery cabbage of China; the spicy mustard cabbage (pak choy) of China and India; the solid-cored red cabbage of Denmark and Germany; or any one of the new hybrid green solid-cored cabbage varieties bred to have a more delicate flavor and texture than cabbages of the past.

I love all these cabbages: I eat them raw, I eat them cooked—but I seldom cook them very long. Cabbage has been much maligned for its strong flavor and odor, but it is the overcooking, not the cabbage, that is the villain. Long cooking may have been necessary to tenderize the tougher old-fashioned varieties, but it's unnecessary for today's more tender hybrids. However, don't overlook the slow braises beloved by French and German cooks. The tougher-textured red cabbage, for example, benefits greatly from a slow braising, as do hearty cabbage stews (such as *Russian-Style Hearty Cabbage Soup*) which develop a mellow flavor from a slow, *gentle* cooking. The secret is to cook cabbage with respect and adapt its cooking time to its age, variety, and the kind of dish you are making.

Our favorite cabbage may be the loose-leaf, crinkly Savoy cabbage with a superior flavor and texture. Russ plants Savoy Ace, the red Ruby Ball hybrid, the green Market Prize, and Early Hybrid Chinese cabbage. He sows seeds for the first of our cabbage crop indoors in March. As we need only a few plants, he places a dozen seeds of each variety (except Chinese cabbage) in 4-inch pots filled with potting soil. When the seedlings are 1 inch tall, he transplants them into individual six-packs, burying them to half their length (which develops sturdier plants). Because Chinese cabbage transplants poorly, he sows seeds directly into peat pots filled with potting soil, which protects the seedlings from transplant shock. Around the first of April, he puts the cabbages in a cold frame outside to harden off.

Cabbage has a better texture and flavor when it's planted in enriched soil, so Russ works compost, well-rotted cow manure, and 10-10-10 fertilizer into the soil before he transplants the seedlings. Then, to help the plants ward off clubroot, he adds ground limestone (about four handfuls to a 6-foot row). He sets out seedlings every 18 inches, leaving 3 feet between rows, and interplants with lettuce seedlings.

Just like broccoli, cauliflower, and other members of the cabbage family, cabbage attracts the cabbageworm caterpillar, and Russ often needs to spray with *Bacillus thüringiensis* at seven- to ten-day intervals.

Some years, Russ sows seeds for midsummer cabbages directly in the garden in early May. After enriching the soil, he plants four or five seeds every 24 inches, thinning to the strongest plants later on in the month. Another sowing of cabbages in June gives us an ample supply throughout the fall. He sows Chinese cabbage seeds either in the spring or mid-July to mid-August because it bolts to seed in hot weather. For some reason, Chinese cabbage also bolts if transplanted, so it's necessary to sow seeds directly in the garden 10 inches apart or to use peat pots so there will be no transplant shock.

Standard cabbage heads often split when they get too much moisture, or grow too fast, so to prevent this (once the cabbage heads form and are growing nicely) Russ cuts along one side of each plant with a spade, slicing down through its root system. This root pruning not only prevents the cabbages from splitting but also stops their growth and ensures fresh garden cabbages over a longer harvesting period.

Harvesting cabbage is no more complicated than cutting off each head from the stem with a sharp knife and tossing the damaged outer leaves into the compost heap. Wash off the cabbage before cooking, and remove the tough outer leaves. You really can't wash the interior leaves of solid-cored varieties until they're sliced or chopped. However, if the outer leaves look clean, don't

worry—you can always rinse the cabbage once it's sliced. Immerse loose-leaf cabbages in water or remove the leaves and rinse them off individually.

I find the easiest way to slice or chop firm-headed cabbage is to quarter the trimmed and washed head, then, using the core as a holder, cut diagonally across the leaves. When I plan to blanch or steam whole cabbage or quarters, I remove most of the core, leaving just enough to hold the cabbage intact while cooking. Elongated loose-leaf varieties, such as Chinese cabbage, are easily sliced across the leaves. Although Chinese cabbage lacks a heavy core, the texture changes toward the top. The 2 inches of leaves found at the cabbage base are, in fact, thick coarse ribs. Gradually, the ribs thin out and become green leaves at the top. I slice the bottom ribs as I would celery (and sometimes cook as I would Swiss chard) and use the tops in salads. The inner leaves are particularly attractive prepared whole, similar to romaine lettuce or endive.

I cook standard solid-cored cabbage every which way, but I do have two favorite methods—one for sliced cabbage and the other for cabbage wedges. A Caribbean hotel owner served me a simple sauté-braise which I now use all the time for sliced cabbage (see *Butter-Braised Cabbage*). I steam rather than boil cabbage wedges, whole cabbage, or leaves, because steaming is faster and the cabbage is less watery. As long as the cabbage is not over-cooked, it holds its color and is positively delicious with simple seasonings such as celery salt or a pat of fresh

butter. The tougher texture of red cabbage is made more palatable by a long braising. On the other hand, Savoy and Chinese cabbages cook quickly. Chinese cabbage is almost a vegetable chapter in itself. I've included a stir--fry and a main-course recipe, but for further ideas peruse some Chinese cookbooks, particularly Irene Kuo's *The Key to Chinese Cooking* or *Chinese Cuisine* and others in the series of books written by Huang Su Huei and translated by Nina Simonds.

Most of the recipes in this section utilize cooked cabbage, but I use raw cabbage a lot and love it. Try wide Chinese cabbage ribs as low-calorie "crackers" for dips; I find my friends are always intrigued by the fresh, clean taste. Coleslaws are a must in this house, with everyone arguing over the best size for the shreds. We eat pickled cabbage, marinated cabbage salads, and, of course, fermented sauerkraut, which—by the way—is said to have originated in China and to have been brought to Europe by Marco Polo. Cooked cabbage can be as basic as my favorite steamed wedges sprinkled with celery salt, or as fancy as cabbage braised with pheasant or baked wrapped in strudel. I can't possibly include all the delightful ways to serve cabbage, but I do hope these recipes will inspire you to experiment on your own.

Marketing

I would not recommend buying Savoy cabbage during the winter. It's edible, but a disappointing contrast to the fresh-picked garden varieties. Often the flavor tastes old and the texture can be limp. Solid-cored green cabbage grown for storage is a better choice. It should feel firm and heavy. Regardless of the type of cabbage the leaves should appear fresh, brightly colored, and blemishfree with no signs of wilt or worm damage.

◇ Steamed Green Cabbage

Cut cabbage into wedges, slice it, or separate the leaves. Bring ³/₄–1 inch of water to a boil in a steamer. Steam cabbage in a steamer basket. Wedges will cook in 6–9 minutes (depending on thickness and size), sliced cabbage will cook in 5–6 minutes, and whole leaves will cook in 3–4 minutes.

◇ Blanched or Boiled Green Cabbage

Bring a large pot of water to a boil, add the cabbage, and let the water return to the boil. Maintaining a steady, gentle boil, cook cabbage wedges for 6–9 minutes (depending upon their size). Drain. If the wedges are to be sliced and reheated, squeeze as much moisture out as possible. Whole leaves will cook in 2–3 minutes.
Note: If you need to remove the outer leaves from a solid-core cabbage for stuffing, etc., either steam or boil the whole cabbage for 10 minutes. The outer leaves may then be removed; the heart will still need to be cooked.

Finishing Touches for Cooked Green Cabbage

- *With Butter:* Simply serve with sweet butter, salt, and pepper to taste.
- *With Seasonings:* Omit butter, and sprinkle with salt and pepper, celery salt, dill, crushed caraway, or any other seasonings you prefer.
- *Sliced:* Reheat sliced cooked cabbage by tossing in butter to evaporate moisture, adding more butter, and then cooking for a few minutes to absorb butter.
- *With Cream:* Evaporate moisture by tossing sliced cooked cabbage with butter; then add heavy cream. Cook until cream reduces and coats cabbage.
- *With Blanched Vegetables:* Sliced cooked cabbage is delicious reheated in butter with other cooked vegetables such as spinach, or any of the greens. Sauté together to evaporate moisture, then braise lightly in butter. See *Mixed Greens Sauté* in *Greens.*
- *Baked in a Cream or Cheese Sauce:* Slice cooked cabbage and squeeze out as much moisture as possible. (Sauté with some butter until moisture evaporates if you wish.) Combine with a cream or cheese sauce and bake in a 350° oven until heated through, approximately 20 minutes. Top with buttered bread crumbs and run under the broiler.

Special Information

Yields
- A firm-headed 2-pound cabbage, trimmed = 1½ pounds sliced leaves = approximately 9–10 cups sliced = 5–6 cups cooked
- A 3-pound cabbage = approximately 14–16 cups sliced or shredded
- A well-trimmed Chinese cabbage = approximately 6–7 cups sliced leaves
- These amounts vary, depending on type of cabbage. Smaller-cored, loose-head cabbages, such as Savoy, have a slightly higher yield.

Storage and Preserving
- Unwashed, firm, compact cabbage keeps up to 2 weeks in the refrigerator; looser-leaf, up to a week. Long-term storage requires high humidity and 32° temperature.
- Sliced cabbage stored in a perforated plastic bag will keep 5–6 days, refrigerated.
- Solid-core cabbage will keep for 4–5 months stored in a humid basement with a temperature of 32°. However, prepare yourself for a strong odor as the cabbage gets older. This can be lessened somewhat by layering in wet sand. Savoy and other loose-leaf cabbages store poorly.

- Cooked cabbage, covered, will keep 1–3 days in the refrigerator. See also *Sauerkraut.*

Hints
- Overcooking ruins cabbage. It causes a mushy texture and a strong taste.
- Make corned beef with cabbage, but cook each vegetable separately and flavor with the cooking juices at serving time.
- Red cabbage has a coarser texture than green cabbage. It must be marinated longer to tenderize when eaten raw, and requires a slightly longer braising time when cooked.
- To retain the bright red color of red cabbage, combine with acids such as wine, apple juice, or vinegar.
- Use a stainless steel knife to cut red cabbage; the cabbage pigment turns blue when you use a carbon steel knife.
- Shred or slice Chinese cabbage and use like any other cabbage, but remember that it has a delicate tartness which makes an excellent addition to stir-fries.
- Use raw Chinese cabbage on a crudités platter.
- When substituting Chinese cabbage for standard cabbage, reduce the cooking time.
- Substitute green cabbage for kale in *Colcannon* (see *Kale*).

Braised Cabbage

Here are two favorite ways to prepare cabbage.

Butter-Braised Cabbage
4–6 Tb butter
2–3 tsp curry powder (optional)
8 cups finely sliced cabbage
Salt and freshly ground pepper

Heat 4 tablespoons of the butter with curry powder (if you want to use it) in a large sauté pan. Add the sliced cabbage and stir to coat with butter. Cover, lower heat, and cook gently for 5–6 minutes, stirring occasionally, or until the cabbage is tender. Season with salt and pepper. Add additional butter if desired. *(Makes 4–5 cups)*

Broth-Braised Cabbage
8 cups finely sliced green cabbage
1/2 cup chicken or beef broth
Salt and freshly ground pepper
2 Tb butter (optional)

Put all ingredients in a covered saucepan, bring to a boil, and cook for 5–6 minutes or until just tender, stirring or tossing occasionally. Or, cook covered in a preheated 350° oven for 20 minutes or longer, until tender. The timing depends on the cabbage variety and the size of the slices. *(Makes 4–5 cups)*
- Substitute wine for broth or butter.
- Use bacon or goose fat rather than butter.

- Pour boiling water over finely sliced green cabbage to tenderize; let stand for a minute and drain. Pat dry and add to stir-fry dishes.
- Select a loose-leaf cabbage, such as Savoy, for stuffed leaves or whole stuffed cabbage.
- Make *Two-Way Squash Slaw* (see *Squash, Winter*), substituting 1 pound sliced cabbage for half the squash.

Microwave
- A 2-pound washed green Savoy cabbage, cut into 8 wedges, placed in a covered dish, will cook tender in 7 minutes.

Leftovers
- Try a cabbage and onion quiche with strips of ham or prosciutto.
- Make *Bubble and Squeak* (the name comes from the noise the cabbage makes when cooking): Combine equal amounts of leftover shredded cooked cabbage and leftover mashed potatoes. Season, then cook in butter in a sauté pan, pressing down like a giant pancake. When brown on the bottom, reduce the heat and cook until heated through. Invert and serve. Add onion or cooked meat if desired.
- Add to soups during the last few minutes of cooking.
- Make a *Cabbage Loaf*.

- Add herbs such as dill, basil, and poppy seeds.
- Add vinegar at the end of cooking time; toss well.
- If you're using red cabbage, always remember to add acid. Braise in wine or try apple cider or apple juice. The braising time will be longer than with green cabbage.
- Add cooked chestnuts.
- Add lightly browned onions.
- Reduce the pan liquids in *Broth-Braised Cabbage*, and fold in sour cream and dill.

Chinese Cabbage Stir-Fry

2 lb Chinese cabbage
1/3 cup dried hot red pepper (optional)
3 Tb peanut oil
2 quarter-size pieces fresh ginger
1/2 tsp sugar
1 tsp salt
2 Tb water or broth

Wash cabbage and cut crosswise into 1–1 1/2-inch pieces. Dice the hot pepper (if you are using it) into 1/2-inch pieces. Heat the oil in a wok or a large frying pan. Stir in the ginger and toss for 1 minute. Add the cabbage and pepper, if you wish, and cook, stirring constantly, for 2 minutes. (Lower the heat if the cabbage begins to brown.) Stir in the sugar and salt; then add the water or broth. Cover, and cook for 2–3 minutes or until the cabbage is tender but still crunchy. *(Serves 4)*
- Season with a few drops of sesame oil.
- Toss in pine nuts or cooked chestnuts.
- Add black Chinese mushrooms (soaked in warm water to cover for 30 minutes) or small ham strips along with the ginger.
- Add pieces of shrimp, crab, or other shellfish.
- Combine 1 teaspoon cornstarch with 1 tablespoon each of soy sauce, rice wine, and vinegar, and stir in at the last until the sauce thickens. Season with sesame oil, if desired.

Sweet-and-Sour Red Cabbage

This cabbage—our traditional accompaniment for Christmas goose—is equally good prepared a day ahead of time.

3–4-lb red cabbage
1 tart apple
4 Tb butter
1 heaping Tb brown sugar
1 cup minced onions
6 Tb red wine vinegar
1 cup beef or chicken broth, or water
1 tsp salt
1/2 cup red currant jelly

Wash, dry, and shred the cabbage. Chop the apple. Melt the butter in a large frying pan and stir in the brown sugar. Add the apple and the onions, cover, and cook over low heat for 4–5 minutes until wilted. Stir in cabbage, add the vinegar, cover, and braise for 10 minutes. Then, pour in the broth or water and salt, and cook, covered, over low heat for 2 hours (or bake in a preheated 300° oven for 2 1/2 hours). Stir in the jelly before serving. *(Makes 6 cups)*

Note: Depending on the freshness of the cabbage the cooking time can be reduced. Start checking texture after 1 hour of cooking.

Cabbage Loaf

2 1/2-lb green cabbage
2 Tb butter
1 Tb oil
Salt and freshly ground pepper
3 eggs
1/2 cup heavy cream
1/2 cup grated Swiss cheese
1 Tb crushed caraway seeds (optional)

Wash, dry, and quarter the cabbage. Shred it into 1/4-inch pieces. Melt the butter and oil in a large pan; add the cabbage. Stir until coated with butter, then cook, covered, over low heat for 8–10 minutes until wilted. Remove the cover and cook for 2–3 minutes over high heat, stirring to evaporate moisture. Cool slightly before seasoning with salt and pepper. Beat eggs and mix with cabbage, cream, cheese, and caraway (if you like). Put in a buttered loaf pan and bake in a preheated 375° oven for 40–45 minutes. Let stand for 10–15 minutes before slicing. Serve either hot or cold. *(Makes a 1 1/2-quart loaf)*

- Make with leftover cabbage. Sauté sliced cooked cabbage in butter and oil to evaporate moisture, about 5 minutes. Then proceed with the recipe.
- Add pieces of ham or sausage.
- Season with herbs or spices.

Marie Caratelli's Steamed Cabbage and Potatoes

2-lb green cabbage
2 large potatoes
1/4 cup olive oil
1 cup sliced onions
Sliced peperoni (optional)
Salt and freshly ground pepper
Broth or water (optional)

Wash cabbage, core, and chop or slice into 1/2–1-inch pieces. Thickly slice the potatoes. Heat the olive oil in a large saucepan; add the onions and peperoni (if you wish); cook until onions are wilted. Add the cabbage and potatoes, then season with salt and pepper. Cover, and steam over low heat for 20–30 minutes or until the potatoes are tender. Stir frequently; if the vegetables start to brown, add some broth or water. *(Serves 4)*

- For a spicy version, sauté some pieces of dried hot peppers along with the onions.

Coleslaw

3/4–1 cup *Mayonnaise* (page 349)
1/2 cup red wine vinegar
1 Tb Dijon mustard
2 tsp sugar
Salt and freshly ground pepper
8 cups finely sliced green cabbage
1 cup grated carrots
1 cup chopped red onions

Combine the mayonnaise, vinegar, mustard, and sugar. Season with salt and pepper. Toss the cabbage with the carrots and onions, then mix thoroughly with the dressing. Taste again, reseasoning if necessary, and marinate, refrigerated, for at least 1 hour. Longer marination tenderizes further. *(Makes 8 cups)*

- Add caraway seeds.
- Add chopped red or green peppers or celery.
- Use both red and green cabbage and marinate longer to tenderize the red cabbage.
- Replace mayonnaise with sour cream; or sour cream and mayonnaise; or a mayonnaise and crème fraîche combination; or thin with yogurt.
- Omit the mayonnaise and use only 1/2 cup vinegar.

Mrs. Peretsman's Diet Coleslaw

2–2 ¹/₂-lb green cabbage
¹/₂ cup chopped onions
¹/₂ cup chopped peppers
¹/₄ cup kosher salt
2 tsp sugar substitute
¹/₂ cup cider vinegar

Wash and chop the cabbage, and mix with onions, peppers, salt, and sugar substitute. Toss with the vinegar and marinate overnight. (*Makes 6–8 cups*)

- For a summer diet coleslaw, mix finely sliced cabbage with red wine vinegar, celery salt, and black pepper. The Italian balsamic vinegar is particularly flavorful.

Wilted Cabbage Salad

2-lb green cabbage
4–5 strips bacon
Salt and freshly ground pepper
3 Tb red wine vinegar

Wash, quarter, and shred the cabbage. Put it in a bowl and cover with boiling water. Let stand for 10 minutes. Meanwhile, cook the bacon crisp. Drain the cabbage and pat dry. Dry out the bowl. Put cabbage in the bowl and season with salt, pepper, and vinegar. Mix in some bacon fat. Taste, and correct the seasonings. Crumble bacon over the warm salad. (*Serves 6*)

Mostly Cabbage Soup

I've eaten many cabbage soups in which the cabbage seemed lost—often the soup had cooked all day. I much prefer cabbage soup to taste like cabbage and to have the leaves firm rather than mushy.

2 ¹/₂–3-lb green cabbage
3 stalks celery
1 large sweet onion
2 leeks
1 lb carrots
3 Tb butter
1 Tb oil
Herb bouquet:
    4 parsley sprigs
    3 crushed cloves garlic
    1 bay leaf
    1 tsp thyme
    8 crushed peppercorns
    Green portions of leek leaves
2 qt water, chicken broth, or a combination of
    both
Salt and freshly ground pepper
2 cups fresh shell beans or cooked dried beans
French or rye bread

Wash and slice the cabbage into ¹/₂-inch shreds. Clean the celery and cut into ¹/₄-inch slices. Peel and slice the onion. Wash the leeks thoroughly and slice the whites, placing some of the green leaves in the herb bouquet.

Peel and diagonally slice the carrots into ¹/₄-inch pieces. Melt the butter and oil in a 4–6-quart saucepan. Stew the celery, onions, leeks, and carrots in the pan for 5 minutes. Add the cabbage and cook 10 minutes longer. Put in the herb bouquet, water or broth, and 1 tablespoon salt. Bring to a boil, then reduce heat slightly and boil gently for 15 minutes. Stir in the beans and cook 15 minutes longer or until the vegetables are tender. Remove the herb bouquet, season to taste, and serve with toasted rounds of French bread or rye bread. (*Makes 3½ quarts*)

- Cook a meaty ham bone along with the vegetables.
- For a heartier version, add other vegetables: sauté sliced turnip along with the onions and carrots; then add ¹/₂–1 pound peeled and cubed potatoes; add cubed winter squash for the last 15–20 minutes. Adjust the cooking time as necessary.
- For a no-fat version, omit the stewing of the vegetables in butter, and simmer them in liquid instead.

Russian-Style Hearty Cabbage Soup

Here's a flavorful blend of cabbage, sauerkraut, short ribs, and vegetables. This soup takes a while to cook, but it is well worth the time. I prefer it served the same day, although it can be served 1–2 days later. Be sure to have some good black bread on hand.

4 lb short ribs
1 meaty shinbone (optional)
1 lb marrow bones
1 large onion
1 large turnip
2 carrots
2 cups beef broth
8 cups water
2 Tb tomato paste
Herb bouquet:
    4 sprigs parsley
    4 sprigs dill
    3 cloves garlic
    1 tsp thyme
    1 bay leaf
2 leeks (white portions only)
2 celery stalks with leaves
Salt and freshly ground pepper
2 ¹/₂–3-lb green cabbage
1 lb sauerkraut
3 Tb oil
3 Tb butter
1 cup finely chopped onions
1 cup finely chopped carrots
¹/₂ cup finely chopped celery
2 cups peeled, seeded, and chopped tomatoes
¹/₄ cup lemon juice
3 Tb sugar
2 cups sour cream
¹/₂ cup chopped dill

Place the ribs, shinbone, and marrow bones in a baking pan. Halve the onion, turnip, and carrots, and add to the pan. Brown in a preheated 500° oven for 20 minutes.

Remove from the oven, and place the meat, bones, and vegetables in a large stockpot. Remove the grease from the baking pan, pour broth into the pan, and cook over high heat until all the brown bits are incorporated into the broth. Add the broth to the stockpot along with the water, tomato paste, herb bouquet, leeks, celery, and 1 tablespoon salt. Bring the broth to a boil, skim, and simmer, partially covered, for 2 hours.

Shred the cabbage into ¼-inch slices. You will have approximately 14 cups. Rinse the sauerkraut in fresh water; squeeze dry. Melt the oil and butter in a large pan, and sauté the chopped onions, carrots, and celery until wilted, approximately 10 minutes. Add the sauerkraut and cook for 2 minutes. Stir in the cabbage and cook over low heat until wilted, about 5 minutes. Add 1 cup of the liquid from the stockpot, partially cover pan, and braise for 30 minutes, checking occasionally to ensure the liquid has not evaporated, adding more if necessary; set aside.

When the stock is cooked, discard the vegetables, shinbone, and marrow bones, and degrease. (The shinbone meat is good for nibbling.) Then add the cabbage mixture along with the chopped tomatoes, lemon juice, and sugar. Simmer 30 minutes longer. Season to taste. Ladle into big bowls, top with spoonfuls of sour cream, and sprinkle with dill. *(Serves 6–8)*

Chinese Lion's Head

Despite the large-size meatballs, this is a delicate dish. The pork mixture is lightened by the gelatin and egg white, and the pork and cabbage flavors mingle. You can make this well ahead of time and reheat over low heat.

3 lb Chinese cabbage
1 package unflavored gelatin
¼ cup consommé
1 egg white
2 lb ground pork
1 Tb dry sherry or rice wine
1 tsp finely chopped fresh ginger
1 tsp chopped garlic
2 Tb minced scallions
3 Tb soy sauce
½ tsp sugar
3 Tb cornstarch
3 Tb peanut oil
1 quarter-size piece of ginger
1 tsp salt
2 cups beef or chicken broth

Wash the cabbage thoroughly and pat dry. Cut crosswise into 2-inch pieces. Soften the gelatin, following the directions on the package, and dissolve in the consommé. Lightly beat the egg white. Combine the pork with the egg white, sherry or rice wine, chopped ginger, garlic, scallions, 2 tablespoons of the soy sauce, sugar, and dissolved gelatin. Mix thoroughly. Chill in the refrigerator for 30 minutes. Dissolve cornstarch in 1 tablespoon soy sauce and 3 tablespoons water; set aside.

In a large pan, heat the oil and toss in the ginger slice;

stir for 30 seconds. Stir in the cabbage to coat with oil, sprinkle with salt, and stir again; set aside. Once the meat has chilled, form 6 giant meatballs. (The easiest way to do this is to toss the mixture from hand to hand to produce a nice round shape.) Completely coat each meatball with the cornstarch mixture. Place two-thirds of the cabbage in a heatproof casserole large enough to hold the meatballs in a single layer. Place meatballs on top of the cabbage. Add any remaining cornstarch mixture to the casserole. Cover the meatballs with the reserve cabbage; add the broth, cover, and simmer for 1 hour. Serve one meatball per person accompanied by the cabbage and broth. (For a thick sauce, boil the liquid until it's the consistency you wish.) To serve as part of a buffet, hold over gentle heat, and provide spoons for guests to scoop off small sections of the meatballs. *(Serves 6)*

Stewed Red Cabbage with Italian Sausage

If you're familiar with only sweet-sour red cabbage, do try this economical, hearty main dish that gives red cabbage a whole new dimension.

6 Tb olive oil
½ cup chopped onions
½ cup chopped celery
½ cup chopped ham
1 Tb chopped garlic
6 cups sliced red cabbage
1 cup peeled, seeded, and chopped ripe tomatoes
1 cup beef broth
½ tsp rosemary
Salt and freshly ground pepper
8 Italian sweet sausages
4 cups cooked white beans
¼ cup chopped fresh parsley

In 2 tablespoons of the oil sauté the onions, celery, and ham until lightly browned. Add 1 teaspoon of the garlic, and cook 1 minute. Add the sliced cabbage and tomatoes; cook until wilted, about 5 minutes. Add the broth, rosemary, 1 teaspoon salt, and pepper to taste. Bring to a boil, reduce heat, and slowly braise, covered, for 30 minutes.

Meanwhile, prick the sausages with a fork to release fat, and brown in a skillet. Add them to the cabbage pot; cook 20 minutes longer. Uncover the pot and reduce the liquid for 5 minutes.

In 4 tablespoons of the oil, cook the remaining garlic until lightly browned. Strain out the garlic bits and heat the beans in the garlic-flavored oil. Mound the beans in the center of a serving platter, sprinkle with parsley, and surround with the cabbage and sausages. (*Serves 3–4*)

Sweet Cabbage Strudel

This "strudel" is easy to make with packaged filo dough, but should you have authentic strudel dough on hand, by all means use it! As the strudel is slightly sweet, serve it as a savory—before, during, or after a meal.

> 1/2 cup raisins
> 4 Tb butter
> 1/4 cup sugar
> 3 Tb lemon juice
> 1 tart apple
> 6 cups shredded green cabbage
> 1/4 tsp salt
> 1/2 cup sour cream
> 10 sheets filo dough
> 8 Tb melted butter
> 1/4 cup finely crushed dried bread or cracker crumbs
> Sour cream (optional)

Plump raisins in hot water for 10 minutes. In a large sauté pan, melt the 4 tablespoons butter, stir in the sugar and lemon juice, and cook for 2 minutes to dissolve the sugar. Grate the apple, and stir in along with the cabbage and salt. Cover pan, stew for 5 minutes, then remove cover and rapidly cook, stirring, for 3–4 minutes to evaporate the moisture; cool slightly. Drain raisins; mix with cabbage and 1/2 cup sour cream. Place a sheet of filo dough on a damp towel. Brush with melted butter and sprinkle lightly with crumbs. Repeat this layering four more times. Then, spread half the cabbage mixture across the narrow end of the dough, leaving a 1 1/2-inch border on both sides and a 4-inch border on the top. (1) First, fold in the side borders, then fold down the 4-inch border. (2) Using the towel, continue rolling the strudel. (You will end up with a pinwheel cross section.) Set

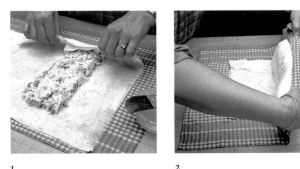

1   2

strudel on a buttered baking sheet, seam side down. Repeat this procedure for the second strudel. Brush both strudels with melted butter, and bake in a preheated 375° oven for 25–30 minutes or until the strudels are crisp and golden brown. Serve with sour cream if you wish. (*Makes 2 strudels*)

- For a nonsweet version, omit the apple, sugar, and lemon. Add 1 sliced medium onion along with the cabbage and the butter, and season thoroughly with salt, pepper, and herbs such as dill or thyme.
- For a luncheon dish, add ham or corned beef strips.
- Use this same filling to stuff *Pierogi*, the Eastern European stuffed dumpling (see *Appendix*).

Stuffed Cabbage Leaves

There are many possible stuffings for cabbage rolls, all of which use the same assembly method. I like this light filling, and find blanching standard cabbage whole makes it easier to remove the leaves. With Savoy cabbage, first remove the leaves and then blanch or steam them.

> 2-lb green cabbage
> 4–5 Tb butter
> 1/2 cup finely chopped carrots
> 1/2 cup finely chopped celeriac or celery
> 1/2 cup finely chopped onions
> 1/2 lb thinly julienned ham
> 1 Tb chopped garlic
> 1 cup thinly sliced onions
> 1 egg
> 1/2 cup fresh bread crumbs
> 1/2 tsp rosemary
> Freshly ground pepper
> 3 cups hot chicken broth
> 1 Tb flour (optional)
> 1/4 cup sour cream (optional)

Core the cabbage, but keep it whole. Blanch it for 6 minutes, or steam it for 10–12 minutes. (Savoy cabbage leaves should be blanched for 2–3 minutes or steamed for 4–5 minutes.) Cool slightly. Remove the 12 best-shaped, largest leaves. Trim the ribs so that they are the same thickness as the leaves and can be easily bent. Finely shred the remaining cabbage. Melt 3 tablespoons of the butter in a sauté pan and cook the carrots, celeriac or celery, chopped onions, and 1 cup of the shredded cabbage for 10 minutes, until wilted but not browned. Add the ham and garlic; cook 5 minutes longer. Place in a bowl, and cool slightly.

While the stuffing is cooling, in the same sauté pan melt 1 tablespoon of the butter and sauté the remaining shredded cabbage and sliced onions for 5 minutes. Strew them in the bottom of a buttered 9 x 13-inch baking dish or one just large enough to hold the cabbage rolls. Beat the egg and combine with the vegetable and ham mixture, the crumbs, and rosemary. Season with pepper. (Salt is usually unnecessary because the ham is salty enough.)

Place a heaping tablespoon of filling on each leaf. Fold over the ribbed end of the leaf, then fold over the two sides and roll up. Place in the dish, the flap side down. Continue until all the leaves are stuffed. Pour the hot broth over them. Cover loosely with parchment paper or aluminum foil, and bake in a preheated 350° oven for 40 minutes, basting occasionally. Serve with just the pan juices or, if you prefer, make a light sauce: Melt 1 tablespoon butter in a sauté pan, stir in the flour, and cook for 2 minutes; pour in the pan liquids (about 2 cups); bring to a boil, then simmer to thicken lightly; stir in the sour cream and reheat without boiling. (Serves 6)

- Substitute cooked rice for the crumbs.
- Add 1 can of tomato paste to the broth before cooking.
- *Ground Meat Stuffing*: Replace the ham with ³/₄–1 pound ground beef or pork, or a combination of both, that has been lightly sautéed and drained of fat. Do not sauté with the vegetables.
- Using the ground meat variation above, add raisins, ¼ cup brown sugar, and sour salt or lemon juice to taste, along with a can of tomato paste, to the broth. Bring to a boil and proceed with recipe.

Whole Stuffed Cabbage

Here's an easy takeoff on a French whole stuffed cabbage. (For an authentic boiled-in-cheesecloth version, see suggestions at end of recipe.) A rounded 8 ½ x 4 ½-inch Pyrex baking dish is essential to form the cabbage, which can be served plain or with a tomato or mushroom sauce.

2–2 ½-lb green cabbage
(preferably Savoy)
1 Tb butter
1 Tb oil
1 cup chopped leeks (white portions) or onions
2 tsp garlic
1 lb Italian sweet sausages
2 eggs

2 cups chopped cooked dark poultry meat (chicken, duck, goose)
1 cup cooked rice
1 ½ cups blanched, chopped spinach, Swiss chard, or greens
½ tsp salt
Freshly ground pepper
1 tsp thyme
¼ tsp allspice
4 slices bacon
2 cups beef broth

Wash the cabbage. Remove 12 of the large outer leaves, and steam for 2–3 minutes; set aside. Steam the rest of the cabbage for 4–5 minutes until wilted, and chop. Set aside 2 cups of this chopped cabbage. Heat the butter and the oil, and sauté the leeks or onions until wilted. Add the garlic, cook for 30 seconds, and set aside. Remove the sausage casings and break up the meat. Beat the eggs and mix thoroughly with the sausage, poultry, the 2 cups reserved cabbage, reserved leeks or onions, rice, greens, salt, and spices. Crisscross 2 strips of the bacon in the bottom of the buttered ovenproof bowl. Pare down the thick ribs of the cabbage leaves until they are as thin as the leaves. Arrange 4–5 leaves overlapping in the bowl (outer edges out) so that the leaf tips are facing the center while the rib ends come up the side edge.

The leaves should overlap and should extend over the edge of the bowl. Spread out a third of the stuffing mixture in the bowl. Cover with 2–3 cabbage leaves and press down. Repeat once again. Then spread the remaining mixture and fold over the cabbage ends. Top with the remaining cabbage leaves, and press down again. Place 2 slices of bacon crisscross across the cabbage. Bring the broth to a boil, and slowly pour it over the stuffed cabbage, easing a knife between the inside of the bowl and the leaves so that the liquid goes down. Cover with aluminum foil and place in a preheated 400° oven.

Bake for 30 minutes. Lower the heat to 350°, and bake 1 hour longer. Remove from the oven, and, tipping the bowl carefully, drain off the liquid. Let the cabbage set 5 minutes; drain again. Then, put a plate on top of the bowl, and invert the molded cabbage. Remove the bacon strips and cut into wedges. *(Serves 8)*

- For the traditional French-style stuffed cabbage, wash the cabbage and fold down the outer leaves to expose the center heart. Cut it away, leaving the outer leaves attached. (Blanch or steam the whole cabbage first, if necessary, to ease detaching the leaves.) Place the stuffing inside the cavity; fold the cabbage leaves around the stuffing, tie securely, and place in a string bag or cheesecloth and tie again. Simmer in broth or water for 2 hours. Remove and cut away the bag.
- If making a round stuffed cabbage seems too much bother, instead make layers with whole leaves and stuffing in a baking dish; proceed as above, serving in squares.
- Vary the stuffing by using ground pork or beef, or bread crumbs instead of rice, etc.

Green Cabbage Relish

2 Tb sugar
²/₃ cup boiling water
¹/₃ cup white or cider vinegar
¹/₂ tsp salt
¹/₂ tsp celery seeds
8 cups finely shredded green cabbage
¹/₂ cup sweet red pepper

Dissolve sugar in water. Mix with vinegar, salt, and celery seeds. Pour over the cabbage and pepper, mixing thoroughly. Cover and marinate for 3–4 hours. It will keep refrigerated 3–4 days. *(Makes 8 cups)*
- Add chopped green pepper or a grated carrot.

Marinated Red Cabbage Relish

As red cabbage is a little tougher than green cabbage, it needs a longer marinating time to become tenderized.

8–9 cups finely sliced red cabbage
1 cup thinly sliced red or sweet onions
¹/₂ tsp mustard seeds
1 tsp celery seeds
2 bay leaves
2 tsp chopped garlic (optional)
2 cups water
1 cup red wine vinegar
2 Tb sugar
2 Tb salt

Mix cabbage with onions, mustard and celery seeds, bay leaves, and garlic (if you wish). Boil the water, vinegar, sugar, and salt until the sugar dissolves. Pour the vinegar mixture over the cabbage, tossing well. The liquid should cover the cabbage. If it doesn't, make up some more vinegar-water marinade. Put the cabbage in a covered jar or bowl. Refrigerate for 2 days, stirring occasionally. It will keep up to 1 week. *(Makes 8 cups)*
- You can add beet juice to the water for a more pronounced red color.

Sauerkraut

Homemade sauerkraut is far superior to the store-bought varieties. Contrary to what you might expect, it's easy to make and an excellent way to preserve a surplus of cabbage.

10 lb very finely shredded green cabbage
6 oz pickling salt

Mix together the cabbage and salt and let stand in large bowls until the juices begin to appear. Then, pack it into a 2-gallon stoneware crock or jar, pressing down hard. To hold the cabbage under the brine, cover with a sterilized plate that just fits into the crock, and weigh it down with a 5-pound weight. (An easy way is a double plastic bag filled with water and tied off.) The cabbage juices will form a brine which should cover the cabbage slices completely. If it is necessary to add more liquid, make a brine of 3 tablespoons salt for each quart of water. Loosely cover the crock with cheesecloth to prevent particles from falling into the brine. Store in a room with a temperature between 60° and 70°. Skim the brine daily. Fermentation is over when the brine stops bubbling—approximately 2–3 weeks. At this point, the sauerkraut is ready to eat, and should be stored in a cooler area where the temperature does not exceed 38°. It will keep for up to 3 months. You could cover the crock tightly, but still keep the plate weighted down below the brine level. If you want to keep the sauerkraut indefinitely, pack in sterilized jars and process in a water bath for 25 minutes. *(Makes approximately 3 quarts)*
Note: Chinese cabbage also makes delicious sauerkraut.
- Add additional seasonings, such as 4–6 juniper berries, 2 bay leaves, or a couple of teaspoons of caraway or cumin seeds.

Carrots

Fresh home-grown carrots have a sweetness and succulence rarely found in carrots that have been stored for some time. When I'm harvesting baby carrots I find them impossible to resist: I'll wipe off a few and crunch on them right in the garden. If their usefulness extended no further, carrots would still merit garden space. But they are one of nature's basic aromatics and garden staples—delightful raw or cooked in countless recipes that benefit from their sweetness and glorious color. What more could you ask of a vegetable?

Ideally, carrots need deep, sandy loam free from rocks and hardpan. Although we have good basic soil, Russ has added peat and sand to improve the texture and drainage—ideal conditions for growing carrots. He plants Pioneer (a relatively new hybrid carrot), the European-style miniature carrots, and a Nantes Half Long, which is a thicker, stump-rooted variety that grows well in all types of garden soil. Russ prefers the wide-row method for growing carrots and sows seeds in a 12–14-inch-wide row into which he has worked 5-10-5 fertilizer. He thins the carrots to only 1 inch apart, letting them grow closely to crowd out the weeds, and sows a carrot crop three times during the season: once in late April after the soil has warmed up, next in June, and finally in late July. Then, as the carrots mature, every other one is harvested, which allows sufficient room for the carrots to grow.

Aside from thinning and regular watering, carrots need little further attention until harvesting time, about eight weeks after the seeds are sown. (The first sowing of carrots often attracts carrot flies, but by the second and third sowings the carrot fly season has peaked.)

We harvest carrots in a leisurely way over a period of several weeks because they hold in the ground quite nicely. With a spading fork, Russ loosens the ground a good distance away from the roots, and then, so that he doesn't damage the roots, twists the carrots gently out of the ground. It's important not to yank, for the brittle tops break easily, leaving the roots in the ground.

I prefer to use carrots as soon as possible after harvesting. Although carrots are one vegetable that can be stored without tremendous damage to their taste, they'll lose sweetness and succulence the longer they're kept.

To store a winter's supply, harvest on a dry day. Lift out the carrots, cut off the foliage near the crowns, and layer the trimmed carrots in boxes of slightly moist sand. Store the carrots in a humid root cellar at temperatures between 35° and 40°.

I treat baby carrots as simply as possible. Their skins are as tender as their flesh and don't need peeling. I rinse them off, or if the roots are particularly dirty, I'll scrub them with a vegetable brush. A small amount of the tops makes an attractive contrast, so I'll leave perhaps ½ inch and blanch them in boiling salted water with a pinch of sugar for 4 minutes. These carrots are divine: the sugar doesn't sweeten the carrots, but merely accentuates their natural sweetness. Increase the "pinch of sugar" for older or storage carrots.

Older carrots don't actually have to be peeled, but their skins are slightly tough and they look more attractive peeled. When you are making carrot ovals, curls, or roll-cuts, always peel or scrape the carrots for looks. Some people prefer to steam unpeeled carrots and slip off the skin after cooking, but I don't find it improves the flavor.

My father was a professional chef and a whiz at preparing food. His method for peeling carrots is one I use all the time: Place the carrot lengthwise cradled in the palm of your hand stem end away. Close your grip slightly to lightly hold the carrot. Using a vegetable peeler, start at the far end of the carrot, and peel toward you. As you peel, turn the carrot by pushing with your thumb to rotate it in your hand. It might take a few tries to get used to this technique, but it is, I'm convinced, the fastest and most efficient way to peel a carrot.

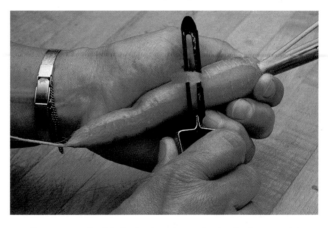

As carrots hold their shape so nicely during cooking, it's fun to vary the way they look. Most usually, I'll make large carrots into "logs"—a good cooking method because the uniformly sized carrots cook evenly. I cut across the length of the carrot, forming even sections. (For example, I'd cut a 6-inch carrot into three 2-inch sections.) Then, I'd make equal-size logs by halving the tip third of the carrot, quartering the middle third, and cutting the remaining third into sixths. The number of cuts varies depending upon size, but it is easy to cut the carrots equally. The cooked carrot logs look attractive stacked like Lincoln Logs or scattered around the plate. Carrots also are pretty sliced into pennies or quarters (which cook in minutes); julienned; cut into extra-thin diagonal slices for cold platters; into wider strips for stews and braises; or into roll-cuts (see illustrations for *Asparagus,* page 4).

1   *penny slice*
2   *julienne*
3   *logs*
4   *diagonal slice*
5   *roll cut*

When our baby carrot supply is gone, I shape large carrots into pretend baby carrots. This technique takes time, but the carrots look so elegant surrounding a roast for a special dinner party. Cut the carrots into 2–3-inch pieces, then trim them into baby carrot shapes, setting aside the scraps for soups or purées. Older carrots often have a tough, woody central core which should be discarded. Cut away the orange flesh surrounding the core and use for a purée or *Mirepoix* (see *Appendix*).

To prepare carrots in advance, regardless of their shapes, I usually blanch them in boiling water—during the day or even the day before when I'm preparing a number of dishes at a time. I cool them immediately in cold water, and finish at serving time.

Steaming works just as well: I use this method when we are going to eat the carrots immediately. When I have other foods cooking in the oven, I'll bake carrots. Braising done at the last minute is a simple treatment that brings out the carrot flavor. Ignore braised carrot recipes that recommend 20–40 minutes of cooking covered—they'll be mush. Garden-fresh and most market carrots do not need to be cooked very long.

Most of the recipes in this section call for cooked carrots. But raw carrots are not only flavorful, they're also loaded with vitamin A. Use them with a *Vinaigrette Sauce* (see *Appendix*), in slaws, and on a crudités platter: a standard French hors d'oeuvre is finely grated raw carrots, marinated in fresh lemon juice with lots of black pepper. Raw carrots also have kept many a dieter sane.

Special Information

Yields
- 1 pound carrots = 3–3 ½ cups sliced, chopped, or grated = 1 ½ cups puréed
- 1 pound carrots = 3–4 servings
- The yield depends upon the amount of waste: ³/₄ pound peeled carrots yields 3 cups chopped carrots

Storage and Preserving

To store
- Remove tops; place in perforated plastic bag or in refrigerator vegetable compartment for up to 2 weeks.
- For longer storage, remove tops and layer in moist sand in a well-ventilated cellar with temperatures between 35°–40°.
- Cooked carrots will keep 2–3 days, refrigerated.
- Whole or sectioned carrots freeze poorly (their texture becomes watery). You can, however, freeze puréed carrots.

Hints
- For a delicious pickled snack, marinate carrot sticks in leftover pickle juice.

- Grate raw carrots into slaws or salads.
- Make julienned carrots: Peel the carrots, then slice into long, flat, thin strips. If you have trouble with a knife, use a vegetable parer. Stack a few of the strips on top of one another, then fold over end to end. Slice down to make fine strips.
- Julienne, blanch, and use carrots as a clear soup garnish.
- Julienne finely, marinate in vinegar or a *Vinaigrette Sauce* (see *Appendix*), and garnish salad plates with mounds of dressed carrots.
- Make carrot curls: Slice a long lengthwise strip from the carrot. Then, with a vegetable peeler, cut long, thin strips from the flat surface. The strips should curl (if not, wrap them around your finger). Drop into a bowl of ice water for an hour or longer.
- Marinate barely cooked carrot slices or logs overnight in a well-seasoned marinade, and serve as an appetizer or relish.
- Add carrots to hearty soups or stews, but only for as long as they need to cook. Don't leave them in for hours on end.

Marketing

Carrots are available year round. I prefer to buy carrots that still have their tops because I know if the tops are fresh, the carrots have been harvested recently. Without the tops, it is more difficult to judge age. One telltale sign, though: old carrots send out a lot of little roots.

Packaged carrots can be fine, but too often I've come upon dried-up, cracked ones. Carrots kept in refrigerated cases or sprinkled with water should be your first choice. Look for crisp, firm flesh and a deep orange color. Deeply colored carrots contain more carotene (which the body converts into vitamin A) than paler-colored carrots.

You can also find packaged miniature carrots. They're not as sweet and moist as garden carrots, but make a pretty addition to a serving platter, and with a touch of sugar and a gentle butter braise they work out well. Don't buy oversize carrots: they probably contain great big unusable cores.

◇ Braised Carrots

Carrots can be braised whole, if small, or cut into any kind of shape. I'm giving you timing for carrot logs approximately 2–3 inches long by 3/8 inch wide, but you must adjust the timing to the size carrots you're preparing. If you cut them into thin disks, for example, the cooking time would be considerably less, while whole small carrots would take a slightly longer time to cook. The carrots' diameter is the deciding factor: test and don't overcook!

Carrots Braised in Butter

Peel carrots and cut into logs. Melt 4 tablespoons butter for each pound carrots in a saucepan and add the carrots, a teaspoon of sugar, salt, and a little water. Bring water to a boil, cover, reduce heat, and cook over gentle heat for 4–6 minutes. Drain and season with salt and pepper or with herbs of your choice.

- Fold in any vegetables you like, such as mushrooms or sliced onions sautéed in butter or barely cooked peas.
- Boil heavy cream and a clove of mashed garlic together until cream is slightly reduced. Barely cover cooked carrots and boil again until carrots are coated with sauce.

Carrots Braised in Broth

Peel carrots and cut into logs. For each pound carrots, add 1 cup beef broth, 1 teaspoon sugar, 1 tablespoon butter, and ½ teaspoon salt. Bring broth to a boil, cover, reduce heat, and cook 4–5 minutes. Remove carrots to a warm plate and reduce the liquids to a light glaze. Pour over the carrots or roll carrots in the thickened liquid.

- *Braised in Broth and Glazed:* Treat the same as above, but increase the butter to 3–4 tablespoons and the sugar to 1½ tablespoons, which will produce a more syrupy glaze.
- *Braised in Vichy Water:* Treat exactly as *Braised in Broth*, but substitute Vichy water for broth.
- *Basic Buttered Carrots:* Treat exactly as *Braised in Broth*, substituting water for broth. Drain and roll in butter, seasonings, and herbs to taste.

- Parsnips and carrots have the same sweet flavor. Substitute carrots in parsnip recipes such as *Parsnip Tart* (see *Parsnips*).
- Mix and substitute. *Cabbage Loaf* (see *Cabbage*) works well with shredded carrots.
- Make fried carrot sticks (see *Salsify*).
- Use to extend meatloaves or meat squares.
- Use carrots in a *Mirepoix* (see *Appendix*) to flavor roasts, braises, and stews.
- Carrots' sweetness helps to tame acidic foods such as the *Marinara Sauce* in *Tomatoes*.
- Add mashed cooked carrots to naturally thicken a sauce while giving a sweet bouquet.
- Substitute carrots in winter squash or turnip recipes, taking into account the carrots' sweetness.
- Experiment with dessert puddings and cakes. The natural sweetness of carrots makes an excellent dessert base.
- Cool barely blanched roll-cut carrots and serve on an appetizer tray.

Microwave

- 1 pound carrots peeled, trimmed, cut into logs, and placed in a covered dish with 2 tablespoons liquid will cook in 4–6 minutes.

Leftovers

- Make a carrot purée, and combine with potatoes or celeriac.
- Mash and reheat with butter and seasonings.
- Use puréed carrots to thicken sauces.
- Use leftover finely chopped carrots in roast beef or corned beef hashes.
- Make breads. See *Carrot Bread*.
- Make a *Savory Carrot Pudding:* Combine 2 cups leftover mashed carrots with a custard (made with 2 eggs beaten with 1 cup milk and seasonings). Add a chopped onion or herbs and bake in a 350° oven for 30–40 minutes. Top with buttered bread crumbs or grated cheese and run under the broiler if desired.
- Make *Chilled Carrot Soufflé*.

◇ *Sautéed Carrots*

This sauté-braise is handy for thinly sliced, julienned, or shredded carrots. Melt butter in a sauté pan, add carrots, salt, and sugar, stir well to coat with butter, cover, and cook over very gentle heat, stirring occasionally until tender. This will take just a few minutes. If you don't want to use butter, simmer the carrots in some liquid, such as the juice and rind of 1 orange. For extra flavor, add finely sliced apples or apricots, or sautéed sliced onions or shallots.

◇ *Baked Carrots*

Carrots bake well, although they take longer to cook this way. Baking is a convenient method when you have other dishes already in the oven. Place the carrots in an ovenproof dish. For 1 pound carrots, cut into logs, sprinkle with 1–2 teaspoons sugar and 1/2 teaspoon salt, and dot with 2 tablespoons butter. Cover and bake in a preheated 400° oven for 30–40 minutes, or a 350° oven for 40–45 minutes. (Size does not make much difference: even shredded carrots will take 40 minutes to bake in a 350° oven as well.)

◇ *Blanched Carrots*

Blanching is a particularly good method to use when you want to prepare carrots ahead of time and finish them later. Undercook (because they will cook further), plunge them into cold water to stop the cooking, drain, and store the carrots in the refrigerator until ready to use. I'm using carrot logs as an example; thinly sliced disks will take only a moment or two, larger chunks longer.

Boil a large pot of water and add salt and 1 teaspoon sugar or more as desired. Drop in carrots, bring back to a boil, and cook 3–4 minutes or until just barely tender. Either chill in cold water, drain, and set aside; or drain and use one of the finishing touches below. Whole carrots, approximately 1 inch across at the base, will cook tender in 8 minutes.

◇ *Steamed Carrots*

Boil 3/4–1 inch water in a pot. Place carrots in a steamer basket or colander over the boiling water. Steam carrot logs approximately 4 minutes until just tender. Whole carrots 1 inch at the base will cook in 10–12 minutes. Flavor the steam water with rosemary, or a little cinnamon and sugar if you like.

Finishing Touches for Blanched or Steamed Carrots

- *With Butter:* Roll in melted butter and season with salt, pepper, and a dash of lemon juice.

- *With Glaze:* Roll carrots in melted butter, sugar, or honey until lightly glazed.
- *With Herbs:* Roll carrots in butter and combine with 1 or more tablespoons chopped herbs such as dill, chives, or fresh rosemary.
- *With Bacon:* Roll in melted butter and sprinkle with coked bacon bits.
- *With Cream:* Roll carrots in butter. Barely cover with heavy cream, and gently reduce cream until it just coats carrots.
- *With Sour Cream:* Roll carrots in butter. Fold in sour cream and heat gently through.
- *With Parmesan Cheese:* Roll carrots in butter and sprinkle liberally with freshly grated Parmesan cheese. Toss with chopped parsley and seasonings.
- *With Peas:* The old standby. Cut carrots in disks. Cook the carrots and peas separately and slightly undercook. Then, braise together in butter for a moment or two to finish cooking.
- *Mashed Carrots:* Cook carrots completely tender, drain, and mash with butter (3–4 tablespoons per pound of carrots), salt, and pepper. Reheat before serving, adding some cream if you like.
- *With Mashed Potatoes:* Combine mashed carrots and mashed potatoes and season to taste. Garnish with chopped chives, dill, or parsley.
- *With a Béchamel or Mornay Sauce* (see *Appendix*): Cover carrots with sauce and bake in a 350° oven until bubbly. Top with buttered crumbs and run under the broiler if desired.
- *With Crème Fraîche* (see *Appendix*): Combine 3/4–1 cup crème fraîche and chopped dill. Roll the carrots in butter, then add the crème fraîche. Bring it to a boil, reduce heat, and boil gently until the crème is reduced and thickened. Season with salt and pepper. (Crème fraîche thickens beautifully and does not separate when cooking.)

Puréed Carrots

Serve plain, flute into mounds for a garnish, or use as a filling for vegetable cases.

> 2 lb carrots
> 3 Tb butter
> 5–6 Tb heavy cream
> Salt and freshly ground pepper

Peel and slice carrots and blanch until tender. Drain, and purée in a food processor or food mill. Return to the heat and beat in the butter, cream, salt, and pepper. Set over low heat in a thick-bottomed pan or place in a double boiler, and reheat, covered, for 10–15 minutes to mingle the flavors. *(Serves 4)*
- Omit cream. Increase butter if you wish.
- Mix with an equal amount of whipped potatoes, 5 tablespoons butter, and 5 tablespoons cream. Whip to blend, and reheat.
- Serve alternating mounds of puréed carrots and puréed parsnips or turnips.
- Combine with grated Swiss or Parmesan cheese to taste and put in a partially baked pie shell. Dot with butter, sprinkle on more cheese, and bake in a preheated 400° oven for 20 minutes or until the crust is cooked. Sprinkle with parsley.

Carrots with Cranberries

Here's a colorful, fresh-tasting garnish for roasted poultry or pork.

> 1 apple
> 1 cup cranberries
> 4 cups grated carrots
> 4 Tb light-brown sugar
> 1/2 tsp salt
> 1/2 cup apple cider
> 2 Tb butter

Grate the apple and wash the cranberries. Combine with the carrots, sugar, salt, and cider. Place in a buttered casserole and dot with the butter. Cover, and bake in a preheated 350° oven for 40 minutes, stirring once. *(Serves 4)*
- *Red Cabbage with Cranberries:* Substitute finely shredded red cabbage for the carrots. Increase baking time to 1 hour or until cabbage is tender.

Carrot and Cabbage Timbales

Carrots and cabbage are an unusual, good-tasting combination. Red cabbage is especially attractive, but you must sauté-braise it longer than green cabbage so that it's tenderized. This is a handy recipe to enliven leftover cooked shredded carrots.

> 3 Tb butter
> 1 Tb chopped shallots
> 1 1/2 cups finely julienned or coarsely shredded carrots
> 1 1/2 cups finely shredded green cabbage
> Sugar
> Salt and freshly ground pepper
> 2 Tb freshly chopped dill
> 4 oz (1/2 cup) cream cheese
> 3 large eggs
> 1/4 cup heavy cream
> 3/4 cup milk
> 1 Tb chopped parsley

In a large sauté pan, melt the butter and sauté the shallots for 1 minute. Stir in the carrots and cabbage, making sure they're coated with butter. Sprinkle with sugar. Cover and cook over very low heat until tender, 5–8 minutes. Season well with salt and pepper, then stir in 1 tablespoon of the dill. Divide among 6 buttered 6-ounce Pyrex dishes. Blend together the cream cheese, eggs, cream, and milk. Stir in 1/2 teaspoon salt and some pepper, and pour over the carrots and cabbage. Place the molds in a deep baking dish and pour boiling water halfway up the sides. Bake for approximately 25 minutes in a preheated 350° oven or until the molds are set. Unmold and serve, sprinkled with the remaining dill and parsley. *(Serves 6)*
- Use 3 cups carrots and omit the cabbage, or vice versa.
- When using red cabbage, sauté 10–15 minutes separately and then combine.

Marinated Carrots

This is a piquant garnish, snack, or salad.

> 1 lb carrots
> 1 tsp sugar
> 1/2 tsp salt
> 2 1/2 Tb white wine vinegar or lemon juice
> 1/2 tsp Dijon mustard
> 1/2 cup olive oil
> 1 Tb chopped shallots
> 1 Tb chopped parsley
> 1 clove garlic, crushed
> Salt and freshly ground pepper

Peel the carrots and julienne, "log," or slice them. Blanch in boiling water with the sugar and salt for 2–4 minutes or until barely tender. Drain. Stir together the vinegar or lemon juice and mustard, beat in the oil, and add the shallots, parsley, and garlic. Pour over the warm carrots. Taste, and season with salt and pepper. Refrigerate for 4–6 hours before serving. *(Makes 3 cups)*

Carrot Slaw

I like this salad slightly sweet, but you can mix and match to taste.

>   6 cups (2 lb) julienned or grated carrots
>   1 cup raisins
>   2/3 cup mayonnaise or a combination of mayonnaise
>   and sour cream or yogurt
>   1 Tb white wine vinegar
>   1 1/2 tsp salt
>   2 tsp sugar
>   Freshly ground pepper

Combine carrots and raisins. Mix together the remaining ingredients and toss with the carrots and raisins. Correct seasonings and refrigerate for several hours before serving. (*Makes 6 cups*)

- For a less sweet version, cut the sugar down to 1 1/2 teaspoons and increase the vinegar to 2 tablespoons. Add 1 teaspoon Dijon mustard. Omit raisins and add 1 teaspoon caraway or poppy seeds. If you wish, add diced peppers, celery, onions, or other vegetables.
- Add toasted sesame seeds or pine nuts before serving.

Carrot Salad Dressings

Julienned carrots make delicious salads. Marinate long enough to tenderize the carrots and allow them to pick up the flavor. If you don't have time to marinate, first blanch carrots until just barely tender.

For 1 pound julienned carrots:

- Finely slice red onions. Toss with carrots and marinate in *Vinaigrette Sauce* (see *Appendix*).
- Combine 1/2 teaspoon cumin, 1/2 teaspoon paprika, and 1/4 teaspoon cinnamon. Mix with a lemon *Vinaigrette Sauce* (see *Appendix*) made with 1 clove crushed garlic. Marinate and toss with plenty of fresh chopped parsley before serving.
- Marinate in a lemon *Vinaigrette Sauce* (see *Appendix*) and 2 tablespoons of chopped fresh mint.
- Mix together 3/4–1 cup sour cream with 1 tablespoon horseradish, 1/2 teaspoon sugar, and 1 teaspoon Dijon mustard. Combine with carrots; marinate. Before serving, season with salt and pepper, and toss with chopped chives or parsley.

Cocktail-Size Carrot Fritters

>   1 2/3 cups flour
>   1 1/2 tsp baking powder
>   3/4 tsp salt
>   2 eggs
>   1/2 cup milk
>   1 1/2 cups shredded carrots
>   1/4 cup grated Swiss or Parmesan cheese or a
>   combination
>   1 tsp chopped dill
>   2 Tb minced onions or scallions
>   Oil or shortening for deep frying

Sift together the flour, baking powder, and salt. Beat the eggs and stir in the milk. Gradually beat in the flour mixture and the carrots, cheese, dill, and onions or scallions. Heat the oil or shortening in a deep saucepan and drop the batter in by rounded teaspoonfuls. Turn until browned on all sides and cooked through. Drain and serve. (*Makes about 3 dozen*)

Sweet Carrot Fritters

Smothered with maple syrup, these are great for a brunch.

>   2 cups flour
>   1 1/2 tsp baking powder
>   1 1/2 tsp salt
>   1/4 tsp cinnamon
>   1/4 tsp nutmeg
>   2 eggs
>   1/3 cup sugar or honey
>   1/3 cup milk
>   1/2 tsp vanilla extract
>   2 cups shredded carrots
>   Oil or shortening for deep frying
>   Confectioners' sugar

Sift together the flour, baking powder, salt, cinnamon, and nutmeg. Beat the eggs, then first add the sugar or honey, followed by the milk and vanilla. Gradually beat in the flour mixture, and stir in the carrots. Heat the oil or shortening, and drop in the batter by heaping tablespoonfuls, turning to brown on all sides. Drain before dusting with confectioners' sugar. (*Makes about 20 large fritters*)

Carrot Soup

Serve this soup either hot or chilled.

>   1 lb carrots
>   1 onion
>   1 leek (white portion only)
>   2 stalks celery
>   5 cups chicken broth
>   1/3 cup rice
>   Salt and freshly ground pepper
>   3/4 cup light cream
>   Chopped dill (optional)

Peel and slice carrots. Peel and chop the onion, and wash and chop the leek and celery. Place the vegetables in a saucepan along with 4 cups of the broth and the rice. Bring broth to a boil, cover pan, and reduce heat. Cook gently for 15–20 minutes, or until the vegetables are tender. Purée a little at a time, adding just enough liquid to blend easily. Add remaining broth if soup is too thick. Taste and season with salt and pepper. Add cream, reheat, and taste again. Sprinkle with dill if you like. (*Makes 1 1/2 quarts*)

- Use 1/2–3/4 pound chopped potato rather than rice. You could also wilt the onion, leek, and celery in 2 tablespoons butter before adding the broth.

Cream of Carrot and Celeriac Soup

This soup has an attractive pale orange color and a subtle, creamy taste.

    1 lb carrots
    1 1/2 lb celeriac
    1/2 lb leeks (white portion only) or onions
    8 cups chicken broth
    1 cup light cream
    Salt and freshly ground pepper

Peel and chunk carrots and celeriac. You should end up with approximately 1 pound celeriac. Wash and chop the leeks or onions. Place the chopped vegetables in a 6-quart saucepan and add 6 cups of the broth. Cover pan, bring to a boil, turn down the heat, and cook gently until the vegetables are tender, 15–20 minutes. Blend vegetables and broth in batches until puréed. Return to the pan, add the remaining broth, reheat, and add the cream. Taste for seasoning and heat just long enough to warm cream. *(Makes 2 1/2 quarts)*

- For a lovely garnish, poach a few scallops, slice them crosswise, and float on top of the soup.
- Decrease the celeriac and increase carrots or vice versa.
- Use celery instead of celeriac.

Marie O'Day's Scotch Broth

It's important to finely dice the vegetables. If you use a food processor, process only small amounts at a time—otherwise you'll end up with mush.

    1 cup barley
    Salt
    3 1/2–4 lb chicken
    6 cups chicken broth
    1 celery stalk
    1 peeled onion
    4 cups finely diced carrots
    4 cups finely diced cabbage
    Freshly ground pepper

Pour boiling water over barley and steep for 1 hour. Drain and cover with fresh water, and add 1 teaspoon salt. Bring to a boil, reduce heat, and simmer until chewy, about 30 minutes. You should now have approximately 4 cups cooked barley. In the meantime, place the cleaned chicken in a large saucepan or soup pot and cover with broth and an additional 6 cups water. Add the celery stalk and onion, and simmer until the chicken is tender. Discard the celery and onion. Remove the chicken, cool slightly, and remove the meat from the bones. Skim the fat from the broth, add the carrots and cabbage, and bring the broth to a boil. Add the barley and simmer for 10 minutes. Add the chicken meat and simmer for 5 minutes longer or until the chicken meat is heated through. Taste. If the chicken stock is too watery, strain out the chicken and vegetables and rapidly reduce the broth until it has the desired flavor. Then add the vegetables and chicken and reheat, correcting the seasonings. *(Makes 3 quarts)*

Quick Chicken and Carrot Fricassee

Carrots are used often in braised dishes but rarely in quantity. The large amount of carrots is essential to the final flavor of this dish.

    2 lb carrots
    Salt
    1 Tb lemon juice
    6 Tb butter
    2 cups sliced mushrooms
    2 Tb chopped shallots
    1 Tb flour
    1 cup chicken broth
    4 whole boned and skinned chicken breasts
        (8 supremes)
    1 Tb chopped fresh tarragon (optional)
    Freshly ground pepper
    1/4 cup dry vermouth
    1 cup heavy cream
    2 Tb chopped parsley

Peel and julienne the carrots. Bring 1/2 cup water, 1/8 teaspoon salt, 1/2 tablespoon lemon juice, and 1 tablespoon butter to a boil. Add the mushrooms, cover, and cook for 2–3 minutes. Drain and set aside. (Save liquid for the next time you make soup.)

Heat the remaining butter in a large sauté pan. Add the carrots and shallots and cook over medium-low heat for 5 minutes, stirring. Sprinkle on the flour, and stir constantly for 2 minutes, until cooked slightly. Stir in the broth. Place the chicken pieces on top of the carrots, and sprinkle with the tarragon (if you like), salt, and pepper. Cover and simmer for 6 minutes. With a slotted spoon, remove chicken and carrots to a warm plate. Add the vermouth to the pan liquids and cook rapidly to reduce slightly. Stir in the heavy cream. Boil rapidly until slightly thickened. Season with salt, pepper, and the remaining lemon juice. Return the chicken and carrots to the pan along with the mushrooms. Coat with sauce, heat through, and sprinkle with parsley before serving. *(Serves 4)*

- For a no-cream version, increase the broth to 1 1/2 cups and serve the chicken and carrots with the pan juices.

Top Steak Roast with Carrots

Top steak roast is my butcher's name for the best rump steak—suitable for roasting or "steaks." Be sure to select a piece will larded with fat. This is an aromatic way of roasting that works equally well with all good cuts of beef, and for veal and pork as well.

    1 1/2–2 lb carrots
    4–5-lb rolled, larded, and tied steak roast
    1 cup chopped onions
    1 cup chopped celery
    Salt and freshly ground pepper
    Herbs (your favorites)
    3 Tb melted butter
    1 1/2 cups homemade beef broth

Peel carrots and cut into long diagonal 1/2-inch-thick slices. Blanch in boiling water for 2 minutes; drain. Set the roast into an oven casserole and place in a preheated 500° oven to sear for 20 minutes. Remove roast from the oven and drain off all accumulated fat. Reduce the oven temperature to 350°. Distribute the onions and celery around and under the roast. Season with salt, pepper, and herbs. Arrange the carrots around and on the roast, and pour melted butter over them. Cover the casserole and cook for 45 minutes. Check the temperature of the meat—it should be 165°. If not done, continue roasting, checking the temperature every 10 minutes. Remove the roast and carrots to a warm platter and degrease the pan. Add the broth and boil down slightly to deglaze the pan. Strain the broth and baste the meat. (*Serves 8*)

• Add blanched, quartered fennel for an anise aroma, or blanched whole leeks, or root vegetables.

Chilled Carrot Soufflé

Sweet carrot desserts were common for centuries, but lately carrots seem to have been relegated to cakes and breads. Here, carrots create a creamy light soufflé just as sweet as any chocolate dessert. I like to use a 2-quart charlotte mold that is 4 inches deep and 7 inches wide, and turn it out onto a serving plate. Or, use a soufflé dish with a collar and serve from the dish.

    1 1/4 lb carrots
    1 Golden Delicious apple
    1/2 cup plus 2 Tb sugar
    2 packages unflavored gelatin
    1 cup apple cider
    4 eggs
    2 tsp cornstarch
    Salt
    1 tsp vanilla extract
    1 1/2 cups half-and-half
    1/4 tsp cream of tartar
    1 cup heavy cream

Peel the carrots and cut into 1/2-inch slices or chunks. Core the apple, leaving the peel on, and cut it into chunks. Combine the carrots, 1 tablespoon of the sugar, the apple, and 1/4 cup water in a small saucepan. Bring the water to a boil, reduce the heat, cover, and cook gently until the carrots are very tender, 15–20 minutes. Drain and purée. You should have 2 cups.

Meanwhile, soften the gelatin in apple cider, then heat to dissolve it. Mix the gelatin into the puréed carrot. Separate the eggs and beat the yolks. Gradually beat in 1/2 cup sugar and continue beating until thickened and pale yellow in color. Beat in the cornstarch, a pinch of salt, and vanilla. Heat the half-and-half and gradually beat it into the egg yolks. Set the mixture over mediumlow heat and, stirring constantly, heat to a temperature of 170° or until the sauce has thickened enough to coat a spoon. Remove from heat and beat until slightly cooled, then combine with carrot and gelatin mixture.

Beat the egg whites until foamy and add cream of tartar and a pinch of salt. Beat until the whites form soft peaks. Sprinkle in 1 tablespoon sugar and continue beating until whites form firm peaks. Fold the whites into the carrot-custard mixture until well mixed in. Chill, stirring occasionally, until cold but not set.

Now, beat the heavy cream until thickened and fold it into the chilled carrot mixture. Line the bottom of the mold with a round of waxed paper. Rinse the mold in cold water. Pour the carrot mixture into the mold, and chill for 5–6 hours.

Run a knife around the edge of the mold. Dip the bottom of the mold into hot water, and invert the serving plate over the mold. Turn and lightly tap the plate on the counter; the soufflé will drop out of the mold. Repeat steps if necessary. Decorate with whipped cream or the following carrot or apple topping. (*Makes a 2-quart soufflé*)

Candied Carrot Topping

    1/3 cup sugar
    1 cup apple cider
    1 cup shredded carrots

Heat together the sugar and the cider, and add the carrots. Cook over low heat until liquid is reduced and barely covers the carrots. Cool carrots in the liquid, then drain and use to decorate the soufflé top.

Apple Topping
4 Golden Delicious apples
¼ cup brown sugar
¼ cup melted butter

Peel, core, and section the apples into 6–8 pieces, depending upon size. Put into an ovenproof pan, drizzle with butter, and sprinkle with sugar. Broil until the apples are lightly browned and tender. Cool. Arrange on top of the soufflé and around the edge of the serving plate.

- For a variation in the soufflé, substitute leftover puréed carrots and eliminate the apple and sugar.
- *Carrot Charlotte*: This uses essentially the same ingredients as above, but eliminates the egg whites and adds additional cream, giving a denser filling for the ladyfinger lining. Line the bottom of the mold with waxed paper. Dip 16 ladyfingers, one at a time, into 1 cup apple cider for 1 second and drain. They should be damp, not wet. Arrange, pressed together, curved sides against the mold. Proceed with the master recipe, eliminating the egg whites. Beat 1 ½ cups of heavy cream (the original 1 cup plus ½ cup) until thickened. Stir one-third of the whipped cream into the carrot custard mixture to lighten it, then fold in the remaining whipped cream. Pour into the ladyfinger-lined mold. Chill for 5–6 hours. Decorate with whipped cream or with the above toppings.

Carrot Cake

Carrot cake was quite the rage a few years ago. I know a Pennsylvania restaurateur who said that carrot cakes were a restaurant quality-test for a while, and the cake formulas were top secret! Now that the craze is over, we can relax with this recipe for a wonderful no-secret carrot cake.

2 cups flour
2 tsp baking soda
2 tsp baking powder
1 tsp salt
1 tsp cinnamon
¼ tsp mace
1 ½ cups sugar
1 ¼ cups oil
4 eggs
3 cups finely shredded carrots
1 Tb finely grated lemon peel
¾ cup chopped nuts
½ cup raisins (optional)

Sift together the flour, soda, baking powder, salt, and spices; set aside. Beat together the sugar and oil. Gradually beat in the eggs and then the flour mixture. Stir in the carrots, lemon peel, nuts, and raisins (if you like). Oil a 10-inch tube pan. Pour in the batter, tap on the counter to release any air bubbles, and bake in a preheated 350° oven for 50–60 minutes or until a toothpick

inserted into the center of the cake comes out clean. Cool on a rack for 15 minutes. Invert and remove from the pan. Cool and frost, if desired, with *Cream Cheese Frosting* (see *Appendix*) or the following *Lemon or Orange Glaze*. (*Makes a 10-inch tube cake*)

Lemon or Orange Glaze
½ cup orange or lemon juice
1 tsp finely grated rind
1 ½ cups sifted confectioners' sugar

Combine ingredients, warm slightly; pour over cake.

- Bake cake for 25–30 minutes in three 8-inch round pans. Frost all three layers or split the layers in half for a 6-layer cake.
- Substitute ½ pound softened sweet butter for the oil.

Carrot-Orange Bars

2 cups flour
2 tsp baking powder
½ tsp salt
½ tsp nutmeg
¾ cup softened butter
½ cup sugar
1 egg
1 tsp vanilla extract
⅓ cup orange juice
2 tsp grated orange rind
½ cup flaked coconut (optional)
1 cup cooked mashed carrots
Orange Glaze (optional: **see above**)

Sift together the flour, baking powder, salt, and nutmeg; set aside. Cream the butter and sugar; beat in the egg and vanilla. Add the flour mixture alternately with the orange juice and rind. Stir in the coconut (if you wish) and carrots. Pour into a greased 8x11-inch baking pan and bake in a preheated 350° oven for 35 minutes. Cool and glaze if desired. (*Makes 20–24 bars*)

Lynn's Pineapple-Carrot Cake

This is a moist, rich cake without being either soggy or heavy.

2 cups flour
1 cup sugar
1 tsp baking soda
3/4 tsp salt
2 tsp cinnamon
3 eggs
1/2 cup oil
3/4 cup buttermilk
2 tsp vanilla extract
2 cups finely shredded carrots
1 cup chopped nuts
1 cup flaked coconut
2/3 cup drained crushed pineapple
Whipped cream (optional)

Sift together the flour, sugar, soda, salt, and cinnamon; set aside. Beat together the eggs, oil, buttermilk, and vanilla. Gradually add the flour mixture to the egg mixture. Stir in the carrots, nuts, coconut, and pineapple. Pour into a well-greased 9x13-inch baking pan and bake in a preheated 350° oven for approximately 40 minutes. Remove from oven. Prick cake with a fork and pour the following *Buttermilk Glaze* over the warm cake. Serve warm or cold, either plain or with whipped cream on the side. *(Makes a 9 x 13-inch cake)*

Buttermilk Glaze
1/2 cup sugar
1/4 tsp baking soda
1/3 cup buttermilk
1/3 cup butter
1 Tb light corn syrup
1/2 tsp vanilla extract

Bring all the ingredients except the vanilla to a boil. Boil gently for 5 minutes. Remove from the heat and stir in the vanilla. Pour over the cake.

Carrot Bread

This is a good recipe for leftover carrots. All you need is a cup of mashed carrots.

1 1/2 cups flour
1 tsp baking soda
1 1/2 tsp cinnamon
1/2 tsp salt
2 eggs
1 cup sugar
1/2 cup oil
1 cup mashed carrots
1/2 cup chopped nuts

Sift together the flour, baking soda, cinnamon, and salt; set aside. Beat the eggs, and beat in the sugar, oil, and carrots. Gradually beat in the flour mixture. Stir in the nuts. Pour into a greased 9x5-inch loaf pan and bake in a preheated 350° oven for 55–60 minutes. Cool 10 minutes in the pan, then turn onto a rack to cool. *(Makes 1 loaf)*

Carrot Yeast Bread

The carrots make a colorful, moist, textured home-style bread.

2 cups orange juice
2 tsp sugar
1 package active dry yeast
1/4 cup honey
1/4 cup vegetable oil
2 tsp salt
4 1/2 cups unbleached flour
2 cups finely grated carrots
2 eggs
2 cups rye or whole-wheat flour

Heat orange juice to 110° or to slightly warm. Stir in the sugar and yeast, and let proof until bubbly. Beat together the honey, oil, and salt. Beat in 1 cup of the unbleached flour, and add the yeast mixture. Add the carrots and eggs, and mix well. Gradually beat in the rye or wholewheat flour and 3 cups of the unbleached flour. Sprinkle the remaining unbleached flour on the working surface and knead the dough until fairly smooth and elastic. Set into a bowl and cover with plastic wrap and a towel. Let rise until doubled in bulk, 1 1/2–2 hours. Punch down and divide in half. Shape, place in two 9x5-inch greased bread pans, and cover loosely with a towel. Let rise for 30–40 minutes. Bake in a preheated 350° oven for 45 minutes. *(Makes 2 loaves)*

Pickled Carrots

This recipe makes crisp carrots; for softer carrots, blanch them for 1 minute before packing in jars.

3 lb carrots
Dill sprigs
24 peppercorns
2 tsp mustard seeds
2 1/2 cups vinegar
1 1/2 cups water
1/2 cup sugar

Peel the carrots and cut them into logs, sticks, or disks. Sterilize 4 pint jars and fill with carrots to within 3/4 inch of the jar top, layering with dill sprigs throughout. Add 6 peppercorns and 1/2 teaspoon mustard seeds per jar. Bring the vinegar, water, and sugar to a boil and cook until sugar dissolves. Pour over the carrots. Either seal and let stand in a cool area or cover and refrigerate for 2–3 days before using. *(Makes 4 pints)*

Cauliflower

Cauliflower takes some care to grow, but I wouldn't have a garden without it. The head, or curd, is actually the undeveloped flower buds of the plant—if they keep growing, they turn into inedible yellow flowers. To prevent this from happening and to let the head grow to its optimum size, we cover (or blanch) the buds.

We start out with seeds of Snow Crown, a standard white-headed variety. Russell sows seeds indoors in March in a seedling tray. Two weeks later, when the seedlings are 1¼ inches tall, he transplants them to 4-inch pots, plunging the seedlings as much as half their length into the soil. This method appears to promote more vigorous root growth. By the third week in April, the seedlings can be placed outside, where they tolerate cool spring weather quite nicely. (Cauliflower likes a neutral soil, so work in some ground limestone if your soil is acidic.)

Russ sets the seedlings 18 inches apart, leaving 3 feet between rows, and places a paper cutworm collar around each stem. By June, when the curd is golfball size, Russ breaks a leaf part way and lets it fall over the curd as a blanching device. If there is any sign of a cabbageworm infestation, he uses applications of *Bacillus thüringiensis*. By late June, the white-headed cauliflower is ready for harvesting. A second crop, directly seeded in July and ready in October, means we always have plenty of this wonderful vegetable for pickling and fresh table use.

If all this sounds like a lot of work, there's a beautiful new no-blanch purple-headed variety, which is actually a cross between cauliflower and broccoli. It cooks faster than conventional cauliflower and has a milder flavor. Its long, broccolilike stems need peeling, unlike cauliflower's short stems, which need peeling only when they're old. The two relatives have different densities: for example, a white cauliflower weighs twice as much as a purple-headed variety. I treat the purple-headed cauliflower as I would broccoli, both in preparation and in cooking. When it is cooked, the head loses its magnificent purple tone and turns lime green, with just a trace of purple on the buds.

Russ sets a few seedlings of the purple-headed variety out in June, and they take forever to mature. But the wait is worth it. Since the plants grow 3 feet tall, they should be in a part of the garden where they won't shade other vegetables. This variety is harvested in fall when the heads turn purple and achieve maximum weight.

Our cauliflower comes from the garden so clean that most of the time I just rinse it off. If your plants harbor insects, soak the heads upside down in some salt water to dislodge them. Use cauliflower right after harvesting, because as it ages, it develops a strong—and sometimes quite unpleasant—odor and taste, and an unattractive brownish tinge.

I like both raw and cooked cauliflower. Raw cauliflower is a great snack, and I always love it on a mixed vegetable appetizer platter. It's good with most dips and is particularly pleasing with sharply contrasting flavors such as anchovies. To prepare cauliflower for a cold platter, crisp the flowerets in ice water in the refrigerator, drain, and pat dry before serving.

The most common way of cooking cauliflower is to break it into flowerets. The curd breaks naturally into fairly large-size pieces, which can easily be broken down again if needed. Trim the flowerets with a paring knife, cut off the ends, and peel the tough stem skin of the older heads. Slightly cutting the stem end makes the flowerets cook faster.

To prepare whole cauliflower, remove the leaves and trim all green from the base, cutting away the thick bottom end. Then hollow out the core to facilitate even cooking.

Either blanching or steaming cauliflower works equally well, so use the method you prefer. For an absolutely white head, blanch the cauliflower, adding lemon juice or milk to the water. I don't mind cauliflower's natural creamy color, so I don't bother with this step. If you're in a hurry, you should blanch cauliflower—steaming does take longer. Also, if a cauliflower is old, blanching releases some of its heavy cabbage taste.

Special Information

Yields
It is difficult to calculate the final weight of the cauliflower "curd" or head, because the weight of the leaves and stems varies so. Before weighing, I trim off the leaves and the heavy bottom stem. Since there seems to be an approximate relationship between the diameter of the curd and its trimmed weight, I think the best way to judge final amounts is to "eyeball" the cauliflower's width or diameter.

- A 5-inch head or "curd" = approximately ³/₄ pound after trimming
- A 6-inch head = approximately 1½ pounds after trimming
- A 7-inch head = approximately 2¼ pounds after trimming
- An 8-inch head = approximately 3–3½ pounds after trimming
- 1 pound trimmed cauliflower = approximately 4½ cups = 4 servings

Storage and Preserving
Cauliflower stores poorly, both raw and cooked—it quickly acquires a strong and unpleasant odor. Store for 2–4 days in a perforated plastic bag in the refrigerator when raw; do *not* store in a sealed container, as cauliflower needs oxygen. Cooked cauliflower becomes mushy and unappetizing even when refrigerated under the best of conditions. My advice is to cook it when you harvest or buy it and eat up any leftovers quickly. Cauliflower also freezes poorly. The flavor is okay but it becomes watery and unappetizing.

Hints
- Make a cauliflower pasta sauce: Cook small flowerets in a thickened tomato and red wine sauce for 10–12 minutes or until tender. Serve on top of pasta in place of meatballs.
- Prepare and cook purple cauliflower like broccoli. But do remember, you get that wonderful cauliflower flavor, too.
- Add cooked cauliflower bits to a rich consommé.
- Add flowerets blanched for 3 minutes to vegetable salads.
- Raw cauliflower makes a delicious crudité platter snack.
- Use brine from *Nana's Mustard Pickle* (see *Tomatoes*) with just cauliflower. Process the same way.

It's important to note that cauliflower quickly passes from being underdone to overdone. Watch closely, for there are few vegetables as unattractive as soggy, mushy cauliflower.

Cauliflower takes preliminary cooking well. Do plunge it immediately under cold water once it's cooked, and drain. When you're reheating cauliflower that gets only a butter and seasonings topping, either steam for 3–4 minutes or heat through in hot water. Usually, however, you'd either be reheating in the oven or sautéing it. All cooking times are approximate, for the actual cooking time depends on the floweret size and the cauliflower's age. Cauliflower accepts a sauté-braise nicely: toss small flowerets or cut-up cauliflower in butter or oil, or a combination of the two, and cover and cook over low heat.

It's also an excellent stir-fry vegetable. Thinly slice flowerets, stir-fry for 1 minute, add 2 tablespoons liquid, cover, and cook for 3–4 minutes.

Marketing

This is an important vegetable to make very sure is absolutely fresh. An old cauliflower is just not worth buying: you can bet your last dollar that it will be foul-smelling when cooked. Look for a crisp, creamy white, fresh-looking curd. Avoid any cauliflower whose curd has become browned. Often markets trim this off. The underneath looks white, but it is a sign that the cauliflower is old, and it will smell and taste strong when cooked. I also do not like to buy cauliflower that has been hermetically sealed, since it has had no chance to breathe and spoils quickly.

Microwave

- 1 pound flowerets cut into 1 1/2–2-inch pieces, placed in a covered dish with 1/4 cup liquid, will cook tender in 6–8 minutes.
- 1 whole, trimmed, and cored 3/4-pound cauliflower will cook in 8–10 minutes.

Leftovers

- Warm chopped cooked cauliflower in butter; add to omelets.
- Add cauliflower and ham bits to a quiche for a complete dinner.
- Turn into a purée, top with cheese, and bake in the oven.
- Purée; make a soufflé or a roulade.
- Add to stews and mash against the side of the pan to thicken naturally.
- Beat into whipped potatoes.
- Make croquettes or patties.
- Make a creamy soup. Wilt some onion and celery in butter, add broth, heat to boiling, add leftover cauliflower, and reheat. Purée, then add cream and butter. Or sauté curry along with onions and celery for a creamy curry soup. Serve hot or cold.

◇ *Blanched Cauliflower*

Whole Cauliflower: Trim and core whole cauliflower. Then boil a large pot of water, adding 1–2 teaspoons salt per quart of water. Add milk or lemon juice to keep the cauliflower white if you like. One trimmed cauliflower weighing 1 1/2 pounds will take approximately 10–15 minutes to cook tender. If you cook cauliflower head down, the top doesn't bob above the surface of the water.

Cauliflower Flowerets: Boil a large pot of water. Drop in the flowerets and return to the boil. The flowerets will cook in 3–6 minutes, depending upon their size.

◇ *Steamed Cauliflower*

Whole Cauliflower: Trim and core the whole cauliflower. Bring 3/4–1 inch water to a boil in a steamer, and put the whole cauliflower, head side up, in a steamer basket or colander over the boiling water. One trimmed cauliflower weighing 1 1/2 pounds takes approximately 20 minutes to cook tender. To be on the safe side, start checking after 12 minutes.

Cauliflower Flowerets: Boil water, as above. Place flowerets in the steamer basket or colander above the water and steam for 6–10 minutes or until just tender.
Note: If you plan to cook the cauliflower further, such as sautéing in oil or butter, or baking in the oven, slightly undercook it.

Finishing Touches for Cooked Cauliflower

My favorite way to finish cauliflower is *Joe Hyde's Cauliflower with Crumbs and Shallots*. I like it so much, I've treated it separately. However, there are many more delicious ways to paint the lily. "W" or "F" (or both) indicates whether the treatment works for whole cauliflower or flowerets, or both.

- *Sautéed* (F): Use just barely tender cauliflower exactly like *Sautéed-Braised* (see page 64), only do not cover and cook. Sauté briefly as in any of those combinations, such as *With Garlic and Oil*, *With Cream*, etc.
- *With Lemon Butter Sauce* (W/F) (see *Appendix*): Coat hot cauliflower and serve.
- *With Black Butter* (W/F): Brown butter (preferably clarified so it doesn't really turn black) in a saucepan until golden nut brown. Pour over cauliflower. Add parsley, if desired. You can also add fresh bread crumbs browned in butter, or add capers and cook for 1 minute before pouring over the cauliflower.
- *Anchovy Sauce* (W/F): Heat 3/4 cup olive oil. Add 12 mashed anchovies, and beat together with oil. Season, and serve as a side sauce with cauliflower. Use butter rather than oil if you prefer.
- *A la Grecque* (F): Slightly undercook flowerets. Drain, and pour over a hot *A la Grecque Marinade* (see *Mixed Vegetables*). Chill before serving.
- *With Hollandaise* (W/F) (see *Appendix*): Coat hot cauliflower and serve. Use 3/4–1 cup sauce per pound of cauliflower.

- *With Mousseline* (W/F) (see *Appendix*): Coat hot cauliflower and serve.
- *With Béchamel* (F)(see *Appendix*): Coat hot cauliflower, and reheat in sauce. Or, coat with béchamel, top with buttered fresh bread crumbs and grated cheese, and bake in a 375° oven until bubbly. Use 1 cup sauce per pound of cauliflower. Add strips of ham or chicken if you wish.
- *With Curry* (F): Make a béchamel sauce as above, adding 1 tablespoon curry powder for each cup of sauce. Add the curry to the butter before you add the flour.
- *With Mornay Sauce* (F) (see *Appendix*): Use 1–1¼ cups sauce per pound of cauliflower. Spread a quarter of Mornay sauce in a baking dish; add cauliflower. Cover with remaining sauce and top with buttered bread crumbs mixed with grated Swiss cheese. Bake in a preheated 375° oven for 20–30 minutes or until bubbly and heated through (or prepare ahead of time and bake later).
- *Baked with Cheese* (W/F): Spread cooked flowerets or set whole cauliflower in a buttered baking dish; top with a grated Swiss and Parmesan cheese mixture. Dot with butter and sprinkle with salt and pepper. Bake for 15–20 minutes.
- *With Brussels Sprouts* (F): Combine cauliflower and just tender Brussels sprouts. Coat with browned butter in which some almonds or water chestnuts have been lightly browned.
- *With Broccoli* (F): Treat as with Brussels sprouts.
- *Parmesan* (F): Place a layer of cauliflower flowerets in a buttered pan; top with tomato sauce, cheese, and herbs and bake as in *Eggplant Parmesan* (see *Eggplant*).
- *Flowerets Fried in Batter* (F): Slightly undercook flowerets. Dip into *Batter* (see *Appendix*) and cook in vegetable oil (sufficient to come one-third up the side of the pan) until crust is golden and browned. Turn and brown on the other side. Then drain and sprinkle with salt. Add some finely grated Parmesan cheese to batter if desired.
- *Fried with Bread Crumbs* (F): Instead of using batter, dip into beaten egg, and then dip in bread crumbs with or without grated cheese. Fry as above in vegetable oil; drain. Salt.
- *Purée* (W/F): Purée cauliflower; beat in butter and a bit of cream to a smooth yet firm consistency. Heat over low heat, stirring; season with salt and pepper. Substitute sour cream and add dill, if desired.
- *Mashed with Potatoes, Then Baked* (W/F): Whip together 1½ cups cooked whipped potatoes, 2 cups mashed cauliflower, 2 beaten eggs, and ¼ cup chopped onion cooked in 4 tablespoons butter. Stir in 1 cup grated Swiss cheese, and salt and pepper to taste. Turn into a greased 1½ quart casserole and bake in a preheated 350° oven for 30 minutes. Sprinkle on another ½ cup grated Swiss cheese or a combination of Swiss and Parmesan cheeses, and bake 15 minutes longer.
- *Whole Stuffed Cauliflower* (W): This is kind of fun. Cook a whole trimmed and cored cauliflower for 10 minutes; drain and cool. Cut out a bowl shape on top of the cauliflower. Chop the cauliflower you have removed (a 7-inch head of cauliflower will give you about 1½ cups). Make a stuffing: in 3–4 tablespoons butter, cook ½ cup chopped onions, 1 minced clove garlic, ¼ cup minced green or red pepper, and ½ cup sliced mushrooms until just wilted. Add chopped cauliflower and 1 cup diced fresh bread. Stir together. Season, and stir in some grated cheese. Pile into the cauliflower cavity and drizzle with melted butter. Sprinkle with Parmesan and bread crumbs, if desired. Bake in a preheated 350° oven for 10–15 minutes or until just heated through. Brown under the broiler, or do ahead and reheat. Make other stuffings, such as one with cubed cooked pumpkin, raisins, pine nuts, and Moroccan spices. Serve a bit of stuffing and a whole floweret from the side of the head.
- *Soufflé* (F): Make a *Béchamel Sauce* (see *Appendix*) with 1½ cups milk. Add ½ cup grated Swiss cheese to the sauce; season well. Separate 6 eggs and slowly beat béchamel sauce into 4 egg yolks. Mix in 2 cups cooked cauliflower; fold in 6 beaten egg whites. Bake in a buttered dish in a bain-marie (or water bath) at 375° for 30–40 minutes. For a smaller amount, see *Spinach Soufflé* (under *Spinach*).
- *Custard* (F): Blanch and drain 1–1¼ pounds small flowerets. Combine 3 beaten eggs, 1½ cups milk, 2 tablespoons melted butter, and salt and pepper. Place flowerets in a buttered 1½-quart baking dish and cover with 1 cup grated Swiss cheese (or a combination of Swiss and Parmesan). Pour custard mixture over top and bake in a preheated 350° oven for 35 minutes or until set.

◇ Sautéed-Braised Cauliflower

- Slice or dice cauliflower, or cut into ¼–½-inch flowerets. Melt a combination of butter and oil (or either one) and toss cauliflower in it until coated. Cover pan, reduce heat to low, and cook for 3–5 minutes, stirring occasionally. (Larger pieces should cook longer.) Sprinkle with herbs and additional butter, if desired, and serve.
- *With Garlic and Oil*: Add a garlic clove when tossing the cauliflower in oil.
- *With Tomatoes*: To larger flowerets, add your favorite tomato sauce or peeled, seeded, and chopped tomatoes combined with fresh herbs such as basil. Cover and simmer as above until flowerets are barely tender.
- *In Vinegar*: Sauté in oil with garlic, add some red or white wine vinegar, then cover and cook until cauliflower is tender.
- *With Peppers*: Toss the cauliflower in butter or oil with strips of red and green pepper. Cover, and cook until tender.
- *With Olives*: Add black olives or large green olives stuffed with pimento.

- *With Cream*: Toss cauliflower in butter and coat with heavy cream. Cover pan and cook until cauliflower is tender. Uncover, and reduce cream so it just coats the cauliflower. Sprinkle with lemon juice; season with salt and pepper.
- *With Nuts*: Sauté cauliflower in butter, cover pan, and braise until barely tender. Uncover, add toasted almonds, walnuts, or pistachio nuts, and sauté over high heat for 1 minute.
- *With Capers or Anchovies*: After sautéing in butter or oil, toss in capers or anchovies and cook for 1 minute before serving.

Molded Cauliflower

If you'd like a fancy presentation with no core to deal with, cook the cauliflower flowerets and mold them back into their original shape. Serve either hot or cold. Choose a bowl slightly smaller than the shape of the raw whole cauliflower.

To serve cold: Blanch flowerets until barely tender, drain, and cool. Arrange the flowerets snugly against the sides of the bowl with the flower tops against the bowl and the stems facing toward the center. Pack the center full of any remaining flowerets or stem pieces. Press down with a weighted plate. After 15 minutes, tip to drain liquid from the bowl. Refrigerate for 2 hours. When ready to serve, remove the weighted plate and place a serving plate on the bowl. Reverse carefully, and unmold. Garnish with hard-boiled eggs, olives, tomatoes, etc. Serve with *Salsa Verde* or a tuna sauce.

To serve hot: Heat the bowl over simmering water, or in the oven if it's ovenproof. Blanch flowerets until just tender, and drain. Butter the inside of the bowl. Arrange the flowerets snugly against the side of the bowl with the flower top against the bowl and the stems to the center. Pack the center with any remaining flowerets or stem pieces. If the cauliflower has cooled, cover bowl with buttered waxed paper and reheat in a 300° oven for 10–15 minutes. Put a warm serving plate on the bowl; reverse onto the plate. Remove bowl. Drizzle with melted butter or serve with any of the sauces for hot cooked cauliflower.

Note: These molds are great fun to do and so pretty. Especially attractive is a mold that alternates white cauliflower with purple cauliflower or broccoli (see the following *Domed Cauliflower-Broccoli Duo*). Vary the portion size by the size of the mold you use. A 3/4-pound cauliflower, placed in a 6 x 2 1/2-inch bowl, serves 2–3 persons.

Domed Cauliflower Duo

Blanch white cauliflower until just tender, approximately 10 minutes. Drain. Blanch purple cauliflower until just tender, approximately 4–5 minutes. Drain. Butter a rounded glass or stainless steel mold, 8 inches wide and 5 inches deep. Line the mold with alternating cauliflower rings. Start with a cluster of white flowerets in the center. (All flowerets should have their buds against the bowl and their stems pointing in.) Then ring a row of purple, then white, and so on to the

top edge of the mold. Fill in the center with smaller pieces. As you fill it, sprinkle the center with salt. Cover with buttered paper or foil, and heat through in a 300° oven for 10–15 minutes. Place a warm plate on top of the mold, invert mold with plate, and remove mold. Serve the domed cauliflower with white butter sauce, brown butter, or any of the sauces mentioned in *Finishing Touches for Cooked Cauliflower*.

- *Domed Cauliflower-Broccoli Duo*: Substitute broccoli for purple cauliflower.
- For smaller domes, cut amounts in half, or less.

Note: 1 1/2 pounds cauliflower flowerets and 1 pound trimmed and peeled purple cauliflower flowerets will serve 8–10 persons.

Marbleized Cauliflower and Broccoli Mold

2 cups puréed cauliflower
2 cups puréed broccoli
4 Tb butter
6 Tb flour
1 1/2 cups milk
Salt and freshly ground pepper
Nutmeg
6 eggs
3/4 cup grated Parmesan and Swiss cheeses

Place the cauliflower and broccoli purées in separate bowls. Make a béchamel sauce: melt butter in a saucepan, stir in flour, and cook for 2–3 minutes. Whisk in milk, season with salt, pepper, and nutmeg, and simmer for 5 minutes longer. Beat eggs. Divide béchamel, eggs, and cheeses between the two purées. Season both mixtures.

Butter a 2-quart mold. Add cauliflower, then cover with broccoli. With a flat knife, swirl the mixtures together to give a marbleized appearance. Cover with buttered waxed paper, and place in a deep baking pan. Pour in boiling water halfway up the sides of the mold. Bake in a preheated 375° oven for 40–50 minutes, or until the mixture is lightly browned at the edges and set in the center. *(Serves 6–8)*

- For a lighter texture replace béchamel sauce and eggs with *Hollandaise Sauce* (see *Appendix*).

Cauliflower Mold with Carrots

Usually, I prefer my cauliflower to look natural, but this is a lovely presentation. It's also an excellent way to use leftover cauliflower—just purée it and proceed.

1 lb cleaned and trimmed cauliflower
5 Tb butter
3 Tb flour
3/4 cup milk
Salt and freshly ground pepper
Nutmeg
1/2 cup carrot slices
1/4 cup heavy cream
3 eggs
1/2 cup grated Parmesan and Swiss cheeses
1/2 cup lightly packed grated carrot

Dice cauliflower into small pieces. Heat 3 tablespoons of the butter in a sauté pan, stir in cauliflower, tossing to coat with butter, cover, reduce heat to low, and simmer for 12–15 minutes until cauliflower pieces are very tender. Purée. In a saucepan, melt 2 tablespoons butter; whisk in the flour. Cook for 2 minutes, then add milk, whisking well to remove lumps. Add 2 teaspoons salt and pepper and nutmeg to taste. Cook over low heat for 5 minutes.

Meanwhile, blanch carrot slices in boiling water for 3–4 minutes. Drain; set aside. Beat together the puréed cauliflower and the sauce. Beat in the cream, eggs, cheeses, and grated carrot. Season. Line the bottom of a buttered 1-quart mold with the carrot slices. Spoon in the cauliflower mixture, and cover with a round of buttered waxed paper. Set in a deep baking pan and pour boiling water halfway up the sides of the mold. Bake in a preheated 375° oven for approximately 40 minutes or until the edges just brown and the mold has puffed up in the center. Cool on rack for 4–5 minutes before turning out of the mold. *(Serves 4)*

- The carrot slices are a decorative touch; omit if desired.
- The heavy cream enriches the mold; omit if desired.

Joe Hyde's Cauliflower with Crumbs and Shallots

The first time I saw this recipe was in my friend Joe Hyde's superb cookbook *Love, Time and Butter*. We serve this dish both at the restaurant and at home. You can fix it way ahead of time and bake just before serving, allowing extra time to warm it thoroughly. The whole head of cauliflower is quite dramatic, but it works just as well with flowerets with the topping scattered over.

1 whole head 7–8-inch cauliflower
4 Tb butter
3 Tb chopped shallots
1 cup fresh bread crumbs

Trim cauliflower and hollow out the core. Blanch until just tender; drain well. Heat butter until it is practically brown. Stir in the shallots and bread crumbs, and cook until the crumbs are brown. Pat mixture evenly all over top of the cauliflower. Bake in a preheated 375° oven for 15–20 minutes or until the cauliflower is hot. *(Serves 6–8)*

Spicy Cauliflower

Cauliflower can take lots of spices and herbs while retaining its own flavor. This easy mixture, inspired by Indian spices, is a piquant accompaniment for grilled meats, mild fish, or veal.

1 1/2 lb cauliflower flowerets
2 tsp ground ginger
2 tsp ground cumin
1 tsp ground cardamom
1 tsp ground coriander
1/2 tsp turmeric
1/4 tsp cayenne pepper
2 tsp salt
Dash of sugar
2 Tb oil
4 Tb butter
1 cup chopped onions
1/2 tsp mustard seeds
1 1/2 cups puréed tomatoes
2 Tb chopped green chilies or pepperoncini (optional)
2 Tb chopped parsley

Trim and cut flowerets into equal-size pieces. Combine spices, salt, and sugar. Heat the oil and 2 tablespoons of the butter in a large sauté pan; lightly brown the flowerets. Remove and set aside. Add the remaining butter and the onions, and cook until the onions are wilted, 5–10 minutes. Add spices and tomatoes. Simmer for 4–5 minutes until sauce is slightly thickened. Add flowerets, stirring until coated with sauce. Add chilies or pepperoncini if you wish. Simmer, covered, for approximately 20 minutes or until the cauliflower is tender. Sprinkle with parsley. *(Serves 4–6)*

Cauliflower Salads

As much as I like to munch on raw cauliflower, I do think cauliflower can overpower a salad unless it is first blanched to soften the texture. Before using cauliflower in a mixed salad, I cut it into bite-size flowerets, blanch for 3 minutes, then immediately cool and drain the pieces. Here's one salad and other salad ideas.

Italian-Style Cauliflower Salad

1 1/2 lb cauliflower flowerets
6 anchovies
1 cup pimento-stuffed green olives (or black)
2 Tb capers
1 clove garlic
1 tsp salt
2 Tb lemon juice
1/2 cup olive oil
Freshly ground pepper

Blanch cauliflower flowerets for 3 minutes; cool and drain. Cut anchovies into pieces and toss with cauliflower, olives, and capers. Mash together garlic and salt; mix with lemon juice. Gradually beat in the oil, then strain. Toss with cauliflower, and season with pepper. Chill and serve. *(Makes 6 cups)*

- Combine blanched, drained, and cooked cauliflower with shrimp and scallions. Dress with soy sauce and sesame oil.
- Combine cauliflower, blanched beans, diced pimento, and sliced ham or chicken. Marinate in a tart mustard *Vinaigrette Sauce* (see *Appendix*).
- Combine 1 tablespoon each finely chopped fresh chervil, basil, chives, and celery. Toss cauliflower with finely sliced red onion and sprinkle with herbs. Dress with oil, vinegar, freshly ground pepper, and salt.
- Mix cauliflower with chopped green pepper, chopped sweet onion, and peeled, seeded, and chopped tomatoes. Combine mayonnaise, sour cream, mustard, and dill; season with salt and pepper, mix until smooth, and combine with vegetables.
- Serve with a tuna sauce.
- Toss with diagonally sliced carrots and chopped fresh dill. Mix in a sour cream or yogurt dressing.

Marinated Cauliflower

Tangy cauliflower is good on an antipasto platter.

1 lb cauliflower flowerets
1/4–1/3 cup chopped fresh basil or 1 Tb dried
1 tsp oregano
1 clove garlic
1 cup white wine vinegar
1/2 tsp mustard seeds
Salt and freshly ground pepper
3–4 Tb olive oil
1–2 Tb chopped parsley
2 Tb chopped scallions (optional)

Blanch flowerets in boiling salted water for 3 minutes. Drain; put in a stainless steel or glass bowl along with basil and oregano. Crush garlic. Bring to a boil the garlic, vinegar, and mustard seeds. Pour over cauliflower, stirring to mix well. Cover. Refrigerate for 8 hours or overnight, stirring once or twice. Correct seasonings. Drain, drizzle with oil, and toss with parsley and scallions. *(Makes 4 cups)*

- For a milder marinade: Slice 1 onion and 2 large pickling cucumbers; add to 1 pound small flowerets in a mixing bowl. Bring to a boil 3/4 cup wine vinegar with 1/2 cup water, 1/2 cup oil, 1 teaspoon salt, crushed garlic, 1 teaspoon prepared Dijon mustard, and 2 whole cloves. Pour over cauliflower mixture. Mix well, cover, and let stand for at least 2 hours, stirring occasionally. Refrigerate; drain before serving.
- Use marinade from *Marinated Brussels Sprouts and Mushrooms* (see *Brussels Sprouts*).

Super-Easy Cauliflower Soup

1 cup chopped white of leeks (or onions)
3 Tb butter
4 cups chicken broth
³/₄–1 lb cauliflower flowerets
1 cup light cream
Salt and freshly ground pepper
1–2 Tb soft butter (optional)
2 Tb chopped fresh dill

Cook leeks (or onions) in 3 tablespoons butter until wilted, 5–10 minutes. Add broth and cauliflower, cover, and simmer over low heat until cauliflower is tender, 10–20 minutes, depending on the size of flowerets. Purée soup; add cream. Reheat, seasoning with salt and pepper. Stir in soft butter for enrichment if you like. Garnish with dill. *(Serves 4–6)*
Note: Omit butter if serving chilled.

- For a curried version, cook 1½ teaspoons curry powder with butter over low heat for 3–4 minutes before adding onions.

Copenhagen-Style Cauliflower Soup

1³/₄ lb cauliflower flowerets
1 Tb lemon juice
4 Tb butter
½ cup finely chopped celery
1 cup chopped white of leeks (or onions)
4 Tb flour
6 cups chicken broth
2 tsp salt
½ cup heavy or light cream
Freshly ground pepper
2 Tb finely chopped chives

Break ³/₄ pound of the cauliflower flowerets into small flowers ½–³/₄-inch across. Drop into boiling salted water with ½ tablespoon of the lemon juice; blanch for 2–3 minutes until just barely tender. Remove, run under cold water, drain, and set aside.

Meanwhile, melt 2 tablespoons of the butter, add the celery and the leeks (or onions), and cook until wilted, 5–10 minutes. Add the flour. Whisk the broth into the mixture, turn heat to high and bring it to a boil, reduce heat, and simmer for 5 minutes. Chop the remaining cauliflower into small pieces. Add the chopped cauliflower and the salt to the broth, partially cover, and simmer for approximately 15 minutes or until the cauliflower is very tender. Purée in a food processor or food mill. Do not use a blender, because you want a less uniform texture. Then, put back in pan, add cream, and season with salt, pepper, and remaining lemon juice to taste. Stir in the reserved flowerets, and reheat. Add the remaining butter, and sprinkle with chives. *(Makes about 2 quarts)*

Lamb with Cauliflower or Kreas me Kounoupidi

3 lb lean lamb (including a few bones)
2–3 Tb butter
1 Tb oil
1 cup chopped onions or white of leeks
1½ cups tomato sauce
½ cup beef broth
1 lemon slice
Salt
1 tsp dried oregano
1½ lb cauliflower flowerets
Chopped parsley
Freshly ground pepper

Cut lamb into 2-inch pieces and brown meat on all sides in butter and oil. Add onions or leeks; cook until lightly browned. Drain off fat and add tomato sauce, broth, lemon slice, 1 teaspoon salt, and oregano. Bring mixture to a boil, cover pan, reduce heat, and simmer for 1 hour. Stir in cauliflower, cover, and simmer for 20–30 minutes longer or until the cauliflower is tender. Season to taste with salt and pepper, and sprinkle with parsley. *(Serves 4)*

Stir-Fried Beef and Cauliflower

1 lb cauliflower
½ lb flank steak or sirloin tips
2 Tb soy sauce
¼ tsp sugar
4 tsp cornstarch
3 Tb peanut or corn oil
2 tsp dry sherry
1 tsp sesame oil
1 clove garlic
1 piece ginger
Salt
½ cup broth or water
3 cups thinly sliced Swiss chard or spinach leaves

Break cauliflower into small pieces or flowerets. Cut steak into ⅛-inch-thick strips (if you semifreeze it ahead, it will be easier to cut thin, uniform slices). Combine 1 tablespoon of the soy sauce, the sugar, and 1 tablespoon of the cornstarch with 1 tablespoon water and 1 tablespoon of the peanut or corn oil. Pour over steak; marinate for 15 minutes. Mix 1 teaspoon cornstarch with 2 teaspoons water; add the remaining soy sauce, sherry, and sesame oil; set aside. Heat the remaining oil in a wok or large sauté pan until very hot; reduce heat slightly. Mash garlic; add to oil along with ginger. Stir in cauliflower pieces, tossing to coat with oil. Add a dash of salt and the broth or water. Cover; steam-cook for 3 minutes. Uncover, spread the meat on top, cover, and steam for 2 minutes. Add the chard or spinach, cover, and steam 1 minute longer. Uncover, turn the heat to high, and toss all together. Add the reserved sauce, and stir for 10–15 seconds before serving. *(Serves 2–3)*

- Replace beef with shrimp.

Celeriac

Celeriac used to be a fairly common vegetable in American cooking. The 1824 Beecher cookbook mentioned it, as did Mrs. Rorer in 1886. In those days, however, celeriac was invariably boiled up and then drenched in cream sauce—so it had limited appeal. This root vegetable fell out of fashion for a while, but today it's once again available, although you'll still have to search for it in most markets.

Celeriac, also known as turnip-rooted celery, celery knob, or celery root, produces a softball-size root with a concentrated celery flavor. I think many people are put off by its appearance: celeriac really is rather ugly—knobby and hairy; its rough exterior thoroughly unappealing. It has been grown for hundreds of years in Europe, where it is particularly popular with the French and Germans. In England, during World War II, celeriac was widely cultivated because it was less trouble than regular celery, would grow in shallow or stubborn soil, and could be stored for winter use. American gardeners should be tempted to follow suit, because celeriac is a vegetable which really makes sense to grow yourself.

Unlike celery, it's easy to raise. You can be assured that your own product will be good, and it's lovely to have on hand to use as you want. You can also experi-

ment with the new varieties offered by seed companies that import European seeds. European varieties of celeriac have more uniform shapes and usable cores than older varieties. (As celeriac is so little known in the United States, little or no hybridizing work is going on here.)

Celeriac has a long growing season of 120 days, so Russ sows seed in individual six-packs in February. He keeps plants in the greenhouse until the third week of May, when he sets them outside. (If you don't own a greenhouse or hotbed, it's best to look for a nurseryman who sells celeriac seedlings.) Russ places the plants 10 inches apart in well-prepared highly organic soil, and waters them well. As the plants develop, he removes yellowed leaves and waters thoroughly at least once a week. Fibrous roots anchor in the earth while the edible round roots form above the ground. (In late summer, sucker shoots will start to sprout from these roots, which should be removed to get good-size bulbs.) The roots can be harvested from mid-September to frost; however, when cold weather arrives, they should be protected by hilling up with earth.

Harvest celeriac when the roots become 2–4 inches in diameter: larger than that, they're woody. Loosen the soil around the roots, then pull them from the ground and remove all leaves except for the little tuft in the center. (If you cut this off, the roots expend their energy producing another set of leaves.)

When I prepare celeriac, I scrub it well, then peel the tough skin, a process that's easier if you remove the skin as you would an orange rind. With a good sharp knife, make a flat cut straight across at either end, removing the hairy roots and the celeriac top at the tuft of leaves, then work around the body, slicing down and around from top to bottom. As celeriac is thick-skinned, you'll end up

with quite a bit of waste—a 1-pound celeriac trims down to approximately ½ pound of flesh. Although the ratio improves as size increases, count on an average 2 to 1 ratio of usable flesh. Similar to vegetables such as Jerusalem artichokes and salsify, celeriac's flesh darkens in contact with air. Therefore, you must immediately place any cut and exposed flesh into acidulated water (water and lemon juice or vinegar) until final preparation.

I cook celeriac both unpeeled and peeled, as both methods have their advantages. Cooking whole unpeeled celeriac eliminates the need for a white bouillon (known as a *Blanc*) (see *Appendix*), but it discolors if left sitting around too long before the final preparation. Wait to peel until just before using it. My preferred method is to peel the celeriac and then braise it or boil it, even though boiling necessitates using a blanc to keep it white. I do not steam celeriac. Steaming whole unpeeled celeriac takes too long, while steamed peeled celeriac darkens.

After spending weeks experimenting with cooked celeriac, I must tell you that in my opinion the very best way to eat it is raw. Served in a well-seasoned dressing, its unusual taste and texture shine, for no other vegetable I know absorbs a coating while maintaining its own identity so well.

Some people love cooked celeriac, but I think cooking alters the appearance and texture: its creamy tan flesh develops a dappled mosaic pattern and the texture becomes mealy and almost glutinous. Also, celeriac does not easily blend with other vegetables when it's cooked and chilled—one reason you should ignore some cookbook advice to serve it in a Waldorf salad or combined with other cold cooked vegetables or meats. The best treatment for cooked celeriac is to serve it alone with a simple sauce or special garnish. One vegetable it combines nicely with is potato, so you'll find several recipes using these two vegetables together.

Special Information

Yields
- 1 pound whole celeriac = approximately ½ pound peeled flesh
- 2 pounds whole celeriac = approximately 1¼ pounds peeled flesh
- ½ pound peeled flesh = 2 cups chopped = 1 cup puréed

Storage and Preserving
- Do not freeze or can celeriac. Trim its fibrous roots and store it, unwashed, for 1 week in the refrigerator, or layer celeriac in sand in a cool cellar, where it will hold for a month or two.

Hints
- Make *Beet and Celeriac Salad* (see variation of *Beets Vinaigrette* under *Beets*).
- Always hold in acidulated water or cook raw peeled flesh in a blanc.
- Use scraps for flavoring or to thicken soups.
- Add small chunks to winter stews.

- Make *Celeriac and Turkey Mornay*: Peel 2 pounds celeriac and boil in a *blanc* (see *Appendix*); slice. Sauté 2 thinly sliced onions in butter. Make 2 cups *Mornay Sauce* (see *Appendix*). Pound 1 pound turkey cutlets until thin. Salt, pepper, and flour, and lightly brown in butter. Layer as follows: sauce; celeriac; sauce; onions; turkey slices; remaining sauce. Bake in a preheated 375° oven for 30 minutes.
- Make a *Jerusalem Artichoke and Celeriac Soup* (see *Jerusalem Artichokes*).

Microwave
- 1 whole 1-pound celeriac takes 8 minutes to cook just tender; 10 minutes to purée soft. Pierce skin so it will not burst.

Leftovers
- Purée for soufflés or soups.
- Add small amounts of raw celeriac salads to a mixed salad platter or stuff into tomatoes.
- Combine leftover celeriac and cooked mushrooms; finely chop. Stuff into raw mushroom caps, broil in oven, and serve as an appetizer course or vegetable.

Marketing

Finding celeriac at the market is still a challenge. Head first for a specialty market. Demand the best quality you can. Occasionally, the celeriac will be old and woody and not worth using. (As a last resort, marinate it thoroughly and salvage it for a raw salad.)

Do not buy soft or withered celeriac. Look for as round a shape as possible: the more gnarled the celeriac, the more you'll have to throw away. Unfortunately, a smooth outer appearance can be deceiving, for celeriac can look fine on the exterior and hide a woody or pulpy interior. That's one reason I feel so strongly that cooks should grow their own celeriac whenever possible.

◇ *Dressings for Raw Celeriac*

Raw celeriac dressed in a flavorful sauce is a classic European hors d'oeuvre. One key step is marination, which both tenderizes the raw celeriac and mingles the flavors. The pieces must be small enough for the liquid to do its work, so julienne the celeriac in thin strips. Marinate for at least 1 hour before serving; 2 or more hours is even better. I have kept celeriac salads for days in the refrigerator and they just seem to improve. Let the cut celeriac sit in a mixture of lemon juice or vinegar, salt and pepper,

and a bit of mustard for several hours, then coat with the final dressing. Or easier still, marinate the celeriac in the final dressing. Celeriac in its numerous coatings can be served as an hors d'oeuvre, on salad platters, or for lunch and dinner courses.

In all of the following dressings mustard plays an important part. Not only does it add taste, but it also seems to help tenderize the celeriac.

The following dressings are for 4 cups julienned celeriac. For that amount, you need approximately 2 pounds whole celeriacs to make 1 pound peeled flesh. Keep the flesh in acidulated water and do not remove until you julienne and coat it with dressing.

Classic Celeriac Rémoulade Dressing
$^1/_2$ cup olive oil
$^1/_2$ cup vegetable oil
3 Tb Dijon mustard
2 Tb wine vinegar
1–2 Tb heavy cream (optional)
Salt and freshly ground pepper
2 tsp chopped fresh tarragon or $^1/_2$ tsp dried

Combine the two oils. Put mustard in a bowl and gradually beat in the oil to make a smooth and creamy emulsion. Slowly beat in the vinegar and lighten the sauce by beating in cream, if desired. Season with salt and pepper and stir in tarragon. Coat celeriac and marinate for 2 hours. (*Makes approximately 1 cup dressing*)

Mustard–Sour Cream Dressing
2 Tb olive oil
2 Tb Dijon mustard
3 Tb *Mayonnaise* (page 349)
$^3/_4$ cup sour cream
Salt and freshly ground pepper
2–3 Tb light cream or milk

Beat oil into mustard. Beat in mayonnaise, followed by sour cream. Season and thin, if necessary, with cream or milk. Taste and add more mustard for a tangier flavor. Mix with celeriac. (*Makes about 1 cup dressing*)
• Replace sour cream with yogurt.

I have always liked the Italian veal with tuna sauce dish, vitello tonnato. This is my version for celeriac.

Tuna Sauce
$^1/_4$ cup tuna in oil
3–4 anchovies
1 Tb lemon juice
1–2 tsp Dijon mustard
$^1/_4$ cup olive oil
$^1/_2$ cup *Mayonnaise* (page 349)
Capers
Cherry tomatoes

Blend tuna and anchovies together to make a paste. Beat in lemon juice and mustard; gradually beat in oil. Fold in mayonnaise. Mix with celeriac and marinate for 2 hours. Garnish with capers and surround with cherry tomatoes. (*Makes about 1 cup sauce*)

Vinaigrette Dressing
1–2 tsp Dijon mustard
Vinaigrette Sauce (page 352)
1 red onion
Chopped parsley
Hard-boiled eggs (optional)
Italian black olives (optional)

Add mustard to vinaigrette to taste. Chop onion and place in a strainer, then run under hot tap water to remove strong taste; pat dry. Combine onion with celeriac and coat with vinaigrette. Marinate for 2 hours. Sprinkle with parsley and surround with egg wedges and olives if you like. (*Makes 3/4–1 cup dressing*)

Celeriac and Apple Salad

1 lb whole celeriac
1/2 cup orange juice
3 firm tart apples
1/2 cup mayonnaise
1 cup chopped celery
1/2 cup chopped walnuts
Salt and freshly ground pepper

Peel and julienne celeriac into matchstick pieces. Toss with orange juice until coated. Peel, core, and chop apples; mix with celeriac. Marinate for 10 minutes, turning often; strain, reserving juices. Place mayonnaise in a large bowl and, little by little, add orange juice marinade until thinned to the point where it coats a spoon thickly. Beat smooth and combine with the drained celeriac, apples, celery, and nuts. Marinate for 2 hours, season with salt and pepper, and serve. (*Makes 5 cups*)

Celeriac-Meat Salad

1/2 lb cooked meat (roast beef, lamb, pork, ham, or salami)
2 carrots
1 cup *Mayonnaise* (page 349)
1–2 Tb Dijon mustard
Lemon juice
1/4 cup heavy or sour cream
Salt and freshly ground pepper
2 lb whole celeriac
Capers (optional)

Julienne meat; peel and julienne carrots. Season mayonnaise with enough mustard and lemon juice to give a sharp tangy taste, then dilute with cream and season with salt and pepper. (Sauce should thickly coat a spoon.) Peel and julienne celeriac. Mix with meat and carrots, and gently stir in mayonnaise dressing. Cover and marinate for at least 1 hour. Before serving, sprinkle capers on top if you like. The salad will keep 2–3 days in the refrigerator. (*Serves 4*)
Note: If refrigerated, bring to room temperature before serving.

◇ Braised Celeriac

Wash and peel celeriac and put in acidulated water as you cut it up. Shape into ovals, logs, or thick slices. (Ovals are particularly attractive: first cut into rectangles, then shape into ovals about 1 1/2 inches long by 3/4 inch wide. Two pounds whole celeriac would give you 12–14 ovals.)

Just before cooking, drain and pat the celeriac dry. For 2 pounds celeriac, melt 1 tablespoon olive oil and 1 tablespoon butter. Add celeriac and cook until browned on all sides. Lower heat, add 1/4 cup beef broth or water, cover pan, and braise for 15–20 minutes or until barely tender. Shake the pan occasionally. Season before serving.

• To glaze, add 1–2 teaspoons sugar while browning.

◇ Boiled Celeriac

Here are two methods for boiling celeriac.

Boiling—Skin On
Wash celeriac. Bring water to a boil in a large saucepan and drop in celeriac; cover pan, maintaining a gentle boil. A 1-pound celeriac will take 45–50 minutes to cook barely tender. Remove from pan, cool, and peel.

Boiling—Peeled
Prepare a *Blanc* (see *Appendix*). Boil the blanc for 2 minutes, then add celeriac. A whole, peeled celeriac will take 25–30 minutes to cook tender; 1/2–1-inch slices will cook in 8–10 minutes; 1/2-inch cubes will take 5–8 minutes.

Finishing Touches for Boiled Celeriac

• *Sautéed Cubed Celeriac*: Melt butter in a sauté pan. Add 1/2-inch cubes of cooked celeriac, shake pan, and sauté until lightly browned, 4–5 minutes. Season with salt and pepper, sprinkle with parsley, and serve at once.

• *Celeriac Cubes in Cream Sauce*: Make a light cream sauce, using the white bouillon as part of the liquid. Fold in cubes of cooked celeriac. Season to taste with salt and pepper and fresh herbs.

• *Baked Celeriac in Tomato Sauce:* Layer slices of cooked celeriac in a buttered dish, using your favorite tomato sauce and a touch of freshly grated Parmesan cheese. Top with additional cheese and bake in a preheated 350° oven for 30 minutes.

• *Celeriac Baked with Potato and Cheese*: Boil equal amounts of potato and celeriac, slice and layer in a buttered ovenproof dish, sprinkling salt, pepper, and grated Swiss or Parmesan cheese between layers and on top of final layer. Pour a combination of hot milk and light cream over the vegetables and bake in a preheated 375° oven for 30 minutes. Run under the broiler to brown the top.

• *Celeriac Baked with Apple*: Layer cooked sliced celeriac in a buttered pie pan, then cover with slices of peeled cored apple. (Slices of celeriac and apple should be 1/4–1/2 inch thick.) Sprinkle with brown sugar and dot with butter. Bake in a preheated 350° oven for 30 minutes.

- *Breaded Celeriac Slices*: Dip cooked celeriac slices into a beaten egg and then into fresh bread crumbs. Sauté in a combination of oil and butter until nicely browned on both sides, approximately 2 minutes per side. Salt and pepper to taste. If you like, grate cheese onto the celeriac slices after they've been turned. The cheese will melt into the bread-crumb coating.

Celeriac with Brown Butter

One of the prettiest ways to prepare cooked celeriac is also the simplest.

    1 lb whole celeriac
    Blanc (page 346)
    3 Tb butter
    1½ Tb chopped shallots

Peel celeriac and cut into wedges (first cut celeriac in half lengthwise, then into fourths, then cut each fourth into thirds). You should end up with 12 wedges from ½ pound flesh. Drop wedges into acidulated water. Boil celeriac in blanc for approximately 8 minutes, until just tender. Drain and place on a warm serving platter. Cook butter in a pan until golden brown, then add shallots and toss with butter for 1 minute. Watch carefully, for the butter can quickly burn. Pour butter over celeriac. *(Serves 4)*

- Substitute turnip for celeriac.

Celeriac with an Avgolemono Sauce

    1 lb whole celeriac
    Blanc (page 346)
    2 eggs
    2 Tb lemon juice
    Salt and freshly ground pepper

Prepare celeriac wedges as in the preceding recipe. When cooked, remove from the blanc and keep warm in a covered dish. Reserve the blanc and keep warm. Lightly beat eggs in a small saucepan; beat in lemon juice, then gradually beat in ½ cup of the reserved blanc. Continue stirring over moderate heat until sauce is slightly thickened. Do not let sauce boil. Season with salt and pepper. Spoon three-fourths of the sauce onto a warm serving plate. Place the celeriac wedges on the sauce in an overlapping row. Pour the remaining sauce down the center of the wedges and serve immediately. *(Serves 4)*

- Celeriac prepared this way can be used with other sauces, such as sorrel, celery, or tomato.

Potato and Celeriac Cake

This cake, or straw mat, usually prepared with potatoes, has a more subtle flavor when celeriac is added. It's important to cut the vegetables just prior to cooking, for if the potatoes are held in water, they lose their starch, the cake holds together poorly, and the celeriac darkens. A no-stick fry-pan or a well-cured iron skillet is a blessing to prevent sticking.

    1 lb whole celeriac
    1½ lb potatoes
    Salt and freshly ground pepper
    8 Tb butter

Peel celeriac and potatoes, julienne in matchsticks, and mix together. (This process is amazingly simple with a mandoline or similar hand machine. The finer the cut the quicker the cake will cook.) Mix salt and pepper into celeriac and potato mixture. Melt 4 tablespoons butter in a 9–11-inch fry pan. When butter is hot, add vegetables, pressing down with a spatula to form a flat cake. Brown over high heat for 2–3 minutes, shaking the pan gently to make sure the cake is not sticking on the bottom. (The cake should move as a unit.) Turn heat to medium and cover pan. Cook for 10 minutes, shaking occasionally; uncover and press down with spatula. Now turn the cake. Either flip the cake (this takes some practice but is fun when you master it) or slide it onto a flat platter and turn the fry pan over on top of it, reversing the cake. Return cake to heat, adding remaining butter, and brown the other side, watching to make sure it doesn't burn. (If the cake is thick and needs additional cooking to become tender, simply reduce the heat, cover, and cook a few minutes longer.) Slide cake from pan and cut into wedges. *(Makes a 9–11-inch cake)*

Celeriac and Parsnip Stew

This filling and hearty "stew" benefits from the sweetness of parsnip. Note that the celeriac darkens after it's cooked, which doesn't affect the taste at all.

    2 leeks
    1 onion
    3 stalks celery
    1 lb whole celeriac
    ½ lb parsnips
    3 Tb butter
    1 Tb flour
    1 cup chicken stock or water
    3 sprigs parsley
    Bay leaf
    ½ tsp thyme
    Salt and freshly ground pepper

Clean leeks, then chop the white and light green sections. Chop onion and celery and combine with leeks. Peel and chop celeriac into ½–1-inch cubes; drop into acidulated water. Peel parsnips and chop into ½–1-inch pieces. Melt butter and add leek mixture, sautéing until golden but not browned. Mix in flour, let cook for 2 minutes, and add drained celeriac, parsnips, stock or water, parsley, bay leaf, thyme, and ½ teaspoon salt. Stir, cover, and cook over medium-low heat, stirring frequently. Cook for 10–15 minutes or until tender. Before serving, remove parsley and bay leaf, and season with salt and pepper. *(Serves 6)*

- Add other cooked vegetables, such as carrots and rutabaga, for a mélange.

Celeriac, Potato, and Cheese Gratin

Here's a celeriac version of Gratin Savoyarde, a French potato-cheese dish cooked with broth.

2 Tb butter
1 lb whole celeriac
3 large potatoes
Salt and freshly ground pepper
2 cups grated Gruyère cheese
1 cup chicken or beef broth

Butter a 1½-quart casserole. Peel celeriac and cut into ⅛-inch slices, placing in acidulated water. Peel and slice potatoes into ⅛-inch slices. Layer potatoes, drained celeriac, and cheese in the following order: put one-third of the potatoes in the dish, cover with half the celeriac, sprinkle on some salt and pepper, and cover with one-third of the grated cheese. Repeat layering, ending with potatoes, and reserving the last third portion of cheese. Salt and pepper the top and dot with butter. Pour in broth, cover, and bake for 45 minutes, then uncover, evenly sprinkle remaining cheese on top, and cook 15 minutes longer. (*Serves 4–6*)

Celeriac and Potato Purée

This celeriac purée is delicious with meats in place of the usual mashed potatoes.

1½ lb trimmed celeriac flesh
½ lb peeled potatoes
Blanc (page 346)
4–6 Tb butter
¼ cup heavy cream
Salt and freshly ground pepper

Chop celeriac and potatoes into approximately ½-inch cubes, placing in acidulated water as you go along. Bring the blanc to a boil, add celeriac and potatoes, and boil until tender, approximately 15 minutes. Drain, purée with butter to taste and cream, and season with salt and pepper. (*Serves 4–6*)

• Make ahead in a buttered 1-quart baking dish. Dot with butter and reheat in a 350° oven for 30 minutes.

Celeriac in the Basque Style

The Basques on the border of France and Spain cook with the onions, peppers, tomatoes, and garlic I love. Celeriac teams well with these fragrant flavors.

2 tomatoes
1 large green pepper
2 small sweet green Italian peppers
1 large onion
1 clove garlic
2 Tb olive oil
3 Tb butter

¼ tsp dried basil or 1 tsp fresh
Salt and freshly ground pepper
Two 1-lb whole celeriacs
1 Tb flour
1 cup beef stock

Peel and seed the tomatoes and cut into thick strips. Blanch peppers in boiling water for 2 minutes, then rinse in cold water. Dry, cut in half, removing the seeds and white membrane, and cut into thin strips. Slice onion; peel and chop garlic. Melt oil and 1 tablespoon butter together. Add onion and peppers and cook over low heat until onion is wilted and golden. Add tomatoes, garlic, and basil. Stir, season with salt and pepper, and set aside. Peel celeriac and cut into ⅛-inch slices, dropping into acidulated water as you go along. (The slices may curl; don't worry about it.) When ready to bake, butter a 9-inch square ovenproof dish and layer drained celeriac, sprinkling each layer with salt and pepper and a bit of flour. Pour on beef stock, then cover with pepper and tomato mixture. Dot with remaining butter. Cover and bake in a preheated 350° oven for 50 minutes, basting occasionally. Uncover and bake for 10 minutes to brown top. (*Serves 4–6*)

Celeriac and Tomato Soup

The celeriac both flavors and thickens this soup.

4 tomatoes
2 ¼–2 ½ lb whole celeriac
3 leeks
1 onion
1 clove garlic
1 large carrot
1 Tb olive oil
2 Tb butter
3 sprigs parsley
6 cups chicken broth
2 cups water
¼ cup chopped fresh lovage (optional)
Salt and freshly ground pepper
Croutons (page 348)

Peel, seed, and roughly chop tomatoes. Peel sufficient celeriac to make 1 ½ pounds trimmed flesh, then cut into ½-inch cubes and drop into acidulated water. Wash and trim leeks and, using only the white and light green parts, thinly slice. You should have 1 ½–2 cups. Chop onion and combine with leeks. Chop garlic. Thinly slice carrot. Heat together oil and butter and sauté leeks and onion until wilted. Add garlic and carrot, and cook for 5 minutes longer. Add one-third of the tomatoes and cook until they are lightly browned on the edges and the juice is evaporated. Add drained celeriac, the rest of the tomatoes, and the parsley sprigs. Cook together for 10 minutes. Add chicken broth, water, and lovage (if you wish). Bring to a boil, reduce heat, and simmer for 30 minutes. Purée, season with salt and pepper, and serve with croutons on the side. *(Serves 8)*

- For a thinner soup, use only 1 pound celeriac and 3 tomatoes.

Cream of Celeriac and Leek Soup

This is a filling soup for a cold winter's night.

3 leeks
1 ½ lb whole celeriac
1 large potato
3 Tb butter
4–5 cups chicken broth
1 cup light cream (optional)
Salt and freshly ground pepper

Wash leeks and slice the white and light green sections until you have approximately 2 cups. Peel and chop celeriac into ½-inch cubes, dropping into acidulated water. You will end up with 3–4 cups. Peel and coarsely chop the potato, and drop into the water with the celeriac. Melt butter in a large saucepan and stir in the leeks, cooking until wilted. Stir in drained celeriac and potato, then add 4 cups broth. Bring the broth to a boil, reduce heat, cover, and simmer for 20–25 minutes or until the celeriac and potato are tender. Pass through a sieve or purée in a food processor or blender. If very thick, thin with light cream and additional broth. Season with salt and pepper. *(Makes 8 cups)*

- Substitute 1 cup onions and 2 stalks celery for leeks.

Celery

My refrigerator never lacks celery, for hardly a day goes by that I don't use this most versatile vegetable. I reach for it as a diet snack, to stretch leftovers into main-course salads, and as a basic aromatic ingredient in stocks, sauces, soups, stews, stuffings, and casseroles. Braised, it becomes an elegant attraction at any dinner party. Considering how much I take for granted a constant celery supply, I was surprised to discover it's a demanding crop, needing just the right soil conditions and preparation to grow well.

Celery does best in a slightly acid, highly organic "muck" soil (a peat bog would be perfect). Our backyard has the ideal spot—a low, swampy area Russ reclaimed. As celery roots can grow 18–24 inches down, he prepares the soil deeply, enriching with plenty of humus and organic matter. This location has adequate drainage, yet holds the moisture necessary to keep the celery from bolting or becoming bitter, stringy, or inedible. Celery also needs soil with a low sodium content, because salt prevents plants from absorbing moisture.

At the Victory Garden and at home, we plant the medium-green summer Pascal celery. Although there are both green and golden kinds of celery—and many varieties of each—most celery grown in the United States is this green or Pascal variety, long considered to be more flavorful. (You can tell the types apart easily: Pascal celery has dark green leaves and large ribs in big, full bunches, while the paler golden celery has white ribs and yellow leaves. It's most often found as packaged celery hearts.)

In late January or early February, Russ starts newly purchased seeds in the greenhouse. He sows seeds early, because celery germinates slowly and seedlings can take as long as three weeks to appear. Cold weather could cause plants to bolt, so Russ waits until outdoor temperatures have risen above 55° before setting plants outside in a sunny, open spot, spacing them 9–12 inches apart in rows 2 feet apart. Throughout the summer, he waters them thoroughly and fertilizes them with a high-nitrogen fertilizer.

We blanch celery, although it's not necessary. In fact, some people prefer the stronger celery taste of unblanched celery. Blanching removes some of the nutrients, but since celery is practically 95 percent water and only a fair source of nutrients anyway, I opt for the more delicate texture and flavor of blanched celery. Russ "planks" the celery the Victory Garden way, by staking boards along both sides of the celery row, leaving only the upper green leaves showing. (Planking can be done in 2-, 3-, or 4-foot sections.) He could get the same results by hilling up to the base of the leaves with dirt, but this method would make the celery more difficult to clean. Commercial growers often keep out light with paper, or grow celery closely together in a block formation, allowing the outer plants to shade and blanch the innermost plants.

In September, approximately four weeks after planking, the celery is ready to harvest, and we remove the boards, exposing the light green, tender, sweet stalks beneath. I cut the plants off at the base and put any damaged leaves into the compost pile. Before using the celery, I give it a good washing and trimming, saving the tops and leaves for salads or flavoring. Celery has no waste—you can use up every scrap.

Celery's high water content causes rapid dehydration, so I put it in a humid, cold environment (approximately 32°) as soon as possible after harvesting and wiping off the dirt.

Peeling or stringing the tough outer celery stalks makes a difference in texture. It's pretty frustrating to try to slice through the pieces and find them still attached by fine strings. When I string celery, I make a slight cut into the end of each stalk, then pull the thin outer layer of flesh down toward the narrow end (1), removing the strings in the process.

(2) Slicing celery diagonally looks especially attractive, and I even think tenderizes it. Depending upon the effect I want, I either cut across the entire stalk or slice it into long, lengthwise sticks before slicing or chopping across on the bias. To julienne, I slice the celery into uniform lengths, (3) cut the lengths horizontally into two or three layers, (4) then cut through the layers to create matchstick-size pieces.

There is only one good way to cook celery. Braising is by far the most delicious way to cook it, because the long slow moisture cooking both tenderizes the celery and enhances its flavor. You can certainly braise celery without blanching it first, but a preliminary blanching takes away celery's "hard edge" and produces a succulently tender vegetable. Since this step takes but minutes, why not aim for the best taste possible? If you have absolutely tender garden celery, feel free to omit the blanching.

I do not recommend either steaming or boiling celery. Steamed celery takes a long time to cook, and you end up with a soft, wilted—rather than tender—texture. Boiled celery, on the other hand, cooks rapidly, but the water leaches out flavor, leaving it tasteless.

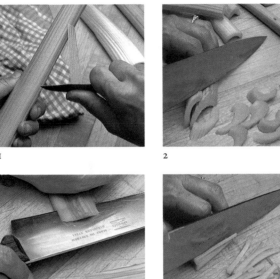

1   2

3   4

Cooking times vary, depending upon the type of celery you use and its age. Garden-fresh blanched celery cooks in far less time than unblanched store-bought celery. Judge the timing as you cook it.

Marketing

Look for firm, crisp, compact stalks. Do not buy any celery with brown or cracked outer stalks; this means the celery is old or has been damaged in shipping. These stalks would be wasted. Celery leaves, which should be fresh and green-looking, indicate the vegetable's general condition as well as being useful for salads and flavoring. Dry or papery leaves could be a sign of freezing injury. Celery should be stored in a refrigerated case, or sprinkled regularly with water to avoid evaporation and wilting.

◇ *Raw Celery*

Raw celery is part of our lives. How would we ever replace the traditional Thanksgiving tray of celery, the celery stirrer in a Bloody Mary, or the dieter's snack? Not to mention the raw celery crunch in tuna, chicken, or egg salads, or main-course salads made with leftover lentils, fish, or meat tossed with celery and a well-flavored mayonnaise or vinaigrette sauce. Here are some of my favorite ways to eat raw celery.

Special Information

Yields

- Expect to need approximately 1⅓ pounds celery in order to get 1 pound prepared usable celery
- 1 pound celery stalks = 4 cups chopped or sliced
- 4 cups raw = approximately 3 cups cooked
- 1 pound prepared = 4 servings

Storage and Preserving

- Store wrapped in a perforated plastic bag in the refrigerator, occasionally sprinkling with water to prevent dehydration. Even so it loses moisture, so it's best used fresh.
- Do not freeze or can.
- Crisping: Wash and trim celery and put in ice water in the refrigerator for 2–3 hours.
- Celery freezes easily. Keep away from the back of the refrigerator where cold may cause partial freezing.
- Use surplus celery in pickling recipes, such as *Nana's Mustard Pickles* (see *Tomatoes*).

Hints

- Use in a *Mirepoix* with chopped carrots and onions (see *Appendix*).
- Keep celery leaves. They're a wonderful addition to salads and enrich the taste of a cooked celery dish.
- Dry extra leaves in a low oven to use later on in soups and casseroles.
- Raw celery enhances vegetable salads such as potato, beet, and mixed, as well as meat and poultry salads, shellfish, eggs, and legumes.

- Use in fish court bouillons, stocks, and soups.
- Use as an aromatic. Stick stalks in or around baked fish.
- Use in stuffings for poultry and fish.
- Make your favorite meat stuffing, stuff braised celery, sprinkle with cheese, dot with butter, and bake.
- Blanch celery halves for 10 minutes, arrange around browned meat or poultry with a browned mirepoix, drizzle with melted butter, and roast until meat or poultry is done.
- Make cocktail tidbits. Braise 1-inch lengths for half the normal time. Cool and dip in beaten egg, then in bread crumbs mixed with finely grated Parmesan cheese. Fry in oil. Salt and pepper to taste and serve.

Microwave

- 2 cups sliced or chopped celery placed in a covered dish with ½ cup liquid takes 8–10 minutes to cook, depending on its tenderness. Use only as a preliminary step. Celery does not microwave well.

Leftovers

- Put leftover braised celery in soups or stocks.
- Add to casseroles during the last 15 minutes of cooking.
- Chop fine and use as omelet filling with minced fresh parsley and chopped tomatoes.

Celery on Its Own

Serve crisped celery stalks:

- with fresh sweet butter and kosher salt.
- sliced and passed with cruets of oil and vinegar, with Dijon mustard on the side.
- with mashed anchovies and olive oil.
- on a crudités platter with tarama or a crudités dressing (see *Crudités* in *Mixed Vegetables*).
- stuffed with a Roquefort and cream cheese mixture lightened with a touch of sour cream.
- with French goat cheese.
  stuffed with seasoned farmer cheese and capers or, fancier yet, cavier.
- with a *Vinaigrette Sauce* (see *Appendix*) made with Dijon mustard. Slice diagonally and marinate for 3 hours before serving.
- in a *Vinaigrette Sauce* made with lemon juice and fresh mint or basil (see *Appendix*). Diagonally slice celery into ½-inch pieces and toss with feta cheese, black olives, and chunks of tuna. Surround with sliced tomatoes.

Celery Antipasto

This refreshing crunchy salad is excellent for luncheon or as part of a relish tray. The marination partially "cooks" the fresh vegetables.

    2 cups celery sliced diagonally ½ inch thick
    1 cup cauliflower in small flowerets
    1 cup carrots sliced diagonally ¼ inch thick
    ½ cup sliced stuffed olives (optional)
    1 Tb capers
    1 Tb wine vinegar
    2 Tb lemon juice
    1 tsp salt
    ¾ cup olive oil (or a combination of olive and vegetable oil)
    1 clove garlic
    Freshly ground pepper

Combine celery, cauliflower, carrots, olives (if you wish), and capers; set aside. Mix together vinegar, lemon juice, and salt; gradually beat in oil to thicken; add garlic and pepper to taste. Combine with vegetables and marinate for 12 hours before serving. *(Makes 4–5 cups)*

- Experiment with additional vegetables such as chunked peppers or button mushrooms, but keep the celery as the main ingredient, increasing amounts as necessary.

Waldorf Salad

Waldorf Salad was created by Oscar Tschirky, the maître d'hôtel of the New York Waldorf Hotel for its opening in 1893. He peeled and cut raw apples and celery into ½-inch squares and mixed the two together with a good mayonnaise. His one warning was to not let any apple seeds mix in. What an easy road to fame! Here's a more recent version.

    3 large firm apples
    2 Tb lemon or orange juice
    4–5 celery stalks
    1–1½ cups walnuts
    1 cup *Mayonnaise* (page 349)
    ¼ cup heavy cream (optional)

Peel and core apples and cut into ½-inch chunks; toss with lemon or orange juice. String the outer celery stalks and slice any large stalks lengthwise; cut into ½-inch dice. Roughly chop walnuts and combine with apples and celery. Pour mayonnaise over ingredients, diluting with cream if too thick, and toss together gently. *(Serves 4–6)*

- Combine apples and celery with lightly whipped cream flavored with Dijon mustard.

Celery Slaw

The tart mustard dressing accentuates the celery taste.

    1 bunch celery (1–1½ lb)
    1 Tb wine vinegar
    2 Tb fresh lemon juice
    2 tsp Dijon mustard
    1½ tsp salt
    1 tsp sugar
    ¼ cup olive oil
    ¾ cup sour cream
    ½ cup chopped red onions

Wash and trim celery and cut into very thin diagonal slices. (You should end up with 4–6 cups.) Finely chop ½ cup celery leaves. Combine vinegar, lemon juice, mustard, salt, and sugar. Slowly, first beat in the oil, then the sour cream. Mix thoroughly with celery, celery leaves, and red onions. Marinate in refrigerator for at least 3 hours. *(Serves 4–6)*

- For a colorful celery/cabbage slaw, add shredded red cabbage. Try other shredded vegetables as well.

Celery and Rice Salad

    ½ cup raisins (optional)
    4 cups cooked rice
    ½ cup *Vinaigrette Sauce* made with lemon juice (page 352)
    Salt and freshly ground pepper
    1 cup chopped celery
    ½ cup chopped scallions
    ⅓ cup chopped celery leaves or parsley

Plump raisins (if using them) for 15 minutes in 1 cup warm water; drain. While the rice is still warm, combine with vinaigrette, and season to taste with salt and pepper. After the rice has slightly cooled, add celery, scallions, celery leaves or parsley, and raisins. Taste and add additional dressing if necessary. Serve at room temperature. *(Serves 4–6)*

- This recipe works equally well with all kinds of cooked legumes. Omit raisins.

◇ *Braised Celery—Plain Version*

I use this plain braise (without any seasoning) whenever I'm going to sauce, brown or stuff the celery, or use it cold.

> *Celery Halves*
> 2 bunches celery
> 1 Tb butter
> 2 Tb lemon juice
> 2–3 cups water or broth

Wash celery and cut in half lengthwise. Cut off celery tops, leaving bunches 6–7 inches long, and blanch in boiling salted water for 10 minutes, then rinse and pat dry. Butter an 8 x 12-inch baking dish; put celery cut side down in the pan, pour over the lemon juice and water until the liquid comes at least halfway up the sides of the celery. First cover with a piece of buttered wax paper, then cover tightly with a lid or aluminum foil. Cook in a preheated 350° oven for 1½ hours or until tender. Test for tenderness; the cooking time will vary depending on the celery size. Remove celery from liquid. Either proceed with a final preparation or boil down the cooking liquids until they are syrupy and pour over celery.
Note: the braising can be done on top of the stove, but make sure the liquid stays at a simmer.

> *Celery Stalks*

Cut into any length and treat as above. Blanch for 5 minutes and braise in water or stock for 20–30 minutes depending on celery age and thickness. This is easiest done simmered in a casserole on top of the stove.

Finishing Touches for Braised Celery

- *With Parmesan*: Drizzle 4 tablespoons melted butter over cut sides of braised celery, then sprinkle with freshly grated Parmesan cheese. Run under the broiler until cheese is lightly browned and bubbly.
- *With Brown Butter*: Melt ½ cup butter in a sauté pan and cook until butter is a nutty brown; pour over celery.
- *With Lemon Sauce*: Beat 4 eggs in a saucepan; beat in 4 tablespoons lemon juice and gradually beat in 1 cup reserved cooking juices or broth. Stir over moderate heat until sauce is slightly thickened; do not let boil. Season to taste and pour over celery halves.
- *Cold Celery with Vinaigrette Sauce* (see *Appendix*): Undercook the celery slightly. Turn the cut sides up while letting cool in their cooking juices. When ready to serve, drain celery well, and dress with a well seasoned *Vinaigrette Sauce*. Decorate with anchovies or pimento.
- *A La Greque*: Braise in à la Grecque marinade (see page 335), instead of water, lemon juice or broth. Prepare as above, cooking until tender, about 1½ hours. For smaller servings, use only the celery hearts, braising for 30–40 minutes, or until tender.
- *Stuffed Stalks*: Cut wide stalks into 4-inch lengths and braise for half the time indicated above. Remove and stuff with fillings of sautéed finely chopped celery,

mushrooms, onion, and seasoned bread crumbs; or crabmeat sautéed in butter and sprinkled with grated Swiss cheese. Dot with butter and bake covered in a preheated 350° oven for approximately 20 minutes, then uncover and run under broiler to brown.

Broth-Braised Celery Halves

This mouth-watering combination of braised celery and beef stock—which needs no embellishment—is my favorite way to fix cooked celery. To braise at a lower temperature, simply extend the cooking time.

> 4 slices bacon
> 2 bunches celery (1–1¼ lb each)
> 1 medium onion
> 1 carrot
> 2 Tb butter
> Salt
> Herb bouquet:
>   Parsley sprigs
>   1 bay leaf
>   ½ tsp thyme
>   4 peppercorns
> 2 cups beef broth
> ½ cup dry vermouth

Blanch bacon in boiling water for 10 minutes. Drain, pat dry, and chop into small pieces. Remove the large outer celery stalks and set aside for other uses. Trim tops so

that celery is 6–7 inches long. Slice celery lengthwise in halves and wash thoroughly. Unless the celery is very tender, blanch it in boiling salted water for 10 minutes. Plunge into cold water to stop cooking and pat dry.

Chop onion and carrot and sauté in butter until just tender. Lay celery cut side down in one layer in a buttered 8×12-inch baking pan. Sprinkle with salt. Then spread bacon, onion, and carrot on top of it. Add herb bouquet and pour on broth and vermouth to halfway up the celery—add more if necessary. (Either heat the broth before adding or bring pan to a simmer on top of the stove.) Cover with buttered waxed paper, then cover tightly and cook in a preheated 350° oven for 1 hour; raise heat to 400°, slightly loosen cover, and cook 30 minutes longer, basting occasionally. (When done, the celery should be tender with the heart retaining a bit of firmness.) Remove it to a warm platter. Boil down the pan liquids to a syrupy glaze and pour over celery. (*Serves 4*)
Note: Cooking time may be less if the celery is especially fresh and tender. Test occasionally.

Broth-Braised Sliced Celery with Shallots

The reduced cooking juices give this braised celery an especially rich flavor.

3 Tb butter
1 carrot
4 cups sliced celery
½ cup chopped celery leaves
12 whole shallots, peeled
1 tsp tarragon
1 tsp salt
½ cup dry vermouth
½ cup chicken, veal, or beef broth
Freshly ground pepper

Melt butter in saucepan. Mince carrot and stir in butter for 1–2 minutes. Add celery, celery leaves, shallots, tarragon, and salt and mix well. Reduce heat, cover pan, and cook for 15 minutes, stirring occasionally. Add vermouth and broth. Cover and cook for 20–25 minutes or until very tender. Uncover pan and reduce liquid to glaze the celery. Check seasoning, adding pepper to taste. (*Serves 4*)
• See main-course recipe, *Chicken with Celery*.

◇ Celery Pieces Blanched and Braised in Butter

Slice or chop celery into ¼-inch diagonal pieces. Blanch for 5 minutes in boiling salted water; drain. Melt 2 tablespoons butter in a saucepan and add celery, stirring until coated. Cover, turn heat to low, and cook for 15 minutes longer or until tender. Season to taste with salt, pepper, and lemon juice if desired.

Finishing Touches for Celery Pieces

• *With Butter*: Omit blanching, then slice or chop celery into ¼-inch pieces. For every 2 cups of celery, use 3 tablespoons butter. Toss celery in butter, cover, turn heat to low, and cook for 20–30 minutes or until tender.
• *With Béchamel*: Mix celery with a *Béchamel Sauce* (see *Appendix*). You'll need 1 cup béchamel for every 2 cups celery.
• *Au Gratin*: Place braised celery in a buttered au gratin dish, cover with *Béchamel Sauce* (see *Appendix*), and sprinkle top with grated Parmesan cheese and buttered bread crumbs. Dot with butter. Cook in a preheated 450° oven for 20–25 minutes or until the top is golden and the dish is bubbly.
• *With Cream*: When celery is braised, remove cover and coat with heavy cream and a touch of Dijon mustard (optional). Reduce heat for a few minutes and serve. Toasted slivered almonds are also nice mixed in with the celery.
• *Puréed with Potatoes*: Make a celery purée by puréeing with an equal amount of boiled potato to desired thickness. Add butter, cream, and seasonings to taste.
• *Stuffings*: Make a stuffing using 2 cups celery and 1 cup onion. Simmer together in butter as above. Cool slightly and then add approximately 2 cups fresh bread crumbs, 1 egg, salt and freshly ground pepper, your choice of herbs, more melted butter if needed to moisten, or chicken broth. Or substitute celery for fennel in *Easy Stuffing for Fish or Poultry* (see *Fennel*).

Stir-Fry Celery

The crisp texture of celery makes it an essential ingredient for stir-fry combinations. Here's one that's even good cold. Consult a basic Chinese cookbook for additional stir-fry dishes using celery.

1 bunch celery
3 Tb oil
Salt and freshly ground pepper
⅓ cup water or broth
Butter (optional)
Soy sauce (optional)

Wash celery well, separating stalks, saving leaves for other recipes. Cut celery into ¼-inch diagonal slices. Heat oil in a wok or large sauté pan, toss in celery, and stir rapidly, turning over in the oil. Sprinkle on the salt and pepper and cook, tossing constantly, for 2–3 minutes. Pour in liquid, turn heat to medium-low, cover, and cook for 2 minutes longer. Remove cover, turn heat to high, and reduce liquid until thickened. Serve as is or add butter or soy sauce to taste. (*Serves 4*)
• Julienne leftover meat, poultry, or shellfish; add during last 2 minutes of cooking.

Scallops with Celery in a Vinaigrette Sauce

This is one of my favorite appetizers at the restaurant. Celery's crispness contrasts pleasantly with the soft texture of fresh poached scallops.

> 1 lemon
> 1 lb baby sea scallops (or large scallops cut into halves or thirds)
> 1 cup very finely chopped celery and celery leaves
> *Vinaigrette Sauce* made with lemon juice (page 352)

Bring a saucepan of salted water to a boil and squeeze in the juice of 1/2 lemon. Pull off any small hard nuggets on the sides of the scallops which would give them a rubbery texture unless removed. Drop scallops into boiling water, immediately turn to a simmer, and poach for 2–3 minutes. Drain. Coat scallops with juice from remaining lemon half. Before serving, toss scallops with celery and leaves and dress with vinaigrette. *(Serves 4)*

Celery Consommé

Make this light clarified soup with celery trimmings. As a base, use chicken or beef broth or a rich homemade fish broth.

> 8 cups chicken, beef, or fish broth
> 4–5 cups celery leaves and stalks
> 1 onion
> Salt and freshly ground pepper
> 2 celery stalks
> 2 peeled carrots
> Lovage sprigs or celery leaves (optional)

Bring first four ingredients to a boil, then simmer covered for 30 minutes. Strain the broth, pressing out vegetable juices; taste for seasoning. Clarify the broth (see page 347) and set aside. Wash celery and peel carrots, julienne them, and blanch in boiling water for 1–2 minutes; drain. Before serving, reheat consommé and add a portion of celery and carrot to each serving. Sprinkle with finely chopped lovage or celery leaves if desired. *(Serves 6)*

Cream of Celery Soup

> 6 Tb butter
> 4 cups chopped celery (1 lb)
> 1 1/2 cups chopped onions or white of leeks
> 1/8 tsp sugar
> 1 lb potatoes
> 6 cups chicken stock
> 1/2 tsp salt
> 1 cup light cream
> Salt and freshly ground pepper
> 1/4 cup chopped celery or lovage leaves

Melt 4 tablespoons butter in a 3–4-quart saucepan, and stir in celery, onions or leeks, and sugar. Cook, covered, over medium-low heat until vegetables are wilted and tender, 15–20 minutes. Meanwhile, peel and chop the potatoes into 1/2-inch dice, and add to pan along with stock and salt. Simmer, covered, until potatoes are tender, about 35 minutes. Purée coarsely in a blender or food processor. Before serving add light cream and remaining butter, season with salt and pepper, and garnish with celery or lovage leaves. *(Makes 2 1/2 quarts)*

- Use 1 cup rice as a thickening, omitting potatoes.
- Serve chilled. Purée finely and omit final addition of butter.

Chilled Celery-Lemon Soup

There's no butter, fat, or cream in this fresh-tasting soup, which works well also as a base for other vegetable soups.

> 3 cups chopped celery stalks and leaves
> 1 onion
> Herb bouquet:
>   1 bay leaf
>   1 clove
>   1/2 tsp thyme
>   1/2 tsp rosemary
>   1/2 tsp lovage or chervil
>   1/2 tsp basil
>   4 parsley sprigs (no stems)
>   4 peppercorns
> 1/2 cup rice
> 1 1/2 tsp salt
> 4 eggs
> 6 Tb lemon juice
> Chopped celery or lovage leaves
> Paper-thin lemon rounds

Slowly boil celery, onion, herb bouquet, and 8 cups water in a 4-quart covered saucepan for 30 minutes. Remove herb bouquet and coarsely purée broth. Add rice and salt, cover, and simmer for approximately 20 minutes or until rice is tender. (Purée again if you wish.)

Beat eggs in a bowl until frothy. Beat in lemon juice, and gradually beat in 2 cups hot celery broth. Whisk this egg-broth mixture back into the hot celery broth and heat, stirring, until soup is slightly thickened, 4–5 minutes. Do not let boil. Cool at room temperature and refrigerate for at least 6 hours. Taste for seasonings before serving. Garnish with herbs and lemon slices. *(Makes 2 quarts)*

- For a richer-tasting version, use chicken broth rather than water.

Chicken with Celery

Although they're cooked together, each ingredient holds its own.

> 4–6 pieces chicken legs and thighs
> 2 Tb oil
> 2 Tb butter
> *Broth-Braised Sliced Celery with Shallots* (page 80)
> 12 large stuffed olives
> 16 cherry tomatoes

Brown chicken pieces in oil and butter; set aside. Prepare *Broth-Braised Sliced Celery with Shallots* up to the point where you add the vermouth and broth. Place chicken on top of celery, add vermouth and broth, and scatter olives around. Cover pan and cook for 25–30 minutes or until chicken is tender. Add cherry tomatoes and cook 5 minutes more. Remove chicken, olives, and tomatoes to a warm platter; keep covered. Boil down pan liquids to lightly glaze celery. Serve celery and chicken garnished with the tomatoes and olives. *(Serves 4)*

Celery Stew

A quickly made stew with good, fresh vegetable flavor.

4 cups celery in ¹/₂-inch chunks
1 sweet red pepper
1 ¹/₂ cups sliced onions
3 Tb butter
1 Tb olive oil
1 clove garlic
¹/₂ tsp celery salt
4 tomatoes
1 tsp chervil
¹/₂ cup chopped celery or lovage leaves or dill
¹/₂ cup hot broth
2 cups cooked white kidney or shell beans
Salt and freshly ground pepper

Blanch celery for 5 minutes in boiling water; drain. Peel pepper if you wish. Slice pepper and cook along with onions in butter and oil until wilted and lightly browned. Chop garlic, add to pan, and cook for 1 minute. Stir in celery and celery salt; cover and cook over medium-low heat for 20 minutes, stirring occasionally. Peel, seed, and chop tomatoes and add along with herbs and broth. Cover pan and cook for 10–15 minutes longer or until celery is tender. Stir in beans and cook until heated through. Season to taste and serve hot. *(Serves 6–8)*

• Add additional broth for a "soupier" stew.

Celery, Cod, and Cream

This version of salt cod had Russ asking for seconds! It's good served with a red cabbage slaw.

1 lb salt cod
1 bay leaf
1 grated onion
4 peppercorns
1 stalk celery with leaves
4 slices bacon or 4 oz salt pork
8 Tb butter
1 cup sliced onions
6 cups diagonally sliced celery
¹/₂ tsp celery salt
6 Tb flour
3 cups milk
1 cup light cream
Salt and freshly ground pepper
1 cup grated Swiss cheese
1 cup fresh bread crumbs

Rinse salt cod and soak in cold water in the refrigerator for 24 hours, changing the water occasionally. Before cooking, rinse again.

Make a poaching liquid of 8 cups water, a bay leaf, grated onion, peppercorns, and celery stalk with leaves. Simmer the liquid, covered, for 10 minutes. Add the cod, bring the broth back to the simmer, cover the pan, and remove from the heat. Let stand for 10 minutes. Drain the cod, and flake into large pieces, removing all bones. Set aside.

Blanch the bacon or salt pork in boiling water for 5 minutes. Drain, pat dry, and dice. Melt 2 tablespoons of the butter in a 3–4-quart saucepan and brown the bacon bits. Add the onions and cook until tender and lightly browned. Stir in the celery and celery salt, then cover the pan and cook slowly until tender, 20–25 minutes, stirring occasionally. Drain mixture and set aside. (The juices would make the final dish too watery.)

Make a cream sauce of 4 tablespoons butter, the flour, the milk, and the cream. Season with salt and pepper. Lightly coat the bottom of an 8-cup baking dish with the sauce, then layer half the celery mixture, half the cod, half the sauce, and sprinkle with half the cheese. Repeat the layers. Lightly brown the crumbs in 2 tablespoons butter and sprinkle over the dish. (The dish may be refrigerated at this point.) Bake in a preheated 375° oven for 30 minutes or until the dish is heated through and bubbly. *(Serves 6)*

• For a heartier meal, add layers of cooked sliced potatoes.

Celery and Rice with Peas

Here the rice is cooked gradually, risotto style.

5 ¹/₂ cups chicken broth
6 Tb butter
1 Tb oil
¹/₂ cup chopped onions
¹/₂ cup finely chopped celery leaves
3 cups finely chopped celery
Salt and freshly ground pepper
1 ¹/₂ cups rice
1 cup shelled fresh peas
¹/₃ cup grated Parmesan cheese (optional)

Bring broth to a boil, turn down to a simmer. Meanwhile, in a 4-quart saucepan, melt 4 tablespoons butter and the oil; add onions and cook over medium heat for 3–4 minutes. Add celery leaves, 1½ cups of the celery, and ¼ teaspoon salt and cook for 5 minutes. Add the rice, stirring to coat with butter; cook for 1 minute or until rice turns translucent. Pour in 2 cups of the simmering stock and boil slowly for approximately 5 minutes, stirring occasionally, until the rice absorbs most of the liquid. Add 1 cup stock and cook, stirring, until it is absorbed; repeat with 1 cup stock and remaining celery. When this cup is finally absorbed, add the fifth cup of stock plus the peas. Cook until all the liquid is gone. (If rice is still not tender, add additional ½ cup of broth and more water as needed.) The whole process should take 25–30 minutes. The peas should be barely tender and the second batch of celery should retain a bit of crunch. Stir in 2 tablespoons of butter and the cheese (if you like). Season to taste. *(Serves 4–6)*

- Omit peas. Add other ingredients such as chopped pimento, peppers, mushrooms, olives, etc.
- Add pieces of cooked chicken, ham, shrimp, crab, etc., for a complete dinner.
- Add spices such as saffron, curry, or freshly grated lemon peel.

Celery Sauce

This sauce is delicious with poached fish, egg on toast, or chicken breasts.

> 2 cups *Celery Pieces Blanched and Braised in Butter* (page 80)
> ½ cup *Béchamel Sauce* (page 346)
> 1–2 Tb heavy cream
> Salt and freshly ground pepper

Combine celery with béchamel, then purée in a blender or food processor, adding heavy cream for consistency. Season to taste and reheat before serving. *(Makes 1–1⅓ cups)*

Corn

Ever since the Pilgrims pilfered a cache of Indian corn, Americans have hankered after this New World vegetable. Today, next to tomatoes, sweet corn is probably our most popular fresh vegetable. We boil it, steam it, bake it, roast it, dry it—use it every which way except as the confection of the Indians, who chewed young ears and stalks and made a candy from the young kernels. For everyday use, the Indians preferred the higher-yielding, and better-storing, field corn. When the early colonists' rye and wheat crops failed, they turned to corn to make such breads as Rhode Island johnnycakes, South Carolina hushpuppies, and the southwestern tortillas.

Sweet corn came into wide table use about a century ago, when seed companies such as Burpee and Harris offered white-kerneled sweet corn for sale. Yellow-kerneled sweet corn, with its higher vitamin A content, appeared at the turn of this century.

Although corn dishes are prevalent in Mexico and South America, in Europe (except for Northern Italy's corn meal polenta) corn is still widely considered an animal food, and fresh sweet corn is a curiosity only Americans eat.

Our family is so fond of sweet corn that Russell has worked out a planting that gives us a three-month yield.

Corn is a heavy feeder, so Russ works plenty of nutrients into the soil before he plants. He turns under a winter rye crop in spring and adds well-rotted animal manure, as well as sand for drainage. About the third week in April, he plants his first blocks of corn. Block planting (in several short rows) aids pollination: since corn is pollinated by the wind, if it were planted in a long, single row, the wind could carry the pollen away, and the corncobs might end up incompletely filled out. Every foot, Russ plants two or three kernels, ultimately thinning to the strongest plant, and sets the rows 2 feet apart. His first planting includes an early variety, such as Sprite, a midseason choice, such as Butter and Sugar, and a late type, such as Silver Queen. Then, at two-week intervals, he sows a second and third planting of midseason corn.

(In the future, you'll be hearing a lot about "sweet gene" corn, a corn hybridized so that each ear of corn contains some kernels with extra sweetness. A typical ear would include 75 percent sweet corn kernels, and 25 percent "sweet gene" kernels, which lack the milky texture and aroma of standard corn, but are sweeter. Watch for names such as Sugar Loaf, Symphony, Bi-Sweet, Golden Nectar, Honeycomb, and Sugar Time.)

When the plants reach knee height, Russ side-dresses with a high-nitrogen 10-10-10 fertilizer. He doesn't believe in spraying corn, so he merely cuts out any worms that appear. We rarely lose an entire ear.

About the second week in July, we harvest our first corn, and with Russ's succession of plantings we have a good supply at least until the end of September.

Corn is ready for harvesting when the end silks have turned brown and dry, and the ears look full and fat. Outer green husks should be folded tightly together. One sure test is to puncture a kernel with your fingernail: ripe corn will spurt "milk" if pressed; underripe corn will contain a watery liquid; overripe corn will have tough-skinned kernels with doughy interiors.

If I could cook corn right in the garden, I would; the faster it gets into the pot after it's picked, the better. I realize this is a fantasy, but remember that corn's natural sugar turns to starch at an astonishing rate, so the sooner you eat corn after picking, the sweeter it's going to be.

Whatever you do, don't pick (or buy) corn and then leave it sitting on the kitchen counter to wilt and lose its sugars in the heat of the day. If you're not cooking it immediately, refrigerate the corn, in its husks, the minute you walk in the door. Should space be limited, shuck the corn and refrigerate it in perforated plastic bags.

By far the best way to eat corn is on the cob. Nine times out of ten, that's how I'll serve it.

To shuck corn, pull the husks down the ear, snap off the stem at the base, and remove the silk around the kernels (a dry vegetable brush is useful here). To cook corn in its husk, pull the husks down the base of the ear without detaching. Remove the silk from the kernels, then replace the husks up around the ear, tying in place if necessary.

Because of my family's enthusiasm for corn on the cob, it took me a long time to appreciate how delicious fresh corn can be in chowders, stews, and custards: all good ways to use up a glut of corn. Don't toss out over-aged or mealy ears of corn—they taste fine in baked corn dishes.

I use both the "cut" and "scrape" methods to remove kernels. The "cut" method removes kernels whole—outer skin and all—while the "scrape" method utilizes just the juices and the inner flesh, while leaving the skin on the cobs. Here's how I do it:

- *Cut Kernels*: Starting at the tip of the ear, run a sharp knife straight down to the stem, leaving 1/8–1/4 inch of pulp behind on the cob. (This prevents you from inadvertently cutting off the tough cob fibers.)

• *Scraped Kernels*: Run a knife down the center of a row of kernels, slicing right down to the end of the ear. Continue until all the rows have been prepared. Place the corn over a bowl. Then, using the back of the knife, push or "scrape" down on the kernels: the flesh and "milk" will spurt out. I go back and forth, up and down the ear until it's finished.

This method works fine for a small amount of corn. If you cook a lot of fresh corn, however, I suggest you invest in a corn scraper. My primitive, but totally satisfactory, scraper is simply a piece of wood on small end legs, with teeth and a dull blade. The "teeth" open the kernels and then the blade scrapes them out, allowing me to clean an ear of corn in seconds.

For a dish like simple sautéed corn, I would use the cut method, while for chowder or puddings, I prefer scraped corn, because the "milky" flesh helps to thicken the broth.

Corn Varieties

These are the corn varieties we've enjoyed:

Burgundy Delight: a midseason, bicolored corn, has burgundy-colored stalks, husks 8 inches long, and well-filled ears with tender kernels.

Butter and Sugar: a midseason bicolored corn with sweet, tender kernels on 7½-inch-long ears.

Seneca Chief: a midseason to late corn; it has good flavor; slender ears; deep, narrow kernels. Good for freezing or canning.

Silver Queen: a late corn; this is the best-flavored white corn. Kernels are always tender and extra sweet. Long, slightly tapered ears have small kernels. Good for freezing or drying.

Sweet Sue: a midseason bicolored corn with large ears, high sugar content. Good for freezing.

Stylepak: a midseason corn, with large ears with golden yellow, tender kernels. Ears fill to the tip, making it a good choice for freezing on the cob.

Sprite: an early bicolored gold and white corn, Sprite has 7-inch ears. It can be planted when the ground is chilly and will take a light frost in spring. Well-filled ears and good flavor for an early corn.

• If you want to grow your own corn for corn meal, hominy, or masa harina, try Hickory King corn. Its huge white kernels are the best for making hominy, grits, corn nuts, and corn meal. Fine for masa harina. Good for roasting ears when picked young.

Marketing

Always buy fresh corn that's just been picked at a local farm, or corn that's been held on ice. Shipped-in corn will have lost sweetness, but will be all right for dishes using cut or scraped corn.

The tip-off for freshly picked corn is the stem. If it is a damp, pale green, the corn has been picked within the day. After 24 hours, the stalk turns opaque and chalky. Longer than that, it turns brown.

Ask for the extra-sweet corn, for it holds sugar longer than other varieties.

◇ *Pennsylvania Dutch Dried Sweet Corn*

Use a sweet variety such as Silver Queen. Blanch corn for 2 minutes. Cut corn from cobs and spread out in a single layer on a baking sheet. Dry in a slow oven (175°) for 12–15 hours, stirring occasionally, or place in a dehydrator and dry until it registers 5° moisture. Kernels should be hard and crunchy, not chewy.

◇ *Corn on the Cob*

Some people prefer corn young and white, while others like it mealy and yellow. Whichever you choose, remember all corn cooks quickly.

Boiled Corn on the Cob

Drop shucked corn into a kettle two-thirds full of boiling water; boil for 4 minutes. The cooking time ranges from 4 to 7 minutes, depending upon the size and age of corn. Remove an ear and taste; it should still be slightly crisp. Serve with butter, salt, and pepper.

Steamed Corn on the Cob

Put 1 inch water in a steamer and bring it to a boil. Place shucked corn on rack and steam for 6 minutes. Cooking time will range from 6 to 10 minutes, depending upon the size and age of corn.

Special Information

Yields

- Kernels *cut* from 6 plump ears = approximately 2 ½ cups whole kernels
- Kernels *scraped* from 6 ears = approximately 2 cups flesh and liquid

Storage and Preserving

- Use as soon as possible after picking. If storing, refrigerate immediately without husking. If husks have been removed, store in perforated plastic bags.
- Refrigerated cooked corn kernels will keep 2–3 days.

Freezing

- Remove husks and silk. Timing from the point when the water returns to the boil, blanch 4 minutes for small ears, 6 minutes for medium ears, and 8 minutes for large ears. Immediately cool in ice water for the same length of time as it was necessary to blanch. Drain; pack whole in bags. You can also blanch, drain, cut off kernels, and freeze in freezer boxes. Frozen corn will last up to a year. Thaw before cooking.

Canning

- Corn cans well, but because it is a low acid vegetable, it's essential to process it for an adequate period of time. Also, can as soon as possible after harvesting for the sugars rapidly turn to starch. See a good preserving book for instructions.

Hints

- Make a frittata—see *American Spinach Frittata* in *Spinach*—substituting corn kernels and adding a bit of sour cream.
- Fold raw corn kernels into scrambled eggs.
- Season fresh corn kernels with salt, pepper, and a pinch of sugar; just before eating, fold into heavy whipped cream.
- Add freshly cut kernels to stir-fry dishes.
- Sauté fresh corn kernels and pieces of chorizo sausage along with boiled small red new potatoes, onions, and peppers.

Microwave

- 4 ears of corn, either in the husk or shucked, placed in a covered dish with 2–3 tablespoons water, take 5–7 minutes to cook.
- 2 cups corn kernels in a covered dish with 2 tablespoons butter take 3 minutes to cook.

Leftovers

- Add leftover corn-on-the-cob kernels to pancake batters, muffins, cornbread, and cornsticks.
- Add to a cold vegetable vinaigrette salad.
- Add kernels to stews or casseroles. I like to save vegetables such as onions, peppers, cauliflower bits, and beans in the refrigerator, and cook them with corn, butter, and herbs in a mixed vegetable braise.
- Add to kidney beans or Boston baked beans.
- Add corn to a cheese quiche, or make individual cocktail tartlets.

Roast Corn on the Cob

Oven Roast: Preheat oven to 375°. Pull down outer leaves without detaching, remove silk from ears, and then wrap leaves back up around corn. Soak in water for 10 minutes, which keeps it from burning or drying out. Place wrapped corn directly on the oven rack and bake for 20–30 minutes.

Foil Method: Remove husks and silk. Brush corn with melted butter. Wrap corn in foil and roast on a hot grill for 15–20 minutes or in the oven for 20–30 minutes.

Grilled Roasted Corn Method: Treat silk and husks as for oven-roasted corn. Grill for 15–20 minutes, turning occasionally.

◇ *Sautéed Corn Kernels*

Using a sharp knife, cut kernels from the cob. Without browning, sauté corn in butter over medium-low heat until cooked through and tender. Add a touch of sugar if the corn is old. Young corn takes 3–4 minutes; older corn, 6–8 minutes. Season with salt and pepper.

Note: If the corn is mealy or thick-skinned, cover and lightly braise. Add a little water if it seems to be dry or sticking.

Finishing Touches for Sautéed Corn Kernels

- *With Cream*: Add cream; reduce until it just lightly coats the kernels.
- *In Broth*: For a low-calorie version, omit butter. Cook corn in 1–2 tablespoons chicken broth.
- *With Bacon*: Cook bacon. Remove, pouring out all but a few tablespoons fat. Sauté corn in bacon fat; before serving, garnish with crumbled bacon.
- *With Leftovers*: Add leftover vegetables or bits of ham and cheese; heat through before serving.

◇ *Creamed Corn*

Proceed as for *Sautéed Corn Kernels*, scraping rather than cutting kernels. After sautéing, add cream and reduce to a thick creamy texture.

◇ *Baked Corn*

Here are some baked corn ideas.

Corn and Swiss Cheese

Combine 2 cups cut kernels with 1 egg, ½ cup cream, salt, pepper, and 1 cup grated Swiss cheese. Bake in a preheated 350° oven for 35–40 minutes.

Baked Corn Layered with Tomatoes

Sauté ¼ cup chopped onions in 3 tablespoons butter. Stir in 1 cup fresh bread crumbs and cook until crumbs are golden. In a baking dish, make 6 layers with 2 cups cut corn kernels, 2–3 large peeled, seeded, and sliced tomatoes, and the bread crumbs, sprinkling with salt and pepper to taste. Pour over ¾ cup light cream (optional). Bake in a preheated 350° oven for 40 minutes.

Succotash

The original succotash, developed by early colonists, was a hearty chicken and corned beef stew containing potatoes, turnips, and whatever dried or fresh corn and beans were available. Certainly a far cry from the simple corn and lima bean dish I call succotash. For a succotash made with shell beans, see *Beans*.

  1 slice blanched salt pork or 1 slice bacon
  1 ½ cups shelled fresh lima beans (2 lb unshelled)
  4–6 Tb butter
  2 cups corn kernels
  Salt and freshly ground pepper

Bring a pot of water to the boil; add the salt pork or bacon and lima beans. Cook until the beans are just tender, 6–10 minutes. Drain, discarding salt pork or bacon. Melt butter in a saucepan, stir in beans and corn, and cook until corn is just cooked through. Season to taste. (*Serves 4*)

- For a creamy version, use 2 cups scraped corn and proceed as above.
- Add a few tablespoons of heavy cream along with the beans and corn.
- Substitute cut green beans for lima beans.

Corn, Tomato, and Hot Pepper Trio

I enjoy the way Mexican cooks combine chili peppers and corn. Add some tomatoes and you have a thick, creamy vegetable stew.

  1 onion
  3 Tb butter
  1 fresh green hot pepper or a 3-oz can
  2 cups peeled, seeded, and chopped tomatoes, drained
  2 cups scraped corn (page 85)
  ¾ cup grated Cheddar cheese
  Salt and freshly ground pepper

Chop onion and sauté in butter until softened. Meanwhile, seed and chop the hot pepper; add along with tomatoes, and cook until liquid is reduced, 15–20 minutes. Add corn; cook 20–30 minutes longer, until thickened. Add cheese, cook very gently another 10 minutes, and season to taste. (*Serves 4–6*)

Corn Pudding

This pudding has a rich corn essence, almost candylike in its sweetness.

    2 cups scraped corn (page 85)
    1 Tb flour (if corn is very milky)
    1 tsp sugar (unless corn is just picked)
    2/3 cup heavy cream
    Salt and freshly ground pepper
    1 Tb butter

Thoroughly combine corn, flour and sugar if needed, cream, and seasonings. Pour into a buttered 4–6-cup baking dish. Dot with 1 tablespoon butter. Bake in a preheated 325° oven for 50–60 minutes. *(Serves 4–6)*

Light Corn Custard

This custard has a delicate, light texture.

    2 cups scraped corn (page 85)
    4 eggs
    1 cup heavy cream
    1 Tb sugar
    1 tsp salt
    1/4 tsp ground white pepper
    Dash nutmeg
    2 Tb melted butter

Combine ingredients, and spoon into a 1 1/2-quart baking dish. Place in a roasting pan; pour boiling water two-thirds up the outside of the baking dish. Bake in a pre-heated 350° oven for 1 hour or until the top is golden and a knife tests clean. Serve immediately. *(Serves 4–6)*
- For a smoother, more uniform texture, purée corn. Add 2 tablespoons flour and proceed as above.
- For an even lighter texture, separate eggs, add yolks to mixture, and fold in whites just before baking.
- Add herbs such as dill, or spices such as curry.

Corn and Chive Soufflé

A particularly delicious and colorful soufflé—see illustration above right.

    2 cups scraped corn (page 85)
    1/2 packed cup Cheddar cheese
    6 egg yolks
    1/4 cup minced chives
    Salt and freshly ground pepper
    8 egg whites
    1/4 tsp cream of tartar

Butter a 2-quart soufflé dish. Blend together corn, cheese, and egg yolks. Add chives and season to taste. Beat egg whites to soft peaks, adding cream of tartar when they become foamy. Stir a quarter of the whites into the corn mixture to lighten it, then fold in the re-maining whites. Pour into the soufflé dish and bake in a preheated 425° oven for 10 minutes, turn heat to 375° and cook for 30 minutes longer. Serve immediately. *(Serves 4)*

Corn Timbales

When these timbales first emerge from the oven, they're puffy, but they sink fast. Either serve them in the cook-ing molds or turn out onto a plate.

    4 eggs
    2 cups scraped corn (page 85)
    1/2 tsp salt
    Freshly ground pepper
    Dash Tabasco sauce
    1/4 tsp sugar
    1/4 cup minced parsley
    2 Tb minced fresh dill (optional)
    1/2 cup grated Swiss cheese
    1/3 packed cup fresh bread crumbs
    2 Tb heavy cream

Beat eggs; mix in remaining ingredients. Spoon into 6 buttered 6-ounce molds. Set molds in a roasting pan, then pour boiling water halfway up the sides of the molds. Bake in a preheated 350° oven for 35 minutes. Before unmolding, run a knife around the edges. *(Serves 6)*
- Cook in a 1 1/2-quart mold. Mixture will take longer to cook, 1–1 1/4 hours. Timbale is done when the filling has pulled away from the sides of the dish.
- Use other cheeses, such as mozzarella or Cheddar.
- Season with your favorite herbs or spices.

Corn Quiche

Tart Pastry (page 351)
8 slices bacon
1–1 1/2 cups grated Swiss or Monterey Jack cheese
1/2 cup minced scallions
4 eggs
1 cup scraped corn (page 85)
1 cup medium cream
3/4 tsp salt
1/4 tsp freshly ground pepper
Dash nutmeg

Line a 10-inch pie pan or quiche form with pastry and partially prebake (see *Appendix*). Cook bacon, and crumble into bits. Sprinkle bacon, cheese, and scallions into pie pan. Beat eggs slightly, then beat in remaining ingredients and pour into pie pan. Bake in a preheated 425° oven for 10 minutes. Reduce heat to 300° and bake for 30–35 minutes longer or until a knife tests clean. Let rest for 10 minutes before cutting. *(Makes a 10-inch quiche)*

Corn Chowder

There are literally dozens of regional corn chowder recipes. I like this scraped corn and cut kernels combination best with fresh corn, but it is almost as good with frozen corn.

4 oz salt pork
1 medium onion
2 cups 1/4-inch potato chunks
2 cups combination chicken broth and water
Salt and freshly ground pepper
2 cups scraped corn (page 85)
1 cup corn kernels (page 84)
1/2 cup heavy cream

Remove rind and cut salt pork into "logs" 2 inches long by 1 1/4 inches thick. Blanch in boiling water for 5 minutes. Drain, pat dry, and cut into 1/4-inch cubes. Sauté in a large saucepan over medium heat until crisp; remove, and drain all but 3 tablespoons fat. Chop onion and cook in fat until softened and golden. Add potatoes, broth, and water, 1 teaspoon salt, and scraped corn. Bring to a boil, lower heat, and cook, partially covered, until potatoes are tender. Stir in corn kernels and cook 5 minutes longer. Add heavy cream; cook until heated through. Season with salt, pepper, and the pork bits if you like. *(Serves 4–6)*

- For a smoother texture, purée corn.
- Add cooked chicken pieces.
- Substitute fish stock, and add pieces of cod or bass 8–10 minutes before serving.

Corn Crêpes with a Tacoese Filling

These crêpes are delicious served plain, but really shine when they're wrapped around a filling. As I'm a taco freak, I enjoy this hot, spicy hamburger filling. Add as many hot spices as you like. Serve with sour cream on the side.

Crêpes
1/2 cup flour (instant is preferable)
1/2 cup medium cream
1 cup scraped corn (page 85)
2 eggs
1/2 tsp salt
Freshly ground pepper
2 Tb melted butter

Put flour in a bowl, and beat in cream with a wire whisk. Add remaining ingredients, mixing well. Let sit for at least 15 minutes before cooking. Meanwhile, make *Tacoese Filling* (below).

Heat a small crêpe or sauté pan. Film with oil so the crêpes won't stick. Ladle out scant 1/4 cup batter, and roll pan to spread the batter to a 6-inch diameter. Brown crêpe lightly on one side, and when it slides easily in the pan, flip over and brown lightly on the other side. Slide onto a warm plate and keep warm while you make the remaining crêpes. When the crêpes are done, place a spoonful of tacoese filling down the center of each crêpe and roll them up. *(Serves 4)*

Tacoese Filling
1 medium onion
2 Tb butter
1 1/2 cups peeled, seeded, and chopped tomatoes
1 Tb finely minced fresh or canned jalapeño peppers (optional)
1/2 cup chopped hot chili peppers
1 tsp salt
1 lb ground beef
3/4 cup grated Monterey Jack cheese

Chop onion and cook in butter until soft and golden. Add tomatoes, peppers, chilies, and salt; simmer for 15 minutes or until tomatoes and liquid are almost evaporated. Meanwhile, brown ground beef. When tomato mixture has cooked, mix in beef and cheese. (Cheese should melt.)

- Cover the rolled filled crêpes with a *Marinara Sauce* (see *Tomatoes*), sprinkle with additional grated cheese, and run under the broiler to glaze.
- Serve with a filling of creamed spinach, or braised chopped kale, or anything you like.
- Make crêpes smaller (3–4 inches wide) and serve as an appetizer with sour cream.
- Lay filled crêpes in a baking dish and cover with a light *Mornay Sauce* (see *Appendix*), sprinkle with grated cheese, and dot with butter. Bake in a preheated 400° oven for 15–20 minutes. Run under broiler to glaze.

Spicy Chicken in Corn Sauce

Serve this tasty supper dish in soup bowls along with fresh bread to sop up the juices.

3 1/2–4-lb frying chicken
2–3 Tb vegetable oil
1 cup chopped red peppers
1 cup chopped green peppers
1 cup chopped onions
1 cup chopped, peeled, and seeded tomatoes
2–3 cups scraped corn (page 85)
3-oz can chopped hot peppers
1 Tb fresh tarragon or 1 tsp dried
1 tsp chili powder
1 tsp salt
Freshly ground pepper

Cut chicken into eight serving pieces. Dry chicken, brown in oil, and set aside. Sauté peppers and onions in oil until softened. Drain oil; return chicken to pan along with remaining ingredients. Cook over low heat, stirring occasionally, until chicken is tender, 30–40 minutes. *(Serves 4)*

- Add 2 tablespoons of sour cream or heavy cream just before serving for extra richness.

Lynn Wilson's Corn and Chicken on Rice

The corn adds a fresh, crisp textural contrast.

2 large chicken breasts (4 halves)
Flour
2 Tb vegetable oil
2/3 cup chopped scallions
1 1/2 cups sliced mushrooms
1 clove garlic
2 cups chicken broth
1/4 cup vermouth or dry sherry
3/4 tsp salt
1/8 tsp freshly ground pepper
1 Tb fresh chopped basil
2 cups corn kernels
2 cups peeled, seeded, and chopped tomatoes
Cooked rice

Skin and bone chicken breasts; cut into 2 x 1/2-inch pieces. Thoroughly dredge in flour. Brown chicken on all sides in oil. Stir in the scallions and mushrooms; cook for 2–3 minutes. Mince garlic; add along with chicken broth, vermouth or sherry, salt, pepper, and basil. Simmer for 10 minutes. Stir in corn and tomatoes. Cook for 5 minutes longer. Serve over rice. *(Serves 4)*

- Substitute turkey, pork, or veal for the chicken.

Corn Fritters

Here are two types of corn fritters: the first, soft and tender; the second, best as a hearty fall meal with the last of the fresh corn.

Soft Delicate Fritters
Serve these as a side dish with main-course meals; or sprinkle with powdered sugar and eat as a dessert.

2 eggs
2 cups scraped corn (page 85)
1/2 tsp salt and freshly ground pepper
2 Tb flour (optional)
1 tsp sugar
1 Tb melted butter
Vegetable oil or clarified butter

Lightly beat eggs; mix with remaining ingredients except oil or clarified butter. Drop by spoonfuls into hot oil or butter, browning on both sides, 3–4 minutes per side. *(Makes 15–20 small fritters or patties)*
Note: The flour is necessary only if corn is very milky.

- Separate 3 eggs. Use 2 egg yolks in mixture. Beat 3 egg whites and fold into batter before frying.

Hearty and Crisp Fritters

These fritters are excellent with glazed ham or served alone for a Sunday night supper along with Vermont maple syrup—or try *Corncob Syrup,* below.

> 1 ½ cups flour
> 2 tsp baking powder
> 1 tsp salt
> Dash freshly ground pepper
> 1 large egg
> ½ cup milk
> 1 Tb melted butter
> 2 cups corn kernels
> Vegetable oil or clarified butter

Sift together dry ingredients. Beat egg; combine with milk and butter and stir into dry ingredients. Add corn. Fry in oil or clarified butter until browned on both sides. *(Makes 15–20 small fritters or patties)*
- For corn and clam fritters, add chopped fresh clams.

Double Cornbread

The scraped corn gives a fresh corn aroma while the corn fragments add texture. You can bake this as corn sticks in the special cast-iron molds designed for that purpose, but cut the baking time down to 15 minutes.

> 1 cup corn meal
> 1 cup flour
> 4 tsp baking powder
> 2–3 Tb sugar (more if you like a sweet cornbread)
> ½ tsp salt
> 1 egg
> ¼ cup melted butter or shortening
> 1 ½ cups scraped corn (page 85)

Combine corn meal, flour, baking powder, sugar, and salt. In a blender, combine egg, butter or shortening, and corn. Then pour over dry ingredients. Beat together until fairly smooth. Place in a buttered 8-inch square baking pan and bake in a preheated 425° oven for 20–25 minutes. *(Serves 9)*
- For even more texture, add ⅓ cup cooked corn kernels to batter.

Corn Pancakes

> 6 ears corn (to make 2–2 ½ cups cut corn kernels)
> 2 cups flour
> 2 Tb sugar
> 2 tsp baking powder
> 1 ½ tsp salt
> Dash freshly ground pepper
> 3 large eggs
> ¾ cup milk
> 2 Tb melted butter

Cut the corn from the cobs and scrape the cobs for additional corn milk. Sift the dry ingredients together. Combine eggs, milk, and butter, and stir into dry ingredients, blending only until moistened. Add corn and corn milk. Cook on a hot griddle or in an oiled frying pan. *(Serves 10–12)*

Baked Dried Corn

This traditional Pennsylvania Dutch dried corn pudding is delicious, and sweeter than most because it's made from Pennsylvania Dutch dry sweet eating corn rather than the flint corn customarily used for corn meal and hominy. You'll find its texture to be halfway between sweet corn and corn meal.

> 1 cup dried corn kernels (page 86)
> 2 eggs
> 2 cups milk
> 1 cup light cream
> 2 Tb melted butter
> 1 tsp salt
> 1 Tb sugar
> ¼ tsp nutmeg

Grind the corn kernels in a blender or food processor. Beat eggs, mix with remaining ingredients, and add corn. Bake in a buttered 1 ½-quart dish in a preheated 375° oven for 55 minutes. *(Serves 4–6)*

Corncob Syrup

This light syrup has a delicate corn aftertaste. Serve it with corn fritters or pancakes.

> 6 corncobs
> 1 qt water
> 1 ¼ packed cups brown sugar

Remove kernels from corn, then break cobs into chunks. Put cobs and water in a saucepan, bring to a boil, and boil uncovered until liquid is reduced to 2 cups (approximately 45 minutes). Discard cobs and strain mixture. Stir liquid and sugar together in a saucepan, bring to a boil, and boil gently, uncovered, until liquid is reduced to 1 cup and is the consistency of maple syrup (approximately 20 minutes). *(Makes 1 cup)*

Cucumbers

I have friends who will never eat cucumbers, even though they love them, because they say cucumbers are bitter and make them burp. The bitterness is no myth, but it is really something of the past.

Bitterness in older cucumber varieties was caused by the so-called bitter gene, part of the genetic makeup of cucumbers. Almost all the research devoted to cucumbers has been aimed at removing this gene. As a result, the new hybrid varieties contain very little bitterness.

If you are harvesting bitter cucumbers, the most likely explanation is that you are growing them incorrectly. Once cucumbers are subjected to stress (such as lack of sufficient water, for example), they tend to bitter up. Select the right kind of cucumber, keep the plants free from anything that might check their growth, and you will be rewarded with perfectly digestible cucumbers that are crisp, refreshing pick-me-ups on a hot summer day.

However, if you want to be on the safe side, there is a trick for removing bitterness. It's almost all concentrated in the leaves, stems, and skin, so remove 1 inch of the cucumber's stem end and peel the skin as well as a thin layer of flesh directly beneath the skin.

I also find that scoring cucumbers with a fork makes the difference between faintly bitter and palatable cucumbers. Try the test yourself. Peel a cucumber. Take two center sections. Score one and leave the other alone. Cut a slice from each and taste. I think you'll find that the scored cucumber is less bitter. (Even if you don't agree, scoring makes them look pretty.) Salting also releases juices.

All this is aimed at making cucumbers as digestible as possible. If you prefer to skip these steps, that's fine.

There are basically three cucumber types: field or standard cucumbers, which grow quite large with a bright green color; smaller pickling cucumbers with a more yellowish cast to the skins; and greenhouse forced varieties, bred to produce fruit in somewhat lower temperatures. The home gardener can grow all three.

Although you can sow cucumber seeds directly in the ground once the weather becomes warm, to ensure an early crop Russ starts the seeds indoors in individual peat pots. He plants Pacer, Victory, Burpee Hybrid, and Sweet Slice (all standard varieties); Liberty Hybrid (a pickling variety); a French cornichon variety; and sometimes a bush type for growing in containers, such as Bush Champion. He sows two seeds 1/2 inch deep per pot, pinches off the weaker of the two seedlings, and keeps them moist in full sun with a temperature of about 70° or better until it's time to transplant them into the garden, usually early in June.

Cucumbers are heavy feeders, so he enriches the soil with some well-rotted manure or compost and adds slow-release fertilizer. He then covers the soil with black plastic mulch (available at any garden center). The mulch warms the soil to 85° by late May or early June, when Russ transplants the seedlings. He cuts a hole right through the plastic mulch, and sets in the plants spaced 24 inches apart. Each plant gets a drink of transplant solution.

The black plastic mulch keeps down the weeds and conserves moisture throughout the summer (more important, it keeps the soil warm). Russ waters the cucumbers faithfully, and in mid-July, the first ones are ready for harvesting. In July, Russ also sows a fresh crop of seeds directly into the soil so that we'll have cucumbers throughout the fall. (At this point, the plastic mulch is unnecessary.)

By the way, if your gardening space is limited, plant cucumbers next to a wire fence or trellis, and they will grow right up it. That's how Russ grew our cornichons last year.

Cucumbers should be harvested frequently because otherwise they become large and seedy. Harvest by twisting the stem and giving a quick snap. The time to pick depends completely upon the variety. A cucumber's mature size varies from the tiny 1–2-inch cornichons to the Asian varieties that grow 20 inches long. Pick standard cucumbers when they reach 5–8 inches; pickling cucumbers smaller (depending upon the variety). Should you miss some cucumbers and they become oversized and yellow, make yellow cucumber pickles (see *Senfgurken*).

Cucumbers are easy to grow, but not so easy to keep. If you have a glut in the garden, the best solution is to pickle them. Because cucumbers are mainly water, once they're harvested, they tend to shrivel very fast. Keep them in a humid spot with a temperature at 45–50° if possible: temperatures over 50° will ripen and turn them yellow—temperatures below 45° will cause damage after 2 days. That's why refrigerating can be only a temporary measure. If you wrap the cucumbers in plastic bags and keep in the hydrator section, they'll hold 1–2 days, but eventually the cold will cause the flesh to collapse and they will become pitted and spotty.

This need for high humidity is the reason you so often find waxed cucumbers. Waxing seals the skin and reduces moisture loss. Because growers and shopkeepers realize the advantages of waxing, it's almost impossible to find unwaxed standard varieties of cucumbers anymore. (Once again the gardener has the advantage.) You can get rid of some of the wax by pouring boiling water over, but this usually doesn't remove it all. So, I recommend peeling waxed cucumbers.

If you are fairly sure your cucumbers are not bitter, don't peel them. Just wash and dry them. When I want a more decorative look, as well as scoring cucumbers, I sometimes peel them at intervals, leaving strips of green skin around the cucumber, so that the slices will have tracings of the skin. I use a paring knife to peel the cucumbers, because I like to remove a little of the flesh beneath the skin, but a vegetable peeler does just as well.

Larger cucumbers, which have larger, tougher seeds than small cucumbers, need seeding. After scoring the cucumbers, I halve them lengthwise, then, with a sharp-edged spoon, scoop out the seeds and watery flesh—leaving cucumber "boats" to use as is, or to then cut in chunks or slices.

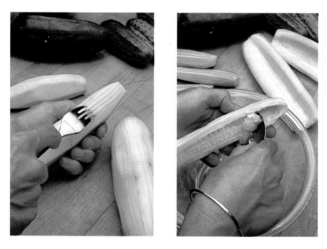

At this stage, I'll frequently salt the cucumbers to remove excess moisture (or more of the bitterness should it exist). I let them sit for at least 30 minutes so that the juices are released, then squeeze lightly. Then I put them in a colander and press down with my hands or a weight, or I press them dry in a clean cloth or towel. If I have grated the cucumbers I will place them in a towel, roll it up, twist the ends in opposite directions, and squeeze out the moisture through the towel. (Use whichever method seems easiest and most suitable to the cut of the cucumber.)

You can also release the excess moisture by blanching; however, that removes some of the cucumber's delicate taste.

Cooked cucumbers are quite delicious—fish and cucumbers being a particularly tasty combination. At the restaurant we serve both cold combinations and hot cucumbers. Occasionally, we'll get sautéed cucumbers back from a patron who won't even try them, but generally people are delighted and surprised to discover the smooth, elegant flavor of cooked cucumbers. You'll notice I prefer to sauté cucumbers, but you can also steam or blanch them.

Marketing

Try to find a grower who has unwaxed, farm fresh cucumbers. Since this is becoming increasingly difficult, be prepared to peel the waxed cucumbers, but don't buy them unless their flesh is firm and crisp.

Look for firm green cucumbers. Avoid any that have yellowed (a sign of age), are shriveled (a sign of dehydration), or look pitted or feel pulpy (a sign that they've been exposed to cold). Larger cucumbers often have large-size seed centers, so pick out the smaller, narrower cucumbers.

You can get pickling cucumbers in the market that are not waxed, because wax interferes with the pickling process. These are fine to substitute for regular cucumbers, because their small seeds are quite edible. Their only disadvantage is color: pickling cucumbers are less green than standard varieties and their skin has a yellow-

Special Information

Yields

Standard Cucumbers
- 2 cucumbers approximately 8 inches long and 2 inches wide = 1 pound
- 1 pound sliced with skins = 4 cups
- 1 pound peeled and seeded = approximately 10 ounces
- 1 pound peeled, seeded, and sliced = approximately 2 cups
- 1 pound peeled, seeded, and sliced, then salted, drained, and pressed = approximately 1 1/3 cups

Pickling Cucumbers
- Five 4–5-inch pickling cucumbers = 1 pound
- Sliced with skins on = 4 cups
- 1 pound cucumbers = 4 servings

Storage and Preserving
- Use as soon as possible after harvesting. Pickling is the best way to store cucumbers for a long time. See the pickling recipes and *Pickling Brine —All-Purpose* in the *Appendix*.

- Because cucumbers dehydrate quickly, store at 45–50° in highly humid conditions (90–95° humidity). Store in perforated plastic bags in hydrator for 1–2 days.

Hints
- Try to find pickling cucumbers during the winter when cucumbers tend to be large, seedy, and waxed.
- Don't seed pickling cukes. Used with their skins on, they have less waste than large cucumbers.
- Scoring with a fork is an attractive decoration which I think releases bitter juices.
- Salting crisps cucumbers for salads.
- Cucumbers have a high water content, almost no calories, and make a great diet snack.
- Make *Cucumber Sandwiches:* Use thin cucumbers with undersize seeds. Peel, score, and thinly slice the cucumbers; salt, and let sit. Meanwhile, thinly slice rounds of homemade bread. Drain the cucumbers; pat dry. Lightly butter the bread or spread with a thin layer of mayonnaise and top with cucumber slices. Add washed and dried watercress and thinly sliced onion (optional). Then, cover with a second

ish cast (which I find perfectly acceptable). Avoid any that are very yellow and have puffy flesh. Because pickling cucumbers are not waxed, they become dehydrated, indicated by shriveled skins and a withered appearance. If they're firm and healthy-looking, they should be delicious.

◇ *Cucumber Salads*

Cucumbers can be both an essential ingredient in a mixed salad and a perfectly delicious salad on their own. When I'm making a mixed salad, I use pickling cucumbers (or small regular cucumbers) because I like to use the whole cucumber—skin, seeds, and all. When I'm slicing the cucumbers directly into a salad just before dressing and serving them, I don't bother with the salting and draining step because the cucumbers keep their garden crispness quite well.

However, when I'm combining cucumbers with other salad ingredients, or serving them on their own, I toss them with salt (or a combination of salt and vinegar) and let them drain in a colander. Then, I press the cucumbers dry and compose the salad. Prepared this way, the drained cucumbers do not water down the dressing.

◇ *Basic Cucumber Salad*

In practically every country where cucumbers are grown, you'll find a cucumber salad—the Austrians and Germans call it *Gurkensalat*; the Danes, *Agurkesalat*; and the Poles, *Salata Mizerja*. Regardless of where it originates, the preparation is very much the same. The cucumbers are first salted to remove the juices and then tossed in a dressing. As salted and drained cucumbers reduce considerably in volume, you'll need to use more cucumbers than with a standard cucumber salad.

I am giving you two alternatives for extracting the moisture, each of which imbues the cucumbers with a different flavor. Just remember to adjust the final dressing to complement these flavors. To remove the salt from wilted cucumbers, rinse them off after they have released their juices and then press dry.

> *Method 1*
> 4 medium or 6 small cucumbers
> Kosher salt

Trim the ends from the cucumbers, peel, and score. Halve lengthwise and scoop out the seeds. Thinly slice the cucumber crosswise. Toss with salt (for every 4 cups of sliced cucumber, use 1/2–1 teaspoon salt) and let stand for at least 30 minutes. Gently press out the moisture. *(Serves 4–6)*

> *Method 2*
> 4 medium or 6 small cucumbers
> 2 Tb wine vinegar
> Kosher salt
> 1/2 tsp sugar (optional)

Prepare as above and toss with combined vinegar, salt, and sugar. Let sit, drain, and press. Adjust final dressing to account for salt, vinegar, and sugar. *(Serves 4–6)*

- *Chopped Cucumber Salad:* Prepare as above. Drain cucumbers and mix with other chopped vegetables for mixed salads or use in recipes such as *Pesto Pasta Salad with Cucumbers*.
- *Grated Cucumber Salad:* Grate, then treat as above; fold into mayonnaise, sour cream, or yogurt dressing for a creamy yet crunchy salad.
- *Julienned Cucumber Salad:* Julienne, and treat as above. Form into mounds to garnish a salad platter.

---

bread round. You can hold these for a while if refrigerated and covered with waxed paper, then covered with a wet towel.

- Make a *Cucumber Grape Salad:* Peel, score, and thinly slice cucumbers. Salt, let rest, then dry. Toss with washed and dried grapes and dress with a *Cream Salad Dressing* (see *Appendix*). Add stemmed watercress, if desired.
- Make decorative *Cucumber Twists:* Wash and dry a cucumber. Score with a fork so that the white flesh alternates with the green skin. Thinly slice the cucumber. Then, starting at the center, cut each slice from the center to one edge. Pull the cut ends away from each other, forming a bow-shaped curl and set on a plate (or sandwich), uncut side up.
- Grate raw cucumbers and drain. Sauté for 1–2 minutes in a curry butter.

Microwave
- 1 pound cucumbers, peeled, scored, and cut into triangular pieces will cook crunchy in 4 minutes.

Leftovers
- Add leftover raw cucumbers to cold salads. Any leftovers in this house usually go into my daughters' tuna fish salad sandwiches.
- Purée leftover cooked cucumbers with whipped potatoes—delicious with melted butter.
- Chop up or grate leftover cucumbers and sauté for 1 minute in butter. Add to the egg mixture in a Western sandwich.

Final Dressings for Cucumber Salad

The basic salad can be varied in any number of ways. The following dressings are sufficient for 4 medium cucumbers.

- *Vinaigrette Sauce:* Toss cucumbers in a *Vinaigrette Sauce* (see *Appendix*). Add chopped shallots or fresh chopped herbs such as dill or mint.
- *Sweet Dressing:* Combine ¼ cup vinegar, 2 teaspoons sugar, salt, and pepper. Beat in ¾ cup oil, or omit oil and combine the vinegar mixture with ½ cup sour cream into which you've folded ¼ cup heavy cream, whipped, and some chopped dill.
- *Soy Sauce:* Mix 2–3 tablespoons soy sauce with 4 tablespoons white vinegar and 1 teaspoon sugar.
- *Lemon Juice:* Toss 3–4 tablespoons lemon juice with 1–2 teaspoons sugar and chopped shallots or red onions. Toss with chopped parsley, mint, or dill and season to taste.
- *Yogurt:* Place 2 cups yogurt in a sieve and drain in the refrigerator for 2 hours or until fairly "dry." Mash 1 clove garlic with ½ teaspoon salt, add 1 tablespoon lemon juice, and beat in 2 tablespoons olive oil. Mix with yogurt, stir in chopped dill and mint (or basil and parsley), and season to taste.
- *Sour Cream:* Combine 1 tablespoon wine vinegar or lemon juice with a touch of Dijon mustard, salt, and pepper. Whisk in ½–1 cup sour cream. Stir in chopped fresh herbs such as dill, basil, or parsley.
- *Mayonnaise:* Dilute homemade *Mayonnaise* (see *Appendix*) with equal parts sour cream, whipped heavy cream, or yogurt. Season with lemon juice, salt, pepper, and fresh chopped herbs.
- *With Crème Fraîche:* For 2 pounds cucumbers, slowly whisk ⅓ cup mustard *Vinaigrette Sauce* (see *Appendix*) into ½ cup crème fraîche (see *Appendix*). Season with salt, pepper, and herbs to taste. Combine with cucumbers and chill. Serve at room temperature.

◇ Combination Salads

Cucumber combination salads can be very pretty and tasty; see *Aunt Pat's Summer Salad*.

- *With Feta Cheese:* Combine chunked, salted, and drained cucumbers with crumbled feta cheese and chopped mint. Dress with a lemon juice *Vinaigrette Sauce* (see *Appendix*).
- *With Peppers:* Toss julienned, salted, drained cucumbers and julienned red and green peppers. Dress with a mustard *Vinaigrette Sauce* (see *Appendix*).
- *With Onions:* Combine finely sliced, salted, drained cucumbers with finely sliced red onions. Add a good wine vinegar and season with salt and pepper. Decorate with wedges of hard boiled eggs.

Aunt Pat's Summer Salad

This salad my sister-in-law made for us twenty years ago is still a summer favorite at our house.

1 lb cucumbers
1 lb zucchini
Salt
Wine vinegar
1½ lb ripe tomatoes
¾ cup chopped red onions
Oil
Freshly ground pepper
2 Tb chopped mint
¼ cup chopped parsley

Peel, seed, and chop the cucumbers. Wash and chop the zucchini. Toss cucumbers and zucchini with 2 teaspoons salt and ¼ cup vinegar. Allow to sit for 30 minutes. Meanwhile, peel, seed, and chop the tomatoes. Drain the cucumbers and zucchini and toss with the tomatoes and onions. Add vinegar and oil to taste, season with salt and pepper, and toss with mint and parsley. *(Serves 4–6)*

Cucumbers with Pasta

Pasta's smooth texture creates just the right foil for cucumber's crunchiness. Here are two cold pasta toppings: one for hot pasta; the other a refreshing pasta salad.

Cold Cucumber-Tomato Topping for Pasta

This topping can be made ahead of time and refrigerated, but bring to room temperature before tossing with pasta.

1 lb cucumbers
Salt and freshly ground pepper
White wine vinegar
1½ lb very ripe tomatoes
½ cup chopped red onions
1 tsp minced garlic
2 Tb chopped parsley
1 Tb chopped fresh basil
¼ cup olive oil
1 lb spaghetti
Grated Parmesan cheese

Peel and seed the cucumbers. Dice the flesh into ¼-inch pieces, and toss with ½ teaspoon salt and 2 tablespoons wine vinegar. Let sit for 30 minutes, and drain. Peel, seed, and dice the tomatoes, and combine with the cucumbers, onions, garlic, herbs, and olive oil. Taste and add more vinegar, salt, and pepper if necessary. Boil the spaghetti in several quarts of salted water until cooked through but still chewy (*al dente*). Toss the hot pasta with the cucumber-tomato mixture. Serve with grated Parmesan cheese. *(Serves 3–4)*

Pesto Pasta Salad with Cucumbers
1 lb cucumbers
Salt
1 lb linguini
2 Tb olive oil
1/2 cup *Pesto Sauce* (page 350)
2 Tb chopped fresh parsley (optional)

Peel and seed the cucumbers and dice into 1/4-inch or 1/2-inch pieces. Toss with salt and let sit. Meanwhile, cook the linguini, drain, cool under running water, and drain again. Toss with olive oil. Drain the cucumbers and press out the moisture. Toss the pasta with the pesto sauce and the cucumbers. If you like, sprinkle with parsley before serving. *(Serves 3–4)*

Cold Cucumber Sauce
Use for cold, poached fish (such as salmon), or as a dip.

1 cup peeled, seeded, and finely diced cucumbers
Salt
1/2 cup heavy cream
1/2 cup *Mayonnaise* (page 349)
2 tsp chopped fresh dill
Lemon juice
Salt and freshly ground pepper

Salt cucumbers, let sit for 30 minutes, and drain. Whip cream, fold together with the mayonnaise, add the cucumbers and dill, and season with lemon juice and salt and pepper. *(Makes 2 cups)*
- Use sour cream or yogurt rather than the mayonnaise and cream.
- Use *Crème Fraîche* (see *Appendix*).
- Add chopped watercress.

◇ *Cooked Cucumbers*
Although people think of cucumbers as a raw vegetable, cooked cucumbers have a unique, subtle flavor. You can blanch, steam, braise, or sauté cucumbers, which is my favorite method and the way we prepare and serve cucumbers at the restaurant. Sautéed cucumbers marry well with delicate fish, chicken, and veal dishes, and, most important, they become tender yet crunchy. Blanching works fine, particularly if you're on a low-fat or salt-free diet—but I do think the flavor lessens. Steaming takes longer and demands constant surveillance because the cucumbers quickly go from an underdone to an overcooked, limp stage.

Sautéed Cucumbers
Peel, score, and seed 1 pound of cucumbers. Quarter lengthwise, cut into triangles or rectangles, then shape the rectangles into ovals if desired. (These steps can be done in advance and the cucumbers refrigerated.) Just before serving, melt 2–4 tablespoons butter in a sauté pan, add the cucumbers, and sauté over medium-high heat, tossing constantly. Reduce the heat if the cucumbers start to brown. The cucumbers will cook through in a few minutes and be tender yet crunchy. Season with salt and pepper, add more butter if desired, and toss with chopped dill. Serve immediately.
- Add 1/4 cup heavy cream or crème fraîche and cook until reduced and cucumbers are coated. Season to taste.

Sautéed-Braised Cucumbers
This is the best method when you want to cook whole cucumber halves and then fill them with a purée. Lightly sauté them in butter, reduce the heat, cover, and cook until cucumbers are tender through yet retain some texture. Fill the halves with an onion soubise, creamed sautéed leeks, mushroom duxelles, or puréed carrots or other colorful vegetables.

Blanched Cucumbers
Prepare as above and drop into boiling water. Quarter pieces cook in 3–5 minutes, halves in 6–8 minutes.

Steamed Cucumbers
Prepare as above and place in steamer with 3/4–1 inch of water. Steam quarter pieces 6–8 minutes, halves 8–15 minutes depending on size.

Sautéed Sliced Cucumbers and Onions

1 lb cucumbers
Salt
1 clove garlic
1 cup finely sliced onions
2 Tb butter
2–3 Tb chopped chives
2 Tb chopped parsley
Freshly ground pepper

Peel, score, seed, and slice the cucumbers. Salt and let stand for 20–30 minutes, then drain and pat dry. Crush the garlic. Cook the onions and garlic in butter until the onions are wilted, about 5 minutes. Add the cucumber and sauté for 2 minutes until cooked through but still slightly crunchy. Remove the garlic. Toss in the chives and parsley and season to taste with pepper and salt. (*Serves 4*)

- After cucumbers are sautéed, add ½ cup heavy cream and cook to lightly reduce the cream. Season as above.
- Omit onions and use peeled, seeded, and chopped tomatoes, first sautéed in butter to evaporate moisture.

Cucumber Mousse

Here's one of our restaurant appetizers which makes a particularly refreshing start to a summer meal. Add additional finely chopped cucumbers to the dressing if you wish. Or serve with an uncooked *Tomato Sauce* (see page 313).

3 lb cucumbers
2 Tb chopped dill or fennel leaves
¼ tsp sugar
1 package unflavored gelatin
2 Tb lemon juice
⅓ cup heavy cream
Salt and freshly ground pepper
3 egg whites
Mayonnaise (page 349)

Peel, seed, and roughly chop the cucumbers. Place in a saucepan with the dill and ¼ cup water. Cover, and gently cook until wilted, about 15 minutes, watching to make sure cucumbers don't burn. Drain and purée in a food processor or sieve. Cool in the refrigerator, then drain once more. Reserve 2 tablespoons cucumber juices. Add sugar to gelatin. Combine gelatin with lemon juice and cucumber juice and heat over simmering water to dissolve gelatin. Combine with the puréed cucumbers. Let cool slightly. Whip cream and stir into cucumber purée. Season to taste. Beat the egg whites until they form soft peaks. Stir one-quarter of the whites into the cucumber mixture, then fold in the remaining whites. Pour into wet 6-ounce molds or into a 1½-quart mold. Chill until set. Unmold and serve with homemade mayonnaise lightened with whipped cream to taste. (*Serves 6*)

- For a strictly dietetic version, omit cream and add 1 additional egg white. This version will fill eight 6-ounce molds.

Tan Abour

This is one of the most refreshing soups for a summer meal—both filling and light at the same time.

2–3 cloves garlic
4 cups yogurt
2 cups minced cucumber
4 tsp white vinegar
4 tsp chopped fresh mint
1 tsp chopped fresh dill
Salt and freshly ground pepper
Cucumber slices (optional)

Mince garlic fine. Stir into yogurt along with remaining ingredients, reserving the cucumber slices. Chill for at least 3 hours. If the soup is too thick, dilute with a little water. Serve garnished with paper-thin cucumber slices. (*Serves 4–6*)

Cream of Cucumber Soup

The best cucumber soup I've ever had is one Julia Child made up in which she uses farina, the baby cereal. We serve this similar version time and again and credit her with its success.

2 lb cucumbers
2 Tb butter
⅓ cup chopped onions or shallots
5 cups chicken broth
1 Tb wine vinegar
½ cup chopped dill
¼ cup quick-cooking farina
Salt and freshly ground pepper
1 cup *Crème Fraîche* (see page 347) or sour cream

Peel and score cucumbers. Slice one-quarter of a cucumber into paper-thin slices and set aside. Seed and roughly chop the remaining cucumbers. Melt the butter and cook the onions or shallots until wilted, for 2–3 minutes; add the chopped cucumbers, broth, vinegar, and ⅓ cup of the dill. Bring the broth to a boil, and whisk in the farina. Simmer uncovered until the farina is very soft, about 20 minutes. Purée. Before serving, reheat the broth, thinning, if necessary, with a bit more broth or water, and correcting seasonings. Whisk in one-half of the crème fraîche or sour cream. Garnish with cucumber slices and a sprinkling of dill. Serve the remaining crème fraîche or sour cream on the side to add to the soup, or add a spoonful with the garnish. For a cold version, chill, and, just before serving, whisk in chilled crème fraîche or sour cream, garnishing as above. (*Serves 4–6*)

- If you don't have farina, substitute ½ pound cubed or sliced potato for the farina for a cucumber vichyssoise.
- Add ½ cup chopped watercress, or substitute 1 cup watercress for the dill.

Baked Stuffed Cucumbers

Braised and stuffed cucumbers are commonplace in Germany and France, but not here. The cucumber makes a pleasant-tasting, noncaloric container for almost any stuffing you might want to make. In this version—a good way, incidentally, to use up seedy cucumbers that really must have the centers removed—they've been filled, braised, and cooled for a picnic take-along or for cold buffet canapés, accompanied by a watercress mayonnaise or a bowl of sour cream seasoned with lemon juice and salt and pepper. (See the variations at end of recipe for a main-course treatment.)

> 6 fat cucumbers (1/2 lb each)
> Salt
> 4 Tb butter
> 1/2 cup chopped onions
> 1 lb ground beef
> 1 egg
> 3/4 cup barely cooked rice
> 1/2–3/4 cup chopped watercress or spinach
> 2 Tb chopped pimento
> 2 tsp dried basil or 2 Tb chopped fresh
> Freshly ground pepper
> 1 cup beef broth
> 1/4 cup dry vermouth

Peel and score the cucumbers. Slice off a 1/2-inch cap at one end; set aside. Using an iced tea spoon or zucchini corer, scoop out all the seeds to hollow each cucumber. Salt the cucumbers and let drain. Heat 2 tablespoons of the butter and cook the onions until wilted. Add the beef and cook until lightly browned; drain. Beat egg and combine with beef mixture, rice, watercress or spinach, pimento, and basil; season to taste with salt and pepper. Dry the cucumbers and stuff. Top the cucumbers with the reserved ends and fasten into place with a toothpick. Pat dry once more.

Heat the remaining butter in an ovenproof casserole or sauté pan. Cook the cucumbers until barely colored on all sides. Heat the broth and vermouth and pour into the dish. Cover and bake in a preheated 375° oven for 35 minutes (or braise on top of the stove if you prefer). Remove casserole from the oven, uncover, and cool in the pan, basting occasionally. When the cucumbers are cool, wrap them individually and refrigerate. Serve sliced in slightly diagonal pieces. *(Serves 4)*

- To serve hot, remove from oven, thickly slice diagonally, and serve with a hot tomato or curry sauce, or thicken the cooking juices with butter and flour.
- Halve and seed the cucumbers and fill with the stuffing. Omit sautéing in butter and braise as above. Top with buttered bread crumbs if you wish.
- Use other stuffings such as a cheese stuffing with equal parts bread crumbs and grated cheese. Combine with chopped herbs, beaten egg, and some sour cream to moisten.

Braised Salmon with Cucumber Sauce

At the restaurant, we often serve sautéed cucumbers to accompany fish. This recipe incorporates cucumber into the sauce that covers thick fish fillets. It works with any fish, but I chose salmon for its beautiful contrasting color.

> 1/2 lb cucumbers
> Salt
> 2–3 Tb chopped shallots
> 1 1/2 lb salmon fillets
> 1 cup dry white wine
> 1 cup fish broth (page 348) or water
> 1/3 cup chopped fresh dill
> 1–2 Tb butter
> 3/4 cup heavy cream
> 1 egg yolk
> Freshly ground pepper

Peel, seed, and finely dice or julienne the cucumbers. Salt and let sit for 20–30 minutes, then drain and pat dry. Set aside. Sprinkle the shallots into a baking dish or a flameproof casserole. Cut the salmon into four 6-ounce serving pieces and place skin side down upon the shallots. Pour in the wine and fish stock or water. Sprinkle with 1/4 cup of the dill. Bring just to a boil on top of the stove, cover, and bake in a preheated 400° oven for 8–10 minutes or until the fish is just cooked through.

Meanwhile, cook the cucumbers for 1 minute in 1 tablespoon of the butter; set aside. Remove the fish to a warm plate and keep warm. Pour the cooking juices into a saucepan and reduce them to 1 cup liquid. Strain and return to the pan. Stir in 1/2 cup of the cream and boil for a few minutes to lightly thicken. Stir in the cucumbers. In a small bowl, beat the egg yolk with the remaining cream. Whisk a bit of the hot liquid into the egg mixture to heat it, then add to the sauce. Heat gently without simmering, or the sauce will curdle. Season to taste with salt and pepper, stir in 1 tablespoon butter if desired. Spoon over salmon and serve sprinkled with remaining dill. *(Serves 4)*

◇ *Pickling Cucumbers*

The art of pickling cucumbers is a book in itself. I'm going to give you a few of my favorite recipes, and refer you to a good pickling book, such as *The Green Thumb Preserving Guide* by Jean Andersen or *The Freezing and Canning Cookbook* by Farm Journal, for further inspiration.

For long-term storage I would recommend the traditional processing methods, but in this house there is no such thing as long-term pickle storage. The entire family is addicted to pickles, to such an extent that it is a real savings for me to crock cucumbers rather than let the girls bring in a few days' supply from the supermarket at $1.59 a jar.

There is no fuss with sterilizing and processing jars. A few large crocks and glass jars are all you need for special equipment: even a deep bowl will do. This is the kind of pickling that can be fitted in between getting breakfast and leaving for work.

Another advantage of the "crock" method is that you can control the amount of sourness. Obviously, the longer the cucumbers stay in the brine, the sourer they become. The standard method is to cover the cucumbers with the brine, put a weight on top, and let sit at room temperature until they reach the degree of sourness you like. Then, transfer the pickles to jars, cover again with the brine, and refrigerate. Once they're removed from room temperature, the pickling rate slows way down—although it does continue—and you can hold the cucumbers at an approximate degree of doneness in the cold of the refrigerator.

The point at which the cucumbers are considered done really depends upon your taste. A rough gauge is that when the pickles have been marinating for two days or longer, and their flesh is still mainly white, they are half-sour. When the cucumbers have marinated longer and their flesh becomes a pale green, they are fully sour. The fermentation time really depends on whether or not you have added vinegar to the brine (which speeds up the action), and upon temperature and bacterial conditions.

The only important consideration is that the cucumbers are covered with the brine and weighted down. How long they cure is strictly up to your taste. If you wish, cover the brine with a piece of cheesecloth to keep it clean, and skim the scum from the surface.

We prefer mild half-sour pickles, which are very crunchy. This means instead of leaving the pickles at room temperature for three or more days, I leave them just overnight and then refrigerate them in jars covered with the brine. The cucumbers continue to pickle (at a much slower rate)—but most important, they remain quite crunchy. Since I am cutting way down on the time spent at room temperature, I add vinegar to the brine to speed up the pickling. Pickle whichever way you like, just remember that if you do not add the vinegar, you should keep the pickles at room temperature longer so that their "sourness" comes from natural fermentation.

Fresh dill is better than dried for pickling cucumbers, and dill with budding flower heads is the best of all possible worlds. When dill is flowering in your garden, cut it and freeze in plastic bags for pickling later on. If you cannot find dill with flower heads, use the fresh stalks and leaves and add some dill seeds. If worse comes to worst, use all dill seeds, about 1 teaspoon of seeds for every 12 cucumbers.

Half-Sour Pickles

In this recipe—the one I described in the general directions—I call for 12 pickling cucumbers, so you can almost pick to order. You can pickle much larger amounts providing you have some big crocks and a family of pickle lovers. Once the pickles are refrigerated in jars, they will keep several weeks, continuing to pickle slightly as they sit.

I've used all sizes of pickling cucumbers for this recipe. We prefer 4-inch-long cucumbers, although I'll sometimes use 3- or 5-inch ones, if necessary. I usually halve them, but they can be left whole or cut into quarters if you wish.

> 12 pickling cucumbers (about 2 1/2 lb)
> 1 large clove garlic
> 6–8 sprigs fresh dill
> 1/4 tsp dill seeds (optional)
> 1 tsp whole pickling spices
> 1/4 cup kosher salt
> 1/4 cup white vinegar
> 2 1/2 qt water

Thoroughly clean the cucumbers. Halve them. Flatten the unpeeled garlic with the back of a knife. Wash the dill. If the dill does not have flower heads, add the dill seeds. (If you have no fresh dill use 1 teaspoon dill seeds.)

Place the cucumbers, garlic, dill, dill seeds, and pickling spices in a crock, glass jar, or bowl large enough to allow at least 2 inches of space between the pickles and the top of the container. Bring the salt, vinegar, and water to a boil and boil 2 minutes. Pour the brine over the cucumbers and weight down with a plate and some heavy cups or cans on top. The brine should be at least 1 inch above the cucumbers. Keep at room temperature overnight, then refrigerate either in the crock or in jars. Fill the jars with the brine and cover until ready. (*Makes 12 pickles*)

- Vary the amount of pickling spices to taste. Omit the dill completely, or add additional garlic for a stronger taste.
- Make pickled green tomatoes exactly the same way, but make a stronger brine with extra salt and vinegar.

Cornichons

The tiny French pickled cucumbers known as cornichons go with pâté as naturally as salt goes with pepper. Their crisp, tart flavor seems to cut the richness of the meat. Commercially pickled cornichons are exceedingly expensive (although a jar does last awhile, because these baby cucumbers are so small). You can try this recipe with small pickling cucumbers, but the authentic way is to use a cornichon cucumber, which is just a miniature variety. Russ had great luck growing them, and we put up all we harvested.

> 3 cups cornichon cucumbers
> 3 Tb kosher salt
> 4 sprigs fresh tarragon
> 1/2 tsp mustard seeds
> White wine vinegar

Wash the cucumbers thoroughly; drain or pat dry. Place in a ceramic bowl and mix well with salt. Let sit for 24 hours. Drain the juices and dry the cucumbers. Either put directly into jars, filling three-quarters full, or place into one large glass jar or crock, leaving a 2-inch space between the cucumbers and the top of the container. Add the tarragon and the mustard seeds. Top with white wine vinegar extending at least 1 inch above the cucumbers. Cover jars (or the large jar) and leave in a cool place for 3–4 weeks. *(Makes 1 1/2 pints)*

Note: Should your harvest be sporadic, pickle as you go along, adding salted, drained, and dried cornichons along with extra spices during the first pickling week of the original batch.

- You can use white wine vinegar with tarragon if you can't get fresh tarragon.

Senfgurken

What gardener doesn't have some of those over-the-hill yellow giant cucumbers that hid under the foliage; and unless they are totally rotten, there is hope yet. Make *Senfgurken*—the German answer to pickled watermelon rind. These pickles are a pleasant accompaniment to meat dishes.

4 large yellow cucumbers (approximately 1 lb each)
1/2 cup kosher salt
3 cups water
1 qt white wine vinegar
1 cup sugar
3 Tb pickling spices
4–5 Tb mustard seeds

Peel cucumbers, halve, and scoop out the seeds. Cut into wide strips or chunks like watermelon rind pickle. Dissolve salt in the water and pour over the cucumbers. Soak for 24 hours, drain, and pat dry. Combine the vinegar, sugar, and pickling spices (placed in a spice bag) and boil for 1 minute. Then place the cucumber pieces into a strainer or basket (in batches if need be) and drop into the boiling liquid. When the liquid returns to the boil, remove the cucumbers and fit them into sterilized jars, filling to within 1/2 inch of top. Divide the mustard seeds among the jars. Cover with the boiling liquid to within 1/4 inch of the top, and seal the jars. Process. Store in a cool place. Serve cold. *(Makes 4–5 pints)*

- If you prefer a sweeter pickle, add up to 2 cups sugar.

One of the more popular dishes we serve at the restaurant is the Turkish specialty *Imam Bayildi*, eggplant sautéed in olive oil and braised with onions, garlic, and tomatoes. *Imam Bayildi* epitomizes why I like eggplant. It's not a fancy dish, nor is it expensive to make, but it's beautiful to look at and is full of the Mediterranean flavors that so complement eggplant. Without a scrap of animal fat, *Imam* is filling—and meaty-tasting—enough to be a meal by itself. (Vegetarians in Asia have relied upon eggplant for centuries as a meat substitute.)

Even if eggplant were inedible (as it was once considered to be), I would still love having it around the house, it is such a beautiful vegetable. Often I'll arrange eggplants on the kitchen counter like a still life, just to enjoy their glorious colors, glossy smoothness, and sensual shapes.

For a long time, gardeners in the North were deprived of growing eggplant because it's a warm-weather crop. Now, short-season varieties have been developed so that even people in Vermont can try. We've experimented with many varieties—including the miniature Italian eggplants and the small white eggplants, beautiful, but rather bland-tasting. We've settled on the standard, all-purpose, large, purple-black eggplant such as Dusky or Black Beauty—occasionally Russ experiments with special varieties developed for containers.

Eggplant cannot be set out in the garden until evening temperatures stay above 55°. In April, Russ sows seeds indoors, 1/2 inch deep in potting soil, two seeds to a peat pot. After the seedlings have grown for a while, he pinches off the weaker of the two seedlings, leaving one plant per pot.

By early June, night temperatures have risen high enough so that Russ can set out the plants. He rotates the growing spot each year to avoid a buildup of the soil-borne diseases that affect eggplant. Russ selects a sunny, well-drained spot and digs 5-10-5 fertilizer into the soil. He then sets out the plants 24 inches apart and feeds them with a transplant solution.

Occasionally, Russ will also plant eggplants in containers filled with sterile potting soil. They make attractive container plants, and the sterile soil guarantees that they won't succumb to the soil-borne disease verticillium wilt.

It's important to pick eggplants at the right stage, for as the fruits age, they can become bitter-tasting with soft flesh and tough skins. Size is no indicator of whether or not the fruits are ready to harvest: I've picked both miniature and standard varieties at the same stage of development. A mature eggplant should have a glossy, taut skin and flesh that is just barely resistant. A good test is to press down on the eggplant gently with your thumb: if the flesh presses in but bounces back, the eggplant is ready for harvesting. If the flesh is hard—with no give— then the eggplant is immature and too young to pick; conversely, if the flesh presses down easily and stays indented, then the eggplant is overripe.

Eggplants bruise easily, so harvest them gently. The stems are sometimes prickly, so you might want to wear gloves or use shears when harvesting. Always cut off the

Special Information

Yields
- 1 pound peeled and cubed eggplant = approximately 4 cups
- 6 cups raw cubed flesh = 3 cups cooked
- 6 cups raw cubed flesh = 2 cups puréed
- 1 1/2 pounds eggplant = 2–2 1/4 cups mashed or puréed flesh
- 1 1/2 pounds eggplant = 4 servings

Storage and Preserving
- Eggplant stores poorly. Its optimum storage temperature is 50°, so don't refrigerate. If you don't have a cool room of 50°, keep the eggplant in as cool a spot as possible, wrapped in a plastic bag with some wet paper toweling or a wet cloth in it to provide humidity. If the weather is hot, you can store the eggplant in the refrigerator, but it will develop soft brown spots and become bitter after a day or two.

Hints
- Salting and draining eggplant cuts down on the eggplant's moisture and the amount of oil needed.
- Top pasta with sautéed eggplant.
- Fold diced eggplant sautéed with hot pepper into scrambled eggs.
- Stuff eggplant with shellfish—shrimp, crab, and lobster all taste wonderful with eggplant.
- Use eggplant cubes in stir-fries: toss salted and drained cubes in a hot garlic-ginger oil for 4–5 minutes, sprinkle with sugar and salt, add a bit of liquid, cover, and cook until soft and tender. Add meat marinated in sesame oil and soy sauce if you wish.
- Sauté eggplant cubes with zucchini or other vegetables and combine with sautéed potatoes and carrot pieces. Reheat before serving.
- Weighting down salted eggplant speeds up the release of moisture.
- Carbon steel knives discolor eggplant: use stainless steel knives instead.
- Drain sautéed eggplant on brown paper; it will absorb excess oil.
- Add cubed eggplant to hearty soups or stews. If the eggplant is sautéed first, the flavor will be richer, but you can also add cubes directly and cook until tender.

eggplant with the cap and some of the stem attached. Eggplant is also perishable, so pick it as close to cooking time as possible. A hot-climate vegetable, it doesn't react well to cold temperatures or refrigeration (see *Preserving*).

Some cooks never peel eggplant; others insist upon peeling. I think it depends upon the recipe: sometimes I peel eggplant; other times I prefer to leave the skin on for color, which is possible only with tender-skinned, young eggplant that is going to cook long enough so that the skin ends up as soft as the flesh. It is disconcerting to eat a smooth chunk of eggplant and then encounter a stringy, chewy piece of skin. Recipes will indicate whether or not the eggplants should be peeled.

Cooks also disagree about whether or not eggplant should be salted. You can certainly cook eggplant without salting, but there's a very practical reason to do so. One thing you learn quickly while cooking eggplant: it drinks up olive oil.

Salted and drained eggplant absorbs much less oil than eggplant that has not received this treatment. Cooking eggplant in less oil is not only a more healthful and more digestible method, it is also much less expensive. Two tablespoons of oil will be sufficient to cook 2 cups salted and drained eggplant, and you'll even have a bit of oil left in the pan. Two cups of unsalted eggplant will need 6–8 tablespoons of oil. I find that a compelling reason to salt eggplant.

Salting also rids eggplant of its excess moisture, which reduces bulk and keeps the eggplant from exuding juices as it cooks. Salting is simply sprinkling cut egg-

plant with salt and placing in a colander for 30 minutes or more. Lightly squeeze out the moisture and pat dry.

I've read that salting helps eliminate eggplant's bitter taste. I have noticed some bitterness in slightly overripe eggplants, but eggplants picked fresh from the garden at the right stage of development don't have these bitter juices.

Do adjust the seasonings of the dish to compensate for the salt on the eggplant. You could rinse off the salt and then dry the eggplant, but I find this a messy solution which does the eggplant more harm than good. If you object to salt, blanch the eggplant. (Also, blanch if you're in a terrible hurry and don't have the 30 minutes or an hour to wait until the salted eggplant is ready.) I don't like blanching because some of the flavor is lost, and do not recommend this treatment unless necessary.

I have no preferred method for cooking eggplant: it is delicious sautéed, broiled, baked, grilled, or steamed. Take a look at the basic techniques and cook eggplant whichever way is best for you. The only way eggplant is not acceptable is raw.

Eggplant is such a versatile vegetable, and is part of the cuisine of so many countries, that I can only hint at the wonderful ways to cook it. For ideas look to Chinese, Japanese, and Midwestern cooks, who often use small eggplants (pictured below), seeds for which are sometimes sold as Italian or Oriental eggplant varieties.

Microwave

- A 1-pound whole eggplant will cook barely tender in 6 minutes (a good stage for scooping out flesh). It will take 8–9 minutes to cook soft enough for puréing. Rotate the eggplant every 2 minutes and watch carefully. Eggplant suddenly goes from a barely cooked to an overcooked stage. One pound cubed eggplant placed in a dish, covered, will cook in 3–4 minutes.

Leftovers

- Use in quiches and omelets.
- Make patties; purée flesh and combine with whipped potatoes, then sauté in butter.
- Make a sandwich stuffing: Sauté in olive oil with mushrooms and onions, stuff pita bread, top with grated cheese, and bake in oven until cheese melts.
- Make *Eggplant Soufflé*. Combine 2 cups puréed or finely chopped cooked eggplant with 2 cups *Béchamel Sauce* (see *Appendix*) and herbs. Beat in 3 egg yolks. Fold in 5–6 beaten egg whites and 1/4 cup finely grated Parmesan cheese. Pour into a prepared soufflé dish with a collar, and bake for 25–30 minutes or until browned.

Marketing

Fresh eggplant is available year round. Regardless of the variety, buy eggplant that has a glossy color, firm taut skin, and flesh that bounces back when lightly pressed. If you press down on the eggplant and the indentation remains, that means the eggplant is too ripe and the inside may be completely brown with oversize seeds. The eggplant should also feel heavy (light eggplants are pulpy). Pick small or medium-size eggplants—they will have fewer seeds and a firmer texture than the larger ones. Dark brown spots or soggy areas are signs of decay. The green caps should always be on the eggplants to protect them from injury.

◇ *Sautéed Eggplant*

This is my favorite way to prepare sliced or cubed eggplant. The eggplant is good plain, or with the addition of a few vegetables, becomes a filling meal.

Sautéed Eggplant Slices

This is the preliminary step for *Eggplant Parmesan* or *Eggplant Rolls*. Or, serve plain with salt and pepper and lemon wedges, or with a sauce, such as *Skordalia* (see *Appendix*). A 2-pound eggplant serves 4. Cut peeled eggplant into 1/2-inch slices. Salt, let drain for 30 minutes, and pat dry.

- *With Oil*: In a sauté pan heat the oil, add the eggplant slices, and sauté until lightly browned on both sides and just tender. Remove, and drain on paper towels. The amount of oil will vary. Allow 1/2–3/4 cup oil.
- *With Flour*: Dip eggplant slices into flour, shake off excess, and sauté in oil as above.
- *With Bread Crumbs*: Coat eggplant slices with beaten egg, then bread crumbs (flavored with herbs or grated cheese if desired). Sauté in oil as above.

Sautéed Eggplant Cubes

A 2-pound eggplant yields approximately 8 cups. Peel eggplant. Cut into 3/4–1-inch slices, then into same-size strips; cube into 3/4–1-inch pieces. Toss with 2 teaspoons salt and let drain for 30 minutes. Pat dry before using. Heat oil in a sauté pan (allow 1/2–3/4 cup oil, but only heat 1/4 cup at a time). Add one batch of eggplant, leaving space between the pieces. Sauté the eggplant for 6–8 minutes or until the eggplant cubes are browned on all sides and tender. Stir the eggplant or shake the pan constantly so the eggplant doesn't burn. (If the eggplant browns before it is completely tender, lower heat, cover the pan, and steam-cook for 2–3 minutes.) Drain in a colander and season with salt and pepper. Finish cooking the eggplant in batches.

Toppings for Sautéed Eggplant

- *With Garlic and Herbs*: Add chopped garlic and herbs (such as basil, oregano, thyme, or rosemary) to the sauté pan during the last minutes of cooking.
- *With Persillade*: After eggplant is cooked, remove from pan, add oil, or reuse the oil drained from the eggplant. Make a *Persillade* (see *Appendix*) in sauté pan, omitting the butter; return eggplant and toss together over medium heat until eggplant is reheated. Stir in fresh chopped parsley, and season to taste with salt and pepper.
- *With Vegetables*: Remove eggplant, and in the same oil, sauté until lightly browned some sliced onions, chunked red or green peppers, cubed zucchini, or other vegetables. Add cooked eggplant and reheat, tossing constantly. Season with salt and pepper and herbs before serving.

◇ *Deep-Fat-Fried Eggplant Fingers*

- *With Batter*: Cut peeled eggplant into 2 1/2 x 1-inch "fingers." Dip into a batter (see *Appendix*) and deep-fry in fat.
- *With Crumbs*: Dip fingers into eggs and bread crumbs and deep-fry in fat.

◇ *Baked Eggplant*

Baking eggplant serves many purposes. A smoky charred taste, which is part of the good flavor of many ethnic recipes, can best be developed by cooking in the coals of a charcoal fire, but when that isn't convenient, try the bake-broil method for a close approximation.

Baked Whole Eggplant

Preheat oven to 400°. Prick eggplant all over with a fork and bake until the flesh is tender. A 1-pound eggplant will cook in approximately 30 minutes; a 1 1/2-pound eggplant will take 40 minutes. Once the eggplant is removed from the oven it continues to cook with inner heat. This is a good method when you want the flesh for puréing.

Baked-Broiled Whole Eggplant

Preheat oven to 400°. Prick eggplant all over with a fork and bake for 20 minutes. Turn on the broiler and set the eggplant under the heat, rotating until the skin is black and blistered. Rub the charred skin off. (If you have difficulty, close the hot eggplant in a paper bag for a few minutes, which will help loosen the skin. Or place under running water.) You can also "char" over a gas flame or on a grill.

Baked Whole Eggplants for Stuffing

Use this method for stuffed whole shells. It's handy for short rounded eggplants. Preheat oven to 400°. Bake eggplants 20–30 minutes, depending on size, until just barely tender. Remove from oven and slice off the stem end just under the cap and set aside. Scoop out the pulp with a sharp-edged spoon, leaving a 1/2-inch thickness of pulp all around. Save pulp for a salad, purée, or stew. If you wish, salt the inside of the eggplants and invert to drain. Wipe out the interior, fill with stuffing, and bake upright, topped with the "caps" in a preheated 400° oven for 30 minutes, or until heated through.

Baked Eggplant Halves

Halve unpeeled eggplant lengthwise and cross-cut the exposed flesh. Sprinkle with salt and drain, flesh side down, for at least 30 minutes. (A weight placed on the eggplant will speed up the time.) Squeeze, and pat dry. Preheat oven to 425°. Brush eggplant with oil and set in a baking pan skin side down. Bake until browned and flesh is tender, 30–40 minutes, depending on size. Rub flesh with garlic, or top with one of the *Toppings* listed below. Or, before baking, you can combine chopped herbs such as fresh parsley and basil, or dill and garlic. Press into slashes on flesh, then brush with oil and bake.

Baked Halves for Stuffing

Proceed as above, but before brushing with oil, run a knife around the skin 1/2 inch in from the edge. Brush with oil, add a little water to the pan, and bake for 15–20 minutes or until just barely tender. Scoop out the flesh. Cool, and fill with stuffing of your choice.

Baked Eggplant Chunks

Cut peeled or unpeeled eggplant into large chunks or wedges. (Cut into quarters, then halve quarters.) Salt, and drain for 30 minutes. Pat dry. Preheat oven to 425°. Oil eggplant and place on baking sheet (skin side down if you're using the skins). Bake for 10–15 minutes, depending on the size, or until the eggplant is tender. Season with herbs or roll in toasted chopped pine nuts or sesame seeds.

Baked Sliced Eggplant

Cut peeled or unpeeled eggplant into 1/2–3/4-inch slices. Salt and drain for 30 minutes; pat dry. Preheat oven to 425°. Dip eggplant into oil and place in a baking pan in one layer or just slightly overlapping. Bake for 5–10 minutes or until barely tender. Brown under the broiler or top with one of the *Toppings* below. Or dip salted dried eggplant slices into a beaten egg and bread crumbs. Place slices flat on a greased baking pan, sprinkle with salt and pepper, and dot with butter. Bake at 450° for 15–20 minutes or until nicely browned.

Toppings for Baked Eggplant

- *With Bread Crumbs*: Spread a *Persillade* (see *Appendix*) or buttered bread crumbs on top of the baked eggplant. Drizzle with oil and run under the broiler to lightly brown.
- *With Cheese*: Sprinkle cooked slices with grated cheese. Drizzle with oil and run under the broiler.
- *With Tomatoes*: Sauté sliced onions and peeled, seeded, and chopped tomatoes until moisture is removed; add a few sliced black olives. Spread on eggplant slices, drizzle with oil, and brown under broiler.
- *With a Pesto Topping*: This is a nice appetizer with halved baked very small eggplant. Cover with *Pesto Sauce* (see *Appendix*) pressed into slashes in flesh.
- *With Herb Butter*: Cover with pats of herb butter and brown under the broiler.

◇ Broiled Eggplant

If you dislike sautéing eggplant in oil, broiling works very well. The disadvantage is that broiled eggplant is not as crisp as sautéed eggplant, since it must be broiled some distance away from the heat in order for the eggplant to cook tender without burning. You could also bake the slices in a 400° oven for 5–10 minutes, depending upon their size, until tender, then brown under the broiler. This works well for the very small varieties of eggplant.

Broiled Eggplant Slices

Peel eggplant and cut into 1/2-inch slices. Salt, and let drain for at least 30 minutes. Pat dry. Brush with oil and set on a broiler pan rack. Set rack about 5 inches from the heating element. Brown eggplant on one side, turn, and brown on the other side. Season to taste. (For a garlic oil: Mash garlic and steep in the oil before using with the eggplant.)

Broiled Eggplant Slices with Bread Crumbs

Dip prepared sliced eggplant into beaten egg, then into bread crumbs, flavored with herbs if you wish. Place the eggplant on a greased broiler pan, and broil at least 5 inches from the heat until lightly browned on both sides. Season to taste.

Broiled Eggplant Cubes

Peel and salt 1-inch eggplant cubes. (If the skin is fresh and tender, do not peel before cooking.) Drain and pat dry. Toss with oil flavored with herbs and/or garlic and skewer either alone or with other vegetables. Broil, turning, until completely browned.

◇ Grilled Eggplant

Grilled eggplant has a delicious, smoky flavor. Use the same treatments as for *Broiled Eggplant*.

Grilled Whole Small Eggplants

Use the small Italian or Japanese varieties. Prick the skins with a fork. Grill over hot coals, turning, until the flesh is soft and the skins charred. Split them open and eat with salt, pepper, lemon juice, and butter.

◇ Steamed Eggplant

Steamed eggplant is the best choice when you're dieting, or when you want to conserve oven space.

Boil 1 inch of water in a steamer. Place a whole eggplant in the steamer basket or a colander, and steam it for 15–30 minutes until tender. The cooking time will depend upon the size of the eggplant. A 1-pound eggplant will cook in approximately 25 minutes, but watch carefully—it suddenly changes from a hard to a cooked stage. Remove the eggplant from the steamer and let rest for a few minutes. Its inner heat will continue to cook the center. Either use the flesh for pulp, eat as is for a dietetic treat, or halve or quarter the eggplant and slash the flesh. Season with lemon, salt, and pepper, or cover with a fresh tomato sauce.

◇ Blanched Eggplant

I rarely blanch eggplant, but when my husband went on a salt-restricted diet, blanching was the best alternative to the salting process. For that reason I use blanching as a first step before further treatment.

Whole Eggplant: Boil water, add eggplant, and cook for 10–15 minutes. To prepare shells, halve lengthwise and scoop out the flesh, leaving 1/2 inch of flesh attached to the skin.

Sliced or Cubed Eggplant: Drop eggplant into boiling water for 1–2 minutes. Remove from the pan and drain.

◇ *Braised Eggplant*

Braised Raw Stuffed Shells

While most recipes for stuffed eggplant use partially baked shells, it is also a common practice to braise stuffed eggplant. Use the following basic preparation, stuffing with any filling you like. For a rice stuffing, use raw rice, but allow room for the rice to expand. The liquid in the braising pan will be absorbed by the rice and eggplant.

Braised Halved Shells

Halve the eggplant lengthwise. Scoop out the center flesh, leaving a ½-inch border of flesh. Salt the eggplant, drain for at least 30 minutes, and fill with stuffing. Arrange halves closely together in a large pan. Pour in liquid (water, water mixed with tomato paste, or broth) one-third of the way up the eggplant shells. Cover the pan, and simmer gently until the eggplants are tender. This will take 30–60 minutes, depending upon the eggplant's size.

Braised Whole Eggplant (with the center flesh)

Remove the eggplant's stem. Peel alternating strips of skin 1 inch wide and 1 inch apart lengthwise, or leave skins intact. Cut 4 equally spaced incisions lengthwise around three-quarters of the eggplant. Make the incisions long and deep, but do not go through the eggplant. Sprinkle with salt, drain for 30 minutes, then gently squeeze and pat dry. Insert stuffing into the slits. Place in a baking pan, uncut side down. Pour in liquid (water, or water mixed with tomato paste) one-third of the way up the eggplant. Cover, and simmer gently for 30–60 minutes, depending upon the eggplant's size. Check the water level occasionally.

Braised Whole Stuffed Eggplant

This is a nice way to fix small round eggplants or the miniature varieties. Cut off the eggplant's cap and set aside. Scoop out the flesh with a sharp-edged spoon, leaving a ½-inch border of flesh. Use the flesh with stuffing such as the *Eggplant Stuffed with Rice* (page 107) or reserve it for another dish. Salt the interior of the eggplant; turn and drain for 30 minutes. Pat dry and stuff. Replace the eggplant cap and stand up in a deep saucepan. Add enough liquid (water, or water and tomato paste) to reach at least one-third of the way up the eggplant. Cover, and simmer 30–60 minutes, depending upon the eggplant's size.

Sautéed Eggplant with Mediterranean Vegetables

Here's a versatile recipe to eat plain or enhance with the basil-garlic purée. Use it to accompany meat or top pasta, or serve it cold as a luncheon dish. Should you have any leftovers, blend them, and serve as a chilled soup, adding tomato juice to thin.

1½ lb eggplant
Salt
6 Tb olive oil
1 cup green peppers cut into ½-inch dice
1 cup red peppers cut into ½-inch dice
1 cup sliced onions
2 cups peeled, seeded, and chopped tomatoes
Freshly ground pepper
2 cloves garlic
½ cup fresh basil leaves

Peel the eggplant and cut into 1-inch chunks. Lightly salt and let drain for 30 minutes; dry. Meanwhile, heat 2 tablespoons of the oil and cook the peppers and onions until tender, but not browned, about 10 minutes. Add tomatoes, and season with pepper. Cook, covered, for 2 minutes, remove cover, and rapidly cook to evaporate the liquid; set aside. Heat the remaining oil in the sauté pan, and sauté the eggplant until lightly browned and tender. Drain oil, stir in the tomato mixture, and cook gently for 5 minutes. (You could serve it at this point.)

Mash together the garlic and ½ teaspoon salt. Finely chop the basil and mash with garlic until it forms a paste. Blend into the eggplant mixture. Reheat and serve. (*Serves 4*)

- Serve cold. Cool, then add ¼ cup chopped parsley and 1 tablespoon olive oil. Garnish with a quartered hard-boiled egg and freshly chopped tomato if desired.
- Make a quiche. Omit the basil-garlic purée. Add cooked crumbled sausage if desired. Beat 8 eggs and combine with 2 cups milk (or half milk and half cream), a dash of Tabasco sauce, and ½ cup grated Swiss cheese. Spoon cooled eggplant mixture into 2 partially baked 9-inch pie shells and pour over the milk mixture. Bake in a preheated 325° oven for 45–60 minutes or until set.

Eggplant, Tomatoes, and Cream

¾–1 lb eggplant
Salt
Oil
1 cup chopped onions
2 Tb butter
2 cups peeled, seeded, and chopped tomatoes
Freshly ground pepper
¾ cup light cream
1 Tb cornstarch
¾ cup grated Swiss cheese

Peel and slice eggplant, salt it, and drain for 30 minutes. Pat dry and place on a baking sheet; brush with oil and broil on both sides until lightly browned. Meanwhile, sauté onions in butter and 1 tablespoon oil until soft and golden. Add tomatoes, cover pan, and cook for 5 minutes. Uncover pan and cook 5–10 minutes to evaporate the juices. In a 1½-quart casserole, layer the eggplant with the tomatoes and onions, and season to taste with salt and pepper. Combine the cream with the cornstarch and pour it over. Top with cheese and bake in a preheated 375° oven for 20–30 minutes or until bubbly and golden on top. *(Serves 4)*

Eggplant-Stuffed Vegetable Cases

For a meal-in-one, stuff red or green peppers, tomatoes, onions, summer squashes, and even turnips with eggplant combined with sautéed ground meats.

1½ lb eggplant
Salt
3 Tb butter
5 Tb oil
1 cup chopped onions
2 tsp chopped garlic
2 cups chopped or ground raw lamb, veal, or beef
½ tsp fresh rosemary
2 tsp tomato paste
¼ cup dry vermouth
½ cup beef broth
¼ cup chopped parsley
½ cup grated Swiss and Parmesan cheeses (optional)
Freshly ground pepper
Vegetables for stuffing
Toasted buttered bread crumbs (optional)

Peel and cut eggplant into ¼-inch cubes. Salt and drain. Heat 1 tablespoon of the butter and 2 tablespoons of the oil in a frying pan and sauté onions until wilted. Add the garlic and sauté a minute longer. Add meat and sauté until lightly colored. Pour off the excess fat. Add the rosemary, tomato paste, vermouth, and broth and simmer gently until the liquid has reduced to glaze. Put mixture in strainer to drain any remaining liquid. Heat remaining oil in a sauté pan. Pat the eggplant dry and sauté until tender, approximately 4–5 minutes, and drain off excess oil. Combine eggplant with meat mixture, parsley, and most of the cheese. Season well with salt and pepper. Hollow out vegetables, blanch if necessary until barely tender, and arrange in an oiled baking dish. Fill with stuffing. Dot each vegetable with a pat of butter and sprinkle with grated cheese or toasted buttered bread crumbs. Bake in a preheated 400° oven until just heated through, approximately 10 minutes. *(Stuffs 6 vegetable cases)*

- Use leftover cooked chopped meats instead of the raw meat.

Vegetarian Stuffed Eggplant Shells

Eggplant is such a "meaty" vegetable you can easily make a hearty meal of it without any meat at all. Here are two ideas for stuffing eggplants, or use one of your favorite stuffings.

Eggplant Stuffed with Mushrooms and Cheese
Two ¾–1-lb eggplants
3 Tb butter
4 Tb oil
2 cups sliced mushrooms
3 Tb flour
1 cup milk
Salt and freshly ground pepper
1 egg
Nutmeg
¾ cup grated Swiss cheese
½ cup grated Parmesan cheese
¼ cup heavy cream (optional)

Prepare eggplants as in *Baked Halves for Stuffing* (page 104). Remove from the oven, cool to handle, and scoop out meat, leaving a ½-inch thickness from outer edge. Chop the flesh into cubes and set aside. You should have about 2 cups. Heat 1 tablespoon of the butter and 1 tablespoon of the oil in a sauté pan. Cook mushrooms until lightly browned; set aside. Heat the remaining oil and sauté the eggplant until lightly browned; drain and set aside.

In a saucepan, heat the remaining butter, stir in the flour, and cook slowly together for 2–3 minutes. Whisk in the milk and bring mixture to a boil. Reduce the heat and, stirring, simmer for 5–10 minutes. Season with salt and pepper. Beat egg. Mix a few drops of the hot sauce into the egg to warm it, and then stir the egg into the sauce along with a dash of nutmeg. Mix together the cheeses. Combine the eggplant, mushrooms, sauce, and three-fourths of the cheese; and taste for seasoning. Add cream to thin out if necessary. Fill the eggplant shells and sprinkle with the remaining cheese. Place in a baking dish and bake in a preheated 450° oven for 10–15 minutes or until the filling is hot and bubbly. Run under the broiler to brown if necessary. *(Serves 4)*

Eggplant Stuffed with Rice
6 small rounded ½-lb eggplants
4 Tb oil
1 cup chopped onions
1 cup chopped, peeled, and seeded tomatoes
1 cup cooked rice
3 Tb pine nuts
½ cup chopped parsley
1 Tb chopped fresh mint
Salt and freshly ground pepper

Bake shells as in *Baked Whole Eggplants for Stuffing* (page 104), but cook for a shorter period of time since they are smaller. Scoop out the flesh, leaving a ½-inch layer of flesh on the shells. Chop 1 cup flesh into cubes and set aside. (Save the remaining flesh for another use.) Heat 2 tablespoons of the oil in a sauté pan, and lightly brown the eggplant. Drain and set aside. In the remaining oil, cook onions until soft, add the tomatoes, and cook to evaporate juices. Then combine with the eggplant, rice, pine nuts, parsley, and mint. Season with salt and pepper. Fill eggplant shells and top with caps. Place in a baking pan, film the pan with water, and bake in a preheated 400° oven for 15–20 minutes or until completely heated through. Serve either hot or cold. *(Serves 6)*

- You could also cook on top of the stove as in *Braised Whole Stuffed Eggplant*, substituting ½ cup raw rice for the cooked rice.

Ratatouille

Here's a specialty of the Provençal area of France, best made in the late summer when all the vegetables are at their glorious peak. Fixed this way, each vegetable should keep its own identity yet combine for a dish that would tempt any appetite. Serve ratatouille hot—or cold as an appetizer as we do at the restaurant. While we garnish with Mediterranean olives, there is a much more unconventional method. My friend Joe Hyde, who trained under the legendary Fernand Point at the Restaurant de la Pyramid in France, says Point served it with a cold soft poached egg on top and garnished it with—catsup!

1 lb eggplant
1 lb zucchini
Salt
1 lb onions
¼ lb green or red peppers
2 lb tomatoes
8–10 Tb good-quality olive oil
1 Tb minced garlic
Freshly ground pepper

Peel eggplant and cut into ½-inch cubes. Wash zucchini and cut into ½-inch cubes. Toss both with salt and let drain for 30 minutes. Meanwhile, slice the onions, clean the peppers, and cut into ½-inch cubes. Peel, seed, and quarter the tomatoes. Dry the eggplant and zucchini. Heat 4 tablespoons of the oil in a large sauté pan, add one batch of eggplant, and brown on all sides. Remove to a strainer set over a pan which will collect the oil draining off the eggplant. Sauté the remaining eggplant, and the zucchini and peppers, using the drained oil and additional oil if needed. Set aside.

In 2 tablespoons of the oil, sauté the onions until wilted and lightly colored. Stir in the garlic and tomatoes, and cover the pan. Cook for 3–4 minutes, uncover pan, and raise the heat. Cook briskly until the juices have evaporated. Season to taste with salt and pepper, and combine with the sautéed vegetables, or layer in a saucepan or casserole. Cover, and simmer for 10–15 minutes, basting occasionally. Uncover, and cook until the juices are reduced. Or layer in a casserole and bake in a preheated 325° oven for 25 minutes, remove, and reduce the juices. Serve either hot or cold. *(Serves 6–8)*

- Use leftover ratatouille in crêpes. Combine 2 cups ratatouille with 1 cup ricotta cheese and grated mozzarella cheese. Spoon on the crêpes and roll them up. Make 2 cups *Mornay Sauce* (see *Appendix*) with Parmesan cheese, and spoon half in a baking dish. Place crêpes, seam side down, on the sauce. Cover with the remaining sauce and bake in a preheated 375° oven for 20–30 minutes.
- Use leftover ratatouille in a tart or pizza. Partially bake the crust. Spoon in a thin layer of tomato sauce. Sprinkle with grated mozzarella and Parmesan cheese. Cover with finely chopped ratatouille. Sprinkle with more grated cheese. Bake in a preheated 425° oven until the crust is baked and the filling is hot.
- Use leftovers in quiches.
- Use leftovers to top pasta.

Eggplant Parmesan

This is an all-time favorite. Homemade tomato sauce is best, but a good-quality canned sauce works just fine.

2-lb eggplant
Salt
3 eggs
1½–2 cups dried bread crumbs
½–¾ cup oil
1 cup grated Parmesan cheese
4 tsp chopped fresh oregano or 1 tsp dried
¾ lb sliced mozzarella cheese
3 cups tomato sauce

Peel the eggplant and slice into ³/₈-inch pieces. Salt and let drain for 30 minutes; pat dry. Beat the eggs with 2 tablespoons water. Dip the eggplant slices first into the eggs, then into the crumbs. Heat ¼ cup of the oil in a large frying pan, and sauté the eggplant slices until golden brown on both sides. Remove and drain on brown paper. Continue cooking the eggplant, using additional oil if needed.

Place half the eggplant slices in a 9 x 13-inch pan. Sprinkle with one-third of the Parmesan cheese, half the oregano, and one-third of the mozzarella cheese. Cover with half the tomato sauce. Repeat the layers. Top with the last of the Parmesan and mozzarella cheeses. Bake in a preheated 350° oven for 30 minutes or until bubbly. *(Serves 6–8)*

- For a change of pace, I use about 1 cup feta cheese rather than the mozzarella and only half as much Parmesan cheese.
- Fresh basil is delicious in place of the oregano.

Red, White, and Blue-Black Eggplant

This colorful dish tastes as good as it looks.

1 lb eggplant
Salt
3 large, ripe tomatoes
6 oz sliced mozzarella cheese
½ cup olive oil

3 cups sliced onions
Freshly ground pepper
3 Tb freshly chopped basil or 2 tsp dried

Wash eggplant, but do not peel. Remove the cap and slice off the other end. Quarter the eggplant lengthwise. Then, slice each quarter again into lengthwise 1/4–3/8-inch pieces. Salt the slices and let drain for 30 minutes. Core the tomatoes, halve, and thinly slice. Cut the cheese into 6 x 1 1/2-inch pieces.

Heat 2 tablespoons of the oil, and sauté the onions until soft without browning, about 10 minutes. Remove from the pan. Pat the eggplant dry, and brown the slices, a few at a time, using most of the remaining oil. Salt and pepper the slices. Lightly oil a 9 x 6-inch 2-quart baking dish. Spread half the onions on the bottom of the pan and sprinkle with half the basil. Starting at one end of the dish, arrange alternate standing layers of 1 slice of eggplant, skin side up, 2 or 3 slices tomato (as best fits across eggplant) and then a slice of cheese against the tomatoes. Repeat these three rows, working down the baking dish. When all have been fitted in, top with the remaining basil and onions. Cover the dish tightly and bake for 40 minutes in a preheated 375° oven. *(Serves 4)*

- Double the ingredients, and use a 9 x 12-inch baking dish. Slightly overlap the ingredients.
- Cut small eggplants in half lengthwise. Slice as above, but do not cut through one end, so as to end up with a fan shape. Salt and drain. Pat dry as above. Fill the individual eggplant fans with tomato and cheese and bake as above.
- Omit cheese for a more dietetic version.

Baby Eggplants with Herbs

This is a good appetizer or part of a cold platter.

3 lb small Oriental-type eggplants (4–6 oz)
Salt
2 tsp finely chopped garlic
1/2 cup oil
1/3 cup red wine vinegar
Pepper
1/2 cup freshly chopped herbs (such as basil or dill)

Wash eggplants, remove caps, and cut into quarters or halves. Salt and let drain for 30 minutes. Pat dry and place in a baking pan. Mix garlic into oil and drizzle over the eggplants. Bake in a preheated 400° oven until the eggplants are browned and tender. Cool slightly in a bowl before tossing with vinegar, pepper, and herbs. *(Serves 4–6)*

Eggplant Appetizer (Baba Ghanoush)

This thoroughly addictive appetizer is the Lebanese version of a recipe popular throughout the Mideast. If you omit the garnish, you have a rich-tasting, yet dietetic dish. Serve it with toasted Syrian bread.

1 1/2-lb eggplant
3 Tb lemon juice
1 tsp salt
2 tsp minced garlic
3 Tb sesame paste (tahini)
1/4 cup chopped parsley
2 Tb olive oil (optional)
1/2 cup toasted pine nuts

Cook the eggplant as in *Baked Whole Eggplant* or *Baked Broiled Whole Eggplant* (page 104) until the flesh is soft. Remove, halve, and scoop out the flesh. You should have 2–2 1/4 cups. Beat in a mixer or food processor, with the lemon juice, until smooth. Mash the salt and garlic together, mix with the sesame paste, and combine with the eggplant. Cool, stir in the parsley, and serve drizzled with olive oil (if you wish) and sprinkled with pine nuts. *(Makes 2 cups)*

- Stir in 1 cup fresh peeled, seeded, and chopped tomatoes and 1/2 cup chopped scallions. Garnish with 1/2 cup finely chopped red peppers and additional chopped parsley.
- *Greek Version:* Omit the sesame paste, olive oil, and pine nut garnish. Blend the puréed eggplant with lemon juice, 2 tablespoons parsley, and mashed salt and garlic. Gradually beat in 1/4–1/3 cup olive oil, bit by bit, to make a delicate purée. Taste for seasoning and sprinkle with additional chopped parsley.
- *With Yogurt or Sour Cream:* Add 3/4 cup yogurt or sour cream to the Greek variation.
- *Turkish Version:* Prepare eggplant as above and mix with lemon juice. Then make a *Béchamel Sauce* (see *Appendix*), using 2 tablespoons flour, 2 tablespoons butter, and 1 cup milk. Add 1/4 cup grated cheese and the eggplant mixture. Stir together and heat through. Serve hot.
- *Rumanian Version:* Prepare the Greek version, adding 1 small grated onion to the eggplant, and replacing the lemon juice with red wine vinegar.
- *With Nuts:* Blend puréed eggplant with 1 1/2 cups ground nuts (such as pine nuts, pecans, walnuts, etc.), 1 teaspoon salt, 2 teaspoons lemon juice, and 1/2 teaspoon allspice. Gradually beat in 1/2 cup olive oil. Season to taste with salt, pepper, and a dash of hot pepper sauce.

Imam Bayildi

I've heard several renditions of the story behind Imam Bayildi—"the priest fainted." One version is that he fainted with pleasure when served these delicious vegetables; another version is that he fainted in horror when he discovered how much expensive olive oil had been used. I'm betting it was a combination of both reasons.

Our restaurant recipe for Imam Bayildi was given to us by one of our customers. There are dozens of other versions, including the second recipe I'm giving you, which uses a different method and is better for smaller eggplant.

Mrs. Papasian's Imam Bayildi
Three ³/₄-lb eggplants
Salt
6 medium large onions
6 large ripe tomatoes
6 cloves garlic
¹/₂ cup olive oil
Freshly ground pepper
¹/₄– ¹/₂ cup parsley

Cut off the stemmed eggplant ends. Peel off strips of skin about 1 inch wide lengthwise at 1-inch intervals. Halve the eggplants lengthwise. Slash the flesh and sprinkle with salt. Place the halves on a platter with a heavy weight on top for at least 30 minutes. Slice the onions into rings. Peel, seed, and rough-chop the tomatoes. Mince the garlic.

Heat 2 tablespoons of the oil and sauté the onions until soft and lightly colored, 5–10 minutes. Add the tomatoes, sauté for 5–10 minutes longer, and set aside.

Squeeze the eggplants and dry them. Heat 4 tablespoons of the oil and sauté the eggplants flesh side down until nicely browned. This will probably have to be done in two batches. Place in a sauté pan that will hold all six halves snugly, or divide into two pans, flesh side up. Gently press the tomato-onion mixture over the eggplants, pressing into the slashes wherever possible. Sprinkle garlic over each one. Season with salt and pepper, drizzle with the remaining oil, and pour in enough water to come about one-third of the way up the sides of the eggplants. Bring water to a boil, cover, and simmer gently until the eggplants are tender. The cooking time will depend upon the size of the eggplants. Start checking after 20 minutes. Cool, sprinkle with parsley, and serve cold. *(Serves 6)*

Martha Coumandaros's Imam Bayildi
6 small eggplants (about 2 lb)
Salt
2 large onions
3 ripe tomatoes
2–3 cloves garlic
¹/₂ bunch Italian parsley
¹/₂ cup olive oil

Stem the eggplants. Cut 4 equally spaced incisions lengthwise around the eggplant. The cuts should be deep and long, but not so deep as to break apart the eggplant. Sprinkle with salt and let stand 30 minutes. Thinly slice the onions lengthwise. Peel, seed, and chop the tomatoes. Sliver the garlic, and coarsely chop the parsley. Pat the eggplants dry. In a large skillet, heat the olive oil and sauté the eggplants just long enough to soften them, turning two or three times. Let cool.

In the same oil, sauté the onions, tomatoes, garlic, and parsley until the onions are wilted. Cool slightly and stuff each eggplant incision. Arrange the eggplants in a casserole or heavy Dutch oven and add the leftover vegetable mixture. Cover and simmer for 30–40 minutes or until the eggplants are tender. Serve either hot or cold. (*Serves 6*)

Caponata

Use this Sicilian specialty on an antipasto platter or as a cold salad. It keeps at least a week refrigerated in a covered jar.

> 2-lb eggplant
> Salt
> 3/4 cup plus 2 Tb olive oil
> 2 cups chopped onions
> 1 cup chopped celery
> 1 cup peeled, seeded, and chopped tomatoes
> 1/2 cup pitted, halved green olives
> 1/4 cup rinsed and drained capers
> 1 Tb pine nuts
> 1/3 cup red wine vinegar
> 1 Tb sugar
> Freshly ground pepper

Peel and cube eggplant into 3/4-inch pieces. Salt and let drain for 30 minutes; pat dry. Heat half the oil in a large frying pan. Sauté half the eggplant until golden brown, 6–10 minutes. Remove eggplant to a strainer and let drain. Add the remaining oil, sauté the rest of the eggplant, and drain as above. In the same oil (or add 2 tablespoons additional oil if necessary), sauté the onions and celery until just tender, then add the tomatoes. Cover the pan and cook for 4–5 minutes, uncover, and cook 5 minutes longer. Add the eggplant, olives, capers, and pine nuts. Heat the vinegar and sugar until the sugar dissolves, and pour over the mixture. Simmer, covered, for 5–10 minutes. Season to taste and cool. (*Makes 7–8 cups*)

- When cool, add 1 cup chunked tuna fish.

Eggplant Salad

> 1 lb eggplant
> Salt
> 1/3 cup oil
> 2 cups peeled, seeded, and chopped tomatoes
> 1/2 cup freshly chopped parsley
> 1/2 cup chopped red onions
> 1/4 cup chopped fresh mint

> *Vinaigrette Sauce* made with lemon juice (page 352)
> Freshly ground pepper

Peel the eggplant and cut into 1/2-inch cubes. Salt the cubes and let drain for 30 minutes. Dry the eggplant and sauté it in hot oil until browned on all sides; reduce heat and cook to just barely tender. Remove to a colander and let drain to remove excess oil. When cool, combine with tomatoes, parsley, onions, and mint. Dress with vinaigrette and season with salt and pepper. (*Serves 4*)

- For a plain eggplant salad prepare only the eggplant and toss with vinaigrette. Add toasted pine nuts or sesame seeds.
- *With Yogurt:* Prepare eggplant as above, omitting everything else but the mint. Toss with yogurt and season with lemon juice, salt, and pepper.

Oriental Eggplant Salad

Marinate the salad for at least 2 hours before serving, and serve chilled.

> 1 lb eggplant
> Salt
> 1/3 cup oil
> 1 tsp minced ginger
> 2 tsp minced garlic
> 1 Tb white vinegar
> 2 Tb soy sauce
> 1 Tb sesame oil
> 1 tsp sesame seeds
> 2 chopped scallions
> 1/4 tsp hot pepper flakes (optional)

Peel and cut eggplant into 3/4–1-inch cubes. Salt, let drain for 30 minutes, and pat dry. Sauté in oil until lightly browned and just barely tender. Place in a colander to remove excess oil. Mash together the ginger, garlic, and 1/2 teaspoon salt. Combine the garlic mixture with the remaining ingredients and toss with eggplant. (*Serves 4*)

- You could also steam the cubes until tender.

Eggplant Sandwiches

These are simply bread-free takeoffs on two childhood favorites: an open-faced cheese and tomato sandwich, and a grilled cheese sandwich. They're easy, fun to make, and very tasty.

> *Open-faced Eggplant, Cheese, and Tomato*
> Salt
> 3/4-inch slice eggplant
> Olive oil
> 1 equal-size slice of mozzarella or Swiss cheese
> 2–3 slices of tomato
> Freshly ground pepper
> Mayonnaise (optional)

Salt the eggplant slice, and let drain for 30 minutes. Preheat the broiler. Dry the eggplant and dip in oil. Place on a broiler rack. Set 5 inches beneath the flame. Brown eggplant on one side, turn and let brown lightly, then top with the cheese and tomatoes. Move closer to heat and broil until cheese melts and the tomatoes are tinged with color." Remove, salt and pepper, or top with mayonnaise. (*Serves 1*)

- Dip in egg and bread crumbs. Sauté until browned on both sides, top with cheese and tomatoes, and run under the broiler.
- Dip in egg and bread crumbs, sauté until browned, then top with 2–3 shrimp sautéed in oil and garlic for 2 minutes. Sprinkle with grated cheese and run under the broiler until the cheese melts.

Grilled Cheese and Eggplant
Salt
Two ¹/₂-inch slices eggplant
1 egg
Seasoned bread crumbs
Oil
1 slice mozzarella, Swiss, or American cheese

Salt eggplant and drain for 30 minutes. Beat egg. Pat eggplant dry; dip in egg, then in crumbs. Heat oil in a sauté pan and brown the eggplant on one side. Turn over one slice, and top with cheese; place the other slice on top, uncooked side facing up. Cook until the bottom is browned; turn with a spatula and brown. The eggplant will have a crisp exterior, a soft interior, and the cheese will be melted in the middle. (*Serves 1*)

Marie Caratelli's Eggplant Rolls

These eggplant rolls are lovely—easy to make and can be prepared ahead of time. Don't leave the garlic out.

1 ¹/₄-lb eggplant
Salt
1 lb ground beef or a combination of beef and pork
¹/₂ cup grated Parmesan cheese
¹/₄ cup chopped fresh parsley
1 tsp minced garlic
1 tsp oregano
3 eggs
Freshly ground pepper
Flour
¹/₂ cup olive oil
1 ¹/₂ cups tomato sauce (homemade if possible)
¹/₂ cup grated mozzarella cheese

Wash eggplant but do not peel. Remove the cap and stem end, and cut into thin slices no wider than ¹/₄ inch. You should have approximately 16 slices. You can obtain larger slices by cutting at a slight diagonal. Salt and let drain for 30 minutes.

Meanwhile, combine the ground meat with ¹/₄ cup of the Parmesan cheese, the parsley, garlic, oregano, and 1 beaten egg. Season with salt and pepper. Pat the eggplant dry. Beat the remaining eggs with 1 tablespoon water. Dip the eggplant slices into the eggs, then into flour. In a large sauté pan, heat the oil. Shake the excess flour off the eggplant and sauté the slices until lightly browned on each side. Place on a brown paper bag to remove the excess oil.

Pour ³/₄ cup of the tomato sauce into a 9 x 13-inch pan. Take an eggplant slice, and place a heaping teaspoon of the meat mixture into the center of the slice. Using a fork, spread the meat mixture over the eggplant in a very thin layer. (The amount of filling used depends upon the

size of each eggplant slice.) Roll the eggplant over the meat like a jelly roll, and place in a baking dish seam side down. Continue filling all the slices. Then drizzle over the remaining tomato sauce. Combine the remaining Parmesan with the mozzarella cheese and sprinkle over the sauce. Cover the pan with aluminum foil and bake in a preheated 375° oven for 25 minutes. Uncover, and bake 10 minutes longer. (*Serves 6–8*)

- Substitute any favorite meatball or meatloaf mixture.

Eggplant and Fish Stew

1 lb eggplant
Salt and freshly ground pepper
6 Tb olive oil
1 ¹/₂ cups sliced onions
1 tsp minced garlic
Saffron
Cayenne pepper
1 bay leaf

4 cups peeled, seeded, and chopped tomatoes
2 Tb tomato paste
3–4 Tb butter
1 1/2–2 lb haddock fillets or other firm-fleshed fish
1/4 cup chopped parsley
1 cup bread crumbs

Peel and cube the eggplant into 1-inch pieces. Salt and let drain for 30 minutes. In a frying pan, heat 2 tablespoons of the oil, and sauté the onions until soft. Add the remaining oil as needed and sauté the eggplant for 5 minutes. Stir in the garlic, a pinch each of saffron and cayenne pepper, the bay leaf, tomatoes, and tomato paste. Cook, covered, 5 minutes; uncover, and cook 5 minutes longer. Season to taste.

Cut the fish into 2-inch chunks; fold into the vegetable mixture along with the parsley. Spoon into a baking dish. Sauté the bread crumbs in butter. Sprinkle over the vegetable-fish mixture, and bake in a preheated 425° oven for 15 minutes or until the fish is tender and the stew is bubbly. *(Serves 4)*

- Turn this into a soup. Add fish stock and simmer on the stove.

Double-Duty Stuffed Eggplant

Here is a double-duty mixture: either fill a mold to present a grand eggplant "cake" or stuff the eggplant shells for individual portions. Serve either with a *Marinara Sauce* (page 317) or a *Béchamel* (see *Appendix*) enriched with egg yolks.

Baked Eggplant Mold
6 eggplants (about 3/4 lb each)
Salt
1/2 cup oil
1 cup chopped onions
2 tsp chopped garlic
1/2 lb Italian sweet sausage
1 lb ground or finely chopped veal (or lamb)
2 tsp cornstarch
1/2 cup beef broth
2 cups peeled, seeded, and chopped tomatoes
2 Tb tomato paste
1 tsp rosemary
1/2 tsp thyme
Freshly ground pepper
3 Tb chopped parsley
2 eggs

Halve the eggplants lengthwise. Slash the flesh, salt, turn upside down, and drain for 30 minutes; pat dry. Brush the flesh with 2 tablespoons of the oil and place in a baking dish, cut side up. Pour 1/4 inch water into the pan and bake in a preheated 400° oven for 15–20 minutes or until the flesh is not quite tender.

Scoop out the flesh, leaving just the skins. Grease an ovenproof bowl or casserole 4 inches high and 6–7 inches wide. Line the mold with the skins (with the black outer skin facing out), and overlap the ends over the mold.

Chop the eggplant flesh and sauté in 2 tablespoons of the oil until lightly browned. Drain and set aside. Heat 2 tablespoons of the oil and cook the onions until wilted and golden. Add the garlic, sausage, and veal (or lamb). Cook until the meat loses color, then drain the fat from the pan. Dissolve the cornstarch in the broth; add to the meat mixture along with the tomatoes, tomato paste, and herbs. Simmer to combine the flavors, 10–15 minutes, then raise the heat and cook to evaporate the juices. Add the eggplant flesh. Season to taste, and add the parsley. Beat the eggs and stir into the eggplant mixture.

Spoon mixture into mold, fold over the skins, cover tightly, and place the mold into a deep-sided baking dish. Pour boiling water into the dish, halfway up the side of the mold. Bake in a preheated 375° oven for 1 1/2 hours. Cool for 10 minutes before unmolding. *(Serves 8)*

Stuffed Eggplant Shells
Prepare the eggplants and bake as in first paragraph of *Baked Eggplant Mold*. Remove from the oven and reduce the temperature to 375°.

Scoop out the center flesh, leaving 1/2-inch thickness of flesh on the skin. Chop the flesh and sauté it in 2 tablespoons of the oil until lightly browned. Drain and set aside. Prepare the meat and eggplant stuffing as in the *Baked Eggplant Mold*, but omit the eggs.

Fill each eggplant shell with the mixture, and place in a greased baking dish. Drizzle with the remaining oil. Bake for 45 minutes in a 375° oven or until completely heated through. Top with bread crumbs or grated cheese and run under the broiler to lightly brown. *(Serves 6)*

- Use cooked leftover meat. First, cook the onion and tomato mixture, then add the meat along with the chopped eggplant.

Moussaka

This is a great dish for a crowd, because you can prepare it ahead of time and bake just before serving.

5–6 lb eggplant
Salt and freshly ground pepper
6 Tb oil
7 Tb butter
2 cups chopped onions
3 lb lamb or a combination of lamb, beef, or veal
2 tsp chopped garlic
4 cups peeled, seeded, and chopped tomatoes (or 3 cups tomato sauce)
3 Tb tomato paste (omit, if using sauce)
1/2 tsp rosemary
1 tsp dill
4 eggs
1 1/4 cups grated Romano cheese
1/2 cup bread crumbs
1/2 cup flour
3 cups milk
4 egg yolks

Wash and slice the eggplant (peel if you wish) into 3/8-inch pieces. Salt and let drain for 30 minutes. Pat dry.

Brush slices with approximately 4 tablespoons of the oil, and broil until lightly browned on each side. Heat the remaining oil and 1 tablespoon of the butter in a large sauté pan. Add the onions and cook until soft and lightly browned. Add the meat and garlic, and cook until the meat loses color. Drain the fat from the pan. Add the tomatoes and tomato paste (or tomato sauce), herbs, and season with salt and pepper. Cook over moderately high heat until thickened and reduced. Beat the eggs. When the meat has slightly cooled, add the eggs and 3/4 cup of the cheese. Oil an 11 x 16-inch or 10 x 15-inch pan. Sprinkle with bread crumbs. Put one-third of the eggplant in the pan, cover with half the meat sauce, follow with another layer of eggplant, then remaining meat sauce, and top with the remaining eggplant. Make a béchamel sauce: Melt 6 tablespoons butter, stir in the flour, and cook for 2–3 minutes. Whisk in the milk, bring the sauce to a boil, reduce the heat, and simmer for 10 minutes, whisking to smooth. Add remaining cheese and season to taste. Beat the egg yolks, stir a small amount of the hot sauce into the yolks to warm them, then whisk the yolks into the sauce. Pour over the eggplant, and bake in a preheated 350° oven for 45–60 minutes. *(Serves 12–15)*

• Add a layer of sliced parboiled potatoes between the eggplant layers.

Pickled Eggplant

1 lb eggplant
2 tsp chopped garlic
1/2 tsp salt
1/2 cup wine vinegar
Freshly ground pepper
1 tsp dried basil
1 tsp dried oregano
Olive oil

Wash the eggplant and cut into 1–1 1/2-inch cubes. Bring 1 inch of water to a boil in a steamer and steam the cubes for 3–4 minutes or until they are barely tender. Remove to a bowl. Mash the garlic with the salt; combine with the vinegar, pepper, and herbs and toss with the warm eggplant. Cool the eggplant, cover, and refrigerate overnight. Before serving, add olive oil to taste. *(Makes 3 cups)*

Endive

One of Russ's proudest gardening moments came the day he brought in his first crop of Belgian endive: I can still see the delight on his face. He had good reason to be excited, for Belgian endive is a time-consuming crop which takes a long time to mature. Before harvesting a single endive, he had to first spend the summer growing plants just for the roots, which were then pulled and stored. Later he repotted and held them in darkness to blanch the new leaves. These leaves were the vegetable we know as Belgian endive.

You might wonder how anyone ever thought to go through this complicated procedure in the first place. Actually, Belgian endive originated as a surprise crop. During the last century, Belgian farmers grew witloof chicory strictly for the roots, which were dried, ground, and used as a coffee substitute. One year, by chance, a crop of roots overlooked in storage started to sprout new whitish leaves. The crop rapidly became a greatly prized delicacy, and serious production began. It was called witloof chicory, or Brussels chicory, after the growing areas around Brussels. In Belgium, endive is still known as witloof; in many other parts of Europe it is often called chicory, while the shoots are known as "chicons." In America we refer to it as Belgian endive.

Because of the large amount of hand labor involved, the production of endive has never caught on in this country, although a few entrepreneurs in the West grow crops for restaurants. As a result, practically all our supply of Belgian endive is still imported from Belgium.

Shipping and labor costs make this vegetable a prohibitively priced luxury item. At today's prices, to prepare a braised endive dish serving eight persons would cost $13.00. I'd say this provides more than an adequate incentive for growing Belgian endive at home.

Seed catalogs list several other kinds of endive, which are really lettucelike salad greens and should not be confused with Belgian endive. Also, ignore regular chicory seeds, for the seeds you want are sold only under the name *witloof chicory*. Growing endive is a lengthy process, but not a tricky one. First, it's necessary to raise the leaf crop. Russ starts by sowing seeds in the garden no earlier than June 1 (earlier sowing causes plants to bolt). He places seeds in rows 2 feet apart, thinning them to 8 inches apart. The garden space isn't wasted, for endive plants have large, decorative leaves creating a foliage background when interplanted with flowers such as zinnias. Plants need at least 100–120 days for good root development, so Russ waits until after the first light frost, but before a heavy frost, before spading up the roots. Then he twists off the leaves and fills a large box with sawdust and buries the roots in it. (Sand or dry peat works as well.) Throughout the winter, as needed, he transfers roots from the holding bin and repots them singly in 8-inch-diameter flower pots, covering each root completely and lightly covering the crown with 1/2 inch of soil. Then he waters thoroughly and inverts another flower pot over it, creating darkness to blanch the shoots, and places both pots in a dark spot—such as under the

greenhouse bench. The roots remain in the dark at a temperature of approximately 50°. Although warmer temperatures will give faster growth, the closed shape of the head is lost: growing in containers never produces the very tight head characteristic of the imported blanched endive grown directly under the ground, in soil heated by underground coils. After three to four weeks, each root planted forms a cylindrical crown of blanched whitish leaves with pale yellow-green tips.

As you can see, it takes months to grow this vegetable from scratch, but what satisfaction and savings!

Before eating, I simply rinse off the leaves quickly and wipe dry. I never soak Belgian endive in water, because this seems to accentuate its bitterness.

Belgian endive is naturally slightly bitter, but that's part of its distinction: I think the bitterness gives a pleasant edge to the crisp texture of the leaves. I've heard that removing the core makes endive less bitter, but, frankly, I don't think it matters much one way or another. I core endive to facilitate separating leaves for a salad or appetizer platter; but when I cook endive whole, the core helps hold the shape of the vegetable.

Some people adore cooked endive and wish it were cheaper so they could serve it more often. I enjoy braised endive but also love it raw. It's absolutely delicious plain or in salads, as it is unlike other salad greens: the heads or chicons have unique cigarlike shapes with crisp, firm, tightly packed leaves and no droopy parts. Each leaf is more like a translucent wide stem than a regular salad leaf. Served whole, or sliced, endive endows a salad with a totally new texture and flavor. And, since endive is about 93 percent water, you can feel free to eat up without worrying about calories—4 ounces of endive has fewer than 15 calories. This water content should be taken into account when cooking endive, however, as the bulk reduces during cooking. For instance, sliced sautéed endive will reduce at a ratio of 4 to 1, necessitating 4 cups raw endive to end up with 1 cup cooked.

There are three basic methods of cooking Belgian endive: braising, steaming, and boiling. I prefer to braise endive, for I find the long slow cooking mellows the flavor. Steaming and boiling are handy first steps for further preparation, but have their disadvantages. Steaming keeps the endive from becoming totally waterlogged and limp, but it does turn gray in the process; boiling in lemon water or a blanc prevents endive from turning dark, but it then becomes quite soggy. In both cases, after the endive has cooked, gently squeeze it to remove any excess moisture.

Marketing

Choose endive wrapped in dark paper, which keeps light from the greens during shipping and prevents them from becoming bitter. Heads should be firm and crisp, and creamy white in color. Any slight browning of outer edges is not serious and can be removed, but endive with completely brown or limp outer leaves should be avoided.

◇ Braised Endive

Whole braised endive can be served plain or prepared as in the *Finishing Touches*.

Oven-Braised Endive

Melt 2–3 tablespoons butter in an ovenproof pan and lightly brown endives. Then arrange in one or two layers and sprinkle with lemon juice; dot with butter and sprinkle with salt and pepper. (For 8 endives, use 3 tablespoons butter and 1 tablespoon lemon juice.) Cover with a sheet of buttered waxed paper and then with a lid or aluminum foil. Bake in a preheated 375° oven for 1¼ hours or until very tender and golden.

Slow Oven-Braised Endive

For even mellower endive, cook longer at a slower heat. Butter an ovenproof casserole and arrange prepared endives in one or two layers. Dot each layer with butter; sprinkle with lemon juice, salt, and pepper. Cover with a sheet of buttered waxed paper, then cover with a lid. Bake in a preheated 325° oven for 1½ hours. Remove the lid and bake 30 minutes longer or until endives are golden and very tender.

- Add ½ cup heavy cream and bake 10 minutes longer.

Stovetop-Braised Endive

Sauté 8 endives in 2–3 tablespoons butter over medium-high heat until lightly colored on all sides. Squeeze on lemon juice, sprinkle with salt and pepper, add ¼ cup water or broth, and cover with buttered waxed paper topped with a lid or aluminum foil. Cook over low heat for 30–40 minutes or until tender. (The outer leaves will be tender and the core still slightly firm.) Cook longer for a softer center.

- For a no-butter version, sprinkle endives with lemon juice, salt, and pepper; pour on approximately ½ cup chicken or beef stock, and cover and cook slowly until tender, 40–50 minutes. Remove cover and boil stock to glaze the endives.

◇ Braised Sliced Endive

Prepare endive this way for stuffings, meatloaves, pies, or quiches. Remove a thin slice from the end of the endives, core, and slice diagonally. Melt 3 tablespoons butter per pound of sliced endives and toss endives in butter to coat completely. Sprinkle with lemon juice and salt and pepper. Turn heat to low, cover pan, and let cook for 10 minutes. Uncover pan, raise heat, and cook until moisture is evaporated and endive is lightly colored, about 10 minutes longer, adding additional butter if necessary. The endive should be golden, tender, and cooked through, yet firmly textured.

Special Information

Yields

- 1 lb = 4 cups cut up
- 4 cups raw sliced = 1 cup cooked
- Count on ½ medium endive per person for serving raw in a salad with other ingredients
- When cooked, use 2 small endives or 1 large endive per person, depending upon the menu

Storage and Preserving

- Use fresh. Do not freeze or can.
- Raw—holds in the refrigerator for 2 weeks. Use cooked refrigerated endive within 2 days.

Hints

- Serve leaves individually on a raw vegetable platter.
- Stuff leaves with fillings such as blue or cream cheese or sour cream (or a combination of these) for appetizers.
- Make a quiche using *Braised Sliced Endive* and crabmeat—or mix endive with feta cheese.
- Cut into 1-inch slices and add to stir-fry dishes.
- Slice crosswise in ¼-inch sections and add to egg or ham salads for crispness.
- Make a spinach and endive salad.
- Combine with creamy cheese dishes to highlight endive's slightly acrid taste.

Microwave

Note: Use the microwave only as a preliminary step—that is, if you are going to give the endive a finishing touch.

- 4 whole 6-ounce endives, in a covered dish with 4 tablespoons liquid (or 2 tablespoons liquid and 2 tablespoons butter), will cook in 6 minutes. Turn once after 3 minutes.
- ½ pound sliced endives, in a covered dish with 4 tablespoons liquid (or 2 tablespoons liquid and 2 tablespoons butter), will cook in 4 minutes.

Leftovers

- Use cooked in stuffings, meatloaves, meat pies and turnovers, and quiches.
- Purée with broad or white beans for an unusual vegetable combination.

◇ *Steamed Endive*

Steam only as a preliminary step for one of the *Finishing Touches*. Clean endives and remove a small slice from the root ends. Bring ³/₄–1 inch water to boil in a steamer and place endives in steaming basket. Steam for 15–25 minutes, depending on the size. The outer leaves should be quite tender while the inner core should be cooked through but still retaining some resilience. Drain, press out excess water, and set aside until final preparation.

◇ *Boiled Endive*

Boil endive only as a preliminary step for one of the *Finishing Touches*. Boil salted acidulated water or a *Blanc* (see *Appendix*). Add endives and cook until barely tender. (A 6-ounce whole endive takes about 10 minutes.) Remove, drain, gently squeeze out water, and proceed with recipe.

Finishing Touches for Braised, Steamed, and Boiled Endive

- *Endive Meunière*: Melt butter and, when foamy, add precooked endives and turn in the butter over medium heat until lightly browned. Remove to a warm platter. Add additional butter to the pan, cook until dark brown, and pour over endive. For braised endives simply pour the browned butter over.
- Stir in finely chopped shallots during the last 30 seconds of browning butter.
- Add finely chopped garlic for the last 10 seconds of browning butter. Do not let garlic brown or it will become bitter.
- *Endive and Cream*: Roll precooked endive in melted butter until golden. Sprinkle with lemon juice and season with salt and pepper. Pour in heavy cream (¹/₂ cup for 8 endives). Shake pan to roll endives in cream, then cover and cook for 5 minutes, without boiling, to intermingle flavors.
- *Endive Halves with Parmesan Cheese*: Slice precooked endives in half lengthwise. Sprinkle with Parmesan cheese, dot with butter, and run under broiler until cheese is brown and bubbly.
- *Endive Wrapped with Cheese and Ham*: Slice large precooked endive in half lengthwise or leave whole if small. Wrap each endive first with a thin slice of Swiss cheese and then with thin slices of ham or prosciutto. Put in a buttered dish and bake in a preheated 400° oven until heated through. Dot with butter and run under the broiler to brown.
- Cover with a light cream sauce and bake at 350° for 20 minutes.
- *Endive in Mornay Sauce*: Make a *Mornay Sauce* (see *Appendix*), 1¹/₂ cups for 8 endives. Spread one-third of the sauce in a casserole, layer the endives, and cover with remaining sauce. Sprinkle with grated cheese and dot with butter. Cook in a preheated 400°

oven until warmed through and then run under the broiler until lightly browned.
- Layer shellfish or wrap in prosciutto or ham before adding sauce.

Endive, Fennel, and Red Pepper Appetizer

Endive is a delightful addition to raw vegetable platters. I often serve endive leaves, fennel sliced diagonally, and strips of red pepper to be dipped into the following anchovy sauce and *Joe Hyde's Russian Dressing* (see *Mixed Vegetables*). One sauce is salty and sharp; the other, sweeter, yet still sharp.

Anchovy Sauce
2-oz tin flat anchovies
1 tsp capers (optional)
¹/₂ tsp freshly ground pepper
2 Tb wine vinegar or lemon juice
³/₄–1 cup olive oil

Mash together until puréed the anchovies, their oil, and the capers. Beat in pepper and vinegar or lemon juice. Then, beating constantly, gradually add oil until the sauce has the consistency of heavy cream. *(Makes 1¹/₄ cups)*
- Add a bit of heavy cream to lighten sauce.

Endive Salads

Endive makes any salad elegant: just one endive added to a plain green salad perks it up. Endive's slightly bitter taste cleans the palate and helps relieve any stuffed feeling after a big meal. The watercress, endive, and mushroom variation is particularly delicious.

Endive Salad with Vinaigrette
4 large or 8 small endives
Vinaigrette Sauce (page 352)

Clean and core endives. Cut across into 1–1¹/₂-inch lengths or leave small endive leaves whole. Toss with vinaigrette. *(Serves 4)*

- Combine with other ingredients such as a bunch of watercress and sliced mushrooms; seasoned julienned cooked beets; crumbled feta or blue cheese; or finely sliced and seasoned radish slices.

Endive, Apples, and Nut Salad

4 endives
2 Golden Delicious or Granny Smith apples
¹/₂ cup walnuts
1 cup *Cream Salad Dressing* (page 347) or *Mayonnaise* (page 349)

Wipe endives clean, core, and cut crosswise into 1-inch pieces. Peel, core, and slice apples; coarsely chop nuts and combine with endive. Toss with cream dressing or mayonnaise. *(Serves 4)*

Endive and Citrus Salad

4 endives
4 oranges or 2 grapefruit
1 cup *Creamy Salad Dressing* (optional; see page 347)

Wipe endives clean, core, and separate leaves. Peel and section oranges, grapefruit, or both. Arrange in alternate decorative circles on serving platters. Serve plain or with dressing. *(Serves 4–6)*

• Flavor heavy cream with Dijon mustard and serve on the side.

Extra-Easy Chicken and Endive

4 Tb oil
4 Tb melted butter
6 chicken legs with thighs attached
6 large endives (more if small)
Salt and freshly ground pepper
12 whole shallots

Combine oil and butter and brush over chicken and endives, covering thoroughly; sprinkle with salt and pepper. Place chicken in a casserole. Peel shallots and arrange around chicken. Top chicken with endives and any remaining butter and oil. Seal casserole with aluminum foil and cover with a lid. Bake in a preheated 375° oven for 1¹/₂ hours. *(Serves 4–6)*

Breast of Veal with Endive Stuffing

This recipe allows you to splurge on endive while balancing its cost with an inexpensive cut of meat. The finished dish looks beautiful, slices easily, and is equally good served hot or cold. The small veal breast I suggest is readily available in supermarkets; for an elegant com-

pany dish, use a larger breast and increase the stuffing amounts (see note following recipe).

2–3-lb bone-in breast of veal
1 lb endives
7 Tb butter
¹/₂ lb boiled ham
1 egg
¹/₄ cup chopped parsley
¹/₂ cup fresh bread crumbs
Salt and freshly ground pepper
2 Tb oil
1 onion
1 carrot
1 bay leaf
¹/₂ tsp thyme
¹/₂ cup vermouth or 1 cup dry white wine
3 cups veal stock or 1¹/₂ cups chicken stock and 1¹/₂ cups beef stock
1 Tb cornstarch (optional)
2 Tb wine, water, or stock (optional)

With a sharp knife, cut out the bones from the veal breast and split a horizontal pocket extending to the far inner edges of the breast. (This is easy, but ask the butcher to do it the first time to see how it goes.) Chop the breast bones into 2–3-inch pieces and set aside. Cut an end slice from the cleaned endives, cut out the cores, and slice diagonally into ¹/₂-inch pieces. You should have approximately 4 cups. In a large pan, melt 3 tablespoons butter until foamy; add endive and cook as in *Braised Sliced Endive* (page 116). The endive will reduce to 1 cup when cooked. Place endive in a mixing bowl. Chop ham into small pieces, beat egg, and add them to the endive along with the parsley and bread crumbs. Season with salt and pepper to taste. Salt and pepper the veal breast pocket. Fill with stuffing; sew together the open edge. (If you are filling the veal breast and then refrigerating for cooking later, make sure the stuffing is cold before putting it into the meat.) The filled breast will measure about 9 x 5 inches.

Heat oil and 2 tablespoons butter. When foamy, add the veal breast, brown on all sides, and place in an oven-proof casserole just large enough to hold the veal and bones. Brown the reserved bones and add to casserole. Chop the onion, slice the carrot, lightly brown, then add to casserole along with the bay leaf and thyme. Pour in vermouth and stock to come at least halfway up the sides of the veal. Bring to a simmer on top of the stove, then

cover and braise on the lower shelf of an oven preheated to 350°. Turn meat once or twice and baste every 20 minutes or so. The meat will be cooked in 1½ hours or when it feels tender with a fork but still retains its shape.

Remove veal to a warm platter, and cover with a piece of foil. Strain cooking liquids, pressing the juices out of the vegetables. (You can purée the carrots and onions and add to the sauce.) Skim off the fat and boil the sauce down to about 2 cups. (If the sauce is too thin, thicken it by combining 1 tablespoon cornstarch with 2 tablespoons wine, water, or stock. Beat paste into sauce and simmer for 2–3 minutes.) Just before serving, beat in remaining 2 tablespoons butter for enrichment. Slice as if you were cutting a loaf of bread. *(Serves 4)*

Note: When stuffing larger breasts, increase ingredients but add equal parts ground veal to ham. Otherwise, the ham would overpower the dish.

- Add sautéed mushrooms or grated cheese to stuffing.
- Double ingredients, stuff an 8–9-pound capon, and braise until capon is cooked through.

Fennel

Although I've seasoned food for years with the herb fennel, it's only recently that I've grown its vegetable namesake, Florentine or Florence fennel. I'm sorry it took me so long to discover this remarkable vegetable.

Florentine fennel, known as finocchio in Italian cooking, looks like a flattened bunch of celery with a fist-shaped bulbous base and feathery blue-green leaves. Cooked, it has a light, delicate anise flavor that makes a good counterpoint to fish, fowl, and bland meats such as veal.

Raw, the anise taste of fennel is even more dominant, and it has a crunchy, celerylike texture. It's a magnificent diet vegetable: in fact, centuries ago, the Greeks called it marathon from their verb *maraino*—to grow thin. No wonder, for fennel has almost no calories—fewer than 30 calories in 3½ ounces. Next time you're contemplating fixing a bowl of celery sticks, prepare fennel instead and satisfy your hunger pangs with its full flavor.

In Italy, fennel is served raw in antipastos, as one of several vegetables to dip in the hot anchovy oil of *Bagna Cauda* (see *Mixed Vegetables*), or is frequently cooked with fish or cheese. The Italians also eat fennel for dessert along with beautifully ripened goat cheese. An Italian friend who dotes on the small underdeveloped shoots at the base of the bulb says their sweetness "cleans" the mouth at the end of a meal. With cheese, or by itself, fennel is a refreshing end to a meal.

Fennel is of top quality for only a limited time in the fall, although it's available through the winter. I think of it as an autumn counterpart to asparagus and look forward to its arrival with the same kind of anticipation. It adds a welcome contrast to the meals of early fall. It comes into season as the garden is winding down, when heavier-flavored root vegetables are abundant, and more delicately flavored vegetables seem to have disappeared. We enjoy fennel while we can, for come frost, it will be a blackened shell, its tender crispness a memory until next year (market fennel always seems coarser with a less deli-

cate texture than the home-grown variety).

Here in Massachusetts we start seeds indoors about four to six weeks before planting outside, although in warmer climates you can sow the seeds directly in the ground. Fennel originated in Mediterranean regions, and needs warmth at all times, so we pick a sunny spot with well-drained fertile soil (heavy soil gives poor results). Fennel is one of the more decorative vegetables with 2-foot-high dill-like leaves fanning out from compact, fleshy bulbs. Russ sets out seedlings in late spring, after all danger of frost is over, and spaces them a foot apart to ensure ample room for root development. When the bulbs reach the size of large eggs, he pulls soil up around the lower stems to blanch them—European gardeners also use cardboard. A month later, the first fennel is ready to harvest and can be enjoyed straight through until frost, although outer stalks can become stringy if held too long. (If this happens, they can be rescued by stringing much as you would celery: cut partway through the top of each stalk and, with the knife, pull away the outside layer of flesh toward the base of the stalk; the strings will come with it.) Harvesting is easiest with a spading fork; merely loosen the soil and carefully lift the fennel out of the ground.

Because it stores poorly, I harvest fennel as I need it. Long storage causes the stalks to dry up, begin to rot, turn brown, or become fibrous, while the interior turns pulpy. Its anise flavor also diminishes somewhat in stor-

age—a reason that store-bought fennel is less flavorful than the home-grown variety.

To prepare for cooking, wash, dry, and trim fennel stalks to the point where they meet the top and sides of the bulb. Leave $1/8$ inch of the base near the root to hold the fennel intact during cooking. Remove dry or pulpy outer layers and save these layers, the stalks, and the edible leaves for flavoring or garnishing. You'll notice I use these trimmings in several recipes, because they give a heightened anise flavor to the completed dish. Now the fennel is ready to eat raw or be cooked.

Fennel adapts well to braising, blanching, and steaming, but for many dishes I prefer a combination of sautéing and braising. Sautéing retains more of the flavor than other methods, and firms the vegetable for the simmering to follow, while the browning adds color and richer flavor. A contrast of lemon often heightens the flavor.

Marketing

Fennel can be difficult to locate, but it's usually available in Italian markets and some city supermarkets between October and March, with November and December being peak months. At Christmas, prices skyrocket and the quantity goes down.

If possible, buy fennel with stalks and leaves attached (although many produce managers cut off all but 2–3 inches so that the fennel keeps longer). Remove the leaves if you're going to store the fennel for any length of time.

Select firm bulbs. Don't buy any with noticeably coarse outer stalks, brownish bases, or deep cracks in the flesh; you'll have to throw most of the bulb away. Test for pulpiness by lightly pressing on the flesh: bulbs should be firm and resist pressure slightly.

◇ *Braised Fennel*

Sautéing before braising keeps the fennel firm and adds flavor and a lovely golden color. Don't omit the minced fennel; it reinforces the anise taste.

> 2 lb fennel (2 bulbs with 1-inch stalks)
> 2 Tb oil
> 2 Tb butter
> 2 whole unpeeled cloves garlic (optional)
> 1 cup minced fennel trimmings
> Salt
> ½ cup white vermouth (optional)
> ½ cup water

Wash and trim fennel bulbs; finely chop enough trimmings to make 1 cup. Halve bulbs to make 4 portions and retain the core to hold the fennel intact. Heat oil and butter in an ovenproof pan large enough to hold the fennel in one layer. When the butter starts to bubble, add fennel and garlic cloves (if you like) and sauté on medium heat for 10–15 minutes, turning to brown on all sides. Add 1 cup of minced fennel the last 5 minutes and let lightly brown. Salt lightly. Pour in vermouth (if you wish) and water, cover, and bake in a preheated 350° oven for 45 minutes. Remove fennel halves and glaze with thickened pan juices. (Reduce liquids by boiling rapidly if necessary before glazing.) (*Serves 4*)

- *Sliced Braised Fennel*: Slice the fennel lengthwise into ½-inch pieces, keeping the core to retain the fan

shape. Proceed as above, sautéing in batches and layering the slices before braising. Add thin slices of ham, cooked sausage, or chicken for a heartier dish.
- Gently simmer on top of the stove, checking after 20 minutes to see if done. Watch to make sure the liquid doesn't boil away.
- Sprinkle the cooked dish with grated cheese and run under the broiler to melt.
- Braise in stock or tomato sauce. Remember, the stronger the stock, the more likely the fennel taste will be overpowered.

Special Information

Yields
- 1 pound fennel with 1-inch stalk = approximately 12 ounces trimmed = 2½–3 cups chopped or sliced = 2¼ cups cooked

Storage and Preserving
- Fennel freezes, cans, and stores poorly. In the refrigerator, it will keep for 3–4 days; stored in a cellar, it will hold 2 weeks at best. Enjoy it fresh.

Hints
- Sprinkle chopped fennel leaves on hot baked oysters or clams.
- Add cooked fennel to omelets, quiches, stuffings, or sauces.
- Use stalks as containers for fish or chicken salad. Separate and steam for 5 minutes to tenderize, then cool and stuff.
- Add stalks to stocks for their flavor.
- Add sliced sautéed fennel to fish chowders.
- Cook fennel in your favorite tomato sauce.
- Place stalks and leaves on barbecue coals as they do in France. The fennel scent permeates the grilled food.
- Slice steamed or blanched fennel, cover with a *Vinaigrette Sauce* (see *Appendix*), and serve chilled.
- Chop raw fennel fine and add to tuna fish sandwiches.
- Slice fennel thin and layer with raw potatoes, cream, and cheese to make a potato au gratin.
- Use stalks as a natural, aromatic "rack" in a roasting pan. Set poultry or meat roast on stalks.

Microwave
- 2 trimmed bulbs each weighing approximately 12 ounces placed in a covered dish with ¼ cup water cook tender in 8–10 minutes.

Leftovers
- Use just like leftover celery.
- Try in meat loaves, hamburgers. Purée and add to soups, custard timbales, soufflés, or mashed potatoes.

◇ *Blanched Fennel*

Wash and trim fennel bulbs, retaining ⅛ inch of the root base to hold the fennel intact. Halve or quarter it if large, but the texture is best when blanched whole. Boil for approximately 10 minutes, depending upon the size and age of the bulbs. (A trimmed 12-ounce bulb will be ready in that time.) Test with a pointed knife. The fennel should be cooked through, yet firm. Drain.

◇ *Steamed Fennel*

Wash and trim fennel bulbs, leaving ⅛ inch of the root base to hold fennel together. Bring 1 inch of water in steamer to a boil, place fennel on rack or in a colander over water, cover tightly, and steam until tender. If you're planning to cook the fennel further, the cooking time will be 8–15 minutes. To serve immediately, test after 20 minutes by pricking with a sharp knife; the cooking time may be another 10–15 minutes. The fennel should be tender yet firm.

◇ *Sautéed Fennel*

Use this slow sauté to prepare fennel for use in soups and stuffings, to sauté with other vegetables, or serve simply as is.

Wash and trim bulbs; quarter without removing the core, which holds the layers together. Then, holding the wedge on a cutting surface with one hand, with the other hand thinly slice fennel around the core. Cook in a butter

or a butter-oil combination over medium-low heat until softened, approximately 15 minutes. Add seasonings and serve.

- For a dietetic version omit butter and cook in stock.
- Add sautéed fennel to pasta along with a sprinkling of olive oil, plenty of fresh grated cheese, salt, and freshly ground pepper.
- Sauté 1 chopped clove of garlic and 1 chopped onion along with fennel. Drain a can of peeled tomatoes and stew with fennel for 5 minutes. Bake with grated cheese with buttered bread crumbs on top at 400° until brown and bubbly.
- Cook in butter until wilted and soft; coat with heavy cream and serve on toast. Sprinkle with chopped upper leaves.

Fast Sauté of Fennel and Mushrooms

Stir-frying retains fennel's anise flavor, and the chopped leaves reinforce the taste as well as adding color.

> 1 large fennel bulb with leaves
> ½ lb whole mushrooms
> 3 Tb butter
> 1 Tb oil
> Salt and freshly ground pepper

Wash and trim fennel, then quarter and thinly slice bulb, discarding core; you should have 2½–3 cups sliced fennel. Mince ¼ cup leaves and set aside. Slice mushrooms the same thickness as fennel. Heat 1 tablespoon butter and the oil, and when foamy, add mushrooms and cook over medium-high heat until browned, about 3 minutes; remove and set aside. Add remaining butter and fennel to pan, and cook over medium heat until fennel is softened but still crunchy. Add mushrooms and stir together for a moment. Season with salt and pepper and stir in minced fennel leaves. *(Serves 4)*

Fennel Mornay

When you need to be away from home all day, make this dish in the morning and pop it in the oven at dinner time. Add bread and fruit and your meal is complete. Don't overcook the fennel; it should stay tenderly crunchy.

> 2 lb fennel bulbs with 1-inch stalks
> 4 slices bacon or ham
> *Mornay Sauce* (page 350)
> ⅓ cup combined grated Parmesan and Swiss cheese
> 4 tsp butter

Wash and trim fennel bulbs and blanch or steam until barely tender, 10–20 minutes, and cool. Halve bulbs, core, then slice or coarsely chop. You should have 4–4½ cups fennel. Cook bacon and crumble, or mince ham fine. Set aside. Make Mornay sauce. Then, butter an oven proof 1½-quart dish, layer half the fennel, sprinkle with half the bacon or ham, cover with half the Mornay sauce, and repeat layers once again. Cover with cheese and dot with butter. Bake in a preheated 400° oven for 15 minutes or until bubbly. Brown under the broiler. *(Serves 4–6)*

Fennel with Parmesan Cheese

Fennel is simply delicious baked with Parmesan cheese.

> 2 lb fennel bulbs with 1-inch stalks
> ½ cup freshly grated Parmesan cheese
> 3 Tb butter
> Salt and freshly ground pepper

Wash and trim fennel bulbs and blanch or steam until tender but firm, 8–15 minutes (or less if freshly picked). Cool to touch and quarter, leaving a thin layer of the core to hold the fennel together, and arrange, cut side up, in a

buttered 1½-quart baking dish. Cover with grated cheese and dabs of butter; season with salt and pepper. Bake in a preheated 400° oven for 20–25 minutes or until the cheese is brown. *(Serves 4)*

Batter-Fried Fennel

Batter-frying seals fennel and gives it a nutlike flavor which goes well with grilled fish and tomatoes. These should be eaten immediately after frying so they don't get soggy.

> 3 lb fennel bulbs with 1-inch stalks
> Vegetable oil
> *Frying Batter* (page 345)
> Salt and freshly ground pepper
> Lemon wedges

Wash and trim fennel bulbs and slice lengthwise through the core, keeping slices ¼ inch thick. Heat 1 inch of oil to 375° in a saucepan or deep-fat fryer. With a fork, dip fennel slices into batter, lifting up to drain any excess batter. Fry until both sides are golden brown. Remove from oil, drain for a moment on brown paper, and keep warm in a low oven while you prepare the remaining fennel. Season with salt and pepper and serve with lemon wedges. *(Serves 4)*

Marinated Fennel

Raw fennel is crisp and unusually delightful-tasting. Serve it instead of celery as part of a crudités platter or à la Grecque (see *Mixed Vegetables*). Stuff it with cheese, or eat plain with salt. Or try this simple marinade.

> 1 lb fennel bulb with 1-inch stalk
> 1 Tb lemon juice
> Salt and freshly ground pepper
> ⅓ cup olive oil

Wash, trim, and quarter fennel, then finely slice it, discarding the core. Mix lemon juice with salt and pepper and gradually beat in oil. Marinate fennel in this mixture, covered, for 2 hours. *(Serves 4)*

Fennel, Endive, and Tomato Salad

This colorful salad shines at a buffet dinner when a leafy green salad might be too bulky and difficult to eat.

> 2 large fennel bulbs with leaves
> 2–3 Belgian endives
> 3 large tomatoes
> 1 recipe *Vinaigrette Sauce* made with garlic (page 352)
> Salt and freshly ground pepper

Wash, trim, and quarter fennel, then finely slice it, discarding the cores. Mince ¼ cup of the feathery leaves, and set aside. Wash and dry endives and slice diagonally into rings approximately ½ inch wide. Peel, seed, and juice tomatoes; halve and thinly slice. Combine all ingredients in vinaigrette. Season with salt and pepper and toss with the minced upper leaves. *(Serves 4–6)*
- Experiment with other vegetable additions such as avocado or radishes.

Cream of Fennel Soup

Fennel is ideal for soups; its delicate flavor is a light beginning for the meal to come.

> 1–1½ lb fennel bulb with 1-inch stalk
> 1 medium onion
> 4 Tb butter
> 2 Tb flour
> 3 cups chicken stock
> 1 egg yolk
> ½ cup light cream
> Salt and freshly ground pepper

Wash, trim, and cut fennel into quarters, reserving any feathery upper leaves to garnish the soup. Then, finely slice or dice, discarding the cores. Mince onion. Melt butter in a 4-quart saucepan and slowly sauté fennel and onion until wilted and softened, approximately 15 minutes. Sprinkle on flour and, stirring, cook for 3–4 minutes. Add chicken stock and, whisking, remove any flour lumps. Bring to a boil, lower heat, and cook for 15–20 minutes to soften slightly, then remove from stove.

In a small bowl whisk together the egg yolk and cream. Gradually add small amounts of the hot soup to the egg mixture to warm. Then slowly add the egg mixture to the soup, whisking constantly. Heat, without boiling, and season with salt and pepper. Garnish with minced fennel leaves. *(Serves 4)*

- For a smoother texture, purée the soup before adding the egg mixture.

Fennel, Bean, and Tomato Soup

My family really appreciates a hearty soup, especially when it's something out of the ordinary—such as this unusual trio of fennel, beans, and tomatoes.

> 1/2 cup dry white beans, such as Great Northern
> 3 lb fennel bulbs with 1-inch stalks
> 4 Tb olive oil
> 4 Tb butter
> 2 cups combined sliced onions and leeks
> 2 cups chicken stock
> 1 bay leaf
> 1 tsp dried thyme
> 2 Tb tomato purée
> Salt
> 2 lb tomatoes
> 2 cloves garlic
> 1/4 cup chopped shallots
> Freshly ground pepper
> Parsley

Add beans to 8 cups of boiling water, cook for 2 minutes, remove from heat, cover, and soak for 1 hour. Wash and trim fennel. Discard the tough outer layers and reserve any feathery upper leaves for garnishing. Then, separate fennel layers and thinly slice the tender inner layers for final garnish; you should end up with 2 cups, set aside. Slice the remaining fennel (approximately 8 cups).

Heat 3 tablespoons olive oil and 3 tablespoons butter in a large saucepan or casserole. Add the onions and leeks and the 8 cups fennel and cook until golden; then cover and cook over low heat until wilted, approximately 15 minutes. Add beans and their soaking liquid plus chicken stock, bay leaf, thyme, tomato purée, and 2 teaspoons salt. Bring to a boil, reduce heat, partially cover, and simmer for 1 1/2 hours, or until the beans are tender. Put through a food mill or food processor, being careful to roughly purée only so that the finished soup will have texture; set aside.

Peel, seed, juice, and dice the tomatoes; mash garlic. Heat 1 tablespoon olive oil and 1 tablespoon butter and sauté reserved 2 cups finely sliced fennel for approximately 10 minutes, until lightly colored but not browned. Add tomatoes, shallots, and garlic, stir together, cover, and cook for 5–10 minutes. Remove cover and cook 10 minutes longer, or until the tomato juices are evaporated. Add to fennel and bean purée, reheat, and season to taste. Garnish with chopped fennel and parsley leaves. *(Serves 8–10)*

- For a heartier meal, during the last 40 minutes of cooking add Italian sausages made with fennel seed, which have been pricked and simmered for 10 minutes to remove fat. Simmer with the fennel and beans, remove, slice, and add just before reheating.
- For a simple fennel and bean soup, use 2 pounds fennel and omit the tomato-fennel mixture. Purée and add cream to taste. Serve hot or cold.

Baked Bluefish with Fennel

The delicate flavors of fennel and fish are mutually enhancing. Serve fennel as a side dish to fish topped with brown butter, stuff it into a whole fish, or, as below, bake it along with fish fillets. I bake the bluefish on top of the fennel so that the fish and fennel flavor each other, but I separate them when serving so that each texture can be enjoyed for itself.

> 2 lb fennel bulbs with 1-inch stalks
> 2 Tb vegetable oil
> 4 Tb butter
> 2 lb bluefish fillets
> 1 Bermuda onion
> 8 flat anchovies
> Salt and freshly ground pepper
> Lemon wedges

Wash and trim fennel and cut into 1/2-inch slices lengthwise. (You should have 8 slices altogether.) Melt 2 tablespoons oil and 2 tablespoons butter in a frying pan and brown fennel. Cook for 10 minutes or until slightly softened, and place in a buttered baking dish. Skin bluefish fillets if you wish and cut into 4 portions. Slice onion into thin rings. Place bluefish on fennel, lay 2 anchovy slices on each portion, and cover with onion; dot with remaining butter and sprinkle with salt and pepper. Bake in a preheated 400° oven for 15–20 minutes, depending upon the thickness of the fish. Then run under the broiler to brown. Serve with lemon wedges. *(Serves 4)*

- Bluefish is a rich dark fish. If you want a more subtle flavor, use striped bass or sea bass and omit the anchovies. Sprinkle with chopped fennel leaves if you have them and serve with a *Lemon Butter Sauce* (see *Appendix*) on the side.

Stuffed Fennel

These fennel boats are particularly nice cooked with a braised bird, especially a succulent capon. Stuffing the capon's cavity with the fennel trimmings flavors the flesh with a delicate perfume. These boats can be cooked, however, just as they are for a satisfying vegetarian dish.

> *Stuffed Fennel Boats*
> 3 large fennel bulbs with leaves
> 1/4 cup chopped parsley
> Salt
> 1 lb whole eggplant
> 3 large ripe tomatoes or half fresh and half canned peeled tomatoes
> 1 medium onion

2 cloves garlic
3 Tb oil
Freshly ground pepper
$^1/_2$ cup chicken stock

Wash and trim fennel bulbs, leaving $^1/_8$ inch of the root base to hold the bulb together. Each bulb should weigh approximately 12 ounces. Chop $^1/_4$ cup of the leaves and combine with parsley; set aside. Save remaining trimmings, stalks, and leaves if you are braising the capon below. Blanch the fennel bulbs in salted water until barely tender, 8–10 minutes. Remove, cool, and then halve lengthwise, and remove the small center layers. Finely chop these fennel layers and set aside. Cut away most of the core, leaving just enough to retain shape. You will end up with 6 fennel halves to stuff.

Peel the eggplant and dice into $^1/_4$ inch pieces. Salt and let drain in a colander for 20 minutes. Peel, seed, and chop tomatoes. If they are pale or out of season, use half fresh and half canned peeled and drained tomatoes. Chop onion and garlic. Dry the eggplant, sauté in oil to lightly brown. Add onion and garlic and cook with eggplant for 2–3 minutes. Add tomatoes, cover pan, and cook for 10 minutes to soften eggplant and release tomato juices. Remove cover and cook 10 minutes longer, or until juices are evaporated.

Stir in the reserved chopped fennel and half of the reserved parsley-fennel mixture; season with salt and pepper to taste. Remove the vegetables and boil down remaining juices to form a glaze. Pour it over the vegetable mixture. Stuff the fennel boats with the vegetable mixture, mounding it up in each boat. (Reserve any extra

stuffing for *Braised Capon with Fennel Boats* or heat separately as a vegetable dish.) Place the boats in an ovenproof dish, add chicken stock, cover, and bake in a pre-

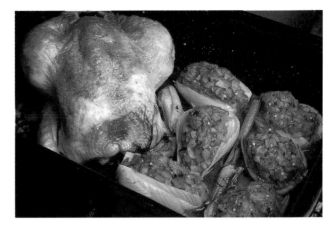

heated 350° oven for 30 minutes. Or braise alongside capon, duck, turkey, etc., during the last 30 minutes of cooking. Before serving, garnish each stuffed boat with a sprinkling of the remaining parsley-fennel mixture. (*Makes 6 fennel boats*)

Braised Capon with Fennel Boats
Fennel trimmings from recipe above
2 onions
8 Tb butter
1 medium carrot
6–7-lb capon
Salt and freshly ground pepper
2 Tb oil
$^1/_2$ cup white vermouth
1 cup chicken stock
1 recipe *Stuffed Fennel Boats*, unbaked

Chop enough fennel trimmings and leaves to make 4 cups. Chop onions. Cook chopped fennel and half the onions in 4 tablespoons butter until wilted, about 10 minutes. Set aside to cool. Chop carrot and combine with remaining onion. Remove fat from cavity of capon, wash and dry capon. Salt and pepper the inside and stuff with the fennel and onion mixture. Truss. Brown capon slowly for 10 minutes in 4 tablespoons butter and oil in a large ovenproof casserole, watching to see that butter does not burn. Cover and put into a 400° oven for 10 minutes to render fat. Remove, pour off fat, and reduce oven temperature to 350°. Set casserole on burner, add chopped onions and carrot, vermouth and stock and any leftover vegetable mixture from *Stuffed Fennel Boats*. Bring to simmer. Cover and cook in oven for 1$^1/_2$ hours or until juices run clear yellow.

Thirty minutes before the capon is done, surround with the stuffed fennel halves. When the capon is cooked, remove from the casserole and keep warm along with the fennel boats. Degrease the pan juices and mash any vegetables in the juice to a pulp. Boil to thicken, if necessary. Carve the capon and serve with fennel boats. Sauce with thickened pan juices.

Note: A 7-pound capon will serve more than 6; increase the fennel and stuffing accordingly. Allow 1 fennel bulb for 2 people.

• A dash of Pernod in the sauce adds to the anise flavor.

Easy Stuffing for Fish or Poultry

1 large fennel bulb with leaves
2 Tb chopped shallots
2 Tb olive oil
2 Tb butter
1 large clove garlic
Salt and freshly ground pepper
Pernod (optional)

Wash and trim fennel, reserving the feathery top leaves, then finely chop, discarding the core. Sauté shallots in olive oil and butter for 3 minutes without browning. Chop 2–3 tablespoons leaves and garlic and add to pan along with fennel; stew slowly, covered, checking occasionally to make sure the mixture doesn't brown, for 20–30 minutes or until tender. Season with salt and pepper and a splash of Pernod if desired. *(Makes 1½–2 cups)*
  • Add 1 egg and bread crumbs for a more substantial stuffing.

Fennel and Cheese for Dessert

Fennel bulbs
One excellent cheese, such as Gorgonzola or a creamy
  goat cheese
Cruet of good-quality olive oil
Salt and freshly ground pepper

Wash and trim fennel bulbs. If small, cut in half; quarter larger ones. Serve with wedges of cheese and pass the oil, salt, and pepper.

Greens

I seriously started cooking with greens only when Russ presented me with some of the different varieties grown in the Victory Garden. Quickly, I discovered that their range of flavors was more diverse than I expected. Collard greens, for example, are quite mild, mustard greens bitter indeed, and most greens fall somewhere in between. I don't know how the delicious broccoli de rabe had escaped my notice all those years. Greens grow fast, come along when little else in the garden is ready, and most important, their slightly sharp yet pleasant flavor sets off other foods quite remarkably.

For the purposes of this section, when I talk about greens I mean leafy vegetables such as beet, collard, and turnip leaves, the Italian broccoli de rabe (also known simply as rabe and rape), mustard greens, and dandelion greens (see *Salad Greens* for other suggestions). Kale, spinach, and Swiss chard are also part of the greens family, but I treat them in individual sections since we devote more garden space to them.

Although we've grown most of these greens in the Victory Garden, their growing requirements differ considerably. I'll give you general thoughts about growing greens here, and refer you to the *Types of Greens* list for more specific growing information.

Most greens tolerate cold temperatures and can be directly sown in the garden once the soil can be worked. They grow fast, often giving a harvest after 1½ months. Successive sowings at 2-week intervals will give you a steady supply throughout the spring and into the summer. An August planting will provide fall greens as well. Because greens are mostly water, water regularly so they don't experience a growth check and become excessively bitter. Although it's tempting to let the leaves grow as big as possible, most greens have a less bitter taste when harvested at a small or medium size.

Harvest by cutting off the outer leaves at the base of the plants. Many greens will continue to produce if you leave the central growing tip untouched.

Before cooking, all greens need a thorough washing in lukewarm water to remove soil and aphids.

I leave young beet, turnip, and mustard leaves whole, only removing any thick stems. Large greens need stemming: fold each leaf together so that the stem is on one side. Then, holding the leaf in one hand, with the other hand pull the stem down. It comes right off the leaf. We pick broccoli de rabe young enough so that it's totally edible. However, as the outer skin tends to be stringy, I always peel the stems—an absolutely essential step and what I consider to be the secret to success with rabe.

Greens are frequently cooked incorrectly. Although they are much appreciated in southern cooking, I think many people shy away from planting and cooking greens because they associate them with mushy gray overcooked vegetables. When greens are cooked too long, they become watery, grayish in color, and limp and soggy. I feel the best way to prepare larger greens is to cook them only for a short period of time in a flavored broth. After experimenting with both water and broth, I have decided that mature greens most definitely benefit from simmering in a ham-flavored bouillon rather than water. This bouillon base achieves optimum flavor and is easy to make (page 130). For example, mustard and turnip greens, which can be bitter almost to a fault if sautéed, retain their bite yet are mellowed by the bouillon. The bouillon also adds a lovely, almost soft aftertaste that makes strongly flavored greens quite palatable.

Don't discard the bouillon after cooking. Southerners call the bouillon "pot likker" and often dunk cornbread in it. Since this liquid is loaded with nutrients and has a smoky ham flavor, it is a natural soup base. To gain

an even stronger flavor and vitamin content, tie up the stems and cook them in the liquid—or boil it down to concentrate flavor.

Large greens are the only vegetable I know that can retain their identity with this kind of smoky flavoring. (Cooking in boiling salted water is all right, but the mature greens will never have as mellow a flavor.) Two exceptions are the milder beet greens and broccoli de rabe, which can be steamed or blanched in plain water.

I usually do not sauté raw greens. However, tiny greens, such as baby beet, turnip, and mustard greens, accept a sauté. Slightly larger greens can be finely sliced and sauté-braised. Steamed greens keep their color and cook in about the same time as blanched greens, but can develop an unpleasant bitter taste.

One warning: greens cook down to one-quarter to one-eighth their original volume, depending upon the type. For larger greens, that's leaf volume minus stems! Note *Yields* under Special Information—each green loses raw bulk at a different ratio.

Although I treat spinach, kale, and Swiss chard as separate entries, substitute them in *Greens* recipes and vice versa. Turnip greens make a good replacement for kale in *Calzone*, kale could be interchanged for collards in *Lentil and Collard Soup*, while any green would be good in *American Spinach Frittata*. Experiment. Once you become accustomed to the amounts needed—and the blanching method—mix and match as you fancy. Above all, remember that greens' unique bite perks up the flavor of more subtle vegetables. To see for yourself, try the *Mixed Greens Sauté*.

Marketing
Look for fresh, springy greens. As greens are largely water, once they are wilted it is difficult to revive them. Do not buy greens that are soft, yellowed, or dried out.

Types of Greens
If I had to classify greens according to their bite, I would start at the mild end of the scale with baby beet greens. Next would be mature beet greens, collards, broccoli de rabe, and dandelion, followed by the sharpest-flavored greens of turnip and mustard. (See also *Spinach; Kale; Swiss Chard.*)

Beet Greens: Look for varieties grown for their leaves. Sow once the ground can be worked, thin, keep well watered, and harvest young. Steam or sauté in butter. (See *Beets* for more extensive directions.)

Broccoli de Rabe: This is an unusual medium-sharp flavored green widely grown in Italy. It has edible stems and small bud clusters. Seeds can be hard to find, but DeGeorgi and Herbst both stock spring and fall varieties. In the Northeast we make 2 sowings. *Spring sowing:* As the plants don't mind crowding, sow seeds closely

Special Information

Yields
- *Whole Baby Beet and Turnip Greens:* Use all of vegetable. 4 cups raw = approximately 1 cup cooked
- *Mature Beet Greens:* 1 pound = 11 ounces trimmed leaves = 8 cups lightly packed = 1½ cups cooked
- *Broccoli de Rabe:* Use the whole vegetable after peeling the stems. 1 pound = 14–16 cups loosely packed = 4 cups cooked
- *Collards:* 2 pounds with stems = 1 pound stemmed. 14–16 cups packed leaves = 3 cups cooked
- *Mustard Greens:* 1 pound = 6 ounces leaves (stems removed) = 6 cups packed leaves = 1½ cups cooked
- *Turnip Greens:* 1 pound = 9 ounces leaves (stems removed) = 9–10 cups packed leaves = 1½–2 cups cooked
- *Dandelions:* 1 pound = 6–8 ounces leaves (stems removed) = 6–8 cups packed leaves = 1½–2 cups cooked
- Allow ½ cup cooked greens per person

Storage and Preserving
- To store greens, leave them unwashed and wrap them in a damp towel. Place them in a perforated plastic bag and refrigerate. By changing the towel occasionally, and keeping it damp, you'll be able to store the greens up to a week.
- Greens freeze well. Wash, then blanch for 2 minutes, drain, and plunge into ice water. Chill for 2 minutes; drain. Pack in freezer containers. Use within 6 months.

Hints
- Wash greens carefully for insects and soil clinging to the undersides of the leaves.
- Most greens are interchangeable in recipes. Be aware that some are stronger-flavored than others.
- Use more than one type of greens in a recipe. Combine stronger-flavored greens such as turnip and mustard greens with milder types such as kale, collards, or spinach.
- Remember that spinach, kale, and Swiss chard are all greens, too (which have their own chapters). Many recipes in those sections work for greens, and vice versa.
- Greens add color and flavor to soups and stews. However, if they are particularly bitter, it is best to blanch them before adding, otherwise they will make the completed dish bitter.
- Use dandelion greens and radish tops in the following greens recipes.
- A cream or velouté sauce mellows bitter greens.

together, thinning to 3 inches apart. Pick in 50 days, or when the buds enlarge. Broccoli de rabe is less stringy on the top 6–7 inches. *Fall sowing:* Sow seeds in August and harvest in mid-October. The foliage is less broad than the spring variety. Blanch or steam both varieties.

Collards: This is a cabbagelike green with large, smooth leaves and a softer, smoother taste than either mustard or turnip greens. We sow collard seedlings in July, spacing them at 3-inch intervals, thinning to 6 inches apart in early August and to 24 inches apart in late August. Each time they are thinned, Russ scratches in some 10-10-10 fertilizer to encourage growth. As long as the plant tip is untouched, collards produce leaves for weeks. Harvest after the first frost. Cook in bouillon.

Dandelion Greens: Look for horticultural varieties that have more tender, longer leaves than wild plants. Dandelions will take acid soils. A year passes before a harvest, so pick a permanent bed for the crop. Sow seeds directly into the ground in late spring and thin plants to 10 inches apart in rows 15 inches apart. Allow the plants to develop roots the first year. During the second spring the plants quickly develop. For the most delicate flavor, blanch the growing leaves by tying at the top. Harvest before the flower buds appear. As the plants have a slightly bitter taste, cook in a bouillon.

Mustard Greens: Sow seed directly in the garden 2 weeks before the last spring frost, and continue successive sowing until the weather gets hot. Thin plants to 10 inches apart in rows 15 inches apart. Mustard needs less water than other greens. The leaves are ready to harvest approximately 1½ months after sowing. For a late fall crop, sow seeds in August. Blanch to cut down on the bitter taste, and cook in a bouillon.

Turnip Greens: Plant varieties developed for greens, such as Shogoin, which matures in 40–50 days. Sow seeds in midspring in rows 12–15 inches apart. Thin seedlings to 2–4 inches apart. For a continuous harvest, sow seeds at 2-week intervals until warm weather. The leaves will be ready for harvesting approximately 5–6 weeks after planting. For a fall crop, sow seeds in late August or early September. Pick young. In fall, an Italian variety called Rapini is available. Cook in a bouillon and expect a sharp taste.

Left to right: collards, mustard greens, dandelion greens, beet greens, broccoli de rabe, turnip greens.

- Young greens and mild greens such as beet greens and broccoli de rabe do not need to cook in a "bouillon." Cook them instead in salted boiling water until barely tender.
- Serve cooked greens with a cruet of red wine vinegar.
- Garnishes enhance cooked greens. Try chopped cooked bacon or chopped onion, served with fried toast pieces.
- Serve cooked broccoli de rabe at room temperature with a good lemon vinaigrette.
- Beet, dandelion, and other young greens are excellent, replacing spinach in *Wilted Spinach Salad* (see *Spinach*).
- Cook baby turnips and greens together (see *Baby Beets and Beet Greens* in *Beets*).
- Top *Sautéed Chopped Cooked Greens* with poached eggs and a grilled ham slice (optional), or use poached chicken breasts with a light *Hollandaise Sauce* (see *Appendix*) topping.
- Substitute broccoli de rabe (either alone or with other greens) for kale in *Turkey Breast with Kale* (see *Kale*).
- Combine blanched broccoli de rabe and cooked fresh shell beans (see *Beans*). Toss together in skillet with olive oil and minced garlic. Add ¼ cup cooking liquid, cover pan, and reheat for 5–10 minutes. Season to taste before serving.

Microwave

Since I believe cooking greens in a flavored bouillon is the best method, I do not normally use the microwave for greens. You can use it, however, as a preliminary "blanch" before further cooking preparations with the stronger flavored greens and also to cook the milder greens and then season or sauce them to taste. All greens keep their color nicely.

- Times vary slightly. For example: ½ pound collard leaves in a covered dish with just the moisture clinging to leaves takes 6 minutes to just tender. Half-pound peeled broccoli de rabe in a covered dish with just the water clinging to its leaves takes 4 minutes to just tender.

Leftovers

- Mix greens into omelets.
- Use in quiches or substitute for kale in *Kale Pie* (see *Kale*).
- Make into timbales or a soufflé as in the *Spinach* recipes.
- Use in dried bean soups.

◇ _Steamed Greens_

I recommend steaming only beet greens and very young mild broccoli de rabe. Boil 1 inch of water in a steamer and place greens in the steamer basket. Steam until done. Mixed sizes of beet greens take approximately 6 minutes, depending on their age and the amount used. Very young beet greens will cook in 3–4 minutes. Broccoli de rabe cut into 2–3-inch pieces will cook in 5–6 minutes, depending upon its age and the amount used.

◇ _Blanched or Boiled Greens_

Use either the following "bouillon" or boiling salted water.

Bouillon: Boil water with 1 medium or 2 small ham hocks, a flavorful ham bone (such as one from a Smithfield ham) or a piece of smoked ham. Use plenty of water so the greens can simmer in the liquid and be adequately covered. If you like, add an onion or crushed red pepper flakes. Simmer for 30 minutes to 1 hour. Remove ham.

Blanch the greens for a short amount of time—it depends on the size and age of the greens. Mature collard leaves take 8–15 minutes to cook, as do most large mature greens. Broccoli de rabe takes 4–5 minutes. Beet greens and young turnip and mustard greens take 5–8 minutes. Baby greens cook in a moment. Judge by eye and taste.

Finishing Touches for Steamed or Blanched Greens

Baby greens need nothing more than draining, a dot of butter, and seasonings to taste. Larger greens benefit from any of the following finishing touches:
- _Cooked Greens Sautéed in Oil and Garlic:_ Chop or slice 3 cups cooked greens, and gently press to remove moisture. Heat 2–3 tablespoons olive oil in a sauté pan and throw in 1–2 whole garlic cloves. Add greens and sauté over high heat to evaporate any moisture, reduce heat, and cook until heated through. Remove garlic cloves, season to taste, and serve.
- _Sautéed Chopped Cooked Greens:_ Chop 3 cups cooked greens. Gently press out moisture. Heat 2 tablespoons butter in a large sauté pan, add 1 cup finely chopped onions, sauté to wilt, and add greens. Cook over high heat to evaporate moisture. Stir in 3–4 tablespoons butter. Cook over low heat for 5–10 minutes, stirring occasionally so that greens absorb the butter. Season to taste and serve.
  To cut down on the butter, braise the greens in either broth or cream. After evaporating the moisture, stir in 1–2 tablespoons flour and cook for a moment. Mix in thoroughly 1 cup broth, milk, or cream. Cook slowly, stirring occasionally, for 8–10 minutes, or until liquid is absorbed. Season and serve.
- _Greens with Béchamel Sauce:_ Prepare greens as in _Sautéed Chopped Cooked Greens_, stopping before braising in butter. Instead, fold greens into a _Béchamel Sauce_ (see _Appendix_). Put into a buttered baking dish, sprinkling the top with either grated cheese or buttered bread crumbs. Dot with butter, and bake in a preheated 375° oven until top is brown and bubbly.
- _Greens with Mornay Sauce:_ Prepare greens as with _Greens with Béchamel_, but use _Mornay Sauce_ (see _Appendix_) rather than béchamel.
- _Ham and Greens with Mornay Sauce:_ Prepare _Sautéed Chopped Cooked Greens_. Place ¼ cup greens into each of 12 ham slices; roll up. Put a few spoonfuls of _Mornay Sauce_ (see _Appendix_) in a buttered baking dish, and line the dish with the rolled ham slices. Cover with the Mornay sauce, sprinkle with cheese, and dot with butter. Bake in a preheated 375° oven until ham is heated through and top is browned.
- Add sliced, sautéed mushrooms to the greens.

◇ _Sautéed Baby Greens:_

Wash and dry raw baby beet or turnip greens. Leave greens whole if very small; cut diagonally if they are larger. Remove stems only if they're dried out or particularly thick. Sauté the greens in a butter-oil combination for 2–3 minutes or until they are wilted and tender. Season with salt and pepper to taste.
- Add shallots, finely minced onion, or garlic to the butter and sauté for a minute before adding the greens.

◇ _Sauté-Braised Greens_

Medium-size greens benefit from this sauté-braise method. I think this is particularly good with beet greens, collards, and broccoli de rabe. Stronger-flavored turnip and mustard greens should be blanched first. Strip the leaves from the stems (except in the case of rabe, which merely needs peeling). Wash greens well, dry, and cut into diagonal strips. Heat butter, oil, or a combination of both in a large sauté pan and add the greens, tossing until they are coated with butter and are starting to wilt. Add a bit of liquid, cover, and braise gently to finish cooking. Uncover the pan and cook until the moisture evaporates. Toss with additional butter or oil, if necessary.
- Add a garlic clove, chopped shallots, or onions to oil before cooking.

Mixed Greens Sauté

This is a lovely combination of both color and flavor, for the vegetables are three shades of green and are both sharp and mild.

> ½ medium (¾ lb) cabbage
> 2 cups blanched collards
> 2 cups blanched broccoli de rabe
> 3 Tb olive oil
> 4 Tb butter
> 2 whole cloves garlic, peeled
> Salt and freshly ground pepper

Divide cabbage in two and blanch in boiling water for 8–10 minutes, until leaves are softened. Cool under cold

running water, then gently squeeze to remove water, and cut into ¹/₂-inch shreds. You should end up with 4 cups. Gently squeeze water out of collards and broccoli de rabe and slice into shreds or diagonal slices. Heat oil and 1 tablespoon of the butter in a large sauté pan, and add garlic, cabbage, and greens. Stir over high heat until moisture is evaporated, add remaining butter, season with salt and pepper, and cook gently for 5–10 minutes, stirring, until heated through. Remove garlic cloves before serving. *(Serves 4–6)*

- For smaller portion omit blanching. Wash, trim, and slice cabbage, and slice cabbage and greens into shreds or diagonal slices. Cook as in *Sauté-Braised Greens* (page 130).
- Braise in broth rather than in butter.
- Add seasonings such as celery seeds.
- Use this mixture in *Calzone Stuffed with Kale* (see *Kale*) or as a replacement for kale in *Turkey Breast with Kale* (see *Kale*).
- Substitute spinach for collards.

Greens with Potatoes and Onions

Here's a handy dish for leftover boiled potatoes and greens.

> 5 Tb butter
> 2 cups chopped cooked greens
> Salt and freshly ground pepper
> 1¹/₂ cups sliced onions
> *Béchamel Sauce* (page 346)
> 2 cups sliced cooked potatoes
> ²/₃ cup grated cheese (such as a combination of Swiss, mozzarella, and Parmesan)

Melt 2 tablespoons of the butter in a sauté pan, add chopped greens, and sauté over high heat until moisture is evaporated. Season to taste with salt and pepper; set aside. In the same pan, melt 2 tablespoons of the butter and sauté the onions until lightly browned. Butter a 9-inch square baking dish. Smooth some béchamel sauce

into the pan. Layer potatoes and sprinkle with salt and pepper. Place onions on top of the potatoes. First, spoon on half the remaining béchamel sauce, then sprinkle on half the cheese. Cover with greens. Pour over the remaining sauce, sprinkle with the remaining cheese, and dot with butter. Bake in a preheated 375° oven for 30 minutes or until heated through and lightly browned on top. *(Serves 4–6)*

- Replace sliced potatoes with sliced cooked turnips. Top with turnip greens.
- Use leftover mashed potatoes. Reheat, then whip with a bit of butter and hot milk. Fold béchamel sauce only into greens.
- Omit the béchamel sauce. Place well-buttered, seasoned greens on the bottom of the dish, and cover with whipped potatoes beaten with butter, milk, and an egg yolk. Dot with butter and bake.
- Top with buttered bread crumbs.

Collards and Rice

Raw collards are mild enough to be added directly to a dish. This quick combination keeps all the nutrients in one pot.

> 2 cups chicken broth
> 1 cup long-grained rice
> 1 Tb butter
> ¹/₂ tsp salt
> 3 loosely packed cups chopped raw collard leaves
> Freshly ground pepper

Boil broth; add the rice, butter, and salt. Stir once, and add collards, handful by handful, stirring constantly. Cover, bring to a boil, reduce heat, and cook until the rice is done, approximately 20 minutes. Season to taste. *(Serves 4)*

- When rice is done, stir in bits of ham or sausage, and heat until just warmed through.

Cream of Broccoli de Rabe Soup

Broccoli de rabe is the Italian green that, as my knowledgeable produce friend Peter says, "has got class." It has a slight bite and adds a pleasant tang to soup.

> 6–8 slices bacon
> 1 cup chopped onions
> 3 cups sliced potatoes
> 6 cups chicken stock
> 2 cups beef stock
> 8 cups peeled and roughly chopped broccoli de rabe
> ¹/₂ cup heavy cream
> Salt and freshly ground pepper

Fry bacon in a large saucepan, crumble, and set aside. Save 2 tablespoons fat, and sauté onions in it until wilted. Add potatoes and stock, bring to a boil, reduce heat, cover, and simmer for 20 minutes or until the potatoes are barely tender. Add broccoli de rabe to broth. Cook for 10–15 minutes or until the greens are tender. Cool slightly, then purée in a blender or food processor. Add cream, reheat, and season to taste. Sprinkle each serving with the chopped bacon bits. *(Makes 2 quarts)*

- You can substitute other greens, such as collards, in this soup, but mature turnip or mustard greens may be too bitter to use without a preliminary blanching.

Lentil and Collard Soup

Greens and legumes are a natural duo. The textures complement each other, and the mild collards do not make the broth too bitter. This soup works equally well with beet greens, Swiss chard, kale, and escarole.

> 2 cups lentils
> 1 qt beef broth
> 1 qt water
> 1 cup chopped leeks
> ½ cup chopped carrots
> 1 small ham hock (optional)
> 2 Tb butter or bacon fat
> ½ cup chopped onions
> ½ cup chopped celery
> 1 Tb chopped garlic (optional)
> 6–8 cups collard leaves sliced in ½-inch strips
> 1 tsp cider vinegar (optional)
> Salt and freshly ground pepper

Wash lentils in cold water and pick over. In a large pot, bring the broth and water to a boil. Add lentils, leeks, carrots, and ham hock (if you wish), and simmer, partially covered, for 30 minutes.

Meanwhile, melt butter or bacon fat in a sauté pan, and cook the onions and celery until wilted and tender, 5–10 minutes. Add garlic (if you like), and stir for 1 minute; set aside. After the lentils have cooked for 30 minutes, stir in the chopped vegetables, collards, and vinegar. Simmer, partially covered, for another 20–30 minutes or until the lentils are tender but not mushy. Season to taste and serve. *(Serves 6–8)*

- For a meal-in-one, add slices of blanched linguica or other sausage, or hot dogs.

Lamb, Tomato, and Greens Stew

This recipe works well with pork, too. Serve the stew with rice.

> 2 lb lamb
> ½ lb smoked sausage or ham
> 3 Tb oil
> 1 Tb chopped garlic
> 1 Tb paprika
> ½ tsp cinnamon
> ½ tsp ground ginger
> 1 tsp salt
> Dash of cayenne pepper
> 2 cups beef broth
> 2½ lb tomatoes, peeled, seeded, and rough-chopped
> 10–12 small white onions
> 3 cups chopped blanched greens

Cut lamb into 1½-inch cubes. Prick and blanch sausage for 5 minutes to release fat; cut sausage (or ham) into ½-inch pieces.

In a large sauté pan, heat oil and lightly brown lamb and sausage (or ham). Add garlic; stir for 1 minute. Then stir in all the spices. Add the broth, bring to a boil, reduce heat, and simmer, covered, for 30 minutes. Uncover, remove fat if necessary, mix in the chopped tomatoes, and simmer, uncovered, for 30 minutes, stirring occasionally. Add onions; simmer 30 minutes longer, or until the tomatoes have cooked into a purée. Gently squeeze the greens to remove moisture; add to the stew. (If they still seem too wet, sauté in 1 tablespoon oil before adding to stew.) Stir together, and cook for another 15 minutes. Season to taste. *(Serves 4–6)*

Smoked Pork Butt Stuffed with Greens

One of the South's most elegant specialties is country ham stuffed with greens. As ham is expensive, I've worked out this plebeian version for everyday meals. Your butcher may balk at removing the bone from a smoked butt, but don't worry: it's easy enough to do yourself. (*Note:* a smoked shoulder works just as well.)

> 1 cup chopped onions
> 3 Tb butter
> 3 cups blanched mixed greens
> ½ tsp crushed red pepper
> Salt and freshly ground pepper
> 1 egg
> 1 smoked pork butt or small pork shoulder

In a large sauté pan, cook onions in butter until wilted and lightly browned. Squeeze moisture out of the greens, rough chop; add to pan, and sauté over high heat to evaporate any remaining moisture. Stir in red pepper, and salt and pepper to taste. Cool slightly, mix in egg, and set aside.

Cover the butt with cold water, bring to a simmer, remove scum, and simmer for 1 hour. Remove from the water and let cool before handling. (The simmering will loosen the meat, making it easy to remove the bone.) Then take a knife, cut down to the bone, and follow it

around, scraping to release the meat. Once you have removed the bone, you are left with practically a butterflied piece of meat. Don't despair. Cut away any little pieces in the center that have become frayed from the boning procedure, chop them, and add to the greens.

Put the stuffing in the center of the meat, roll or fold up the sides of the meat, and sew together with kitchen string. (You can do this ahead and bake later on.) Or, wrap the ham in a double layer of washed cheesecloth, and simmer instead. Roast in a preheated 325° oven for 1½–2 hours or until the shoulder is tender. Apply a favorite glaze if desired. *(Serves 4–6)*

- If you don't want to bother boning the butt, cut slits in the meat and stuff the slits.
- For a lovely cold buffet dish, use a 10–12-pound smoked ham. Soak overnight (or follow package directions), scrub, and bring to the simmer as above. Simmer for 1 hour. Remove. When cool enough to handle, cut slits in the flesh and pack with stuffing, or bone as above. If you bone the butt, double the stuffing. Wrap ham in a double thickness of cheesecloth or washed linen and simmer until tender, approximately 18 minutes per pound. If serving cold, let cool in the cooking liquid, drain, and refrigerate.

Double-Duty Fowl with Greens

A nice fat fowl, a rich broth, and greens form the base for either a soup or a casserole.

Broth and Meat Base
5–6-lb washed fowl
1 large ham hock or a piece of smoked ham
5 qt liquid (½ chicken stock and ½ water)
1 Tb salt
1 celery stalk
1 onion with 3 cloves stuck in it
Herb bouquet:
　6 parsley sprigs
　1 bay leaf
　1 tsp thyme
　2 cloves

Put fowl and ham in a large pot, cover with liquid, and bring to a boil. Skim, then add salt, celery, onion, and herb bouquet. Simmer, partially covered, for 2–2½ hours or until the fowl is completely tender and the flesh is falling off the bones. Remove the fowl and degrease the stock. (If you have time to refrigerate the stock, the fat will solidify and you can lift it right off.) Remove the chicken flesh from the bones and break into pieces. Take the ham meat from the hock. Set both aside.

Greens Soup
2–3 lb mild greens
½ cup rice or farina
Salt and freshly ground pepper
Broth and Meat Base (see above)

Boil broth until reduced to 4 quarts to concentrate flavor. Wash and trim greens; cut into large julienne, and slowly add to boiling broth. After greens have wilted, sprinkle in the rice, stirring constantly. Cook for 15–20 minutes, adding the chicken and ham pieces during the last 5 minutes until heated through. Season to taste. *(Serves 6–8)*

Chicken and Greens Casserole
1½ lb carrots
Salt
1 tsp sugar
2–3 lb greens
3–3½ cups broth from *Broth and Meat Base* (see above)
½ cup chopped onions
10 Tb butter
Salt and freshly ground pepper
4 hard-boiled eggs
6 Tb flour
½ cup heavy cream
½ cup cottage cheese
Reserved chicken and ham pieces from *Broth and Meat Base* (see above)
½ cup grated Swiss or a combination of cheeses

Peel carrots, julienne into 2-inch pieces, and boil in salted water along with sugar for 3–4 minutes. Drain; set aside. Wash, trim, and blanch greens in broth. Drain greens, saving broth. Firmly squeeze greens to remove liquids; chop. In a large frying pan, sauté onions in 3 tablespoons of the butter until wilted and lightly browned. Raise heat, add greens, and cook until moisture is evaporated. Season with salt and pepper; set aside. Slice eggs.

Make a velouté sauce: Melt 6 tablespoons of the butter and stir in the flour. Cook for 2–3 minutes. Whisk in 3 cups broth and the heavy cream, and bring to a boil. Reduce heat and simmer for 15 minutes. Add additional broth if sauce becomes too thick. Purée the cottage cheese and beat into the velouté sauce. Place a layer of greens in a buttered medium-size casserole; cover with one-third of the sauce. Arrange chicken and ham on top and cover with half the remaining sauce. Top with egg slices; cover with remaining sauce. Sprinkle with cheese, and dot with remaining 1 tablespoon butter. Bake in a preheated 375° oven for 30 minutes or until brown and bubbly. *(Serves 6)*

Pork Chops with Broccoli de Rabe

The slightly sharp broccoli de rabe is much used in Italy with sweet meats such as pork.

Four 1½–2-inch-thick pork chops
2 Tb oil
2–3 cloves garlic
Sprig of fresh thyme or ½ tsp dried
⅓ cup beef broth or wine
¼ cup chopped shallots
4 Tb butter
Salt and freshly ground pepper
2–3 cups blanched chopped broccoli de rabe (page 130)
1 cup halved water chestnuts (optional)

In a large frying pan, brown pork chops in oil for 2–3 minutes on each side. Drain fat, and add garlic, thyme, and broth or wine. Sprinkle shallots over chops; dot with 2 tablespoons of the butter. Season with salt and pepper. Cover, and slowly cook for approximately 20 minutes, basting occasionally.

Meanwhile, cook the broccoli de rabe over high heat in the remaining butter to evaporate moisture, tossing to coat with butter. Add to pork chops along with the water chestnuts, basting with the pan juices. Cover until broccoli de rabe is heated through and chops are done, 5–10 minutes, then season to taste. *(Serves 4)*

• Substitute turnip or other greens for the broccoli de rabe.

Broccoli de Rabe with Penne

Use any large tubular pasta. For a milder taste, blanch the broccoli de rabe and toss in hot olive oil before adding to pasta.

1 lb broccoli de rabe
½ lb penne (tubular pasta)
6 Tb olive oil
1 Tb chopped garlic
½ cup white vermouth or water
Salt and freshly ground pepper
2 Tb butter
½ cup freshly grated Parmesan cheese

Wash and peel broccoli de rabe, trimming off any large stalks. Leave whole or halve if large; set aside. In a large pot of salted water, boil penne for 8–10 minutes or until *al dente.*

Meanwhile, heat oil and garlic in a large sauté pan. Add broccoli de rabe and toss to coat with oil. Pour in vermouth or water, turn heat to low, cover, and steam-cook for 6–8 minutes, stirring occasionally. Uncover, reduce pan juices, and season to taste. When pasta is done, drain and toss with butter. Place on a warm platter, laying broccoli de rabe on top. Sprinkle with Parmesan cheese and pepper. *(Serves 4)*

Broccoli de Rabe with Spaghettini

Here's an easy all-in-one skillet meal based on a recipe of Edward Giobbi's, whose book *Italian Family Cooking* teems with delicious recipes using fresh ingredients.

1 lb broccoli de rabe
1 large red sweet pepper (optional)
½ lb spaghettini
1 Tb chopped garlic
6 Tb olive oil
2 cups water or chicken stock
2 Tb butter
Salt and freshly ground pepper
Parmesan cheese

Wash and peel broccoli de rabe, and cut into 2–3-inch pieces; set aside. Peel the pepper, and thinly slice. Break spaghettini into 2–3-inch pieces. In a large sauté pan, cook garlic in oil for 1 minute. Add pepper, cook slightly, and stir in rabe, spaghettini, and water or stock. Cover and cook over medium low heat, stirring frequently, for approximately 10 minutes, adding additional water if necessary. When broccoli de rabe is tender, and spaghettini cooked, remove the cover, reduce any pan liquids, and stir in butter. Season to taste and serve with Parmesan cheese. *(Serves 4)*

Jerusalem Artichokes

I first came upon Jerusalem artichokes one glorious fall day years ago on a family visit to Plimoth Plantation—a museum village in Massachusetts re-creating daily life in Pilgrim times. While we were there the "residents" were preparing dinner. We clustered around a lamb roasting on a spit, its fat sizzling and dripping into a pan wedged into the embers below. One of the residents threw several strange-looking tubers into the hot fat, where they rolled and bubbled around. Suddenly, he reached over, forked some out, and thrust them at us to eat. That may have been the best biteful of chokes I've ever tasted. The contrast of the crisp skin with the moist, slightly sweet interior was a revelation.

It was fitting that we first tried chokes at Plimoth Plantation, because they're a native American food introduced by the Indians to the settlers. This Indian staple, sunroot, grew wild throughout North and South America and was cultivated by Indians along the East Coast. Explorers took chokes back to Europe as a novelty, where they quickly became popular and widely grown. In some areas they were known as Canadian potatoes, while in France they were called Topinambours after a tribe visiting France at the time the chokes were introduced. Although no one is certain how the more common name "Jerusalem artichoke" came about, it's most likely a mispronunciation of the Italian word *girasol*, which means "turning to the sun" (a trait of sunflowers), combined with artichoke—for their flavor resembles that of the more familiar globe artichoke. In any case, Jerusalem artichokes never came from Jerusalem and are not related to the globe artichoke.

The plant is a 6–10-foot-tall perennial sunflower with yellow blossoms that also make attractive flower arrange-

ments. The thin stems grow in clusters and are a nutritious cattle fodder. (For this reason, during the 1930s the federal government tried to interest farmers in raising Jerusalem artichokes, but to no avail.) Their roots spread out in all directions, bearing knobby, edible tubers at their tips. They're virtually indestructible, easy to grow, and thrive under almost any conditions. Plant them in a secluded spot of their own in the garden—unchecked, they can become a pest, spreading with abandon and shading other garden crops.

Tubers are available from several mail order companies such as Burpee and Gurney's, but supermarket or health-food store tubers grow equally well. In Europe, where they have a cultlike following because of their dietetic qualities, it's possible to buy large, smooth, named varieties of Jerusalem artichokes, but currently, American catalogs offer no choice of varieties.

When tubers of Jerusalem artichokes grow wild in heavy soil they are smaller and less firm than those grown in garden loam rich in potassium. With good soil, yields can reach 10 pounds of tubers per plant. Tubers can be planted in either fall or spring: just cut into pieces and plant 6 inches deep and 18 inches apart. Major growth takes place after the flowers bloom, so wait to harvest chokes until stalks have died down, which is early to mid-October in Massachusetts. Some people consider the flavor of chokes sweeter when they've been tempered by frost, but our experience has been that an early harvest makes no difference to the flavor.

I harvest chokes with a spading fork, digging about 6 inches away from the base of the plants, prying up their entire root system, and then collecting any tubers left in the ground. Hunt as I may, I never find all the chokes from a plant. Even small pieces broken off start new plants the following year: once you have a planting of chokes, they're yours for life.

Jerusalem artichokes store poorly, for their thin skins rapidly lose moisture. The best way to store them is to leave them in the ground and dig up as needed. If this is impossible, see notes under *Storage and Preserving*.

Jerusalem artichokes' flavor and texture change dramatically from the raw to cooked stages, making them as versatile as two different vegetables. Raw chokes taste crisp and crunchy, with a texture like water chestnuts. They're best served sliced for dips or in salads where their sweet, delicate flavor is not overwhelmed. Cooked, the chokes' interior becomes moist, sweet, and starchy with a texture somewhat like cooked chestnuts and a nutty flavor reminiscent of globe artichokes.

Preparation for cooking is simple. All you need to do is wash them well. As they can be very knobby, a brush is helpful to get around the protrusions and into crevices. You can cook chokes either with or without their skins. Cooking the chokes in their skins helps hold the flesh intact and makes them easier to peel—the cooked skins slip right off like beet skins do—however, the flesh will darken. To retain the natural creamy white color of chokes, I peel them first, drop them in acidulated water, and cook them in a *Blanc* (see *Appendix*), which is simply a flour and lemon mixture. It's no trouble to make, and the chokes look much more attractive.

Special Information

Yields
- 1 pound raw chokes = 13 ounces peeled raw = 3 cups sliced or chopped raw
- 1 pound raw chokes cooked in skin and peeled = 2 1/2 cups sliced or chopped cooked
- 1 pound raw chokes = 1 1/2 cups cooked mashed chokes without skins

Storage and Preserving
- Store in wet sand in a damp cellar with a temperature of around 34°. For short-term storage, wipe them off without washing and place in a perforated plastic bag in the refrigerator, where they'll keep for at least 2 weeks before softening and shriveling.
- Do not freeze or can chokes. Freezing turns the flesh black and destroys texture. Canning turns them into mush.
- Chokes pickle well. In the American South, Jerusalem artichoke pickle is a culinary standby. See *Jerusalem Artichoke Pickles*, page 141.

Hints
- Sliced raw chokes can be added to any cooked vegetable just before serving. Heat through to add a crisp texture to the completed dish.
- Slice or grate into salads.
- Try *Choke Chips* with cocktails. Slice chokes paper thin and drop into hot fat. Fry just to brown, drain on a paper bag, salt, and serve.
- Substitute chokes for water chestnuts in a bacon and choke appetizer. Cook bacon until almost done but still pliable. Cut chokes into 1/2-inch cubes and wind bacon around, then skewer with toothpicks and run under broiler for 1 minute. Don't leave them too long or the chokes will cook. They are crunchy and much cheaper than water chestnuts.
- Never cook chokes in an iron pot. They will turn black.
- To restore crispness to chokes that have been in storage, soak in ice water.

Microwave
- 1 pound whole cleaned chokes in a covered dish takes 5–6 minutes, depending on size.

Leftovers
- Add mashed cooked chokes to soups or stews to thicken them.
- Combine with mashed potatoes or turnips for a purée.

When I'm serving chokes whole with butter and salt, I bake them; when puréeing or serving with hollandaise, I steam them. For all other preparations, aside from sautéing, I cook them in the blanc mentioned above. *Chokes quickly turn to mush if they are overcooked for even one minute*, so time your cooking carefully.

Jerusalem artichokes have two unusual characteristics, one less agreeable than the other. First, as they pass through the large intestine, bacterial reaction can be fierce, sometimes causing gastric distress and flatulence. My family has this problem, while other people have no reaction at all: so go easy the first time you eat chokes. Second, Jerusalem artichokes contain no starch, making them low in calories. Their sugar is in the form of inulin, a substance poorly absorbed by the body, which means they can be eaten by dieters and diabetics with impunity.

Marketing

Many supermarkets and health-food stores now sell Jerusalem artichokes, usually packed in 1-pound plastic packages labeled "Sun Chokes." Good-quality chokes are firm to the touch with a clear brown golden skin and no bruise marks. Look for the smoothest chokes you can find: the knobbier they are, the harder to clean and peel and the greater the amount of waste.

◇ *Whole Baked Jerusalem Artichokes*

This is the closest I get to the Plimoth Plantation chokes without stoking up the outside grill. Either bake, unpeeled, in the drippings of a roast or film a pan with vegetable oil and roll the chokes in it. Bake in oven, remove, and eat with butter, salt, and pepper. In a 350° oven,

medium-size chokes will take approximately 30 minutes; in a 400° oven, about 20 minutes. The cooking time varies depending on the oven temperature and the artichoke size. If you're cooking different-size chokes, put the large ones in first, and the smaller sizes 5–10 minutes later.

◇ *Whole Steamed Jerusalem Artichokes*

Bring water to a rapid boil in a steamer. Put in chokes, unpeeled, cover, and steam 12–20 minutes, depending upon the size of the chokes. Watch them carefully: they continue to cook after they're removed from the pan, so remove the moment they feel tender when pricked with a knife.

◇ *Whole Boiled Jerusalem Artichokes*

Bring a saucepan of water to a rolling boil and immerse unpeeled chokes. After the water boils for a second time, the small chokes will take 12–15 minutes, larger ones up to 25 minutes. As they vary greatly in size, watch carefully and test often. Eat either with or without skins.

Jerusalem Artichokes with Hollandaise

This is a sinfully delicious way to eat chokes. I like to serve them as a separate course, surrounding a ramekin of hollandaise sauce. We just cut them into chunks and dip into the sauce. Serve peeled or unpeeled—they're delicious either way.

> 1 lb whole steamed or boiled Jerusalem artichokes (see above)
> *Hollandaise Sauce* (page 348)

While the chokes are steaming or boiling, make the hollandaise sauce. Serve immediately. *(Serves 4)*

Sautéed Raw Chokes

This simple sauté retains all the crispness of raw chokes.

> 1 lb Jerusalem artichokes
> 2 Tb lemon juice
> 3 Tb butter
> ½ Tb vegetable oil
> Salt and freshly ground pepper
> 2 Tb finely chopped parsley (optional)

Thinly slice chokes (leaving skins on if you prefer) into 1 quart water to which the lemon juice has been added. Just before cooking, drain and dry chokes. Heat butter and oil in a sauté pan, add chokes, and cook over medium to high heat, turning frequently so that they brown on all sides, approximately 5 minutes in all. The chokes are done when they're lightly browned on the outside and tender inside. Season with salt and pepper and sprinkle with parsley if you like. *(Serves 4–6)*

• Toast sesame seeds and add to sauté a minute before serving.

Stir-Fry Chokes and Broccoli

Chokes and broccoli are a colorful and delicious combination. Add the raw chokes at the last moment so they remain crisp.

    1 bunch fresh broccoli
    1/2 lb Jerusalem artichokes
    2 Tb lemon juice
    1 Tb cornstarch (optional)
    1/4 cup water (optional)
    1 Tb soy sauce (optional)
    3 Tb peanut oil
    1 1/2 tsp finely minced ginger root
    1/2 tsp salt
    2/3 cup chicken stock or water
    2 Tb butter

Wash broccoli, remove flower buds from stalks, peel, and cut into 1-inch-diameter pieces. Peel stalks, slice down, and cut into 1 1/2-inch pieces. Slice chokes into rounds and keep in 1 quart water to which the lemon juice has been added. If you wish to thicken the finished dish, mix together cornstarch, water, and soy sauce and set aside.

Heat oil until very hot, add ginger, and stir for 10 seconds. Add broccoli and cook for 2 minutes, stirring, until all sides are coated with oil and slightly cooked, then add salt and stir for another minute. Pour in stock or water, bring to a boil, cover pan, turn heat to medium, and braise the broccoli for 5–10 minutes or until tender but still crisp. Meanwhile dry the chokes. When the broccoli is tender, uncover and reduce remaining liquid to 3 tablespoons, then add butter and chokes. Stir for 30 seconds or just to warm through. If you fancy a sauce, add the cornstarch mixture along with the chokes and stir until the stock is thickened. *(Serves 6–8)*

- With the addition of 1/2 pound meat or poultry you have a full meal. Thinly slice the meat, sauté in hot oil, set aside, and follow recipe as above, returning meat to pan just before chokes and butter. You may wish to increase the amount of sauce.

Lacy Jerusalem Artichoke Pancakes

There's no flour in these delicious German-style pancakes and they have the fullest possible Jerusalem artichoke flavor. Grate artichokes with a fine grater just before cooking, do not shred them, and serve immediately, for they lose flavor and texture if they stand around.

    1/2 lb Jerusalem artichokes
    2 Tb lemon juice
    2 eggs
    1/2 tsp salt
    Freshly ground pepper
    Butter
    Vegetable oil
    1 cup sour cream (optional)
    Homemade applesauce (optional)

Wash and peel chokes and place in 1 quart water to which the lemon juice has been added. Beat together eggs, salt,

and pepper. Drain and dry chokes and grate directly into egg mixture. Heat equal amounts of butter and vegetable oil over medium-high heat, in a sauté pan, preferably nostick. (The amounts of butter and oil depend on how many pancakes are cooking at a time. A 6-inch pan would call for a tablespoon each of butter and oil.) Stir grated choke and egg mixture and ladle out approximately 1/4 cup per pancake, which will spread to about a 3-inch diameter. Cook until browned on each side, 8–10 minutes in all. Serve immediately with sour cream or homemade applesauce. *(Makes eight 3-inch pancakes)*

- Grate 1 small onion into batter.
- Cut down on the chokes and add another grated vegetable such as carrot, potato, or salsify.
- Add a bit of finely julienned celeriac, or sprinkle chopped fresh green herbs into batter.

Glazed Jerusalem Artichokes

Shaped into ovals and glazed, these Jerusalem artichokes are festive enough for a party. Save the trimmings for soup.

    1 lb Jerusalem artichokes
    2 Tb lemon juice
    1/2 cup water or stock
    2 Tb butter
    Salt and freshly ground pepper
    1 Tb sugar

Wash and peel chokes and place in a quart of water to which the lemon juice has been added. When all are peeled, shape them into ovals approximately 1½ inches long and ¾ inch wide. Place in a single layer in a sauté pan. Add water, 1 tablespoon butter, ½ teaspoon salt, and pepper. Bring water to boil, then reduce heat and simmer uncovered, turning the ovals frequently to cook evenly. Cook for approximately 15 minutes or until tender and the liquid is reduced. (If, when the artichokes are cooked, the liquid has not reduced, pour out all but a few tablespoons.) Add 1 tablespoon butter and the sugar, turn heat up, and roll chokes around to brown and glaze on all sides. Check seasoning and serve immediately. *(Serves 4–6)*

Jerusalem Artichokes with Cheese and Cream

This creamy casserole can be made in advance and reheated just before serving.

⅔ lb Jerusalem artichokes
3 Tb lemon juice
Blanc (page 346)
3 Tb butter
2 Tb flour
¼ cup heavy cream
Salt and freshly ground pepper
½ cup grated Swiss cheese

Wash, peel, and dice chokes into ½-inch pieces. (You should have 2 cups.) Keep in water diluted with 2 tablespoons lemon juice until ready to use. Make blanc, bring to boil, add chokes, reduce heat to a simmer, and cook approximately 10 minutes or until chokes are tender. Drain, reserving cooking liquid. Melt 2 tablespoons butter, add the flour, stir, and cook for 2 minutes without browning. Remove from heat, whisk in 1 cup of the cooking liquid, and cook for 10 minutes longer. Thin, if necessary, with more cooking liquid. Then, add cream, 1 tablespoon lemon juice, and salt and pepper to taste, and cook 1 minute longer. Butter a 1-quart baking dish, fold drained and dried chokes into sauce, pour into casserole, and sprinkle with grated cheese and remaining 1 tablespoon butter. Place casserole in a preheated 425° oven and bake until bubbly. Run under the broiler to brown cheese. *(Serves 4)*

- For a Mornay sauce, increase cheese to 1 cup and fold ½ cup cheese into cream sauce. Sprinkle with remaining cheese.
- Leftover cooked ham, tongue, or chicken added to casserole will make it hearty enough for a main course.

Puréed Jerusalem Artichokes in Tomato Shells

The choke filling stuffs four large tomatoes, sufficient for a complete luncheon or dinner accompaniment or, with patience, a couple of dozen cherry tomatoes on an appetizer tray.

4 large tomatoes
1 lb Jerusalem artichokes
3 Tb butter
2 Tb heavy cream
¾ cup combined grated Parmesan and Swiss cheeses
Salt and freshly ground pepper

Slice tomatoes in half, gently squeeze out seeds and juice, and set aside. Steam whole artichokes until tender, then peel and purée in a food processor or food mill. Add 1½ tablespoons butter, the cream, and ¼ cup grated cheese. Mix well and season with salt and pepper.

Place choke mixture in tomato shells, and top each tomato with remaining cheese and butter. Bake in a preheated 400° oven for 10 minutes, then run under the broiler to brown. *(Serves 4)*

Lynn Wilson's Marinated Jerusalem Artichokes

Put this together the night before or early in the morning for a crisp marinated salad that can be served by itself or as part of an antipasto platter. Make the marinade and slice the chokes right into it, and you'll have no need for acidulated water.

1 onion
1 clove garlic
2 Tb chopped fresh chervil
1¼ cups vegetable oil
¼ cup olive oil
¾ cup tarragon vinegar or lemon juice
½ tsp thyme
½ tsp salt
Freshly ground pepper
1 lb Jerusalem artichokes

Thinly slice onion and crush garlic. Combine with remaining ingredients except chokes. Wash chokes and slice, peeled or unpeeled, into marinade. Cover and refrigerate for at least 12 hours. Serve cold. *(Makes 3 cups)*

Jerusalem Artichokes Vinaigrette

Cooking the chokes in a blanc preserves their creamy color. Or, just steam or boil whole chokes and slice warm: the color will change, but the flavor is the same either way. My family particularly likes this salad warm, but it can be chilled as well.

4 slices bacon
1 lb Jerusalem artichokes
2 Tb lemon juice
Blanc (page 346)
2 Tb chopped shallots
Vinaigrette Sauce (page 352), flavored with celery salt
2 Tb chopped parsley

Cook bacon until crisp, crumble, and set aside. Peel and slice artichokes into a quart of water to which the lemon juice has been added. Bring blanc to a boil, add artichokes, reduce heat, and cook for 5–6 minutes or until tender. Drain and dry the chokes.

Fold chokes and shallots into vinaigrette sauce. Let stand to absorb flavors, then sprinkle with parsley and bacon. *(Serves 4–6)*

- Prepare as above and cool. Fold in *Mayonnaise* (see *Appendix*) and other chopped ingredients such as celery, olives, and so on.

Radish, Jerusalem Artichoke, and Watercress Salad

This is an especially handsome salad with its contrasts of red and green. Note that the chokes should stay in acidulated water while the radishes keep best in ice water until used.

> 1/3 lb Jerusalem artichokes
> 2 Tb lemon juice
> 1 bunch radishes
> 2 bunches watercress
> *Vinaigrette Sauce* (page 352)

Wash and slice chokes into water acidulated with lemon juice. Wash radishes and keep in ice water. Wash watercress, removing any thick stems, dry, and break into bite-size pieces. Lightly dress with a little vinaigrette. Drain and slice radishes; drain and pat dry chokes. Combine chokes and radishes in vinaigrette and serve on watercress. *(Serves 4)*

Jerusalem Artichoke Soup

This is Russ's favorite choke recipe. I pass by celeriac en route to harvesting chokes in our garden. Combine the two (see variation at end of recipe) for a delicious soup.

> 1 lb Jerusalem artichokes
> Lemon juice
> 1 medium onion
> 2 stalks celery
> 1 leek
> 2 Tb butter
> 1 1/2 Tb flour
> 3 cups chicken broth
> 1 cup medium cream
> Salt and freshly ground pepper
> 1/2 cup sour cream
> Chopped chervil

Wash, peel, and coarsely dice chokes, dropping them into water acidulated with 2 tablespoons lemon juice as you prepare them. Chop onion, celery, and leek and cook in butter over low to medium heat for 10–15 minutes until softened. Sprinkle on flour and cook, stirring, for 3–5 minutes.

Add chokes and broth and bring to boil, then cover and simmer for 15–20 minutes or until all the vegetables are tender. Purée mixture in a blender; return to sauce-pan, add cream, and reheat. Season with salt, pepper, and lemon juice to taste and serve with a spoonful of sour cream and a sprinkling of chopped chervil on top. *(Serves 4–6)*

Note: If artichokes are knobby and hard to peel, steam for 10 minutes, then slip off skins and add chokes to soup. The simmering time will be less.

- *Jerusalem Artichokes and Celeriac Soup*: Add a peeled and chopped celeriac to the soup along with the chokes and chicken broth. Simmer slightly longer until the celeriac is tender. Add broth if necessary.
- Both versions can be served cold. Chill the soup base and add cream just before serving.
- If you are cutting down on calories, replace cream with additional broth.

Jerusalem Artichoke Cheese Soup

This thick soup has less cheese than a traditional cheese soup, allowing the Jerusalem artichoke flavor to dominate. Add more cheese if you prefer. Serve with toasted thin black bread triangles. With a salad, you have an unusual and filling meal-in-one.

> 1 lb Jerusalem artichokes
> 2 Tb lemon juice
> 2 stalks celery
> 1 medium onion
> 6 Tb butter
> 2 1/2 cups chicken broth
> 3 Tb flour
> 1 1/2 cups medium-sharp Cheddar cheese
> 2 tsp dry mustard
> 1/2 cup cream
> Salt
> Cayenne pepper
> 1 tsp Worcestershire sauce

Wash, peel, and roughly chop chokes and keep in water to which lemon juice has been added until ready to use. Chop celery and onion and cook in 2 tablespoons butter until slightly wilted, approximately 10 minutes. Add chokes and 1 1/2 cups chicken broth, cover, and cook for 10–15 minutes or until vegetables are cooked through. Purée in a blender, food processor, or food mill.

In a medium-size saucepan, melt 4 tablespoons butter, add flour, and cook for 2 minutes without browning. Remove from heat and whisk in 1 cup broth, then cook for 5 minutes. Add cheese and mustard and stir until blended. Stir in choke mixture and cream and cook until soup is heated through. Season with salt, cayenne pepper, and Worcestershire sauce. *(Serves 4–6)*

Note: For a thinner soup, add additional chicken stock.

Gibelotte of Rabbit and Chokes

Gibelotte at one time meant only a stew of game, but now it refers to a rabbit and white wine stew. Chokes substituted for the traditional potatoes make the dish less heavy. If you haven't tried rabbit before, please do; it's available in most supermarket frozen food sections. The flesh is drier than chicken, with a unique taste all its own.

> ¼ lb lean bacon
> 6 Tb butter
> 2 ½–3-lb rabbit
> 2 medium onions
> 2 carrots
> 2 cloves unpeeled garlic
> 2 Tb flour
> 1 ½ cups dry white wine
> 1 ½ cups chicken broth
> 1 lb Jerusalem artichokes
> 2 Tb lemon juice
> 2 Tb vegetable oil
> 18 cherry tomatoes
> 18 stoned black olives, or green olives
> *Beurre Manié* (optional; see page 346)
> Parsley

Dice bacon and parboil for 5 minutes, then drain and dry thoroughly. Cook in 2 tablespoons butter until lightly browned, remove bacon pieces and set aside. Wash rabbit, pat dry, and cut into serving pieces. Finely chop liver (if it's included) and set aside. Sauté rabbit in 2 tablespoons butter and bacon fat. While the rabbit is cooking, chop onions, carrots, and garlic and add to pan. Don't let the vegetables brown. When the rabbit is nicely browned on all sides, turn heat to medium, sprinkle on flour, and turn rabbit until flour is lightly browned. Pour in wine and broth and scrape up pan juices, adding extra water if needed to cover rabbit. Bring to a boil, reduce heat, and simmer, covered, over low heat until rabbit is tender, approximately 30 minutes, or longer, depending upon the age of the rabbit.

Meanwhile, cut peeled chokes into pieces (ovals are especially attractive) and drop into water acidulated with lemon juice. Save the choke trimmings for soup. Drain and dry chokes and sauté in 1 tablespoon butter and oil until nicely browned; set aside. In the same pan, melt 1 tablespoon butter and lightly sauté the cherry tomatoes, then the olives and diced liver in turn.

After the rabbit has been cooking for 20 minutes, check it and if it's just about ready, add the chokes and cook with the rabbit for 10 minutes. Remove rabbit and chokes to a warm plate. Strain the cooking juices and vegetables, pressing down on the vegetables with a wooden spoon. Return rabbit and chokes to the casserole, adding cherry tomatoes and olives. Keep warm in a low oven while you thicken the sauce. Skim the fat from the sauce, then boil until thickened. The sauce should be thick enough to coat the rabbit. If necessary, thicken with beurre manié. Add chopped liver and pour sauce over rabbit and vegetables. Reheat until the dish is warmed through. Chop parsley and sprinkle over dish. *(Serves 4)*

- Substitute chicken for rabbit.

Jerusalem Artichoke Chiffon Pie

> *Tart Pastry* (page 351)
> 1 lb Jerusalem artichokes
> 1 package unflavored gelatin
> ¼ cup water
> ¼ cup light-brown sugar
> ¾ tsp cinnamon
> ½ tsp nutmeg
> ½ tsp ground ginger
> ½ tsp salt
> 3 large eggs
> ½ cup light cream
> 1 Tb granulated sugar
> 1 cup heavy cream

Bake a 9-inch pie shell and cool. Cook and purée the chokes—you will need 1¼ cups of purée. Dissolve gelatin in water. In a double boiler stir together the light-brown sugar, spices, and salt. Separate the eggs and beat yolks with light cream until well blended, then mix into sugar mixture. Add gelatin and puréed chokes; stir together and cook until thickened, approximately 20 minutes. Remove and chill mixture in refrigerator until it mounds on a spoon but is not firmly set. Beat the egg whites, adding the granulated sugar when soft peaks have formed. Continue beating until glossy—do not overbeat—and fold into choke mixture. Fill the pie shell and chill until set. Whip heavy cream and serve on side. *(Makes a 9-inch pie)*

Jerusalem Artichoke Pickles

This is an excellent way to use up all the chokes in your garden to make way for next year's crop. I prefer a light pickling solution that doesn't mask the crisp taste of the vegetables. You could omit the cauliflower, but I find it adds a soft contrast to the crisp chokes.

> 2½ lb Jerusalem artichokes
> 2 Tb lemon juice
> 1 lb cauliflower (optional)
> Pickling salt
> 4 cups cider vinegar
> 1 cup white vinegar
> 1 cup water
> 2 cups sugar
> 1 ½ tsp celery seeds
> 1 ½ tsp turmeric
> 2 tsp mustard seeds
> 1 ½ tsp dry mustard
> 1 large green pepper
> 1 large red pepper
> 1 large onion

Peel and cut the chokes into ½-inch chunks and drop into water acidulated with lemon juice. Cut up the head of cauliflower, break flowerets into ½-inch pieces, and peel and cut the stems into ½-inch cubes. Crisp the vegetables in a brine solution made this way: Cover the chokes and cauliflower with water to see how much wa-

ter you need, then drain the vegetables, saving the water, and mix into it ⅓ cup pickling salt per quart. Place the vegetables in this brine and soak for 24 hours.

Combine vinegars, water, sugar, celery seeds, turmeric, mustard seeds, and dry mustard, in a stainless steel or enameled saucepan and bring to a boil. Stir to dissolve sugar, reduce heat, and let simmer for 3 minutes. Remove from heat.

While the brine is simmering, coarsely chop the peppers and onion. Drain the chokes and cauliflower, rinse them well to remove salt, and drain again. Combine chokes, cauliflower, peppers, and onion and pack into clean hot jars, following manufacturer's directions. Ladle in hot brine, a bit at a time, making sure it runs through the vegetables. (Putting a long, sterilized skewer in the jar and moving it around helps the syrup flow through the vegetables.) Fill to ⅛ inch of the jar top, seal, and process in a hot water bath for 10 minutes. Set in a cool place for at least 1 week before serving. *(Makes 3 quarts)*

Kale

On a blustery winter day, it's not uncommon to find me out in the garden, brushing the snow off the kale I plan to fix for dinner. Kale is one of those exceptionally hardy vegetables that withstand even severe frost. Our kale planting provides us with greens from November to February. Just to look out on the barren garden and see kale's beautiful curly leaves makes me feel the gardening year is not yet over. I find its slightly sharp taste a pleasant change of pace from the sweetness of other winter vegetables, such as parsnips, carrots, and rutabagas. Even so, its flavor isn't the least bit overpowering, and unlike other greens, kale holds its texture when cooked. Although it can look tough as shoe leather, it actually cooks tender, yet crisp, in minutes.

With all these virtues, kale is also an easy vegetable to grow—much easier than cabbage, for example. Russ plants a short row of Dwarf Blue Curled Vates kale in July. He sows seeds every inch, thinning to one plant every 8 inches once the seedlings reach ¾ inch tall. A dozen plants are plenty for our needs. Kale benefits from

moisture while germinating, so to prevent the seedlings from drying out under the hot summer sun, he covers the row with burlap until the seedlings emerge. Throughout the growing season, he keeps the plants thoroughly watered.

The plants are relatively pest free, with the exception of aphids in August—which can be controlled by washing off with a hose. (Be sure to wash the undersides of the leaves where the aphids hide.)

We don't harvest kale until after a frost, which improves its flavor. As the plants grow from the inside out, we leave the inner leaves to grow and harvest just the outer leaves, snapping the stems off at the base of the plants.

Because kale is mostly water, it wilts once picked and stores poorly. It's best to keep it in the garden until you need it.

The leaves not only harbor aphids but also collect soil, and should be carefully washed before cooking. Place the kale in a sink filled with tepid water. Dunk the leaves up and down until clean, running them under the tap if necessary.

Baby-size kale leaves can be cooked stem and all. For larger leaves, I remove the stems by pulling down along the leaves. I fold each leaf lengthwise so that the insides touch and then bend back the stem and pull down. The stems go right to the compost heap.

Although it's largely a matter of personal taste, I think kale tastes best when blanched. Blanching removes the slight hard edge that remains when it's steamed or sautéed. (If I have young kale leaves, I will simply sauté them.) I recommend blanching, sautéing, and steaming, in that order. Since kale isn't a harsh vegetable, it doesn't need the bouillon treatment I use with other greens to "mellow" their taste. In fact, you can drop kale directly into a soup, and it won't "bitter" the broth as other greens do. This method also retains the nutrients, for kale is an excellent source of vitamin A. Because it holds its texture, finely shredded kale looks particularly appetizing floating in a clear consommé or Chinese soup.

After the initial preparation, you can substitute kale for all the recipes in *Greens*. For example, kale is delicious in *Cream of Broccoli de Rabe Soup*—and vice versa, broccoli de rabe can replace kale in *Turkey Breast with Kale*. You can see the opportunities for exchanging.

Marketing

Kale is sold throughout the winter at most markets. Select dark green leaves with some "bounce" to them. Avoid yellowed, wilted leaves or those that look old: if kale is held too long after picking it sometimes develops a hard, bitter taste it doesn't have when first harvested.

◇ Blanched Kale

Boil a large pot of salted (1 1/2 teaspoons per quart) water, add washed and trimmed kale, and boil for approximately 4–5 minutes, or until kale is barely tender. (The cooking time depends on the size and age of the kale.) As the kale wilts by a ratio of approximately 4 to 1, you may have to add it in batches.

◇ *Steamed Kale*

In a steamer, bring 1 inch of water to a boil. Place the kale in a steamer basket. Cover and steam for 4–5 minutes, depending on the kale's age and size and the amount in the steamer. The kale is ready when it is limp but still retains some texture.

Note: For finishing touches for cooked kale, see *Finishing Touches for Steamed or Blanched Greens*, page 130.

◇ *Sautéed Kale*

It is difficult to sauté large batches of kale because it's so bulky and reduces so much. I chop or shred mild young kale for sautéeing. In a large sauté pan, heat olive oil or a combination of oil and butter. Toss in well-dried kale and turn for 2–3 minutes, stirring frequently. Add the kale by handfuls if necessary. If desired, add a garlic clove. Season to taste and serve.

- For older kale cover pan and steam-braise for 5–6 minutes or until tender.
- Combine with shredded cabbage and treat as above.

Portuguese Kale Soup

This is one of my favorite soups.

1 lb kale
1 lb potatoes
1 lb smoked sausage (linguica or chorizo)
1 cup chopped onions
1/2 cup chopped carrots
2 tsp chopped garlic
2 Tb olive oil
2 Tb butter
2 qt chicken broth or combination of beef and chicken
3 lb peeled, seeded, and chopped tomatoes
1 1/2 cups cooked kidney beans
Salt and freshly ground pepper

Strip the leaves from washed kale, and cut diagonally into wide slices. You should end up with 6–8 cups of lightly packed kale. Wash, peel, and chop potatoes, and keep in cold water. Prick sausage; blanch in boiling water for 5–10 minutes to release fat. Drain; cut into 1/2-inch slices; set aside. In a large saucepan, sauté onions, carrots, and garlic in oil and butter, cooking until softened, about 5 minutes. Add potatoes and broth, and simmer, partially covered, for 15–20 minutes or until the potatoes are cooked. Mash the potatoes against the side of the pot (or

Special Information

Yields

- 1 pound kale with stems = 6–8 ounces leaves = 8 cups raw = 2 1/2 cups cooked, lightly packed
- 4 cups finely chopped raw kale will wilt in cooking to barely 1 cup

Storage and Preserving

- There's no need to freeze kale, as it keeps fresh in the ground. Just push aside the snow and harvest all winter long. You *can* freeze it, however. Wash, stem, and blanch the leaves for 2 minutes. Cool and pack in freezer containers. Refrigerated, unwashed kale will keep 3–4 days wrapped in a perforated plastic bag. The outer leaves will yellow if you hold it too long.

Hints

- Wash well in warm water; aphids hide in those curly kale leaves.
- For a pretty and flavorful accent for omelets and quiches, add shredded or chopped kale sautéed in olive oil for 2–3 minutes.
- Add chopped or sliced raw kale directly to hearty soups and stews for the last minute of cooking. It's nutritious, has a pleasant texture, and leaves no bitter aftertaste as do some greens.
- Take a broth, add rice, potatoes, legumes, or barley, and add plenty of shredded raw kale for an inexpensive hearty soup.

- Add raw finely sliced young kale to salads.
- For more ideas, see hints in *Greens* and *Swiss Chard*.
- Use in stuffings.

Microwave

- 1/2 pound trimmed and washed young kale leaves placed in a covered dish will cook tender in 4 minutes.

Leftovers

- *Russ's Favorite Scrambled Eggs*: Take leftover kale, chop medium-fine, and sauté in butter with some chopped onions or shallots. Add beaten eggs and grated Romano cheese. Stir and cook until eggs are done. You can also add bits of ham or the occasional shrimp.
- Purée leftover kale and mix with puréed potatoes or parsnips.
- Finely chop; add to hamburger patties or meat loaves along with an egg and seasonings.
- Fry blanched Italian sausages in olive oil; stir in chopped kale and cook alongside sausage.
- See *Greens* and *Swiss Chard* for other ideas.

Wash, trim, and blanch kale (page 143). Drain, gently squeeze out water, and chop finely. Set aside. Peel potatoes; boil in salted water.

Meanwhile, heat 2 tablespoons of the butter in a frying pan and gently stew the leeks until tender, 5–10 minutes. Add the chopped kale and sauté over high heat, stirring to evaporate excess moisture. Turn the heat to low, add 2 tablespoons of the butter and slowly cook the leeks and kale for 5–10 minutes longer. Season with salt and pepper to taste.

In a small frying pan, brown the onions in the remaining butter. When the potatoes are tender, drain and mash them. Whip in the kale and leek mixture and 1 teaspoon salt. Heat cream or milk and gradually beat in until mixture is smooth, creamy, yet firm. Season with salt and pepper. Reheat if necessary, and mound in a hot dish. Make a depression in the center and pour the browned onions and butter in the well until they spill over the side. *(Serves 4–6)*

- If you wish to cut down on butter, simmer the leeks in milk until they are soft, and cook the onions in less butter.
- Omit the browned onions.

Kale Pie

Double recipe *Tart Pastry* (page 351)
1 lb kale
4 Tb butter
1/2 cup chopped onions
1 tsp chopped garlic
6 cooked Italian sausages
4 eggs
2 cups shredded mozzarella cheese or a combination of mozzarella and Parmesan
1 cup ricotta or cottage cheese
1 tsp salt
Freshly ground pepper
1/3 cup light cream
1 egg beaten with 1 tsp water

Take one-half of the pastry and partially bake a 10-inch pie shell. Blanch kale (page 143), gently squeeze, and roughly chop. Sauté in 2 tablespoons of the butter over high heat to evaporate moisture; set aside. In the same pan, sauté the onions in the remaining butter until wilted; add the garlic and stir for 1 minute. Combine with kale; cool.

Slice sausages into 1/4-inch pieces. Combine eggs, cheeses, salt, pepper, and cream. Fold in the kale and sausages. Pour into partially baked pie shell and cover with a top crust made from the remaining dough. Crimp edges, cut decorative steam vents, and brush pastry with egg glaze. Bake in a preheated 350° oven for 1 hour. *(Serves 6–8)*

purée with some of the broth and return to the pot). Stir in tomatoes and kidney beans, and simmer for 10–15 minutes. Add the kale and sausage, cook 5–10 minutes longer, and season to taste. *(Serves 6–8)*

- Omit kidney beans. Use only 1/2 pound potatoes, and mash as above. Add cooked small new potatoes cut in half.
- Use cooked sweet Italian sausage and omit blanching.

Colcannon

Since kale grows so well in cold areas, it's no wonder that it has a long culinary history in Scotland and Ireland. Colcannon is traditionally eaten at Halloween, and symbols of fortune are placed within its whipped mound. Traditional treasures are a golden ring (you will marry within the year), a sixpence (you will become wealthy), a thimble (you will be a spinster), or a button (you will remain a bachelor). Do tell your guests what's in store, or *your* fate will be a lawsuit for someone's broken tooth.

1 lb kale
1 1/2 lb potatoes
8 Tb butter
1 cup finely chopped leeks
Salt and freshly ground pepper
1/2 cup finely chopped onions
1/2–3/4 cup light cream, milk, or combination of both

Calzone Stuffed with Kale

My daughters are wild about these delicious Italian bread pockets. You can use plain kale, kale with other greens, kale and potatoes, kale and sausage meat, or even (heaven forbid) omit the kale and use a favorite substitute.

> 4 cups blanched kale (page 143)
> 2 cloves garlic
> 6 Tb olive oil
> 1 Tb butter
> 1/2 tsp rosemary
> Salt and freshly ground pepper
> 1 package active dry yeast
> 1/2 cup tepid water
> Pinch of sugar
> 4 cups all-purpose flour
> 1/3 cup lukewarm water
> 1/2 cup lukewarm milk
> 6 slices mozzarella cheese
> 1/4 lb Genoa salami, diced
> 1 egg

Chop kale and garlic. Sauté kale in 3 tablespoons of the olive oil over high heat until moisture is evaporated, stirring frequently. Reduce heat, stir in garlic, butter, and rosemary, cover, and simmer for 5 minutes. Season with salt and pepper and set aside to cool.

Dissolve the yeast in 1/2 cup tepid water; add a pinch of sugar, and let stand for 10 minutes or until the yeast is foamy. Sift the flour and 1 teaspoon salt together in a large bowl; pour in the yeast. Combine water and milk. Work flour into yeast, gradually adding liquids until dough is smooth and soft. (You can put dough ingredients in food processor and process until mixture forms a soft mass on blade.) Place on a floured board, knead for 1 minute, form into a ball, and place in a floured bowl. Cover with plastic wrap and let rise in a warm place until doubled in bulk (1 1/2–2 hours). Knead for 2–3 minutes; divide into 6 portions and roll each portion into 8-inch-diameter rounds, 1/8 inch thick. Brush with olive oil. On each dough circle, place 1/2 slice mozzarella cheese on the

lower half; top with 1/2 cup kale, spreading the kale to within 1 inch of the edge. Sprinkle with diced salami, then top with 1/2 slice of cheese. Moisten the edges of the dough with water, then fold the top half over the stuffing, making a turnover shape. Press the edges securely together and crimp the outer rims with a dull

knife edge. Place calzones on baking sheets, cover, and let rise for 1 hour. Beat egg with 1 teaspoon water and glaze calzones. Bake in a preheated 375° oven for 25 minutes. *(Serves 6)*

- Mix cooked hot sausage with kale.
- Vary the cheeses and greens.
- Make cocktail-size calzones for buffets.
- For a crispy crust omit second rising.

Lamb, Kale, and Barley Stew

> 3/4 cup barley
> 2–2 1/2 lb lean lamb stew meat and a few neck bones
> 2 cups beef broth
> 1 cup chopped onions
> 1 cup chopped white portion of leeks
> 1 stalk celery with leaves
> 1 bay leaf
> Salt
> 1/2 lb carrots
> 8 cups sliced raw kale
> 1 1/2 Tb Worcestershire sauce
> Freshly ground pepper

Boil barley in water to cover for 2 minutes, remove from heat, and let stand for 1 hour. Drain, rinse, and set aside. Cover lamb and bones with water and bring to a boil. Then discard water, rinse off meat, and rinse out the pan to remove the scum. Cover lamb with broth and water; add barley, onions, leeks, celery, bay leaf, and 1 tablespoon salt. Bring to a boil, skim scum, and reduce heat. Cover and simmer gently for 1 hour, or until lamb is tender. Peel and slice carrots and add to stew. Cook, covered, for 10–15 minutes. Uncover, add kale, and cook, uncovered, 10 minutes longer. Season with Worcestershire sauce, salt, and pepper. (*Serves 4–6*)

- Substitute potatoes or turnips for barley. Before adding the carrots, mash some of the potatoes (or turnips) against the pot side to thicken the stew.

Turkey Breast with Kale

Credit to Jane Doerfer for sharing her method of butterflying and stuffing a turkey breast. She does an elegant version using greens, ham, and hard-boiled eggs. Here, I've made a simpler filling which presents attractive mosaic slices, delicious either hot or cold. Serve plain, with the pan juices, or with a light hollandaise sauce.

> ¹/₄ lb mushrooms
> 6 Tb butter
> ¹/₄ lb ham or prosciutto
> 3 cups blanched or steamed kale (page 143)
> 1 cup chopped onions
> 1 egg
> ³/₄ cup ricotta or cottage cheese
> Salt and freshly ground pepper
> 4–6-lb boned turkey breast
> 4 slices bacon

Wipe and slice mushrooms, and cook in 2 tablespoons of the butter until lightly browned, about 5 minutes. Chop ham, and lightly brown; set aside. Gently squeeze water from kale and chop into medium-fine pieces. In 2 tablespoons of the butter, cook onions until slightly wilted. Add kale and cook over high heat, stirring to evaporate moisture. Reduce heat, add remaining butter, and cook gently for 5 minutes until kale absorbs the butter. Cool slightly.

Beat egg; combine with kale, mushrooms, ham, and cheese. Season with salt and pepper; set aside.

Lay the turkey breast flat, skin side down. I keep as much of the skin as possible to help hold roll together—remove only heavy fatty sections. Pull out the tendons from the 2 fillets on each side of the breast and fold the fillets over to the outside. You want to "butterfly" the turkey meat and make it as uniformly thick as possible. At the thickest part, slice into the breast parallel with the skin, cut almost all the way through, and flip it over to enlarge the total piece. Once you have evened out all the thick sections as much as you can (and don't be afraid of poking, prodding, and filling in gaps, for the meat adheres when it cooks), cover the breast with waxed paper and pound to flatten it a bit more. Now you should have a "butterfly" or free-form rectangle in front of you, with

the widest part running east and west. Salt and pepper the meat. Place the stuffing across the widest section, forming a long round about 2–3 inches in diameter. Bring

both sides of the turkey together around the stuffing and sew together with kitchen string. The roll will be approximately 12–14 inches long. Lay the turkey roll in the center of a buttered sheet of aluminum foil. Lay strips of bacon on top of the roll, and roll up in the foil. Bake in a preheated 425° oven for 40 minutes. Turn heat down to 350°, uncover the roll, and cook for 30 minutes longer. (*Serves 6–8*)

- Use other greens, such as broccoli de rabe or *Mixed Greens Sauté* (see *Greens*) or a combination of both.

Kohlrabi

Kohlrabi looks like something straight out of a science fiction movie, with its spherical shape and leaves jutting out into space. Although it resembles a root vegetable, the globular shape of kohlrabi is actually a swollen above-ground stem. In Central Europe and Asia, kohlrabi is a commonplace vegetable, but in America you'll find it mostly in midwestern German and Eastern European communities. Yet it's a wonderful, unusual vegetable, well worth cultivating. The leaves, which are delicious cooked, have an earthy flavor with a hint of cabbage. The stems are good either raw or cooked. The raw stems have a crisp, sweet—yet tangy—flavor very similar in taste to delicate radishes. Cooked kohlrabi stems take on mild turnip and celeriac, artichoke, cabbage, and even Jerusalem artichoke overtones.

The name is German: *Kohl* means cabbage, and *rabi* turnip, and that's exactly what it is—a cross between a cabbage and a turnip.

Kohlrabi is easy to grow and is rarely bothered by insects. It comes in purple and white (really light green) varieties which taste the same. If you prize the leaves as much as the stems, select Purple Vienna kohlrabi. The recently introduced Grand Duke kohlrabi grows larger than old-fashioned varieties before it becomes fibrous or pithy, and is a good choice for that reason.

The most important factor in growing kohlrabi is plenty of moisture. If kohlrabi experiences a growth check, regardless of the final size of the stem, it will be pithy and tough. Kohlrabi is a cool-weather crop which grows best before temperatures climb (hot weather also makes it pithy). In mid-April, Russ sows a pinch of seeds at 4-inch intervals directly in the garden. In 2 weeks, he thins to single plants and a month later side-dresses the kohlrabi with 5-10-5 fertilizer. By mid-June, when the swollen stems reach golfball size, the kohlrabi can be harvested. Harvest kohlrabies small. We prefer them no larger than 1–2 inches, when they are sweet without any older heavy taste. Unless you've planted Grand Duke kohlrabi, larger kohlrabies tend to be fibrous and tough with a pronounced cabbage flavor. The leaves are also best harvested young: larger leaves yellow and toughen.

Before the leaves can be cooked, you'll need to remove the ribs (even the smallest leaves have tough ribs). Fold over each leaf, hold it in one hand with the rib facing inward, and with the other hand pull off the rib. That's all there is to it.

Whether or not you peel the stems before cooking depends upon your final preparation. Cooked kohlrabi has more flavor when it's first cooked, then peeled. I use this method for any basic cooking preparation with finishing touches. Trim the leaves, wash and cook the stem, then start removing the skin at the kohlrabi base where it is thicker. With a sharp paring knife, slice off the end and pull off the skin—it comes easily, especially near the top where the skin is thinner. The filaments directly under the skin come off as well. When I'm serving kohlrabi raw or directly adding it to a soup or stew, I peel all around the stem with a sharp paring knife as if I were removing an orange skin. You can prepare it ahead of time and refrigerate for a few hours without any problems.

Either boiling or steaming kohlrabi works equally well. However, if you're cooking more than 2–3 kohlrabies, boiling takes less time than steaming. For maximum flavor, don't remove the skins before cooking. If you do, you'll lose a little flavor and a bit more of the kohlrabi flesh.

By the way, over-the-hill kohlrabi is salvageable—although the compost heap is the best place for the leaves. Without peeling, quarter the stems, steam or boil them until tender, and purée. Sieving removes all the pithy filaments and skins. The easiest way to purée is with a food mill, as the tender flesh goes through the sieve while the fibers and skin remain in the mill. Serve the purée plain, make *Whipped Kohlrabi and Potato*, or use as a creamy soup base.

You'll notice that many of the recipes I've given you for kohlrabi call for the stems and leaves to be cooked together. But both leaves and stems are delicious cooked alone and can be substituted in other recipes in this book. Try raw kohlrabi stems in *Radish* recipes, or cooked in the *Turnip*, *Celeriac*, and *Jerusalem Artichoke* recipes. You can use the leaves in *Greens* or *Spinach* recipes (but remember that they have a firmer texture and slightly sharper flavor than spinach). The sautéed kohlrabi leaves recipe is a lovely accompaniment to any of the basic kohlrabi recipes or with *Swedish Meatballs with Kohlrabies*.

Special Information

Yields
- 1 pound kohlrabi with leaves = approximately 4 bulbous stems 1½–2 inches wide
- 1 pound kohlrabi with leaves removed = approximately 8 bulbous stems 1½–2 inches wide
- 1 pound peeled stems = approximately 10–12 ounces flesh = 3–4 servings
- 1 pound cooked, mashed kohlrabi stems = approximately 1 cup
- ½ pound trimmed kohlrabi leaves = approximately 8 cups lightly packed = 1 cup cooked and chopped

Storage and Preserving
- Separate the leaves from the stems before storing. Refrigerate, unwashed, in perforated plastic bags. The leaves will keep 2–3 days while the stems will hold for up to 1 week. For longer storage, layer kohlrabi in moist sand in a cool cellar.
- Whole kohlrabi freezes poorly because the texture breaks down. You can freeze puréed kohlrabi, but it will discolor.

Hints
- Small kohlrabies have the most delicate flavor and texture.
- Use raw kohlrabi in stir-fry dishes.
- Add small or chunked kohlrabi to stews and hearty soups; cook for 20–30 minutes until tender.

- Serve raw kohlrabi as a low-calorie snack. It tastes like a cross between radishes and white turnips. When substituting kohlrabies for white turnips, remember they have a more delicate, less assertive flavor than turnips.
- For maximum flavor, leave the skins on while cooking, peel, and then use whole, quartered, cubed, or sliced in the final preparations.
- Combine with colorful root vegetables, such as winter squash, to perk up kohlrabi's color.
- Mix grated raw kohlrabi with your favorite salad dressing.

Microwave
- 4 trimmed kohlrabies approximately 2½ inches in diameter, weighing 1 pound, with skins, placed in a covered dish with 2 tablespoons liquid, will cook done in 8 minutes. Allow a range of 6–9 minutes depending on size.

Leftovers
- Add peeled cooked kohlrabi to mixed vegetables or casseroles; heat through.
- Mash kohlrabi; mix with potatoes. Form into patties and fry in butter.
- Thicken sauces or soups with puréed kohlrabi.
- Slice kohlrabi and fry in butter.

Marketing

You want small, firm kohlrabies with tender skins and fresh, crisp-looking leaves. They should be held in a refrigerated case or on ice to prevent wilting. Avoid at all costs kohlrabies larger than 2 ½ inches—or you'll probably end up with pithy flesh, rubbery leaves, and an old taste. Also pass by any split or cracked kohlrabies.

◇ *Raw Kohlrabi*

Raw kohlrabi's delicate radishlike flavor makes it an excellent substitute in radish recipes. In addition, here are some of my favorite ways to serve raw kohlrabi.

- Cut into cubes and dip into soy sauce and sesame seeds for a low-calorie snack.
- Use on a crudités platter or slice directly into salads.
- Grate or finely chop, season with red wine vinegar, salt, and pepper, and use to garnish a composed salad plate.
- Substitue it for celeriac in cold preparations such as *Celeriac Rémoulade* (see *Celeriac*).
- For a coleslawlike salad with a sweet, mild cabbage taste, mix raw grated kohlrabi with your favorite dressing. Because kohlrabi is watery, salt it, let stand for a minute, then gently squeeze to remove moisture before mixing into dressing.

◇ *Boiled Kohlrabi*

Trim kohlrabies without peeling. Cover stems with water, add ½ teaspoon salt and butter if desired, and bring to a boil. Reduce heat and boil gently until tender. Stems from 1 ½ to 2 inches will cook tender in approximately 30 minutes. After cooking, peel skin and proceed with the recipe.

◇ *Steamed Kohlrabi*

Bring ¾–1 inch water to a boil in a steamer. Trim kohlrabies, but do not peel; place in a steamer basket or colander, and steam, covered, until tender. Kohlrabies 1 ½–2 inches in diameter will cook in 30–35 minutes. Peel and proceed with the finishing touches.

◇ *Baked Kohlrabi*

When you're baking other items in the oven, cook kohlrabi along with them. Place trimmed, unpeeled (or peeled) kohlrabi in a covered dish with 2–3 tablespoons liquid. Bake at 350° for 50–60 minutes or until tender.

Finishing Touches for Cooked Kohlrabi

- *In Butter:* Roll kohlrabi in butter, season with salt, pepper, and lemon juice (if desired), and sprinkle with parsley.
- *In a Cream Sauce:* This is the standard recipe for kohlrabi. Make a *Velouté Sauce* (see *Appendix*), using the cooking liquids if possible, and combine with cubed, sliced, or small whole cooked kohlrabies. Heat through, and add nutmeg and seasonings to taste. Top with grated cheese if desired and run under the broiler.
- *With Cheese:* Make a *Mornay Sauce* (see *Appendix*) and treat as in preceding cream sauce.
- *With Sour Cream:* Coat with sour cream; heat through. Garnish with chopped dill.
- *With Flavored Butters:* Melt butter in a sauté pan and stir in curry powder, fresh herbs, or finely minced shallots or garlic. Add cooked kohlrabi, and roll in the butter. Season with salt and pepper.
- *Glazed:* In a sauté pan, make a butter-sugar caramel glaze. Roll kohlrabi in the mixture until lightly coated.
- *Puréed:* Purée kohlrabi in a food mill or food processor. (If you use the processor, sieve to remove any pithy strands.) This is a good method for older kohlrabi. Add some cooking liquids, if desired, or heavy cream. Flavor with butter, salt, and pepper, and serve with buttered crumbs.

◇ *Sautéed Grated Kohlrabi*

This is certainly the quickest way of cooking kohlrabi, as well as the most delicious. Follow the directions for *Grated White Turnips* (page 328). Sautéing in butter seasoned with curry is equally good. I have found it best to grate by hand on the largest holes of the grater.

Butter-Braised Sliced Kohlrabi

The mirepoix gives a lovely flavor.

> 1 ½ lb kohlrabies
> 4–6 Tb butter
> *Mirepoix* (page 349)
> Salt and freshly ground pepper

Peel and slice kohlrabies into ¼-inch pieces. Heat 2 tablespoons of the butter and sauté the mirepoix until wilted, add the kohlrabies, and lightly brown for about 5 minutes. Add remaining butter and season with salt and pepper. Cover, and slowly cook until kohlrabies are tender, 20–25 minutes. *(Serves 4)*

- Substitute chopped onions for the mirepoix or omit completely.
- Julienne kohlrabies or shape into ovals, changing the cooking time, depending upon their size.

Broth-Braised Kohlrabi

1 1/2 lb kohlrabies
2 Tb butter
2 cups chicken or beef broth
Lemon juice (optional)
Salt and freshly ground pepper

Peel and slice kohlrabies into 1/4-inch pieces. Heat the butter and sauté kohlrabies over medium-high heat, tossing frequently, for 5 minutes or until lightly browned. Add the broth. Partially cover, and simmer until barely tender, approximately 20 minutes. Remove the cover, raise heat, and cook for 4–5 minutes, until the broth reduces and just coats the kohlrabi slices. Sprinkle with lemon juice if you like and season with salt and pepper. *(Serves 4)*

- After the initial 20-minute cooking period, add 1/4 cup heavy cream. Boil down until kohlrabies are glazed with sauce. Season, and sprinkle with parsley.
- Sauté a *Mirepoix* (see *Appendix*) in butter and add kohlrabi slices. Brown, and continue as above.

Sautéed Kohlrabi Leaves

2 lb kohlrabi leaves
4–6 Tb butter
Salt and freshly ground pepper
Lemon juice (optional)

Using only young leaves, wash and derib enough leaves to end up with 1 pound. Blanch in a large pot of boiling salted water until just wilted, 4–5 minutes. Place leaves under cold water to stop them from cooking, squeeze dry, and chop. Heat 2 tablespoons of the butter in a sauté pan and add the chopped kohlrabi. Cook over medium-high heat, stirring constantly, until all the moisture is evaporated. Then, add enough butter to coat and cook for 5–10 minutes longer. Season with salt, pepper, and lemon juce to taste. *(Serves 3–4)*

- Substitute kohlrabi leaves for spinach in *Creamed Spinach* (see *Spinach*).

Whipped Kohlrabi and Potato

This lighter version of whipped potatoes has a bit of tang from the kohlrabi.

1 lb potatoes
2 lb kohlrabies
3–4 Tb butter
2–3 Tb heavy cream
Salt and freshly ground pepper

Peel potatoes and cut into chunks. Trim kohlrabies; quarter larger sizes, leave small ones whole. Boil the potatoes and kohlrabies in separate pans of salted water until tender, 20–25 minutes. Drain. Skin and purée the kohlrabies. (Larger, older kohlrabies need to be sieved after puréeing to remove any fibers.) Whip the potatoes, and add to kohlrabi. Whip together with butter and cream. Season with salt and pepper. *(Makes 3–4 cups)*

Kohlrabi Dumplings (or Gnocchi)

You need a food processor for this recipe.

1 1/2 lb kohlrabi stems
1/2 lb kohlrabi leaves
14 Tb butter
1 cup ricotta cheese
Nutmeg
2 tsp salt
Freshly ground pepper
3/4 cup flour
3 large eggs
1 1/4 cups grated Parmesan cheese

Cook the kohlrabi stems, peel, and roughly chop. Set aside. Wash and derib the leaves, then blanch in a large pot of salted boiling water until just wilted, 4–5 minutes. Drain, squeeze dry, and chop leaves. Sauté in 1 tablespoon of the butter until all moisture evaporates. Place in food processor along with chopped kohlrabi and ricotta cheese; purée. Heat in a saucepan, seasoning with a pinch of nutmeg, 1 teaspoon salt, and pepper to taste. Set aside, keeping warm.

In a saucepan, bring 1 cup water, 6 tablespoons of the butter, and 1 teaspoon salt to a boil. Remove pan from the heat and add flour, beating vigorously with a wooden spoon to combine. Return mixture to the heat and beat until the mixture leaves the sides and bottom of the pan and films the bottom of the pan. Beat for 2–3 minutes longer to evaporate moisture. Remove mixture from the heat and beat in the eggs, one by one, making sure each is absorbed into the mixture before adding the next. Add the warm kohlrabi mixture along with 3/4 cup of the Parmesan cheese. Taste, and correct seasonings.

Bring a pan of salted water at least 3 inches deep to a simmer. Flour your hands and form kohlrabi mixture into 1–1 1/2-inch dumplings. Drop them into the barely simmering water, and gently roll them around to cook evenly. The dumplings will sink to the bottom, then float to the top while they cook, and will be ready in 15 minutes. Using a slotted spoon, remove dumplings and drop into a basin of cold water to firm. When the dumplings sink to the bottom, remove from the water and place them on a towel to dry for at least 10 minutes. (You can do this step ahead of time; if you're refrigerating the dumplings, dry about 30 minutes, then place between waxed paper and store them. They'll keep 2 days.)

Melt 7 tablespoons butter. Brush a baking dish with 3 tablespoons of the butter and arrange the dumplings in a single layer. Drizzle remaining butter over them and sprinkle with the remaining 1/2 cup Parmesan cheese. Bake in a preheated 350° oven for 15–20 minutes or until the dumplings are hot. *(Makes about thirty 1–1 1/2-inch dumplings)*

Kohlrabi Soup

This subtly flavored soup is good served either hot or cold.

> 3 lb kohlrabies
> 1 lb celeriac
> 1/2 lb potatoes
> 2 Tb butter
> 1 cup chopped onions or whites of leeks
> 2–2 1/2 qt chicken broth
> 1 cup light cream
> Salt and freshly ground pepper
> Nutmeg

Peel and chunk kohlrabies, celeriac, and potatoes. In a large saucepan, heat the butter and cook the onions or leeks until wilted, about 5 minutes. Add the vegetables and 2 quarts of broth, bring to the boil, reduce heat, and simmer until the vegetables are tender, 25–30 minutes. Place some of the vegetables and broth into a blender and purée until completely smooth; repeat until all the vegetables and broth are combined. Return to the heat; add the cream, salt, pepper, and a dash of nutmeg. Thin with additional broth if desired. (*Makes 2 1/2 quarts*)

- Add chopped kohlrabi leaves along with the vegetables.

Kohlrabi and Chicken Stew

This is delicious served on top of butter-coated barley, couscous, or rice.

> 3–4-lb chicken
> 2 lb kohlrabies
> 3/4 lb carrots
> 4 Tb butter
> 4 cups sliced onions
> 1 cup peeled, seeded, and chopped tomatoes
> 2 tsp salt
> 1 tsp freshly ground pepper
> Pinch saffron threads
> 1/4 tsp turmeric
> 1/2 tsp cinnamon
> 2 tsp ground coriander
> 1 qt chicken broth or water
> 4 sprigs parsley

Wash chicken, dry, remove fat, and cut into serving pieces. Peel and trim kohlrabies, separating the leaves from the flesh. Leave kohlrabies whole if small; cut into 1-inch chunks if large. Wash and derib the leaves, then cut into 1/4-inch strips. (You'll need 2–3 cups of julienned leaves.) Peel the carrots, and slice diagonally into 1/2-inch-thick pieces.

In a large saucepan, heat the butter and sauté the onions, tomatoes, salt, and spices for 4–5 minutes. Add the chicken and cook for 5 minutes. Add the broth or water and parsley. Bring broth to a boil, reduce heat, cover, and simmer for 20 minutes. Add the kohlrabies, cover, and simmer for 15 minutes. Then add the carrots, cover, and sim-

mer for 10 minutes. Finally, add the kohlrabi leaves and simmer, uncovered, 10 minutes longer or until all the vegetables are completely tender. (*Serves 6*)

- Add other chunked vegetables, such as squash or zucchini.
- Try kohlrabi leaves combined with julienned cabbage.

Lamb-Stuffed Kohlrabies

This Central European specialty is especially pretty made with small kohlrabies. It makes an unusual luncheon, light supper, or buffet dish. Count on 3–4 kohlrabies per person as a main course.

> 24–30 small (1 1/2–2-inch) kohlrabies with leaves
> 5 Tb butter
> 1/2 cup minced onions
> 1/2 tsp minced garlic
> 2 eggs
> 1 lb ground lamb
> 1 cup fresh bread crumbs
> 1 1/2 tsp salt
> Freshly ground pepper
> 1 tsp rosemary
> 1/4 cup chopped parsley
> 2 cups chicken or meat broth
> 2 Tb flour
> 1/2 cup sour cream

Wash and derib kohlrabi leaves. Chop enough to make 1 1/2 cups. Peel the kohlrabies, cutting slices off the bottoms so they will sit straight. Trim the tops and hollow out the centers, leaving shells 3/8 inch thick. Finely chop some of the pulp to make 1 cup. Combine with 1 cup of the chopped leaves; set aside. In boiling salted water, blanch the hollowed kohlrabies for 5 minutes. Drain upside down. Melt 2 tablespoons of the butter and sauté the onions until wilted; add garlic, and cook 30 seconds longer. Set aside.

Beat the eggs; add lamb, onions, garlic, bread crumbs, salt, pepper, rosemary, parsley, and the remaining ½ cup chopped kohlrabi leaves. Use the mixture to stuff hollowed kohlrabies, mounding it on top of each kohlrabi. Butter a baking dish, place the kohlrabies in it in a single layer, and strew the bottom with the reserved chopped kohlrabi pulp and leaves. Boil the broth and pour into the pan. Cover the pan and bake in a preheated 325° oven for 40–45 minutes or until the kohlrabies are tender. Remove them to a warm plate and cover to keep warm.

Reduce the pan liquids to 1½ cups. Melt 3 tablespoons butter and stir in the flour; cook for 2 minutes. Beat in the reduced liquids and add the sour cream. Bring to a boil and cook until thickened. Season to taste and coat stuffed kohlrabies. (Kohlrabies can be reheated in sauce.) *(Serves 8)*

Note: Grind your own lamb from the shoulder or neck pieces, or ask your butcher to do this.

- Stuff larger kohlrabies (if they are not pithy) and extend the cooking time to 1–1¼ hours.
- Use different spices, such as sweet Hungarian paprika, in the stuffing and sauce.

Swedish Meatballs with Kohlrabies

This is fun to do with tiny kohlrabies. Make chopped sautéed greens out of the leaves and serve as a side dish along with sliced glazed carrots. Serve the meatballs and kohlrabies on rice or noodles.

> 1 lb 1-inch kohlrabies
> 1 egg
> 1 lb ground beef
> ½ lb ground pork
> ½ cup minced onions
> ¾ cup fresh bread crumbs
> 1 Tb minced parsley
> 2 tsp salt
> ½ tsp freshly ground pepper
> 1 tsp Worcestershire sauce
> ½ cup milk
> 2 Tb butter
> 2 Tb oil
> ¼ cup flour
> 2 tsp sweet Hungarian paprika
> 2 cups beef broth
> 1 cup sour cream

Peel and trim the kohlrabies; set aside. (You should have about 12.) Beat the egg and add the beef, pork, onions, bread crumbs, parsley, 1½ teaspoons of the salt, ¼ teaspoon of the pepper, Worcestershire sauce, and milk. Form mixture into 1-inch balls. Heat the butter and oil, and brown the meatballs. Remove the meatballs, and stir the flour into the pan fats; cook for 2 minutes. Stir in the paprika, ½ teaspoon salt, and ¼ teaspoon pepper; whisk in the broth until combined, then whisk in the

sour cream. Return meatballs to sauce along with the kohlrabies. Cover and cook for about 20 minutes or until the kohlrabies are tender and the meatballs are cooked through. *(Serves 6)*

Kohlrabi Pickle Chips

This refrigerator bread-and-butter pickle recipe works equally well using pickling cucumbers instead of young kohlrabi.

> 1½–2 lb small kohlrabi, trimmed
> 3 small onions (about ½ lb)
> ¼ cup pickling salt
> 2 cups vinegar
> ⅔ cup sugar
> 1 Tb mustard seeds
> 1 tsp celery seeds
> ¼ tsp turmeric

Peel and thinly slice kohlrabi and onions. Mix salt with 1 quart of ice water, pour over the vegetables, and soak for 3 hours. Drain, rinse, and place in a bowl. Bring remaining ingredients to a boil, cook for 3 minutes, and pour over the vegetables. Cool, cover, and refrigerate for 3 days. *(Makes 1 quart)*

Leeks

I find it puzzling that leeks remain virtually unknown in the United States, while in Europe they're a cooking staple, prized for their versatility and subtlety. Here they're relegated to exotic vegetable status and sold in a few metropolitan regions—usually at prohibitive prices. There's no reason for this: they're easy to grow and are known as "poor man's asparagus" in Wales. I find them indispensable for cooking in dozens of ways from stocks, soups, appetizers, salads, and vegetables to main courses.

What sets them apart from other members of the onion family is their subtlety. Leeks have a milder, more refined flavor than onions and are easier to digest. They enhance and meld flavors together as few other ingredients can do: when I serve a dish cooked with leeks, my guests can't identify the leek flavor—they just ask what makes it so delicious. Some people will tell you that leeks aren't worth growing because onions can always be substituted for the leeks in a recipe. That's wrong. All the delicacy of the finished dish would be lost. At the restaurant I prepare an elaborate lobster stew in which leeks are a crucial ingredient. I never serve it when leeks aren't available, for onions would destroy the delicate taste of the lobster.

Leeks could be as common as onions (as they are in France, Belgium, England, and Wales, where they're worn in the hat on St. David's Day) because they're easy to grow and virtually pest free. We've grown them successfully in the Victory Garden and at home for years, starting with seedlings of Giant Musselburgh, a proven variety that's been around most of this century. Leeks have a long growing season, so it's best to start with plants, either those you grow from seed or seedlings from a commercial source. In late January or early February at our place, Russ plants seeds in a 6-inch standard pot filled with potting soil. (He doesn't use a flat because it's not deep enough to allow for sufficient root development.) Six weeks later, when the ground can be worked, he transplants the tiny, grasslike seedlings 6 inches apart into a 12-inch-deep trench filled with 3 inches of compost. A month later he begins filling in the trench around the plants, gradually blanching them. Repeating this every 6 weeks, he scratches in some 5-10-5 fertilizer each time, because leeks are heavy feeders. This continual hilling up is important because the longer the white, blanched portion of the leek, the greater the yield of edible vegetable. Our leeks are easier to clean than those at the market because Russ is careful not to mound the earth so high that it works its way down into the leaves. By July, our first scallion-size thinnings can be harvested for salads, or for such recipes as *Baked Scallops and Leeks*, while the remaining plants continue to mature until harvest time in mid-fall.

We harvest many of our leeks by late fall. The rest Russ mulches heavily before the ground freezes, allowing us to dig them up throughout the winter. Leeks are biennial plants that set seed the second year. Wintering-over can be tricky, for leeks should be harvested the moment they start growing again in spring; otherwise, they'll get ready to set seed, their stalks will become hard and woody, and the leeks will be useless for cooking. (This hard, woody core forms the base of the seed stalk.)

The best time to harvest leeks is when they're 1½ inches in diameter. Larger than this, they become tougher and stronger flavored, fine for soups or stews, but not for recipes in which delicacy of texture and flavor is essential. Harvest with a spading fork, or barring this, ease out of the ground with a twisting motion. (If you have heavy soil, don't pull leeks out by force—chances are you'll end up with a slimy bunch of leaves and a decimated plant.) Trim the leeks right in the garden, saving the blanched white base up to the point where the green begins to shade into white, and relegating the upper dark green leaves to the compost pile. (These leaves have very little flavor and are not worth saving.) Trim the roots, leaving ½ inch at the base of the plant.

Leeks' broad, flat leaves easily collect soil and grit, making it imperative to clean them carefully. Unless you're cooking leeks whole, wash them like this: remove

any withered outer leaves, and cut off and discard the green upper leaves down to the point where the dark green begins to pale. Quarter lengthwise to within 1½ inches of the base, and gently fan out the leaves so that grit is easy to remove. Fill your sink or a deep pot with lukewarm water and plunge the leeks upside down a number of times. If the leeks are extra gritty, let them soak or clean in lukewarm water under the tap. To clean whole leeks, slit down one side to within 1½ inches of

the base, then gently spread out the leaves and run under lukewarm water. They'll stay whole during cooking: serve cut side down.

I cook leeks every which way, but when serving them whole I braise them because I think braising best retains their texture and flavor. However, boiling and steaming are also useful, especially as a first step for a completed dish with a heated sauce or marinade. Whatever method you use, take into account what I call the "repose" time. When you drain hot leeks, if you do not immediately plunge them into cold water, they continue to cook. Remember this when testing for tenderness, and if necessary, remove leeks slightly underdone. Overcooking ruins leeks. They become mushy, almost slimy, and fall apart easily.

Marketing

At the market pick out straight, cylindrical plants with clean bases and fresh, moist upper green leaves. Avoid any with dried-out leaves (a sign they're not fresh) or bulbous bases (a sign they may be woody). Woody leeks are the bane of the cook in the spring, when commercial-

Special Information

Yields
- 2 pounds leeks = 1 pound cleaned = approximately 4 cups chopped leeks = 2 cups cooked chopped leeks
- Count on ½ cup cooked leeks per portion

Storage and Preserving
- Store leeks unwashed with roots attached. Keep them dry; wet, they turn brown and begin to rot. I've held refrigerated leeks for 2 weeks with no loss of quality, but past that point they deteriorate. When you're refrigerating leeks, loosely wrap in plastic so other foods don't pick up their aroma. For longer storage, the best method is to mulch them in the garden before the gound freezes and dig them as needed. You can store harvested leeks in a cold, dry area.
- Don't can or freeze leeks. Freezing softens them; they lose all texture and may pick up a bitter taste. Freeze only cooked leftovers for soups, and use up within 3 months.

Hints
- If you're flavoring a soup with leeks, don't throw them out. Purée and put them back into the soup to thicken it.
- Drain leeks thoroughly, or they'll be watery.
- Sprinkle with grated lemon rind.
- For a quick bouquet garni of fresh herbs, sandwich herbs in a split leek and wrap with string—easier and quicker than wrapping in cheesecloth.

- Cook pencil-size leek thinnings and use in salads or for garnishes.
- Make a *Leeks à la Grecque* appetizer. Make the marinade in *Mixed Vegetables à la Grecque* (see *Appendix*). Bring the marinade to a boil in a stainless steel pan. Add leeks and enough boiling water to cover two-thirds of the leeks. Simmer for 8–10 minutes. When leeks are tender, remove them and boil down the marinade to ¾ cup. Pour over leeks and refrigerate before serving.

Microwave
- ½ pound trimmed leeks, placed in a covered dish, will cook tender in 6–8 minutes. However, as the outer layers will be chewy and the inner layers soft and mushy, I don't recommend cooking them this way.

Leftovers
- Use in any casserole in place of onions or garlic.
- Any leftover leeks are delicious in soups such as lentil or fish chowder.
- Add grilled, peeled sweet peppers to leftover marinated leeks for a completely new salad.
- Combine raw hamburger with leftover chopped braised leeks for very light, moist meatballs.
- Use in sandwiches. Top lightly toasted Syrian bread with a tomato slice, chopped cooked leeks, and mozzarella cheese. Run under the broiler to melt cheese.
- Reheat cooked chopped leeks in butter. Combine with equal amount mashed potatoes. Delicious!

ly wintered-over leeks are for sale in northern markets. These leeks are fine if they've been harvested correctly, but harvested late, they ought to be discarded, not sold. If you end up with a batch of woody leeks, don't throw them out; march right back to your market and complain. Young leeks are now being shipped from California, Mexico, and Florida during the spring, so your produce manager ought to be able to locate a good supplier.

◇ *Whole Braised Leeks*

I like to present these as part of a fall vegetable platter along with sautéed baby carrots, quartered beets, and tiny whole Brussels sprouts. The braising time depends upon the leeks' diameter and age. I've had ³/₄-inch-diameter leeks ready in 8 minutes, while older leeks double that size have taken up to 30 minutes. Just keep testing. Leeks are ready when their bases can be easily pierced by the point of a sharp knife.

Trim leeks but keep whole and slit down one side to within 1 inch of base. Fan out the leaves, run them under lukewarm water to dislodge the grit, and drain thoroughly. I would use about eight ³/₄–1-inch-diameter leeks to serve 4. In a large sauté pan, melt butter (4 tablespoons for 8 leeks) and roll leeks around until they're completely covered with butter; cook until barely colored. (It may be necessary to do this in two batches.) Layer leeks in the pan and pour over water or stock halfway up their sides (2–3 cups liquid for 8 leeks). Bring to a boil, turn down heat, partially cover, and simmer until tender. Pour off any accumulated liquid and serve, saving braising liquid for sauces or soups.

You can also cook the leeks in a 350° oven after they've been browned in butter. Just add stock or water, partially cover with aluminum foil, and cook until leeks are tender and glazed, 50–60 minutes. (The reason they're partially covered is to let steam escape. Uncovered, they'll brown, while totally covered they'll become limp and unappealing.)

- When the first leeks in your garden are the size of fat scallions, harvest, and braise as above. They'll take but a few minutes to cook.
- Cook in less liquid. By the end of the cooking time it will almost totally evaporate—the leeks will turn golden and have a stronger flavor.

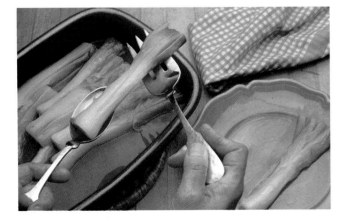

- You can braise or "poach" leeks with just broth and omit the butter.

Finishing Touches for Whole Braised Leeks

- *In Cream Sauce:* Use the braising liquid to make a cream or cheese sauce. Cover the cooked leeks with the sauce and run under the broiler.
- *In Tomato Sauce:* Cover with 2 cups fresh *Marinara Sauce* (see *Tomatoes*), using braising liquid to dilute sauce. Serve hot or chilled. If chilled, remove from refrigerator 30 minutes before serving to come to room temperature. Serve with olives and lemon wedges.

◇ *Whole Boiled Leeks*

Trim and wash leeks. Add to boiling water and cook until barely tender, about 12 minutes for 1¼-inch recently harvested leeks. Drain well.

- Try topping with a cream, cheese, or fresh tomato and onion sauce, with a black olive garnish.
- See *Leeks Vinaigrette*.

◇ *Whole Steamed Leeks*

Trim and wash leeks. Bring 1 inch of water to boil in steamer. Add leeks and cook until tender, approximately 15 minutes for 1¼-inch leeks. Cooking time will be determined by the size and age of the leeks. Remove from steamer, drain, and sauce or simply roll in melted butter and seasonings.

- Whole baby leeks, ½ inch in diameter or less, are delicious steamed or boiled. Clean and tie in bundles and cook for just a few minutes. Pour lemon butter over and eat like asparagus.
- Try the sauces mentioned under *Whole Boiled Leeks*.

◇ *Chopped Braised Leeks*

Chopped braised leeks not only are delicious but also can be prepared quickly—a big plus when you need a vegetable on the table within 15 minutes. This basic preparation is found later on as an ingredient in other recipes.

> 6 Tb butter
> 4 cups chopped leeks
> 2 large stalks celery, chopped (optional)
> Salt and freshly ground pepper

Melt butter in a saucepan and add leeks and celery (if you wish). Stir vegetables to coat with butter, and cover pan. Cook over low heat for 8–10 minutes, checking to make sure they don't stick to the pan and burn. Season with salt and pepper. (*Serves 4*)

- Try in timbales. Just replace the spinach mixture in *Spinach Timbales* (see *Spinach*) with the chopped mixture above.
- For a less buttery dish, use 3 tablespoons butter and 1 cup chicken broth or water while braising. When leeks are cooked, remove cover and reduce liquid. Season and serve.

- Pour ¹/₂ cup heavy cream and ¹/₃ cup feta cheese over the cooked leeks and stir until cheese melts and leeks are coated with sauce. Serve on sautéed buttered toast for a Sunday night supper.
- Sliced or julienned leeks accept the same treatment.

Leeks Vinaigrette

In France, leeks are so plentiful and inexpensive that they're prepared in hundreds of ways. One popular way is leeks vinaigrette, a piquant, classic appetizer, which also makes an excellent summer luncheon dish. I serve leeks with toasted rye bread: my family finds the textural contrast between the smooth leeks and the hard edge of the bread very pleasant. Use summer's early leeks for this recipe.

Butter
Eight ³/₄-inch leeks
2–3 cups water or chicken broth, or combination of both
Salt and freshly ground pepper
Vinaigrette Sauce (page 352)

Clean and trim leeks to equal lengths and place in a large buttered pan. Pour broth halfway up their sides. Bring to a boil, immediately lower heat, partially cover, and cook until tender. Leeks this size will take 8–15 minutes, depending upon their age. Remove from liquid and drain. Season to taste. While still warm, cover with vinaigrette. Serve lukewarm or chilled. If chilled, remove from refrigerator 30 minutes before serving. *(Serves 4)*

Leek Tartlets

I often make these unusual leek tartlets for an appetizer course. Through the years I've varied the filling, adding crab, cheese, or meats, but I always come back to the simplicity of leeks. No one can decipher the leek taste; they just ask for more.

Butter
Tart Pastry (page 351)
2 cups *Chopped Braised Leeks* (page 157), cooled
2 large eggs
1¹/₂ cups heavy cream
Few drops hot pepper sauce
Salt and freshly ground pepper

Butter twenty-four 2¹/₂-inch tartlet molds or muffin tins about ¹/₂ inch deep. Roll out pastry dough ¹/₈ inch thick and cut with a cookie cutter ¹/₂ inch larger in diameter than your molds. Line with pastry and prick with a fork. Partially fill each mold with a tablespoon of the leeks. Beat eggs with cream, season with hot pepper sauce, salt, and pepper, and add a tablespoon to each mold. Mix with a fork so that eggs, cream, and leeks blend together.

Bake in a preheated 425° oven for 15 minutes or until nicely browned. Let rest for 1 minute before unmolding. Serve hot. *(Makes 24 tarts)*

- Add cheese, tiny bits of ham, or sausage for a heartier appetizer.
- *Rutabaga Tartlets:* Substitute 1¹/₂ cups diced rutabaga for leeks. Sauté the rutabaga in butter, cover, and cook over very low heat for 20–30 minutes or until soft but still retaining shape. Mix with ¹/₂ cup crumbled feta cheese, combine with remaining ingredients, and proceed with recipes as given above.

Leek Tart

Leek tart is a specialty of the Alsace region of France, along the Rhine River. Take it along on a picnic, or bake it for a Sunday night supper.

8 slices bacon (optional)
2 cups *Chopped Braised Leeks* (page 157), cooled
10-inch pastry shell, partially baked (page 351)
4 large eggs
1¹/₂ cups cream
³/₄ tsp salt
¹/₄ tsp sugar
Dash hot pepper sauce

Cook bacon until crisp, cool, and crumble into bits. Spread leeks evenly in pastry shell and sprinkle bacon bits over. Mix eggs, cream, salt, sugar, and hot pepper sauce, and pour over leeks, mixing with fork to distribute egg mixture throughout. Bake in a preheated 425° oven for 15 minutes, then turn oven down to 300° and bake an additional 30 minutes, or until a knife inserted into the center comes out clean. Remove and let sit for 15 minutes. *(Serves 8)*

- Prick ¹/₂ pound kielbasa or chorizo sausages and cook in boiling water for 5–10 minutes to release fat. Slice into very thin diagonal slices and layer on top of tart before baking.
- Slice olives, peeled red peppers, and anchovies in any combination on top before baking.

Leek and Potato Soup

This perfectly simple, humble soup is wonderful for supper on a cold, wet day. Or, when friends arrive unexpectedly and you're caught with nothing in the house, in minutes you can fix a delicious company soup with leeks and potatoes from the garden. Some cooks use water, but I think chicken stock gives a richer flavor. Try both ways and see which you prefer.

4 oz butter
5 cups chopped leeks
2 stalks celery, chopped
1 large onion, chopped
3–4 cups roughly chopped potatoes
2 qt chicken stock or water
1–2 cups heavy cream
Salt and freshly ground pepper

Melt the butter in a saucepan, add the leeks, celery, and onion, and stew slowly until golden and soft, about 10 minutes. Don't let the mixture brown. Add potatoes and chicken stock or water; cover and bring to a boil. Reduce the heat and simmer until potatoes are cooked through —anywhere from 20 to 40 minutes, depending on the potatoes' age and how finely they're chopped. Mash vegetables or roughly purée in a food processor or food mill. Heat the cream and add to the soup, along with salt and pepper to taste. *(Serves 4–6)*

- The soup, minus cream, keeps very well in the refrigerator and freezes beautifully. Reheat and add cream at serving time.
- If you're using canned chicken stock, a squeeze of lemon juice will give it a fresher taste.
- Have too few leeks? Add an onion.
- Add leftover vegetables after potatoes have cooked.
- Add rough-chopped fresh vegetables to first butter simmer.

Vichyssoise

Vichyssoise was invented by a French chef, Louis Diat, more than fifty years ago when he was head chef at the New York Ritz Carlton. One day, he needed a new cold soup recipe and was inspired by memories of his mother's leek and potato soup, which she would often cool with milk. Diat changed milk to cream, chilled it, added some minced chives, and named it after Vichy, a spa close to his boyhood home. It's been a mainstay on restaurant menus ever since.

    Leek and Potato Soup (preceding recipe)
    2 cups heavy cream
    3–4 Tb finely chopped fresh chives

Purée leek and potato soup so that it is totally blended. Use full 2 cups of cream. Add cream and chill. Serve with a sprinkling of chives on each portion. *(Serves 4)*

Leek and Barley Soup

This hearty soup brings together two neglected soup ingredients—barley and leeks. As all of the vegetables are puréed, it's a good way to use up your tougher late fall leeks.

    2 oz barley
    8 cups chicken stock
    1 onion
    3 stalks celery
    6 cups chopped leeks
    1 cup finely chopped carrots
    6 Tb butter
    1 cup cream
    Salt and freshly ground black pepper

Blanch barley in 1 quart boiling water for 5 minutes; drain. Put 5 cups chicken stock in a large saucepan, add barley, cover, and simmer until cooked through, 1–1 1/4 hours.

Meanwhile, chop onion and celery. Stew the onion, celery, leeks, and carrots in the butter over low heat until the vegetables are soft and golden. Add the remaining stock and simmer for approximately 10 minutes or until tender. Roughly purée the vegetables. When the barley is cooked, add the leek mixture to it, then add cream and seasonings to taste. *(Serves 4–6)*

- For a richer version, beat 1 egg yolk with the cream, add stock to warm, and stir into the soup.

Stir-Fried Shrimp and Leeks

Only leeks will do here, for their mild flavor accentuates the delicate taste of the shrimp, while their pale green color is a perfect foil for the shrimps' coral tones. Stir-frying with salt and sugar is a Chinese trick which keeps the leeks bright green and smooth-textured.

    1 lb whole leeks
    1 lb medium raw shrimp
    1 Tb very dry sherry
    1 1/2 Tb light soy sauce
    1 tsp salt
    3/4 tsp sugar
    2/3 cup peanut or vegetable oil
    1 quarter-size piece of fresh ginger, minced
    1 clove garlic, minced

Trim and wash the leeks. Either cut into very thin diagonal rounds or finely julienne into 1½–2-inch strips. Peel and devein the shrimp and set aside. Mix sherry, soy sauce, ½ teaspoon salt, and ¼ teaspoon sugar together and set aside.

Heat oil in a wok or skillet to 375°, or until a small cube of bread browns immediately. Scatter in shrimp, a few at a time, and toss for a minute to whiten and blister, almost like searing a roast. Strain, reserving the oil, and place shrimp on paper towels to drain. Return 2 tablespoons oil to the pan, reheat, and stir in leeks. Sprinkle with ½ teaspoon salt and stir for 1 minute. Add ½ teaspoon sugar and stir for another 2 minutes. Add ginger and garlic, toss and sauté for 30 seconds. Return shrimp to pan along with the sherry–soy sauce mixture, cover, and cook for 1 minute. Uncover and stir for 2 minutes, and serve very hot. (*Serves 4*)

- For more sauce, add ¼ cup water or chicken stock to the soy sauce–sherry mixture, and thicken just before serving with 1 tablespoon cornstarch dissolved in 2 tablespoons water.
- Substitute chicken meat for the shrimp or use just the leeks.
- Try finely julienned turnip cooked with the leeks, put the cover on and steam for 2–3 minutes.

Leeks and Chicken Breasts

Last year, after a wonderful European business trip, we arrived home to find ourselves satiated with rich foods. It was fall and the leeks were ready. I put together this dish and it was just right for us—it's quickly made, light, and quite beautiful to look at.

 4 whole chicken breasts (to make 8 trimmed pieces)
 2 cups *Chopped Braised Leeks* (page 157)
 Salt and freshly ground black pepper

Bone chicken breasts, making sure you remove the tendons, and save the bones for broth. Place braised leeks in a sauté pan with extra butter if needed. Heat, then lay the chicken breasts on top, cover, and cook over low heat. The chicken will poach on top of the leeks and be ready in 8–10 minutes. Uncover and season with salt and pepper. Serve the chicken on its bed of braised leeks. (*Serves 4*)
Note: Watch to ensure that the leeks don't burn. It may be necessary to add a few tablespoons of chicken stock or water.

- Chicken legs and thighs are equally good, but will take longer to cook, 25–30 minutes.
- Try making with julienned leeks and carrots. Just blanch the carrots and add to the leeks along with the chicken.
- Slivers of leftover ham or tongue are also a nice addition with the chicken. Experiment.

Baked Scallops and Leeks

This subtle preparation of scallops and leeks is one of my favorite recipes: it's elegant yet simple to make. I prefer to cook with the more delicate baby sea scallops, but they can be hard to find; large sea scallops will do almost as well. If possible, use leek thinnings from your garden, so they'll be almost the same size as the scallops.

 Six ½-inch-diameter leeks
 1½ lb scallops
 8 oz butter
 3 Tb finely chopped shallots
 ¼ cup fresh bread crumbs

Clean leeks, keeping them whole, then tie together with kitchen string and plunge into boiling salted water. Cook for 5 minutes, or just until tender. Run under cold water, pat thoroughly dry, and cut into ½-inch rounds.

Examine your scallops carefully. If they have nugget-like side protrusions (which formerly connected the flesh and shells), pull them off, for they will cook up like rubber bands and ruin your dish. Cut large scallops into ½-inch pieces. Wipe the scallops dry. Butter 4 scallop shells or small au gratin casseroles and divide scallops and leeks evenly among them. Melt remaining butter in a small saucepan, add the shallots, and cook until they're lightly colored, approximately 3 minutes. Pour shallot butter over the scallops and leeks and sprinkle lightly with bread crumbs. Bake in a preheated 400° oven for 15 minutes, then remove and run under the broiler briefly to brown the crumbs. (*Serves 4*)

Leek and Pork Pie

Traditional meat pies, chock full of meat and gravy, can be very solid and indigestible. That's not the case here: the leeks predominate, resulting in a pie that's very filling yet not too heavy. I use lard in the pastry, which guarantees a flaky, richly flavored crust. The pie may be cooked early in the day and reheated later.

 4 thick slices bacon
 1 onion, sliced
 9 Tb butter
 2 Tb oil
 2 lb cleaned leeks
 4 stalks celery
 2 lb lean pork
 1 cup flour
 Salt and freshly ground pepper
 1 clove garlic, minced
 1 bay leaf
 Pinch of rosemary
 2 cups dry white wine or broth
 3 cups combined chicken and beef broth
 ½ lb whole mushrooms
 Shortcrust Pastry (page 351)
 1 egg

and cook until the broth reaches a consistency thick enough to lightly coat the pork and vegetables. Mix broth with the casserole contents and cool before covering with pastry.

Preheat oven to 400°. Prepare shortcrust pastry, roll out, and cut into shape 1 inch larger than the top of your casserole. Fit over casserole, crimping pastry edges as if you were making a pie crust. Beat egg with a teaspoon of water and paint an egg glaze on the dough. Cut an air hole or slits, and paint again with egg glaze. Bake for 30 minutes and serve hot. *(Serves 6)*

- Cook with beef or lamb. As they may become tender faster, check simmering mixture after 1 hour. If you use leftover meats, simmer all the ingredients for 30 minutes, add leftover meat, and bake as directed.
- Prunes go well with pork. Soak for 1–2 hours, or until plumped, and add to casserole along with mushrooms.

Cockaleekie

This old Scottish recipe combines an old fowl and coarse end-of-season leeks for a flavorful and inexpensive meal. Fowl is much cheaper than roasting or frying chicken and has better flavor in any dish calling for long simmering. The prunes are traditional, and impart a distinctive slightly sweet taste to the broth. Omit them if this doesn't appeal to you.

6-lb fowl
3 lb leeks, washed and trimmed
6 parsley sprigs
1/2 tsp thyme
1 bay leaf
6 peppercorns
1 qt chicken or beef stock or water
1/2 lb prunes (optional)

Put fowl into casserole and surround with half the leeks. Tie parsley, thyme, bay leaf, and peppercorns in cheesecloth and add to casserole. Add stock or water to cover. Bring to a boil, skim, reduce heat, and cook, partially covered, for 2–3 hours or until the chicken meat is falling off the bone. Remove leeks and chicken from broth. Cool chicken and then remove meat from bones in large chunks. Degrease broth.

Purée leeks in a food processor or put through a food mill. Return purée to broth and simmer to reduce and thicken broth. Chop remaining leeks into 1/2-inch rounds, add to broth, and cook for 20 minutes. Add chicken meat and prunes (if you like); cook for another 15 minutes. Serve as is or remove prunes before serving. *(Serves 6)*

- For a clear broth, do not add puréed cooked leeks. Save for another meal.
- Simmer a 2-pound piece of shin beef with the chicken for a chicken-beef stew.
- Add 1/3 cup rice in final 15 minutes.

Cut bacon into 1/4-inch strips and blanch in boiling water for 10 minutes to remove excess saltiness. Drain, rinse in cold water, and dry thoroughly. Cook onion in 1 tablespoon butter and 1 tablespoon oil until tender, then turn up heat to brown, which will give a nice color and flavor to the pie.

Cut the leeks and celery into 2-inch sections, then sliver into matchstick-size pieces. (This sounds time-consuming but goes quickly with a good sharp knife, and even faster with a food processor with a julienne attachment.) Melt 6 tablespoons butter in a saucepan, stir in leeks and celery, and cook slowly until tender, approximately 10 minutes.

While leeks and celery are cooking, heat 1 tablespoon oil in a saucepan and cook bacon until crisp, remove from pan, and save the fat. Cut pork into 1 1/2-inch cubes, toss in 1/2 cup flour seasoned with salt and pepper, shake off excess flour, and brown in bacon fat.

Pour off excess fat from pork; add leeks and celery, browned onion, bacon, garlic, bay leaf, and rosemary. Cover with wine and broth and bring to a boil; turn down the heat and simmer, covered, for 1 1/2 hours. In the meantime, melt 2 tablespoons butter in a frying pan, sauté mushrooms until lightly browned, and set aside.

Reserving the broth, place the contents of the saucepan and the mushrooms into a 2-quart ovenproof casserole about 3 inches deep. Mix 1/2 cup flour with enough water to make a thin paste. Whisk into simmering broth

Okra

People either like okra or they can't stomach it because of its slimy texture when cooked. But it is this mucilaginous character that makes okra capable of thickening any liquid it is cooked in. Okra is really best when stewed or simmered, which allows its juices to lightly thicken a dish, although it can be simply sautéed, steamed, or boiled (and some people do like it that way). By the way, the mucilaginous texture is caused by the sugar-carbohydrate ratio within the plants, which are part of the mallow family.

There's nothing controversial about the flavor of okra: it has a subtle taste similar to that of eggplant. In fact, foods that go well with eggplant also match up nicely with okra. Okra complements tomatoes, peppers, corn, lamb, ham, bacon, and other smoky meats—and is enhanced by spices such as coriander. It's also particularly delicious combined with shellfish, and with fish and fish stock.

Although okra is usually associated with southern cooking, there's no reason that it can't be grown successfully in the North. Anywhere cucumbers and eggplant prosper, you can grow okra.

In mid-April, Russ sows 2 seeds per peat pot. Because the seed surfaces are hard, he lightly rubs a piece of sandpaper over them before planting, making it easier for the seeds to germinate. Once the plants start growing, he pinches out the weaker seedlings, leaving just one plant per pot. In June, he sets the plants out in the garden, 18 inches apart, in well-drained, fertile soil. Okra is quite ornamental—eventually the plants reach 4 feet tall with attractive foliage and yellow blossoms with red centers that flower before the pods appear. The pods are the edible portion of the plants. By July, the first okra is ready for harvesting.

Okra must be harvested daily, or at least every other day, to keep the pods from turning fibrous and woody, and to keep the plants producing. For the highest-quality okra, pick pods when they're no longer than 2–2 1/2 inches, breaking off the stems immediately above their cap-shaped tops. Remember, the more you pick, the more you get. One warning: avoid touching the leaves if possible. Commercial harvesters wear long sleeves and gloves to pick okra. The leaves give some people a rash that I'm told is similar to having a batting of fiberglass rubbed against your body.

Do you remember gathering milkweed pods as a child, touching their fuzzy surfaces, blowing the inside fluff into the air, and having your fingers become sticky? Well, okra has those same properties. The surface fuzz is easy to deal with: wash the pods, and with a small, stiff brush, remove the fuzz. (Scraping with a paring knife works equally well.) Then, remove the stem and peel the cap of the okra, concentrically. Don't cut into the interior flesh, or you'll release the juices. Of course, if you're cutting up the okra, you don't have to be quite as careful—the juices will come out the moment you cut into the pods.

When you sauté okra, the juices "rope" and form a spiderweblike string on the surface of the pods, which dries up somewhat as the okra continues to cook. There's nothing harmful about this roping—it's merely the way the protein in the okra reacts to heat, and it doesn't affect the flavor of the dish at all. So ignore it.

Frankly, I don't like okra cooked plain. I can't warm up to its soft, gummy interior. But a friend raised in the South disagrees: she boils up the pods, laces them with melted butter and lemon, and considers them a special treat. So don't take my word for it—try okra plain, too—you might like it.

Marketing

The best okra is the freshest okra, so if you're restricted to market purchases, select bright green pods no longer than 2 1/2–3 inches. Feel them—they should be tender and easily snapped. Old pods get fibrous and woody, and darken when exposed to air.

◇ *Stewed Okra with Vegetables*

The best way by far to cook okra is to stew it with other vegetables. By this, I mean a gentle braising to tenderize the okra, release its juices, and mingle its flavors with the vegetables. There's no need for a long cooking period culminating in mushy grayish okra, although simmering in a stew or soup doesn't hurt its mellow flavor. For the basic technique, see *Okra and Tomato Stew*. My next choice would be to cook it in a microwave (see *Microwave*).

◇ *Blanched Okra*

Wash and trim whole okra pods. Drop in a large pot of boiling salted water and cook for approximately 5 minutes until tender. Drain.

◇ *Steamed Okra*

Wash and trim okra. Boil 3/4–1-inch of water in a steamer. Place pods in a steamer basket or colander. Steam for 5–6 minutes. Remove and drain.

Special Information

Yields
- 1 pound okra = 10–12 ounces trimmed = 3–4 cups sliced
- 1 pound = 3–4 servings

Storage and Preserving
- Pick just before cooking, because the pods lose their bright green color and toughen up in storage. If you must store okra, spread the pods out flat, without washing, and place in a perforated plastic bag in the refrigerator. (When okra is stored wet, it molds on the outside and becomes even slimier inside.) A day or two in the refrigerator is all the storing okra will take. Freeze any you can't use by then.

Freezing
- Freeze only young, tender okra. Wash, and trim off stems, leaving caps whole. Blanch in boiling water for 4 minutes. Cool in ice water for 4 minutes. Drain, and loosely pack in freezer bags. Will keep 6–8 months.

Pickling
- See *Pickled Okra*.

Hints
- Use cut okra pieces to thicken soups or stews.
- Add to stewed vegetables.

- Use sliced cooked okra in omelets and quiches. Use with tomatoes for the best results. Tomatoes' acidity cuts the mucilaginous texture of okra, while the flavors are complementary.
- Put okra in *Ratatouille* (see *Eggplant*). Sauté as you would the eggplant and pepper, and add to the stewing vegetables.
- Do not purée okra. It comes out thick, gluey, and messy.
- Cook sliced okra in butter along with onions and ham. Combine with cooked rice and use to stuff hollowed-out tomatoes. Bake for 10 minutes at 400°.

Microwave
- If you have a microwave oven and want to eat okra plain, I definitely recommend this method over both blanching and steaming. For some reason, the okra is drier and not as mucilaginous cooked in the microwave. One pound stemmed and washed okra, placed in a dish with only the water clinging to it, takes 6 minutes to cook covered.

Leftovers
- Add to egg dishes such as omelets and quiches.
- Reheat with cooked rice, or sauté with cooked potatoes.

Finishing Touches for Blanched and Steamed Okra

- *With Butter and Lemon:* Drain okra; lightly sauté in butter and lemon juice. Season to taste.
- *With Tomatoes and Cucumbers:* Cool okra in cold water. Drain and pat dry. Cut into ¼–½-inch slices; combine with chopped tomatoes and cucumbers.
- *With Vinaigrette:* Dress with a lemon *Vinaigrette Sauce* (see *Appendix*). Serve chilled.
- *Deep-Fried Okra:* Slightly undercook okra. Cool, drain, and pat dry. Roll in bread crumbs or corn meal, and fry in hot oil. Drain on paper towels; season with salt and pepper.

◇ Sautéed Okra

When sautéing raw prepared okra, it's best to use clarified butter (or butter and oil). Okra picks up a bitter taste when it browns too much, and clarified butter helps prevent this from happening. Wash whole okra, dry it well, and remove the stems and the caps, without cutting into the flesh. Melt clarified butter in a sauté pan and toss the okra pods in the butter. Sauté over moderate to high heat for 2–3 minutes, reduce heat to low, cover, and sauté, tossing often until just tender. Season to taste.

- *Curried Okra:* Add curry powder to the clarified butter and cook for 1 minute before adding okra.
- *Sweet and Sour Okra:* Mix equal parts lemon juice and sugar, approximately 2 tablespoons of each per ½ pound okra. After the initial sauté, add the lemon-sugar mixture. Stir for 1 minute. Add ½ cup water, lower heat to medium, and, tossing constantly, reduce liquids until thickened. When the sauce is syrupy, the okra should be tender.

Fried Okra

Our good friend John Fitch insisted that we try this method of preparing okra. He has served it at many a meal while working in Atlanta, Georgia, and swears it is by far the best way to enjoy okra. He holds that the crisply cooked exterior nicely balances the super soft interior. Judge for yourself.

1 lb okra, preferably 1–2 inches long
2 eggs
½ cup milk
1 tsp salt
Vegetable oil
1 cup crushed cracker crumbs
Salt and freshly ground pepper

Wash and dry okra; remove stems. Beat eggs, milk, and salt. Heat 1 inch of vegetable oil in a saucepan. Dip okra into the egg mixture, then into crumbs, coating thoroughly. Fry in the hot oil until crisp, lightly browned, and just tender. Drain on paper towels. Serve sprinkled with salt and pepper. (*Serves 4*)

Okra Soup

Notice how the okra thickens the broth in a light, subtle manner.

½ lb okra
3 Tb butter
1 cup chopped onions
½ cup chopped celery
½ cup chopped minced green peppers
½ cup minced carrots (optional)
2 cups roughly chopped, peeled, seeded tomatoes (or use canned)
7 cups chicken stock (preferably homemade)
½ cup raw rice
1 cup small lima beans
2 cups corn kernels
1–1½ cups minced chicken (optional)
Salt and freshly ground pepper

Wash, dry, and stem okra and cut into ¼-inch slices. Heat butter in a large saucepan; cook onions, celery, peppers, and carrots (if you wish) until wilted, 5–10 minutes. Add okra; sauté for 5 minutes, stirring until the "roping" of the mucilage diminishes. Add tomatoes and chicken stock. Bring to a boil, stir in rice, reduce heat, and simmer covered for 10 minutes. Add lima beans. Simmer 10 minutes longer. Add corn and chicken (if desired); heat through for approximately 5 minutes. Season

to taste and serve. *(Makes 2 quarts)*
- Omit beans and corn; slightly increase the amount of okra.
- Experiment with different vegetable combinations, such as chopped summer squash or green beans, retaining the okra for thickening.
- Make a shellfish soup. Replace chicken stock and chicken with shellfish stock and crabmeat or shrimp.

Okra and Tomato Stew

Okra and tomatoes are the ideal combination, as the tomatoes' acidity offsets okra's somewhat gluey texture. Use this simple stew as a base for other vegetable combinations, or eat as is.

> 1 lb okra
> 1 lb tomatoes
> 1 clove garlic
> 1 small hot red pepper (optional)
> 2 Tb butter
> 1 Tb vegetable oil
> 1 cup chopped onions
> 1/2 cup chopped celery (optional)
> Salt and freshly ground pepper

Clean and trim okra; cut into 1/2-inch pieces. Peel, seed, and chop tomatoes. Finely mince garlic and chili pepper (if using it). Heat butter and oil in a sauté pan. Stir in the okra, onions, and celery (if you wish); sauté until lightly colored, about 10 minutes. Add garlic, tomatoes, and chili pepper; sauté 3–4 minutes longer. Reduce heat, and simmer for 10–15 minutes or until the okra is tender. Season to taste and serve. *(Serves 4–6)*
- Cook bacon in fat instead of butter and oil; top with crumbled bacon.
- For a main course, add 1/2-inch cubes of sautéed cooked ham. Serve with rice.
- Use other vegetables, such as thin rounds of carrots, corn, lima beans, or small green bean pieces.

Okra and Lamb Stew

> 2 lb okra
> 2 lb lamb neck and shoulder
> 1 lb eggplant
> Salt
> 1 green pepper
> 2 Tb butter
> 2 Tb plus 1/4–1/2 cup oil
> 1 cup chopped onions
> 3 tsp chopped garlic
> 1 tsp coriander
> Freshly ground pepper
> 6 cups peeled, seeded, and roughly chopped tomatoes
> Juice of 1 lemon (optional)

Wash, trim, and dry okra; cut large okra into 1-inch chunks. Cut lamb into 1 1/2-inch chunks. Peel eggplant, cut into 1-inch chunks, and sprinkle with salt. Set aside to drain. Chop pepper into 1-inch chunks. Melt butter and 2 tablespoons oil in a large saucepan. Sauté onions until lightly browned, then add garlic. Stir for 30 seconds. Add lamb and brown. Stir in coriander, 2 teaspoons salt, and pepper. Add tomatoes. Bring stew to a boil, reduce heat, cover pan, and simmer for 30 minutes.

Meanwhile, heat 1/4 cup oil in a large sauté pan. Lightly sauté okra. Drain in a colander. Brown eggplant, then pepper, adding additional oil if needed. After lamb has cooked 30 minutes, add the vegetables and simmer for 50–60 minutes longer. Taste for seasonings and add lemon juice if desired. *(Serves 4–6)*
Note: You can just as easily bake covered in a preheated 325° oven.
- Substitute other meats—but lamb is particularly nice with okra.

Baked Okra and Ground Beef Casserole

Here's a good do-ahead recipe which is also quite delicious served cold.

> 1 clove garlic
> 9 Tb butter
> 3 Tb oil
> 1 cup chopped onions
> 2 lb ground beef or lamb
> 2 cups crushed tomatoes
> Salt
> 1/4 tsp cayenne pepper
> 1 tsp dill
> 2 eggs
> 1 cup grated Parmesan cheese
> 2 lb okra
> Freshly ground pepper
> 1/2 cup flour
> 3 cups milk
> 4 egg yolks

Chop garlic. Heat 1 tablespoon of the butter and 1 tablespoon of the oil; sauté onions until soft and lightly browned. Add garlic and meat and cook until the meat is just cooked through. Drain fat; add tomatoes, 1 teaspoon salt, cayenne pepper, and dill, and cook over moderately high heat for 4–5 minutes to thicken. Place in a bowl; cool slightly. Beat 2 eggs. When mixture has cooled, stir in eggs and 1/2 cup of the cheese; set aside.

Wash, dry, and stem okra; cut into 1/4-inch slices. Heat 2 tablespoons of the butter and 2 tablespoons of the oil and, stirring constantly, sauté okra until very lightly browned, about 10 minutes. Season with salt and pepper; set aside.

Melt 6 tablespoons of the butter, stir in the flour, and cook for 2–3 minutes. Whisk in milk, bring to a boil, reduce heat, and simmer for 10 minutes. Strain through a sieve if sauce is thick or lumpy. Beat in remaining cheese and 4 egg yolks. Season with salt and pepper. Butter a 9×13-inch baking dish. Spread half the meat mixture in the dish, cover with the sautéed okra, and top with the remaining meat. Cover with the sauce. Bake in a pre-heated 350° oven for 45–50 minutes. Serve hot or cold in squares. *(Serves 8–10)*

- Substitute ½-inch-cubed, salted, and drained eggplant for okra.

Shellfish Gumbo

You'll find myriad versions of gumbo, varying in cooking time (1 to 8 hours), in stock base (fish, chicken, or meat), and in ingredients (crab, shrimp, or chicken), but all gumbo contain okra! Indeed, the word "gumbo" comes from the African word for okra, Ochinggombo, and has over the years come to represent the name of this famous southern dish rather than the vegetable itself. This is a simple version, but I have retained the traditional roux, which is a must for an authentic gumbo. The roux can be made in advance, stored in the refrigerator, and reheated at will. Although I give ham-stock directions, you can substitute a homemade fish stock or canned broth.

½ lb ham chunk
1 ham hock
1 lb veal bones with meat
¾ cup flour
½ cup oil
1 lb okra
3–4 Tb bacon fat or oil
1 Tb butter
1 tsp minced garlic
1½ cups chopped onions
1½ cups chopped green peppers
½ cup chopped celery
1½ cups peeled, seeded, and chopped tomatoes
1 tsp hot pepper sauce
½ tsp cayenne pepper
1 tsp Worcestershire sauce
1 bay leaf
½ tsp thyme
Salt and freshly ground pepper
1 lb crabmeat
1½–2 lb raw peeled medium shrimp
2 Tb filé powder
4 cups cooked warm rice

Cover ham, ham hock, and veal bones with 3 quarts water. Bring to a boil, cover, reduce heat, and simmer for 2 hours. Strain and reduce stock to 2½ quarts. Set aside.

Make a roux: Combine flour and oil in a heavy 4–6-quart saucepan. Cook, whisking constantly, until the flour turns a rich mahogany red-brown color. This will take 15–20 minutes over medium-high heat. (*Note:* Cooking over a very low flame gives a lovely mellow flavor with less risk of burning, but takes a great deal longer.) Set aside.

Trim and cut okra into 1-inch pieces. Heat bacon fat or oil in a deep sauté pan or saucepan and sauté okra for 5–10 minutes, or until lightly browned and the "roping" has stopped; drain. In same pan melt butter, add garlic, onions, peppers, celery; cook until wilted. Stir in toma-toes and reserved ham stock, bring to boil, reduce heat, and simmer 10 minutes.

Stir the roux and, if it has cooled, reheat over low heat, stirring constantly. Whisk the warm ham stock and vegetables into the warm roux to combine well. Add okra, hot pepper sauce, cayenne pepper, Worcestershire sauce, bay leaf, thyme, 1 teaspoon salt, and pepper. Stir in ½ pound crabmeat, and simmer, partially covered, for 1 hour. Add shrimp and remaining crabmeat. Simmer 5 minutes, remove from heat, cover, and let steep for 5 minutes longer. Add filé powder just before serving. Serve surrounding a mound of rice in individual bowls. *(Serves 8)*

- Substitute fish stock for ham stock. Add 1–1½ pounds chopped smoked sausage when you add the okra to the stock.
- Depending on your budget, add lobster meat, or cleaned soft-shelled crabs.
- Add or substitute chicken or well-flavored ham.
- Reduce the amount of roux for a thinner texture.

Pickled Okra

1½ lb freshly picked, small, young okra
3 cloves garlic
3 small hot peppers
1½ tsp dill seeds or 3 good-size sprigs fresh dill
3 tsp mustard seeds
2 cups vinegar
1½ cups water
3 Tb pickling salt or kosher salt

Wash okra well, removing fuzz and stems. Leave the caps on; do not cut into the pods. In each of 3 pint jars, place 1 garlic clove, 1 hot pepper, ½ teaspoon dill seed or 1 sprig, and 1 teaspoon mustard seeds. Pack okra evenly into the jars, alternating tips and caps up and down so they fit in snugly. Bring vinegar, water, and salt to a boil and pour over okra up to within ½ inch of the jar rim. Fasten lids and process in a hot water bath for 5 minutes. (Put jars on a rack in a kettle; cover with boiling water, topping by 2 inches. Bring the water to a boil, cover kettle, and boil for 5 minutes.) Remove jars and cool. Let sit for 4 weeks before using. *(Makes 3 pints)*

Onion Family

If I went through every recipe in this book, I would be hard pressed to find many that did not contain onions or another member of the onion family. Cooks around the world flavor dishes with the pungent taste of onions; in addition, many members of the onion family are delicious and attractive vegetables to serve on their own. They come large and small, sweet and sharp, and can be cooked just about every which way. What versatility— and what a list to choose from—chives, scallions, onions, shallots, garlic, and leeks. Leeks, however, are such an important part of my cooking that I've treated them in a separate entry.

So let's talk about each of the other members of the family one by one, as the techniques for growing and preparation vary.

Chives

We grow chives in our herb garden. Unlike most members of the onion family, the stalks of chives are used for cooking rather than the bulbs. I use chives raw in salads and chopped in dishes where their delicate size and fragrance is particularly suited, such as soufflés or feather-light omelets. I find them irresistible for seasoning a very light dressing for scallops or a raw fish appetizer.

They're easy to start from seed. Just sow seeds in a 6-inch pot filled with potting soil—maybe 20–30 seeds per pot. Don't thin the seedlings, just put them out in a clump in the ground. Within two years, this small clump will have become large enough to divide and give sections to friends. Garden centers also sell clumps of chives for transplanting. Garlic chives—which have a garliclike flavor—can be grown exactly the same way.

To harvest, with garden scissors I simply cut them off 2 inches from the bottom, preferably before they flower. Although the chive blossoms are a lovely purple, once chives flower, the stalks thicken and the flavor becomes harsher.

Scallions or Bunching Onions

These garden-fresh onions are equally good raw—tossed in a salad—or cooked. As part of a crudités platter (see *Mixed Vegetables*), their brilliant green color accents the entire dish while their slight sharpness sets off the more mellow tastes of other vegetables. They are particularly beautiful and tasty in stir-fry dishes, where, because of their size, they cook with lightning speed. No wonder scallions are more popular than storage onions in China and Japan.

Scallions are easy to grow. Russ sows Beltsville Bunching onion seeds directly in the garden in mid-April. He sows them thinly because he will get almost 100 percent germination. Eventually he thins the scallions 3 inches apart. Scallions grow rapidly, but as they're shallow-rooted they should be well weeded and given an inch of water a week until they're ready to harvest, when the tops are 6–8 inches long. Scallions will lift right out of well-tilled ground, but if they are stubborn, dig them up with a hand fork.

To trim, I simply pull off the outer, tougher layer of skin and trim the scallion at the base and midway up the green section. I use all the white bulb and the portion of green that is light-colored and tender. Then I either chop or julienne them to serve raw (or leave whole for the crudités platter) or use in a cooked dish. Scallions are wonderful with egg dishes—not only for flavor but for color. What would a Western sandwich be without scallions?

Onions

Most supermarkets carry some fresh green onions and the familiar storage red and white and yellow onions, but for the greatest variety grow your own.

Onions are not hard to grow, but it is important to remember that they are light-sensitive and their bulbing is triggered by the number of daylight hours. You should check with your county agent or garden center operator to see which varieties do best in your area. (For example, the Beltsville Bunching onion we use for scallions in Massachusetts is grown for mature onions in the South.) Also, decide whether you want to use the majority of your onions immediately or for storage and select seeds accordingly. You can also grow onions from sets, but the advantage of starting with seeds is the wider choice among the hundred of varieties. We use both seeds and sets. Sets are immature onion bulbs that have been stored over winter. They start growing again as soon as they're placed in the ground.

Onions take forever, so Russ sows seeds indoors around mid-February for seedlings to set out in mid-April. We try different varieties, like Spartan Sleeper (a good yellow keeper), the cylindrically shaped imported Owa, the red Bermuda onion, the new Carmen, and Sweet Spanish.

Russ sows seeds in 6–8-inch-deep pots so the roots have ample room to develop. If the onions are "reaching" before it's time to set them out in the garden, he'll trim the tops with scissors.

In mid-April, when he transplants the seedlings to a sunny spot in the garden with light soil and good drainage, he'll set them 1–2 inches apart and give a drink of transplant solution. As the onions develop, we'll harvest every other one to eat as scallions so the final spacing will be 3–4 inches apart. Russ also plants onion sets at this time because they will come along faster to use early.

During the shorter daylight hours of spring, the onions develop their roots and tops (and need cool, moist conditions to do well). Once the daylight hours increase to the number that the particular onion variety needs to fully develop, the onions' growth is concentrated in the bulbs. Day-length sensitivity is the reason it's important to sow onions early in the year for large bulbs.

Although onion varieties have been bred to accentuate certain characteristics (such as good storage capabilities), all onions can be harvested as fresh green onions or allowed to mature to the stage where they can be held for winter storage. (Botanically, green and dried onions differ only in the stage at which they are harvested.)

Green Onions

Green onions are a step further along in the growing stage than scallions. The green onions pulled at midsize are special treats: their bulbs have grown to 1–2 inches across and they still have beautiful thick green stalks. If need be, I'll store them in plastic bags in the refrigerator, where they'll keep at least two days in good condition.

I prepare green onions the same way for cooking as I would scallions; however, I cut off the stalks about 1½ inches above the bulbs. One of our favorite summer dishes is marinated lamb accompanied by a side dish of these onions.

Storage Onions

We let the garden onions fully mature before harvesting and curing for storage. When the onion foliage collapses, it's a sign that the onions are fully mature, but we let the foliage turn brown before harvesting. Once the foliage has dried and withered, the onions are ready to harvest for curing. (The closer to winter the onions mature, the better the chance that they'll keep through the winter but they must be pulled before frost.)

We dig up the onions, let them dry in the sun for a few days, then brush off the soil, bag them in open mesh onion bags (some folks braid them), and store in a cool, dry place (see *Preserving*). We store our harvest in a cool, dry garage where they keep nicely during the winter. Once inside the house, however, they sprout at room temperature. (I use them anyway and cut off the sprouts.)

Our storage onions include the small white onions that were part of every Thanksgiving and Christmas dinner I can remember. Creamed white onions are good, but they're even better braised in broth. They are an essential vegetable in the beef stews and fricassees I prepare, but I always cook them separately and then add them to the dish so they are cooked just right.

The all-purpose storage onion we see at the stores has a firm crisp texture and the strongest flavor of any member of the onion family. This makes it the best choice for dishes that require long cooking because the flavor is assertive enough to hold its own.

Large sweet onions such as Sweet Spanish store less well, but their more delicate taste makes them a good choice for salads and cooked dishes in which you want a more subtle flavor. I like them in fish chowders where their flavor doesn't overpower the fish; or in onion soups, where their natural sugar caramelizes, giving the soup its rich brown color and extraordinary flavor. They, along with the glowing red Bermuda onion, are my choice for raw preparations, especially for onion sandwiches, sliced paper thin with sweet butter and kosher salt. Use slices to top hamburgers or batter-fry rings as well.

To prepare small white onions: I drop them into boiling water, let them roll around for 30 seconds to a minute, and quickly place into cold water. This loosens the outer skin so it slips right off. If you trim either end just a bit with a sharp knife, the outer layer will peel off without disturbing the lower layers. This is really worth doing because it preserves the onion layers—while peeling with a knife often results in cuts two or three layers deep, resulting in an unattractive onion.

I always cut a crosshatch or X in the root so the onion cooks more evenly. Once the onions are prepared this way, they are ready to cook.

To prepare standard onions: I cut off a thin slice at either end of the onion and remove the outer layer of skin. To slice, I halve peeled onions lengthwise from tip to root. Then, with the flat side down, I begin slicing straight down at the curved side of the onion. I think this

method exposes more of the onion to the cut. To dice, I peel and halve it as above and place flat side down on a cutting surface. I slice the onion vertically but do not cut into the root. Keeping the root end intact holds the onion together while you cut. Then, slice horizontally across the onion, again keeping the root intact. Finally, cut down across the onion into dice.

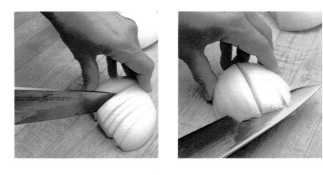

I try to prepare onions just before cooking because if they sit around once cut, the flavor suffers. If you must prepare the onions ahead of time, freeze them in a plastic bag, and they'll be fine for cooked preparations. (This works for shallots as well.)

As much as I like food processors, I do not recommend chopping onions in them. Processors release so much of the juices that the onions' crisp texture is lost and they get an acrid flavor.

Here's a trick for using strong raw onions in salads. Put the chopped or sliced onions into a strainer and pour boiling water over them. Rinse in cold water and pat dry. You'll find that the sharpness is gone and the onions haven't wilted—they're still crunchy.

I wish I could pass along an equally useful trick to avoid weepy eyes when peeling onions. I really don't know the answer. I've tried holding bread in my mouth, a burnt match, and even wearing my daughter's ski sunglasses. Nothing really worked—although the bread technique was best. Some onions are stronger than others, and if you get a particularly strong batch I think the best answer is to grin and bear it.

Shallots

Shallots are the most "elegant" member of the onion family because of their delicate shape, color, and flavor. I've been asked: "Why use shallots instead of onions?" The answer is shallots not only have a lovely mild flavor, but—most important—they are quite tender and cook quickly. For that reason they are ideal for cooked sauces such as the *White Butter Sauce* (see *Appendix*) we use in the restaurant all summer long or raw in a *Mignonette Sauce* or in *Peter McGhee's Shallot and Avocado Salad*.

Shallots are grown from bulb divisions (cloves) set into the ground up to their growing tip in early spring. Russ spaces them about 2 inches apart and keeps them well watered and weeded during the growing season. Similar to other members of the onion family, once the tops die down, the shallots are ready to store, but (like onions) they can be used at any time during their de- velopment. We dig them as we would onions, dry them in the sun, and store in a cool, airy place. They won't keep more than a month or two without sprouting. Shal- lots form heads like garlic, and the number of cloves varies considerably.

To prepare shallots I cut off both ends, remove the thin outer skin, then slice or dice them as I would onions. At the restaurant we use literally pounds of shal- lots. The kitchen staff would peel them patiently, but they got tired mincing all those small bulbs. As a last re- sort, they turned to the food processor. For some reason, shallots do not exude juices quite the way onions do when processed with a fast on-and-off motion. While hand chopping is the best, use the processor when you need to chop a large amount of shallots.

Garlic

I happen to adore garlic and use any excuse I can think of to include it in recipes. It gives foods a pungent, enticing flavor unique in the culinary world.

The most amazing aspect of whole garlic is how it changes when cooking; slow braising refines its raw harshness into a delicate aroma. *Chicken with Lots of Gar- lic* is a wonderful example: the whole garlic cloves cook down to the consistency of soft butter and spread just as easily. They taste mellow and soft, quite unlike potent, strong raw garlic.

There is absolutely no reason to cook with powdered garlic. Fresh garlic is available just about everywhere. The dried powders and salts have a strong unpleasant aftertaste not present with fresh garlic. Although the oils in garlic leave an aroma on your breath, enjoy garlic when you don't have to worry about people around you.

Garlic can be tricky to grow. During the first three weeks it is growing, it needs a great deal of water. Water every 3–5 days, and continue until you see the stalks emerging from the ground. Garlic also needs full sun to mature properly—if there is any shade whatsoever, you will not have good-size bulbs.

As garlic has a long growing season, northern gardeners should plant in fall so that the root systems develop before the ground freezes. Put the cloves a mini- mum of 3 inches apart, 1–2 inches deep. Mulch around the garlic in the winter. Come spring the garlic comes right up and grows throughout the summer. (In other sections of the country, plant the cloves in early spring.) Once the leaves start to turn brown, stop watering and the cloves will keep on growing. When the tops die down, harvest by gently digging up with a pitchfork, and

Special Information

Yields

- 1 pound onions = 4 cups sliced = 2 cups cooked and wilted = 3–4 servings
- 1/2 pound grated onions = 1 cup
- 1 pound scallions = 8–10 ounces trimmed = 2–2 1/2 cups chopped
- 1 pound small 1 1/2-inch white onions = approximate- ly 14 onions
- 1 shallot = approximately 1 tablespoon chopped
- 1 clove garlic = approximately 1 teaspoon chopped

Storage and Preserving

- Your seed catalogs will list the varieties best for storage. It is important to let the foliage brown naturally before storing. If there is any moisture left in the foliage at all, the onions will not store well. Once the onions have dried, put them in mesh bags and hang up so that the air goes through. Store in a cool, dry place (not the refrigerator and most cellars are too damp). Ideal temperatures are 40°–50°. Heat and moisture make them sprout. Store shallots the same way, but they will not keep as long and will start to sprout.
- To store chives or scallions, put them in a plastic bag in the refrigerator, where they'll hold 2–3 days with- out becoming limp.

Freezing

- I freeze chopped onions, chives, or scallions all the time, but I use them only in cooked dishes because they are limp and only contribute flavor. It's a good way to use up chopped onions when you have too many.

Hints

Scallions

- Make a scallion and mushroom soup: sauté 2 cups sliced mushrooms and 3 cups chopped scallions in 2–3 tablespoons butter to wilt. Add 3 cups hot chicken broth and 1/4 cup raw rice; simmer until rice is tender. Purée, add 1 cup combined cream and sour cream. Reheat and season.
- Put scallions and chives in herb omelets and salads.
- Garnish a meat platter with trimmed 5–6-inch scal- lions lightly sautéed in butter.
- Spread thin ham slices with softened cream cheese or a combination of cream cheese and Roquefort cheese. Trim a scallion to the ham slice width, place at one end and roll up the ham, jelly-roll fashion. Cut the roll into 3/4-inch slices. Stand on end so that you can see the scallion center. Serve as appetizers.
- Scallions are excellent in stir-fries because they cook quickly and stay green. Chopped ginger, chopped garlic, and scallions are an unbeatable combination with stir-fried shrimp or crabmeat, or stir-fry the three alone to top grilled fish.

let dry on the ground for a day or two. Dig only during a dry period. You can braid the dried stalks and hang the garlic on your wall where it will be decorative and handy.

By the way, specialty seed houses carry elephant garlic with cloves that are larger and milder than standard varieties.

The harvested garlic consists of several cloves, each of which is wrapped in its own skin, and then all the cloves are enclosed in a common outer skin. The whole grouping of cloves is the garlic "head."

How strong the garlic ends up depends upon how it is treated. Whole unpeeled garlic is the mildest, as it releases less of its potent juices, mashed garlic is the strongest, while minced or sliced garlic falls somewhere in between.

When you need to peel several cloves at a time—as in *Garlic Pipérade Soup*—try this easy method: drop the cloves into boiling water for 30 seconds to 1 minute, rinse them under cold water, drain, and peel. The skins will come off easily.

To peel just a few cloves, give them a good whack with the flat side of a heavy knife; the skins almost "pop" off. I use a garlic press infrequently, preferring to hand-mince with a sharp chef's knife. I do believe that squeezing garlic through a press gives it an acrid aftertaste you don't get with hand-chopping (not unlike the onion processor problem). I use a small paring knife to slice garlic, or dice it with a large chef's knife. For puréed garlic to use, for example, in a vinaigrette sauce, I mash the garlic in a mortar with a little salt, which helps purée it. If you don't own a mortar, mash the garlic and salt together on a board with the flat side of a knife. It works like a dream.

Marketing

- Chives are often sold in pots. Put them on a sunny windowsill during the winter and transplant to your garden come spring. Growing chives indoors can be tricky. Cut them frequently so they don't flower. Keep well watered and give them a feeding of liquid house plant fertilizer once a month.
- Scallions or green onions should have a bright green

- *Scallion Decorations:* Trim the root and the green portion of a scallion to within 1½–2 inches from the base. Remove the outer skin. Cut down toward the base to form a fringe.
- *Pickeled Scallions:* Trim, salt, and let sit overnight. Wash off the salt and place the scallions in sterilized jars. Pour over your favorite hot vinegar brine, seal, and marinate for at least 3 days.

Shallots

- Remember that shallots give a gentle onion flavor and cook quickly. That makes them a good choice for sauces.
- *Scallops Vinaigrette:* Make a lemon juice *Vinaigrette Sauce* with Dijon mustard (see *Appendix*). Omit the garlic and add chopped tarragon or chervil. Add chopped shallots. Poach scallops for 1 minute and marinate in lemon juice to "cook." Drain and toss with the shallot vinaigrette and chopped parsley. Substitute other lightly poached shellfish for scallops.
- Cook giant shallots like small white onions but remember they will cook faster.
- Cut 1½–2 pounds swordfish into thin 3-inch pieces. Dust with flour and sauté in 4–5 tablespoons butter to brown on both sides. Add ½ cup chopped shallots, 2 cups sliced mushrooms, 1 tablespoon lemon juice, 1 cup dry white wine, and 1½–2 cups heavy cream. Season with salt and pepper. Cook to reduce and thicken liquids.
- Make *Broth-Braised Sliced Celery with Shallots* (see *Celery*).
- Shallots give enormous pleasure both for their subtle taste and for their delicate pink beauty. See *Peter McGhee's Shallot and Avocado Salad* (see page 180).

Onions

- Substitute cooked onions for cabbage in *Cabbage Loaf* (see *Cabbage*).
- Don't throw out your onion peels. Put them into the stock pot, where they'll add a pleasant color.
- Bake eggs in blanched onion shells, along with a little cream, grated Swiss cheese, salt, pepper, and butter. Bake at 400° until the eggs are set, 12–18 minutes.
- Use onion rings in *Tempura* (see *Mixed Vegetables*).
- Use chopped or sliced onions and leftover potatoes for *Hash Brown Potatoes* (see page 215).
- Make crispy onions for curries or snacking. Thinly slice onions and separate into rings. Soak in salted ice water for 30 minutes to crisp. Drain, and pat dry. For every 1½ cups onions, heat ½ cup oil. Add the onions and cook, stirring, until crisp and brown. Watch carefully, for the onions brown suddenly. Drain on brown paper. Season with salt if you wish.
- Hold a piece of bread in your mouth to absorb some of the strong vapors while peeling onions.

color and a firm texture. Part of their appeal is their crisp texture, so never buy limp scallions.

- Storage onions should feel firm and hard and have no signs of sprouting. A soft storage onion is probably spoiled.
- Shallots are hard to find in good condition. Often markets will let them sit around for weeks until they are withered and sprouting. Mail order specialty shops may be better places to buy shallots. Although you can still use sprouted shallots, they are not as delicate-tasting as the younger ones. Dried-up shallots are a total loss.
- Garlic heads should be firm and fat. There is nothing more irritating than dealing with itsy-bitsy garlic cloves. Don't buy any that look yellowed or dried out or are soft and flabby.

Raw Onions

We eat raw onions with gusto for good reason: they bring a bite, or tang, to everything from a tossed salad to a cheeseburger. Some of my favorite ways of serving raw onions are:

- Trimmed scallions on a crudités platter.
- Chopped scallions or chives garnishing a salad or an omelet.
- Chopped chives as a cold soup garnish.
- Thinly sliced red or sweet Spanish onions crisped in salted ice water for an hour or so. Drain, pat dry, and dress with *Vinaigrette Sauce* (see *Appendix*).

- Slice large ripe tomatoes and alternate with slices of Bermuda onion. Drizzle with a good-quality olive oil and sprinkle with freshly cut basil. Season with salt and pepper.
- Butter crustless bread and put thinly sliced sweet Spanish onions and watercress between the slices. Cut the bread into rounds for a fancy party.
- Rounds of red onion to top hamburgers.
- Thinly slice sweet onions and crisp in ice water if you wish. Toss with cut anchovies and capers. Dress with *Vinaigrette Sauce* (see *Appendix*) with plenty of black pepper and oregano.
- Finely chopped shallots are delicious in salads and dressings.

Cooking with Onions

Onions can be cooked in so many ways—braised, boiled, steamed, baked, sautéed, deep-fried, grilled, pressure-cooked, and cooked in a microwave. They are a vegetable that can be appreciated when barely cooked and also develop flavor when cooked for a long time. The cut of the onion and the recipe are really the determining factors. No one likes a small white onion cooked to a mush, but how about a large sliced onion sauté-braised to a creamy purée tasting of the essence of onion! I most often braise small white or yellow onions, or I'll roll them in butter until lightly browned and bake them along with a roast. One of my favorite easy elegant meals is thinly sliced sautéed calves' liver served with golden sautéed onion slices. My daughters dote on batter-fried crisp onion rings, while Russ favors the mellow full flavor of a

Special Information
(Continued)

- Crosshatch the roots of small onions before cooking to even the cooking time.
- Use small (1-inch) white onions for an à la Grecque vegetable. Peel and simmer in à la Grecque broth (see *Mixed Vegetables*) until tender.
- Add braised small onions to fricassees.
- Add brown braised small onions to beef stews.
- Try *Baked Peppers, Potatoes, and Onions* (see *Peppers*).
- Adding a dash of lemon juice or vinegar to the water in which onions are cooking helps keep them white.
- As onions age they become stronger-flavored.
- The juice is the most potent part of the onion. To extract juice, grate the onion.
- Make an onion frittata. Sauté 4 cups sliced onions in 2 tablespoons butter until wilted and golden. Substitute onions for spinach and onions in *American Spinach Frittata* (see page 265).

Onions and Garlic

- To remove onion (and garlic) smells from your hands, rinse in cold water, then rub with tomato

juice or salt; rinse and wash with soap and water.
- Some people have luck removing garlic and onion odors from the mouth by swirling lemon juice around, then chewing parsley.
- When you're storing cut onions or garlic in the refrigerator, cover them with plastic wrap or a glass top, or their odors will permeate everything.

Garlic

- Mashed garlic is essential in vinaigrette salad dressings.
- Stud lamb or pork roasts with garlic slivers for flavor.
- Use in pasta recipes, such as *Spaghetti with Clam Sauce*: chop garlic and shallots. Cook for a moment in butter, add clams, cook for 1–2 minutes, and toss with cooked spaghetti and chopped parsley.
- String garlic cloves (like popcorn) and marinate in a bottle of oil for a garlic oil.
- Arrange as many whole, unpeeled garlic cloves as you wish under and around chicken or lamb roasts. The garlic fragrance permeates the meat and you can use the cooked garlic to spread on bread.

soubise. If you are cutting down on fats, prepare small onions simply by boiling or steaming; broth-braise large onions, or bake whole onions in their skins. Serve with herbs, seasonings, or lemon juice.

When I add onions to a stock, I don't cook them first. But when I add chopped or sliced onions to a dish, I usually sauté them in butter first. This may sound like an unnecessary (and fattening) step, but I do believe the onion texture is softened and the taste enriched. Plus, some of the strong vapors diminish by this initial cooking. If you don't want to cook in butter, bake the onions or simmer gently in a bit of wine or broth.

◇ *Boiled Onions*

Use small white or yellow onions. Whole scallions also can be boiled; cut the cooking time to a few minutes. Peel the onions (see page 169). Cover with water, add salt, and bring the water to a boil (or drop into boiling salted water). After the boil is reached, cook for 10–20 minutes, depending upon their size. Do not overcook. Drain and serve with seasonings and melted butter or prepare as in *Finishing Touches for Cooked Whole Onions*.

◇ *Steamed Onions*

Use small white or yellow onions, or scallions. Peel the onions (or remove peel after steaming if you prefer). Steam for 15–25 minutes, depending upon the onion size. Flavor the steaming liquid if you wish with herbs such as thyme or tarragon. Prepare as in *Finishing Touches for Cooked Whole Onions*.

◇ *Braised Small Onions*

Small white onions are best braised, which can be done one of two ways. Either method produces good eating onions, but each serves different purposes: white braised onions are best for creamed onions or chicken or veal fricassees; brown braised onions are an attractive roast accompaniment, or a good addition to brown stews such as a beef bourguignon. Regardless of how you braise the onions, first peel them (see page 169). Then, cut a cross-hatch or X in the roots so that they will cook more evenly.

White Braised Onions

1 lb peeled small onions
1/2 cup light-colored broth, water, or white wine
2 Tb butter (optional)
1 bay leaf
2 parsley sprigs
Salt and freshly ground pepper

Put all the ingredients into a saucepan. Bring the liquid to a boil, cover the pan, reduce heat, and cook gently until onions are tender. Shake the pan occasionally. Check the liquid level and add more if necessary. Cook for 15–25 minutes, depending on the onions' size. (Onions 1–1 1/2 inches in diameter will take about 20 minutes.) If the onions are to cook in another dish, undercook them slightly. (*Serves 4–6*)

- Make *Garlic-Stuffed Mushrooms*: Remove mushroom stems and chop them. Chop garlic. Cook the mushroom caps in oil for 5–6 minutes. Remove and drain. Sauté the chopped stems in oil, add the garlic, and cook 30 seconds. Mix with chopped parsley, season to taste, and stuff into caps. Sauté bread crumbs in the oil and spoon over the top. Either brown under the broiler or chill and serve cold.
- Prepare mushroom caps as above. Gently boil garlic cloves until tender, 15–20 minutes. Remove the peel (it will pop off) and blend the garlic with softened butter and sautéed chopped shallots (optional). Fill the mushroom caps with the purée and sauté a few minutes more or top with grated cheese and broil until the cheese melts and lightly browns.
- Fill artichoke bottoms as you would mushroom caps (above).
- Beware! If garlic browns, it tastes strong and bitter.
- Make *Garlic Bread*: Mash garlic and mix with softened butter. Slice a loaf of crusty bread three-quarters of the way through and spread each slice with the garlic butter. Wrap in aluminum foil and bake in a preheated 350° oven, about 15 minutes.
- Brown butter, toss in chopped garlic and swirl, off heat, for 30 seconds; pour over sautéed fish.

Microwave

- 1 pound onions (3 medium peeled) placed in a covered dish will cook tender enough to stuff in 4 minutes; in 5 minutes they will be softened.
- 1 pound small white onions, peeled and placed in a covered dish with 1 tablespoon water, will cook in 6 minutes.
- 1/4 pound (24–30) scallions 6 inches long will soften in 2 minutes.
- Don't cook garlic in a microwave. The cloves will soften in 4 minutes but lack the mellow flavor produced by long slow cooking.

Leftovers

- Freeze leftover raw onions to use in cooked dishes.
- Leftover cooked onions will keep in the refrigerator for a few days to be incorporated in stews or soups.
- Mash leftover chopped garlic with Dijon mustard and refrigerate to use in salad dressings.

Brown Braised Onions

2 Tb butter
1 Tb oil
1 lb small peeled onions
1/2 cup brown broth, red wine, or water
1 bay leaf
2 parsley sprigs
Salt and freshly ground pepper

Heat the butter and oil in a sauté pan, and add onions. Gently sauté them until browned. Add the remaining ingredients. Bring the liquid to a boil, cover the pan, reduce heat, and gently cook until tender, 15–20 minutes. (*Serves 4–6*)

Note: Once the onions are browned, you can put them in a pan with the cooking fat and bake in a 350° oven until tender. Baking is a practical treatment when you are cooking a roast. Toward the end of the roasting period, add the browned onions to the roasting pan and cook along with the roast. Turn occasionally.

Finishing Touches for Cooked Whole Onions

- *In Butter*: Roll onions in butter, then sprinkle with chopped parsley or freshly chopped herbs.
- *In Cream*: For white braised onions. Combine 1 cup *Béchamel Sauce* (see *Appendix*) with 1/4 cup heavy cream. Fold in the onions, heat through, and season with salt and pepper. Enrich with additional butter if desired. (My mother always made a béchamel sauce using the juices remaining in the onion pan. If you have 1/2 cup liquid from the pan, use 2 tablespoons flour, 2 tablespoons butter, 1/2 cup liquid, 1/2 cup milk, and 1/4 cup heavy cream. Cook like a béchamel sauce and season with salt and pepper. Fold in onions as above.)

- *Glazed Onions*: Melt butter and sprinkle with sugar. Roll the onions in the mixture and cook until lightly glazed. Or add sugar to braising liquid. As the liquid reduces, it will provide a glaze.

◇ Baked Onions

Onions Baked in Their Skins

All onions can be baked in their skins. Rub the onions with oil. Cut a slice from the root end so they stand upright in the pan. Prick with a fork to keep them from bursting, and film the pan with liquid so they will not stick. Bake along with other foods at 350°, 375°, or 400°. When I am baking onions alone I bake at 375°. The cooking time varies tremendously, depending upon the density of the onions. Sweet Spanish and Bermuda onions will cook in less time than firm, tightly layered yellow onions. A rough timetable is

Small white onions	50–60 minutes
2 1/2–3-inch onions	1–1 1/4 hours
4-inch onions	1 1/2 hours

Onions are done when they compress when pinched. Peel skin and serve with butter and seasonings.

Baked Small White or Yellow Peeled Onions

Sauté in butter to lightly color or rub with oil. Put in oven with roast or alone in a pan with a bit of liquid to keep from sticking. Bake at 375° until tender, time depending on size. Roll around occasionally. Spring onions are delicious this way. See *Onions Baked in Foil.*

◇ Onions Baked in Foil

Peel onions, score, or prick with a fork. Season with butter, soy sauce, or whatever flavoring you prefer. Wrap in foil and bake in a preheated 375° oven or on the edge of a grill. The cooking time depends on the size: medium-size yellow onions will take 50–60 minutes to cook. Onions cooked on the grill may become charred: remove the charred portion and eat the inner flesh with butter.

◇ Grilled or Broiled Onions

Onions can be cooked under the broiler or are delicious cooked on the outdoor grill. For small white and yellow onions, blanch to peel and thread on skewers. Roast over coals, basting with oil, butter, or a marinade sauce. If you cook these under the broiler, keep 5–6 inches from the heat and turn occasionally.

- *Grilled Onion Slices*: Peel and slice onion in half horizontally, or cut into thick slices. (Hold together with small skewers if necessary.) Brush with butter, oil, or a marinade. Cook on the grill to char on both sides, basting occasionally.
- *Grilled Spring Onions*: Peel 1–2 1/2-inch-wide onions, leaving 1–2 inches of green stem. Blanch in boiling water for 2–3 minutes to tenderize slightly, drain,

and pat dry. Rub with oil and cook under a broiler 5–6 inches from the heat, or on an outdoor grill, turning occasionally.

◇ *Deep-Fat-Fried Onions*

Cut onions into rings. Dip into batter or egg, and crumbs or flour. Heat fat to 320° and cook the onion rings until lightly browned. Drain on paper towels.

◇ *Sautéed Onions and Scallions*

Use sliced or chopped onions. This can be either a light sauté or a sauté-braise in which the onions cook for a long slow time. Melt butter—or butter and oil—add onions, and cook slowly until softened and golden. As the onions cook down to a golden color, and then turn brown if you wish, the flavor mellows yet intensifies. Therefore, if you are cooking onions for a quiche or tart filling, it is far better to let them cook for 20 minutes or more to develop their flavor rather than to cook to just wilted. This is also true when cooking onions for onion soup: in that case, add some sugar to almost caramelize the onions, giving flavor and color to the soup.

Scallions also can be sautéed in butter and cooked to just tender. Do not overcook or they will lose their shape.

Broth-Braised Onion Rings

Braised onion rings make a simple, flavorful garnish for main-course meats and poultry. I like this plain version with pot roasts and even steaks; the following sweet-and-sour version goes well with pork and game.

1 lb onions
3/4 cup beef broth
1 tsp sugar
1 Tb butter
1 bay leaf
1/2 tsp thyme
Freshly ground pepper
1 clove garlic (optional)
Salt

Peel and slice the onions into rings and place in a saucepan. Combine with the remaining ingredients, reserving the salt. Bring the broth to a boil, cover, reduce heat, and cook gently for 45 minutes, stirring occasionally. Remove the cover, and if there is too much liquid, reduce by boiling gently for 10–15 minutes, adding salt if necessary. Serve as a side garnish. (*Makes 2 cups*)

Sweet-and-Sour Broth-Braised Onion Rings

1 lb onions
3/4 cup beef broth
1/2 tsp Dijon mustard
2 Tb wine vinegar
2 Tb sugar
1 clove garlic
1 bay leaf
Freshly ground pepper
1/3 cup raisins
Salt

Cook as in preceding recipe. (*Makes 2 cups*)
• Use small whole onions prepared for cooking.

◇ *Onion Shells*

Stuffed onions can be filled with all sorts of meat and vegetable combinations. I prefer to use onions at least 3 inches across—3 1/2–4-inch onions are preferable. These "fat" onions give you a good-size cavity to stuff. Peel the raw onion and cut a flat slice off the root end so it stands evenly. Then, cut off a flat slice from the onion top. With a sharp knife, cut a cone shape into the body of the onion. Then, with a melon scoop or a sharp-edged teaspoon, hollow out the inside, leaving approximately 3/8 inch of flesh on the side walls and on the bottom. Be careful; sometimes the center core will pull out right down to the base of the onion, leaving a hole in the bottom. If you scoop from the middle to the outside, this is less likely to happen, but if it does, plug hole with a piece of onion.

The blanching time is just long enough to wilt the onion, and the type of onion determines the length of blanching needed: red Bermuda onions or sweet onions soften quickly because their onion layers are not as dense as those of yellow onions. Once the onions are hollowed, drop them into boiling salted water and blanch for just 3–5 minutes. The onions should be just barely tender and definitely holding their shape. Remove the shells and drain upside down on a rack.

Very pretty shells can be made with great big onion halves. Use 4-inch Bermuda or Spanish onions. Trim the two ends; peel and halve onions. Core the halves just as you would a whole onion above and blanch in boiling water. The blanching time depends on whether or not they will be cooked further. If the onions are to be stuffed and cooked in the oven, blanch just long enough to soften slightly. If I am using them as cooked containers, I blanch the onions until they are tender enough to eat. Drain upside down and pat dry. These shells are especially nice filled with other cooked vegetables, such as creamed baby onions, topped with grated cheese and browned under the broiler. Stuff with glazed baby onions tossed with fresh peas, or fill with individual servings of broccoli Mornay.

If you have the patience, small onions can be cored and stuffed for appetizer portions.

I have read suggestions for stuffing shells without blanching. that doesn't work well because the onion shells take longer to cook than their filling. I've also heard of people who blanch the whole onion for 10 minutes, then remove the insides. That works, but I find it cumbersome because the onion layers tend to slip and slide.

Onions Stuffed with Wild Rice

Wild rice is expensive, but a little goes a long way in this recipe. I use medium-size onions and arrange them around roasted poultry.

> Six 3-inch onions
> 1/2 cup wild rice
> 1/8 tsp fennel seeds
> 6 Tb butter
> 2 cups sliced mushrooms
> 1/2 cup fresh bread crumbs
> 2 Tb chopped parsley
> 1 Tb chopped fennel leaves
> 1/2 cup grated Swiss and Parmesan cheeses
> 2–3 Tb heavy cream
> Salt and freshly ground pepper
> 1 cup beef or chicken broth
> 1/2 cup dry white wine (optional)

Prepare onions as in *Onion Shells* (page 175). Chop the pulp. You should have 1 1/2–2 cups. In a small pan, place the rice, 1 cup water, the fennel seeds, and 1 tablespoon of the butter. Bring the water to a boil, cover, and simmer for 20–25 minutes. Uncover pan, drain, and put the rice in a bowl. Melt 2 tablespoons of the butter in a sauté pan and cook the chopped onion pulp until wilted and golden, 5–10 minutes. Remove from the pan and add to the rice. Add 1 tablespoon of the butter to pan and sauté the mushrooms until wilted; raise the heat to brown

lightly and evaporate the moisture. Combine with the rice along with the bread crumbs, parsley, fennel leaves, 1/4 cup of the cheeses, and the cream. Season with salt and pepper. Stuff onion shells, mounding slightly on the tops. Sprinkle with the remaining cheese and dot with butter. Place in an ovenproof pan and pour in hot broth and wine (if you like). Bake in a preheated 375° oven for 40–50 minutes. Check occasionally, and cover with aluminum foil if the onions become too browned. (*Serves 6*)

Soubise

Soubise is a classic French onion-rice braise that cooks to a soft, buttery consistency. It's absolutely delicious served as a vegetable or layered in a casserole (see suggestions following recipe). I prefer Sweet Spanish onions for this preparation.

> 1/2 cup rice
> 2 lb onions
> 6 Tb butter
> 2 Tb oil
> Salt
> 3–4 Tb heavy cream (optional)
> 1/2 cup grated cheese (optional)
> Freshly ground pepper
> Lemon juice

Drop rice into boiling salted water, boil for 5 minutes, and drain. Peel and chop the onions. Heat the butter and oil in a baking dish; stir in the onions, then the rice and 1/2 teaspoon salt. Mix to coat well with butter and oil. Cover the pan and place in a preheated 325° oven. Bake for 45–60 minutes or until the rice is completely tender and the onions are soft and golden. Stir occasionally. Mix in the cream and cheese if you wish, adding salt, pepper, and lemon juice to taste. (*Makes 4 cups*)

- To use as a layer in a casserole, after the onions and rice are cooked, beat in 2 egg yolks. Omit the cream and cheese and season as above. Then layer in whatever casserole you choose to include it in and bake according to directions. See following suggestion.
- Make a layered ham, spinach, and soubise casserole in a *Mornay Sauce* (see *Appendix*). First, make a bed of cooked chopped spinach. Sprinkle with Swiss and Cheddar cheeses. Fill ham slices with soubise and fold each over like an envelope; set on the spinach, seam sides down. Spoon any remaining soubise around the ham and top with Mornay sauce and some grated cheese. Bake in a preheated 375° oven until bubbly, about 25–30 minutes.

Parslied Onions and Dried Beans

I adore this combination of parsley, onion, and lemon flavors. Prepare this as a side vegetable dish or add chicken (see variation at end of recipe) for a meal-in-one. I have used many varieties of legumes, such as black-eyed peas, kidney, Great Northern, and white Italian beans.

6–8 oz flat-leafed Italian parsley
6–8 oz curly parsley
4–6 oz dill
1 large lemon
2 cups chicken or beef broth
2 Tb butter
1 Tb oil
6 cups sliced onions
½ tsp curry powder
4 cups cooked dried beans
Salt and freshly ground pepper

Wash and dry the parsley and dill. Remove any thick stems and chop into ½–1-inch pieces; set aside. Halve the lemon and squeeze the juice; set aside. Put the halved lemon and broth in a small saucepan. Bring the broth to a boil, lower heat, and simmer, covered. In a large saucepan, heat the butter and oil and cook the onions until wilted and golden. Stir in the curry powder, parsley, and dill. Add the broth and lemon halves. Cook slowly to tenderize the parsley and slightly reduce the broth. (If you cover the pan, the parsley loses some of its brilliant color.) Stir in the beans and the lemon juice and heat through. Remove lemon halves. Season with salt and pepper. (*Serves 6–8*)

- Add more broth for a soup consistency.
- *Chicken, Onions, and Beans*: Poach a chicken in water and chicken broth to cover, and add seasonings. When chicken is cooked, remove and bone. Skim fat from broth and reduce to 2–3 cups. Follow the recipe above, using the broth and adding the boned chicken meat along with the beans.

Escalloped Onions

3 Tb butter
8 cups sliced onions
Salt and freshly ground pepper
Nutmeg
1½ cups heavy cream
Grated Swiss cheese (optional)

In a large saucepan, melt the butter and stir in the onions. Cover and cook until wilted, about 5 minutes. Uncover and cook, stirring, for 5–10 minutes, until golden. Season with salt, pepper, and a dash of nutmeg and spoon into a buttered baking dish. Pour over the cream, sprinkle with cheese (if you like), and bake in a preheated 375° oven for approximately 30 minutes or until bubbly and lightly browned. (*Serves 4–6*)

- Before baking, top with buttered bread crumbs.
- Use small whole pearl or white onions. Parboil or braise for 5 minutes before placing into casserole. Dot with butter, then add cream or cheese.
- Alternate layers of onions and thinly sliced potatoes. Cover with cream, or a cream and milk combination, and bake for 45 minutes or until the potatoes are tender.
- Add blanched vegetables such as sliced celery or carrots; the ratio of onions to vegetables is up to you.

Baked Garlic

This is an absolutely heavenly way to enjoy garlic. Remove the outer skin covering the whole garlic head. The easiest way to do this is to make a slight cut all around the circumference of the head about ½ inch up from the base. The upper skin then peels off easily, leaving the whole head intact with each clove covered by skin.

Garlic heads
Butter
Salt and freshly ground pepper
Olive oil
Crusty French bread
Goat cheese

Set the garlic heads in a baking dish, using 1 head per person, and top each with 1 tablespoon butter. Sprinkle with salt and pepper and drizzle with olive oil. Place in a preheated 250° oven for 30 minutes, then baste and add just enough water to film the pan bottom. Cover and bake another 1–1½ hours or until the cloves are tender. Serve with fresh crusty bread and a good French goat cheese. Each person squeezes the soft garlic out of its skin and spreads on the bread (with or without the cheese).

- *Puréed Garlic*: Squeeze out the soft garlic and purée it with a bit of soft butter. Season with salt and pepper.
- Purée the garlic with potatoes and Jerusalem artichokes.

Onion Sauce

This is a béchamel sauce flavored with sweet onion. It is a lovely silky sauce for delicate-flavored foods and perfect for baked-in-cream dishes.

4 cups chopped or sliced sweet onions
Salt
5 Tb butter
1/4 cup flour
2 cups milk
Freshly ground pepper

Stir onions and 1/2 teaspoon salt into butter, cover and cook to wilt and tenderize, approximately 20–25 minutes. Stir in flour and cook for 2–3 minutes. Remove from heat and whisk in milk. Bring to a boil, reduce heat and cook gently for 15 minutes, stirring occasionally. Purée in a blender. Season to taste and reheat.

Simple Shallot Sauces

Deglazing the cooking juices from a sauté pan with a bit of liquid gives you a simple, flavorful sauce. Adding shallots makes the sauce even more delicious.

For Beef
1–2 Tb finely chopped shallots
1/4 cup dry vermouth
3/4 cup beef broth
2 Tb butter (optional)
Salt and freshly ground pepper

After sautéing steaks or beef patties or slices of calves' liver, remove the meat from the pan and pour off all but 1 teaspoon of the fat. Add the shallots and sauté for 1 minute. Pour on the vermouth and scrape up any cooking juices in the bottom of the pan. Add the broth and boil until the sauce reduces and thickens almost to a syrup. Remove the pan from the heat and beat in the butter, if

you like, to enrich it. Season to taste with salt and pepper and pour over the meat. (*Serves 2*)

- *With Red Wine*: Use half broth and half red wine.
- *With Cream*: Omit the butter. Reduce the broth to a thick glaze and pour in 1/2 cup heavy cream. Reduce by boiling until thickened.
- *With Cognac*: Substitute cognac for vermouth. Pour cognac in the pan, flame, add broth, and reduce to a thick glaze. Add 1/2 cup heavy cream and boil until thickened. This is particularly good with sautéed steak that has had green peppercorns pressed into the sides. (You can omit the broth and just thicken with heavy cream.)

Note: Meat pans may be simply deglazed by pouring off the fat, sautéing the shallots, adding liquid to scrape up the congealed pan juices, and boiling down to intensify flavor and to thicken.

For Poultry
2 Tb finely chopped shallots
1/4 cup dry vermouth
3/4 cup poultry stock, such as chicken, turkey, or duck
2 Tb butter (optional)

Remove the poultry from the pan, pour off the fat, add shallots, and sauté for 1 minute. Add the vermouth and scrape up the pan juices. Add the stock and boil until thickened and almost syrupy. Remove from the heat and beat in the butter. (*Serves 2*)

Shallot Butter Sauce
This is an excellent quick sauce when you lack pan juices. Pour over sliced London broil or English-cut roast beef.

8 Tb butter
6–8 Tb chopped shallots

Heat butter in a deep saucepan. Let it get brown (but not black) and remove the pan from the heat. Immediately drop in the shallots. The hot butter will cook them. Take care, the cold moist shallots in the hot butter will cause it to bubble way up. Spoon over sliced beef. (*Serves 2*)

Onion and Garlic Butters

Shallots, scallions, chives, and garlic added to butter make an easy and tasty garnish for broiled fish or meat. At the restaurant, we garnish steaks with a shallot butter, use garlic butter for broiled swordfish, and add escargot butter (so called because it is the classic French butter to serve on snails) to clams. Simply beat the softened butter with the ingredients and chill in a bowl for later use, or make a roll with aluminum foil as follows:

The technique is easy: once the butter is softened sufficiently to beat, mix in whatever seasonings or herbs you like. Then, with a spatula, form a long sausage of the butter approximately 1 1/2 inches round down the first third of a sheet of aluminum foil lined with waxed paper. Fold one edge of the foil over the butter and roll the butter across the remaining foil. Once the foil is rolled around the butter, twist the foil ends in opposite direc-

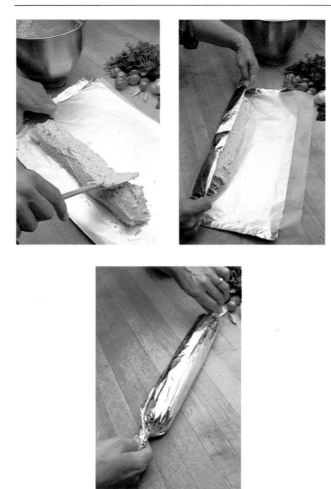

tions. This evens out the roll. The flavored butter can now be chilled or frozen. When it is firm, slice pieces to place on cooked fish or meat.

Escargot Butter

1 lb butter
3–4 cloves garlic
$^1/_4$ cup finely chopped parsley
$^1/_4$ cup finely chopped shallots or chives

Soften butter to room temperature. Finely chop the garlic. Add remaining ingredients, beat together, and chill in a bowl or make a butter roll as explained above. (*Makes a 12-inch roll*)

- *Garlic Butter*: Omit shallots and add more garlic.

- *Shallot Butter*: Omit garlic and add more shallots.
- *Chive or Scallion Butter*: Omit garlic and increase the chives or add scallions.
- Add lemon juice to any of the above butters.
- *Clams with Escargot Butter*: Allow 5 clams per person. Set on heatproof dishes and dot each clam with $^1/_2$ teaspoon *Escargot Butter*. Sprinkle lightly with bread crumbs. Brown under the broiler or place in a preheated 400° oven for 5–6 minutes and then run under the broiler. (*Makes enough for 4–6 dozen clams*)

Garlic Marinades

Garlic "makes" a marinade. Two of my favorite marinades are for lamb and shrimp. I marinate chunks of lamb for a shish kebab or marinate butterflied leg of lamb. Once the meat sops up the flavorful sauce, all it needs is grilling on the outdoor barbecue or under the broiler. Extra-large shrimp, marinated, then sautéed in butter with a bit of the garlic-flavored oil marinade, make a fantastic scampi.

Shrimp Marinade

$^1/_2$ cup olive oil
$^1/_2$ cup vegetable oil
$^1/_3$ cup lemon juice
2 Tb tomato paste
$^1/_4$ cup chopped parsley
1 Tb dried oregano
$^1/_2$ tsp salt
2 Tb chopped garlic
$^1/_2$ tsp hot pepper sauce

Whisk all the ingredients together. Pour over 3 pounds peeled shrimp and marinate in the refrigerator for at least 3 hours. (*Makes 1–1$^1/_4$ cups*)

Lamb Marinade

$^1/_2$ cup olive oil
$^1/_2$ cup vegetable oil
$^1/_2$ cup fresh lemon juice
4 cloves garlic
1 tsp salt
1 tsp oregano
1 tsp rosemary
1 cup thinly sliced onions
10 bay leaves
$^1/_4$ cup chopped parsley

Beat together the oils and lemon juice. Peel and smash the garlic and add to oil mixture along with other ingredients. Toss with 5 pounds cubed lamb or spread over a butterflied 7–9-pound leg of lamb. Marinate for at least 8 hours in the refrigerator. Baste with the garlic marinade during grilling. (*Makes about 2 cups*)

- Baste pork with garlic marinade. Mash 2–3 cloves garlic and 1 teaspoon salt; combine with 1 teaspoon crushed rosemary, $^1/_2$ teaspoon thyme, and a dash of allspice. Beat in $^1/_4$ cup olive oil.

Aïoli—Garlic Mayonnaise

Aïoli is to southern France what *Skordalia* (see *Appendix*) is to Greece. This mayonnaise-garlic mixture is great stirred into fish soups such as *Mediterranean Bourride* (see *Potatoes*) or as an accompaniment to grilled or batter-fried vegetables or poached fish or lamb.

    ¼ cup fresh bread crumbs
    1 Tb lemon juice
    6 cloves garlic
    Salt
    2 cups olive oil
    6 egg yolks
    2 tsp Dijon mustard (optional)
    Freshly ground pepper

Moisten the bread crumbs with the lemon juice, then squeeze thoroughly. The bread should be damp. Chop the garlic. Place in a mortar along with the bread crumbs, ¼ teaspoon salt, and a few drops of oil (if necessary) and mash into a smooth paste. Beat in the egg yolks. Place in a mixing bowl and gradually beat in the oil until you have a thick mayonnaise. Beat in the mustard, if you like, and season with salt and pepper. Thin, if necessary, with hot water or fish stock. (*Makes 1½–2 cups*)
  • Add 2–3 tablespoons finely chopped pimentos.
Note: When stirring aïoli into a soup, you can add additional warmed beaten egg yolks to further thicken the soup. Do not boil after egg yolks are added.

Rouille

Rouille is similar to aïoli but has more of a zing, and is best served with fish soups containing tomatoes and saffron such as *Straight Wharf Fish Soup* (see *Tomatoes*). The basil is not necessary, but is one of my favorite summer herbs and adds something special.

    6 cloves garlic
    Salt
    ⅓ cup drained pimento
    ⅓–½ cup chopped basil leaves
    3 egg yolks
    ¾ cup fresh bread crumbs
    ¾–1 cup olive oil
    Hot pepper sauce
    Freshly ground pepper
    Fish broth (optional)

Chop the garlic and place in a mortar with ¼ teaspoon salt. Mash, then mash in the pimento and basil. (This step will take 4–5 minutes.) Add the egg yolks and bread crumbs and mash to a paste. Add a few drops of olive oil if necessary. Transfer to a mixing bowl or processor. Gradually beat in the oil until mixture is thick. Season with hot pepper sauce, salt, and pepper. Thin, if you wish, with hot water or fish broth. (*Makes 1½–2 cups*)

Mignonette Sauce

Once you've served this with raw clams and oysters, you'll throw out your cocktail sauce.

    ¾ cup red wine vinegar
    ¼ cup finely chopped shallots
    ¼ cup finely chopped parsley
    2 Tb coarsely ground black pepper
    Dash of white pepper
    Dash of salt

Combine the ingredients and let stand for a while before serving. (*Makes 1 cup*)

Cold Herring and Onion Appetizer

Every year we go to Martha's Vineyard Island for the herring run and pickle herring from scratch. The taste of onions and herring together is one of my loves. Here's an easier way to enjoy that combination.

    2 lb (about 6) fresh herring or mackerel fillets
    1 carrot
    3 cups thinly sliced onions
    1½ cups dry white wine
    ⅔ cup white wine vinegar
    Herb bouquet:
        4 sprigs parsley
        1 tsp thyme
        2 bay leaves
        6 peppercorns
    Salt
    Lemon wedges
    Olive oil (optional)

Score the fillets so they will lie flat and place skin side down in a large (12-inch) skillet. Coarsely grate the carrot and combine with the onions, wine, vinegar, herb bouquet, and 1 teaspoon salt. Pour over fish, cover, and bring to a boil. Reduce heat and cook gently for 5 minutes. Remove from heat and let steep, covered, for 10 minutes. Remove herb bouquet and lift fillets to a shallow glass dish. Spoon onions over fish and pour liquid over all. Cool, then refrigerate. Liquid will gel in 3–4 hours. Serve with lemon wedges and oil if you like. (*Serves 6*)

Peter McGhee's Shallot and Avocado Salad

My friend Peter insists on absolutely fresh top-quality ingredients prepared in their simplest and purest form. His combination of the delicate sharpness of shallots with meltingly smooth avocado is an exquisite example of his culinary philosophy. This salad alone justifies a large garden crop of shallots.

    1 large or 2 small ripe avocados (approximately ¾ lb)
    2 Tb lemon juice
    ¼ cup chopped shallots
    2–3 Tb *Vinaigrette Sauce* made with lemon juice (see page 352)

Peel and seed avocado. Slice vertically from end to end in thin wedges. Dip each wedge into lemon juice to keep from darkening. Arrange wedges in a slightly overlapping line on a serving platter. Arrange the shallots in a strip down the center of the avocado. Spoon over the vinaigrette to taste. (*Serves 4*)

Brandade

Here's a classic garlic dish that keeps them begging for more. This has the best texture when prepared in a mortar, but a mixer is convenient and works just fine.

2 lb dried cod
1 large baking potato
1 onion
3 cloves garlic
Salt
1–1 1/2 cups half-and-half cream
1–1 1/2 cups olive oil
Freshly ground pepper
Lemon juice

Soak the cod for 24 hours in cold water, changing the water frequently. Drain. The fish should have gained a fresh fishlike texture and have lost its salty taste. Bake the potato.

Place the cod in a saucepan and cover with water. Grate the onion and add it to the water. Bring the water to a simmer, remove from the heat, cover, and let the fish

steep for 10–15 minutes. Drain, and skin and bone the fish. Purée the garlic with 1/4 teaspoon salt; set aside. Skin the potato and set aside.

Warm the half-and-half cream and olive oil separately. Flake the warm cod into a mixing bowl, and add the garlic and warm potato. Beat the mixture, adding the warm cream and warm oil alternately, a bit at a time, until the mixture resembles fluffy white whipped potatoes. The consistency should be smooth and spreadable, but not runny. Season to taste with salt, pepper, and lemon juice. Serve either warm or cold. (*Serves 6*)

Note: To serve warm: Reheat over a low flame, stirring. Serve surrounded by triangles of bread sautéed in olive oil. Garnish with watercress or parsley sprigs and black olives. To serve cold: Chill and mound in tomato shells or on lettuce accompanied by hard-boiled eggs, tomato slices, and a fresh basil garnish.

Onion Soup

A homemade onion soup brings one of the best classic dishes to your table for pennies. The long slow cooking of the onions is the secret for maximum flavor.

3 lb onions
4 Tb butter
1 Tb oil
1 tsp sugar
Salt
3 Tb flour
2 qt beef broth (homemade if possible)
3/4–1 cup dry vermouth or white wine
Freshly ground pepper
1/4 cup cognac (optional)
Croutons Made from Toasted French Bread (page 348)
Grated Swiss cheese

Finely slice the onions. Melt the butter and oil in a large heavy saucepan. Stir in the onions until coated with butter, cover the pan, and slowly cook for 15 minutes, stirring once or twice. Uncover, stir in the sugar and 1 teaspoon salt, and cook about 30 minutes longer until onions turn a rich brown color (regulate the heat and stir frequently so that the onions brown, not burn). Add the flour and cook, stirring, for 2–3 minutes. Remove from the heat and whisk in the broth and vermouth. Bring to a boil, lower heat, and simmer, partially covered, for 30 minutes. Season with salt and pepper. Just before serving, stir in cognac if you like. Top with croutons and sprinkle lavishly with grated cheese. (*Serves 6–8*)

• *Gratinéed Onion Soup*: Butter a large ovenproof tureen (or individual tureens). Place a layer of *Croutons Made from Toasted French Bread* (see *Appendix*) in the tureen; cover with about 1/4 pound sliced Swiss cheese. Pour in the soup, top with more bread, and sprinkle with 1 cup grated Swiss cheese combined with 1/4 cup Parmesan cheese. Drizzle with a tablespoon of olive oil or melted butter. Bake in a preheated oven at 425° for 30 minutes.

Creamy Onion Soup

Here's a variation on the traditional brown onion soup. Serve it with croutons if you like.

 2 lb onions
 3 Tb butter
 1 Tb oil
 1 cup thinly sliced carrots
 1 tsp curry powder
 ¼ cup rice
 2 cups chicken broth
 2 cups milk
 2 cups light cream
 Salt and freshly ground pepper
 2 egg yolks
 1 egg
 Chopped chives

Thinly slice the onions. In a large saucepan, heat the butter and oil; add the onions and carrots. Cover and cook, stirring occasionally, for 10 minutes. Uncover, stir in curry powder, and cook for 1 minute. Add the rice and broth. Bring the broth to a boil, reduce the heat, cover, and simmer until the rice, onions, and carrots are tender, 10–15 minutes. While the vegetables are cooking, heat the milk and cream. Add to vegetables and simmer for 5 minutes. Season with salt and pepper. Beat the egg yolks and egg together in a small bowl. Pour in a little hot liquid to warm the eggs, then whisk eggs into the soup. Cook over low heat, stirring, until slightly thickened. Sprinkle with chives. (*Makes about 2 quarts*)

 • Purée soup before adding the seasonings and eggs.
 • Omit eggs, and enrich with butter instead.

Garlic Pipérade Soup

The bread thickens this stew while the twenty cloves of garlic cook down to a mellow trace.

 20 garlic cloves
 2 cups sliced onions
 1 cup sliced peppers
 3 Tb oil
 3 cups peeled, seeded, and sliced ripe tomatoes
 2 cups beef broth
 3–4 slices crustless dark bread
 Salt and freshly ground pepper
 Grated cheese (optional)

Blanch the garlic in boiling water for 30 seconds, run under cold water, and drain. Peel and slice the garlic cloves. Cook the onions and peppers in oil for 10 minutes until wilted and golden. Add the garlic and tomatoes. Cover the pan and cook over low heat for 30 minutes. Pour in the broth and heat to the boiling point. Break bread into large pieces and add to the soup. It will disintegrate and thicken the soup. Adjust the amount of bread to the thickness you desire. (I like this soup thick, but Russ prefers it thinner.) Add more broth if necessary. Season to taste. Serve with grated cheese if you wish. (*Serves 3–4*)

Cream of Garlic Soup

 20 large cloves garlic
 1 small onion
 2 cloves
 1 bay leaf
 ¼ tsp thyme
 1 tsp salt
 5–6 Tb olive oil
 2 egg yolks
 1 cup grated Swiss and Parmesan cheeses
 Croutons Made from Toasted French Bread (page 348)

Blanch the garlic in boiling water for 30 seconds, place under cold water, and drain. Peel. Stud the onion with the cloves. In large saucepan, place garlic, onion, bay leaf, thyme, salt, and 2 tablespoons of the oil. Cover with 1 quart water. Bring water to a boil, cover, and cook at a gentle boil for 40 minutes. Strain the soup, pressing the garlic through a sieve into the soup. Beat together the egg yolks and ¼ cup of the cheese. Gradually beat in 3–4 tablespoons oil until you have an emulsion. Beat in some hot soup and then whisk the emulsion into the soup and cook gently until heated through. Serve with remaining cheese and croutons. (*Serves 3–4*)

Pissaladière

In France, you'll find dozens of onion tarts from the creamy Alsatian version to this sinfully good Mediterranean braised onions and anchovies tart. Use a standard pie pastry or even a pizza dough for the base if you like. See variations at end of recipe for a creamy quiche. Don't rush the onion cooking time: long, slow cooking means a more flavorful tart.

 Tart Pastry (page 351)
 6 cups sliced onions
 1 clove garlic, chopped (optional)
 ¼ cup olive oil
 Salt and freshly ground pepper
 ¼ cup grated cheese (optional)
 1 can flat anchovy fillets
 16 pitted black or green Mediterranean olives

Make a 10-inch tart shell and partially bake. In a large, heavy saucepan, cook the onions and garlic (if you like) in oil very slowly for 30–45 minutes or until completely tender and golden. Do not let brown. Season with salt and pepper. Cool. You should end up with approximately 3 cups onions. Arrange onions in the tart shell and sprinkle with cheese if you wish. Arrange anchovy fillets radially fanning out from the center, and decorate with the olives. Bake in a preheated 400° oven for 15–20 minutes or until filling is hot and the pastry browned. Cut into 6 wedges for luncheon servings. For appetizer servings, cut a circle in the tart 2½ inches in from the outer edge. Then cut small sections from the outer rim and inner circle so as to have 15–18 appetizer-size pieces. (*Makes a 10-inch tart*)

 • Some people like to add tomatoes to this tart. I have

enjoyed a stunningly good pissaladière made with equal parts cooked onions and a thick fresh tomato sauce. Combine the tomatoes and onions and prepare as above.

- *Onion Quiche*: Incorporate the braised onions into a quiche, using a 10-inch deep pie shell instead of a tart shell. Sprinkle the shell with ½ cup grated Swiss cheese, top with the braised onions, and sprinkle with another ¼ cup grated cheese. Beat 2 eggs with 1 cup light cream and season with a dash of Tabasco sauce, Worcestershire sauce, and salt and pepper. Pour over onions and bake in a 375° oven for 45–50 minutes. For a smoky flavor sprinkle crust before filling with ¼ pound cooked crumbled bacon.

Joe Hyde's Swordfish with Garlic

One of the most aromatic and mouth-watering dishes we serve at the restaurant originated with my dear friend, Joe Hyde. This is a simple-to-cook and imaginative way to serve swordfish. Don't allow the garlic to brown or it will become bitter.

1 ½ lb swordfish
10 Tb butter
Salt and freshly ground pepper
Flour
2 Tb chopped garlic

Slice the swordfish into four 6-ounce steaks. You want thin, wide swordfish pieces. Heat 4 tablespoons of the butter in a heavy sauté pan (or two if needed). Add salt and pepper to the flour and lightly coat the swordfish. Shake off excess. When the butter is bubbly and lightly browned, add swordfish and cook until medium brown. Turn over and cook the other side. Depending upon the thickness of the swordfish, this step will take 6–8 minutes. The fish must be barely cooked through; if you cook it too long, it will dry out. Remove fish to a warm plate. Wipe out the pan with paper towels and return to heat. When the pan is hot, add the remaining butter and cook until it is dark brown. Toss in the chopped garlic, remove pan from heat, and swirl the garlic quickly to cook slightly. Pour over the swordfish and serve. (*Serves 4*)
Note: I prefer to use Wondra flour for coating fish because it doesn't leave any cakey coating.

Baked Fish with Onions

Here's a hearty meal that is lovely served with whipped potatoes. For a more dietetic version, see variations at end of recipe.

2 Tb oil
5 Tb butter
6 cups sliced onions
5 Tb flour
2 cups milk
1 cup half-and-half cream
Salt and freshly ground pepper
1 cup grated Swiss and Parmesan cheeses
1 ½–2 lb cod fillets
½ cup fresh bread crumbs

Heat oil and 2 tablespoons of the butter and cook onions to soft and golden, stirring often. This will take at least 20 minutes. Stir in the flour and cook for 2–3 minutes. Whisk in the milk and cream, bring to a boil, reduce heat, and simmer for 15 minutes. Season with salt and pepper.

Spread one-third of the onion sauce in a casserole, and top with one-third of the cheese. Cover with the cod fillets, then sprinkle on one-third of the cheese. Pour over the remaining sauce and sprinkle with the remaining cheese. In the remaining 3 tablespoons of butter, sauté bread crumbs until golden; cover the casserole with them. Bake in a preheated 400° oven for 20 minutes or until the bread crumbs are golden and the casserole is bubbly. (*Serves 4*)

- Sauté 3 cups onions and 3 cups julienned celery or fennel. Prepare as above.
- Omit making the cream sauce. Smother the fish with the cooked onions, top with anchovies, and drizzle with oil.

Calves' Liver with Onions

5 Tb butter
1 Tb oil
4 cups thinly sliced onions
1 ½ lb thinly sliced calves' liver
Flour
Salt and freshly ground pepper
Red wine (optional)
Lemon wedges (optional)

Heat 2 tablespoons of the butter with the oil, and cook onions slowly for at least 20 minutes, stirring occasionally, until wilted and golden. When the onions are cooked, heat the remaining butter in a sauté pan. Lightly dust the liver with flour, salt, and pepper and sear over high heat until browned on both sides. Arrange the liver slices on a bed of onions. Deglaze the pan, if desired, with red wine and pour over the liver, or serve with lemon wedges. (*Serves 4–6*)

Kidney with Shallots

1 veal or beef kidney
Flour
Salt and freshly ground pepper
7 Tb butter
¼–⅓ cup chopped shallots
2 Tb red wine vinegar

Remove the kidney's fat and skin and slice thinly. Season the flour with salt and pepper and lightly dust the kidney pieces. Sauté kidney in 3 tablespoons of the butter until seared and browned. Remove to a warm plate. Heat remaining butter in the pan. When it begins to turn brown, add the shallots, swirling in the pan constantly. When the butter turns dark brown, pour in the vinegar and boil for a few seconds. Pour over the kidney slices. (*Serves 3–4*)

- Use sliced lamb kidney, thinly sliced calves' liver, or small whole chicken livers.

Chicken with Lots of Garlic

The only limit to the quantity of garlic is how much you can peel without fainting. You could skip peeling and squeeze the buttery garlic out of its skin, although the chicken will lose some of the garlic perfume. Serve with slices of dark bread upon which you can spread the garlic like butter.

> 3–4 heads of garlic
> 4–5 stalks celery
> 6 leg and thigh chicken portions
> ⅓ cup olive oil
> 12 peeled small white onions (optional)
> 1 Tb chopped fresh tarragon, or ½ tsp dried
> Salt and freshly ground pepper

Separate the garlic heads into cloves, and blanch in boiling water for 1 minute. Run the cloves under cold water, drain, and peel. Wash the celery, dry, and cut into ¼x3-inch lengthwise strips. Rub the chicken with oil and place into an oiled casserole. Top with the peeled garlic cloves, celery, onions (if you like), and tarragon. Pour over any remaining oil and sprinkle with salt and pepper. Cover *tightly* and bake in a preheated 375° oven for 1½ hours. (*Serves 4*)

Sausage-Stuffed Onions

Replace the sausage with any ground or leftover meat. I have even used leftover creamed cooked codfish.

> Four 3½-inch onions
> ½ lb Italian sweet sausage meat

> 3 Tb butter
> 2 tsp chopped garlic
> ¼ cup chopped fennel or celery
> ¼ cup chopped sweet red pepper
> ¼ lb Swiss chard leaves
> ½ cup fresh bread crumbs
> 1–2 Tb heavy cream
> Salt and freshly ground pepper
> 1 cup beef broth
> ½ cup dry white wine (optional)

Prepare the onions as in *Onion Shells* (page 175). Chop and reserve 1½ cups pulp; freeze any extra for another day. Brown the sausage, and set aside to drain. In a sauté pan, heat the butter and add the reserved onion pulp. Sauté for 5 minutes until wilted. Add the garlic, fennel or celery, and sweet pepper; cover and stew for 5–10 minutes.

Meanwhile, wash and dry the chard leaves, and slice or chop them. You will have approximately 3 cups. Uncover the onions, add the chard, and stir until wilted, 2–3 minutes. Raise the heat and cook until the moisture evaporates. Combine with the sausage, bread crumbs, cream, and salt and pepper to taste. Mound the mixture in the onion shells, set into a baking dish, and pour the broth and wine (if you wish) into the bottom. Bake in a preheated 375° oven for 40–50 minutes. Check occasionally, and if the top is getting too brown, cover loosely with foil. Before serving, remove the onions to a warm platter, and reduce the pan juices if desired. Pour over the stuffed onions. (*Serves 4*)

- Top with buttered bread crumbs or grated cheese before baking.

Pork Stew with an Onion Sauce

This goes nicely with egg noodles.

> 2 lb pork
> ¼ cup flour
> Salt and freshly ground pepper
> 4 Tb butter
> 1 Tb oil
> 6 cups sliced onions
> 2 tsp chopped garlic
> 1 Tb tomato paste
> Herb bouquet:
>> 1 bay leaf
>> 1 tsp thyme
>> 4 sprigs parsley
> ½ cup dry vermouth
> 1–1½ cups veal or beef broth
> 1 Tb cornstarch (optional)
> 2 Tb chopped parsley

Trim pork and cut into 1½-inch cubes. Combine flour, salt, and pepper. Toss the pork in the flour; then shake off any excess flour. Heat 2 tablespoons of the butter and the oil and brown the pork on all sides; set aside. In the same pan, add 2 tablespoons of the butter, stir in the onions and cook until wilted and lightly colored. Stir in the garlic and tomato paste. Add the browned pork and the herb bouquet. Pour in the vermouth and 1 cup of the broth. Cover and simmer on top of the stove or in a preheated 350° oven for 1–1¼ hours or until the pork is fork tender. (Add the remaining broth if necessary.) Remove the herb bouquet and skim the fat. If the liquid is too thin, remove the meat to a warm plate and thicken the liquid either by reducing by boiling or mixing in 1 tablespoon cornstarch. Replace the meat in the onion sauce and serve sprinkled with parsley. (*Serves 4*)

- Make with beef, veal, or defatted and skinned pieces of duck or goose.
- During the final minutes of cooking, add vegetables such as mushrooms simmered for 2–3 minutes in lemon water, or small blanched carrots.
- For a smoother sauce, when you simmer the browned pork, add one peeled and sliced medium potato and cook along with other ingredients. When the pork is cooked, remove to warm plate. Remove the herb bouquet, skim fat and purée the onions, potato, and liquid. Season and serve over pork.
- Make an old-fashioned smothered beef. Use chunks of beef and only ½ cup liquid. Add additional liquid during cooking if necessary, but the onions should exude enough liquid so that this will be unnecessary.
- Make a casserole: Layer meat and onions and top with thinly sliced onions. Pour on the broth and bake for 1 hour. Sprinkle with grated cheese and bake another 30 minutes.

Mrs. Culler's Onion Dinner Rolls

2 packages active dry yeast
3 eggs
4 ½–5 cups flour
½ cup vegetable shortening
½ cup sugar
2 cups chopped onions
2 tsp salt
7 Tb butter

Dissolve the yeast in ¼ cup warm water. Let stand for 10 minutes. Beat eggs and combine with 2 ½ cups flour, 1 cup warm water, shortening, sugar, and salt. Using a mixer, beat at medium speed for 2 minutes. Stir in the remaining flour to make a soft, slightly sticky dough. Cover, and let rise until doubled in bulk. Punch down. Refrigerate 6 hours or overnight in the same bowl.

Remove from the refrigerator 3 hours before baking. Sauté 1½ cups onions in 2 tablespoons butter until wilted and golden; cool. Divide the dough in half. Roll each half into a ½-inch-thick rectangle. Spread each rectangle with 2 tablespoons softened butter, then spread with onions. With the long side facing you, roll into a jelly-roll shape. Cut into 1-inch slices. Place cut side down into greased 2-inch muffin tins. Cover and let rise until doubled in bulk. Melt the remaining tablespoon of butter and brush over the tops; sprinkle with remaining ½ cup raw onion. Bake in a preheated 400° oven for 12–15 minutes. (*Makes about 30 rolls*)

Parsnips

I think of parsnips almost as a garden candy. Because cold temperatures seem to intensify the natural sugar present in parsnips, they can develop a sweet, nutty flavor unlike any other vegetable. We hadn't even thought of raising parsnips, however, until Russ tasted one grown in the Victory Garden plot, and discovered that this crisp, delicious vegetable bore no resemblance to the overcooked, mushy parsnips he had tasted in stews of his youth. Now he's become such a parsnip fanatic that each year he adds a little extra space to the parsnip row.

Parsnips break the rule that only the youngest vegetables are the most tender—our mature parsnip roots grow sometimes 20 inches long, yet stay as tender as can be. (These parsnips have been among our most successful hostess gifts—one giant parsnip feeds a family of four.)

Our success with parsnips is directly attributable to the way Russ prepares the soil. Their long roots become malformed or fibrous when they're obstructed by rocks, clay, heavy soil clumps, or shallowly prepared beds. To combat this, we use an ingenious planting system both at the Victory Garden and at home.

Every 9 inches along the row, Russ rotates a crowbar until it forms a deep, cone-shaped hole, 16–18 inches deep and 5 inches across. Then, he fills each hole with sifted

compost or soft soil, plants three or four *fresh* seeds (parsnip seed loses viability rapidly) ½ inch deep and adds a pinch of radish seed. The radishes serve to break the ground and mark the row, and will be harvested before the parsnips need thinning.

We've had good luck with Harris Model and Hollow Crown as well as Avon Resistant, which, as its name implies, is resistant to canker disease.

Parsnips need a long, relatively cool growing season. In New England, optimum growing conditions are to plant in the spring, have a mild summer, and harvest after the first frost or in the following spring. Parsnips germinate slowly, often taking three to four weeks before they come up. Four to eight weeks after planting, we thin to the strongest plant in each hole and side-dress with 5-10-5 fertilizer. Throughout the summer, we need only water and cultivate plants. Before winter, we've learned through bitter experience to mark the parsnip row. Early one spring, Russ forgot where they were and rototilled under our entire remaining crop—a grim day in the Morash household.

It's possible to harvest parsnips anytime they've achieved any size but I prefer to leave many of them undisturbed in the ground and dig them in the spring, when I think they have reached optimum sweetness. They are like leeks, "garden treasure," buried in the ground to be dug up when the ground thaws.

Harvesting requires some care. Since the roots grow deeply, they must be carefully removed with a spading fork. The best storage is to keep them in the ground until needed, but it is possible to layer them in damp sand or store in a cool root cellar.

To prepare parsnips for cooking, simply wash off dirt and peel if desired. Usually it's not necessary to remove the central core, which looks just like that of a carrot, only paler. Really giant parsnips sometimes need coring, because although the core is tender, it can lack the nutty taste of the flesh. Taste and see. Any parsnips that have been stored awhile should be checked for pithiness, and cored if necessary.

Unless I'm steaming parsnips, I always peel or scrape them, and, if necessary, chunk them before cooking. I don't peel steamed parsnips, as the skins slip off easily once cooked. Supersize parsnips need sectioning, while smaller ones can be cooked whole or halved. Whole parsnips tend to cook unevenly: the tip cooks through before the thicker top. To avoid this, cut them up as evenly as possible, gauging the cooking time by the diameters. I add any narrower sections halfway through the cooking process.

My favorite way to cook parsnips is to slice them thin and sauté in butter: they're just delicious. There's not much difference between boiling and steaming them; for all-purpose cooking I usually boil because it's the fastest, easiest method and leaves delicious cooking liquids for sauces. The rich yet delicate taste of parsnips enriches many winter stews and soups: simply drop chunks into the liquid for the last 15–20 minutes of cooking. Remember how sweet they are and take this into consideration when determining amounts. Or cook them alongside a roast, and baste with the pan juices. Whichever method you use, don't overcook parsnips. They cook faster than you might think, so watch them like a hawk.

Marketing

In some areas, you can buy freshly dug parsnips from local farmers. Usually you'll have to settle for market parsnips packaged in plastic bags. Look for smooth roots that are firm and well shaped, indicating proper storage. Poorly stored parsnips become shriveled or flabby with pithy or decaying flesh. Occasionally, I've had bad luck with waxed parsnips, whose thick wax coating hid pithy texture and soft spots. Don't buy any you have doubts about. As far as I'm concerned, they have absolutely nothing in common with the sweet morsels we pull from the garden.

Special Information

Yields
- 1 pound = 2–3 servings
- 1 pound unpeeled = 1 1/2–1 3/4 cups whipped or puréed, depending on amount of waste

Storage and Preserving
- Harvest and store in sand or leave in ground throughout winter in cold climates, digging up as needed.
- Parsnips will keep in the refrigerator unwashed in a perforated plastic bag 4–5 weeks.
- Freeze cooked purées.

Hints
- Cut up and add to stews and hearty soups during the last 15–20 minutes.
- Cook in braised casseroles and mash into sauce before serving to thicken and flavor it.
- Grate for puddings as in *Lynn Wilson's Rutabaga Pudding* (see *Turnips and Rutabaga*).
- Add grated raw parsnips to salads.
- Slice raw parsnips into long, thin pieces and use as a "cracker" for dips.
- Make parsnip chips just like potato chips (see *Potatoes*).
- Substitute parsnips for potatoes in *Stampfenbohnen* (see *Beans*).
- Julienne equal amounts of parsnips and carrots. Boil together until just barely tender, drain, and add to a clear homemade chicken consommé for an elegant first course.
- Cut parsnips into logs. Drop into boiling water for 1 minute; drain and cool. Coat with *Frying Batter* (see *Appendix*) and fry in hot oil (375°) until golden brown, 4–5 minutes. Drain on brown paper; serve.
- Cut large parsnip into slices and drop into boiling water for 1 minute; drain. Prepare as in *Old-Fashioned Scalloped Turnips* (see *Turnips and Rutabaga*). Alternate with potatoes if desired.
- Julienne and use as in *Celeriac with Mustard–Sour Cream Sauce* (see *Celeriac*).
- Purée with pumpkin.

Microwave
- 1 pound peeled parsnips, cut into 1-inch chunks and placed in a covered dish with 2 tablespoons liquid, cooks tender in 4 minutes; in 6 minutes, cooks to purée softness.

Leftovers
- Shape mashed parsnips into croquettes and fry in oil, or mash and use in *Sautéed Parsnip Patties*.
- Slice chunks; reheat in butter, sprinkling with sugar to glaze.
- Combine with other leftovers, bind together with a cream sauce, and use as a main-dish pie topped with a crust or baking powder biscuits.

◇ *Boiled Parsnips*

Peel parsnips, cut into chunks, cover with water in a saucepan, and add 1 teaspoon salt. Bring to a boil, partially cover, and cook slowly until barely tender. The cooking time varies, depending on the size of chunks and the freshness: ½–1-inch chunks will cook tender in approximately 5 minutes. Count on 8–10 minutes to be soft enough to purée.

- Cut peeled parsnips into 3-inch log or baton lengths about ½ inch thick. Cook in boiling water until tender, 4–5 minutes.

◇ *Steamed Parsnips*

Peel parsnips, if you like, cut into chunks, and put into a steamer basket. Place over 1 inch of boiling water, then cover and steam until tender. One- to 1½-inch chunks will cook tender in 8–10 minutes, and in 12–15 minutes will be tender enough to purée. Whole small parsnips 1–1½ inches wide and approximately 6 inches long will take the same time as equal-size chunks. (The widest diameter determines the cooking time.) Logs or batons cook in 5–8 minutes.

Finishing Touches for Cooked Parsnips

- Roll in melted butter and season with salt, pepper, and herbs.
- Dress with browned butter. For each pound parsnips, heat 6 tablespoons butter. Cook butter until dark brown and pour over parsnips.
- Roll in melted butter, sprinkle with sugar, and cook until glazed.
- Roll drained parsnip chunks in a melted butter/curry powder mixture; cook slowly for 2–3 minutes until parsnips absorb the curry taste.
- Drain boiled parsnips, saving the cooking liquid. Make a *Béchamel Sauce* with half the cooking liquid and half cream (see *Appendix*). Reheat parsnips in sauce before serving. Or add grated cheese to sauce before reheating.
- Prepare equal-size parsnips and carrot logs. Serve with melted butter, arranged side by side.
- Arrange steamed whole parsnips in a baking dish: For each pound parsnips dot with 2–3 tablespoons butter and ⅓ cup light-brown sugar mixed with orange or grapefruit juice to moisten. Bake in a preheated 400° oven for approximately 15 minutes, until nicely glazed, basting occasionally.
- Roll parsnips in heavy cream; reheat, adding fresh herbs to taste.
- Roll parsnips in sour cream mixed with chopped preserved ginger and some of its liquid, reheat. Preserved or stem ginger can be found in Oriental food markets.
- Whip or purée. See *Puréed Parsnips*.

Sautéed Parsnip Slices

My favorite parsnip recipe couldn't be simpler.

1½ lb parsnips
2–3 Tb butter
Salt and freshly ground pepper

Peel and thinly slice parsnips and sauté in melted butter until lightly browned. This will take 5–8 minutes, depending on the thickness of the slices. (For a softer center, reduce the heat slightly, cover, and steam-cook for a minute or two.) Season to taste and serve. (*Serves 4*)

- For a darker brown color, sprinkle with a bit of sugar.
- Coat with heavy cream.
- Before adding parsnips, add 1 teaspoon good curry powder to butter.

Puréed Parsnips

It has become very fashionable to serve some sort of vegetable purée with dinner. Puréing makes the delicate sweet taste of parsnips even more prominent. Unlike other root vegetables, they retain a light, silken texture when puréed. I serve them plain or use as a filling for other vegetables. They're also good in soufflés, timbales, and pies. This purée can be served immediately or reheated over simmering water or in a covered casserole in a preheated 325° oven for 15–20 minutes. (Reheating intensifies the flavor.)

2 lb parsnips
1 tsp salt
3–4 Tb butter
⅓ cup heavy cream
Salt and freshly ground pepper

Peel parsnips and roughly chop them. Cover with water and add salt. Bring to a boil, cover, and cook slowly for 7–10 minutes, or until tender; drain. Purée with butter in a food mill or processor. Add cream, and season to taste. (*Makes about 3 cups*)

- *Plain Purée*: To prepare a plain purée as an ingredient in further recipes, cook as above, but omit butter, cream, and seasonings.
- *Puréed Parsnips and Potatoes*: Boil peeled chunked potatoes and parsnips together. (Use half as much

potato as parsnip.) Purée with butter and cream and add curry or herbs to taste.

- Cook with equal amounts of turnip or rutabaga, then purée with sour cream or yogurt.

Vegetables Stuffed with Parsnip Purée

Cherry Tomato and Parsnip Garnish

Remove cherry tomato tops and scoop out inside; cut thin slices off the bottoms so that the tomatoes will sit flat. Salt the insides of the tomato cases and drain upside down. Fill with parsnip purée and bake in a preheated 350° oven until heated through. Use to garnish a roast.

- For a vegetable course, stuff medium tomatoes. Bake in a preheated 350° oven for approximately 30 minutes. Then top with grated cheese and run under the broiler.

Zucchini Halves

Halve zucchinis and hollow out the centers. Blanch halves in boiling salted water for 3–4 minutes until barely tender. Brush with melted butter, then fill with purée. Dot with butter, or buttered fresh bread crumbs, sprinkle with Parmesan cheese, and bake in a preheated 350° oven for 25–30 minutes until heated through.

Mushroom Caps

Brush mushroom caps with melted butter and fill with parsnip purée. Sprinkle with grated Swiss cheese or fresh herbs and dot with butter. Bake at 375° for 15 minutes or until caps are tender and stuffing has become lightly browned.

Parsnip, Potato, and Carrot Purée

1 lb parsnips
3/4 lb potatoes
1/2 lb carrots
1 small onion
Salt
4 Tb butter
Freshly ground pepper
1/2 cup heavy cream

Peel parsnips, potatoes, and carrots; chop into 1/2-inch cubes. Cover vegetables with water, add a peeled onion and 1 teaspoon salt, and bring to a boil. Cover pan and cook slowly until vegetables are barely tender, about 10 minutes. Drain, discard the onion, then purée with butter. Add salt, pepper, and cream to taste. Serve immediately or reheat over simmering water for 20 minutes. (*Makes about 4 cups*)
Note: For a slightly intensified flavor, sauté cooked vegetables in butter for a moment before puréeing.

- To bake, add 1 beaten egg to the mixture and place in a greased casserole or use to stuff vegetables. Dot with butter and bake in a preheated 350° oven for 30 minutes or until heated through.
- *Parsnip Timbales:* Use less cream to give a thicker consistency. Watching carefully, cook purée to remove excess moisture, then add 4 beaten eggs. Fill buttered 8–10 ramekins with mixture and put in a pan with boiling water coming halfway up the sides of ramekins. Bake in a preheated 325° oven for 20–30 minutes or until set. Unmold and serve.

Sautéed Parsnip Patties

Whipping parsnips, either by hand or mixer, retains their somewhat fibrous texture. They're delicious with butter, or can be converted into croquettes. These patties are lovely served with homemade applesauce.

1 1/2 lb parsnips
1 small onion
6 Tb butter
2 Tb flour
1/2 cup milk
Salt and freshly ground pepper
1 Tb chopped chives (optional)
2 eggs
1 cup fresh bread crumbs
2 Tb oil

Peel and roughly chop the parsnips. Cook until tender; whip (do not purée). Finely chop the onion and brown lightly in 4 tablespoons butter. Stir in the flour and cook for 2–3 minutes without browning. Meanwhile, whisk milk into the onions off the heat; then cook until just thickened. Stir in parsnips and season with salt, pepper, and chives (if you wish). Chill mixture for 2 hours.

Beat eggs and set aside. Form parsnips into patties (the mixture will be slightly soft); dip into the beaten eggs and then into the bread crumbs. (At this point, the patties may be refrigerated again.) Sauté patties in 2 tablespoons butter and 2 tablespoons oil, adding additional butter and oil if necessary. (*Serves 4*)

- Add grated cheese either to mixture or to bread crumbs.

Baked Parsnips with Fruit

This easy dish is particularly good served with poultry and game birds.

1 lb parsnips
2 apples
1 orange
3 Tb melted butter
2 Tb brown sugar
3 Tb orange juice

Peel parsnips and cut into logs. Peel and core apples; cut into 8 wedges per apple. Slice unpeeled orange into 1/4-inch slices, cutting 4 or 5 slices in half. Combine butter, sugar, and orange juice, and mix with parsnips, apples, and orange. Put into a buttered baking dish, cover, and bake in a preheated 325° oven for 30 minutes, stirring occasionally. Uncover and bake 15 minutes longer to glaze. Baste with juices and serve. (*Serves 4*)

Parsnip-Soffritto Soup

Here, the Mediterranean flavors of tomatoes, onion, and garlic meld with the sweet nuttiness of parsnip to produce a delicately flavored soup.

  1 large onion
  1 clove garlic (optional)
  1 1/2–2 cups peeled and seeded fresh or
        canned tomatoes
  4 Tb olive oil
  Salt
  1 lb parsnips
  2 carrots
  6 cups chicken broth
  Freshly ground pepper
  Chopped chervil or parsley (optional)

Finely chop onion, garlic (if you use it), and tomatoes. Heat oil and gently cook onion until wilted but not browned, approximately 5 minutes. Add garlic, if you like, and tomatoes, sprinkle with salt, cover and cook for 5 minutes, uncover and cook until the liquid has evaporated and the mixture has thickened, 15–20 minutes. (This is the soffritto.)

Peel and cut parsnips and carrots into 1/4-inch slices. Heat chicken broth in a 3–4-quart saucepan. Add soffritto, parsnips, and carrots to broth and bring to a boil; reduce heat and simmer, covered, until vegetables are tender, approximately 10 minutes. Season to taste and serve garnished, if you like, with chopped chervil or parsley. (*Makes 2 quarts*)

- Simmer a fowl; use both the broth and the meat in the soup.
- Drop cooked meatballs into the soup; heat through before serving.

Parsnip Chowder

This traditional New England recipe is well worth preserving. My main modification is the short cooking time, for some old cookbooks recommend boiling for 1–2 hours!

  4 slices bacon
  1 small onion
  1 lb parsnips
  1/2 lb potatoes
  1 tsp salt
  1 cup milk
  1 cup medium cream
  Freshly ground pepper
  2 Tb butter

Blanch bacon in boiling water for 5 minutes; drain and dice. Chop onion. Peel parsnips and potatoes and dice into 1/2-inch pieces. Place potatoes into water to keep from discoloring. Brown bacon bits in a 3-quart saucepan. When crisp, remove from pan and set aside. Cook onion in bacon fat until wilted and lightly browned, about 5 minutes. Meanwhile, boil 3 cups of water. When the onion is cooked, add parsnips and potatoes, pour over just enough boiling water to cover. Add 1 teaspoon salt. Bring to a boil, reduce heat, cover, and simmer for 15 minutes or until the vegetables are tender. Heat the milk and cream and add to the vegetables; reheat together. Add pepper and more salt, if desired, to taste; stir in butter just before serving and garnish with bacon bits. (*Makes 6–8 cups*)

- *Fish and Parsnip Chowder:* Poach 1–1 1/2 pounds white fish fillets (such as cod) and use the poaching liquid to cook the vegetables. Add the cooked fish along with the milk.
- *Chicken and Parsnip Chowder:* Use a simmered chicken and broth in the same way.
- Add small amounts of other vegetables, such as corn.

Cream of Parsnip Soup

This rich parsnip essence has a texture similar to that of pea soup. A cup suffices as a soup course, but with the addition of chunks of ham, you have a complete supper.

  1 lb parsnips
  1 onion
  2 Tb butter
  1 peeled clove garlic
  1 Tb flour
  1/2 tsp turmeric
  1/2 tsp ground coriander
  4 cups beef stock
  Salt and freshly ground pepper
  1/2 cup light cream (optional)
  2 Tb chopped chives

Peel and chop parsnips. Chop onion and sauté in butter in a 3-quart saucepan for 3–4 minutes, until wilted and lightly colored. Stir in parsnips and garlic, and cook for 2 minutes, turning to coat with butter. Cover, turn heat to low, and cook for 5 minutes. Uncover, stir in flour and spices, and cook for 2 minutes. Off heat, gradually stir in the stock, then bring to a boil, cover, reduce heat, and cook slowly for 10–15 minutes or until parsnips are very tender. Purée, then reheat in a saucepan, adding 1 cup water if soup is too thick. Season with salt and pepper and cream if desired. Serve garnished with chopped chives. (*Makes 5 cups*)

Parsnip, Carrot, and Chicken Casserole

1 lb parsnips
½ lb carrots
Salt
7 Tb butter
6 Tb flour
1 cup chicken broth
½ cup heavy cream
Freshly ground pepper
1–1½ lb cooked chicken
¾ cup buttered fresh bread crumbs (optional)

Peel parsnips and carrots, and cut into ½×3-inch logs. Cover carrots with 6 cups water and 1 teaspoon salt and bring to a boil. Cook for 2 minutes, add parsnips, and cook for 5 minutes or until tender. Drain vegetables, saving the water. Melt 6 tablespoons butter, stir in flour, and cook over low heat, stirring, for 3 minutes; do not let brown. Mix some of the cooking liquid with chicken broth to make 4 cups total. Remove flour mixture from heat and whisk in 3 cups liquid and the cream. Return to heat and simmer for 10–15 minutes to thicken and mellow flavor; season with salt and pepper. (Add more liquid if sauce becomes too thick.) Combine with cooked chicken and reserved carrots and parsnips and turn into a greased baking dish. Dot top with butter, sprinkle with buttered fresh bread crumbs if desired, and bake in a preheated 400° oven for 20 minutes or until heated through. (*Serves 4*)

- Add sautéed or poached whole mushrooms to mixture along with chicken.
- Heat mixture, put into a greased casserole, and top with baking powder biscuits. Bake in a preheated 450° oven about 12 minutes, to cook biscuits.

Grated Parsnip Salad

3 cups grated raw parsnips
½ cup grated carrots
½ cup chopped celery
½ cup chopped green peppers
½ cup thinly sliced radishes
¼ cup *Vinaigrette Sauce* (page 352)
⅓ cup mayonnaise or sour cream
Salt and freshly ground pepper

Combine the vegetables, mix with vinaigrette, add mayonnaise or sour cream, and season to taste. (*Makes 4–5 cups*)

Parsnip Tart

Try other citrus fruits as well.

Tart Pastry (page 351)
4 Tb orange marmalade
1½ cups puréed cooked parsnips
4 eggs
¼ tsp salt
½ cup heavy cream
4 Tb orange juice
1 Tb lemon juice
1 grated orange rind
3-oz package cream cheese, softened
6 Tb sugar
4 Tb finely chopped toasted almonds or walnuts

Prepare pastry to fit a 10-inch tart pan; partially bake and let cool. Heat marmalade until softened and coat the inside of the pastry shell with it. Mix together all ingredients, reserving 4 tablespoons sugar and the nuts. Pour mixture into the crust and bake in a preheated 400° oven for 15 minutes. Combine the 4 tablespoons sugar and nuts and sprinkle them over the tart; bake for 15 minutes longer or until filling is set. Cool before serving. (*Makes a 10-inch tart*)

- *Sliced Orange Topping:* Slice 1 large unpeeled orange paper-thin. Mix together ⅔ cup sugar and ¾ cup water and bring to a boil. Drop orange slices into the mixture and simmer for 15 minutes; cool. Decorate the top with the glazed orange slices.

Parsnip Pie

Parsnips are delicious in desserts because of their natural sweetness. The cream lightens the texture, but the pie is equally delicious without it.

Tart Pastry (page 351)
2 lb parsnips
2 Tb softened butter
1/3 cup light-brown sugar, lightly packed
1 tsp lemon juice
1 tsp lemon rind
2 eggs
1/2 tsp cinnamon
1/4 tsp mace
1/4 tsp nutmeg
1/4 tsp ground cloves
1 cup sour or heavy cream (optional)

Roll out pastry to fit a 10-inch pie pan, partially bake, and cool. Peel and chunk parsnips, and cook until tender; whip or purée. You should have approximately 3 cups parsnips. Cool slightly. Beat in butter, sugar, lemon juice and rind, eggs, spices, and cream (if desired). Pour into pie shell and bake in a preheated 350° oven for 40–50 minutes, or until filling is firm. (*Makes a 10-inch pie*)

Parsnip Muffins

1 cup whipped cooked parsnips
1 egg
1/2 cup milk
1 1/2 cups flour
1/3 cup sugar
2 tsp baking powder
1/2 tsp salt
1/4 tsp nutmeg
1/2 tsp cinnamon
1/4 tsp ground ginger
Dash of ground cloves
1/4 cup butter

In a large mixing bowl, mix together the parsnips, egg, and milk. Sift the dry ingredients. With a pastry blender, cut in the butter. Add the parsnip mixture, stirring only until the ingredients are combined. Fill 8 greased muffin cups. Bake in a preheated 400° oven for 20 minutes. Serve warm. (*Makes 8 large muffins*)

Parsnip-Pecan Cake

Serve this cake warm with applesauce, or cool it and serve plain or frosted.

1 1/4 cups salad oil
1 1/4 cups sugar
2 cups flour
1 Tb baking powder
1 Tb baking soda
2 tsp cinnamon
1/4 tsp salt
4 eggs
3 cups grated raw parsnips
1 1/2 cups finely chopped pecans

Thoroughly combine oil and sugar. Sift together dry ingredients. Add to oil and sugar mixture, alternating with eggs, beating well after each addition. Mix in parsnips, then pecans. Pour into a buttered 10-inch tube pan. Bake in a preheated 325° oven for 1 hour and 10 minutes. Cool in the pan for 10 minutes before removing. (*Makes a 10-inch tube cake*)

Peas

Just like sweet corn, peas should be harvested and cooked in the same breath. Once picked, their sugar rapidly turns to starch, and even a two-hour lag between garden and table significantly diminishes their sweetness. That's why frozen peas, or even fresh market ones, never taste the same as home-grown peas rushed to the table and savored in season.

Although peas freeze well, I think they lose texture, so I prefer them fresh. The high point of the New England harvest is the traditional Fourth of July pea and salmon feast. At the restaurant, I always feature fresh salmon, accompanied by new peas and baby potatoes. Our customers rave about the fresh peas, which I continue to serve even though it takes the whole staff

Russ Morash and Bob Thompson inspecting Sugar Snap peas.

hours to shell enough peas for 150 people, plus extra for nibbling.

At home we grow both the common or garden pea (which needs shelling) and the edible-podded or sugar pea (which can be eaten whole). Garden peas come in both bush and tall varieties. Most years our choice is Little Marvel, a low-growing, prolific variety that matures over a three-week period and grows well on short vines that need only minimal support. Little Marvels produce a big, sweet crop.

Although we love garden peas, it's hard to bother with them since we discovered the new Sugar Snap peas—edible-podded peas that look just like garden peas, with fully developed peas and pods. We harvest Sugar Snaps over a four- to five-week period. For Chinese stir-fries, we grow Oregon Sugar Peas, thin-skinned snow

peas, with underdeveloped flat peas. These peas mature over a three-week period. (We don't dry peas, but should you wish to try, Early Alaska makes a wonderful split pea soup.)

The moment the ground is workable, at the end of March or the beginning of April, Russ plants peas. Peas thrive in cool weather and once germinated will tolerate damp early spring conditions quite well. Similar to other legumes, peas take nitrogen from the air with the aid of soil bacteria, so before planting, Russ coats the seeds with a powdered legume inoculant to aid this process. He sprinkles the seeds approximately 1 inch apart in a 6-inch-wide by 3-inch-deep trench, covers them with $\frac{1}{2}$ inch of soil, and presses it down lightly. This thick sowing gives a higher pea yield and a dense foliage which helps to hold up the plants as they grow. Throughout the spring, as the peas grow, he adds soil to the trench. (The trench holds water, and the thick layer of soil keeps the roots cool.)

All peas benefit from support, which keeps them from rotting on the ground and lets the pods hang straight down, making them less misshapen and easier to pick. In the past, Russ simply used bits of brush for stakes, but now that he's planting such a large Sugar Snap crop—which needs 5–6-foot high bracing—he uses post and chicken wire support for all the peas. By mid-June, the first peas are ready, and the harvest continues for three to five weeks. The snow peas come along first, followed by the garden peas, and finally the Sugar Snaps. We pick daily, the moment the peas mature, pulling the plumpest peas first. Peas do poorly in hot weather. For a while, we tried planting a fall crop in August, but had mixed results, so now we limit our fresh pea crop to the spring.

Harvesting peas is a two-handed job: using only one hand, you might pull up the entire plant. Holding the plant stem in one hand, pull the pods off with the other. When you're freezing garden peas, do it in several small operations. The plumpest peas should be gathered before the pods start to wrinkle on the stem. If you wait until all the peas mature, many will be too old and will taste starchy and mealy.

Once you've gathered peas, prepare them immediately if possible. I may occasionally complain, but way down deep I like shelling peas. There's no more relaxing afternoon than kibitzing with family and friends while shelling peas. You can't speed up the process, so just make up your mind to relax and enjoy it.

To shell garden peas, snap off the top of the pod and pull the string down the side, pushing open the side seam in the process. The peas pop right out. Although Sugar Snap pods are edible, both sides need stringing: snap off the stem tip toward the flat side of the pod, and gently

pull downward. The strings come right off. Snow peas need only the stem tip removed, although some varieties require stemming.

The secret of success with peas is to barely cook them. Merely a moment in a hot pan is all that's necessary for superb cooked peas.

Marketing

Whatever happened to fresh peas? I find it astonishing that 95 percent of all the peas grown in the United States end up either frozen or canned. You owe it to yourself to find a source for fresh peas, but don't expect them to taste as sweet as those from the garden. A farm stand, with continuous pickings, is your best bet. Whatever the variety, look for a bright green color and crisp flesh, with pods that snap, not bend. Old peas look scalded, spotted, or limp and bedraggled. Never buy shelled peas—they'll taste old.

Special Information

Yields

Garden Peas
- 1 pound whole peas = 1–1 1/3 cups shelled peas
- 1/2–3/4 pound whole peas = 1/2–3/4 cup shelled peas = 1 serving

Sugar Snap Peas
- 1 pound Sugar Snap peas = 4–5 cups strung peas = 4–6 servings

Snow Peas
- 1 pound = 3 servings

Storage and Preserving

Short-Term Storage
- Refrigerate unwashed peas in a perforated plastic bag. They will keep for 4–5 days.

Long-Term Storage
Peas freeze beautifully.
- *Frozen Garden and Snow Peas:* Shell peas; blanch in boiling water for 2 minutes. Immediately drain and place in ice water for 2 minutes. Drain. Loosely pack in freezer bags, making sure all air is removed, label, and freeze.
- *Frozen Sugar Snap Peas:* Blanch for 2 minutes and chill in ice water for 5 minutes. Place in a single layer on trays; freeze. Package, once frozen. Sugar Snap peas will keep for 9 months to a year, but should be added only to cooked dishes, as, once frozen, they are no longer crisp.

Hints
- All peas benefit from a touch of sugar if they are not perfectly sweet.

Garden Peas
- Add raw shelled peas to stews, soups, and mixed vegetable braises during the last minutes of cooking.
- Add blanched shelled peas to risotto.
- Add blanched shelled peas to plain rice. Sauté equal amounts of peas and cooked rice in butter or curry butter for a Sunday night supper.
- Put blanched peas in fresh vegetable salads.
- Peas are particularly good (and pretty) with veal and salmon.

Sugar Snap Peas
- Delicious as part of a crudités platter or use as party tidbits. Arrange on a platter—let guests string them.
- Coat with a tempura batter (see *Vegetable Tempura* in *Mixed Vegetables*) and deep-fry.
- Add to stews and hearty soups during the last 2–3 minutes.

◇ *Braised Peas in Butter*

When I'm serving peas immediately, my favorite method of cooking is to sauté them quickly in butter. Clarified butter is best, if you have it on hand, but regular butter will do. Don't let the pan get too hot or the peas will brown.

For each cup of peas, melt 1–2 tablespoons butter. Toss the peas in the butter until they are heated through yet barely cooked. Cover the pan for just a moment to braise them (keeping the cover on too long deadens their beautiful color). Young peas, Sugar Snaps, or snow peas need only to be tossed for 2–3 minutes in the hot butter. Older peas do best with a slightly longer braising.

◇ *Blanched Peas*

This is as good a method as braising, but takes a bit more time. When you need to cook peas ahead of time, or use them cold in a salad or composed plate, this is the best way.

Boil a large kettle of water, adding 1 teaspoon salt per quart of water. (For 2 1/2 cups shelled peas, use 4–6 quarts water.) Drop peas into water and bring back to a second boil as quickly as possible. Depending on their age and size, Sugar Snap peas and snow peas will blanch in 1 minute or less. (Older peas take 2 minutes, but no longer.) Shelled garden peas will blanch in 2–4 minutes. They should still retain texture. If you're eating them immediately, drain them, season, and top with pats of butter. If you're using them cold, run cold water into the pot to immediately cool the peas, or drop them into a kettle of cold water. Once the peas are cooled, drain well and set aside.

◇ *Steamed Peas*

Steaming peas works well, but takes longer to do, and the color is not as bright. Bring an inch of water in a steamer to a boil; add the peas. Cover, and steam until just tender. Snow peas will take 2–3 minutes; garden and Sugar Snap peas, longer, depending upon their size and age.

◇ *Blanched and Braised Method for Overaged Peas*

Should you have a crop of overaged peas, blanch as above, then melt 2 tablespoons butter per cup of shelled garden peas, add a bit of sugar, and season with salt and pepper. Braise peas over low heat for 5–10 minutes or longer to tenderize them. For 3–4 cups shelled peas, you will need approximately 6 tablespoons butter and 1–2 tablespoons sugar.

Finishing Touches for Cooked Peas

- *With Onions:* Add equal amount of tiny boiled onions to peas. Reheat in butter.
- *With Ham:* Add 1 cup lightly sautéed julienned ham or prosciutto to 3–4 cups shelled peas.
- *With Mint:* Add 1 tablespoon finely chopped mint to 3–4 cups shelled peas.
- *With Cream:* Coat with heavy cream; reduce the cream until it just coats the peas.
- *With Nuts:* Add 1/2 cup toasted almonds or pine nuts to 3–4 cups shelled peas.
- *With Mushrooms:* Add 1 cup sautéed sliced mushrooms to 3–4 cups shelled peas.
- *With Rice:* Combine equal amounts of cooked rice and peas. Add butter and seasonings to taste.
- *With Crabmeat:* Sauté 1/2 pound crabmeat with 4–5 tablespoons butter and 1 tablespoon chopped shallots. Reduce 3/4 cup heavy cream to lightly coat crab. Fold in 2 cups blanched peas. Serve on toast triangles topped with thin broiled ham slices.
- *With Cucumbers:* Sauté 2–3 cups diced cucumber, add 1 1/2 cups blanched peas and 1 tablespoon chopped dill, and reheat in butter.
- *Stuffed Vegetables:* Fill hot cooked turnip or onion cases with sautéed peas.
- *With Ham or Bacon:* For a smoky taste, braise peas with a strip of bacon or ham. Or add crumbled bacon.
- *With Chicken:* Add peas to chicken cooked in tomato sauce.
- *In Vegetable Salads:* Use cooled blanched peas in mixed vegetable salads.
- *With Red Onion:* Toss cool blanched peas with a chopped red onion and equal parts mayonnaise and sour cream.

- Cook rapidly. Cooking longer than 2 minutes opens pea pods and diminishes the sweet flavor.
- Use in à la Grecque or vinaigrette vegetable platters.
- Sauté sliced Sugar Snap peas in butter for 1 minute; add to omelets or quiches.

Snow Peas
- A few snow peas add crunch to stir-fry dishes. Add during last few minutes of sauté.

Microwave
- 2 cups shelled peas with 2 tablespoons liquid in a covered dish cook tender in approximately 5 minutes.
- 1 pound snow peas with 2 tablespoons liquid in a covered dish cook tender in approximately 8–10 minutes.

Leftovers
- Add to omelets, quiches, or frittatas with ham or mushrooms.
- Add to cold mixed salads.
- Mix with leftover rice for rice croquettes.
- Use in *Pasta Primavera* (see *Mixed Vegetables*).
- Use in a cold pasta salad.

- *With Limas Vinaigrette:* Toss 2 parts blanched peas with 1 part cooked small lima beans in a *Vinaigrette Sauce* (see *Appendix*). Add some chopped celery or peppers if desired.
- *With Pesto:* Use cooled blanched peas and diced cucumber in a pesto spaghetti (see *Appendix* for *Pesto Sauce*).

Note: Many of these ideas work equally well with leftover peas.

Braised Peas with Lettuce in the French Style

Here's the classic French way to cook peas. The long braise gives a totally different taste and texture to the peas. Use older peas and see how they mellow. You can almost eat them with a spoon.

1 head Boston or Buttercrunch lettuce
1/2 cup chicken broth or water
8 Tb butter
1–2 Tb sugar
2–3 sprigs parsley
1/2 tsp salt
3 cups shelled peas

Clean and trim lettuce, cut into quarters, and place in a saucepan along with chicken broth, 6 tablespoons butter, sugar, parsley, and salt. Bring to a boil, stir in peas, cover, and return to the boil. Reduce heat and cook slowly for 15–20 minutes or until peas are very tender, tossing several times. (When the peas are done, the cooking liquid will be almost evaporated.) Remove lettuce and parsley. Toss peas with remaining butter; serve with the lettuce if desired. (*Serves 4–6*)

- Parboil small white onions for 5 minutes and add to pan with peas.
- Shred lettuce; add chopped scallions or onions. Make a bed of the lettuce in the pan and proceed as above, serving the peas with the shredded lettuce.
- Use shredded lettuce. When the peas are tender, and the juices are evaporated, add 3–4 tablespoons heavy cream and cook until cream is thickened, lightly coating the vegetables.

◇ *Puréed Peas*

When peas get oversize and mealy, rather than discarding them, turn them into a tasty purée.

Cook the peas until tender; then purée in a food processor or blender, or use a food mill. Put in a saucepan over high heat and shake pan until moisture has evaporated. Add butter, seasonings, and a bit of cream if desired. If the skins are particularly tough, put the peas through a Mouli strainer or use the following recipe.

◇ *Joe Hyde's Skinned Peas*

Here is a foolproof way to remove tough pea skins. I use this method only when the peas have extraordinarily thick skins, and I want to use them for a purée or cream soup.

For every 5–6 cups shelled peas, add 1 teaspoon baking soda. Cover with water, and bring to a gentle boil. Skim the foam and cook gently until peas are tender. The skins float to the top, where you can skim them easily. Drain peas and purée or stew in butter.

Peas and Carrots '80s Style

1 lb Sugar Snap peas
1 lb carrots
Salt
2–3 tsp sugar
6 Tb butter
Freshly ground pepper

String peas. Peel carrots, and cut into logs approximately 3 inches long by 1/2 inch thick. Bring 3 quarts water to a rolling boil. Add 2 teaspoons salt and 2 teaspoons sugar, and drop in the carrot logs. Cook at a medium boil until barely tender, 4–8 minutes; drain. (If preparing ahead of time, run cold water into pan to immediately stop cooking; drain. The carrots will be tender but will still retain crunch. Refrigerate until ready to serve.)

Melt 3 tablespoons butter in a large sauté pan, add carrots, and roll them in butter until coated. Sprinkle with sugar, if a light glaze is desired, heat through, and season with salt and pepper. Stack the carrot logs down the center of a warm platter; keep warm. Meanwhile, melt 3 tablespoons butter in a large sauté pan. Stir in peas, cover pan, and cook over medium heat for 2–3 minutes to barely cook peas, shaking pan occasionally. Do not let them brown. Serve peas flanking the carrots. (*Serves 4–6*)

Spicy Peas and Rice

1 cup shelled peas
3/4 cup chopped onions
6 Tb butter
1 Tb finely minced garlic
10 whole cardamom seeds
10 whole allspice berries
10 whole cloves
2-inch cinnamon stick
3 cups rice
6 cups water or a combination of water and broth (hot)
1/2 cup yellow raisins (or more to taste)
1/2 cup blanched almonds (or more to taste)

Blanch peas; set aside. Sauté onions until wilted in 4 tablespoons of the butter. Add garlic and spices, cook for 1–2 minutes, stir in rice, and sauté for 5 minutes longer. Add hot water, cover, bring to a boil, reduce heat, and cook slowly until liquid is absorbed.

Meanwhile, plump the raisins for 5 minutes in hot water; drain. Sauté the almonds in 2 tablespoons butter. When the rice is cooked, stir in the plumped raisins, sautéed almonds, and peas. Cook for a moment until heated through. (*Serves 4–6*)

Dried Beans and Peas

During the fall and winter, use frozen peas, and add the defrosted peas 2–3 minutes before serving. The pinquito bean is a pea-size pink bean that turns a lovely maroon color when cooked, contrasting beautifully with the green peas.

2 cups dried pinquito beans (or substitute pinto)
1/2 cup bacon fat or blanched salt pork
1 1/2 Tb chopped garlic
2 cups chopped onions
4 cups beef broth or combination of water and broth
1 cup tomato sauce
1 lb smoked sausage, such as kielbasa
2 Tb dried tarragon
2 1/2–3 cups shelled peas
Salt and freshly ground pepper
1 pimento, sliced

Soak beans overnight in cold water, or cover with boiling water and let stand until cool; drain. In a large saucepan, put beans, bacon fat or salt pork, half the garlic, half the onions, broth, and tomato sauce. Mix thoroughly, bring to a boil, lower heat, and slowly cook, covered, for 2 hours or until the beans are just beginning to turn tender.

Meanwhile, prick sausage, blanch in boiling water for 5 minutes to reduce grease, then slice into 1/2-inch pieces. When the beans have reached the *al dente* stage, add the remaining garlic, onions, sausage, and tarragon.

Simmer another 30–60 minutes, or until the beans are done, adding additional water if necessary. Stir in the peas and cook for 5–6 minutes or until the peas are cooked through. Season with salt and pepper, and garnish with pimento. (*Serves 6–8*)

- For a barbecue version, omit tarragon and use 3–4 teaspoons chili powder and 1/2 teaspoon cumin. Add hot pepper sauce to taste.
- Add cooked corn kernels along with peas for an unusual and colorful succotash.

Sugar Snap Pea and Shrimp Appetizer

Serve at room temperature.

1/2 lb Sugar Snap peas
16 cooked shrimp
1 lemon

String and blanch peas (see page 195). Slice each shrimp lengthwise. For each serving, arrange 12 peas in 4 groups of 3 peas each, separating each section of peas with 2 shrimp slices. Garnish with a lemon wedge in the center. (*Serves 4*)

Nage with Fish and Peas

This is an excellent first course when rich dishes are following. "Nage" is a vegetable-flavored court bouillon. I have combined the nage with a fish stock to create a delicate broth in which to cook the fish and peas. The firm texture of the peas adds so much to the soup.

2–2 1/2 lb peas
1 qt *Fish Stock* (page 348)
1 qt *Vegetable-Flavored Broth (Nage)* (page 352)
Salt and freshly ground pepper
2 lb fish (cod, haddock, monkfish, or combination of white fish)
1/2 lb sea scallops

Shell peas; you should have 2–3 cups. Bring the fish stock to a boil, lower heat, and cook gently until reduced to 2–3 cups. Heat vegetable nage, add to fish stock; taste and adjust seasoning. Reduce a bit more to concentrate flavor if need be. Cut fish into 1 1/2–2-inch chunks, and large sea scallops into 2 or 3 pieces. Poach fish gently in broth until just cooked, about 5–7 minutes. After 3 minutes add the scallops and peas. They will take 3–4 minutes to cook. Correct seasonings and ladle broth, fish, and peas into individual bowls or into a soup tureen. (*Serves 6–8*)

- You can use blanched peas and add 1 minute before serving to just heat through.
- If you don't have fish stock, use just the vegetable nage. The fish will flavor the broth. Or, add a cup of bottled clam broth.
- Omit fish and fish stock. Use the vegetable nage with vegetables alone. Add other vegetables to the peas, such as finely chopped celery and carrots, corn kernels, or fresh beans. Cook in nage or blanch first and add.

Fresh Pea Soup

When we have a bumper pea crop, I make this fresh pea soup.

1 carrot
1 cup sliced onions or leeks, or combination of both
4 Tb butter
3 cups shredded lettuce
1/2 tsp sugar
3 cups chicken stock
2 cups water
Salt
4–5 cups shelled peas
1/2 cup heavy cream
Freshly ground pepper

Finely chop carrot. Sauté onions or leeks and carrot in 3 tablespoons butter until tender but not browned, 8–10 minutes. Add lettuce and sugar; gently braise for 5 minutes. Add chicken stock, water, and 1 teaspoon salt; bring to a boil. Reduce heat and cook for 5–10 minutes. Add peas, and cook until they are very tender, approximately 10 minutes longer. Purée soup. Thin with additional stock if necessary. Stir in cream and remaining butter, and season to taste. (*Serves 6*)

- To serve cold, omit final butter enrichment.
- Add a touch of mint along with lettuce. (Go easy, or the mint flavor will dominate.)

- For a heartier version, blanch 4–6 pieces of bacon for 4 minutes. Then, using 2 tablespoons oil rather than butter, cook onions, leeks, carrot, and bacon. Continue as above.
- For greater texture, cook peas in broth, then purée. Chop other vegetables and bacon fine; cook separately from peas. Combine with peas and broth; heat together before serving.
- If the peas are big with thick skins, treat first as in *Joe Hyde's Skinned Peas.*

Maltese Scampi

This is a gloriously colored dish. The peas' vivid green sets off the bright pink shrimp, the blue-black mussels, the creamy white scallops, and the sienna-colored sausage. At the restaurant, I serve Maltese Scampi on a bed of rice (see *Easy Rice Pilaf* in *Appendix*) and guarantee that it tastes as good as it looks; garnished with parsley sprigs, lemon wedges, and sautéed cherry tomatoes.

1 1/2–2 lb large raw shrimp (14 per lb)
　　　or 5 to 6 shrimp per serving
Shrimp Marinade (page 179)
1/4 lb smoked sausage (kielbasa or chorizo)
1–1 1/2 lb peas
1/2 lb baby sea scallops
1 lb mussels
6 Tb butter

Peel and devein shrimp. Add shrimp to marinade and marinate for 4 hours or overnight.

Prick sausage with a fork; blanch in boiling water for 5 minutes to release fat. Cool, slice diagonally in 1/4-inch pieces, and set aside. Shell peas, blanch for 1 minute and cool; set aside. Remove side muscle from scallops; set aside. Wash and scrub mussels, removing beards.

When you are ready to cook, remove shrimp from marinade, heat butter, and sauté shrimp over high heat until pink on one side, about 3 minutes. Shake the pan occasionally. Turn shrimp; add scallops, sausage, and mussels. Sauté for 2–3 minutes longer, or until the shrimp, scallops, and sausage are lightly browned and the mussels have opened. Add the blanched peas during the last minute of cooking. (*Serves 6*)

Pasta with Peas

2 cups shelled peas
1 cup heavy cream
3 Tb butter
1 lb fettucini
3/4 cup freshly grated Parmesan cheese
Salt and freshly ground pepper
Nutmeg

Blanch peas, drain, and cool. In a large saucepan, heat 3/4 cup cream and butter for 2–3 minutes, until cream has slightly thickened; set aside. Meanwhile, boil pasta in salted water until barely tender. Drain, then toss with cream and butter over low heat. Add remaining cream, cheese, and peas; season with salt, pepper, and a dash of nutmeg. Toss until sauce is lightly thickened. (*Serves 4–6*)

• Add sliced sautéed mushrooms.
• Add tuna or chicken chunks heated in a butter/shallot mixture.
• Add prosciutto.

Peas with Sautéed Veal or Lamb Hearts

I'm delighted that veal and lamb hearts are increasingly more available in our markets, for they are economical and delicious. This is a good recipe for kidneys, too.

1 1/2 cups peas
1 lb veal or lamb hearts (4 hearts)
1/2 lb mushrooms
4 Tb butter
Salt and freshly ground pepper
1/3 cup chopped shallots
1/3 cup dry vermouth
2 Tb Calvados (or applejack) or cognac
1 cup heavy cream

Blanch peas; set aside. Clean hearts, removing any fat or membrane; cut into halves and then into 1/2-inch slices.

Slice mushrooms. Heat 2 tablespoons of the butter in a large frying pan, add hearts, and sprinkle with salt and pepper. Cook over high heat, stirring constantly, for 2–3 minutes, until the meat is lightly browned, yet still pink inside. Remove to a strainer and drain juices.

Sauté the mushrooms in the remaining butter until they turn light brown; remove, and add to hearts. Sauté shallots for 1 minute. Add vermouth and Calvados or cognac to pan, scrape all the bits on the bottom of the pan, and reduce until sauce forms a glaze. Add half the cream, and reduce until thick. Stir in hearts, mushrooms, and peas. Add just enough cream to coat the hearts and vegetables, then gently cook until heated through. Do not let the sauce boil or the hearts will toughen. Correct seasonings, and serve immediately. (*Serves 4*)

Two Easy Stir-Fries

When our daughter, Vicki, had her first apartment at college, she requested recipes for some extra-easy and economical dishes. These fit the bill. Though fresh peas taste best, frozen peas work nicely.

Hamburger and Peas
1 1/2 cups shelled peas
2 tsp cornstarch
3 Tb peanut oil
1 lb ground beef
1/2 lb mushrooms, sliced (optional)
2 Tb soy sauce
1 Tb very dry sherry
1 tsp sugar

Blanch peas (see page 195); set aside. Dissolve cornstarch in 1 tablespoon water. Heat oil, add the ground beef, broken up, and brown. Remove beef, drain off all but 2 tablespoons oil, and sauté mushrooms (if you are using them) until lightly browned. Combine with beef, soy sauce, sherry, and sugar. Lightly mix in peas; cook for 3–4 minutes. Stir in the cornstarch, and cook until sauce is lightly thickened. (*Serves 4*)

• Add chopped onion; sauté with beef.

Pork and Peas
Use either snow peas or garden peas.

3/4 lb boneless pork
2 tsp cornstarch
2 Tb soy sauce
3 tsp dry sherry
4 Tb vegetable or peanut oil
1/2 lb snow peas (1 1/2 cups) or 1 1/2 cups blanched
    garden peas
1/2 lb fresh bean sprouts
1/2 tsp salt
Sugar
1/4 cup broth or water
1 tsp sesame oil (optional)

Cut pork into 1 1/2-inch-long by 1/4-inch-thick strips. Dissolve cornstarch in 1 tablespoon water; mix in 1 tablespoon soy sauce and 1 teaspoon sherry, and pour over pork, tossing to coat thoroughly. Marinate pork for 20–30 minutes.

Heat 2 tablespoons oil in a wok or large frying pan until very hot; stir in peas and sprouts; add salt and a pinch of sugar. Cook for 2 minutes, tossing continuously; remove with a slotted spoon. Heat 2 tablespoons oil; cook the pork, stirring until lightly browned. Add broth or water, cover the pan, and braise for 2 minutes. Uncover, add the vegetables, remaining soy sauce and sherry, and ½ teaspoon sugar, and stir for 1–2 minutes longer, adding sesame oil if desired. (*Serves 4*)

Peppers

Each summer, Boston's Italian North End comes alive with one religious festival after another: colored lights festoon the streets, and vendors hawk slush, fried dough, and my favorite grilled pepper and sausage sandwiches. During the hundreds of years since people first cooked peppers over coals, cooking may have become refined, but nothing matches the sweet, smoky taste charring creates. It's absolutely the best way to cook peppers.

As there are literally hundreds of varieties, classifying peppers can become confusing, but basically all peppers are either sweet or hot-tasting. Regardless of how they taste, they are all members of the Capsicum family. The familiar green bell-shaped pepper, for example, is a sweet pepper, as are most bell peppers. Hot peppers, which many people call chili peppers — or chilies — range in size from that of a small cherry tomato to long, skinny types. Although many people consider any red pepper a hot pepper, color has nothing to do with it. The degree of heat in a pepper depends upon the amount of the heat compound, capsaicin, it contains. Capsaicin is lodged in heat pustules located in the pepper's interior ribbon of tissue and its seeds. When you remove the tissue and seeds, you greatly decrease the pepper's pungency.

Rather than indicating how hot a pepper is, a red color indicates ripeness. The bell peppers at the supermarket start out green and turn red when fully ripened, as do yellow banana peppers. When fully ripe, sweet peppers become sweeter. Yellow can also be the color of a mature pepper: Cubanelle peppers are first green, then yellow.

Countries that have the long growing season that many peppers require have developed whole styles of cooking around them. I couldn't possibly do justice to the Mexican and South American recipes for hot peppers, and suggest you look at Diana Kennedy's excellent book *The Cuisines of Mexico*. What's more, only a few hot pepper varieties really grow successfully in northern climates. We can grow Anaheim, good for tacos and

chilies, and the hotter Jalapeño, but the cayenne, one of the hottest of all, doesn't do well here. (By the way, cayenne peppers are dried and ground for cayenne pepper, and various kinds of hot peppers are dried for chili powder. The cooking of Hungary is based on the sweet rose paprika, made from dried, ground sweet peppers.)

Experiment with some of the different varieties of peppers, such as the elongated banana-type peppers which form the base of my favorite Italian sandwich. Thick-walled bell peppers are excellent for stuffing, the thinner-skinned varieties are good in a delicate salad, and small 1–1½-inch round cherry peppers are fine for pickling and a pretty addition to a crudités platter. Study the seed catalogs and pick varieties that do well in your area.

We grow Gypsy, a tapered, sweet yellow All-American winner; Calwonder and Lady Bell, good, blocky bell peppers; Sweet Banana and Cubanelle, tapered sweet peppers that are good for frying; and one of the hot pepper varieties.

Peppers are cranky to grow. If the temperature is too cold, they won't flower; if it's too hot, they won't set fruit (the reason they often don't set fruit in midsummer).

Russ sows seeds in six-packs indoors in mid-April for plants to transplant outdoors in late May or early June when the ground has warmed up and danger of frost is gone. He uses a black plastic mulch to keep the ground warm under the peppers. He cuts holes in the plastic and

sets the plants 18 inches apart. Peppers also do well in containers because they don't have extensive root systems. During the summer he keeps them well watered.

By early July we are picking our first peppers. You can leave peppers on the vine and harvest as needed; as they mature and turn color they will become sweeter and their texture will soften. We continue to harvest throughout the summer and well into October. To harvest, we twist off the fruit, taking a little of the stem, or cut it with shears. Don't yank—you could pull up the plant. Harvesting can be spread over a number of weeks because peppers hold well on the vine.

Without any question, you can eat fresh peppers without removing their skins. Either halve them, remove the seeds and tissue, and cut into the size you prefer, or cut a cap off the top, remove the seeds and veins with a sharp-edged spoon, and blanch and stuff them. That's a perfectly fine way to prepare peppers for any dish. Unpeeled peppers are delicious raw in salads, cooked alone, or in combination with other vegetables and meats.

There is, however, another dimension to peppers that have been charred and peeled which gives them a totally different taste. Compare the taste of a pimento strip with that of an unpeeled red pepper and you will see what I mean. The charred pepper becomes slightly cooked and the charring of the skin seems to impregnate the pepper with a taste that plays up its natural smokiness and sweetness—quite unlike the taste of oven-cooked peppers. Treat these peppers simply so that you can appreciate their subtle flavor in recipes such as *Peeled Peppers in Oil*.

I used to consider peeling peppers the world's biggest chore, and avoided it whenever possible. I just hadn't learned the simple method I'm going to pass on to you. This procedure might sound time-consuming, but you can cook other foods while the peppers char.

Peeling Sweet Peppers

Start with the thickest-fleshed peppers you can find because they're easier to peel and you lose less flesh than with thin-walled peppers.

Lay the peppers in a broiler pan, and broil until their skins blister (2–3 minutes). With a tong or long fork, slightly rotate them and continue turning until the

peppers are completely charred, then pop them into a paper bag. Close the bag and let the peppers sit in it for 15–20 minutes: the charred skin steams loose from the

flesh. Then, holding each pepper over a bowl, slit down one side, open it up, and discard the seeds, ribs, and stem. Cut the pepper into 2–3 pieces, and peel off the loosened skin with a paring knife. The bowl collects the pepper juices, which can be used to store the peeled peppers if you wish. Or, drain the skinned and seeded peppers on a rack.

If you have a gas stove, you could also char the peppers over the flame, or you can use an open grill.

Peeling Hot Peppers

Hot peppers are charred exactly the same way, but remember the capsaicin contained in the tissue and seeds. If you get it on your hands and rub your eyes or nose, you will get a painful stinging sensation. Also, most hot peppers have thinner skins than large sweet peppers and it is trickier to remove the skin from the thin flesh. Since many hot peppers are small, peeling them can be a time-consuming task. You can dilute the pungency by soaking the hot peppers in water or a mild vinegar and water solution for 30 minutes. Once peppers are peeled, they can be held in cold water.

Peppers take to sautéing, braising, roasting, and grilling like ducks take to water. I blanch peppers for a few minutes before stuffing or if I want to tenderize the flesh before grilling, but that is one of the few times their flesh hits water. You can also steam peppers before stuffing.

Special Information

Yields

Sweet Bell Peppers
- Peppers approximately 4 x 3 inches: 3 peppers per pound
- 1 pound peeled and seeded sweet bell peppers = ½ pound flesh = 1–1¼ cups
- 1 pound raw bell peppers cleaned, trimmed, and thinly sliced = approximately 4 cups

Sweet Italian Peppers
- Peppers approximately 6 x 1½–2 inches: 6 peppers per pound

Hot Peppers
- Peppers approximately 3–6 inches long and ½–¾ inch in diameter: approximately 20 peppers = ½ pound

Storage and Preserving

Whole fresh unwashed peppers will keep in the refrigerator 3–4 days. Ripe red peppers will spoil faster. Peeled peppers stored in a covered container will keep 1–2 days.
- *Freezing:* Clean, seed, and mince the peppers. Do not blanch. Freeze in covered freezer boxes. The frozen peppers will be soft, but will be fine for soups or casseroles where flavor is the prime consideration
- *Drying Hot Peppers:* If you have a cool, dry, airy spot (such as an attic), you can dry peppers as they do in the Southwest. Wait until the peppers turn red; string together on button thread (which is stronger). Sew through the stems, stringing the peppers loosely. Hang in an attic or spare room (your cellar is probably too humid and they would mold).
- *Pickling:* See *Preserved Vinegar Peppers*. Check in a basic preserving book for other methods.

Hints

- Select thick-fleshed peppers for peeled peppers; otherwise you will find yourself with little left.
- Remember that peeled peppers have a more intensified flavor and softer texture than unpeeled peppers.
- For a great snack, spread a layer of large-sized taco or corn chips on a cookie sheet. Top liberally with a mixture of grated Cheddar and Monterey Jack cheeses. Sprinkle with peeled, chopped hot peppers to taste. Place 3–4 inches beneath the broiler flame and cook until the cheeses have melted over the chips and are just beginning to turn brown. Remove and separate into individual pieces.
- See *Ratatouille* in *Eggplant*.
- Make a special hero sandwich using peeled peppers. On a 2-foot loaf of Italian or French bread, arrange ¼ pound each of prosciutto, Genoa salami, and either mortadella or capicola. Add a layer of tomato slices, Provolone cheese, and plenty of peeled red peppers. Top with pitted black olives, a sprinkling of oregano, and drizzle with olive oil and red wine vinegar. Press together, wrap in aluminum foil or a damp towel, and refrigerate. Leave for at least 2–3 hours, and then cut into serving slices.

Marketing

Look for firm, shiny peppers with no signs of dehydration and good color (pale color denotes immaturity). Remember the red ones will be at their ripest stage and will not keep as well as green peppers. Pick up the peppers: the lighter the pepper in relationship to its flesh, the more chance that the pepper has dehydrated.

◇ *Sautéed Peppers*

This is the way I most often prepare peppers. Cut cleaned peppers into strips, dice, or chunks. Sauté in butter or olive oil until tender. The cooking time depends upon the size and thickness of the flesh—it could be anywhere from 3 to 10 minutes, depending upon size.

- Combine julienned sweet red peppers with julienned summer squash or zucchini. Sauté until tender.
- Combine peppers with sliced onions. Sauté until tender.
- Combine peppers with onions and tomatoes; see *Pipérade.*
- Combine with other vegetables. Sauté peppers with or without onions, add sautéed chunked or sliced salted and drained summer squashes or eggplant. Cook until the vegetables are tender. Season with salt, pepper, and herbs to taste. Combine with a tomato sauce if desired.
- Combine peppers; onions; cubed raw potatoes; peeled, chopped, and seeded tomatoes; herbs and seasonings. Cover and cook together until potatoes are tender, and the mixture is soft and moist.

Finishing Touches for Sautéed Peppers

- Combine sautéed peppers, onions or garlic, and eggs; or incorporate into an omelet or frittata.
- Combine sautéed peppers and onions, add mushrooms (optional), and use to cover a pan-fried steak. Season with a hot pepper sauce if desired.
- Combine sautéed peppers with corn, or a combination of corn and fresh lima beans.
- Combine sautéed peppers with cooked white or kidney beans; sauté together and season to taste.
- Combine sautéed peppers and onions with cubed cooked potatoes. Add herbs, salt and pepper, and additional oil and butter if needed. Sauté until lightly browned.
- Garnish grilled sausages, hot dogs, or hamburgers with sautéed peppers.

- Combine peeled, seeded, and finely chopped cucumbers with minced hot peppers. Coat with sour cream or yogurt and season to taste with salt and pepper.
- *Piquant Mussels Vinaigrette:* Steam mussels in white wine until they open. Save broth for soup. Toss the warm mussels in a *Vinaigrette Sauce* (see *Appendix*) along with finely minced hot and sweet peppers, finely minced shallots, and chopped parsley. Serve at room temperature.
- Use *Preserved Vinegar Peppers* as a sauce base: scrape out the seeds, chop peppers into small pieces, and whirl in a blender with a bit of the brine to make a smooth sauce.
- Don't rub your eyes after cutting hot peppers.
- Peppers are loaded with vitamin C.
- Use pieces of pepper on a crudités platter, or in a mixed vegetable grill.
- Dust chicken pieces with flour and dry mustard; drizzle with oil and soy sauce. Season with salt and pepper, and add pepper chunks and lemon slices. Bake in a preheated 375 ° oven until tender.
- Peeled large sweet peppers make a good substitute for hot peppers in a stuffed chili recipe such as chili rellenos. Or roll and bake them in a tomato sauce. Add chopped hot peppers for some heat.
- Make an easy soup: Sauté 3 cups diced sweet peppers, 1 cup diced onions, and 1 small minced hot pepper in butter with 1 teaspoon chili powder until wilted. Add 1 1/2 cups corn. Sauté 1–2 minutes, add 4–6 cups chicken broth, bring to a boil, and simmer for 5 minutes. Serve with whipped cream or sour cream on top.
- Add sliced raw peppers to mixed green salads or chop them and add to tuna, chicken, and meat salads.

Microwave

- Cut-up peppers will cook in 4–6 minutes to a crisp, tender stage. In 8–10 minutes, they will become quite soft.
- Stuffed peppers cook well in the microwave oven. It retains the peppers' bright color while quickly heating the filling. Prepare 4 peppers as for stuffed peppers, and place the empty shells in the microwave for 2 minutes. Remove the shells, stuff them with a cooked stuffing, and return to the microwave. Cook 7–8 minutes longer or until the stuffing is hot.

Leftovers

- Peppers are sublime added to egg dishes, omelets, quiches, frittatas, even as a base for baked eggs.
- Add cooked peppers to sandwiches, such as an egg Western, or to any hot sandwich—meatball, steak, sausage, or hamburgers.
- Peppers and tomatoes have a natural affinity. I make a quick tomato sauce by sautéing leftover peppers, onions, and superripe tomatoes. Puréed, it tastes great.
- Use to top pizza.

◇ *Grilled or Broiled Pepper Pieces*

Halve the peppers, clean the insides, and cut into wide strips or chunks. Dip the pieces into oil. Place them on a grill or broiler pan about 4 inches from the heat. Brown one side, turn, and brown the other side. A thick-fleshed pepper will be tender in 5–6 minutes or less. If the peppers are part of a shish kebab or mixed vegetable grill, coat them or marinate in a sauce before cooking.

Note: Some people like to first parboil the peppers for 2 minutes and then oil and grill them. This is necessary only if they are immediately on top of the heat source and will be cooking quickly.

◇ *Baked Pepper Pieces*

Clean peppers, and cut into strips or chunks. Rub them with oil and bake in a preheated 400°–425° oven until tender; see *Baked Peppers, Potatoes, and Onions*.

◇ *Baked Stuffed Peppers*

To ensure that stuffed peppers are extra tender, give them a preliminary blanching. Clean the peppers, remove the tops, and blanch the pepper shells and tops for 4–5 minutes. Then, drain well and fill with stuffing. Bake in a preheated 375° oven for approximately 20 minutes or until the skins are tender and the filling is heated through.

◇ *Oven-Braised Stuffed Peppers*

This method works well for stuffed peppers that contain a raw ingredient, such as rice. Prepare peppers as in *Baked Stuffed Peppers*. Place the stuffed peppers in a casserole, pour in some liquid, cover, and bake in a preheated 400° oven for 15 minutes. Reduce the heat to 350° and continue baking until the peppers are tender, approximately 20 minutes.

Note: You can also cook the peppers on top of the stove, bring the liquid to a boil, reduce the heat, and cook gently until tender.

◇ *Pepper Cases for Stuffing*

Thick-fleshed, sweet, firm bell peppers are perfectly shaped for stuffing. Choose peppers that have an even end and will stand up without tipping over. If your large peppers are irregularly shaped and might topple, halve them lengthwise. Cut the tops off whole peppers and set aside. Scoop out the insides with a sharp-edged spoon. Cut halved peppers lengthwise and scoop out the seeds. Blanch the pepper cases in boiling water for 3–5 minutes. Remove and run under cold water to stop the cooking process. Drain well and pat dry before stuffing. Season the pepper cases with salt and pepper before filling.

You can also cook stuffed peppers without a preliminary blanching, but blanching starts the tenderizing process and cuts down on the baking time. This means the filling does not become overcooked.

A pretty embellishment is to blanch and bake the tops with the peppers for a high hat to top the stuffing.

A less familiar taste is stuffed peeled peppers. Peel the peppers, roll them up around a stuffing, then bake or braise them; or try Mexican-style stuffed hot peppers. Split the peeled peppers but keep the tops intact. Remove the seeds and veins and stuff the peppers. Press closed and pat dry. Coat the peppers lightly with flour, dip into a light batter, and fry in oil until lightly browned. Heat through, if necessary, in an oven or in a saucepan on top of the stove.

Note: The stuffings can be any combination of cooked vegetables, rice, meats, poultry, or even fish.

Stuffed Pepper Suggestions

Note: The stuffings below will fill 6–10 pepper cases, depending on size of peppers.

Chili-Stuffed Peppers: See recipes.

Leftover Meat and Rice Stuffing: Cook 1 cup chopped onions and 1 teaspoon chopped garlic until wilted; combine with 1½–2 cups cooked rice, 2 cups cooked chopped or ground meat or sliced cooked sausages, beaten egg, and salt, pepper, and herbs to taste. Blanch the pepper cases, stuff, and bake in a preheated 375° oven for 20 minutes until heated through. Top with buttered bread crumbs or grated cheese. Add chopped tomatoes or tomato sauce to moisten.

Zucchini or Eggplant and Lamb Stuffing: Peel, cube, salt, and drain a 1½-pound zucchini or eggplant. Cook 1 cup chopped onion and 1 teaspoon garlic until wilted, add 2 cups ground lamb, and cook until lightly browned; pour off the fat. Add 1 cup peeled, chopped tomatoes or 1 cup wine or broth. Season to taste. Cover and simmer for 10 minutes, uncover, and cook for 10–15 minutes longer to evaporate liquid. Set aside. Heat oil in a pan. Pat the zucchini or eggplant dry and cook until lightly browned on all sides. Combine with the lamb mixture, and season to taste with salt, pepper, and freshly chopped herbs. Fill the pepper cases and bake in a preheated 375° oven for 15–20 minutes until heated through.

Vegetable Stuffings: Revitalize yesterday's vegetables in stuffed peppers. Fill cases with ratatouille or succotash, or combine a vegetable mixture with reduced tomato sauce, then fill and bake as above. For a puréed version, mash vegetables such as eggplant and combine with lots of grated cheese, 2–3 beaten eggs, and fresh bread crumbs and seasonings. Stuff cases and bake as above.

Tuna Stuffed Peppers: Sauté 1 cup chopped onions and 1 teaspoon chopped garlic in olive oil. Combine with 1–1½ cups fresh bread crumbs, flaked tuna fish (or any leftover fish—swordfish is nice), capers, and peeled, chopped red peppers or pimentos. Season with salt, pepper, and herbs. Fill cases and drizzle with olive oil. Bake in a preheated 375° oven for 20–25 minutes, basting, if necessary, with oil or wine. Serve hot or cold.

Sausage Stuffing: Sauté 1 cup chopped onions and 1 teaspoon garlic in 3–4 tablespoons butter. Add 1½ cups cubed, salted, drained, and chopped squash. Sauté until lightly browned. Combine with 1½–2 cups cooked sausage meat and 1 cup fresh bread crumbs. Moisten with melted butter or a beaten egg. Season to taste and stuff peppers. Bake in a preheated 375° oven for 20–30 minutes.

Edith Wilson's Tomato and Crumb Stuffing: Use this mixture with small peppers as a garnish for a roast. Sauté 1/2–1 cup chopped onions in 4–6 tablespoons butter until wilted and golden. Stir in 1 1/2 cups fresh bread crumbs. Add 1 1/2–2 cups peeled, seeded, and chopped ripe tomatoes, 2–3 tablespoons grated Parmesan cheese, and salt and pepper to taste. Stuff pepper cases and bake in a preheated 375° oven for 20 minutes or until heated through.

Rice and Herbs Stuffing: Sauté 1 cup chopped onions in olive oil until wilted. Stir in 1 cup raw rice; cook until just lightly colored, 2–3 minutes. Add 2 cups chicken broth and 1 teaspoon each sugar, salt, and allspice. Bring broth to a boil, cover pan, and simmer 15–20 minutes or until the rice is tender. Toss with 1/4 cup chopped parsley combined with mint. Add 1 cup peeled, seeded, and chopped tomato bits if desired. Season to taste with lemon juice and pepper. Add toasted pine nuts (optional) and/or raisins. Stuff pepper shells and cook as above.

Rice and Cheese Stuffing: Cook rice as for preceding stuffing. Stir in at least 1/2 pound grated cheese. Stuff pepper cases and bake in a preheated 375° oven until heated through and cheese is melted (about 15 minutes).

Pepper Cases for Cold Salads

Blanch the peppers until tender. Run under cold water, and drain well. Fill with cold pasta salad, rice salad, fish, meat, or fowl salad, cabbage salad, etc.

Pepper Cases for Buffets

Garnish a buffet table with small pepper shells stuffed with cooked vegetables. Cook the peppers until tender and fill with cooked red cabbage, creamy leeks, chunks of sautéed shellfish, or mushroom duxelles topped with bread crumbs and cheese. Serve hot.

Red Pepper and Zucchini Sauté and Salad

At some point every summer our garden is overloaded with zucchini and peppers. Here's a dual-purpose combination.

Sautéed Peppers and Zucchini
2 lb sweet red peppers
2–3 lb zucchini
1/4 cup olive oil
1 tsp minced garlic
Salt and freshly ground pepper

Peel the peppers and cut into 1-inch pieces. Wash and trim the zucchini. Quarter lengthwise and then cut into 1-inch pieces. Salt and drain. Pat dry. Heat the oil and sauté zucchini for 4–5 minutes, until lightly browned and barely softened. Stir in the garlic, cook 30 seconds, then add the peppers. Heat together for 2–3 minutes. Season with salt and pepper to taste. Serve hot. (*Serves 4–6*)

• Julienne the vegetables and treat as above. Reduce the cooking time.

Cold Pepper and Zucchini Salad
2 lb sweet red peppers
2–3 lb zucchini
1/4 cup olive oil
1 tsp minced garlic
1/3 cup wine vinegar
1–2 tsp soy sauce
1 Tb sugar
1/4 cup *Toasted Sesame Seeds* (page 351)

Prepare the peppers and zucchini as above. Heat the vinegar, soy sauce, and sugar until the sugar dissolves. Toss with the vegetables, and marinate at least 6 hours. Serve cold tossed with the sesame seeds. (*Serves 4–6*)

Pepper and Cheese Bake

Peeled peppers are an excellent choice for mixed baked dishes because they have a soft texture, no sharp-edged skins, and are subtly but distinctly flavored. Add a salad and you have a meatless supper.

2 lb thick-fleshed peppers
1/2 lb Cheddar cheese
1/2 lb Monterey Jack cheese
2 Tb butter
2 cups chopped onions
2 cups corn kernels
Salt and freshly ground pepper
Chopped fresh hot pepper (optional)
4 eggs
1 cup light cream

Peel peppers (see page 201). Keep each pepper in one flat piece if possible. Drain well. Roughly grate the cheeses, and combine: you should have approximately 4 cups.

Heat the butter in a sauté pan and cook the onions until wilted and golden; add corn and sauté lightly to coat with butter and remove any moisture. Season to taste with salt and pepper.

Butter an 8 x 8-inch baking dish. Pat the peppers dry. Place half the peppers across the dish and sprinkle with a little chopped fresh hot pepper if you like. Top with one-third of the cheese. Spread the corn and onions over the cheese and top with one-third of the cheese. Cover with the remaining peppers. Add more chopped hot pepper if you wish, then cover with the remaining cheese. Beat eggs, combine with cream, and season with salt and pepper. Pour over the top and bake in a preheated 425° oven for 10 minutes; reduce the heat to 350° and bake 20 minutes longer. (*Serves 6–8*)

- Omit the corn, and add more peppers.
- Substitute other sautéed vegetables, such as eggplant slices, for the corn and onions.

Baked Peppers, Potatoes, and Onions

Here is probably one of the easiest recipes in existence, both pretty and good to eat. A heavy green olive oil such as the Sicilian Amastra is preferable.

1–1 1/2 lb green and red peppers
1 lb potatoes
1 large sweet onion
1/4 cup olive oil
Salt and freshly ground pepper

Wash and clean the peppers and cut into 1 1/2–2-inch pieces. Peel the potatoes if thick-skinned; I prefer to use unpeeled new potatoes. Cut the potatoes into 1-inch slices or chunks. Peel the onion and cut into chunks. Place everything in a shallow ovenproof dish and pour over the oil. Rub the vegetables with the oil. Sprinkle with salt and lots of pepper. Bake in a preheated 425° oven for approximately 30 minutes or until the potatoes are tender. (*Serves 4*)

- Add sausages that have been pricked and blanched in water to release their juices.
- Add chicken pieces which have been rubbed with oil, or with an oil and garlic mixture.

Hot Pepper Sauce

How hot this sauce turns out depends upon the type of hot peppers you use. I prefer medium hot cherry peppers. To change the strength, increase or decrease the amount of peppers. I use this sauce to top omelets, chicken, beef, and other meats. Occasionally, I'll stir some into soups and stews for extra zing.

1 cup chopped hot peppers
1 clove garlic
2 cups fresh tomato pulp
1 tsp wine vinegar
1 Tb oil
1/2 cup chopped onions
1 cup chicken or beef broth
Salt

Roughly purée peppers, garlic, tomatoes, and vinegar in a food processor or blender. Heat the oil in a saucepan and cook the onion until wilted. Add the pepper mixture and broth. Cover the pan, and cook for 5 minutes. Then uncover and gently boil for 30 minutes until thickened, stirring occasionally. Season with salt. (*Makes 2 1/2 cups*)

- Substitute peppers from *Preserved Vinegar Peppers* for fresh peppers.

Sweet Pepper Sauce

This is a subtly flavored garnish for individual vegetable custards—picture it with a spinach timbale—or served with cooked eggs, fish, or poultry.

1 1/2 lb sweet red peppers
2 Tb olive oil
1 cup chopped onions
1/4 cup chopped celery with leaves
1 tsp minced garlic
1 1/2 cups peeled, seeded, and chopped tomatoes
1/2 tsp thyme
Salt and freshly ground pepper

Peel the peppers (see page 201) and cut into strips. Heat the oil, and sauté the onions and celery until wilted and golden. Add the garlic and cook 30 seconds, then stir in the peppers, tomatoes and thyme. Season with salt and pepper. Cover the pan and cook 5 minutes; uncover and simmer 15–30 minutes or until thickened. The cooking time depends upon the tomatoes' juiciness. Purée smooth in the blender, food processor, or food mill. Taste for seasoning before serving. (*Makes about 2 1/2–3 cups*)

Peeled Peppers in Oil

Peeled peppers and the best-quality olive oil are all you need for a superb appetizer or antipasto selection. Accompany with anchovies, and decorate with black olives, capers, and hard-boiled egg wedges if desired. Serve with a thick-crust, no-salt Tuscan-style white bread.

2 lb red and green thick-fleshed peppers
Good olive oil
Salt

Peel peppers (see page 201) and cut into strips. Mix with olive oil and season lightly with salt. The peppers can stay in the oil for 2–3 days. (*Makes 2–2 1/2 cups*)

- Mash garlic and salt and beat in the oil; coat the peppers with the flavored oil.
- Make a *Vinaigrette Sauce* (see *Appendix*) and use to marinate the peppers. Or spice up a lemon vinaigrette sauce with 1/4 teaspoon each cumin and paprika, a dash of cayenne, salt, and pepper.
- Toss the pepper strips with lots of pitted or sliced olives, then marinate in the oil.
- Use the marinated peppers in green salads, or rice or pasta salads.

- Cook the peppers lightly in the oil and toss with hot pasta, grated cheese, and seasonings.
- Purée any leftover peppers with tuna fish and capers to taste. Gradually add enough olive oil to make a thick sauce to garnish sliced tomatoes, cold meats, or hot pastas.
- See *Sweet Pepper Sauce*.

Guacamole

Roll guacamole in a warm tortilla with sour cream on the side, or serve as a snack with toasted crisp tortillas and sour cream.

> 2–3 hot peppers
> 2 Tb minced onion
> 1/2 tsp ground coriander or 2 tsp freshly chopped
> 1/4 tsp salt
> 2 large ripe avocados
> 1–2 Tb lime or lemon juice

Mince the hot peppers and mash together with onion, coriander, and salt. Mash the avocado flesh with lime or lemon juice and combine with the pepper mixture. Serve immediately or keep from turning dark by covering with a layer of oil, mayonnaise, or sour cream. (*Makes 1 1/2–2 cups*)

- Fold in the sour cream cover when serving.
- Add chopped, peeled, and seeded red or green tomatoes.
- Add minced scallions.
- Mash garlic with hot peppers and onion.

Pepper and Tuna Antipasto

> 3 lb green and red sweet peppers
> 7 oz tuna fish, flaked
> 2 Tb capers
> 1 tsp chopped garlic
> 1/2 teaspoon salt
> 1 Tb lemon juice
> 1/4 cup olive oil

Peel peppers, julienne, or cut into 1-inch pieces. Combine with tuna and capers. Mash the garlic with salt, stir in the lemon juice, then add the oil. Toss with the pepper-tuna mixture. Serve at room temperature. (*Serves 4*)

- Add chopped anchovies, and cut down on the salt.
- Add minced hot peppers.

Pepper Slaw

> 1 1/2–2 lb red and green sweet peppers
> 4 cups thinly sliced cabbage
> 1 Tb finely minced fresh hot peppers (optional)
> 1–2 tsp celery seeds
> *Vinaigrette Sauce* with mustard (page 352)
> Salt and freshly ground pepper

Clean peppers and cut into fine strips or julienne them. Combine with cabbage, hot peppers (if you like), and celery seeds. Toss with vinaigrette and season to taste with salt and pepper. Marinate for 2–3 hours before serving. (*Serves 6–8*)

- Peel the peppers (see page 201) for a totally different taste. Remember to double the amount of peppers because they reduce by half in the peeling.
- Add finely julienned carrots.
- Sometimes I load this with sliced olives.

Pepper-Tomato Soup

Add hot peppers if you wish.

> 1 cup chopped onions
> 1/2 cup finely chopped carrots
> 1/2 cup finely chopped celery
> 1 Tb oil
> 2 Tb butter
> 1 tsp minced garlic
> 4 cups peeled, seeded, and chopped tomatoes
> 1 Tb wine vinegar
> 1 tsp sugar
> 1–2 pieces dried orange peel
> 2 lb sweet peppers (red, green, or a combination)
> 4 cups beef stock
> Saffron
> 1/4 cup rice
> Paprika
> Cayenne
> Salt and freshly ground pepper
> Hot pepper sauce (optional)

Cook the onions, carrots, and celery in the oil and butter until the vegetables are wilted and tender and the onions are golden. Stir in the garlic, tomatoes, vinegar, sugar, and orange peel. Cover the pan and cook 5 minutes; uncover, and cook until the mixture becomes a fairly thick purée. This will take 15–30 minutes, depending upon the water content of the tomatoes. Meanwhile, peel the peppers (see page 201) and cut into strips. (You should have 2–2 1/2 cups.) When the tomato mixture is ready, process it in a food processor or put through a large sieve, leaving it coarsely textured. Mix in the stock and a pinch of saffron, and bring the stock to a boil. Add the rice, peppers, a pinch of paprika and cayenne, and salt and pepper to taste. Lower the heat and cook gently, covered, approximately 15 minutes or until the rice is tender. Taste and season again if necessary, adding hot pepper sauce if desired. (*Makes 2 quarts*)

Creamy Fish Stew

Here is an easy-to-make, adaptable stew. Eliminate the mussels or use only peppers or leeks (see variations at end of recipe). The more butter you add, the richer this stew becomes. Serve it with crusty French bread for dunking in the sauce.

2 lb sweet red peppers
1 lb leeks
2 lb white fish combination, such as cod, haddock, bass, monkfish, etc.
18–24 mussels
6 Tb butter
Salt and freshly ground pepper
2 cups heavy cream
1 ½ cups dry white wine
Saffron (optional)
Chopped parsley or fennel leaves

Peel the peppers (see page 201), and cut into thin julienne strips. Wash the leeks thoroughly, removing the dark green tops. Thinly julienne the leek whites. Skin the fish and cut into chunks. Scrub the mussels if you are using them.

In a large deep saucepan, heat 4 tablespoons butter, stir in the leeks, cover, and cook over low heat for about 10 minutes, stirring occasionally. The leeks should be wilted and tender. Uncover, add the peppers, and cook for 2–3 minutes. Season with salt and pepper.

Add 1 cup cream. Cook 5 minutes, until cream reduces and absorbs pepper-leek flavors. This can be made ahead to this point. When ready to cook, place the mussels and wine in a saucepan along with a pinch of saffron. Cover the pan and bring the wine to a boil, lower the heat slightly and cook only until the mussels open, about 3–5 minutes. Keep the mussels in their shells, lift out of the liquid, and keep warm. Strain the juices and reduce to approximately 1 cup. Add the remaining cream and heat for 3–4 minutes.

Place the fish pieces on top of the pepper-leek mixture, pour on the cream-broth, taste for seasoning, and add the remaining butter. Cover pan, and cook 5–8 minutes or until the fish is just tender. Add the mussels and cook another minute or two to just reheat them. Sprinkle with parsley or fennel. (*Serves 4*)

- If you omit mussels, reduce 2 cups of fish stock or dry white wine or combination of both by half.
- Cook large raw shrimp in their shells along with the fish.
- Bake, covered, in 400° oven if you wish.
- Place in individual bowls, cover, and bake.
- Make with all peppers or all leeks.

Pipérade

A Basque specialty, pipérade is an omelet that incorporates a garnish of peppers, onions, and tomatoes. This vegetable combination need not be limited to eggs. Try it cooked with meat, fish, or fowl.

The Pipérade Garnish
½ lb green peppers (or 2 cups thinly sliced pepper strips)
3 Tb olive oil
2 cups finely sliced onions
1–2 tsp minced garlic (or more to taste)
3–4 cups peeled, seeded, and julienned tomatoes
½ tsp basil
½ tsp oregano (optional)
Salt and freshly ground pepper

Clean the peppers and cut into thin strips. Heat the oil and cook the onions and peppers over low heat for 5–8 minutes until wilted. Add the garlic, stir for 30 seconds, then top with the tomatoes, herbs, and salt and pepper. Cover the pan, and cook gently for 5 minutes to release the tomato juices. Uncover and cook until almost all the moisture is gone. Set aside and keep warm.

- Substitute ½ pound sliced sweet red peppers for the tomatoes, and cook uncovered until tender.

The Omelets
6 Tb butter
1 cup julienned ham (optional)
12 eggs
Salt and freshly ground pepper

Heat 2 tablespoons of the butter in an omelet pan. Sauté the ham (if using it) until lightly browned, remove, and set aside. Beat the eggs with salt and pepper. Heat 2 tablespoons of the butter and pour in half the eggs. Stir rapidly with a fork, shaking the pan constantly. Stir only until the eggs begin to set and are creamy throughout. Spread with half the pipérade, top with half the sautéed ham strips, then fold over and onto a hot platter. Repeat the process. (*Serves 4*)

- Make one giant omelet. Either fold it over as above or top with the pipérade and ham strips, sprinkle with cheese, and run under the broiler before serving.

Bluefish Baked with a Pipérade Garnish

2 lb bluefish
1 Tb butter
2 Tb oil
Flour
Salt and freshly ground pepper
1 recipe slightly undercooked *Pipérade Garnish* variation with red and green peppers (see above)
½ cup dry vermouth
4 flat anchovies (optional)
One half recipe *Aïoli* with pimento variation (page 180) (optional)

Skin the fish and cut into four serving pieces, approximately 8 ounces each. Heat 1 tablespoon butter and the oil in a sauté pan. Lightly flour and season the fish pieces and sauté in the hot butter and oil quickly on both sides without browning; you want to "seal" the flesh. Remove the fish from the pan.

Butter a baking dish large enough to hold the fish or butter 4 individual au gratin dishes. Place the fish in the baking dish and cover with the pipérade mixture. Add the vermouth and top with the anchovies (if desired). Cover the dish with aluminum foil and place in a preheated 400° oven for 15–20 minutes, depending upon the thickness of the fish fillets. Uncover the pan, remove fish and pipérade garnish to warm plates. Either boil down the cooking juices and pour over the fish, or beat a bit of the hot cooking juices into aïoli and serve on top or to the side. (*Serves 4*)

- White fish such as striped bass, halibut, or haddock are equally delicious, as are chicken breasts. Dot with butter before covering and baking.
- Cook on top of the stove if you prefer. Allow more liquid in the pan by increasing the amount of vermouth to 1 cup or using more fish stock. Cover the pan and cook over gentle heat until the fish is cooked through, 8–15 minutes. Reduce the juices as above.

Chicken with Peppers

1–1 1/2 lb sweet red or green peppers (or a combination)
3 1/2–4 lb chicken
1 lb sweet Italian sausages
2–3 Tb oil
2 cups sliced onions
1 tsp minced garlic
4 cups peeled, seeded, and chopped tomatoes
1/2 tsp oregano
1/4 tsp thyme
Salt and freshly ground pepper
1/2 cup green olives stuffed with pimento (optional)

Clean the peppers and slice into 1/2-inch pieces. Clean the chicken, removing any fat, and cut chicken into 8 serving pieces. Pat dry. Prick the sausages with a fork and blanch for 5 minutes in boiling water. Remove, drain, and cut into 1/2-inch slices. Heat 2 tablespoons of the oil in a large deep sauté pan and sauté the sausages until browned; set aside. In the same pan, sauté the chicken pieces until lightly browned; set aside. Add peppers, lower the heat, and cook without browning until barely tender; set aside. Add 1 tablespoon oil if necessary, sauté the onions until wilted and golden. Add the garlic, cook for 30 seconds, then add tomatoes, herbs, and salt and pepper to taste. Cover the pan and cook 5 minutes to release the tomato moisture. Uncover and cook until juices reduce, approximately 10 minutes. (The time depends on the amount of moisture in the tomatoes. The sauce should be thick, for the chicken juices will dilute it.) Add the chicken and cook slowly for 20 minutes, or until the chicken is cooked through. Uncover the pan, and add sausage pieces, peppers, and olives (if desired). Cook 5 minutes longer until mixture is heated through. Taste for seasoning before serving. (*Serves 6*)

Pork and Peppers

This dish is most attractive when you use a combination of red and green sweet peppers.

2 lb boneless pork loin (approximately 8 inches long)
1/2 tsp rosemary
1/2 tsp thyme
1/8 tsp allspice
2 tsp chopped garlic
Salt
6 Tb oil
1 1/2 lb sweet peppers
1–1 1/2 cups sliced onions
1 cup dry white vermouth
Freshly ground pepper

Trim off any fat from pork and cut into eight 3/4–1-inch slices. Crush the rosemary and thyme and mix with the allspice. Mash together the garlic and 1 teaspoon salt; mix with the crushed herbs. Beat in 2 tablespoons of the oil. Brush the pork with this marinade and set aside for 3–4 hours.

When you're ready to cook, clean the peppers and cut into 1/2-inch strips. Heat 2 tablespoons of the oil and brown the pork pieces. Lift pork into a baking dish. If necessary, add 2 tablespoons additional oil and sauté the peppers and onions for 5 minutes until slightly tenderized. Strew them between the pork slices in a baking dish. Pour the fat from the pan. Add the vermouth; let boil for a moment until all browned bits in pan are incorporated; pour over pork and peppers. Season with salt and pepper. Bake in a preheated 375° oven for 25–30 minutes or until the pork is tender, basting occasionally. Pour the cooking liquid into a small saucepan and boil rapidly until lightly thickened. Pour over meat. (*Serves 4*)

- Use pork or veal chops instead of the loin.

Chili-Stuffed Peppers

Peppers can be stuffed with almost as many food combinations as there are kinds of peppers. This recipe makes approximately 6 cups chili, enough to stuff 6 large peppers or a few more smaller peppers.

>6 large peppers
>1–2 small hot peppers
>2 Tb oil
>1 ½ cups chopped onions
>1 ½ cups chopped sweet peppers
>1–2 tsp minced garlic
>1 lb ground beef
>1 ½–2 cups peeled, seeded, and chopped tomatoes
>1 Tb chili powder
>1 tsp sugar
>Salt and freshly ground pepper
>2 cups cooked kidney beans
>1 cup grated Monterey Jack and Cheddar cheeses
>   (optional)

Prepare pepper shells (see *Pepper Cases for Stuffing*, page 204). Clean and finely mince the hot peppers. In a large deep sauté pan, heat the oil and add onions and the chopped sweet and hot peppers. Cook until wilted and softened; stir in the garlic and cook 30 seconds. Push vegetables to one side and lightly brown the beef, breaking it up with a fork. Pour fat from the pan. Stir in the tomatoes, chili powder, and sugar. Taste, and season well with salt and pepper. Cover the pan, and cook for 5 minutes. Add the kidney beans, and cook slowly for 15–20 minutes until thickened. Taste again for seasoning.

Oil the baking dish. Salt and pepper the pepper shells, and fill with the chili mixture. Top with grated cheese if you like. Bake in a preheated 375° oven for 20 minutes or until heated through. (*Serves 6 or more*)

- Use your favorite chili mixture. This is a good recipe for leftover chili.
- Make a Spanish-style stuffing: Omit the beans. Add ½ cup raisins, ¼ cup chopped stuffed olives, and ½ cup toasted blanched almonds or pine nuts; season

with cinnamon and cloves. Add cooked rice if desired.
- Omit beans and use chunks of meat rather than ground beef.

Preserved Vinegar Peppers

My Italian friend Marie's mother had great wooden barrels full of her "vinegar peppers," which she used throughout the winter. Here is her preserving method and some cooking suggestions. This is an easy way to store the final pepper harvest, your own "peck of pickled peppers."

Use a covered container. Wash it thoroughly to make sure it is sterile. Wash the peppers, leave them whole, and put in the container. You can use any size or shape peppers: either hot or sweet works equally well. Make a *Pickling Brine* (see page 350) with a clove or two of garlic, and a sprig of fresh herbs (Marie's mother used mint!). Cover the peppers with the brine, cover, and keep in a cool place at least 2 weeks or place in jars and process in a boiling water bath for 15 minutes. Rinse well before using.

- Clean and stuff large vinegar peppers just like fresh peppers. Try a combination of fresh bread crumbs, parsley, grated Romano cheese, and raisins moistened with a little milk, 1 egg, and seasoning to taste. Stuff the peppers, drizzle on a bit of oil, and bake for approximately 30 minutes in a preheated 350° oven.
- Use small vinegar peppers whole in an antipasto plate, or cut up larger ones, seeds and all. Add minced garlic and thinly sliced onions. Dress with olive oil and use in salads.
- Sauté pieces of vinegar peppers with sausages, potatoes, or whatever you like. Or, brown pork strips, add bay leaves and vinegar peppers, and cook together.

Potatoes

Have you ever tried marble-size new potatoes boiled in their skins and topped with a pat of fresh butter? These first potatoes of the year—new potatoes' most delicate form—are a treat we anticipate eagerly each summer. I once saw a Rhode Island potato farmer sell these tiny potatoes in one-pound bags for almost the price of prime beef: his nongardening customers had never seen potatoes that size.

I've heard people refer to new potatoes as if they were a special variety to grow. Although small red potatoes are

often equated with new potatoes, any freshly dug potatoes that haven't been stored are new potatoes.

We'd grow potatoes just to have new potatoes on hand, but that's not the only reason. Many of our favorite potato varieties are unavailable commercially, such as the European kipfel potatoes, known here as yellow ladyfinger potatoes, brought to the Midwest by European immigrants. These waxy, firm potatoes cooked are absolutely delicious in salads and sautés. Irish Cobbler, another favorite, has fallen into disrepute in the market-

place because of its deep eyes—but its flavor is wonderful.

Also, the trend in potato breeding is to produce disease-resistant, all-purpose potatoes. This means that many of the commercially produced potatoes (with the exception of Russet types) have a medium starch content. The amount of potato starch really governs how well potatoes work in recipes. When you grow your own potatoes you can include varieties to cover all culinary needs.

If you prefer mealy-textured potatoes, plant starchy varieties with what potato breeders call high specific gravity. Seed catalogs usually list these as baking potatoes. Any Russet types will be good bakers. High-starch potatoes are also good mashed, because of their light and dry qualities; and in French fries, best made with low-moisture potatoes, so you get a crisp exterior and a fluffy interior.

On the other hand, low-starch potatoes have a firmer texture and are good choices for boiling, potato salads, sautés, or au gratin dishes where you want the potato shape to stay intact, and where mealy or loose-textured potatoes would break down and become mushy. For example, a low-starch variety, such as Green Mountain,

is an excellent choice for potato chips because the potatoes crisp right up and hold their shape. Most red potato varieties, such as Norland or Pontiac, are low in starch and are best boiled or fried.

All-purpose medium-starch varieties such as Kennebec, Katahdin, or Superior can be used for either boiling or baking, but their baked texture will be more watery than a standard baking potato. They are excellent in a dish like Straw Mat Potatoes where you need some starch to hold the potatoes together, yet enough firmness to hold the shape.

A quick starch content test is to rub together cut potato halves. The starches show up as a white froth. Stick the surfaces together and hold up the potato: the halves of a starchy potato will adhere, while a low-starch potato will not hold together at all. You can almost tell the amount of starch by the length of time the halves hold together. Remember that all potatoes, regardless of their initial starch content, lose sugar and become starchier as they age. Potatoes are also lower in calories than most of us realize—fewer than 100 calories for an average-size potato. It's the butter and sour cream that add calories, not the potato.

Special Information

Yields

- 2 large russet baking potatoes = 1½ pounds
- 2 medium-size baking potatoes = 1 pound
- 3 medium-size boiling potatoes = 1 pound
- 10–12 small new potatoes (1–1½ inches) = 1 pound
- 3 pounds baking potatoes baked and mashed = 6 cups
- 1 pound potatoes sliced = 2½–3 cups = about 2 cups mashed

Storage and Preserving

- Do not freeze potatoes: they become watery.
- Late-season potatoes store well in a cellar once they have been cured: let the skins toughen, otherwise the potatoes could shrivel and become soft shortly after storage. After harvesting, place in the sun for 2–3 hours to dry, brush off the soil (don't wash), and store in the darkest part of your cellar. An ideal storage temperature is 45–50°. If the temperature is too high, potatoes tend to soften, shrivel, and sprout. Temperatures that are too low cause the starch in the potatoes to turn to sugar, giving them a sweet taste. (Should this happen, hold the potatoes at 70° for a week or so, and the sugar will convert back to starch, making the potatoes edible again.) Potatoes properly stored should last all winter long. It is a good idea to layer the potatoes with newspapers so if one turns bad, it won't spoil the whole lot.

Hints

- Try to use the type of potatoes with starch qualities best suited for the recipe.
- Thicken a soup or stew with a potato, which will disintegrate and give body to the liquid.
- Make a *Swiss Raclette:* Boil potatoes (preferably new potatoes). Melt a 2–3-pound chunk of Gruyère or Raclette cheese in a pan on top of a stove or over a fire's coals, gradually melting the outer layer. As the cheese melts, scrape it warm onto plates with the potatoes. Eat together accompanied by sweet gherkin pickles or sweet pickled vegetables.
- Make a new potato, knockwurst, and sauerkraut casserole. Cook 2 pounds thick sliced new potatoes with 1 cup sautéed onions, paprika, and caraway and ½ cup water for 10 minutes. Top with 2 cups sauerkraut and 6 knockwurst cut into ½-inch slices. Cover and cook another 10 minutes or until potatoes are tender. Serve with a bowl of mustard laced with sour cream.
- Serve small boiled potatoes with an *Aïoli* sauce (see *Onions*).
- Add raw potato chunks to stews and hearty soups during the last 20–30 minutes of cooking.
- Keeping peeled potatoes in cold water prevents them from discoloring; however, it also releases their starch.
- Roll boiled potatoes over heat to "dry out."
- See *Baked Peppers, Potatoes, and Onions* in *Peppers*.

Potatoes are a cool-climate vegetable; they do best when temperatures average slightly below 70° during the growing season. Early in spring, Russ buys certified seed potatoes grown from plants inspected for disease. As potatoes are host to more than 60 types of disease, this is very important. (Don't be tempted to recycle leftover supermarket potatoes, because many have been chemically treated to inhibit sprouting and they won't grow.) Russ purchases approximately 10 pounds of potatoes for each 100-foot row, selecting early, midseason, and late varieties, such as Norland, Irish Cobbler, Kennebec, and Katahdin.

The ideal seed potato is the size of an egg (with sprouts), but this is difficult to obtain at garden centers, which frequently sell larger seed potatoes to be dissected. Russ cuts the potatoes into sections with at least three healthy eyes per piece. After dipping the cut surfaces into agricultural sulfur to help resist fungus diseases, he sets them out in the full sun on the windowsill for two weeks until they form calluses. Although there is some labor involved, the reward is slightly earlier "new" potatoes.

By the way, a new development from major seed companies that may appeal to some home gardeners is growing potatoes from seed. As yet, however, the number of varieties available is quite limited, so we still plant potatoes the way our grandfathers did.

As soon as the ground can be worked in the spring, he digs a flat-bottomed trench 6–8 inches wide and 4–5 inches deep, and scratches in some 5-10-5 fertilizer. He places the cut sections, sprout sides up, about 12 inches apart and covers them with a 3-inch layer of soil. (Or, he'll use whole small potatoes of the desired variety thrown intact into the same-size trench.) Throughout the summer, as the plants grow, he mounds them with more soil.

Potatoes need at least 1 inch of water per week, which is best applied all at once, since intermittent watering is probably the major reason for malformed potatoes. The plants might look fine, but the tubers actually stop growing until they obtain moisture, and end up knobby or with dumbbell shapes. Oblong potatoes are less likely to become malformed.

I steal my favorite marble-size potatoes around the first of July while the plant is growing vigorously, trying

to keep the roots undisturbed. Later, after most of the foliage has died down, the potatoes are ready to harvest. Dig the potatoes with a pitchfork, sufficiently away from the main vine to avoid piercing or slicing the tubers.

Before preparing to cook, wash the potatoes thoroughly and remove the eyes. I peel potatoes just like carrots, by holding the potato in one hand and, while I'm rotating it, removing the peel with a vegetable peeler. Sometimes, when I'm peeling loads of potatoes, I find it faster to use a paring knife and peel around the potatoes. After doing a television segment on *Leek and Potato Soup*, I received a letter from a viewer who liked the recipe but was upset I had peeled the potatoes—she never peeled potatoes even for mashing. I certainly can appreciate the desire to retain as many nutrients as possible, but think it's a trade-off. Baby potatoes boiled in their skins make the best possible potato dish, but older, tough skins in mashed potatoes are unappealing. The decision to peel or not depends upon the recipe, but you can decide for yourself.

Potatoes peeled in advance should be kept in cold water so they won't darken. The water leaches out some of the starch, but unless starch is needed to "glue" slices together, this doesn't matter. In Europe potatoes are sold in outdoor markets all peeled and stored in buckets of water. What a convenience for the working housewife!

Microwave

- 4 large baking potatoes (3 pounds) placed directly in the oven will cook done in 16–18 minutes, but I find some potatoes turn gummy in the center.
- 2 pounds boiling potatoes placed in a covered casserole with ¼ cup water will cook done in 10–12 minutes.
- 6 small (1½–2-inch) new potatoes placed in a covered casserole with ¼ cup water will cook in 8–10 minutes.

Leftovers

- Use cooked sliced potatoes in quiches and omelets.
- Make a *Mashed Potato Soup*. Sauté chopped onions in butter; whip in potatoes and broth, heat and add cream to taste. Sprinkle with chives or other herbs. Add mashed leftover root vegetables if available.
- Use leftover mashed potatoes in cakes, yeast bread, and doughnut recipes (see *Lynn's Chocolate Potato Cake* and potato bread and doughnut recipes).
- Use to thicken sauces or stews.
- See *Boiled Potatoes Twice Around*.
- Make a potato luncheon omelet with sliced potatoes, onions, green peppers, olives, and eggs. Prepare as in *Pipérade* in *Peppers*.
- Simplify the basic *Shepherd's Pie for a Crowd* recipe, using leftover potatoes, lamb and gravy.

Marketing

Buy firm, heavy potatoes with smooth skins and no signs of discoloration or spotting. The depth of the potatoes' eyes is no indication of quality, even though they're harder to peel. (Some of the most flavorful potatoes, such as Irish Cobbler, have deep eyes.)

Often you'll buy potatoes that look perfectly fine on the outside, but when you cut them open, they're discolored or have a ring of rot. That's black rot disease, which cannot be detected by external appearance.

For baking or boiling, select equal-size potatoes so they will cook in the same amount of time. Idaho Russets are the best baking choice. They are grown under ideal conditions and are the finest of the russet potatoes.

Seed Potato Mail Order Varieties

Here are some of the seed potato varieties available from seedsmen. Note that some old favorites such as *Green Mountain* and *Red Bliss* are rarely stocked because they are too susceptible to diseases. Look for a local source for them.

- *Bake King:* A midseason russet-type potato that has an oval shape and white skin with slight russeting. It's strictly for baking and matures earlier than most other baking potatoes.
- *Chippewa:* A midseason, white-skinned oblong potato that is a heavy yielder. It stays white when cooked and is a good northern choice.
- *Colorado Long:* A midseason, white-skinned potato that resists blight.
- *Early Gem:* A rough-skinned early potato that resists scab, although it is subject to cracking in clay soils.
- *Early Ohio:* An old-fashioned potato that's good for either boiling or frying.
- *Fingerlings:* A fingerlike yellow-fleshed potato that is about 1 inch in diameter and 2–4 inches long. Its waxy texture makes it a unique salad and frying choice.
- *Irish Cobbler:* An old standby with deep eyes, a round shape, and white flesh.
- *Katahdin:* A medium to large all-purpose, medium-starch midseason potato that has white flesh.
- *Kennebec:* A late potato that has smooth white skin and resists blight and mosaic. It's a good all-purpose, medium-starch keeper.
- *Norland:* An early, low-starch red-skinned potato that has white flesh and heavy bearing capabilities.
- *Red La Soda:* A slightly waxy, all-purpose potato that has bright red skin and flesh that stays white after cooking. It's adaptable to many soils and climates.
- *Red Pontiac:* A midseason, red-skinned potato that is best for boiling—it becomes soggy when baked. It's a long keeper.
- *Russet Burbank:* Famous as the Idaho potato—has good baking and frying capabilities. It's difficult for the home gardener to grow because it needs a steady supply of just the correct amount of water.
- *Superior:* An all-purpose potato that has an oval shape and white flesh. It's a disease-resistant early-mid-season choice.
- *White Cobbler:* Another old-fashioned variety with good flavor.

◇ Boiled Potatoes

Few foods can match a freshly dug new potato boiled until tender, eaten with some sweet butter, coarse salt, and freshly ground pepper. Boiled baby new potatoes, skins on, are my favorite way of serving potatoes.

Whether you boil potatoes in their skins or peel them first depends completely upon the recipe. New potatoes' tender skins don't need to be removed before boiling. When I'm boiling potatoes for mashed potatoes or chunking big potatoes to be served with butter and herbs, I peel them first. Remember that low-starch—or waxy—potatoes are really best for boiling: baking potatoes tend to disintegrate, while old starchy potatoes become soggy and gluey.

Occasionally, I'll flavor the boiling water. Thirty minutes before adding the potatoes, I simmer garlic, an herb bouquet, onion—or all three—or exotic spices in the cooking water. The flavoring essence permeates boiled potatoes.

Cooking times for boiled potatoes are approximate, as the time depends upon potato size, variety, and the amount of potatoes in the pot. Usually, I boil potatoes 1½–2 inches in size. I rinse them off, cover with water, add salt (1–1½ teaspoons per quart of water), bring the water to a boil, and cook until tender—they'll take 15–20 minutes after the water has returned to a boil. Drain the potatoes, roll them gently over heat to dry, and serve. Or roll in butter to glaze.

Finishing Touches for Boiled Potatoes

- *With Cream:* Slightly undercook the potatoes. Peel and slice them while warm. (If you prefer, peel and slice raw potatoes, boil them to just barely tender, and drain.) Place the slices in a sauté pan; season with salt, pepper, and herbs if desired. Barely cover with cream and cook until the cream reduces and just coats the potatoes. The amount of cream depends upon the quantity of potatoes. One pound potatoes would need ½–⅔ cup cream.
- *With Sour Cream:* Drain new potatoes and immediately slice. For each 2 pounds potatoes, fold in 1 cup sour cream and toss with chopped fresh dill, salt, and pepper.
- *Caramel Potatoes:* Peel 1–1½ pounds baby potatoes while they're still warm. Cook ¾ cup sugar and ¼ cup water in a saucepan until it turns a golden caramel. Stir in 6–8 tablespoons butter; add the potatoes. Roll the potatoes around in the caramel-butter until coated.
- *Roasted in Butter:* Boil the potatoes only until half cooked. Peel, and thickly slice. Sprinkle with salt and pepper and pour melted butter over until lightly coated. You'll need approximately ¼ cup of butter

per pound of potatoes. Bake in a preheated 375° oven, tossing occasionally, until tender and glazed.

- *In Mornay Sauce:* For every 3 pounds potatoes make 2 ½ cups cheese sauce (see *Mornay Sauce* in *Appendix*). Fold into potatoes, top with buttered bread crumbs, and bake in a preheated 375° oven for 20 minutes, or until hot.

◇ *Boiled "Salt" Potatoes*

These are delicious if you're not on a low-sodium diet. Place small new potatoes in a pot and cover with cold water. Pour kosher salt into the pot until the potatoes begin to float. (One pound potatoes will take about 1 cup salt.) Bring water to a boil and cook at a gentle boil approximately 15 minutes or until tender when pierced with a fork. Drain. The potatoes will have a white salt cast to their skin. Dip them into melted butter and bite in!

◇ *Boiled Potatoes Twice Around*

Whenever I boil potatoes, I usually boil extra, because we enjoy cooked leftover potatoes—especially the firm, waxy new potatoes. Russ always asks for home fries with his weekend breakfasts, and I think of the leftover potatoes crisply fried in butter and served for the staff dinners at the restaurant.

Home Fries

Cook sliced leftover cold boiled potatoes in butter until browned (an iron skillet works best). Sprinkle with salt and freshly ground pepper. For 2 cups sliced potatoes, use 2–3 tablespoons butter or bacon fat.

"Staff Potatoes"

At the Straight Wharf, we melt plenty of butter in an iron skillet and sauté chopped onions until light golden brown. Then we add sliced cold cooked potatoes and sauté until brown. By then, the onions are good and dark. Season with salt and freshly ground pepper. Turn these into Lyonnaise potatoes by cutting onions into rings, sautéing in butter, then combining with the sautéed potatoes and seasoning to taste.

Hash Browns

Heat butter (or bacon fat and butter) in a heavy skillet. (You would need 4–6 tablespoons fat for every 2 pounds potatoes.) Add diced cold boiled potatoes, press down, forming a cake, and cook to brown the bottom. To add more butter, place pats on top of the potatoes and let it melt in. Sprinkle with salt and pepper. If the potato cake is thick, cover the pan so it will steam for a minute or two. Then, invert onto a plate; add additional butter to the skillet if necessary, return the potatoes, and cook the paler side until browned. (If you make small cakes, you have hash brown patties.)

You can make hash browns without bothering to form a cake. Add the diced potatoes, do not press down, and stir until the potatoes are completely browned. Add heavy cream and cook down to form a crust. Season.
Note: A bit of vinegar added to the skillet adds flavor and helps the browning process.

Sliced Potatoes with Eggs

This is a great brunch dish. Lightly sauté sliced boiled potatoes and place in a buttered casserole. Top with slices of mozzarella or Swiss cheese. Carefully break eggs over the cheese. Season with salt and freshly ground pepper. Pour over just enough heavy cream to coat the eggs. It will run off and down into the potatoes. Sprinkle the top with grated Parmesan cheese and dot with butter. Bake in a preheated 400° oven for approximately 15 minutes or until the eggs are set and the dish is hot. Add herbs as desired. If you prefer, omit the cream, drizzle with butter, and sprinkle with Parmesan cheese.

See also, in this section, *Potato Dauphinoise, Potato Gratin à la Savoyarde,* and *Naomi Morash's Old-Fashioned Scalloped Potatoes.*

◇ *Steamed Potatoes*

I find steaming takes the least time when you have just enough potatoes to cover the bottom of the steamer basket. For larger quantities, the time increases, so I'm more likely to boil the potatoes instead. However, steaming is perhaps the best way to preserve the actual texture of the potatoes, so I recommend steaming equally as much as boiling. I steam whole small new potatoes in their skins, and I peel larger new potatoes and cut them into rounds or ovals. Shaped potatoes steam particularly nicely, for they really retain the exact shape that you cut. Bring water to a boil in a steamer and set the potatoes in the basket. Cover, and steam until tender. Potatoes approximately 1 ½ inches in diameter or cut rounds will steam tender in 12–15 minutes; whole 2-inch potatoes will cook in 15–18 minutes. The cooking time depends upon the amount of potatoes in the pot. You could also cut the potatoes into thick slices and steam them. Sprinkle with chopped parsley and fresh herbs and serve with melted butter, salt and pepper.
Note: Older potatoes will take slightly longer to cook; avoid very starchy potatoes.

◇ *Baked Potatoes*

What could be more American than apple pie? Perhaps baked potatoes! Certainly the Idaho Russet baking potato is justifiably famous, and baked potatoes are a staple of restaurants. I have never understood the necessity for cooking baking potatoes in aluminum foil. An oven-baked potato cooks to a mealy softness inside and keeps a crispy exterior. Why cause the skin to soften to a limp rag inside the foil? I have wrapped potatoes in foil, but only on hiking trips. Tossed in the coals of the evening fire, the foil holds in a wonderful charred aroma.

All types of potatoes bake well, but by far the best baking potato is the Idaho Russet. Its dry mealy interior remains white when done. Other potatoes can be baked exactly the same way, but the textures will not be the same. For example, I like to bake small new potatoes for appetizers because their firm texture is just the right contrast to the soft sour cream and salty caviar that tops them.

Baked Whole Potatoes

Scrub and dry the potatoes. If you wish, rub the skins with oil for a less crisp, more tender exterior. Bake in a preheated 400° or 450° oven until tender. The cooking time depends completely upon the potato size. Pierce with the point of a sharp knife to test for doneness. At 450°, a large baking potato will bake in 40–50 minutes. When done, cut a cross in the top. Squeeze the bottom of the potato to push up the flesh. Dot with butter and serve with a choice of toppings, such as sour cream, chopped red onion, scallions, or chives.

Small Baked New Potatoes

Try these as a cocktail party treat. Bake 1½–2-inch unpeeled potatoes at 400° for 20–25 minutes until tender. Remove from the oven and, when they're cool enough to touch, split in half. Serve warm as a canapé topped with caviar or at room temperature with sour cream and caviar.

Baked Stuffed Potatoes

Once potatoes are baked, scoop out the flesh into a warm bowl. Blend with butter, seasonings, grated cheese, and some cream. Heap into the shells, sprinkle the tops with additional cheese and butter, and place back in the oven. Bake the potatoes until browned on top, about 10 minutes. (You can vary the stuffing ingredients: use chopped chives or other herbs, a curried cream, etc.)

Baked Potato Chunks

Bake potato chunks alone or with other vegetables, at a very high heat, 450°–475°, so the potatoes brown as they soften. Place the potatoes in a shallow pan with garlic cloves (optional). Drizzle over olive oil or oil and butter and rub to coat potatoes. Large chunks will cook through in approximately 30 minutes. Turn and baste the chunks with oil every 10 minutes. Often, I add chunks of onion or whole small onions, chunks of peppers, or even blanched sausage. Sprinkle liberally with fresh cracked pepper and coarse salt.

Baked Sliced Potatoes

Peel and thickly slice potatoes, and rub with oil or butter. Arrange in a shallow pan, sprinkle with salt and bake in a very hot (450°–475°) oven until golden and tender.

Pan-Roasted Potatoes

Peel and parboil small whole potatoes or large chunked potatoes for 5 minutes. Rub them with oil and place in a pan to bake, either with a roast or alone. Depending upon their size, they will be done in a 400° oven in 30–40 minutes or in a 350° oven in about 45–55 minutes. Turn occasionally.

Baked Potato Skins

After you've scooped out the mealy insides, here's a real treat! Cut baked potato skins into strips or large pieces, butter and salt, and bake in a 450° oven until crisp. In upstate New York, where my daughter is in school, this is how they're served: leave about 3/8 inch of the potato flesh on the skin, and add grated cheese, crumbled bacon, butter, salt, and pepper. Broil. You get a crisp top with a soft skin and potato flesh underneath.

◇ Sautéed Potatoes

Use firm, low-starch potatoes, which will hold their shape without becoming mushy. Yellow waxy fingerling potatoes are ideal for sautéed dishes, as are any fresh new potatoes. Use baby new potatoes whole; cut up larger ones. Stored all-purpose potatoes that have not gotten too old and starchy will also work.

Cut equal-size olives or rounds so they will cook in the same amount of time. Use the potato scraps for soups or boil them up and use for breads, etc. As in *Straw Mat Potatoes*, clarified butter really makes a difference. Butter combined with oil works all right, but you run the risk of overbrowning the potatoes.

For every 2 pounds potatoes, use 4–6 tablespoons clarified butter or a combination of butter and oil. Peel and shape the potatoes. Pat dry. Heat the butter and roll the potatoes in it until seared, 1–2 minutes on each side. This step keeps the potatoes from adhering to the pan as they cook. Cover the pan and simmer the potatoes in the butter, shaking the pan occasionally, for 10–15 minutes, or until the potatoes are tender and golden brown. Sprinkle with salt and pepper and fresh herbs of your choice such as chopped parsley, chervil, or savory. If you wish, roll potatoes around in more butter before serving. For a fancier look, cut potatoes into small balls with a potato ball cutter, and cut down on the cooking time. You could also dice or slice the potatoes and cook the same way.

Sautéed with Garlic

For additional flavor, cook some minced garlic along with the potatoes.

Sautéed in Oil

Peel the potatoes and cube or cut into thick slices. For every 2 pounds potatoes, heat 4–6 tablespoons olive oil. Add one unpeeled crushed garlic clove, stir in potatoes, and sauté until potatoes are seared and lightly browned. Season with salt (for additional flavor, add sage), cover the pan, lower the heat, and cook until tender, stirring occasionally. Sprinkle with additional salt (optional) and coarsely ground pepper. During the last 5 minutes of cooking, you can add peeled, sliced sweet red peppers (see *Peppers*). Then you can go one step further, and pour in beaten eggs for a potato-pepper frittata. Add sliced olives and ham if you like, cook over low heat until eggs firm. Sprinkle with cheese and run under the broiler.

◇ Mashed Potatoes

People disagree about the best way to mash potatoes. When I was growing up, my mother either riced potatoes or mashed potatoes with an old-fashioned potato masher, using an up-and-down, rather than circular, motion. She moistened the potatoes with the cooking liquid rather than milk or cream, and added sweet butter, salt, and pepper. My husband and children prefer potatoes mashed and then whipped with a whisk into a creamy, airy purée with plenty of butter and milk. I don't use an electric beater or a food processor for I think they make the potatoes gummy.

Boil potatoes until cooked through. Drain, dry out over low heat, and put through a ricer, or mash with a potato masher. Add cooking liquid, milk, or cream, and stir, beat or whisk in butter and seasonings. Baking potatoes will give a light, dry result.

Note: Before combining the potatoes with cream, butter, and seasonings, set some aside to use in *Large Mashed Potato Cake* or *Potato Doughnuts*.

My Mother's Riced Potatoes
Peel baking potatoes, cut them up, and boil until tender. Drain them and put through a ricer into a saucepan. Reheat for a moment, stirring, to remove excess moisture. Then stir in a bit of the cooking liquid, milk, or cream, and flavor liberally with sweet butter and plenty of salt and pepper.

Riced Potatoes with Onions
My mother's best riced potatoes were those that she laced with buttery onions. Follow above technique. For every 3–4 cups riced potatoes, chop one onion and sauté it slowly in butter until wilted and coated with butter. Then turn up the heat, and cook medium brown. Mound the potatoes in a hot serving dish and pour over the butter and onions. Ambrosia!

Mashed Potatoes with Leeks
Combine equal amounts of warm mashed potatoes and *Chopped Braised Leeks* (see *Leeks*), season and serve hot. Or cool mixture, roll into balls and sauté to light brown on all sides. Dip in egg milk mixture and fine crumbs before sautéing, if you like.

Stampfenbohnen
For a mashed potato and green bean combination, see *Beans*.

Mashed Potato Pancakes
Use cold leftover mashed potatoes. Beat in an egg if desired. Add chopped chives or other herbs if you wish. If the potatoes are very moist, stir in a little flour. Shape into 3/4–1-inch-thick patties and sauté in butter until lightly browned on both sides.

Light-as-a-Feather Mashed Potato Pancakes
For every 2 cups warm mashed potatoes, beat in 2 egg yolks; season with salt, pepper, and herbs. Beat 2 egg whites separately until they form firm but not dry peaks and then fold in. Cook in butter on a hot griddle until browned.

Mont d'Or Potatoes
Beat 2 pounds mashed potatoes with 4–6 tablespoons butter and 3/4 cup hot milk. Add salt, pepper, and herbs to taste and 3 egg yolks. Beat 3 egg whites until they form firm but not dry peaks, and fold in. Spoon the mixture into a buttered baking dish, sprinkle with grated cheese, and dot with butter. Bake in a preheated 400° oven for 15–20 minutes.

Mashed Potatoes with Cheese
Mash potatoes and mix with butter, salt, pepper, a bit of cream, and plenty of grated cheese. Heap in a mound, sprinkle with melted butter and additional grated cheese, and brown in a hot oven.

Bubble-and-Squeak
For a mashed potato and cabbage combination, see *Cabbage Leftovers* (page 43).

Large Mashed Potato Cake
Mash 2 pounds potatoes, and season with salt and pepper. Beat in approximately 4 tablespoons butter and chopped chives or herbs to taste. Melt 1 tablespoon butter and 1 tablespoon oil or clarified butter in an 8-inch round ovenproof pan or skillet, put the mashed potatoes into the pan, and press down with a spatula. Bake in a preheated 400° oven for 30–40 minutes, pressing the cake down occasionally. Invert onto a warm ovenproof plate, sprinkle the top with grated cheese, and dot with butter. Brown under the broiler.

Mashed Potato Omelet
Mash 1 pound potatoes with salt, pepper, and butter. Beat 5–6 eggs, add sautéed onions or mushrooms if desired, and mix with potatoes. Pour into a well-buttered round baking pan and bake in a preheated 325° oven until the eggs are set, approximately 40 minutes.

Mashed Potatoes with Puréed Root Vegetables
Combine equal amounts of warm mashed potatoes with puréed rutabagas, turnips, parsnips, or celeriac. Beat together over medium heat to evaporate moisture. Add butter, salt, and pepper to taste.

Mashed Potatoes with Garlic
This is a luscious combination I first made from a recipe of Julia Child's, and it has become a staple. Make 1 1/2 pounds riced potatoes. Meanwhile, make a garlic cream by simmering 1 head of peeled garlic cloves in a covered saucepan along with 2 tablespoons butter until tender, about 20 minutes. Beat in 1 tablespoon flour, cook for 2 minutes, and whisk in 1/2 cup cream and seasonings. Bring the cream to a boil, cook for 1 minute, and purée.

Add this purée to the potatoes and heat together to evaporate moisture. Beat in butter, salt, pepper, and additional cream if desired.

Potatoes Duchesse

These are a lovely addition to a party dinner. For every 2 cups riced or mashed potatoes, beat in 3 egg yolks, 2–3 tablespoons butter and 2 tablespoons heavy cream. The mixture should be fairly firm. Season to taste. Pipe through a large rosette tube into a decorative border or individual rosette mounds. Brush the tops with melted butter or an egg glaze made with 1 egg and 1 tablespoon water. Brown in a 400° oven for 20 minutes or broil 5–6 inches from heat to brown top lightly. Arrange around a roast or on individual plates.

Potato Croquettes

Make *Potatoes Duchesse* and chill. On a floured board, shape heaping tablespoons of the mixture into cylindrical or cone shapes. Dip in beaten egg, then dry bread crumbs; chill to firm and set the coating. Deep-fry until completely browned in fat heated to 375°. Remove and drain on brown paper before serving.

◇ Deep-Fat-Fried Potatoes

We rarely fry potatoes in deep fat because proper deep-fat frying requires absolutely fresh oil: otherwise, the food picks up off-tastes and becomes heavy and greasy-tasting. Sometimes I'll save the oil for a second frying, but never use it more than twice. Using a fresh batch of oil every time you fry food is expensive, so I don't do it often (except for an occasional batch of French fries for my daughters). Remember, the oil must be absolutely fresh. I think peanut oil is the most suitable, for it is taste-less, then my next preference would be a good light vegetable oil. Second, the potatoes should have what potato breeders call "high solids" or a low moisture content. This is important because, unless you cook almost all the moisture out of the potatoes, they will quickly "limp" out after cooking. Starchy potatoes, such as Idaho Russet Burbank potatoes have "high solids" and, in fact, absorb less oil than higher-moisture varieties.

French Fries

I used to watch my father make French fries in his restaurant: they were the only deep-fat frying he did. Early in the day, he would prepare the first step and then finish frying them to order. Separating into 2 steps makes deep-fat frying possible for entertaining, because the final cooking time takes just a minute or two before serving. It's not necessary to use a frying basket or special deep-fry pot—just more convenient.

Cut peeled potatoes into lengthwise 3/8-inch (or less) strips. Place the frying basket in the oil and heat the oil to 325°. (A hot basket won't cool down the oil when it's submerged.) Pat the potatoes dry. To avoid sticking, rinse them off, pat dry, and fry. Lift out the basket and insert a small layer of potatoes. Lower the basket into the oil and stir so that the potatoes do not stick together. The natural moisture of the potatoes will come out in the fat, causing bubbles to appear. When you first add the potatoes, the bubbles could come over the edge of the pot. So, to prevent dangerous burns or an overflow, dip the basket in and out until the bubbles are contained within the pot. The bubbles also indicate how much moisture is left in the potatoes. When they just about disappear, you have a nice crisp fry. Cooking most of the moisture out of the potatoes pretty much guarantees that they won't become limp before serving (which should be as soon as possible after they are ready). If you like French fries with crisp exteriors and moist interiors, remove them from the fryer while you can still see bubbles. Cook the potatoes for 2–3 minutes until cooked through but not browned. Lift out and drain in the basket. If you have more potatoes to fry, drain the potatoes on brown paper or in another basket. Continue frying until all the potatoes are cooked. Cool until ready to serve.

Just before serving, reheat the oil to 375°. Place the potatoes in a basket and cook for 3–5 minutes or until they are nicely browned and the fat has almost stopped bubbling, indicating that the moisture inside the potatoes is almost gone. During this second cooking time, the bubbles will be smaller, as there is little moisture left in the potatoes. The potatoes will be crisp. Drain on brown paper, salt, and serve immediately.

Note: Fry potato rounds in the same way.

Potato Chips

Peel potatoes (low starch varieties will not disintegrate when thinly sliced). Slice paper-thin, or pare strips with a vegetable parer for extra-thin chips. (You can fry the skin parings as well!) Soak in cold water for 15 minutes, changing the water once, to remove starch so the slices won't stick together. Pat dry. Heat the oil to 375° and place a handful of slices in the frying basket. Lower into the oil and cook—stirring or shaking the pan to move the chips around—until the bubbles disappear, the color is good, and the chips are nice and crisp. Drain, place on brown paper, and salt. The chips can be dried out and stored in a closed jar.

• Substitute sweet potatoes or parsnips.

◇ Potato Gratins or Scalloped Potatoes

When I think of potato casseroles, I consider the French gratins and the old-fashioned American scalloped potatoes. Regardless of the origin, the principle is the same: thin, layered, raw potato slices cooked in a liquid. Many gratins are made with milk and cream; some with naught but broth. Vary the recipes by using different flavorings: adding cheese, other vegetables, or even sliced or chopped smoked meats.

I usually make the layer of potatoes relatively thin, usually no higher than 1 inch, which assures even cooking and coating of the potatoes. To end up with discernible potato slices in the gratin, I use low-starch potatoes, and rinse and pat them dry before layering. This is certainly not a hard-and-fast rule. Some people prefer gratins in which the potatoes have "melted" together, creating a softer texture. In that case, don't rinse the starch off the potatoes. I am including a few favorite versions, but know full well every cook has a favorite potato casserole!

Potato Dauphinoise

This is a classic of French cooking. The eggs are optional—you can make the gratin with just cream or a cream-milk mixture.

> 1 clove garlic
> 3 lb boiling potatoes
> 6 Tb butter
> Coarse black pepper
> 3 eggs
> 2–2 1/2 cups light cream
> Salt

Peel and halve the garlic. Rub thoroughly over the inside of a 10×14-inch gratin dish. Peel the potatoes and cut into 1/8-inch slices, drop into cold water, swish around, and dry. Melt the butter and pour into a baking dish. Evenly arrange the potatoes in the dish. Sprinkle with a generous amount of coarsely ground pepper. Beat the eggs with cream and 1–2 teaspoons salt, and pour over the potatoes. The cream should just cover the potatoes. Bake in a preheated 375° oven until brown, approximately 50 minutes. (*Serves 6–8*)

- Make a *Béchamel Sauce* (see *Appendix*) using 8 tablespoons each flour and 10 tablespoons butter and 4 cups milk. Add seasonings, which could include chopped herbs, curry mustard, etc. Peel and slice the potatoes and layer in a casserole as follows: béchamel sauce, potatoes, and grated cheese. Repeat layering and bake in a 400° oven for 30 minutes.
- For a less rich version, omit the eggs.
- Add grated cheese: either omit or reduce the number of eggs.
- Top with buttered bread crumbs.
- Substitute other vegetables, such as sliced carrots or rutabagas, for some of the potatoes.
- Add chopped or sliced onions which have been lightly sautéed in butter.
- Shred prosciutto or smoked ham, and place in a layer before adding the potatoes.
- Cut down on the potatoes, and layer ham, cooked onions, and potatoes. Add cream and bake as above.

Potato Gratin à la Savoyarde

If gratins with cream seem too rich, layer and cook them with broth.

> 3 lb potatoes
> 4 cups thinly sliced onions (optional)
> 6 Tb butter
> Salt and freshly ground pepper
> 1 Tb chopped fresh rosemary
> 1–1 1/2 cups grated Swiss cheese
> 2 cups beef or chicken stock

Peel and cut the potatoes into 1/8-inch slices; drop in cold water. Sauté the onions (if you are using them) in 4 tablespoons of the butter until wilted and golden. Melt the remaining butter and pour into a 10 x 14-inch oval casserole. (If you are omitting the onions, pour all the butter into the casserole.) Dry the potatoes. Spread half the potatoes in the casserole. Season with salt, pepper, and 1 1/2 teaspoons rosemary. Top with half the onions and one-third of the cheese. Repeat once, ending with the remaining two-thirds cheese. Pour broth halfway up the potatoes. Place in a preheated 425° oven and bake for 30–40 minutes until the potatoes are tender, the top is brown, and the liquid is almost gone. (As the onions will exude moisture, you may need to pour off the cooking liquid and boil it down. If you are omitting the onions, cover three-quarters of the potatoes with broth, and boil down the liquid if necessary.) (*Serves 6–8*)

- *Potatoes à la Boulangère*: Omit the cheese. Bake sliced potatoes and onions in broth under a leg of lamb. Set the lamb on top of the vegetables. The meat juices add to the flavor.

Naomi Morash's Old-Fashioned Scalloped Potatoes

When I got married, Russ said he hoped someday I could make scalloped potatoes like his mother's. She always cooks them in a deep-dish casserole and lets the flour thicken the sauce.

> 2 1/2 lb boiling potatoes
> 1 large onion
> 1/4 lb sharp Cheddar cheese
> Salt and freshly ground pepper
> 4 Tb flour
> 6–8 Tb butter
> 3–4 cups milk

Peel and slice the potatoes into 1/8-inch pieces; drop into cold water. Peel and thinly slice the onion. Roughly grate the cheese. Butter a deep 2 1/2–3-quart casserole dish. Dry the potatoes. Divide the ingredients into fourths and in the following order, layer the potatoes and season with salt and pepper; add the onion slices, sprinkle with flour, and dot with butter; top with cheese. Repeat this layering three times. Pour over just enough milk to cover the potatoes. Cover the dish and place in a preheated 350° oven. Bake for 45–60 minutes or until the milk comes to the boil and bubbles. Remove the cover and bake for another 30–45 minutes or until the potatoes are tender and the top is browned. (*Serves 6–8*)

Blender Potato Pancakes

Potato pancakes comes in all types from the delicate, lacy German version (see *Lacy Jerusalem Artichoke Pancakes*, page 138) to these smooth breakfast pancake look-alikes. Serve with applesauce, homemade berry or beach plum jelly, or even maple syrup.

    2 cups chopped raw potatoes
    4 eggs
    2 Tb melted butter or oil
    ²/₃–1 cup flour
    1 ½ tsp salt
    ½ cup milk
    ½ cup chopped onions

Pat the potatoes dry. Place the eggs in a blender or food processor; whirl for 5 seconds. Add butter or oil to machine along with ²/₃ cup flour, salt, and milk. Blend to incorporate the flour. Add the onions and potatoes and blend until puréed. If the mixture looks too thin for pancakes, add 3–4 tablespoons more flour. Pour onto a greased, hot skillet, and cook approximately 2 minutes on each side. (*Makes twenty-four 3–4-inch pancakes*)

- *Potato Crêpes*: Leave the batter thin. Pour about ¼ cup batter into an oiled, slope-sided 6-inch pan. Make crêpes (see *Spinach Crêpes* under *Spinach* for directions). Fill with warm applesauce or spinach, or roll with mirabelle (plum) jelly and sprinkle with powdered sugar.

Grated Potato Pancakes

These are less fragile than *Lacy Jerusalem Artichoke Pancakes* (see page 138) and quite tasty.

    1 lb potatoes
    2 eggs
    1 tsp salt
    ⅛ tsp freshly ground pepper
    2 Tb flour
    ¼ cup grated onion
    1 Tb heavy cream
    1 cup vegetable oil

Peel the potatoes, grate, and squeeze dry in a towel. Beat the eggs and mix with the potatoes and remaining ingredients except oil. Heat ¼ cup of the oil in a frying pan (or enough to cover the pan bottom) and add 2–3 tablespoons batter per pancake. Spread thinly. Fry about 2 minutes, turn pancakes, and fry the other sides. (Sides should be well browned.) Continue frying until all the batter is used. Serve hot. (*Makes 10–12 pancakes*)

Straw Mat Potatoes

Mat potatoes are easy and fun to make: you can vary the thickness of the "mat" from finely julienned to a heavier hand-cut, and the texture from a soft center with crispy skin to completely crunchy. And who would be bored "flipping" the potatoes? Three tricks make this dish easy rather than frustrating. First, using starchy potatoes (a baking potato or older boiling potato is fine) that hold together is essential. (Try flipping a pan full of potato sticks that aren't clinging together!) Second, a Teflon pan is a definite advantage. The "slide" that Teflon allows makes up for two years' apprentice flipping. Third, cook the mats in clarified butter, which removes the possibility of a burnt-butter brown. (I have used butter and oil when I didn't have clarified butter on hand.) Cut the potatoes into matchstick juliennes with a food processor, the julienne disk attachment of a Mouli grater, or a French mandoline, or hand-cut them into larger sticks (the method I prefer). While I prefer a thicker julienne cut, many people like a very fine julienne. Regardless of the cut, the technique is the same. If you must julienne the potatoes ahead of time, hold them in cold water to avoid discoloration. Just remember to use very starchy potatoes so you still have some starch left after draining. Press them in a towel to get rid of as much moisture as possible.

This recipe fits an 8-inch Teflon pan, which is a good size for practice flipping. Once you become expert, you can make larger 10-inch, 12-inch, or 14-inch mat potatoes. Be prepared to make more than one round: these potatoes are so good, a recipe for four could easily serve only two.

    1–1¼ lb baking potatoes
    4–6 Tb *clarified butter* (page 347) or butter and oil
    Salt and freshly ground pepper

Peel the potatoes and cut them into ⅛-inch slices, then into ⅛-inch strips. Pat dry; but do not rinse. (A slight discoloration doesn't matter; the potatoes will become white again when they're cooked.) Heat 4 tablespoons butter, and spread the potato sticks over the pan bottom. You will have a ½–¾-inch-thick mat. Press down with a spatula, and season with salt and pepper. Cook until the underside is browned, shaking the pan occasionally, and press down with the spatula to help form the mat. Soon, the potatoes should move as one when you shake the pan. In just a few minutes, the underside will be lightly browned. Turn down the heat slightly, cover, and cook for 5–6 minutes to tenderize the center. Now comes the fun: remove the cover, shake the pan to ensure that the potatoes are moving as one, and, with an upward-for-

ward shake, flip the mat over onto its raw side. (You could always use a plate to reverse the mat potato, but that's not dramatic.) Add the remaining butter if necessary. Raise the heat and brown the other side. If the potatoes need further cooking, lower the heat and cook uncovered, 5 minutes longer or so. Sometimes I flip the mat over a few times just to recrisp the sides. (*Serves 4*)

Note: You can make these ahead, and reheat by sautéing both sides in the frying pan. The potatoes taste good, but never as good as when freshly made.

- *Vegetable Surprise Filling*: Include a thin layer of another vegetable in the mat, such as golden browned onions, creamed leeks or corn, or grated and stewed parsnips or carrots. Cool the vegetable. When assembling the mat, put a layer of potatoes in the pan, spread with the second vegetable, and cover with the remaining potatoes. Proceed as above.
- Make straw mat potatoes with two-thirds potatoes and one-third julienned celeriac, turnip, or kohlrabi. Combine and cook as above.
- Make individual servings. Butter individual muffin tins or small tart pans generously. Pack the potatoes into the mold. Turn upside down into hot clarified butter and brown as above, with the tin serving as a cover. When you are ready to turn the potatoes, slide a wide spatula under each portion, lift out, and turn over. Run a knife around the edge, turn the potatoes back onto the spatula, and slide into the pan, uncooked side down. Continue cooking, as above, until all the potatoes are cooked through. These small mats can also have a surprise filling as above.
- Make a crisp pancake of potatoes. Spread a thin layer of julienned potatoes in pan. Cook to brown, flip, and cook other side. Making the thin layer and omitting the covered cooking gives a totally different texture. Quite nice.

Potatoes Anna

This is one of the most beautiful potato dishes. Its requirements are similar to those of *Straw Mat Potatoes*: boiling potatoes starchy enough to hold together and form the "cake" but not so starchy that they become mushy. Use clarified butter, which makes the difference between overbrowned potatoes that stick to the pan and a smooth effortless production; and a heavy skillet to distribute heat evenly (a Teflon one makes life very easy).

3 lb boiling potatoes
1/2–2/3 lb melted *clarified butter* (page 347)
Salt and freshly ground pepper

Peel the potatoes and cut into 1/8-inch slices. Pat dry. Heat 1/2 cup of the butter in a heavy, ovenproof 8-inch straight-sided saucepan, and keep over medium heat while you arrange the potato slices. Line the bottom of the saucepan in a slightly overlapping circular arrangement. When you have formed one layer, drizzle over more butter, and sprinkle with salt and pepper. Make another layer of potatoes going in the opposite direction. Continue building up the potato layers, drizzling each layer with butter and seasoning with salt and pepper. Shake the pan occasionally to make sure that the bottom potatoes are not sticking. Press down on the potatoes

with a heavy skillet that fits inside the saucepan. (This helps hold the slices together.) Cover the saucepan tightly and bake in a preheated 425° oven for 25 minutes. Remove the cover and press down on the potatoes again. Cook, uncovered, another 25 minutes—or longer if necessary. Potatoes should be tender with brown edges. Tilt the pan to pour out the excess butter. Shake the pan to ensure the potatoes are loose, run a knife around the edge, and invert onto a warm serving plate. (*Serves 6*)

Potato Dumplings

These traditional accompaniments to sauerbraten go just as well with plain old pot roast and gravy.

4 large baking potatoes (approximately 3 lb)
4 Tb softened butter
2 eggs
1/2 cup dry bread crumbs
2 tsp salt
Freshly ground pepper
1/4 tsp nutmeg
2 Tb finely chopped parsley
Chopped fresh herbs (optional)
Flour

Bake the potatoes. Peel, then rice or mash them. You should have approximately 6 cups flesh. Beat in the butter, eggs, bread crumbs, salt, pepper, nutmeg, parsley, and other herbs if you like. Beat in 3 tablespoons to 1/2 cup or more flour until you have a dough that can be shaped. The amount of flour depends upon the moisture content of the potatoes. Form into 1 1/2–2-inch round balls. Drop into simmering salted water at least 2 1/2–3 inches deep. Do not crowd. The dumplings will fall to the bottom of the pan. Stir them gently so they won't stick. Once the dumplings float to the surface, gently simmer them for about 10 minutes. Then, remove one dumpling with a slotted spoon and test it. The center should be firm and not gooey. Drain and serve surrounding a roast. (*Makes 20–24 dumplings*)

- Brown 1 cup dry bread crumbs in butter. Roll the cooked dumplings in the bread crumbs.
- Many dumpling fanciers place small croutons in the dumpling's center as a textural change. Poke 1 or 2 into each dumpling while you shape them.
- Slice leftover dumplings into halves or thick slices. Reheat by sautéeing in butter on either side; or coat with crumbs or chopped fresh herbs and sauté until lightly browned and heated through.

Potato Gnocchi

These dumplings, made with a pâte à choux mixture, are a lighter version of *Potato Dumplings*. For gnocchi based on ricotta cheese and flour, see *Kohlrabi Dumplings (or Gnocchi)* (page 156).

2 lb baking potatoes
3/4 cup butter
Salt
Freshly ground pepper
Nutmeg
1 cup flour
3 eggs
1 cup grated Parmesan cheese
1/3 cup spinach or watercress purée (optional)

Bake potatoes; scoop out and mash the flesh. You will have about 4 cups. Keep warm over simmering water. Heat 1 cup water and add 6 tablespoons of the butter, 1 teaspoon salt, 1/4 teaspoon pepper, and a pinch of nutmeg. Bring water to a boil, remove from the heat, and beat in the flour. Return to low heat, and beat quickly until the mixture forms a ball. Make a depression in the mixture and beat in the eggs, one at a time. Combine this pâte à choux mixture with the potato flesh, 1/2 cup of the cheese, and the purée (if you like). Season with salt and pepper. Flour your hands and form 1 1/2–2-inch round dumplings. Drop them gently into a large pot of simmering salted water; do not crowd. The gnocchi will fall to the bottom and then float to the surface. They should cook done in about 15 minutes. When ready, the gnocchi will swell and be firm. Remove them with a slotted spoon and drain on a towel. (To prepare ahead of time, drop into cold water until firmed, drain, dry for 20 minutes,

then refrigerate.) Place the gnocchi in a buttered shallow baking dish. Melt remaining butter and drizzle it on top. Roll gnocchi gently in the butter, sprinkle with the remaining cheese, and reheat in a preheated 375° oven for 15–20 minutes. Run under the broiler to brown if you wish. (*Makes 24–30 dumplings*)

Kâthe's Potato Salad

I vividly remember my mother making potato salad: with one hand, she would hold the steaming potato skewered on the end of a fork. With the other, she deftly pared off the skin with a knife. When the potatoes were peeled, she sliced and dressed them with a vinaigrette sauce while they were still good and warm so they absorbed the dressing. If the potatoes don't get to sop up that flavoring while they're warm, they really don't taste as good. I use low-starch potatoes because I want the slices to stay firm, and use new potatoes whenever possible. I cook them until just tender: remember that even when the potatoes are drained, they are still cooking with internal heat.

>5 lb boiling potatoes (preferably new potatoes)
>Salt
>1 cup chopped red or sweet onions
>*Vinaigrette Sauce* (page 352)
>Freshly ground pepper
>2 Tb chopped parsley
>1/2–1 cup *Mayonnaise* (page 349)
>1 1/2 cups chopped celery (optional)
>1 cup chopped dill pickle (optional)

In a large saucepan, cover the potatoes with water, add salt, and bring the water to a boil. Cook at a gentle boil, partially covered, until the potatoes are barely tender. (New 3-inch potatoes will cook in 12–15 minutes after they come to a boil. Times vary, depending upon the potatoes' age and size.) Drain. While they are still hot, peel the potatoes. Fresh new potatoes need not be peeled at all. Slice the potatoes and toss with onions and vinaigrette, using enough dressing to seep into the potatoes. Season with salt and pepper, and let stand for at least 30 minutes to absorb the dressing. Mix with parsley and mayonnaise to taste. (I often omit the mayonnaise and just dress the salad with the vinaigrette.) My mother added nothing else to her salad, but Russ likes the crunch of celery, and Vicki, the sharpness of pickle. Both are optional and can be added along with the mayonnaise. Season again before serving. (*Makes about 3 quarts*)

Note: When I'm making more than 2–3 pounds of potato salad, I put the potatoes in two or more bowls when folding in the dressing and/or mayonnaise. This helps keep breakage of slices to a minimum.

- To cut down on oil, moisten the hot potatoes with 1/2 cup broth mixed with 2 or more tablespoons vinegar.
- Cook and slice baby red potatoes, leave on the peels, and dress when warm with vinaigrette, a fine olive oil, or olive oil and vinegar. Serve tossed with freshly chopped parsley and salt and pepper.
- Add other ingredients such as diced hard-boiled eggs, diced pimentos for color, diced green or red peppers, capers, diced olives, etc.
- For a party, coat the salad top with a thin mayonnaise layer applied with a long metal spatula. Decorate with peppers, eggs, olives, chopped parsley, or herbs.

- *Potatoes with Pesto*: Slice or chunk potatoes while hot and dress with a flavorful olive oil. (Use 1 tablespoon per pound of potatoes.) When the potatoes have cooled down, toss them with *Pesto Sauce* (see *Appendix*) and serve.
- *Hot German Potato Salad*: When the potatoes are removed from the heat and are too hot to handle, fry 1/2 pound bacon until crisp. Remove bacon and crumble. Peel and slice the potatoes. Sauté 1/2 cup chopped onion in the bacon fat until golden. Add 1/3 cup of vinegar and 3/4–1 cup broth. Bring the liquids to a boil, cook for 2 minutes, and pour over the warm potatoes. Season with salt and pepper and sprinkle with parsley. Stir in bacon.

Fish Chowder

This chowder wouldn't be the same without firm textured, waxy potatoes.

>4 oz salt pork
>2 lb potatoes
>6 Tb butter
>2 cups chopped onions
>2 cups chopped leeks (white and light green portions)
>1 cup chopped celery
>6 cups *Fish Broth* (page 348)
>Salt and freshly ground pepper
>2 lb white-fleshed fish, such as cod, haddock, or bass
>2 cups light cream
>2 Tb chopped parsley

Cut salt pork into 1/4-inch pieces and blanch for 5 minutes in boiling water; drain and pat dry. Peel potatoes and dice into 1/2-inch pieces. Place in cold water until ready to use. In a heavy saucepan, sauté the salt pork until it is lightly browned and the fat is rendered. Discard fat, add the butter, onions, leeks, and celery, and sauté until wilted, 8–10 minutes. Add the potatoes and fish broth, bring to a boil, and simmer until the potatoes are tender (about 15 minutes). Season with salt and pepper. (This can be made ahead and refrigerated. Reheat before continuing.) Cut the fish into chunks and add to the pan. The fish will cook in just a few minutes, depending upon the size of the chunks. Add the cream, heat, taste again for seasoning, and sprinkle with parsley. (*Serves 4*)

- *Mediterranean Bourride*: Omit the salt pork and butter and substitute 4–5 tablespoons olive oil. Sauté the vegetables in oil; add 2 cloves minced garlic and 1–2 teaspoons saffron threads. Cook as above with 8 cups of fish broth. Omit cream. Put the cooked vegetables and broth through a food mill. Pour this puréed soup over the fish and cook 4–5 minutes or until the fish is tender. Distribute the fish over garlic-flavored *toasted French bread rounds* (see *Appendix*). Stir 1 cup or so of *Aïoli* (see page 180) into broth and pour over the fish and bread. Serve remaining aïoli on the side.
- Add a few scallops for additional texture.

Potato and Sorrel Soup

The ultimate potato soup has to be *Leek and Potato* (see page 158), but this is a close second.

1 ½ lb boiling potatoes
1 lb sorrel leaves (page 345)
2 Tb butter
1 cup chopped leeks (white portion)
6 cups chicken broth
Lemon juice
Salt and freshly ground pepper
½–1 cup heavy cream

Peel and roughly chop the potatoes. Hold in cold water. Wash the sorrel leaves and remove the heavy ribs running up the leaves (for the technique, see *Spinach*). Fold the leaves over and slice into very thin shreds. You should have 5–6 cups. Heat the butter and cook the leeks until wilted. Drain the potatoes and add to a saucepan along with broth and 3 cups of the sorrel. Cook approximately 20 minutes or until the potatoes are tender; purée. Return to the saucepan and reheat. Taste for seasoning, adding lemon juice, salt, and pepper. Stir in the remaining sorrel and cook until barely wilted. Add cream to taste. Serve either very hot or chilled. If serving hot, enrich with more butter if desired. (*Makes 2 quarts*)

Note: I don't throw out the sorrel stems, but cut them into 3–4-inch lengths, wrap in washed cheesecloth, and add them in with the potatoes and the broth. They add flavor, and the cheesecloth bag is easily removed before the puréeing step.

- Substitute lovage for the sorrel.
- For more delicate herbs like chervil, cook the soup, purée, and add 3 cups chopped herbs just before serving so they barely cook through.

Delicate Older Potato Soup

I devised this soup one day to use up some older potatoes. You end up with the potatoes' nutrients and thickening abilities without relying upon them for top-quality texture: the other vegetables give texture. This soup is a bit like a beetless borscht. Add some beets if you like.

2 lb boiling potatoes
8 cups chicken broth (or a combination of broth and water)
½ cup heavy cream
4 Tb butter
2 cups chopped onions
3 cups julienned carrots
½ tsp sugar
6 cups julienned cabbage
½ cup finely sliced lovage (optional)
Salt and freshly ground pepper

Peel the potatoes and chop them into large hunks. Cook until tender in the broth. Remove the potatoes, reserving the broth, and mash with the cream.

Meanwhile, melt the butter in a large saucepan and cook the onions until wilted and golden. Stir in the carrots and sauté until almost tender, then sprinkle with sugar. Add the cabbage and cook until wilted. Stir in the lovage (if you have some). Whisk the mashed potatoes into the broth, add the sautéed vegetables, and heat together for 5 minutes. Taste and season with salt and pepper before serving. (*Makes about 3 quarts*)

Savory Potato Pie

Not only is this pie savory, it also uses savory (one of my favorite herbs), which is good in meat pies and with potatoes. Serve the pie piping hot or chilled for a picnic.

Double recipe *Tart Pastry* (page 351)
2 lb potatoes
1–2 Tb freshly chopped savory (or 1 tsp dried)
2 Tb chopped fresh basil
1 Tb chopped chives
6 Tb butter
Salt and freshly ground pepper
½ cup grated cheese (optional)
1 egg beaten with 1 tsp water
1 egg yolk
5 Tb heavy cream

Line a 9-inch pie pan with half the pie dough. Peel the potatoes and cut into ⅛-inch slices (you should have approximately 6 cups). Combine the herbs. Layer one-third of the potatoes in a pie shell. Sprinkle with one-third of the herbs, dot with one-third of the butter, and season with salt and pepper. Sprinkle with one-third of the cheese, if you like. Repeat this layering twice. Cover with the remaining pie dough, moisten the edges, and make a decorative edging. Cut a ¾-inch round hole into the center and insert a round nozzle. Paint the crust with egg-water and, with a sharp knife, make a decorative design. Bake in a preheated 425° oven for 30 minutes, cover the crust with foil if it gets too brown, and turn heat to 350°. Cook 10 minutes longer, or until the potatoes are tender (check by sticking a knife into the funnel hole). Beat the egg yolk with cream and pour into the hole, shifting the pie pan to distribute the cream. Cook the pie 4–5 minutes longer to set the cream-egg custard. (*Makes a 9-inch pie*)

Swedish Potato and Anchovy Casserole (Jansson's Temptation)

2 large yellow onions
20 Swedish anchovy fillets
4 Tb butter
2 lb boiling potatoes
Freshly ground pepper
1 ½–2 cups light cream

Finely slice the onions. Drain and chop the anchovies. Sauté the onions in butter until wilted and golden. Peel the potatoes. Cut into ¼-inch slices and then cut the slices into ¼-inch strips lengthwise. Pat dry. Arrange half the potatoes in a buttered 1½–2-quart casserole or au gratin dish. Cover with half of the onions, all of the anchovies, the remaining onions, and top with the remaining potatoes, sprinkling the layers with pepper to taste. Barely cover with cream and bake in a preheated 375° oven for 50 minutes or until the potatoes are tender. (*Serves 4*)

Lamb Shanks and Potatoes

Here is a simple family dinner with flavors reminiscent of Greek cooking.

12 small new potatoes or 4–5 large boiling potatoes
4 lamb shanks
Salt and freshly ground pepper
2–3 Tb olive oil
2–3 lb lamb bones (optional)
1 cup sliced onions
1½ cups sliced celery
1 tsp chopped garlic
2 bay leaves
2 Tb dried mint
2 tsp basil
2 cups chopped tomato pulp
1 cup beef or chicken broth
2 Tb lemon juice

Peel the potatoes; if they are large, cut into chunks. Put into cold water. Sprinkle the lamb shanks with salt and pepper. In a flameproof casserole, heat the oil; brown the shanks, remove, and brown the bones. Remove the bones and pour off most of the fat. Over medium heat, brown the onions and celery for 2–3 minutes, add the garlic, and stir for 30 seconds. Add the browned lamb, bones, bay leaves, herbs, tomatoes, broth, and lemon juice. Bring to a simmer; cover first with aluminum foil, then with a cover. Place in a preheated 350° oven and bake for 1–1½ hours or until the lamb is almost tender. Remove the cover, skim the fat, raise the heat to 400°, and add the potatoes. Cook 30 minutes longer, or until the potatoes and lamb are tender, basting occasionally. Lift out the shanks and potatoes to a warm plate. Skim the fat and purée the vegetables and cooking liquids. Serve as a sauce with the lamb and potatoes. (*Serves 4*)

• For a simple meatless version, flavor the potatoes only with lemon juice, butter, and broth. Peel 2 pounds potatoes, cut into ½-inch strips or thick slices, and place in a shallow pan. Combine ¼ cup butter, ¼ cup lemon juice, and 1½ cups broth. Pour over the potatoes to cover, adding additional broth if necessary. Bake in a preheated 400° oven until potatoes are tender, turning them occasionally.

Shepherd's Pie for a Crowd

This is an absolutely delicious meal for a crowd. Shepherd's pie got a bad name when it was used to disguise dried-up meat that belonged in a stockpot—not a casserole. This version is moist, and fills all my require-

ments for a company dinner, especially when it is served with a platter of boiled baby onions, carrots, and green beans. First, almost everyone likes mashed potatoes (and very few turn up their noses at lamb); second, this easy-to-serve dish does not need to be carved or sawed at, either by hostess or by guest; third, I like a meal that doesn't wear me out on the day of the party. All the long cooking on this can take place the day before and the final dish assembled before the doorbell rings. Finally, the most important part: shepherd's pie is plain, good food. Of course, you can halve this recipe for a family meal. I'll divide the steps into the initial braising of the lamb (which can be done a day ahead) and the final assembly of the pie.

Braising the Lamb
2 lamb shoulders
4 Tb oil
4 cups roughly chopped onions
2 cups roughly sliced carrots
1 cup roughly sliced celery
1½–2 cups dry white vermouth
Salt and freshly ground pepper
7–8 cups beef broth
2 cups chopped ripe tomato pulp
1 Tb tomato paste
2 bay leaves
1½ tsp thyme
3 cloves garlic, peeled
6 sprigs parsley

Have the butcher bone and roll the lamb shoulders. Save the bones. Heat the oil in a large casserole at least 12 inches wide; 14 inches is better. (If you don't have a casserole that size, brown the shoulders one at a time and transfer them to a deep roaster for the final cooking.) When the shoulders are browned, remove them and brown the bones. Remove the bones and pour out all but 2 tablespoons of the fat. Add the onions, carrots, and celery and brown for 2–3 minutes, stirring. Stir in the vermouth and loosen the brown bits in the pan. Add the browned lamb and surround it with bones. Sprinkle with salt and pepper. Add broth three-quarters of the way up the meat, along with the tomato pulp, tomato paste, bay leaves, thyme, garlic, and parsley. Bring the broth to a simmer on top of the stove, cover the pan with aluminum foil, and cover with a lid. Place in a preheated 350° oven, cook for 10 minutes, then reduce the heat to 325°. Cook the lamb until tender—approximately 2 1/2 hours—turning the shoulders once. Remove from pan and set aside. Strain the braising liquid, pushing against the vegetables to extract their juices, and degrease the liquid. If holding for a while, cool the liquid slightly, place the lamb back in the liquid, and refrigerate.

Preparing the Pie
Cut the cooled lamb into small pieces, discarding the fat. You should have approximately 12 cups chopped lamb.

> 2 cups sliced carrots
> 3/4 lb butter
> 8–9 lb baking potatoes (approximately 12 large bakers)
> 4 cups chopped onions and white of leek
> 1 Tb minced garlic
> 1 cup flour
> 9 cups braising liquid (add additional beef broth if necessary)
> 2 Tb tomato paste
> 2 Tb red wine vinegar
> 12 cups chopped lamb
> Salt and freshly ground pepper
> 2 cups heavy cream
> 1/4 cup chopped parsley
> 1 cup grated cheese (half Parmesan and half Swiss)

Cook carrots with 1 tablespoon of the butter in 1/4 cup water, covered, until tender. Drain and purée to have 1 cup purée. (This step is not absolutely necessary, but the puréed carrot gives a pleasant flavor and additional body to the sauce. Sometimes I double the amount of carrots to add 2 cups purée.) Bake the potatoes in a preheated 450° oven until tender, approximately 50 minutes.

While the potatoes bake, make the sauce for the pie. Melt 4 tablespoons of the butter and cook the onions and leeks until wilted and golden, 8–10 minutes. Stir in the garlic; cook for 30 seconds. Gradually stir in the flour; cook for 2–3 minutes. You should have about 9 cups of braising liquid; if not, add enough beef broth to make 9 cups. Off heat, whisk the braising liquid into the flour-onion mixture; return to heat and bring to a boil, and cook, whisking constantly to dissolve the flour, until thickened. Stir in the tomato paste, puréed carrots, vinegar, and lamb. Season with salt and pepper. When the potatoes are cooked, halve them lengthwise. Scoop the potato pulp into a bowl. (Save the skins for broiling or baking with cheese [see page 216]. They could be served at the same party as a cocktail snack.) Mash 1/2–1 cup of the potatoes into the sauce to thicken. Either rice or mash the remaining potatoes with 1/2 pound butter and the heavy cream. Season with salt and pepper.

To assemble, I use one large pottery oven-to-table 18 x 12 x 3-inch dish. However, you can easily divide the mixture between two or three attractive baking dishes. Combine the chopped parsley with the meat and sauce, and ladle into the dish. Spread over the mashed potatoes, spreading them with a spatula or flat knife. Sometimes I decorate the sides with potato rosettes formed with a

pastry bag. Sprinkle the top of the pie with cheese and dot with the remaining butter. Bake in a preheated 400° oven for 20 minutes or until the top is golden and bubbly. (*Serves 20 or more*)

- Make with leftover meats, such as a pot roast, leg of lamb, or veal, or a combination of meats. Use a good stock to moisten the meat and always use freshly cooked potatoes: leftover potatoes add nothing.
- Thicken the sauce with mashed turnip or rutabaga.
- Add other vegetables, such as sautéed mushrooms or green peppers.
- A friend makes this with ground lamb shaped into small patties, cooked like hamburger, and placed in a good stock.
- You can brown and braise the shoulders with the bones in, but you need large pans to do so.

Jane's Potato Bread

This dense, hearty bread is ideal for thick sandwiches. The water in which the potatoes cook adds flavor and improves the bread's texture.

> 2 packages active dry yeast
> 2 cups lukewarm potato water
> 1/4 cup sugar
> 1 Tb salt
> 1 cup cooled mashed potatoes
> 1/2 cup softened butter
> 7 1/2–7 3/4 cups all-purpose flour

In a large bowl, dissolve the yeast in the water; stir in the sugar and salt. Beat in the potatoes, butter, and 3 1/2 cups of the flour; work together until smooth. Add 4 cups of the flour (the dough will be stiff). Knead on a floured surface until smooth, approximately 10 minutes. Place in a greased bowl, invert the dough, and let rise for 1 hour, or until the dough is doubled in bulk. Punch down the dough, wait 15 minutes to relax the gluten in the flour, then turn onto a floured board. Divide the dough in half and shape into 2 loaves. Place in 2 greased 9 x 5-inch bread pans. Let rise until dough doubles in bulk. Bake in a preheated 400° oven for 30–40 minutes. Cool before slicing into thick pieces. (*Makes 2 loaves*)

Potato Doughnuts

Here's a heavy, textured, old-fashioned doughnut recipe.

> 2 1/2 cups flour
> 4 tsp baking powder
> 3/4 tsp salt
> 3/4 tsp nutmeg
> 1/2 tsp cinnamon
> 2 eggs
> 1 cup mashed potatoes, at room temperature
> 1/4 cup milk
> 2 Tb melted butter
> 2/3 cup sugar
> Fat for deep frying
> Cinnamon sugar (optional)

Sift together the dry ingredients. Beat the eggs; then beat in the potatoes, milk, butter, and sugar. Beat in the dry ingredients. The mixture will be soft and sticky. Chill for 45–60 minutes, until it can be handled easily. On a floured board, roll out to approximately ³/₄ inch thick. Cut with a 2 ¹/₂–3-inch doughnut cutter. Heat fat to a temperature of 375°, drop in doughnuts, and cook for 2–4 minutes or until browned. The doughnuts sink and then float to the top. Sprinkle with cinnamon sugar if you wish. (*Makes about 18 doughnuts*)

Lynn's Raised Potato Doughnuts

The yeast gives these doughnuts a light texture.

1³/₄ cups milk
¹/₂ cup butter
1 package active dry yeast
³/₄ cup plus 1 teaspoon granulated sugar
6 ¹/₂ cups flour
1 tsp salt
1 ¹/₂ tsp nutmeg
1 cup mashed potatoes
3 eggs
Fat for deep frying
Confectioners' sugar

Scald the milk and stir in butter until melted. Set aside to cool. Dissolve the yeast with 1 teaspoon granulated sugar and ¹/₄ cup warm water. Sift together 6 cups flour, salt, and nutmeg; set aside. Combine the milk and yeast mixtures and beat in ³/₄ cup granulated sugar and mashed potatoes. Beat the eggs and stir them in, then gradually stir in the flour. Add the remaining ¹/₂ cup flour if necessary to make a workable dough. Let rise until doubled in bulk. Punch down and roll ¹/₂ inch thick on a floured surface. Cut with a 2 ¹/₂–3-inch doughnut cutter and place doughnuts and holes on a floured cookie sheet. (Life is easier if you roll out on a floured cookie sheet—then you don't have to transfer from board to sheet.) Let rise 1 hour. Cook in deep fat preheated to 375° for 2–4 minutes. Sprinkle with confectioners' sugar before serving. (*Makes 30–36 doughnuts*)

Lynn's Chocolate Potato Cake

Potatoes make this cake moist and rich.

4 oz unsweetened chocolate
1 tsp vanilla extract
2 cups cake flour
1 tsp baking powder
¹/₂ tsp baking soda
¹/₂ tsp salt
¹/₂ tsp cinnamon
1 cup butter
1³/₄ cups sugar
4 eggs
1 cup mashed potatoes
1 cup buttermilk

Melt chocolate with the vanilla; cool slightly. Sift together the flour, baking powder, soda, salt, and cinnamon. Cream the butter and sugar and beat in the eggs one by one. Add the chocolate and mashed potatoes. Beat in the dry ingredients alternately with the buttermilk. Pour into a greased 13×9-inch pan and bake in a preheated 350° oven for approximately 40 minutes (or bake in 2 round 9-inch pans for 30–35 minutes). Cool before frosting. (*Makes a 13 x 9-inch cake or two 9-inch layers*)

Frosting
3 oz unsweetened chocolate
1 ¹/₂ tsp vanilla extract
1 lb confectioners' sugar
Dash of salt
¹/₂ cup softened butter
Hot milk
Chopped walnuts

Melt chocolate and vanilla; let cool slightly. Cream the sugar, salt, and butter. Add just enough hot milk to make a spreadable consistency. Beat in the melted chocolate. Spread on the cake and sprinkle with chopped nuts.

Pumpkins

Drive past a country farm stand in autumn, and you'll see piles of field pumpkins destined to be carved into Halloween jack-o'-lanterns. They're marvelous-looking, but don't be fooled—their stringy, watery flesh makes them poor eating. For cooking, you want eating varieties, sometimes known as sugar pumpkins, smaller in size, with finer-grained flesh and a sweeter, more delicate flavor than field pumpkins. You probably won't find eating pumpkins listed as such in seed catalogs, but the tip-off is phrases such as "fine-grained flesh" or "good for pies."

Pumpkins do make excellent pies and other desserts. They're members of the squash family and can be substituted in most of the winter squash recipes as well as many of the sweet potato recipes. I've given you many choices for desserts, but pumpkin cooking shouldn't stop there. In other parts of the world, pumpkins are a standard vegetable: Latin American cooks use them in casseroles; Russian cooks combine pumpkins, fruits, and meats, and northern African cooks include pumpkins in many recipes.

Although sugar pumpkins are smaller than field pumpkins, they carve up just the same for decorating. Russ plants Cinderella, a bush jack-o'-lantern type, and

Spirit Hybrid, a fine-fleshed pumpkin for pies. As pumpkins are heavy feeders, Russ takes a bushel basket of cow manure and inverts it where he wants his pumpkin hills. Then he works it into the soil, mounding up the soil and manure in the center. The hills, 10 feet apart to allow for ample vine growth, are about the size of a half-bushel basket. In each hill, he plants six seeds in three groups of two and thins to the three strongest plants.

With this good start, there's little else to do until September when the pumpkins are ready to harvest. Russ says it's quite important to never prune the vines. He lets two fruits grow on each vine and removes the rest of the blossoms (but not the leaves) to encourage the plants to put their vigor into the remaining fruit.

When the pumpkins turn orange, they're ready to be harvested. Use shears to cut them off, because if the stem pulls away, rot sets in faster. Preparing pumpkin is simple. If you're using the whole pumpkin wash it well, cut a "lid" off the top of the pumpkin, and scoop out the seeds and stringy pulp. (Hold on to the seeds—they make delicious snacks.) I find the easiest way to scrape out the pulp is with a dime-store thin-edged soup spoon. The spoon works like a scraper and its curve has the same contour as the pumpkin. Once the pulp is removed, you're ready to cook.

If you want to use only the flesh, cut off the top and also cut across the bottom so that the pumpkin stands flat on the counter. Then, as if you were cutting off an orange skin, cut down under the skin from top to bottom, and work your way around the pumpkin. This goes much

faster than cutting the pumpkin into chunks and then peeling them. Then, halve the pumpkin and scrape out the seeds and pulp.

For pumpkin purée, it's best to steam chunks, because boiling would rob them of some of their subtle flavor. When pressed for time, you can certainly boil pumpkin (the cooking time is half as long as steaming), but be sure to drain the flesh well. Regardless of how I cook pumpkin, I always drain it after cooking, and once again after puréeing to remove excess moisture. Baking pumpkin produces a dried texture, but it takes longer than steaming.

Marketing

Ask for eating, or sugar, pumpkins. They're often more spherical in shape and are considerably smaller in size, usually weighing less than 7 pounds. The pumpkins should have a bright orange color and the stem should be attached, which prevents spoilage. Dehydration is a sign of poor storage conditions.

Special Information

Yields

- A 4-pound whole pumpkin = 2 pounds raw flesh (and 6 ounces seeds)
- 1 pound raw peeled pumpkin = approximately 4 cups raw chunked or lightly packed grated pumpkin = approximately 2 cups cooked puréed drained flesh

Note: A pumpkin will trim down to approximately one half its weight; however, as the size of the pumpkin reduces, I think you get slightly more pumpkin flesh for your money.

Storage and Preserving

- Fresh pumpkin will keep for 1–2 months in a dry, ventilated attic with temperatures in the 50–55° range. Lower temperatures can cause chilling injuries.
- Pumpkin chunks will keep in the refrigerator in a perforated plastic bag for at least a week. Don't leave them at room temperature or the flesh will dehydrate.
- For longer storage freeze cooked pumpkin: cook, purée, and package in freezer boxes. Use within 6 months.

Hints

- Use pumpkin shells as serving containers for cooked vegetables. Cook as in *Whole Baked Pumpkin* and fill with your favorite mixture. This is great fun to do with an oversize Hubbard or Banana winter squash, too.
- Make *Fried Pumpkin Slices*: Halve pumpkins lengthwise; peel. Slice ¼-inch pieces across pumpkin and dip in an egg beaten with 1 teaspoon milk or cream, then in either a mixture of bread crumbs, Parmesan

cheese, and salt or a mixture of flour, sugar, and cinnamon. Fry in vegetable oil, turning once, until tender.
- Substitute small sugar pumpkins in acorn squash recipes.
- Cook pumpkin with hot peppers, tomatoes, and corn; then combine with cooked pinto beans for pumpkin Mexican style.
- Substitute for winter squash. See *Winter Squash, Hints.*
- Use puréed pumpkin, rather than flour, to thicken gravy.
- Try a *Pumpkin Custard Pie:* Make your favorite custard filling and add cooked sieved pumpkin (approximately 1 cup cooked pumpkin to 5 eggs and 1¾ cups milk or cream).
- Make a *Pumpkin Sherbet* following the basic instructions for *Tomato Sherbet* in *Tomatoes.*
- Substitute pumpkin for squash in *Old-Fashioned Squash Pie* (see *Winter Squash*).

Microwave

- Pumpkin, cut into 1½–2-inch chunks in a covered dish, will cook tender in 8 minutes.

Leftovers

- Add puréed pumpkin to mashed potatoes.
- Cook leftover pumpkin chunks or pumpkin purée with broth and finely chopped stewed vegetables such as onions, tomatoes, and celery. Add some cream for an unusual cold-weather soup.
- See *Winter Squash, Leftovers.*

◇ *Steamed Pumpkin*

Peel pumpkin and cut into 1 1/2–2-inch chunks. Boil 3/4–1 inch water in steamer, place pumpkin in steamer basket or colander, and cover. Steam for 15–20 minutes, depending upon the size of the pumpkin chunks.

Use the steamed pumpkin in a purée, serve plain with melted butter, or glaze as in *Steamed Squash* (see *Winter Squash*).

◇ *Boiled Pumpkin*

Peel pumpkin and cut into 1 1/2–2-inch cubes. Boil a large pot of salted water and add pumpkin when the water comes to a rapid boil. The pumpkin will cook in 8–12 minutes.

◇ *Baked Pumpkin*

If you're baking the flesh for puréeing, use any of the three following methods:

Cut into Pieces: Cut pumpkin into 3–4-inch pieces. Leave the skin intact. Place in a covered casserole and bake for approximately 40 minutes at 375°. Cool before peeling off the skin. Purée.

Halved: Split a small 2–4 1/2-pound pumpkin, and clean out the seeds and pulp. Put flesh side down in a baking pan with a bit of water. Bake at 350° for 1 1/2 hours or until the flesh is tender.

Chunked—Moisture Method: Follow the directions for *Winter Squash* (see page 286).

Baked Pumpkin Halves

Wash a 2-pound (or smaller) pumpkin, halve lengthwise, and remove the seeds and pulp. Brush the flesh with melted butter, and place, flesh side down, in a baking pan with a little water. Bake at 350° for 40–50 minutes. Turn and baste with butter and/or sugar or honey, and cook for another 10 minutes.

Whole Baked Pumpkin

A whole baked pumpkin is splashy-looking as well as being good to eat. Bake a pumpkin whole, slice it in wedges, and eat as is, or use it as a container for your favorite vegetable or meat mixture. Fill a whole pumpkin with filling and bake it. (See *Lynn's Bread Pudding Baked in a Pumpkin Shell*.) Experiment.

For just plain pumpkin eating, wash a 2 1/2–3-pound sugar pumpkin; cut off the top, saving the lid and the stem for a handle. Scrape out the seeds and pulp, wipe out the inside, then brush with melted butter and/or sugar or salt. Replace the lid and bake in a 350° oven for 35 minutes. Coat the inside flesh once again with butter, sugar, or salt and bake another 10–15 minutes or until it is fork tender. Either slice into wedges and serve plain or fill with a cooked stuffing.

◇ *Pumpkin Seeds*

Pumpkin seeds are a bonus snack included in every fresh pumpkin. We often combine the seeds with raisins and nuts or dried fruits for a nutritious nibble. Here are two easy ways to prepare them.

Plain Roasted Pumpkin Seeds

Separate seeds from pumpkin pulp, but do not wash. For every 2 cups of seeds, use 2 tablespoons mild vegetable oil and 1–2 teaspoons salt. Combine and spread out on a cookie sheet. Bake in a 250° oven until the seeds are dry, approximately 1 1/4 hours.

Curry-Roasted Pumpkin Seeds

Separate seeds from pumpkin pulp. Combine 3–4 tablespoons curry powder, 1 1/2 cups warm water, 1 tablespoon lemon or lime juice, and 1 teaspoon salt. Bring to a boil to dissolve the curry powder; add pumpkin seeds. Simmer mixture for 5–10 minutes. Drain, place on an oiled cookie sheet, and bake in a 250° oven for 1–1 1/4 hours or until the seeds are dried out.

Easy Pumpkin Scramble

1 Tb vegetable oil
3 Tb butter
3/4 cup chopped onions
1 clove garlic
2 cups peeled, seeded, and chopped tomatoes
1 cup corn kernels
1 cup lima beans
2 1/2 cups pumpkin cut into 1-inch chunks
1/4 cup water or broth
Salt and freshly ground pepper

In the oil and 1 tablespoon of the butter, sauté onions until wilted, about 5 minutes. Add garlic, tomatoes, corn, lima beans, pumpkin, and water or broth. Cook over medium-low heat until the vegetables are tender, 15–20 minutes. Remove garlic, season with salt and pepper, and add remaining butter if desired. (*Serves 4*)

Puréed Pumpkin, Parsnips, and Cannellini Beans

4 Tb butter
1/2 cup chopped carrots
1/2 cup chopped white of leek
1/2 cup chopped celery
1 tsp chopped garlic

1 bay leaf
Salt
4 cups chopped pumpkin
2 cups chopped parsnips
1/4 cup chicken broth
2 cups cannellini white beans, cooked and drained
    (or use canned beans)
2 eggs
1/4 cup heavy cream
Salt and freshly ground pepper
1/4 cup grated Swiss cheese

In 2 tablespoons of the butter, cook carrots, leeks, and celery until wilted, 5–10 minutes. Add garlic, bay leaf, 1 teaspoon salt, pumpkin, parsnips, and broth. Bring broth to a simmer, cover, and cook over very low heat, stirring occasionally, until pumpkin and parsnips are tender, approximately 15 minutes. Add beans. Cook 5 minutes longer. Remove cover, and cook over high heat, stirring, to evaporate any moisture in the pan. Purée vegetables. Beat the eggs and cream; beat into pumpkin mixture; season to taste. Pour into a buttered medium (2-quart) casserole, sprinkle top with cheese, and dot with remaining butter. Bake in a preheated 425° oven for 20–25 minutes or until purée is heated through. (*Serves 8–10*)

• Bake in a partially precooked pumpkin shell: Clean a 4–5-pound pumpkin; brush interior with melted butter; sprinkle with salt. Cook at 400° for 30 minutes, then fill with purée and bake until pumpkin is completely tender. Serve both the purée and the pumpkin slices.

Pumpkin Shell Stuffed with Rice

A cooked pumpkin makes an attractive serving container as well as holding the heat. You can either prepare your favorite mixture and reheat it for the last half hour in the shell or, as I suggest here, stuff the completely cooked shell with the hot mixture made from another pumpkin and serve with a pumpkin sliver on the side.

3-lb sugar pumpkin
2 Tb melted butter
Salt
2 1/3 cups chicken broth
6 oz long-grain rice and wild rice combination
3 Tb butter
1 1/2 cups pumpkin cut into 1/2-inch cubes
1/2 cup chopped onions
1 cup sliced mushrooms

Cut off pumpkin lid, and clean out inside. Brush interior with melted butter; sprinkle with salt. Put lid back on pumpkin and bake in a preheated 350° oven for 1 hour or until the flesh is completely tender; set aside.

Meanwhile, bring the broth to a boil. Add rice, 1 tablespoon of the butter, and 1 teaspoon salt. Simmer, covered, for 15 minutes. Add pumpkin cubes and cook until liquid is absorbed, approximately 10 minutes; drain.

Melt 2 tablespoons of the butter in a sauté pan; cook onions until soft. Add mushrooms, cook until lightly browned, and thoroughly combine with rice. Stuff the pumpkin with the rice mixture. To serve, dish out the rice, then slice the pumpkin into wedges and serve alongside. (*Serves 6*)
Note: If you make the rice mixture ahead of time, cook the pumpkin for 30 minutes, add the rice, and continue cooking pumpkin until done. The rice will reheat in the pumpkin.
• Add pieces of meat and vegetables, such as sautéed chopped spinach.

Pumpkin with Soup Inside
I love making this dish. It's easy, attractive, and every vegetable comes straight from our fall garden.

7–8-lb pumpkin (sugar pumpkin if possible)
4 Tb melted butter
Salt and freshly ground pepper
1 cup minced white portions of leeks (or onions)
1/2 cup minced carrots
1/2 cup minced celery
4 cups beef broth
1 cup peeled, seeded, and chopped tomatoes
1/4 cup rice
Bay leaf
1 cup sour cream (optional)
3 Tb chives (optional)

Cut a lid from pumpkin (leaving the stem on as a handle). Clean it out. Melt 2 tablespoons of the butter and brush it on the pumpkin interior. Then, sprinkle with salt and pepper. Replace lid and place pumpkin in a large pan or oven-to-table container. Bake in a preheated 400° oven for 20 minutes.

Meanwhile, sauté minced vegetables in 2 tablespoons butter until wilted, 5–10 minutes. Add broth; heat to boiling point. Add tomatoes and season to taste. Place rice in the pumpkin. Add boiling broth and vegetable mixture, and float bay leaf on the top. Cover, and bake for 45–60 minutes, or until the pumpkin is tender, but not soft. Place on a serving dish. To serve, ladle out the soup, scraping out a portion of pumpkin flesh with each serving. Garnish with sour cream and chives, if desired. (*Serves 6–8*)

- Omit rice; add other chopped vegetables, such as parsnips and turnips (add 20–30 minutes before serving), or zucchini (add 5–10 minutes before serving).
- For a lightly thickened soup, substitute 2 tablespoons farina for the rice.
- Add ½ cup hot cream to enrich just before serving.
- Make in a larger pumpkin, and double the ingredients. Remember that a large pumpkin's flesh may be stringy and not as sweet.
- For a more delicate version, heat chicken broth with the minced vegetables. Omit tomatoes and rice. Add finely julienned strips of cooked chicken and prosciutto ham. Cook the broth in the shell; decorate with finely sliced green scallions.

Turkey Dinner Swan Song Soup

Russ's favorite Thanksgiving "leftover" is rich vegetable soup made from the turkey carcass. The fall garden contributes just about everything for this soup, thickened by our mellow pumpkins.

The Broth
1 large turkey carcass
1 cup chopped carrots
1 cup roughly chopped celery
1 cup roughly chopped onions
2 tomatoes, halved and seeded
Herb bouquet:
    6 parsley sprigs
    1 tsp thyme
    1 bay leaf
    6 peppercorns
Salt
Leftover gravy (optional)

Finishing the Soup
2 lb pumpkin, cut into ½–1-inch chunks
½ lb carrots
1 lb tomatoes
½ lb Brussels sprouts
½ cup rice
Chunks of leftover turkey meat
Freshly ground pepper

Cut up turkey carcass and cover with 2–3 quarts water. Add chopped carrots, celery, onions, 2 tomatoes, herb bouquet, 1 tablespoon salt, and leftover gravy if you have it. Bring water to the boil, partially cover, reduce heat, and simmer for 2 hours. Strain the broth, pressing the vegetable juices into the broth. Remove any flesh from the bone and set aside. You should have about 3 quarts liquid. Put the broth into a large saucepan, and add 1 pound of the pumpkin. Boil broth gently until reduced to 8–10 cups, approximately 45 minutes.

Meanwhile, peel and thinly slice the carrots; peel, seed, and chop the tomatoes; trim the Brussels sprouts (halving if large, keeping whole if small). When the broth has reduced, mash pumpkin against the sides of the pot to thicken the soup. Or remove, purée with a bit of the broth, and return to the pan. Season to taste. Add the rice and the remaining pumpkin; cook for 10 minutes. Add the carrots, tomatoes, and leftover turkey; add reserved meat from the carcass if desired. Cook for 5 minutes longer. Add the Brussels sprouts; cook for 5–10 minutes or until the sprouts are barely tender. Season with salt and pepper. (*Makes 3 quarts*)

- Leftover puréed pumpkin or squash can be used to thicken soup. Omit 1 pound of the raw pumpkin.
- Use other vegetables. Replace rice with chunks of cooked potatoes or small soup noodles.
- *Purée of Rutabaga Soup:* Peel and cut 2 pounds rutabaga into ½-inch dice and substitute for pumpkin. Cook until soft (approximately 25 minutes) and purée with a bit of the broth. Return to soup, add rice, and cook until rice is barely tender, about 15 minutes.

Beef Stew with Pumpkin in a Pumpkin Shell (or Carbonada Criolla)

This is my version of a South American specialty. You don't need the pumpkin shell, but it looks so pretty and is a good way to use those big field pumpkins.

10–12-lb field pumpkin
5 Tb butter
⅓ cup sugar
2-lb sugar pumpkin
2–3 peaches or pears
1½–2 lb stew beef
1 Tb vegetable oil
1 Tb chopped garlic
1 cup chopped onions
1 cup sliced carrots
½ cup chopped green pepper
4 cups beef broth
1½–2 cups peeled, seeded, and chopped tomatoes
Herb bouquet:
    1 bay leaf
    ½ tsp oregano
    6 sprigs parsley
Salt
¾ lb white potatoes

³/₄ lb sweet potatoes
1 lb zucchini
1 ¹/₂ cups corn kernels, or 2–3 corn on the cobs cut into ¹/₂-inch rounds
Freshly ground pepper

Clean out the field pumpkin: Slice a lid and save the seeds for snacks. Melt 3 tablespoons of the butter, and brush it on the pumpkin interior. Sprinkle sugar on the interior, turning the pumpkin so that the sugar adheres to all surfaces. Cover pumpkin with lid, and bake in a pre-heated 375° oven for 45 minutes.

Clean the sugar pumpkin, peel the flesh, cut into ¹/₂-inch cubes, and set aside. You should end up with 1–1 ¹/₄ pounds. Meanwhile poach, peel, and seed the peaches or pears. Cut them into quarters and set aside. (You can use canned fruits as long as you drain them.)

Cut beef into 1½-inch chunks. Heat oil and 2 table-spoons butter, and brown meat. Remove meat; add the gar-lic, onions, carrots, and green pepper; cook for 5 minutes, until wilted. Add the meat, broth, tomatoes, herb bou-quet, and 2 teaspoons salt. Cover and simmer for 15 min-utes. Cut white potatoes and sweet potatoes into ½-inch cubes; add to pan along with pumpkin. Cover and cook for 30 minutes. Purée 1–1½ cups of the vegetable mixture along with some of the liquid. Put back into the stew to thicken the broth. Cut zucchini into ½-inch slices, add to stew along with corn and peaches or pears. Cook for 5 minutes. Season to taste and place into the field pumpkin. Bake for 15 minutes. Ladle the stew from the pumpkin (if the field pumpkin is not too stringy, scrape some of its flesh into the stew). *(Serves 6)*

- Eliminate the sweet potatoes and/or white potatoes, adding additional pumpkin.
- Add leftover vegetables, such as whole baby onions or green beans, during the last 5 minutes of stove-top cooking.
- Substitute some dried apricots plumped in warm water or rum for the fresh fruit (or add them as well).

Pumpkin Brûlée

This absolutely divine dessert is best made well ahead of time. Everyone warns about how hard it is to get a good almost-but-not-burnt-brown-sugar topping, but this method has always worked for me. You must finely purée the pumpkin, and use a refrigerator-to-oven dish. You will end up with a crisp sugar caramel on top of a velvety cream custard.

3 cups heavy cream
2 tsp vanilla or rum
6 egg yolks
6 Tb superfine sugar
³/₄ cup finely puréed cooked pumpkin
¹/₄ tsp cinnamon
Pinch salt
¹/₂ cup brown sugar

Scald cream and vanilla or rum. Beat egg yolks and super-fine sugar until lightly colored and thick; beat in pump-

kin, cinnamon, and salt. Slowly whisk in the hot cream. Pour into a 6-cup or an 8 x 8-inch refrigerator-to-oven dish. Place into a baking pan, and pour boiling water halfway up the sides of the dish. Bake in a preheated 350° oven for 45–60 minutes, until the custard is set (the time depends upon the height of the baking dish). Chill for 8 hours, or overnight.

Preheat broiler, and place an oven rack 8–10 inches below it. Sieve the brown sugar and sprinkle it evenly over the custard. Place dish in a large pan, and surround it with ice cubes. Place on the broiler rack, and, watching carefully, let the brown sugar heat until it just begins to bubble, brown, and melt. Remove from the broiler; cool for 10 minutes. Return to the broiler and repeat the pro-cess. The sugar should become very brown, but not burnt. Remove pumpkin brûlée from oven, and chill for 2 hours. *(Serves 6)*

- Cook the custard in a double boiler over simmering water. Stir until the mixture coats a spoon (163°). Pour into a dish and refrigerate. Proceed as above.

Chilled Pumpkin Soufflé

After a heavy dinner, serve this light pumpkin dessert.

1 package unflavored gelatin
¹/₄ cup orange liqueur
4 eggs
6 Tb sugar
2 cups puréed cooked pumpkin
1 Tb grated crystallized ginger
1 tsp cinnamon
¹/₂ tsp ground ginger
¹/₄ tsp allspice
¹/₄ tsp cream of tartar
1 cup heavy cream
Candied orange slices or slivered crystallized ginger
(optional)
Raspberry sauce (optional)

Oil a band of waxed paper, long enough to encircle a 1-quart soufflé dish, place around so that the paper extends 2 inches above the dish, and tie it. Sprinkle gelatin over the liqueur and place over simmering water, stirring to dissolve the gelatin. Separate the eggs. Beat the egg yolks, gradually adding 4 tablespoons of the sugar until the yolks are pale yellow and thickened. Add the pumpkin, grated ginger, and spices. Mix in the gelatin.

Beat the egg whites until foamy, add the cream of tartar. Continue beating; as whites thicken, gradually add the remaining sugar. Beat whites until glossy. Stir a quarter of the whites into the pumpkin mixture to lighten it, then fold in the remaining whites. Whip the cream and fold into the whites. Pour into the prepared soufflé dish and chill until set, preferably overnight. Remove collar; decorate with candied orange slices or slivered crystallized ginger if you like. This is lovely served with a raspberry sauce. (*Serves 6–8*)
Note: You could also serve this in individual long-stemmed goblets.

Super-Easy Pumpkin Mousse

1 package unflavored gelatin
2 Tb orange juice
1 cup heavy cream
1/2 tsp vanilla extract
4 egg yolks
5 Tb sugar
1 1/2 cups puréed cooked pumpkin
1 tsp cinnamon
1/2 tsp nutmeg
Grated orange rind (optional)

Over simmering water, dissolve gelatin in orange juice. Scald 1/4 cup of the cream and vanilla. Beat egg yolks and sugar until thick and lemon-colored. Gradually add the hot cream, then the pumpkin and spices. Beat in gelatin and orange rind. Whip the remaining cream; fold into

the pumpkin mixture. Fill individual dishes or a 1 1/2-quart mold. Chill thoroughly. (*Serves 6*)

Chilled Pumpkin and Sweet Potato Dessert

This rich vegetable dessert is similar to one we had in the Caribbean Islands. It's good for a large buffet party because you need only a sliver to satisfy a sweet tooth.

2 lb peeled raw pumpkin
2 lb puréed cooked sweet potatoes
1/3 cup rum
1/2 tsp ground ginger
1 tsp cinnamon
1/2 tsp ground cloves
4 Tb butter
3/4 cup sugar
3 eggs
4 Tb flour
1 tsp salt
1 cup coconut milk
Whipped cream
Sour cream

Grate the pumpkin, and combine with sweet potato, rum, and spices. Cream butter and sugar; beat in eggs. Whisk together flour, salt, and coconut milk until smooth. Thoroughly beat into pumpkin mixture. Pour into a well-buttered 9 x 3-inch round casserole. Bake in a preheated 350° oven for 2–2 1/4 hours or until the mixture is completely set. Cool on a wire rack, making sure it is completely cool before unmolding. Chill. Remove from refrigerator shortly before serving to just take the chill off. Serve with bowls of whipped cream and sour cream. (*Serves 16–20*)
Note: You can buy canned coconut milk in some areas. If not, use a real coconut. Crack open, and remove the shell and brown skin from the flesh. Grate the white flesh and squeeze through a fine towel to extract the milk. You will probably get 1/4–1/2 cup milk. Then pour 1/2–3/4 cup boiling water over grated meat and let set for 5 minutes. Squeeze again to make the 1 cup required.
- If raw pumpkin is out of season, use equal parts of puréed *cooked* sweet potato and puréed *cooked* pumpkin. It makes a slightly denser texture.
- Substitute canned diluted pina colada mix from a liquor store for coconut milk.

Lynn's Bread Pudding Baked in a Pumpkin Shell

To the Pilgrims, "pumpkin pie" meant a custard cooked right in the pumpkin shell. What a good idea! I serve it with whipped cream, fruit, or a brandy sauce.

4–5-lb short, wide sugar pumpkin
2 Tb melted butter
1/3 cup plus 2 Tb sugar
2 cups milk
1/4 cup butter

2 cups stale bread in ¼– ½-inch cubes, crusts on
    (3–4 slices)
3 eggs
⅔ cup raisins
¼ tsp salt
1 tsp cinnamon
½ tsp nutmeg

Clean out pumpkin, making a lid. Brush the inside with melted butter and sprinkle with 2 tablespoons sugar. Put lid back on, place in a baking pan, and bake in a pre-heated 350° oven for 20 minutes.

Make the bread pudding: scald the milk; add ¼ cup butter and ⅓ cup sugar. When the butter melts, pour the mixture over the bread cubes. Let stand for 5 minutes. Beat eggs; mix in raisins, salt, cinnamon, and nutmeg. Combine with bread, and fill the warm pumpkin. Return to oven, uncovered. Bake for 1½–1¾ hours or until the custard is set. The custard will puff up above the opening, but will sink down as it sets. Let stand for at least 10 minutes before serving. Slice into wedges to serve, much like a big wedge of pie or cake. (*Serves 8–10*)

Pumpkin Ginger Ice Cream

I love spices with pumpkin and perhaps my favorite is ginger. Here the pumpkin gives the ice cream a soft peach-orange color while three forms of ginger add flavor. You may omit the crystallized ginger if you wish.

1½ cups light cream
1 tsp minced fresh ginger
2 oz (approximately ½ cup) crystallized ginger
¼ cup light rum or pear liqueur
6 egg yolks
1 cup sugar
1 Tb powdered ginger
¼ tsp nutmeg
⅛ tsp ground cloves
Dash of salt
1½ cups puréed pumpkin, chilled
1½ cups heavy cream, chilled

Bring light cream to a boil, remove from heat and add fresh ginger. Cover and let steep for at least 2 hours or refrigerate overnight. Finely chop crystallized ginger, if using, and cover with rum or pear liqueur. Set aside. When cream and ginger have steeped together strain out the ginger and reheat cream. Beat egg yolks with sugar, spices, and salt to form the ribbon. Gradually beat in the hot cream. Pour into a heavy bottomed saucepan. Stirring constantly, heat until very thick, about 180°–185°. Remove from heat, stir to cool, and chill well. When chilled beat in pumpkin and heavy cream. Pour into container of a freezing machine and freeze according to manufacturer's directions. Drain crystallized ginger pieces. When mixture has churned for 15 minutes (or ¾ of the time allowed for freezing) stop the machine and stir in the drained ginger pieces. Process another 5 minutes or until mixture is ready. Pack ice cream into containers, top with a piece of plastic wrap, cover and freeze. (*Makes generous 1½ quarts*)

Pumpkin Cheese Pie

1⅓ cups graham cracker crumbs
1 cup plus 2 Tb sugar
1½ tsp cinnamon
¼ cup melted butter
3 eggs
1 tsp vanilla extract
9 oz softened cream cheese
1½ cups puréed cooked pumpkin
½ tsp nutmeg
¼ tsp ground cloves
1 cup sour cream

Stir together the graham cracker crumbs, ¼ cup of the sugar, and ¼ teaspoon of the cinnamon. Mix in the melted butter, and pat mixture into a deep 9-inch pie dish. In a large bowl, beat together the eggs and ¾ cup of the sugar until light and fluffy. Add the vanilla and cream cheese; beat until smooth. Stir in the pumpkin, 1 teaspoon cinnamon, nutmeg, and cloves. Pour into the pie shell and bake in a preheated 350° oven for 40 minutes. Remove; let stand for 5 minutes. Combine the sour cream, 2 tablespoons sugar, and ¼ teaspoon cinnamon. Spread on top of the pie, and bake at 450° for 5 minutes. Chill pie before serving. (*Makes a 9-inch pie*)

• Substitute pulverized ginger snaps for the graham

cracker crumbs.

- For a ginger flavor add ¹/₂ cup finely pulverized crystallized ginger. Substitute ginger extract for vanilla.

Pumpkin Chiffon Pie

¹/₄ cup softened butter
³/₄ cup dark-brown sugar
4 egg yolks
1 tsp cinnamon
¹/₂ tsp nutmeg
¹/₂ tsp ground ginger
¹/₄ tsp salt
2 cups puréed cooked pumpkin
¹/₂ cup heavy cream
5 egg whites
1 partially baked 9-inch pie shell made from
    Tart Pastry (page 351)

Cream the butter and sugar until light and fluffy. Beat in the egg yolks, cinnamon, nutmeg, ginger, salt, pumpkin, and cream. In a clean bowl, beat egg whites until peaks are firm but not dry. Stir one-quarter of the whites into the pumpkin mixture to lighten it, then fold in the remaining whites. Pour into the pie shell, and bake in a preheated 350° oven for 45–50 minutes, or until just firm. Cool to room temperature before serving. (*Makes a 9-inch pie*)

- Fold ¹/₂ cup grated coconut into the pumpkin mixture.

Pumpkin-Cranberry Cookies

These are soft, cakelike cookies.

¹/₂ cup softened butter
1 cup sugar
1 tsp vanilla extract
1 egg
1 cup puréed cooked pumpkin
2 ¹/₄ cups flour
2 tsp baking powder
1 tsp baking soda
¹/₂ tsp salt
1 tsp cinnamon
1 cup cranberries
1 Tb grated orange peel
¹/₂ cup chopped nuts

Cream butter and sugar until light and fluffy. Beat in vanilla, egg, and pumpkin. Sift together flour, baking powder, baking soda, salt, and cinnamon; beat into pumpkin mixture. Halve cranberries, and stir into mixture along with orange peel and nuts. Drop by rounded teaspoonfuls onto a greased cookie sheet. Bake in a preheated 375° oven for 10–12 minutes. (*Makes 36 cookies*)

- Substitute chocolate chips for cranberries.

Pumpkin Muffins with Raw Grated Pumpkin

1 ¹/₂ cups flour
¹/₂ cup sugar
2 tsp baking powder
¹/₂ tsp salt
¹/₂ tsp cinnamon
¹/₂ tsp nutmeg
¹/₄ cup soft butter
1 egg
¹/₂ cup milk
1 cup finely grated pumpkin

Sift together the flour, sugar, baking powder, salt, cinnamon, and nutmeg. Add the butter, egg, milk, and pumpkin, and cut with a pastry blender until just mixed (which makes a lighter muffin than if it is beaten together). Fill greased muffin tins almost full; bake in a preheated 400° oven for approximately 20 minutes. (*Makes 8 large or 12 medium-size muffins*)

- Add raisins or nuts.
- Top with brown or cinnamon sugar.

Cranberry Pumpkin Muffins

These muffins are heavier than *Pumpkin Muffins with Raw Grated Pumpkin*, but are tasty and attractive. They will not rise as high as standard muffins.

1–1 ¹/₄ cups cranberries
2 cups flour
1 cup sugar
¹/₂ tsp baking powder
1 tsp baking soda
1 tsp salt
1 tsp cinnamon
¹/₂ tsp allspice
¹/₂ cup butter
2 eggs
1²/₃ cups cooked puréed pumpkin

Halve cranberries; set aside. Sift together flour, sugar, baking powder, baking soda, salt, cinnamon, and allspice. Add butter, eggs, and pumpkin, and mix together with a pastry blender until just combined. Stir in cranberries. Fill 18 greased muffin cups almost full. Bake in a preheated 350° oven for 35 minutes or until a toothpick inserted into the center comes out clean. (*Makes 18 medium muffins*)

Grated Pumpkin Bread

1 cup raisins
¹/₄ cup rum, cognac, or warm water
3 eggs
³/₄ cup sugar
1 cup vegetable oil
2 ¹/₂ cups grated raw pumpkin
1 tsp vanilla extract
2³/₄ cups flour

2 tsp cinnamon
1 tsp mace
1 tsp salt
1 tsp baking powder
1 tsp baking soda

Cover raisins with rum, cognac, or water to plump. Beat eggs, then thoroughly mix in sugar, oil, pumpkin, and vanilla. Sift together remaining ingredients. Mix into pumpkin mixture, beating well. Drain raisins and stir into the batter; pour into a greased and floured 9 x 5-inch loaf pan. Bake in a preheated 350° oven for 1–1 1/4 hours or until a toothpick inserted into the center comes out clean. Cool on a rack for 15 minutes before turning out of the pan. (*Makes 1 loaf*)

• Substitute 1 cup halved cranberries for raisins.

Toni Greenwald's Pumpkin Yeast Bread

This bread's golden autumn color makes a beautiful accompaniment to *Pumpkin with a Soup Inside.*

8 1/2–9 cups unbleached all-purpose flour
2 packages active dry yeast
1/4 cup lukewarm water
1/4 cup sugar
1 3/4 cups milk
1 Tb salt
1/4 cup butter
2 cups puréed cooked pumpkin

Sift flour; set aside 2 1/2 cups. Dissolve yeast in water, stir in 1 teaspoon of the sugar, and let stand for 6–7 minutes. Scald milk, pour into a large bowl, and stir in the salt, butter, and remaining sugar. Cool to lukewarm; add yeast. Beat in the 2 1/2 cups flour, mixing until smooth, then beat in the pumpkin. Add 6 cups flour (the dough will be slightly wet). Spread some of the remaining 1/2 cup flour on a board, turn the dough onto it, and let rest for 10 minutes. Knead for 10 minutes. Place in a buttered bowl and cover with plastic wrap or a clean towel. Let rise until doubled in bulk; punch down and let rest for 5 minutes. Shape into 2 loaves, place in buttered bread pans, and let rise until doubled in bulk. Bake in a preheated 400° oven for 35–40 minutes. (*Makes 2 loaves*)

Radishes

Round about May, when both the root cellar and the garden look pretty sparse, I'm grateful for radishes. Suddenly, I have a fresh vegetable that's good for salads, soups, as a cooked side dish, or a zesty dip as pleasing to see as it is to eat. This versatility is much prized in Europe and the Orient, where radishes are in great demand.

On our honeymoon in France, we discovered what's become an all-time favorite luncheon: buttered French bread topped with young red radishes, to be devoured, stems and all. At a Munich beer hall, we whetted our appetites on the giant white radishes accompanying our steins of beer. The Chinese and Japanese eat prodigious quantities of fresh, cooked, and pickled radishes.

Some exotic varieties are finding their way into American seed catalogs. But before you rush out and buy every packet in sight, I have some caveats about growing radishes.

Radishes are reputed to be a fast, easy vegetable to grow: one so foolproof even a child will succeed. But the truth is that too often the results are disappointing. Maybe radish seed packets should carry the warning: "Watch out for root maggots, underdeveloped roots, and a fiery aftertaste"—all common radish problems.

First, you'll have to deal with the root maggot larvae that hatch from fly eggs. Drenching the soil in the growing area with the pesticide Diazinon works. However, an even better solution is to keep flies from landing near the plants in the first place. Nylon mosquito netting, fastened to wire hoops placed over the crop, keeps the varmints out.

Another problem: leafy foliage paired with minuscule roots (or all tops and no bottoms) is a matter of climate. Radishes need 6 hours of daily sun and unchecked growth to develop correctly. Sow, fertilize, cultivate, water—and keep your fingers crossed.

You can control the third problem of a bitter or fiery aftertaste by timing your planting so that your radishes mature in warm, not hot weather.

At the Victory Garden, as at home, we plant both spring and fall radish varieties: spring varieties include the red All-America winner Cherry Belle; the scarlet and white French Breakfast; the round Burpee White; and the long White Icicle. Spring radishes need cool weather, quick growth, and harvesting before the weather turns hot.

In April, or when the soil warms up, Russ prepares a row 16 inches wide by 6 feet long, works in some 5-10-5 fertilizer, sows seed ½ inch apart (eventually thinning the seedlings to 1 inch apart), and covers the bed with nylon netting. The radishes can be harvested 30–45 days later. He sows successively until a month before the temperatures reach the 80s, then he stops. These frequent small plantings are preferable because radishes get woody and pithy if held too long in the ground. (Radishes are also useful as markers for slower-germinating crops.)

During mid-late summer, Russ plants a fall radish crop. We like the black-skinned 3½–4-inch-diameter Round Black Spanish—a good storage choice—and the 5–6-inch-long White Chinese, the mildest fall radish. Fall radishes thrive on the opposite of spring growing conditions: warmth to germinate and cool weather in which to

Special Information

Yields

- 1 bunch of radishes with greens weighing approximately ½ pound = 1½ cups packed greens and about 18 radishes
- ½ pound whole radishes = 2 cups sliced
- 1½ pounds radish greens = 8 cups packed down

Storage and Preserving

- Use radishes fresh. Do not freeze or can.
- *Spring Radishes:* Harvest as needed. Before refrigerating, remove tops and package separately in a perforated plastic bag. Keep roots refrigerated; they will hold about 1 week.
- *Fall Radishes:* Store as above. For long-term storage, pack in wet sand in a cool, dry place—they will last almost all winter.

Hints

- Crisp radishes in ice water.
- Slice raw into salads.
- Garnish main courses with steamed whole radishes.
- Simmer slices for 1 minute and add to clear meat or poultry consommé.
- *Radish Rémoulade*: Peel, grate, or julienne black radish. Treat just as *Celeriac Rémoulade* (see *Celeriac*).
- *Radish Pancakes*: Use radishes in *Lacy Jerusalem Artichoke Pancakes* (see *Jerusalem Artichokes*) or add chopped scallions as well. Serve with sour cream.
- Add radish greens to hearty mixed vegetable soups. Mix grated radishes with a bit of sour or whipped cream to use in place of horseradish garnish.
- Add grated fall radishes to carrot or cabbage slaws.
- Use sliced spring radishes or julienned or rolled-cut fall radishes in stir-fries.
- Cook julienned fall radishes and serve alone or on a mixed salad platter along with julienned beets, carrots, or other vegetables.

Microwave

- ½ pound sliced radishes placed in a covered dish with 1 tablespoon water or butter cooks in 4 minutes.

Leftovers

- Add to mixed vegetable soups.
- Add finely chopped cold radish salad to *Gazpacho* (see *Tomatoes*).

grow. As the radishes take 60–90 days to maturity, we end up with a fall crop that can also be stored for winter use. When storing, we either mulch the crop in the ground (just like parsnips), or hold radishes inside layered in sand.

When I prepare radishes, I save the greens for *Radish Top Soup*. Then I wash, dry, and refrigerate the greens and roots separately. To crisp radishes, soak in ice water for a few hours, which is also the proper way to store radish roses or other radish fantasies.

You don't need to peel the thin, tender skin of spring radishes, but the more thick-skinned, pungent fall radishes should be peeled for the most delicate flavor.

I only recently began experimenting with cooked radishes, and discovered they have a mellow, delicate flavor similar to that of white turnips. I cook them either thinly sliced or whole. Using a food processor certainly eliminates tedious slicing, but if you don't own a machine, a hand-held slicer works equally well.

Steam whole radishes in a steamer or in a bit of water and butter. It's not necessary to boil radishes because they steam-cook so rapidly. Cooked red radishes turn an appealing delicate pale pink color. If, like my two daughters, you don't favor raw radishes, you may be surprised—as they were—to find how much you enjoy them cooked.

Marketing

In season, you should be able to find locally grown radishes with attached greens. Trim and keep them refrigerated or hold in ice water. Out of season they'll usually be topped and bagged in plastic. Buy firm, crisp, medium-size radishes: larger ones can be woody or pithy. Avoid any that are soft or mottled.

◇ *Steamed Radishes*

Place cleaned radishes in a steamer basket over 1 inch boiling water. Steam until just tender, 8–12 minutes, depending upon size.

◇ *Steam-Boil Method*

Place radishes in a saucepan with 1 tablespoon butter (optional) and ⅓ inch water. Bring water to a boil, cover, and reduce heat. Depending upon size, radishes will steam tender in 5–10 minutes. If radishes are larger, add additional water so that it doesn't boil away.
- Roll-cut fall radishes and steam as above.

Finishing Touches for Cooked Radishes

- Roll in butter and season with salt and pepper.
- Roll in butter, add heavy cream, and cook rapidly, reducing the cream to coat the radishes.
- *Creamed Radishes*: Cover radishes with a cream sauce made with 2 tablespoons flour, 2 tablespoons butter, 1 cup cooking liquid (adding additional water if

needed), ½ cup heavy cream, and seasonings to taste. Reheat and serve.

◇ *Sliced Sautéed Radishes*

Sauté sliced radishes in butter for 1 minute. Lower heat, cover pan, and simmer until just tender, 3–4 minutes. Season with salt, pepper, and herbs.
- Julienne fall radishes and treat as above.

◇ *Whole Raw Baby Radishes*

Without a doubt, this is my favorite way to eat radishes. I pull the first young radishes, wash them off, and serve them—tender leaves and all.

Radishes, leaving tender stems and leaves
Softened sweet butter
Kosher salt

Arrange radishes on a plate along with crocks of butter and kosher salt. Using the stems as handles, dip the radishes first into butter, then sprinkle with salt.
- *Radish Sandwich:* Spread French bread with softened

butter, top with radishes, and sprinkle with kosher salt. It's heaven!

- *With Herb Butter:* Finely chop your favorite fresh herbs, mix with softened butter, and serve as above.
- *With Anchovy Butter:* Finely chop anchovy fillets, mash into softened butter, and serve in a crock as a dip.

◇ Radishes with Vinaigrette

Tossing sliced radishes and other vegetables in a simple *Vinaigrette Sauce* (see *Appendix*) creates a quick, easy summer salad. Here are a few combinations to start you thinking.

- *Radishes and Celery:* Combine equal amounts of sliced radishes and finely sliced celery. Toss with vinaigrette; sprinkle with chopped egg.
- *Radishes and Green Beans:* Mix together sliced radishes and very small cooked green beans. Toss with vinaigrette; garnish with toasted pine nuts or slivered almonds.
- *Radishes, Carrots, and Dill:* Combine thinly sliced radishes, thin diagonally sliced carrots, and fresh chopped dill. Dress with vinaigrette.
- *Radishes with Feta Cheese:* Combine 4 cups thinly sliced radishes, 1/2 pound crumbled feta cheese, sliced black olives (optional), and chopped scallions or fresh mint. Dress with a vinaigrette made with lemon juice, and marinate for 30 minutes or longer. Serve as salad or as a pita bread sandwich filling.

Susan Mayer's Radish Dip

If you have a bumper radish crop, don't despair. Save the tops for *Radish Top Soup,* and make this tasty dip out of the roots. Serve it with crackers or raw vegetable crudités.

4 cups washed and trimmed radishes
1 cup softened cream cheese
1/2–3/4 cup sour cream
2 Tb chopped chives
Salt and freshly ground pepper
Hot pepper sauce (optional)

Dry radishes thoroughly. Roughly chop in a food processor or by hand. (The size of the chop depends on how chunky you want the dip.) Beat together cream cheese, sour cream, and chives, and combine with radishes. Season with salt, pepper, and a dash of hot pepper sauce if you like. (*Makes 1 quart*)

- Replace some of the radishes with other chopped vegetables such as peppers, carrots, and scallions.

Radish Salad

Radishes add a zing to most raw vegetable combinations or are good alone, dressed with vinegar, salt, pepper, and sugar. (The sugar is a holdover from German radish salads I knew as a child.)

3–4 Tb wine vinegar or lemon juice
1 tsp sugar
1 Tb salt
4 cups thinly sliced radishes
Freshly ground pepper

Mix together vinegar, sugar, and salt; toss well with radishes. Marinate for 1 hour, drain, and add pepper to taste. (*Serves 6–8*)

- For more dressing, toss in *Vinaigrette Sauce* (see *Appendix*).
- Add fresh chopped herbs, such as dill.
- *Radish and Cucumber Salad:* Prepare equal amounts of radishes and peeled, seeded, and thinly sliced cucumbers. Marinate separately, as above, combine and add chopped fresh dill and a mixture of sour cream and whipped heavy cream if desired.
- *Radish and Cabbage Salad:* Combine radish slices with finely shredded raw cabbage. Prepare as above, omitting the sugar and adding chopped red onion and celery salt. Serve plain or dress in mayonnaise thinned with heavy cream.
- *Radish and Yogurt Salad:* Prepare radishes as above. Dress with yogurt combined with 2 cloves garlic mashed with 1 teaspoon salt.
- *Radish and Onion Salad:* Add 1 chopped small red onion or chopped scallions. Prepare as above. Fold in sour cream before serving.

Radish Top Soup

Don't throw out your radish greens. Believe it or not, those fuzzy leaves can be transformed into a smooth green soup, with a hint of watercress flavor. This can be either an elegant creamy first course or a simple supper.

6 Tb butter
1 cup chopped onions or white leek portions
8 cups loosely packed radish leaves
2 cups diced peeled potatoes
6 cups liquid (water, chicken stock, or combination)
Salt
1/2 cup heavy cream (optional)
Freshly ground pepper

Melt 4 tablespoons butter in a large saucepan, add onions or leeks, and cook until golden, approximately 5 minutes. Stir in radish tops, cover pan, and cook over low heat until wilted, 8–10 minutes.

Meanwhile, cook potatoes until soft in liquid along with 1 teaspoon salt. Combine with radish tops and cook, covered, for 5 minutes to mingle flavors. Purée finely in a food processor or food mill. Add heavy cream if desired and enrich with 2 tablespoons butter. Season to taste with salt and pepper. Serve hot. (*Serves 4–6*)

- To serve cold, omit butter enrichment.

Spring Radish, Chicken, and Scallion Dinner

½ lb whole trimmed red radishes
8–10 large scallions
2 carrots
1 onion
2 celery stalks
4 cups chicken broth
2 ½–3-lb frying chicken
1 cup dry white wine or vermouth
Salt
Herb bouquet:
 1 bay leaf
 ½ tsp thyme
 ½ tsp tarragon
 4 sprigs parsley
¼ cup heavy cream
½ lb plus 1 Tb butter
Juice of 1 lemon
Freshly ground pepper

Wash radishes; set aside. Wash and trim scallions, leaving 1–1½ inches of green. Chop carrots, onion, and celery. Combine chicken broth and 2 cups water, add the chopped vegetables, and simmer for 15–20 minutes. Strain broth, setting aside 2 cups.

Meanwhile, wash and cut chicken into serving pieces and arrange in a large saucepan or casserole. Pour in wine and remaining broth to cover (adding additional broth or water if needed). Lightly salt, add herb bouquet, then bring to a boil, reduce heat, cover, and slowly simmer chicken (or poach in a 325° oven). After 15–20 minutes, remove light meat; keep warm while dark meat finishes (5–10 minutes longer).

While chicken is cooking, boil down 2 cups reserved broth to ¼ cup. Heat cream; keep warm. Add 1 tablespoon cream to broth; boil again until slightly thickened. Cut ½ pound cold butter into tablespoons. Over low heat, add butter to broth reduction tablespoon by tablespoon, whisking constantly. (The sauce will thicken to a mayonnaise consistency.) As you are whisking, squeeze in the lemon juice. After butter is incorporated, beat in remaining warm (not hot) cream. Season and hold over warm water.

Ten minutes before the chicken is cooked, steam-boil radishes with 1 tablespoon butter and ⅓ inch water until tender. Blanch scallions until tender in boiling salted water, 2–3 minutes; drain.

Remove chicken (saving broth for other uses). On individual plates, arrange separate portions of chicken, scallions, and radishes. Spoon the sauce over. It will just lightly cover the chicken and vegetables, allowing the delicate creamy chicken, light green scallion, and pale rose radish colors to show through. (*Serves 4*)

Radish Garnishes

I have spent many an enjoyable hour carving up radishes to decorate a platter. Here are two easy-to-do garnishes.

Radish Roses

Cut off the radish roots and trim the stems, leaving just a few inner leaves. Using a sharp paring knife, start at the root tip and cut out 5–6 thin "petals," continuing down to ¼ inch from the stem. Do not detach the skin. If you wish, cut a second petal layer, starting once again at the root tip and spacing the new "petals" evenly between the first cuts. Chill the radishes in ice water for a few hours so the petals will open and curl.

Radish Fans

Use oval radishes if possible. With a sharp paring knife, make 5–6 parallel crosswise cuts three-quarters of the way down the radishes. Chill in ice water for several hours; the radishes will fan out.

Radish Condiments

Radishes and Oranges

This makes a cool accompaniment to hot dishes or a curry dinner.

 3–4 oranges
 2–3 cups thinly sliced radishes
 Lime or lemon juice

Remove white pith from oranges and cut into sections; combine with radishes. Marinate in lime or lemon juice. (*Makes 4 cups*)

Radishes Chinese Style

Try these as part of a Chinese dinner or as a snack.

 2 Tb soy sauce
 2 Tb white vinegar
 1 Tb sugar
 2 Tb sesame oil
 4 cups sliced radishes

Combine soy sauce, vinegar, sugar, and oil; mix with radishes. Cover, refrigerate, and marinate for at least 1 hour. (*Makes 4 cups*)

Salad Greens

Although produce markets magically bring us fresh salad greens year around, nothing beats strolling out to the garden and selecting an assortment of lettuces for the evening meal. I might pick pungent, dark green arugula, some delicately flavored pale green Bibb, or a cascade of loose-leaf ruby lettuce, filling my basket to the brim with salad greens of different textures, hues, and flavors.

Even though everyone is familiar with the crisp iceberg lettuce beloved by market growers, there are several other groups of lettuce worthy of notice. Iceberg is only one of the round cabbage-type varieties, which also include soft-leafed or butterhead lettuces, such as Boston, Bibb, and Buttercrunch. Recently we've enjoyed two varieties Russ found in Europe, Reine de Mai and Unrivaled. Cos or romaine lettuces grow erect with large crisp ribs and a sharper flavor than cabbage types. And there are open-heart, loose-leaf types with spreading leaf rosettes, such as Oak Leaf, Black Seeded Simpson, Ruby and Salad Bowl.

The gardener has a distinct advantage because he can try greens seldom available at the market. Corn salad, also known as lamb's lettuce or mâche, is popular in Europe. One of the best salads I ever ate was prepared by my aunt in Germany: tiny corn salad leaves dressed with the purest of oil and vinegar. Corn salad has an almost nutty flavor and an exceedingly delicate texture. Many import seed companies sell seeds. The Europeans also favor arugula (rocket), with its tart mustardy flavor—a good foil for subtler greens.

Chicory family members provide a nice sharp addition to the salad bowl or make unusual cooked vegetables. Chicories include the curly loose-leaf endive chicory, Belgian endive (treated in a separate entry), and the broad-leafed endive escarole.

When dandelion greens are young (their least bitter stage) they are refreshing served alone, mixed with other greens, or in a wilted salad. (For growing and cooking suggestions see *Greens*.) And don't overlook the just-right bitterness of watercress for salads.

Most lettuce varieties thrive and grow rapidly in cool weather, so Russ gets a jump on the season by starting an assortment indoors in March to move into the garden in mid-April. We particularly like the butterheads, such as Buttercrunch and Little Gem, and the loose-leaf Oak Leaf. Last year, the Victory Garden tested many imported European varieties with great success.

Russ sows seeds in a 4-inch pot filled with potting soil and lightly covers the seeds with milled sphagnum moss. After a few days, the seedlings appear, and after

Front basket, clockwise: Romaine, Buttercrunch, Iceberg, Escarole. Rear basket: looseleaf lettuces, Ruby and Black Seeded Simpson. Behind baskets: King Crown (r.), Royal Oak Leaf (l.)

two weeks, Russ transfers them to six-packs filled with potting soil. In mid-April, he sets them out in the garden, spaced 8 inches apart, and keeps a supply of seedlings on hand to interplant with slow-growing crops. At that time of the year, the ground is also warm enough to directly sow seeds in the garden.

Russ prepares the row by scratching in some 10-10-10 fertilizer, sows seeds into a 1/2-inch deep furrow, and covers lightly with soil. He thins the seedlings and keeps them well watered so they won't dry out. To ensure a constant supply of tender young lettuce he sows a few seeds regularly throughout the summer.

Summer lettuce planting is tricky, as many varieties go to seed in hot weather. Slowbolt, Matchless, and Summer Bibb are good summer choices. In mid-August, Russ sows seeds for a fall crop. (Arugula and corn salad have special growing requirements; see page 244 for more information.)

As salad greens are delicate, to enjoy them at their best, prepare them carefully. Wash lettuce by filling the sink with lukewarm water and plunging the whole lettuce heads into the water. Let them sit for a while, and if you're not preparing them whole, cut out the cores so the leaves float freely. I wash each leaf individually because I really dislike gritty salads. (The exception is iceberg lettuce, which has such tightly formed leaves this treatment is unnecessary. After removing the large outer leaves, simply rinse off the main heart of the lettuce.)

Once the lettuce is clean, discard any blemished leaves and spin-dry the rest. Before the advent of lettuce spinners, I would stand in the yard and swing a string bag around and around to remove moisture. During cold weather, I'd pat each leaf dry. The lettuce spinner has simplified my life—what a great invention! My favorite

spinner has a loop with a string attached. All you have to do is put the washed lettuce in the spinner, and pull out the string. The basket spins, the string recoils, and the moisture flies off the lettuce.

Once the leaves are prepared, they're ready to use or store. I put some lettuce in a plastic bag, add some paper towels, more lettuce, and continue this layering of leaves and paper towels. The towels absorb moisture and keep the lettuce from getting brown and soggy. To store the lettuce longer than a day, replace the paper towels with new dry ones, and it will stay crisp a second day—but don't go longer than that.

Never cut lettuce for tossed salads, because this discolors and bruises the leaves. Rather, tear them (which is also prettier). A touch of the stronger-flavored greens such as escarole and arugula (see *Salad Ideas*) adds a bite and texture that otherwise would be missing. Although you can make a salad of these greens by themselves—they can be quite strong unless they are very young. For salads, I'll use every variety of lettuce but iceberg, a good lettuce for many purposes but too tasteless and hard-textured for tossed salads. (Iceberg is a good choice for shredded greens, Greek or Cobb salads, or sandwiches that need a lettuce that will stand up—and it's also a good cooked wrapper for other foods.)

At one time, I ate salad either before or during the meal. Now I find a tossed green salad after a meal the ideal pause between the main course and dessert. Do try salad after a main course and see how refreshing it is.

Although we mainly enjoy lettuces in salads, it's fun to cook them as a special vegetable. I'll occasionally braise the soft-textured lettuces or use them to wrap other foods. Braising lettuces in broth produces a very mellow flavor: in Europe braised lettuce is a very popular dish. Lettuce leaves make excellent wrappers for meat, fowl, fish, or vegetable stuffings. Braise the rolled filled leaves and eat hot, or marinate and eat cold. When lettuce is used to wrap stuffings it keeps the filling moist and is a delicate—and pretty—skin as well.

The lettuces I most often cook are those with the toughest texture and sharpest taste, such as escarole, chicory, and dandelion greens (also see *Belgian Endive*). Cooking softens their flavor, transforming them into very palatable food. Chicory's flavor is better when sautéed rather than blanched or steamed. Sautéing does involve cooking in fat, however, so if you're trying to eliminate fats from your diet, blanch or steam lettuces, drain, and dress with lemon juice or herbs and salt and pepper. A neighbor always boils chicory and then loads it with butter: I prefer to sauté the raw chicory in butter or oil and omit the boiling. I think there is a remarkable improvement in flavor.

Blanch lettuces when you have an extra-bitter crop. Drop them in boiling water for just a few minutes to leach out the strong taste and then drain, pat dry, and sauté. Blanching is also a necessary first step for preparing lettuce leaves for stuffing, as it softens the leaves just enough so you can roll them or form them around a filling. Use the large outer leaves of butterhead or iceberg lettuces—the butterheads end up with soft, silky textures, while iceberg results in a crisper dish.

Two European Salad Greens

Arugula (Rugula, Roquette, or Rocket Cress)
Arugula is a sharply flavored green popular in Italy. It grows best in the spring and fall. Sow as soon as the

Special Information

Yields
Lettuce bulk varies, depending upon the lettuce variety.
- 1 pound romaine lettuce = 20 leaves or approximately 16 cups of pieces
- 1 pound iceberg or butterhead lettuce = 10 cups pieces and 8 cups shredded
- 1 pound chicory = 12 cups pieces and 10 cups packed
- 1 pound raw lettuce = 4–5 2-cup servings
- 5 cups raw lettuce (approximately ½ pound) reduces to approximately 1 cup cooked lettuce
- Allow ½ cup cooked lettuce per serving
- 1 whole braised lettuce = 1 serving

Storage and Preserving
- Leave lettuce whole, and store, unwashed, in a plastic bag in the refrigerator. It should keep in good condition for 2–3 days.
- Dry washed lettuce thoroughly and store between layers of paper toweling, in a perforated plastic bag in the refrigerator. It will keep 2 days if stored correctly.

Hints
- Tear, rather than cut, lettuce into pieces; cutting discolors the edges.
- Always wait to toss greens with salad dressing until just before serving.

- Refrigerate greens; they turn limp quickly.
- Do not store lettuces with apples, pears, cantaloupes, or other foods that give off ethylene, which produces russet spotting.
- Prepare wilted lettuce salads as you would *Wilted Spinach Salad* (see *Spinach*).
- Use to wrap whole fish and fish fillets.
- Add sliced crisp lettuces, such as iceberg, to stir-fries.
- Use sautéed wilted greens in quiches: try a dandelion quiche.
- Make a watercress and *Cream of Cucumber Soup* (see *Cucumbers*).
- Make a lettuce purée by stewing 1 pound sliced lettuce in butter and shallots. Sauté lettuce in butter; cook rapidly to evaporate moisture. Combine with ½ cup cooked potato, then purée with butter and a bit of heavy cream. Reheat and season to taste.
- Substitute arugula or watercress for kohlrabi in *Kohlrabi Dumplings* (see *Kohlrabi*).
- Add sliced or chopped lettuce to soups and stews at the end of cooking.
- Use lettuce to roast a "no-fat" small chicken. Season the cavity, put a pierced lemon in the cavity, and

ground can be worked—around mid-April—in a row and cover with fine soil. Thin to 4 inches apart. Make successive sowings. Harvest 5–6 weeks after sowing. Sow seeds in late August for a fall crop.

Corn Salad, Lamb's Lettuce, or Mâche

Corn salad is a popular European salad green. In France, gardeners sow seeds in late fall which come up during the beginning of spring for a crop 8 weeks later. Broadcast corn salad in wide rows and thin for salads. Sow a fall crop in August.

Marketing

Buy crisp, firm lettuce with bright-colored leaves that show no signs of wilting or decay. Avoid overly watered lettuce. Check for browning edges. When lettuce has not been trimmed of very large outer leaves, remember you're paying for them.

roast chicken, breast side down, on a bed of old or outer lettuce leaves. The leaves provide moisture but no fat and keep the bird from sticking to the pan.

- Shred iceberg lettuce as a base for the elegant salad Crab Louis. Top lettuce with fresh crabmeat, garnish with wedges of hard-boiled egg and olives, and dress with *Joe Hyde's Russian Dressing* (see *Mixed Vegetables*) which you have lightened by folding in whipped cream.
- Combine cooked sharp lettuces such as escarole with pasta and grated cheese. Toss together or layer and bake topped with buttered bread crumbs.

Microwave

I do not recommend cooking lettuces in the microwave oven. I found poor color and some bitterness that was not evident when cooking by another method.

Leftovers

- Use leftover lettuce in soup.
- Cook and add to quiches.
- Slice raw leftover lettuce into salads to be used in egg or tuna fish sandwiches.

Compare lettuces by feeling the heft of them: even though the outer size is the same, some firm-headed lettuces will feel lighter because they have looser inner leaves. Choose a heavier head, you'll get more for your money. However, if they are very hard, they may be overmature.

◇ *Lettuces in Salads*

Vary two or three lettuce varieties in salads, both for looks and for texture. I accent Bibb lettuce with crisp romaine and sharp arugula; or toss red ruby lettuce leaves with Boston lettuce and top with small Belgian endive spears. Often I add fresh garden herbs or a thinly sliced white mushroom garnish. I decorate or make a border with lettuce, use it as a base for a composed salad, or make a "chiffonade" garnish for a salad platter by taking well-washed and dried lettuce leaves, folding them over on themselves, and slicing into thin strips.

Most lettuces are easily bruised and need gentle handling. Refrigerate washed and dried lettuce until serving time. I like to use small whole leaves, or I tear larger leaves into small leaf sizes. Sometimes it's possible to rearrange washed and dried butterhead lettuce leaves into a semblance of the original head, by opening and exposing the inner creamy leaves. In this case, serve the dressing on the side and dribble it across the leaves rather than tossing them.

I always wait to dress salads until just before I serve; otherwise the greens become soggy and limp. Most people put too much dressing on their salad. For 8 lightly packed cups of lettuce leaves, I use only 3–4 tablespoons of vinaigrette. If you use more dressing the lettuce absorbs too much oil and becomes greasy.

When I add additional ingredients to salad greens, such as cucumbers or green beans, I like to dress each ingredient separately and then combine, because then I know the entire salad is seasoned properly. When I serve salad on individual plates, I mound each portion in the center; how a salad looks makes such a difference!

My favorite tossed green salad dressing is a simple *Vinaigrette Sauce* (see *Appendix*), which can be altered by using different oils and vinegars. I'm partial to the heavy dark green Sicilian Amastra oil, which I combine with a lighter oil, or the delicate Colavita olive oil. Often I combine olive oil and vegetable oils for a lighter dressing. Be sure to ask for "first pressing virgin" or "extra virgin" oils because they're higher-quality. Walnut and hazelnut oils from specialty shops stand up to the strong, tart tastes of lettuces such as chicory or arugula (but nut oils become rancid quickly).

A good wine vinegar is fine for most salads, but it's fun to have a supply of different vinegars on hand. For a change of pace, I've tried the Italian Balsamic, as well as dill, tarragon, pear, and strawberry vinegars. Some salads, such as the *Greek Salad* with its mint and feta cheese flavors, go nicely with a lemon vinaigrette sauce.

We never use any dressing but a vinaigrette for tossed green salads, but occasionally I serve quarters of different lettuce varieties arranged on a platter, accompanied by side dishes of Roquefort or Russian dressing.

When I dress a salad using cruets of oil and vinegar, I first lightly coat the leaves with oil, sprinkle with vinegar to taste, season with salt and pepper, and toss together. Remember that a vinaigrette dressing is the simplest and best way to appreciate lettuce. When dressings become too complex or overpowering, you taste the dressings, not those crisp garden greens.

◇ Composed Salads

Lettuce forms a base or surrounding ring for many salads in which cold foods are combined and presented in artful arrangements. You can use such diverse foods as duck breast or pasta, or even arrange leftovers from the refrigerator. Two attractive main-course composed salads are *Salade Niçoise* or *Salmagundi* (see *Beans*).

I have a few important tips for all composed salads. The greens must be fresh and crisp and must not be dressed until just before serving. The best composed salads contain a careful selection of complementary ingredients. It is important to dress or marinate each ingredient separately so that the flavorings are just right.

Some possible toppings for greens are:
- Colorful vegetable juliennes blanched until just lightly tenderized (about 1 minute).
- Peeled, seeded, and chunked tomatoes and cucumbers marinated in wine vinegar and salt, along with feta cheese chunks drizzled with an herb-flavored vinaigrette.
- Julienned meats and poultry dressed separately and arranged in individual mounds.
- Chunks or flakes of fish arranged in mounds.

◇ Tossed Green Salad

Wash and dry 2–3 types of salad greens. Combine and top with any of these garnishes:
- Belgian endive spears
- Finely sliced mushrooms
- Watercress leaves
- Alfalfa sprouts
- Paper-thin sliced cucumbers
- Paper-thin sliced small zucchini
- Chopped fresh herbs such as dill, basil, chervil, chives
- Avocado slices dipped in lemon juice
- Baby spinach leaves
- Edible flower petals (such as nasturtiums or chive flowers)
- Chopped hard-boiled eggs
- Crumbled Roquefort cheese
- Chopped or julienned scallions
- Crumbled bacon

Dress with *Vinaigrette Sauce* (see *Appendix*) just before serving. Season with salt and pepper.

A Special Tossed Green Salad

Toss washed lettuce with *Vinaigrette Sauce* (see *Appendix*). Warm a slice of good-quality French goat cheese in the oven or under the broiler (on a low rack) until it is just beginning to melt. Place on top of the salad. The contrast of the warm cheese and the cool greens is wonderful. Tossing a green salad with vinaigrette and then topping with crumbled Roquefort cheese is also perfectly delicious.

◇ Lettuce Wedges

Select compact lettuce, trim the heads, wash, and pat dry. Cut lettuce into quarters or sixths. Depending upon its size, arrange on a platter and serve with a choice of dressings, *Creamy Roquefort* and *Yogurt Herb Dressing* (see *Appendix*) or *Joe Hyde's Russian Dressing* (see *Mixed Vegetables*).

◇ *Watercress Salads*

Watercress, which grows in marshy wetlands, is an elegant, colorful addition to a tossed salad. It is also delicious served by itself, and is one of the salads I'm addicted to. (Watercress seeds are available, but unless you have marshland conditions with fresh running water you will have no success.)

- *Watercress and Beet Salad:* Wash and dry watercress, removing the thickest stems. Thinly slice or julienne cooked beets. Just before serving, arrange a garnish of beets and crumbled cooked bacon on top of watercress. Toss with a strong mustard *Vinaigrette Sauce* (see *Appendix*), season with salt and freshly ground pepper, and serve.
- *Watercress and Endive Salad:* Combine equal parts of watercress and Belgian endive spears. Toss in a *Vinaigrette Sauce* (see *Appendix*). Season with salt and freshly ground pepper, and serve. Garnish with sliced mushrooms if you like.
- *Watercress and Mushroom Salad:* For 4 cups watercress, use ⅓ pound thinly sliced mushrooms and approximately 2 tablespoons *Lemon Vinaigrette Sauce* (see *Appendix*). Just before serving, toss together watercress and mushrooms with vinaigrette. Season with salt and freshly ground pepper to taste, and serve.
- *Watercress with Fruits:* Just before serving, top watercress with sliced pears or apples. Mash bleu cheese into *Vinaigrette Sauce* and toss all together.

◇ *Arugula Salad*

Arugula's earthy, mustardlike taste appeals to some people so much that they can make a whole meal out of just this salad. You can substitute arugula in watercress salads. Wash and dry the arugula. Chop garlic and toss with arugula. Use Sicilian Amastra oil or a good strong green olive oil and a red wine vinegar. Dress with oil, a bit of vinegar, and season with salt and pepper.

◇ *Corn Salad*

For something special, dress corn salad with a walnut oil dressing. Serve with wedges of ripe pear and creamy French goat cheese. The walnut oil accentuates the nutty taste of corn salad.
Note: Substitute arugula.

Dandelion Salad

Use only young and tender dandelion leaves; older greens can be tough and bitter.

½ lb dandelion leaves
2 hard-boiled eggs
1 tsp Dijon mustard
¼ cup lemon juice
Salt
½–⅔ cup olive oil
4–5 strips bacon
2 Tb wine vinegar
Freshly ground pepper

Wash the dandelion greens thoroughly by soaking in lukewarm water. Wash twice if necessary. Trim off any tough stems and dry well. Remove the egg yolks and mash in a bowl with mustard, lemon juice, and ½ teaspoon salt. Gradually beat in the oil. Finely dice the egg whites. Brown the bacon, drain on brown paper or paper bags, and crumble. Pour out bacon fat and add the vinegar to the pan. Just before serving, heat the vinegar and deglaze the pan. Toss the greens with dressing to coat, season with salt and pepper, add egg whites and bacon, and toss with the hot vinegar. *(Serves 4)*

- Omit the eggs, mash a garlic clove or two with salt, then combine with lemon juice, mustard, and oil.
- Omit mustard (and eggs if you like). Mash 5–6 chopped anchovies and proceed as above, adding additional chopped anchovies if you like a strong anchovy taste.
- Make a plain dandelion salad with the tossed greens and a vinaigrette sauce made with a richly flavored green olive oil or walnut oil.

Caesar Salad

This is my most favorite salad—it requires nothing more than fresh ingredients. Julia Child researched the history of this salad as created by Caesar Cardini in his restaurant in Tijuana, Mexico. He used only whole small and medium interior leaves, no anchovies (they were a later addition)—instead he added a dash of Worcestershire sauce. I appreciate his method of serving the salad with whole leaves, but I save that presentation for elegant dinner parties. Ordinarily I use every scrap of romaine, and break larger leaves across their width into good-size pieces. I enjoy anchovies, but my family is not as exuberant about them as I am, so I serve them as a garnish.

1 lb romaine lettuce
1 egg
1 garlic clove (optional)
Salt
½–⅔ cup good-quality olive oil
6–8 flat anchovies (optional)
1 lemon
½ cup freshly grated Parmesan cheese
Worcestershire sauce (optional)
Freshly ground pepper
Garlic Croutons (page 348)

Immerse lettuce in a sink of water. Remove leaves and wash thoroughly. Keep the small leaves whole and break the larger leaves crosswise into large pieces. The pieces should not be bite-size—this salad should be served with both a fork and a knife. Spin the lettuce dry, layer it with paper towels, and refrigerate wrapped in a plastic bag until ready to use. Boil a small pan of water. Drop in an egg and boil for 1 minute, then remove. Cut up the garlic clove (if you are using it) and mash it with 1 teaspoon salt. Whisk the olive oil into the garlic and salt. Halve the anchovies and place in a small bowl or plate.

When you are ready to serve, assemble all the ingredients. Place the romaine in a large salad bowl, pour on oil to coat, and toss well. Break the egg into the salad. Toss well again. Squeeze the lemon and pour in the juice; toss again. Add the Parmesan cheese, a dash of Worcestershire sauce (if you wish), and salt and pepper to taste. Add the croutons, and toss one last time. Serve with the anchovies as a garnish if you like. *(Serves 4)*

- Use only small or medium leaves of two 1-pound heads of romaine. Save the larger leaves for another salad. Serve 5–6 whole leaves per serving.

Greek Salad

A tart lemon vinaigrette and mint are essential in this salad.

    8 cups mixed lettuces
    2 cucumbers
    3 large ripe tomatoes
    3 scallions
    8–12 pepperoncini (optional)
    16 black Greek olives (optional)
    1 1/2 cups feta cheese
    Lemon Vinaigrette Sauce (page 352)
    2 Tb chopped fresh mint or 1 Tb dried
    Salt and freshly ground pepper

Wash, dry, and break the lettuces into bite-size pieces. Peel, score, and slice the cucumbers. (Seed if necessary.) Cut tomatoes into wedges. Chop the scallions. On each of 4 plates, arrange the lettuce, then distribute equally the cucumbers, tomatoes, and pepperoncini and olives if you like. Sprinkle with scallions. Break the feta cheese into chunks and distribute on top. Combine the vinaigrette and mint. Season well. Just before serving, pour dressing over the salads. *(Serves 4)*

- I often use cherry tomatoes, cut in half, and scored and sliced tender pickling cucumbers. Sliced radishes are nice.

◇ Sautéed Lettuces

I do like sautéed lettuces, particularly the sharply flavored varieties, and most often use the Italian treatment of sautéeing in olive oil (or olive oil and garlic) until the leaves are wilted and tenderized. Amazingly enough, this method softens the flavor of the sometimes bitter lettuces, making it unnecessary to blanch ahead of time. Use clarified butter, or a combination of oil and butter if you prefer. As the lettuces exude moisture, turn the heat up to high at the end of the sauté-braise to dry them out. All lettuces can be sautéed, although softer-textured lettuces do not stand up quite as well as the escaroles and chicories. I will give you an example for chicory, but you must adjust the timing for softer-textured lettuces.

Sautéed Chicory

Wash, dry, and chop 1 pound chicory. Heat about 1/4 cup olive oil in a large saucepan and add 1–2 teaspoons chopped garlic. Cook for 30 seconds (do not let brown) and add the chicory. Stir well to coat with oil. Cook, stirring, for 6–7 minutes until wilted and tenderized. When the chicory is tender and reduced, turn the heat to high to evaporate the moisture in the pan. Season to taste. The pound of chicory will have reduced to 2 cups.

Finishing Touches for Sautéed Lettuces

- Add heavy cream (1/2 cup or more as needed) *after* moisture is evaporated. Cook until the cream is reduced and coats the lettuce. Season with salt and freshly ground pepper.
- Add any of the following items to cooked lettuces, but heat through before serving. These ingredients are especially good for escaroles and chicories: anchovies; sliced black or green olives; toasted pine nuts; chopped sorrel leaves; and capers.
- Sauté chopped onions in oil before adding the garlic. Proceed as above.
- Add cooked shell or dried beans or refreshed canned Italian white beans to cooked sharply flavored lettuces or dandelion greens. Heat together before serving.

◇ Blanched Lettuces

Blanching is best when you want to avoid fats, need to wilt lettuces to use as wrappers, or wish to remove excessive bitterness.

- *Blanched Trimmed Lettuce:* Boil a pan of salted water, drop in the lettuces, and cook until just tender. Cooking time varies, depending upon the texture of the lettuces and the amount cooked at any one time. For example, 1/2 pound chicory will blanch in 4–5 minutes. *Do not cover the pan—you will lose color.*
- *Blanched Individual Leaves:* Drop into boiling salted water and press into the water with a perforated spatula: the leaves tend to float. Blanch 1 minute and remove with a spatula to a pot of cold water. The cooking time varies somewhat: some heavy leaves will take 2 minutes to blanch, thin leaves will be blanched in 30 seconds. Cool in the water, and remove to a dry towel. Pat dry. If blanching ahead of time, store the leaves between layers of toweling.

◇ Steamed Lettuces

Steaming has both advantages and disadvantages. The lettuce flavor is more pronounced when steamed, but the color is less bright because the lettuces tend to gray up or become darker. Boil 3/4–1 inch water in a steamer and place the lettuces in a basket or colander above the water. Cover the pan. One-half pound chicory will cook tender in approximately 8 minutes. The cooking time varies depending upon the lettuces' texture and the amount in the pot.

I do not steam individual leaves because they lose too much of their color.

Finishing Touches for Blanched or Steamed Lettuces

Drain before applying the finishing touches.
- Toss with anchovies or capers.
- Toss with herbs, such as chervil or lovage.
- Toss with lemon and seasonings.

Broth-Braised Lettuce

It's amazing that a vegetable that looks as light and airy as lettuce takes so long to braise. But the slow cooking produces an enticing liaison of vegetables and broth. I like escarole best, although you can use Boston or Bibb lettuce or chicory.

4 slices bacon
4 heads escarole
1 medium onion
1 carrot
4 Tb butter
Salt and freshly ground pepper
2 cups beef broth
Herb bouquet (optional):
    6 sprigs parsley
    1 bay leaf
    1/2 tsp thyme

Drop bacon into boiling water and simmer for 10 minutes. Drain, dry, chop, and set aside. Trim the lettuce base, and remove core and outer bruised or damaged leaves. Careful cleaning is absolutely necessary here! Gritty braised lettuce is a disaster. I part the leaves to let water run down among them, then fill the sink with warm water and soak the lettuces head down before plunging them up and down until they are clean.

Boil a large pot of water, plunge the lettuces in it, two at a time, let the water come to a boil, and cook the lettuces 2 minutes. Then place in a sink of cold water to cool down. (This is just to wilt them.) Drain. Halve lettuces lengthwise (or, if heads are small, leave them whole) and gently squeeze out the excess moisture. Fold the cut side in half on itself and set aside. Chop the onion and carrot, and sauté in 2 tablespoons of butter for 5 minutes.

Butter a baking dish the correct size to hold the lettuces, snugly. Spread the carrots, onions and blanched bacon in the pan and arrange the lettuces on top. Sprinkle with salt and pepper. Partially cover the lettuces with the beef broth and 1/2–1 cup water. Add herb bouquet. Bring broth to a simmer on top of the stove, cover lettuces with waxed paper, then cover with a lid or aluminum foil. Bake in a preheated 350° oven or simmer on top of the stove for 1 hour, checking occasionally to see that the liquid maintains a simmer. Remove the lettuces and herb bouquet and boil the liquid down to 1/2

cup. It will be syrupy. Beat in 2 tablespoons butter to thicken. Pour over lettuce. (*Serves 6–8*)

Stuffed Broth-Braised Lettuces

Here is an economic and filling stuffing, but you can use any favorite stuffing the same way. I like butterhead lettuces, such as our own Boston lettuce, which are also available year round in the markets. Pick heads that will trim down to 1/2 pound each. You can serve these lettuces with *Joe Hyde's Creole Sauce* (see *Appendix*) diluted with a few tablespoons of pan juices.

6 heads Boston lettuce
2 eggs
2 cups cooked smoked tongue (or ham, poultry, cooked meat)
2 cups fresh bread crumbs
2 Tb chopped parsley
2 Tb chopped shallots or scallions
2 1/2 cups broth, chicken or beef or combination
Salt and freshly ground pepper
4 Tb butter
1 cup sliced onions
1/2 cup sliced carrots
Herb bouquet (optional):
    6 sprigs parsley
    1 bay leaf
    1/2 tsp thyme

Trim and thoroughly wash the lettuces, leaving heads whole. Blanch in boiling water for 1–2 minutes—pushing down with a slotted spoon—and plunge into cold water. Drain and gently squeeze out moisture. Beat the eggs. Dice the meat and combine with eggs, bread crumbs, parsley, and shallots or scallions. Moisten with a tablespoon of broth, and season with salt and pepper. Mix again. Slice lettuces lengthwise without cutting through the cores and the bottom few leaves. Separate the center leaves and fill each lettuce with equal amounts of stuffing, tucking into the leaves wherever possible. Close each lettuce and tie with a string. Melt 2 tablespoons butter in a pan just large enough to hold the lettuces snugly. Sauté the onions and carrots for 5 minutes until wilted. Place lettuce bundles on top of vegetables. Add the optional herb bouquet and remaining broth. Bring the broth to a simmer, cover with waxed paper or parchment, cover with a lid, and cook at a simmer for 1 hour. (Or cook in a 350° oven, regulating the heat to keep at a simmer.) When the lettuces are done, remove, then drain. Cut the strings and keep warm. Boil down the cooking liquid to 1/2 cup and strain. Beat in 2 tablespoons butter to thicken slightly. Spoon over lettuces. (*Serves 6*)

Lettuce Custard

While the *Chicory Tian* that follows is particularly suited to chicory's sharp taste, this custard suits the milder flavors of butterhead, loose-leaf, and crisp lettuces. I usually combine lettuce varieties and find it an excellent way to use up the large outer leaves I've set aside when choosing inner leaves for a salad.

> 2 lb lettuce leaves
> 2 Tb butter (clarified if possible)
> ¼ cup grated Swiss or Parmesan cheese, or a combination
> Salt and freshly ground pepper
> Nutmeg
> 4 eggs
> 1¼ cups heavy cream

Wash, dry, and chop the lettuce. In a large saucepan, melt the butter and stir in the lettuce. Cover for 2 minutes until wilted, remove the cover, and cook over medium heat about 5 minutes, stirring occasionally, until completely wilted and tenderized. Then raise the heat and cook until any moisture evaporates—about 5 minutes. Drain and cool slightly.

Place lettuce in a bowl and mix in the cheese. Season with salt, pepper, and nutmeg. Beat the eggs, add the cream, and combine with lettuce. Butter a deep 1½-quart mold or casserole. Line bottom with buttered waxed paper. Pour in the custard. Place in a deep baking pan and pour boiling water halfway up the side of the mold. Bake in a preheated 350° oven for 45–50 minutes. Cool for 5 minutes before running a knife around custard. Unmold onto a warm plate. (*Serves 6–8*)
Note: This recipe also makes 8 individual 6-ounce custards. Cut down on the cooking time.

Chicory Tian

A tian, named after the earthenware container in which it is baked, is basically a gratin containing greens, garlic, and rice. You can substitute escarole or a variety of lettuces, spinach, and chard. This dish is also delicious served cold.

> 2½ lb chicory
> ⅓ cup plus 3 Tb oil
> 1 cup chopped onions
> 2–3 tsp chopped garlic
> ½ cup sorrel leaves (optional)
> Salt
> ½ cup rice
> ¾ cup grated Parmesan cheese
> Freshly ground pepper
> ½ cup fresh bread crumbs

Wash, dry, and chop the chicory. In a large saucepan, heat ⅓ cup of the oil and cook the onions until wilted, about 5 minutes. Add the garlic, stir for 30 seconds, then add the chicory, ½ pound at a time, stirring to coat with oil. Cook the chicory until slightly wilted. Add the sorrel (if you are using it), and cook until tender, about 7–8 minutes.

Meanwhile, bring salted water to a boil, add the rice, and cook 5 minutes. Drain. When the chicory is tender, lift it out of the pan and place it in a bowl. You should have approximately 5 cups. (Do not let the chicory completely drain, because you'll need some liquid to continue

cooking the rice.) Add the rice to the chicory along with ½ cup of the cheese. Season with salt and pepper. Put in a buttered 1½-inch-deep baking dish. Mix remaining cheese with the bread crumbs and sprinkle on top. Drizzle with the remaining olive oil and bake in a preheated 400° oven for 30–40 minutes. (*Serves 6–8*)

Warm Shrimp and Lettuce Salad

This is a colorful and different first course.

> 3 types of lettuces: Boston, ruby, romaine, or arugula
> 4 Tb butter
> 24 peeled raw medium shrimp or 40 small ones
> 8 chicken livers
> *Vinaigrette Sauce* (page 352)
> Small sprigs of chervil, dill, or mint

Select small lettuce leaves. Wash, pat dry, and arrange on 4 plates. Heat 2 tablespoons of the butter and sauté the shrimp until pink, then arrange on top of each platter. Sauté the chicken livers in butter until brown but still pink in the centers. Put two chicken livers in the center of each plate. Pour out butter in the pan, then deglaze the pan with vinaigrette. Pour the warm vinaigrette over the salads and decorate with herb sprigs. (*Serves 4*)

Lettuce and Oyster Appetizer

Here's an elegant and unusual appetizer.

> 8 large outer leaves of butterhead lettuce
> 24 oysters and their liquid
> 2 Tb melted butter
> *Lemon Butter Sauce* (page 346)

Drop lettuce leaves into boiling water for 30–60 seconds to slightly wilt. Drop into cold water, drain, and thoroughly dry. Spread them out and arrange 3 oysters in a row at the stem end of each leaf. Roll up, jelly-roll fashion, and place in a large sauté pan seam side down. Add the oyster liquid and the butter. Cover pan and bring liquids to a boil, reduce heat, and poach the packets for 2–3 minutes or until the lettuce is heated through and the oysters are plumped. Remove them with a slotted spoon, holding them above the pan for a moment to drain, and place 2 rolls on each of 4 warm plates. Spoon the lemon butter sauce around them and serve immediately. *(Serves 4)*

- Use iceberg lettuce (which gives a crunchier texture), spinach, or Swiss chard leaves.

Lettuce Leaf Dolmathis

Use thicker leaf lettuces in place of the traditional grape leaves of this Near Eastern appetizer.

>12 large lettuce leaves
>1 cup finely chopped onions
>3 Tb butter
>1 Tb sugar
>1 Tb salt
>1 Tb pepper
>1 1/2 cups rice
>1/2 cup chopped fresh herbs, such as dill and parsley
>Lemon juice
>Pine nuts
>1 1/2–2 cups chicken broth
>Olive oil (optional)

Trim lettuce leaves, blanch for 1 minute, and cool. Pat dry and set aside. Sauté onions in butter with sugar, salt, and pepper until wilted. Set aside. Meanwhile, blanch rice in boiling water for 5 minutes, drain. Mix with onion and add herbs. Taste and season with lemon juice and additional salt and pepper if necessary. Add pine nuts to taste.

Spoon mixture on leaves and roll, tucking in the ends and allowing some room for the rice to expand as it cooks further. Place seam sides down in a baking dish and pour over enough chicken broth to cover. Simmer for 30–40 minutes or until the rice is cooked through and tender. Cool lettuce rolls in the broth and drain. Sprinkle with olive oil if desired, and serve at room temperature. *(Serves 6)*

Hot Meat Filling

You will need 1 1/2–2 cups stuffing for 12 leaves. Grind 1–1 1/2 cups meat (lamb is particularly good); add bread crumbs, seasonings, and finely chopped celery and onions wilted in butter and moistened with broth. Blanch the leaves 1 minute, cool, and pat dry. Place about 2 tablespoons stuffing mixture on each lettuce leaf and roll up jelly-roll fashion, tucking in the ends. Place in a buttered baking dish, pour in enough broth to cover the pan bottom, and dot rolls with butter if desired. Cover with parchment or waxed paper, bring broth to a boil, then reduce heat to a simmer. Cover with a lid and cook until heated through and tenderized, about 30 minutes. (Bake in the oven at 350° for 30–40 minutes if you wish.) A nice touch is to strew julienned carrots and leeks on the bottom of the baking dish before topping with lettuce rolls. Serve the cooked julienned vegetables as a bed for the lettuce. *(Serves 6)*

Lettuce Soup

Here's a good way to use up the large outer leaves of lettuce.

>1 head lettuce or 3–4 cups leaves
>1 cup finely sliced onions or white of leeks
>1 cup julienned celery or fennel
>1/2 cup julienned carrots
>4 Tb butter
>2 Tb flour
>6 cups chicken or beef broth
>Salt and freshly ground pepper
>1/2 cup grated Parmesan cheese

Wash the lettuce and finely slice. Set aside. Sauté the onions or leeks, celery or fennel, and carrots in the butter until barely wilted. Stir in the flour and cook for 2–3 minutes. Add the broth, bring to a boil, and boil gently for 10 minutes. Add the lettuce and cook 5–8 minutes longer, or until the lettuce is tender. Season with salt and pepper. Serve with the Parmesan cheese on the side. *(Serves 4–6)*

- Add 1/4 cup rice or small pasta along with the broth.
- Cook until quite soft, purée, and add cream.

Arugula Soup

Here is a simple, satisfying way to enjoy this mustardy green. Note the "peasant" variation at end of recipe.

>2 cups arugula leaves
>1 lb potatoes
>1 lb leeks
>2 qt water or chicken broth
>Salt and freshly ground pepper
>1/2 cup heavy cream (optional)

Wash and dry the arugula. Set aside. Peel and chop the potatoes. Wash leeks, slice the white portion, combine with potatoes and add to water or broth and 1 tablespoon salt. Simmer for 25 minutes or until the vegetables are tender. Add the arugula and cook 10 minutes longer. Put through a food mill or purée in a processor (or a blender if you prefer a very fine texture). Season to taste, reheat, and serve. Add cream if desired. *(Serves 4–6)*

- *Peasant Style*: Do not purée. Serve with crusty toasted French or Italian bread rounds floating on top. Drizzle bread with olive oil and grated Parmesan cheese.
- Substitute watercress for arugula.

Escarole Soup

Escarole keeps its texture in a soup. Although this version has meatballs, they're not necessary. To eliminate fats, sauté the meatballs in a nonstick skillet before adding to the soup. However, you do lose the "dumpling" texture of the simmered meatballs.

1 egg
1 lb ground beef (or half pork and half beef)
1/2 cup fresh bread crumbs
3/4 cup grated Parmesan cheese
2 Tb chopped parsley
1 tsp minced garlic (optional)
Salt and freshly ground pepper
2 qt beef broth (or a combination of chicken and beef broth)
1/3 cup orzo pasta
2 heads escarole (1 1/2–2 lb)

Beat egg and combine with ground meat, bread crumbs, 1/4 cup of the cheese, parsley, and garlic (if you like). Season with salt and pepper. Form into 3/4-inch balls. Heat broth to boiling point and drop in the meatballs and the orzo. Cover pan and simmer for 15 minutes.

Meanwhile, wash escarole well and slice or chop into large pieces. Uncover the pan, add the escarole, and cook for 10 minutes or until wilted and tender. Serve with the remaining grated cheese. (*Serves 6–8*)
- Add diced carrots and celery.
- Substitute potatoes or cooked dried beans for the orzo.

Lettuce Pie

Select lettuces with some texture and bite. I often use outer escarole and chicory leaves, saving the inner hearts for salads. You can also incorporate leftover raw greens.

Double recipe *Tart Pastry* (page 351)
3 lb chicory, escarole, or a combination of lettuces
1/2 cup olive oil
1 Tb chopped garlic
12 black olives
1/4 cup toasted pine nuts
Salt and freshly ground pepper
1/4 lb peperoni (optional)
1 egg

Roll out 1/2 of the pie dough to 1/8-inch thickness, line a 10-inch pie plate, and partially bake. Set aside. Wash the lettuce, dry, and chop. In a large saucepan, heat the oil, add the garlic, and cook for 30 seconds. Gradually add lettuce. As it wilts, it will fit in the pan. Stir to coat with oil. Lower the heat and cook, uncovered, until tender. Sauté for about 10 minutes, stirring. Turn up the heat to evaporate any moisture in the pan.

Meanwhile, slice the olives, add to pan along with pine nuts, and season with salt and pepper to taste. Let cool. Slice the peperoni (if you are using it) paper-thin. Spread out half of the lettuce mixture in the pie shell. Add a layer of peperoni, then cover with the remaining lettuce. Roll out the remaining dough, and cover the pie. Seal the edges, flute, and prick the top. Brush the pastry with ice water, or an egg glaze made by beating the egg with 1 tablespoon water. Bake in a preheated 375° oven for 40 minutes or until the crust is golden brown. Serve either warm or at room temperature. (*Serves 6–8*)
- Use as a filling in *Pissaladière* (see *Onions*). Decorate with olives.
- Omit peperoni, substituting 5–6 chopped anchovies. Mix in.
- Substitute grated cheese for peperoni.
- Use the lettuce filling in quiches or pizzas.

Chicory Soufflé

You can use any lettuce in a soufflé, but the best choices are chicory, escarole, or romaine, which have the most assertive textures and flavor. Don't rule out arugula, dandelions, or a combination of any of these. The egg whites should be at room temperature for maximum volume.

5 1/2–6 Tb butter
1/4 cup grated Parmesan cheese
1/2 lb chicory
3 Tb chopped shallots or scallions
6 egg yolks
4 1/2 Tb flour
1 1/2 cups milk
1/2 cup grated Swiss or Cheddar cheese
1/2 tsp Worcestershire sauce
3–4 drops hot pepper sauce
Salt and freshly ground pepper
8 egg whites

Butter a 2-quart soufflé dish, completely coat with Parmesan cheese, and tie a buttered aluminum foil collar around the outer rim of the dish. Refrigerate until ready to use. Wash the chicory, and slice or chop into pieces. In 2 tablespoons of the butter, cook shallots or scallions until wilted, 2–3 minutes. Add the chicory with the water clinging to the leaves. Cover the pan and cook over low heat for 4–5 minutes until wilted. Remove cover, raise heat, and cook, without browning, until moisture evaporates, about 5 minutes longer. Set aside. You should have 1 1/4 cups chicory.

Beat the egg yolks and set aside. Heat the remaining butter and stir in the flour. Cook for 2–3 minutes. Whisk in the milk. Bring mixture to a boil, whisking, and boil for 1 minute. Beat a small amount of the hot liquid into the egg yolks to warm them slightly, then beat the egg yolks into the hot sauce. Stir in the lettuce, Swiss or Cheddar cheese, Worcestershire sauce, hot pepper sauce, and salt and pepper to taste. Let cool slightly.

Beat the egg whites until they form stiff peaks that still look moist, not dry. Stir one-quarter of the whites into the soufflé mixture to lighten it, then fold in the remaining whites. Pour the mixture into the soufflé dish, tap lightly on the counter, and smooth the top. Bake in a preheated 375° oven for 30 minutes or until the top is nicely browned; the inside should still be creamy. For a firmer texture, cook an additional 5 minutes. (*Serves 6*)

Lettuce-Wrapped and Stuffed Fillets of Fish

At the restaurant we make stuffed fish encased in brioche dough. Here, lettuce leaves seal together and wrap the fish in a mummylike layer of bright green. The same treatment works nicely with whole stuffed fish, but you will have to contend with the bones.

8–10 large outer leaves of iceberg lettuce
1/2 lb escarole
2 Tb olive oil
6 Tb butter
1 tsp minced garlic
1/2 cup fresh bread crumbs
Salt and freshly ground pepper
2 Tb chopped shallots
2 fillets of fish, 1 lb each
1/2–3/4 cup dry white wine or vermouth
1 cup heavy cream

Blanch the lettuce leaves for 1 minute, cool, drain, and lay out on a towel; pat dry. Wash, dry, and finely chop the escarole. Heat the oil and 2 tablespoons of the butter, and add the garlic. Cook for 30 seconds. Add the escarole and cook until wilted and tender, 6–7 minutes. Turn up the heat for a moment to evaporate the moisture. Add the bread crumbs and season with salt and pepper. Cool.

Sprinkle shallots in a buttered long ovenproof dish. On top of the shallots, arrange the lettuce leaves in two rows slightly overlapping in the center. Skin fish if desired. Place one fish fillet down the center, skin side down. Season with salt and pepper. Spread the stuffing across the fish, then top with the second fish fillet, skin side up. Salt and pepper the second fillet. Fold in the let-

tuce leaves on both sides, encasing the fish, and tuck in the ends. The fish should be completely encased in the lettuce. Pour in enough wine to cover the bottom of the dish, and dot with 1 tablespoon of the butter. Top with parchment or waxed paper. Cover with a lid or aluminum foil, and place in a preheated 400° oven. Bake for approximately 20 minutes, depending on the thickness of the fillets.

Meanwhile, reduce the cream to 3/4 cup. When the fish comes out of the oven, pour the cooking juices into a small saucepan; reduce by half. Add the cream and reduce to a syrup consistency. Off the heat, beat in the remaining butter. Season to taste and serve with the fish. (*Serves 6*)

- Use any lettuce with a broad outer leaf.
- Vary the stuffing: use spinach, mushroom duxelles, or a celery stuffing.
- Make a *White Butter Sauce* (see *Appendix*).

Lettuce Packets of Sole and Smoked Salmon

The lettuce provides moisture so the fish doesn't dry out, and wraps the fish in a very pretty package.

8 large leaves of butterhead or a crisp lettuce
Four 6-oz fillets of gray sole, skinned
Salt and freshly ground pepper
8 paper-thin slices smoked salmon
2–3 Tb chopped shallots or white of leeks
3/4 cup dry white wine or vermouth
3 1/2 Tb butter
1/2 cup heavy cream
Lemon juice (optional)

Blanch the lettuce leaves in boiling water for 1 minute, pushing down with a perforated spatula. Using the spatula, place the lettuce in a bowl of cold water. Drain on towels and pat dry. Lightly score the dark side of the fillets and place on work surface scored side up. Season with salt and pepper. Place 2 salmon slices on each fillet, then fold the ends up and over, forming an envelope. Wrap each fillet in 2 lettuce leaves, tucking in ends.

Sprinkle shallots or leeks in a buttered sauté pan. Place lettuce packets seam side down in the pan. Pour in the wine and dot each packet with 1 teaspoon of the butter. Cover with parchment or waxed paper and then cover the pan. Bring the wine to a boil and simmer for about 8–10 minutes. (Or, bake in a preheated 400° oven for 10–12 minutes.) Remove the fish packets to a warm platter. Strain the pan juices, add the cream to them, and boil until reduced to a medium-thick consistency. Off the heat, beat in 2 tablespoons cold butter. Season with salt and pepper and lemon juice if desired. Serve with fish packets. (*Serves 4*)

- Omit the salmon and use other stuffings such as fish mousse or fresh chopped herbs and butter.
- If you wish, serve with the pan juices or make a *Lemon Butter Sauce* (see *Appendix*).
- For an elegant touch add a dollop of caviar.

Watercress Sauce

This makes a pretty sauce for poached or sautéed chicken breasts. If you're sautéeing the breast, deglaze the chicken pan drippings with the ½ cup white wine before adding it to the shallot-butter sauce base.

2 bunches watercress, approximately 1 lb
3 Tb butter
2 Tb chopped shallots
½ cup white wine
1 cup heavy cream
Salt and freshly ground pepper
Lemon juice (optional)

Wash and thoroughly dry the watercress. Remove the heavy stems, and roughly chop the leaves. Heat 1 tablespoon of the butter and stir in the watercress. Lower the heat, cover, and cook until tender, 2–3 minutes. Place in a food processor and chop into fine small pieces (or chop finely by hand). In 1 tablespoon of the butter, cook shallots until wilted. Stir in the wine and boil rapidly until reduced by half. Add the cream and, once again, cook rapidly until the sauce has a thick consistency. Add the watercress and reheat. Season to taste with salt and pepper. Off the heat, beat in the remaining butter. Add drops of lemon juice if desired. (*Makes about 1½ cups*)

Salsify

Salsify (opposite page) and scorzonera (at right) are rarely found in America outside of Italian and French markets, although they are widely grown in Europe. Americans just aren't familiar enough with these unusual root vegetables to demand them as a commercial crop.

Although their skin color, leaf, and root shapes differ, salsify and scorzonera cook up almost identically, so I am treating them as one in this section. When a recipe calls for salsify, you can always substitute scorzonera. These vegetables—members of the daisy family—are easy to grow and are seldom bothered by pests or diseases.

Salsify, a biennial, is savored for its roots and the second year's crop of young shoots. Even though salsify resembles parsnips in color and shape, it is not as sweet, but has a more delicate texture. Because of its faint oysterlike taste (which is accentuated by cooking) salsify is often nicknamed "oyster plant." Some say its flavor suggests coconuts and artichokes, while others swear it tastes like asparagus. I guess it's all in your taste buds!

Salsify's distant relative, scorzonera—or black salsify—has brownish black skin and longer, more slender roots. (I've cooked Belgian scorzonera that had roots 12–14 inches long.) In much of France and Italy, scorzonera is the vegetable you'll be given when you ask for salsify. Because of its darkly pigmented skin, scorzonera fell

out of favor in Victorian times; however, many people consider its flavor more delicate and superior to that of salsify. Although I find the flavors similar, scorzonera's coconut flavor is more pronounced and is especially noticeable in a purée or when eaten raw. By the way, scorzonera contains inulin. As with Jerusalem artichokes, some people may end up with gastric distress. Don't eat too much at any one time until you find out whether or not you're affected.

Because salsify and scorzonera are rarely grown, even by the home gardener, the seeds can be hard to find: large seed companies such as Burpee, Stokes, and Harris carry

the Mammoth Sandwich Island salsify, while DiGeorgi stocks scorzonera.

Both vegetables are deep-rooted and need deeply cultivated soil: stones and/or heavy manuring cause root forking. To make life simpler, Russ forms planting holes with a crowbar, just as he does with parsnips. In late April or early May, he rotates a crowbar in the soil until he has formed a cone-shaped hole 16–18 inches deep and 3 inches across. He spaces the holes 9 inches apart, fills each hole with sifted compost or soft soil, and sows three seeds 1 inch deep in each hole. When the seedlings are 2 inches high, he thins to one seed per hole. During the summer, the plants need no further attention other than regular weeding and watering. (Watering is most important during dry weather, because without water, the plants tend to go to seed.)

We wait until mid-October to harvest the roots. As the taproots grow deep (particularly in scorzonera), it is important to lift them carefully out of the ground, taking care not to puncture or bruise them. With a spading fork, we loosen the soil near the plants and then dig each root out of the ground. We're careful to not pull on the roots because they bleed easily, affecting storage.

The best possible time to harvest salsify and scorzonera is just before cooking—they wither quickly unless you are storing in sand. Once you dig the roots, wash them well and they are then ready to prepare. If you must hold them, brush off the dirt and refrigerate in a perforated plastic bag.

If you want to store the vegetables inside, dig up the entire crop in October and store in damp sand in a humid cellar. Or, if your climate permits, mulch and store in the ground. The mulch protects the vegetables, which can be dug as long as the ground is workable. Should you decide to winter over the roots, the second spring let the shoots, or "chards," grow 5–6 inches long. (Blanch by covering with a flowerpot.) Cut them and cook like asparagus, or use the raw leaves in a salad, where they'll taste a bit like Belgian endive.

As the flesh of both salsify and scorzonera darkens when exposed to air, they should be placed immediately in acidulated water when you're peeling before cooking. I find it easiest to cut into 4–5-inch lengths, pare rapidly with a vegetable peeler or paring knife (removing as little skin as possible), and drop into the acidulated water until cooking time. You can also cook the vegetables before peeling: cut them into 4–5-inch lengths and drop into boiling water. After the vegetables cook, rinse under cold water and push off the skins. (The scorzonera skin peels off like strips of bark.) If the vegetables are even the slightest bit overcooked, the flesh adheres to the skin and you end up with a lot more waste. Don't use the cooking water for a sauce if the scorzonera roots haven't been peeled.

When you're using raw salsify or scorzonera in a recipe remember that the flesh will immediately darken unless you grate directly into an acidic dressing or into a batter to be cooked up right away. I don't eat either as a raw vegetable because their flavors are enhanced by cooking.

Although both salsify and scorzonera can be formed into logs or slices and sauté-braised, the most practical initial preparation is to boil or blanch in acidulated water or in a mixture called a *Blanc* (see *Appendix*). Often I don't bother with this mixture—it does keep the flesh white, but when you add lemon juice to the cooking water, the flesh retains an attractive creamy color. Steaming works equally well, but the vegetables darken slightly.

Once salsify and scorzonera are boiled, blanched, or steamed, they can be finished any number of ways—but do choose sauces which accentuate, not overpower, their delicate flavor.

Marketing

Salsify and scorzonera are not commercial crops. Your best bet is to cultivate a home gardener who grows them as a crop. Should you find a farm stand that carries them, make sure the vegetables have received proper storage. Unless they have been stored in a cool, damp place, they wither and lose their mild flavor. Judge the roots as you would carrots or parsnips: they should be firm and crisp, not limp and soft.

◇ Blanched or Boiled Salsify

Wash salsify or scorzonera, peel (see page 255), cut into 3–4-inch lengths, and keep in acidulated water. Boil salted water and add lemon juice or make a *Blanc* (see *Appendix*). Cook the salsify at a gentle boil for approximately 10 minutes or until just tender. Slices or logs will cook faster, in approximately 7 minutes. If you are planning to purée or mash, cook until soft, about 15 minutes or slightly longer.

◇ Steamed Salsify

Bring 3/4–1 inch of water to a boil in a steamer. Place washed sections of peeled or unpeeled salsify or scorzonera in a steamer basket or colander. Steam for 10–15 minutes or until barely tender.

Finishing Touches for Blanched or Steamed Salsify

- *With Butter:* Roll cooked salsify in melted butter and season with salt, pepper, and drops of lemon juice.
- *With Cream:* Roll in butter as above, add cream, and cook rapidly to thicken and coat the salsify.
- *With Browned Butter:* Cook butter until darkly browned but not burned. Pour over drained cooked salsify.

Special Information

Yields

- 1 pound salsify or scorzonera = approximately 3/4 pound trimmed and peeled = approximately 3 cups logs or 2–2 1/2 cups cooked and diced = 1 1/3 cups puréed
- 1 pound = 3 servings

Storage and Preserving

- Salsify dehydrates quickly. Do not store at room temperature, but keep, unwashed, in a perforated plastic bag in the refrigerator, where it will hold 3–4 days.
- Do not freeze.
- Store in the ground until ground freezes. Before a winter frost, dig up the salsify and layer in sand in a cool cellar. Or mulch heavily and store in the ground as you would parsnips.

Hints

- Use a stainless steel knife when cutting to avoid discoloration.
- Put peeled salsify into acidulated water to prevent discoloring.
- Add to hearty soups or stews. Add cooked salsify during the last few minutes of cooking. Add raw salsify for 1 hour of cooking: see *Sautéed-Braised Salsify— Whole Pieces.*

- Substitute grated salsify for Jerusalem artichokes in *Lacy Jerusalem Artichoke Pancakes* (see *Jerusalem Artichokes*).
- Use the cooking liquids in cream sauces.
- Use in mild-flavored dishes, such as those made with fish, chicken, or veal.
- Substitute salsify in many of the Jerusalem artichoke, carrot, and parsnip recipes, but do select mild-flavored recipes.

Microwave

- 1 pound salsify, peeled and cut into logs and placed in a dish with just the water clinging to it, will cook tender in 6–7 minutes.

Leftovers

- Combine puréed or whipped salsify with whipped potatoes.
- Purée, add an egg, make patties, and sauté them in butter.
- Use chopped salsify in a hash; see *Turkey and Salsify Hash.*
- Reheat with other cooked vegetables or use in cold salads.

- *With Garlic:* Make browned butter, add minced garlic, swirl around the pan, and pour over cooked salsify. Sprinkle with parsley.
- *Glazed:* Roll salsify in melted butter, lightly sprinkle with sugar, and cook until glazed.

- *With Béchamel Sauce:* Drain cooked peeled salsify, saving the cooking liquid. (This is not for scorzonera that you have cooked unpeeled.) Slice, if desired. For 4 cups make *Béchamel Sauce* (see *Appendix*), using half cooking liquid and half cream. Reheat the salsify in the sauce. Or bake it in a 1 quart casserole until the sauce is bubbly. Top with buttered bread crumbs or grated cheese and pats of butter. Heat in a

450° oven for 10 minutes to brown the top.
- *With Root Vegetables:* Prepare salsify and carrot logs or salsify, parsnips, and carrots. Cook, then combine with butter and herbs; or serve side by side.
- *With Cheese and Cream:* See *Jerusalem Artichokes* (page 139), substituting 2 cups salsify for the Jerusalem artichokes.
- *With Mornay Sauce:* Make a *Mornay Sauce* (see *Appendix*) and combine with 1½ pounds cooked salsify. Bake in the oven until hot and bubbly.
- *With Vinaigrette Sauce:* Drain cooked salsify and, while still warm, pour over well-flavored *Vinaigrette Sauce* (see *Appendix*). Either eat warm or chill and return to room temperature before serving.
- *With Poulette Sauce:* See *Salsify Poulette.*

◇ *Sautéed-Braised Salsify*

Sliced Salsify

Wash, peel, and slice salsify and drop into acidulated water. When ready to cook, remove salsify from water and pat dry. Melt butter in a sauté pan and add the sliced salsify. Turn in butter for 30 seconds until coated, squeeze over some fresh lemon juice, and turn the salsify in the juice. Cover and cook over low heat for 7–8 minutes, stirring occasionally so that the salsify does not burn.

Whole Pieces

Peel thin salsify or scorzonera so you will have long, round sticks, approximately ³/₄ inch thick. Cut these sticks into 2–3-inch pieces and place in acidulated water. Just before sautéing, drain and pat dry. Brown the salsify in butter, cooking over medium heat for approximately 10 minutes. Add ¼ inch of beef or chicken broth, and cover. Braise the salsify until tender, about 5–10 minutes, adding more broth if necessary.

Finishing Touches for Sautéed-Braised Salsify

- *Glazed:* Sprinkle with sugar and cook until lightly glazed.
- *With Broth:* Before covering pan, add ½ cup chicken or beef broth and cook salsify almost tender; remove cover and cook until broth is reduced and just coats the salsify.
- *With Onion:* Sauté sliced onion in butter until lightly browned. Add sliced salsify and proceed as above.
- *With Cheese:* Sprinkle salsify with finely grated Parmesan cheese.

Salsify Purée

This is one of my favorite purées. It's amazingly delicate and is a lovely accompaniment to other purées as well as an excellent filling for vegetable shells.

1 lb salsify
Acidulated water or *Blanc* (page 346)
2–3 Tb butter
3–4 Tb cream
Salt and freshly ground pepper
Lemon juice

Wash and peel the salsify, drop into acidulated water, then chunk it and cook in blanc or boiling acidulated water until tender. (Cook until very tender or the purée will be grainy.) Drain, and finely purée with butter and cream. Add salt and pepper to taste, and drops of lemon juice. Reheat over a double boiler for 10–15 minutes to concentrate the flavor. (*Makes about 1⅓ cups*)
- Omit the cream and beat the purée with an egg. Chill until firm and drop spoonfuls of the mixture into hot butter. Press down, forming small patties, and fry on both sides.
- Combine with an equal amount of whipped potatoes and pipe into vegetable shells.

Salsify Poulette

This slightly tart sauce that goes so well with mussels and shellfish also emphasizes the "oyster" flavor of salsify.

1 1/2 lb salsify
Acidulated water or *Blanc* (page 346)
Lemon juice
2 Tb butter
2 Tb flour
1 cup milk
2 egg yolks
Salt and freshly ground pepper
2 tsp chopped parsley

Wash and peel the salsify and drop into acidulated water. When ready to cook, slice into diagonal pieces or into logs. Drop into the blanc or boiling acidulated water, and cook until just tender, 8–10 minutes, depending upon size. Drain the cooked salsify, saving 1 cup cooking liquid, and set aside in a warm bowl.

Melt the butter, blend in the flour, and stir over medium heat for 2–3 minutes without browning to cook the flour. Remove from heat and beat in the reserved cooking liquid and milk, whisking until smooth. Return sauce to the heat and bring to a slow boil. Boil sauce for 2–3 minutes to thicken; reduce the heat and simmer for 10 minutes, stirring occasionally. Beat the egg yolks in a small bowl, gradually beat in a little of the hot sauce to warm the eggs, then add eggs to the hot sauce. Reheat, without boiling, then stir in lemon juice to taste, about a tablespoon. Season with salt and pepper, and stir in the chopped parsley. Mix with salsify and reheat, if necessary, but do not boil. (*Serves 4*)

Fried Salsify

Fried salsify is a delicious hot appetizer to serve with drinks. Prepare it with either a crumb or a batter coating.

With Crumbs
1 lb salsify
Acidulated water or *Blanc* (page 346)
2 eggs
1 tsp salt
1 cup dried bread crumbs
1/4 cup grated Parmesan cheese (optional)
1/2 cup flour
Vegetable oil

Wash and peel the salsify, cut into logs, and place in boiling acidulated water or blanc. Blanch for 6–7 minutes, until just barely tender. Cool and drain. Beat eggs in a shallow dish and stir in salt. Combine bread crumbs and cheese on waxed paper. Dip salsify logs into flour, shake, dip into egg, then roll in the crumb-cheese mixture. In a deep fryer or deep saucepan, heat 3 inches oil to 375°. Lower the salsify into the oil and deep-fry until crisp, about 1 minute. Drain and serve, sprinkled with additional salt if desired. (*Serves 3–4*)

- Marinate the blanched salsify in an oil and lemon

Vinaigrette Sauce (see *Appendix*) for 15 minutes. Then proceed with flour, eggs, and crumbs.

With Batter
1 lb salsify
Batter: Use *Lemon Juice Batter*, or *Beer Batter* (see *Appendix*)
Salt

Prepare and cook salsify as above. Coat with batter and deep-fry until batter is lightly browned. Season with salt. (*Serves 3–4*)

- Substitute carrot sticks or parsnips, etc.

Cream of Salsify Soup

Call this Oyster Bisque and mystify your friends.

2 lb salsify or scorzonera
Acidulated water
3/4 lb potatoes
2 Tb butter
1/2 cup chopped onions
6 cups chicken broth
1/2 cup light cream
Salt and freshly ground pepper
Chervil or lemon balm sprigs (optional)

Peel salsify or scorzonera and cut into 1-inch chunks; drop into acidulated water. Peel the potatoes, cut into 1-inch chunks, and hold in water until ready to use. Melt the butter in a 3–4-quart saucepan and cook the onion until wilted. Add the salsify, potatoes, and chicken broth. Bring to a boil, reduce the heat, and cook, covered, until the vegetables are soft, 15–20 minutes. Purée very fine in a blender or put through a sieve. Add cream, reheat, and season to taste. Garnish with sprigs of chervil or lemon balm if you like. (*Serves 6*)

Salsify with Seafood

The subtle flavors of fish and salsify mesh for a light and lovely meal.

1 1/2–2 lb salsify
Acidulated water or *Blanc* (page 346)
2 lb thick fish fillets (haddock, cod, or bass)
3 Tb butter
4 Tb oil
1 cup finely sliced onions
1 cup finely sliced carrots
1 cup finely sliced sweet red peppers
1 cup finely sliced green peppers
1 tsp chopped garlic
Salt and freshly ground pepper
Flour
1 Tb fresh thyme or tarragon (optional)
1/2 cup dry vermouth or white wine
1 cup fish or chicken stock
1/4 cup chopped parsley

Wash and peel salsify; cut into logs and drop into acidulated water. Blanch in boiling salted lemon water or

blanc for 10 minutes. Drain and set aside. Cut fish into serving pieces. In a large sauté pan, melt butter and 1 tablespoon of the oil. Add the onions, carrots, and peppers. Sauté over medium heat, stirring, until lightly colored and wilted, 5–6 minutes. Add the garlic and salt and pepper; sauté 2 minutes longer. Remove the vegetables from the pan and set aside.

Heat the remaining oil in the pan. Dip the fish into flour and shake to remove excess. Sauté in oil 1–2 minutes on each side to lightly brown, removing pieces once they brown. Return sautéed vegetables to the pan, place the fish on top of them, and strew with the salsify. Season with salt, pepper, and herbs. Pour in the wine and broth, cover, and simmer for 8–10 minutes or until the fish and salsify are tender. Pour liquids into a small saucepan and rapidly boil down to reduce. Arrange the fish and vegetables on a plate and baste with the reduced juices. Garnish with parsley before serving. (*Serves 4*)

- Substitute 2 cups peeled, seeded, and chopped tomatoes for the peppers.

Veal and Salsify Ragout

2 lb salsify or scorzonera
Acidulated water
2 lb leeks
2 lb stewing veal
Salt and freshly ground pepper
Flour
3 Tb butter
3 Tb oil
Juice of 1/2 lemon
1/2 cup dry vermouth or white wine
3 cups veal or chicken broth
Herb bouquet:
    4 sprigs parsley
    1 tsp thyme
    1 bay leaf

Wash and peel the salsify or scorzonera and cut into 2-inch lengths. (If thicker, cut into 3/4-inch logs.) Drop into acidulated water. Remove green portions of the leeks, wash the white portions well, and slice. You should have 4 cups. Cut the veal into 2-inch pieces, season with salt and pepper, dust with flour, and shake off the excess.

Melt the butter and oil in a large saucepan or deep sauté pan and brown meat; set aside. Drain salsify or scorzonera, pat dry, and brown in oil and butter over medium-low heat, adding lemon juice and seasoning with salt and pepper. Cook about 10 minutes, turning to lightly brown all over. Remove. Add the chopped leeks, toss with pan juices, cover, and slowly cook for 5 minutes without browning. Add the wine and broth, bring to a boil, return the meat and salsify or scorzonera to the pot, and add the herb bouquet. Season with salt and pepper and bring broth to a boil. Partially cover, lower heat, and gently simmer for 1 hour. The pan juices will thicken; however, if you want a thicker sauce, drain the pan juices into a saucepan and reduce by boiling. Taste for seasoning, and pour over meat mixture. (*Serves 4–6*)

- Substitute chicken, duck, or goose for veal. Skin and defat the poultry and cut into pieces before flouring. Extend the cooking time for goose if necessary until the meat is tender and just about ready to fall off the bone.
- Add garlic or blanched, diced, and sautéed salt pork for a more robust flavor.
- Use as a filling for a meat pie.

Turkey and Salsify Hash

Try this with leftover turkey and leftover salsify; or cook the salsify and use any leftover poultry or meat. Serve with leftover gravy if you have any on hand.

1/2 cup butter
1 cup chopped onions
1/2 cup chopped sweet red pepper
1 tsp chopped garlic (optional)
3 cups chopped cooked salsify
4 cups chopped cooked turkey
3 Tb chopped parsley
1/2–3/4 cup cream
Lemon juice
Salt and freshly ground pepper

Melt 2 tablespoons of the butter, sauté onions and red pepper until slightly wilted, and add garlic (if you wish). Scrape into a bowl along with the salsify, turkey, parsley, enough cream to moisten, drops of lemon juice, and salt and pepper. Heat the remaining butter in a large sauté pan and cook mixture over medium heat until heated through, turning to blend. Brown lightly. (*Serves 4*)

Spinach

Spinach is the first crop we plant; the day the seeds go into the ground symbolizes the real beginning of spring to me. In a few weeks we'll be savoring the thinnings in salads and other early-season recipes where only the tenderest of leaves will do. This tenderness, of course, is the main reason we grow our own spinach. As with so many other vegetables, commercial spinach is bred for shipping, with thicker, tougher leaves suitable only for recipes in which tenderness isn't crucial. While browsing through a seed catalog the other day, I noticed a commercial variety described as having leaves rugged enough to withstand long-distance travel. That's why I cook with home-grown spinach whenever possible.

We've tried numerous spinach varieties both at the Victory Garden plot and at our home, but we keep coming back to these three: Melody, with fairly smooth upright leaves, making it easy to clean; Bloomsdale, an old-fashioned type popular for more than eighty years; and a recent introduction, America, a thick-leafed, crinkly variety that holds in good condition two weeks later than most spinach before bolting to seed. On occasion, we've also grown New Zealand spinach, which has the advantage of thriving in hot weather when standard spinach

cannot be grown. Served raw, it's rather bland, but cooked it's much like the spinach we know. Two other spinachlike greens, Malabar spinach and Tampala, also flourish in hot weather, but I find their flavor no match for spinach.

Russ prepares a spot for spinach in the fall so, come spring, he'll be able to plant the day the ground thaws a couple of inches. He broadcasts the seeds—almost as if he were sowing lawn seeds—onto a 16-inch-wide raised bed which warms up quickly and has room for lots of thinnings. I thin whole plants, leaving the remaining plants to mature. When this early crop is finished in late spring, we wait until August before planting a fall crop which stays in good condition until December.

Remember that spinach has a water content of 80–90 percent, making it wilt easily and be very perishable. Don't wash spinach before storing, for even if it's dried, some water lurks on the leaves, causing them to rot.

Unfortunately, spinach is gritty. Those crinkly leaves that look so beautiful in the garden trap soil and dust, necessitating careful cleaning before serving. I take my time in washing, for there's no shortcut to absolutely clean spinach: biting into particles of grit can ruin an otherwise pleasant meal. I dump unwashed spinach into a sink filled with lukewarm water. (At first I used lukewarm, rather than cold, water because I disliked getting my hands cold. I quickly learned that dirt floats off faster in lukewarm water, making it the major key to really clean spinach.) Then I remove the roots, placing the leaves on the drainboard. After cleaning the sink and refilling it with lukewarm water, I dunk the leaves until they come clean or, if necessary, run them under the tap. I repeat this until no grit is left in the sink, then whirl the leaves in a salad spinner or dry them in an absorbent towel. The spinach is now ready to be cooked, or can be refrigerated for a short time, wrapped in paper towels.

When I cook young spinach, I keep the stems, for they add texture to the finished dish. Older spinach stems, which tend to be woody or tough, get tossed right into the compost heap. To stem spinach quickly and easily, fold each leaf over lengthwise along its stem so that the underside faces you. Holding the leaf in the center, rip off the stem with your other hand. Often the stem breaks off near the leaf tip, which is perfectly fine, because by then it's too small to matter.

Cooked properly, spinach has a lovely taste and appearance. I like the way its dark green color picks up other food colors and the liaison it creates with fish, cheese, and poultry. I usually blanch spinach, because that way it retains its beautiful color and tart pleasant flavor. Occasionally, when I'm cooking a small amount of spinach, I'll steam it, or sauté it without blanching. All methods work well and can be interchanged in recipes calling for cooked spinach.

Whatever you do, however, don't let the spinach become waterlogged. When spinach sits around in water even a moment too long, all the nutrients start to leach out and it becomes gray and flavorless. I suspect that many people who claim to dislike spinach actually overcook it, ruining its texture and flavor, while other people who object to the taste of spinach really don't like its smooth texture. Add contrast by garnishing with something crunchy, such as croutons or pine nuts, and I wager you'll like the result. Spinach is slightly acidic, creating a pungent aftertaste I happen to like. If this bothers you, cooking spinach with lots of cream and butter neutralizes the acidity, resulting in a richer-tasting, subtler vegetable.

Marketing

Find a store that sells unbagged spinach. (Often packaged spinach has a high proportion of stems and damaged leaves.) Buy only dark green spinach with fresh bouncy leaves. If you are able to find only packaged spinach, be sure to open up the cellophane and discard any damaged leaves before refrigerating.

Special Information

Yields
- 2–3 pounds fresh spinach = 2 cups cooked spinach. The weight varies, depending upon age, water content, and variety
- 1/2 cup cooked spinach = 1 serving

Storage and Preserving
- Store, grit and all, in your vegetable bin, where the spinach will stay in good condition for 3–4 days.
- Frozen spinach is handy, particularly in recipes where it's used as one of several ingredients. Count on 1 1/2 pounds fresh spinach for each pint of frozen spinach, or 1 bushel (18 pounds) for 12–16 pints. Clean and stem the leaves, blanch for 2 minutes in boiling water, cool, and pack in freezer containers.

Hints
- Don't cook in aluminum. The spinach picks up an acidic taste and becomes grayish.
- Use for fillings, or make a roulade. See *Rutabaga Roulade*.

- Chiffonade leaves and add to soups for the last few minutes.
- Add young leaves to tossed green salads.
- Use sautéed or creamed spinach as a bed for other foods. Try topping with oysters, poached eggs, chicken breasts, or fish fillets.

Microwave
- 8 ounces of trimmed spinach leaves, placed in a covered dish with just the water clinging to the leaves, will cook tender in 3 minutes.

Leftovers
- Combine leftover spinach with grated Cheddar or Swiss cheese. Heat together and serve on toast.
- Puréed spinach adds color to *Potato Gnocchi* or to homemade pasta.
- Add to omelets.
- Make a puréed spinach soup.

◇ Blanched Spinach

Boil 6 quarts salted water. Add spinach bit by bit, so that the water keeps boiling. After it has come to a second rolling boil, count on 2–5 minutes to cook, depending upon the spinach's age. Then, immediately place in the sink and let cold water run into the pot—the spinach

won't flow over the side. When the water is cold, drain and squeeze the spinach to remove all the water. At this point the spinach can be reheated or refrigerated for later preparation. (See *Finishing Touches*.)

◇ Steamed Spinach

Boil 1 inch of water in a steamer or pot, and place the washed and trimmed spinach into the steamer basket or colander with just the water clinging to its leaves. Place in pot and cover. Do not overcook: 2 pounds of fresh spinach should take 8–10 minutes. (My colander will only take 1 pound at a time, which reduces steaming time to 5 minutes.) Remove from pot, cool slightly, and squeeze out excess moisture.

Finishing Touches for Blanched and Steamed Spinach

- *Buttered Spinach:* Cook spinach in butter over high heat until moisture evaporates (3–5 minutes). Season with salt and pepper before serving. (Two cups blanched spinach will take 3–4 tablespoons butter.)
- *Sautéed Chopped Spinach:* Chop 2 cups blanched or steamed spinach. Chop 2 tablespoons shallots or 1 onion. In a large skillet melt butter (approximately 2 tablespoons for 2 cups spinach) and sauté shallots or

onions until they soften and barely turn yellow. Add spinach and raise heat to medium high, stirring constantly. After the moisture has evaporated, add additional butter (approximately 3 tablespoons per 2 pounds spinach) and cook slowly for 5–10 minutes, stirring often, until spinach absorbs all the butter. Season with salt and pepper and top with another tablespoon of butter.
- *Creamed Spinach:* Coarsely chop 2 cups blanched spinach. Melt 2 tablespoons butter in a heavy skillet, add spinach, and cook over high heat, stirring constantly until moisture evaporates. Turn heat to medium and stir in 1 tablespoon flour, stir for a minute to cook flour, and lower heat. Stir in 1 cup heavy cream and cover the pan. Cook until the spinach has absorbed all the cream, about 15 minutes. Season with salt and pepper before serving. Serve plain or garnish with minced chives, or a pinch of nutmeg or chopped mint leaves.
- *Spinach with Cream and Garlic:* Simmer a peeled clove of garlic with 1 cup cream for 15 minutes. If cream cooks down, add more milk or cream to bring back to 1 cup. Add to spinach and proceed as with *Creamed Spinach*, above.

Whole Sautéed Spinach

Early in the season when spinach leaves are tiny and tender, we look forward to the taste of young spinach just turned in butter.

2 lb spinach
4 Tb butter
1–2 Tb olive oil (or butter)
1 garlic clove (optional)
Salt and freshly ground black pepper

Wash spinach and let drain. In a large frying pan, melt butter olive oil over medium-high heat, and sauté garlic (if you are using it) until it just has a tinge of brown; remove. Add spinach and sauté for 3–4 minutes, stirring often with a wooden spoon until the spinach absorbs the butter. Season with salt and pepper. (*Serves 4*)
- For older sliced spinach leaves, sauté in oil and butter, cover pan, and let cook 3–4 minutes to completely tenderize.

Sauté of Spinach and Celery

I love cooked celery and am always on the lookout for new ways to serve it. One evening I tried the soft bite of spinach with the crunchy texture of celery. My family approved—I hope you will too.

2 lb spinach
5 large celery ribs
4 Tb butter
2 Tb vegetable or olive oil
1/2 cup chopped onions
Salt and freshly ground pepper
Nutmeg

Wash and stem the spinach. Young tender spinach leaves can be cooked whole; larger leaves should be stemmed and sliced diagonally into 1-inch strips. Cut celery diagonally into ¼-inch slices.

Heat 2 tablespoons butter with the oil in a large frying pan; add celery and onions and sauté, stirring occasionally, for 5 minutes or until barely tender. Remove with a slotted spoon and set aside. Add spinach and remaining butter to pan, cooking until just wilted, about 4 minutes. Return celery and onions to the pan and stir until well mixed. Season with salt, pepper, and a dash of nutmeg. (*Serves 4*)

- Add herbs such as parsley or sweet marjoram.
- For a gratin add enough heavy cream, sour cream, or yogurt to the spinach mixture to coat the vegetables. Sprinkle with grated cheese, dot with butter, and place under broiler until cheese is lightly browned and cream is bubbly.
- For a richer sauce reduce 2 cups cream to 1 cup. Stir in, and cook with spinach 1 minute to coat.
- Try other vegetable combinations such as spinach and lettuce, or summer squash, grated cucumber, or mushrooms. They all taste good.

Stir-Fried Spinach with Ginger

Soy sauce and ginger give this sautéed spinach a Chinese touch. Its sharp flavor contrasts nicely with the sweet taste of a pork roast or chops.

    2 lb fresh spinach
    1 small onion
    3 Tb peanut oil
    1 clove garlic
    2 slices ⅛-inch-thick ginger
    Salt
    1 Tb very dry sherry
    1½ Tb soy sauce
    1 tsp sugar

Wash and trim spinach and cut leaves into wide strips (or tear into 2-inch squares). Chop onion. Heat oil in a large frying pan or wok, and add onion, garlic, and ginger. Stir-fry on high heat for 1 minute. Add spinach, sprinkle with a pinch of salt, then stir for 3 minutes. Add sherry, soy sauce, and sugar; turn heat down to medium, cover, and cook 3 minutes longer. Remove ginger and garlic and serve immediately. (*Serves 4*)

- Add ½ pound sliced mushrooms when spinach goes in.

Spinach Soufflé

Spinach soufflé is so pretty that its wonderful taste seems like an extra bonus. It's also a surprisingly easy workday recipe if you prepare the spinach/egg yolk base in the morning and then need only to fold in the beaten egg whites just before baking. Serve plain or with my fresh *Marinara Sauce* (see *Tomatoes*).

    1 cup blanched spinach
    5½ Tb butter
    3 Tb flour
    1 cup hot milk
    3 egg yolks
    Salt and freshly ground pepper
    5 egg whites, at room temperature
    ¼ tsp cream of tartar

Butter a 1½-quart soufflé dish. Chop spinach very fine and sauté in 3 tablespoons butter until moisture is removed; set aside.

Melt 2½ tablespoons butter in a saucepan and add flour; cook together slowly for 2 minutes without browning. Remove pan from heat, stir in 1 cup hot milk, and beat well. When mixture is smooth, return pan to heat and cook for about 4 minutes. Remove from heat to beat in egg yolks, spinach mixture, then salt and pepper. Cool.

Start beating the egg whites at low speed. When they become frothy increase the mixing speed and add cream of tartar. Beat just until the egg whites hold their shape on the back of a spoon. Watch carefully—you do not want them to become glossy and overbeaten.

Mix a quarter of the whites into the spinach mixture. Now, gently but quickly, fold in the rest of the whites. Don't try to get them 100 percent mixed, or you'll remove some of the air and end up with a much flatter soufflé. Pour into the soufflé dish and place in a preheated 400° oven. Immediately turn the oven down to 375° and bake for 25–30 minutes. The soufflé is done when it's puffy and lightly browned. Serve immediately. (*Serves 4–6*)

- Use other greens or lettuces in place of spinach.

Spinach Timbales

Timbales, from the Arabic word for drum, *thable*, are filled molds; in this case, spinach bound with custard. As they're not as fragile as soufflés, you don't have to worry about watching them sink or slump as you serve them. I use small, inexpensive Pyrex glass molds, which come in all sizes, so I can tailor the portion to my guests' appetites. Timbales are a blessing to anyone who works, as they can be made ahead, refrigerated, and cooked at the last minute. They also reheat nicely.

    2 cups blanched spinach
    1 small onion
    5 Tb butter
    Salt and freshly ground pepper
    Nutmeg
    1½ cups milk or combination of milk and light cream
    4 eggs
    ½ cup grated Swiss cheese

Chop spinach very fine. Chop onion. Melt 2 tablespoons of the butter in a saucepan and add onion. Cook until just soft and yellow, not brown. Add spinach and cook until moisture is evaporated, then add 3 tablespoons butter and stew until butter is absorbed by the spinach. Season with salt, pepper, and a pinch of nutmeg. Add milk and cook for a moment until slightly warmed. Lightly beat eggs and mix in; add cheese. Stir until thoroughly combined.

Butter 4 individual molds or a 6-cup mold. Pour mixture into mold(s) and place in a pan into which you add boiling water to at least halfway up the sides of the mold(s). Place in a preheated 325° oven for 20 minutes. (The larger mold may take 30–40 minutes to cook, depending upon its shape.) The molds are done when a toothpick inserted in the center comes out clean. Unmold and serve. (*Serves 4*)

- Use other greens, lettuces, or combination of both in place of spinach.

Fresh Spinach Salad

Every time I turn around, another restaurant has opened with brushed brick walls, natural woods—and spinach salad on the menu. I'm afraid many of these restaurant owners are using large, tough spinach as a substitute for iceberg lettuce, and they are giving raw spinach a bad name. The only way to make a decent spinach salad is to use tiny, tender leaves—nothing else will do—and, here, of course, home gardeners have all the advantages.

I like spinach best freshly picked and served with a vinaigrette sauce. I also admire the contrast between the dark green of spinach and the pale green of endive. Some days I'll lunch on spinach salad with chopped hard-boiled eggs, cheese, and bacon bits. Or I add another green, sliced mushrooms, and radishes.

Do experiment, but try one plain salad first.

    2 lb fresh young spinach
    1 clove garlic
    1 1/2 tsp salt
    1/4 tsp Dijon mustard
    2 Tb lemon juice
    1/2 cup olive oil
    1/2 cup corn oil

Wash, trim, and dry spinach and, if necessary, crisp in the refrigerator. Mash the garlic and salt together. Stir in the mustard and lemon juice, and gradually beat in the oils. Pour dressing over spinach to coat; toss well. (*Serves 4*)

- Add 1/2 pound washed and dried endive.
- For a main-course salad, add 6 slices crumbled cooked bacon, 1/4 cup freshly grated Parmesan cheese, and 2 finely chopped hard-boiled eggs.

Wilted Spinach Salad

    3 lb fresh spinach
    1 small onion
    6 slices bacon
    2 tsp sugar
    1/2 tsp salt
    1/2 tsp dry mustard
    1/2 cup cider vinegar
    Freshly ground pepper

Wash and stem spinach, dry, and place in a serving bowl. Chop onion. Cook bacon until crisp, remove from pan, and crumble into bits. Discard all but 2 tablespoons of the bacon fat; add onion, and cook until just soft. Add sugar, salt, mustard, and vinegar. Heat until sugar is dissolved, pour over spinach, grind pepper over, toss, and garnish with crumbled bacon bits. (*Serves 6*)

Oysters and Spinach in White Butter Sauce

My complaint about most baked shellfish appetizers, such as Clams Casino or Oysters Rockefeller, is that the stuffing overwhelms the shellfish flavor. When I cook oysters I still want to experience as much of their fresh sea taste as I can. Here, the spinach and oysters retain their separate identities, but together they add up to something very special. The binder is my old favorite butter sauce.

    White Butter Sauce (page 346)
    12 oysters in the shell
    Rock salt or aluminum foil
    2 cups blanched spinach
    3 Tb butter

Prepare white butter sauce and keep warm. Open oysters and place half shells on rock salt or crumpled heavy gauge aluminum foil in a large baking pan. The rock salt or foil steadies the oysters and absorbs excess heat.

Chop spinach. Heat butter in a frying pan and add spinach, stirring over medium-high heat for a few minutes to evaporate moisture. Lower heat and braise for 5 minutes to soften spinach and incorporate butter. If the spinach seems dry, add a bit of the butter sauce. Keep warm.

Put oysters in a preheated 450° oven and bake for 4 minutes, or just until plumped up. Remove and cover each with 1–2 tablespoons of spinach mixture, depending upon the size of the shells. Add only enough spinach to cover the oysters with a nice even layer. Coat with butter sauce and serve immediately. (*Serves 4*)

Fresh Spinach Soup

Reserve the most tender leaves you can find for this fresh spinach soup—a favorite both at home and at the restaurant.

    3 cups blanched spinach
    1/2 cup shallots, scallions, or onions
    1 clove garlic
    6 Tb butter
    6 cups chicken broth
    Salt and freshly ground pepper
    Dash of nutmeg
    Plain *Croutons* (optional; page 348)
    Grated Jarlsberg cheese (optional)

Roughly slice spinach. Slice shallots or onions and chop garlic. Melt 2 tablespoons butter in a 4-quart saucepan. Sauté shallots over low heat until soft and yellow, add garlic, and cook for another moment. Add 4 tablespoons butter; when it's melted, add spinach. Turn up heat and sauté spinach for 5 minutes or until all the butter is absorbed. Add broth, then bring to a boil and simmer. Cook for 15 minutes. Just before serving season with salt, pepper, and nutmeg. If you wish, garnish with toasted bread rounds sprinkled with cheese. (*Serves 6*)

Cream of Spinach Soup

This spinach soup utilizes tough old spinach leaves that otherwise would be relegated to the compost pile. It makes a hearty fall lunch or light supper.

    2–3 lb fresh spinach
    4 Tb butter
    1/2 cup minced onions
    6 cups chicken broth
    1 cup potatoes
    1 cup heavy cream
    Salt and freshly ground pepper

Trim spinach and slice diagonally. In a large saucepan melt butter and sauté onions until soft and golden. Add the spinach and cook until wilted, about 5 minutes. Meanwhile, heat broth to boiling and coarsely chop potatoes. When the spinach is limp add broth and potatoes. Cook until potatoes are soft, about 20 minutes. Cool the mixture slightly and put through a food processor, blender, or food mill to break up the spinach and potatoes. Don't totally purée; you want the texture of spinach and potato bits in the soup. Return to the saucepan, add cream, reheat, and season with salt and pepper. (*Serves 6–8*)

American Spinach Frittata

Frittata, the Italian open-faced omelet, should be firm, but not dry, and the secret is cooking over very low heat. At the restaurant when we have a staff dinner at 5:30 p.m., a favorite dish for both those who prepare it and those who eat it is a giant frittata. Chopped onions, leftover potatoes, vegetables, or diced ham are all sautéed in a great big 20-inch skillet. Two dozen or more beaten eggs are poured over and topped with grated cheese. Gentle cooking produces a delicious meal for 20 plus. Here is a smaller version.

    1 onion
    9 Tb butter
    2 cups blanched spinach
    8 eggs
    1/2 cup grated Jarlsberg or Swiss cheese
    1/2 cup grated Parmesan cheese
    1/2 tsp salt
    Freshly ground black pepper

Slice onion; in a skillet melt 3 tablespoons of the butter and add onion; sauté until yellow and soft. Add spinach, stirring to separate leaves, and sauté for 4–5 minutes or until nicely coated with butter; remove from stove. Beat

eggs lightly, and combine thoroughly with the spinach mixture, cheeses, and seasonings. Melt remaining butter in a 9-inch skillet (nonstick if possible); when the butter foam subsides, turn the heat down and add the egg mixture. Cook over very low heat, covered, for 10 minutes or until set. Place under the broiler to lightly brown the top. Then loosen edges and cut the frittata into pie-shaped wedges, or slip out onto a warm round platter to serve. (*Serves 4–6*)

Note: You can also put the frittata in an ovenproof skillet, cook lightly on top of the stove for 2–3 minutes until a crust is formed, then bake at 400° until set, approximately 5–10 minutes.

- Combine vegetables and herbs, such as basil with zucchini; tomatoes and marjoram; and mushrooms, peppers, summer squash, and chives or parsley. Let your imagination and the state of your garden dictate the choice.

Mrs. Avis's Greek Spinach Pie

Years ago, when my daughters and I were active in Campfire Girls, one of the mothers brought a wonderful Greek spinach-cheese pie to a potluck awards dinner and shared the recipe with me. When I first cooked it, Russell was delighted, and to this day he considers spinach pie an enormous treat.

    6–7 cups blanched spinach
    1 medium onion
    1/2 lb butter
    6 large eggs
    2 lb ricotta or cottage cheese
    1/2–1 lb crumbled feta cheese
    Salt and freshly ground pepper
    1/2 lb filo dough (if frozen, thaw to room
       temperature)

Chop spinach and dice onion. Melt 2 tablespoons butter in a large frying pan and sauté onions until soft. Add spinach, then turn up heat and cook until all moisture is gone. Remove mixture from heat. Melt remaining butter in a small pan.

Beat eggs and mix in cheeses. Add spinach mixture; season with salt and pepper. Carefully spread the filo

dough out flat and cover with a moistened dish towel so that the separate sheets don't become brittle. Butter a 15 x 10-inch baking pan and place a sheet of the dough on the bottom of the pan. Brush lightly with melted butter and continue layering sheets of dough, buttering each sheet until you have a stack of 10. The dough should just fit the pan. If it doesn't, tuck in any excess dough, it doesn't have to be terribly neat. Spread the spinach mixture evenly on top and stack with another 10 sheets of dough, buttering them as before.

Bake in a preheated 375° oven for 15 minutes; turn oven down to 350° for an additional 30 minutes. If the top layer begins to get too dark, cover with brown paper. Remove from oven and let rest for 15 minutes before cutting. (*Serves 12 as main course, 16 as appetizer*)

Note: Filo, or phyllo, dough is available in many supermarket frozen food sections. Strudel dough could be substituted.

Spinach Crêpes

This crêpe batter is one we prepare at the restaurant because it can be mixed up and used right away, unlike conventional batters. The secret? Instant flour, which may be more expensive than regular flour but worth it in time and convenience. If you use regular flour, increase the amount to 3 cups total, strain batter through a fine sieve, and refrigerate for at least an hour, allowing the flour particles to swell, resulting in lighter crêpes.

Crêpe Batter (makes 30 crêpes; refrigerate or freeze extra crêpes)
2 cups instant flour
1/2 cup all-purpose flour
6 large eggs
1 1/2 cups cold milk
1 1/2 cups cold water
3/4 tsp salt
6 Tb melted butter or 3 Tb melted butter and 3 Tb vegetable oil

Sauce
2 cups medium cream
1 cup heavy cream
4 Tb cornstarch blended with 4 Tb milk or dry vermouth
1 cup grated Swiss cheese
1/2 tsp salt
Freshly ground black pepper

Filling (sufficient for 15 crêpes)
2 cups *Sautéed Chopped Spinach* (page 262)
1/2–1 cup grated Swiss or Parmesan cheese or combination of both
2 Tb butter

Whirl all batter ingredients (except butter) in an electric blender or food processor at high speed for 1 minute, or place flours in a bowl and gradually blend in eggs, liquid ingredients, and salt and butter with a whisk or electric beater. Mix in cooled melted butter. Oil a 6-inch fry pan with sloping sides and heat it until it's just beginning to smoke. (A well-seasoned pan or Teflon is a big asset.) Wipe pan. Remove from heat, pour a scant 1/4 cup batter into the center, and quickly tilt the pan back and forth so that a thin film of batter covers the entire surface of the pan. Place back on heat and cook crêpe for approximately 1 minute or until it moves slightly when you shake the pan. Turn over and continue cooking another 30 seconds: this less attractive side is the side you fill. Slide the crêpe onto a plate and cook the rest of the batter, greasing the pan lightly when necessary. The crêpes may be stacked after they have cooled for a minute or two.

To make the sauce, cook the two creams and cornstarch over medium heat, stirring constantly, because the sauce thickens fast. Add 1 cup grated Swiss cheese and stir until melted. Season with salt and pepper.

Mix a third of this sauce into the spinach. Place a tablespoon of filling across the lower third of a crêpe and roll up. Put into a buttered au gratin dish or into one large buttered baking pan, with the seam down. Repeat, using all spinach mixture. Thin sauce, if necessary, by stirring in some milk, then spoon over the crêpes. Sprinkle with grated cheese, dot with butter, and bake in a preheated 375° oven for 20 minutes. Run under broiler, if necessary, to brown the top. (*Serves 4–6*)

- Spinach crêpes are a marvelous way to use up small bits of leftovers that by themselves would go to waste. Fold bits of chopped ham or chicken into the spinach; add fresh mushrooms lightly sautéed in butter or even some crisp bacon.
- For a less rich dish, use a milk-based white sauce and less cheese.
- Substitute sautéed chopped greens or broccoli.

Spinach and Fish Paupiettes

Take just-picked garden spinach and absolutely fresh fish, add a mouthwatering butter sauce, serve with absolutely plain boiled new potatoes, and you have a delicious meal. I like this recipe because the two ingredients join together but still retain their own unique tastes. As far as I'm concerned, that's exactly what good eating is all about.

> 3 cups blanched spinach
> 1 medium onion
> 7 Tb butter
> Salt and freshly ground pepper
> Nutmeg
> 1 ½ lb fillets of flounder or any flat fish
> *White Butter Sauce* (page 346)

Finely chop spinach, and set aside. Chop onion fine, and sauté in 2 tablespoons of the butter until golden but not browned; add spinach. After moisture has evaporated from spinach, stir in 3 ½ tablespoons butter and season carefully with salt, pepper, and a dash of nutmeg.

Butter four 10-ounce Pyrex glass molds or molds of approximate size. Cut fish fillets lengthwise and score the outside flesh (the darker side)—which will counteract the natural curl of the fish. Divide fish into four portions and line the molds, placing the white flesh against the outer sides of the molds and the less attractive darker scored sides in the centers. Fill molds with equal amounts

of spinach; dot with the remaining 1½ tablespoons butter. Set into a baking pan deep enough for water to reach halfway up the sides of the molds. Add boiling water and place in a preheated 400° oven covered with a sheet of aluminum foil (or individually covered). Cook for 15–20 minutes.

While the fish is cooking, make the butter sauce. Remove timbales from the oven and drain by holding a small plate over each mold and tipping out the juices. Unmold the timbales onto serving plates and lightly coat with butter sauce. (*Serves 4*)

- If you have no fresh fish supplier, frozen fish adapts very nicely to this particular recipe.
- For a richer version, add raw fish to the spinach mixture before filling the timbales. Buy an extra ¼ or ½ pound fish, grind or chop it, and mix into the spinach.
- For a more custardlike consistency, add 2 beaten eggs and a bit of cream to the spinach.
- Mix other greens, such as sorrel, with the spinach; two-thirds spinach and one-third sorrel would give a lemon flavor.
- Instead of butter sauce, make a sauce out of the fish juices. Melt 2 tablespoons butter; add 3 tablespoons flour, then 1 cup fish liquid. Let cook for 10 minutes, and add ¼ cup heavy cream.

Rolled Flank Steak
Stuffed with Spinach

Flank steak stuffed with spinach is a beautiful and economical dish.

1 1/2 lb flank steak
5 Tb butter
4 Tb flour
3 cups hot beef broth
1 cup red wine
2 carrots
1 stalk celery
1 bay leaf
1/4 tsp thyme
Pinch of sugar
1 clove unpeeled garlic
Salt and freshly ground pepper
2 cups *Sautéed Chopped Spinach* (page 262)
1/2 cup chopped pitted black olives (optional)
1 Tb vegetable oil

Score flank steak in a diamond-shaped pattern, then place between two pieces of waxed paper and pound as flat as possible with a rolling pin, mallet, or the flat edge of a cleaver. Set aside.

In a heavy saucepan, melt 3 tablespoons butter, stir in flour, and cook slowly, stirring constantly, for 10–15 minutes, until the flour is a rich, nutlike brown. Remove from heat, whisk in hot broth, return to heat, and simmer until slightly thickened. Add wine to sauce. Chop carrots and celery and add to sauce along with herbs, sugar, and garlic.

Lay out the flattened flank steak and season with salt and lots of freshly ground pepper. Spread the spinach evenly over it up to 1 inch of the edge of the steak. Sprinkle chopped olives (if you wish) on the spinach. Roll the steak up firmly and tie in several places with kitchen string.

Melt 2 tablespoons butter with the oil in a frying pan over high heat. When the butter foam subsides put in flank steak and brown on all sides. Place in casserole just large enough to hold the steak and the sauce.

Pour sauce over beef, adding additional broth or water to ensure that the meat is covered. Bring to a boil on top of the stove and place in preheated 375° oven.

Cook for 1 hour, turning occasionally. Beef should be cooked through at the end of this time. If not, cook until a sharp knife easily goes through to the center of the roll.

Remove meat roll to a carving board and keep warm. Reduce the sauce for 10–15 minutes or until it is the thickness you want. Slice the meat into 3/4-inch slices, arrange overlapping slightly, and pour sauce over the meat. (*Serves 4–6*)

- If you wish, replace olives with chopped onions sautéed in a little butter.
- For an Italian-style dinner, brown the beef roll and simmer in a *Marinara Sauce* (see *Tomatoes*).

Turkey Florentine

Whenever you see the word "Florentine" in a recipe, it means spinach. As prices skyrocket, turkey breast comes into its own, for it has the same delicate qualities of veal at one-third the price.

1 1/2–2 lb fresh turkey breast
Salt and freshly ground pepper
1/2 cup flour
2 tsp vegetable oil
11 Tb butter
2 cups hot turkey or chicken stock
1/2 cup heavy cream
1/2 cup grated mozzarella cheese
1/4 cup grated Parmesan cheese
2 large egg yolks
1/2 lb fresh mushrooms
2 cups *Sautéed Chopped Spinach* (page 262)

Cut raw turkey breast into 8 slices, which is easier to do if the breast is frozen for an hour beforehand and if you cut at a slight angle. Place each piece of turkey between 2 sheets of waxed paper and pound with a rolling pin or a flat cleaver. Salt, pepper, and lightly flour the turkey. Heat oil and 3 tablespoons butter in a large frying pan and quickly sauté turkey on both sides. Remove and set aside.

Melt 4 tablespoons butter and add 5 tablespoons flour off the heat. Stir until well blended and cook over low heat for 3 minutes. Remove from heat, pour in hot stock, and whisk well to blend. Return mixture to stove and bring to a simmer, stirring constantly. Cook for 2–3 minutes until sauce thickens, stirring occasionally. Add cream. Combine cheeses, add 1/2 cup to the sauce, and stir until cheeses melt. Beat the egg yolks together in a small bowl, add 3–4 tablespoons of the hot sauce to the eggs until they are heated through, then pour the egg mixture into the sauce. Stir until well blended and season with salt and pepper. Slice the mushrooms and sauté in 2 tablespoons butter until lightly browned.

Butter a 9 x 12-inch baking dish and place a very thin film of sauce on the bottom. Stir approximately 1/3 cup of the sauce into the spinach. Spread along the bottom of the baking dish and layer with mushroom slices, then another thin film of sauce, and turkey slices, and the rest of the sauce. Sprinkle with remaining cheese and dot with 2 tablespoons butter. Bake for 20 minutes in a preheated 375° oven. If you wish, run it under the broiler to brown just before serving. (*Serves 4*)

- Try sliced raw chicken breast or slices of veal cut from the leg.
- Simmer a fowl, use the broth for the sauce, and substitute the cooked fowl for the turkey. Don't sauté the fowl, but cut into thin pieces and season a little more heavily than you would with turkey.
- For vegetarians: layer poached eggs with spinach and sauce. Bake to just heat through.

Squash (Summer)

Most people plant too much summer squash and harvest it too late. They end up with quantities of giant squashes, desperately looking for anyone to whom zucchini might still be a treat.

This won't happen to you if you plant a small amount of squash (and I mean one to three plants, total) and harvest it young. When summer squash is cooked young, it has a crisp, yet tender flesh, soft and digestible seeds, and a delicate flavor. I am bemused by the thousands of recipes currently in print for doctoring up overaged squash. I think more tons of newsprint have been devoted to answering this question than any other vegetable cooking topic. Even large squash has a chance if simply cooked. A perfect example is *Sautéed Grated Squash*. We serve this frequently at the restaurant and even our regular customers never tire of it.

Summer squashes are gourds, as are winter squashes, but unlike winter squashes, which are harvested mature with hard outer skins and tough seeds, summer squashes are harvested at an immature stage. Their skins and seeds are edible. (Although I doubt a gardener exists who hasn't had a few summer squashes get so big and tough as to render the skins inedible.) The summer squash family

includes a number of different varieties. The most common are the yellow crookneck and straight neck; the green zucchini, originally imported from Italy and known as courgettes in France and England; and the lesser-known small, pale green scalloped squashes called patty pan (or cymlings in the South). There's an even smaller dark green version called Scallopini. We grow all three summer squash varieties. Zucchini merits special

attention because it has a more delicate—yet distinctive—taste than other summer squashes. The saucer shape of patty pans is so unique that it is fun to include them in your garden.

In addition, Kuta is a new squash variety which can be harvested at different stages of development as both a summer and a winter squash. In the South, you'd have good luck with chayotes (known as christophene in the Caribbean and vegetable pear or mirleton in the South). Substitute this bland tropical squash in all summer squash recipes.

I can't emphasize strongly enough that the average family doesn't need more than one to three plants. Russ plants Early Golden Summer Crookneck yellow squash; the green Elite or Aristocrat zucchini and the golden Gold Rush Hybrid zucchini; and Early White Bush patty pan squash. He likes to rush the season, so he sows seeds indoors in late April, six weeks ahead of planting time, two seeds to a peat pot about $1/2$ inch deep. He lets the seedlings develop and then pinches off the weaker plant. Squashes like a fairly sweet soil, so he makes sure that the soil is not acidic. In early June, when the ground is warm enough for the squashes, Russ prepares the soil with compost and then sets out each plant surrounded by a 4-foot space. He gives them a drink of transplant solu-

tion or diluted fertilizer to get them off to a good start. The spacing is important because the plants need plenty of air around them so they don't develop mildew. If your space is limited, most of the seed houses now list bush squash varieties that require less space.

Few insects or diseases attack squashes, but Russ keeps an eye out for the squash vine borer, which, as its name suggests, bores through the vine, causing it to wilt. When this happens, he locates the pest and cuts it out.

By mid-July, the summer squashes are ready to harvest. They grow so rapidly that it's necessary to pick every day.

We harvest the squashes when they're less than 4 inches long. At that point, their skins and seeds are most tender, and their flavor most subtle. Very few commercial growers harvest a crop at this stage. Also, since squashes grow overnight, when you harvest them small and tender, you will use up many more and are less likely to be found wandering around the neighborhood trying to palm off baskets of oversize squashes.

All is not lost, however, should summer squashes become larger than 3–4 inches. You can make my favorite grated summer squash preparation with any size squash. If it is really giant and has an impossibly tough skin, peel and seed the squash and use only the flesh.

Special Information

Yields

- 1 pound squash = 4 cups grated = 2 cups salted and squeezed
- 1 pound squash = approximately 3 1/2 cups sliced or chunked
- 1 pound squash = approximately 1 1/4–1 1/2 cups mashed

Storage and Preserving

- Summer squash dehydrates rapidly, so refrigerate in a perforated plastic bag immediately after harvesting. The squash should keep in good condition 3–4 days.
- Cooked squash, refrigerated in a covered container, will keep 2–3 days. Do not try to store summer squash. It freezes poorly, turning mushy because of the high water content. However, you can freeze puréed squash (for *Squash Fritters*) or soups.
- Both zucchini and summer squash make good pickles. See *Evelyn Higginbotham's Zucchini Pickles*.

Hints

- Summer squash and eggplant have similar cooking characteristics and can be frequently interchanged in recipes. Both are best drained and squeezed of excess water. See eggplant recipes such as *Eggplant, Tomatoes, and Cream; Ratatouille; Eggplant Parmesan; Red, White, and Blue-Black Eggplant; Eggplant Sandwiches*.

- Use oversize squashes as containers. We've had a few grow so big I turned them into "watermelon baskets." Cut a cover or a decorative top and handle, core and clean the interior, and brush with a lemon-oil mixture. Fill with salads or crudités, or blanch barely tender and fill with hot mixtures.
- Zucchini peel makes a beautiful salad plate garnish. Run a lemon zester down the sides of a zucchini to form long, thin threads.
- Use raw for snacks. Julienne for a crudités platter, or grate directly into salads.
- Make a simple Italian zucchini soup. Dilute homemade *Marinara Sauce* (see *Tomatoes*) with water, then add zucchini and onion slices cooked in garlic-flavored oil. Reheat and serve with grated cheese on the side. For a heartier version, cook potatoes in the tomato "broth."
- Layer blanched squash slices alternately with chopped onion cooked with buttered bread crumbs. Repeat two or three times and top with butter. Heat in a 350° oven until hot and bubbly.
- For an unusual, attractive appetizer, stuff blanched baby patty pan squash with buttered fresh bread crumbs sautéed with garlic and fresh herbs. Heat through and serve.
- Harvest squash blossoms as in *Winter Squash*. They are delicious in *Tempura* (see page 337).

Harvest by cutting the stems from the plants gently with a paring knife. Don't try to twist or pull them off—you may end up tearing the skin and damaging the plants. As summer squashes are mainly water, they dehydrate rapidly. Harvest just before cooking and keep in the refrigerator in a perforated plastic bag until cooking. Don't forget that squash blossoms are delicious to eat. See *Winter Squash* for information on harvesting blossoms.

Properly grown small summer squashes are used skin and all, so there is very little waste. Larger squashes need to have their skins and seeds removed: slice lengthwise, and scoop out the seeds with a spoon. Also, large squashes often have dry or pulpy flesh which should be discarded. Use only the flesh that is still moist and crisp. Don't be afraid to throw giant squashes on the compost heap if they are too far gone for cooking. If that seems too wasteful, convert them to containers (see *Stuffed Squash*).

Before preparing squashes, wash them thoroughly (using a scrub brush if necessary) and cut off their stems.

As summer squashes are so watery, when they're cooked this water comes out and can make a soggy mess of your preparation. Thus, it is best to remove as much water as possible before cooking. You can do this two ways: salting or blanching. The method you should use depends upon the final preparation of the vegetable. For example, I salt grated squashes, but blanch whole squashes.

This preliminary salting or blanching might seem unnecessary and yet another bothersome step. Of course you don't have to do it, but I guarantee you will notice a difference in the consistency of the final dish.

Salting is the best method for grated, thinly sliced, or julienned squash. I prefer to use kosher or sea salt. Lightly salt the squash, place in a colander, and let stand for 30 minutes. Some water will exude during the resting period, but you will be amazed at how much more will come out during squeezing. If you are restricting salt intake, rinse off the squash before squeezing it.

- Sautéed sliced squash makes a pretty quiche or frittata. I especially like cubed browned potatoes with cubed browned zucchini and plenty of black pepper.
- Try a summer squash tian. Substitute grated zucchini for the chicory in *Chicory Tian* (see *Salad Greens*). I use half grated zucchini and half Swiss chard or spinach.
- Make *Summer Squash à la Grecque*. Cut squash into 1-inch-thick slices and cook in a hot marinade à la Grecque (see *Mixed Vegetables*) for 3–5 minutes. The squash should be undercooked, for it will continue to cook in the marinade. Pour marinade over the squash and any other vegetables you are using and cool.
- Cut summer squash into chunks and add to stews and hearty soups at the end of the cooking time so that they retain texture and do not become soggy.
- Don't overcook!
- Make a zucchini bed for crabmeat. Prepare *Sautéed Grated Squash* and place in a casserole. Top with lumps of fresh crabmeat. Bake in a 375° oven until crab is *just* heated through. If you like, brown 4–6 tablespoons butter and pour over crabmeat.
- Try to keep patty pan squashes as close to their original shape as possible when cooking. Cook baby patty pan squash whole.

- Use patty pan squash disks to garnish a plate. Blanch squash, slice across the circumference, and then sauté.
- Stuff large patty pan squash (if they're not pulpy). Core the centers and stuff them to retain their shape.

Microwave
- 1 pound whole squash or chunks placed in a covered pan with 3 tablespoons water will cook tender in 4–6 minutes.

Leftovers
- Mash squash and use in a soufflé, or in patties.
- Refry, and add to omelets or frittatas.
- Cut leftover raw squash into small pieces and add to tuna fish salad for texture.
- Freeze puréed squash for winter meals. Grate or chop the squash. Sauté chopped onions in butter and add squash; cook until tender. Purée with just enough chicken broth so the blender works easily (or enough to make a thick liquid). If you use a food processor, you do not need the broth. Freeze. Use as a soup base by adding more broth, or combine it as is with other soups or stews. Make a hearty winter soup by using purée as a base for pasta, beans, and root vegetables.
- Make *Mashed Squash Fritters*.

Take a handful of grated squash and firmly squeeze out *only* as much moisture as comes easily. Those vegetable juices are an integral part of the squashes, so don't wring them dry. For sliced and julienned salted squash, pat out the moisture as best you can.

Blanching is the best method to remove moisture from whole squashes. Drop them into boiling water. The cooking time will depend on size: small squashes blanch in 2–4 minutes; medium squashes will take 6–8 minutes; large squashes to be hollowed out and stuffed might take 10 minutes; and giant squashes up to 20 minutes.

Your aim is not to cook the squashes, but merely to get them to the point where the flesh begins to yield to the touch. The squashes should still be firm, not soft. After blanching whole squashes, you can immerse them in ice water, then drain and hold. I use this method when I later cut the squashes into chunks or slices, or halve them for stuffing.

Once you have salted or blanched the squashes, you can refrigerate them to prepare later on.

I cook summer squashes many different ways, often depending upon the way I've cut them. My favorite is sautéing because it best accentuates the flavor of squash. Other times I'll steam, boil, bake, grill, stuff, or deep-fry. Remember, simple cooking is best.

Marketing

Buy small squash—the larger they become the more risk you take. Certainly, any squash larger than 8–10 inches is best to avoid. Patty pan squash are best under 3 inches (after 4 inches they are really beyond the pale). Look for small, firm squash with skin easily pierced by a thumbnail, indicating that the vegetable is still immature. The seeds should be soft enough to eat and the flesh tender and moist, yet crunchy. The squash should have the right heft: it should feel heavy, not light. A light squash might mean a loss of moisture and a pulpy interior. The skin should be glossy and bright. Withered or limp-looking squash will have lost texture and probably flavor.

◇ Sautéed Summer Squash

Sautéing best brings out the flavor of summer squash. I either grate the squash or cut it up, salt, drain, and sauté. Or, I blanch the whole squash (eliminating the need to salt) and cut up before sautéing. I sauté squash in many different ways—grated, chunked, thinly sliced—and each method has such subtle differences that I've written them up as separate recipes (see pages 273–75). In the recipes, I'll suggest my favorite cutting methods and the finishing touches that seem most appropriate. Note that clarified butter is preferable for sautéing to keep squash from browning. I sauté the squash until it's tender yet slightly crunchy.

◇ Steamed Summer Squash

Steam the squash whole or, if large, halve lengthwise in order to best preserve its texture. Bring 3/4 inch water to a boil in a steamer. Place the whole squash in a steamer basket or colander; cook until just tender. Check by piercing with a fork or knife point. The cooking time depends upon the diameter of the squash. A 1 1/2–2-inch-diameter squash will cook in 10–15 minutes. Chunks will take 5–10 minutes.

◇ Boiled Summer Squash

Boiling is a practical method for older squash. Boil whole or in halves to retain maximum texture. Drop whole squash into boiling water; cook until just tender. The cooking time depends on the squash's diameter. A 1 1/2–2-inch squash will cook in 10–15 minutes. Chunks will cook in 5–10 minutes.

Finishing Touches for Steamed or Boiled Squash

- *In Butter:* Cut steamed or boiled squash into chunks or slices and reheat in butter, or butter and lemon juice. Sprinkle with herbs, salt, and pepper.
- *Mashed Squash*: Cook squash until tender, drain, mash, and drain again. Add butter, salt, pepper, and herbs to taste. Beat in finely grated cheese if you wish.
- Pat dry halved and blanched squash and sprinkle with generous amount of grated feta, Swiss, or Cheddar cheese. Cover with buttered bread crumbs or dot with butter. Run under the broiler until browned and crusty.

◇ Baked Squash

Baking squash works best when the squash are very young and small. Halve the squash, butter them, and top with fresh bread crumbs which have been sautéed in butter and mixed with chopped herbs. Place in a pan with a film of water to prevent the squash from sticking and bake in a preheated 350° oven until the squash are just tender. The cooking time depends on their size. The flesh should be just tender. Run under the broiler to lightly brown, if desired.

Baked Squash Fans

Slice young squash down lengthwise, without cutting through the tip. Open the slices and spread with a garlic or herb butter. Push the slices together (the butter acts like a glue) and bake in a preheated 400° oven in a buttered pan with a film of water on bottom. As they cook, the squash slices will open into fanlike shapes. Cook until tender and season with salt and pepper, or sprinkle with cheese and run under the broiler to brown the top edges.

◇ *Broiled Summer Squash*

I sometimes broil large slices of summer squash. I coat them thoroughly with a garlic oil and broil on both sides until tender. I serve plain or substitute for eggplant in *Eggplant Parmesan* (see *Eggplant*). I cut very small squash in half, brush with oil, and broil 6 inches below heat to brown and cook through.

◇ *Grilled Summer Squash*

Small squash halves are fun to grill. Oil them and place on the grill. Cook about 3–4 minutes on the hottest part of the grill, then turn and place in a less hot spot away from the coals to finish cooking. This will take at least 8–10 minutes, or longer. Baste with oil or with a marinade.

Skewered summer squash chunks that are basted with oil or a marinade go well with other skewered summer vegetables with a mixed grill or lamb shish kebab.

◇ *Stuffed Summer Squash*

Summer squashes are ideal stuffing containers. All squashes use the same principle, but techniques vary somewhat. Stuffings can be vegetables, meat, fish, fowl, or cheese (see *Eggplant*). The stuffings in *Eggplant* and in *Summer Squash* are interchangeable.

Wash and trim the squash. Either blanch the whole squash in boiling salted water until tender, but firm enough to hold its shape, and then cut in half—or halve, hollow out the centers, and cook the halves in boiling salted water until barely tender. The cooking time depends upon the size of the squash. For example, whole 5–6-inch "boats" will cook in 3–5 minutes, depending upon their diameter.

Giant squash—more than 10 inches long—may take 15–30 minutes to cook. For really giant monsters, cut out a top (just as you would in *Giant Stuffed Banana Squash for a Crowd*; see *Winter Squash*), and hollow out the large inedible seeds inside. Boil as above. Use these large squashes hot as containers for other cooked vegetables or stews; use cold for salads.

Regardless of their size, run squashes under cold water to stop the cooking action, drain, pat dry, and continue with the recipe. If the squashes are almost tender and will be filled with a cooked stuffing, the oven cooking time will be only long enough to heat through all the ingredients. If the squashes are to be heated separately and used to hold precooked ingredients, brush the "boats" with melted butter, and heat in a preheated 400° oven (with a film of water on the bottom of the pan) until heated through. Fill with hot filling. In the fall I like to fill summer squash boats with a winter squash purée.

The pale green scalloped patty pan squashes are also attractive containers for stuffing, but they should have a light stuffing that doesn't overpower the delicately flavored squash. Cut a small top out of the rounded side of each 3–4-inch squash. Then, with a melon baller, scoop out the inner flesh and seeds, and set aside for filling. Blanch the patty pans until almost tender, 4–8 minutes. Drain, butter the insides, and fill with a pre-cooked stuffing. Cook until the filling is heated through and the squash is tender, 20–30 minutes.

Patty pan squash also make lovely containers for grated squash. Blanch as above, drain, and brush with melted butter. Then sauté grated squash, coat with some heavy cream or crème fraîche (see *Appendix*), and add herbs and seasonings. Fill the patty pans with the squash mixture, dot with butter and grated cheese (optional), and bake until the squash are tender and the filling is heated through. Make small individual squashes or cut the larger 4-inch ones into servings.

By the way, you can buy a zucchini corer, which is similar to an apple corer, only longer. Select straight, even-diameter squash, large enough to retain at least a ½-inch wall of flesh once the core is removed. When you push the corer through end to end, you create a hollow interior for stuffing. Blanch as you would whole squash, drain, pat dry, and stuff. Once the squash are cooked, cut into rounds. The contrast of the dark skin, flesh, and center filling is quite pretty if you want to take the time.

◇ *Deep-Fried Summer Squash*

Wash and trim the squash. Cut into long slices or strips. Place in a colander, sprinkle with salt, and let drain for 30 minutes. Pat dry. Use one of the following coatings, and deep-fry in hot fat. Serve with salt and pepper and lemon wedges. Or deep-fry parsley sprigs and serve as a garnish.

In Flour: Dip into flour, shake off excess, and deep-fry in hot oil until golden brown, 2–3 minutes.

In Egg: Prepare as above. Dip into flour, shake off, then coat with beaten egg. Deep-fry in hot oil until crisp.

In Crumbs: Dip into flour, eggs, then bread crumbs. Fry in hot oil until browned and crisp.

In Batter: Make a light batter of ¼ cup oil, ½ cup water, and ¾ cup flour. Let stand for a few minutes, then fold in a beaten egg white. Dip the prepared squash into this batter and fry in hot oil. For other batters, see *Appendix*.

Sautéed Grated Squash

2 ½ lb summer squash
Salt
4 Tb butter
Freshly ground pepper

Wash and dry the squash. Trim the ends. Grate on the largest holes of a grater or in a food processor. Salt, and let drain for 30 minutes. If you wish, rinse to remove the salt. Firmly, but gently, squeeze the moisture from the squash. Heat the butter in a sauté pan and cook the squash for 3–5 minutes until tender, stirring to coat with butter. Season with pepper and salt, taking into consideration the salt already on the squash. (*Serves 3–4*)

- Sauté whole peeled garlic for 30 seconds, then add the squash.
- Sprinkle with freshly chopped herbs, such as basil, dill, or mint.
- Combine grated yellow and zucchini squashes; add grated red pepper for color, if you like.
- Sauté finely chopped onions, shallots, or scallions in butter until wilted, then add squash.
- Sauté the grated squash for 2 minutes, sprinkle with salt and pepper, and add 1 cup heavy cream. Cook gently until the cream reduces and coats the squash. Vary the flavorings with herbs such as rosemary and tarragon—or spices such as curry.
- Combine squash with more assertively flavored vegetables, such as greens. Use equal amounts of squash and blanched, chopped spinach, kale, broccoli de rabe, turnip or mustard greens, or Swiss chard leaves. If the other vegetables are young and tender, you need only to julienne or chop them finely before sautéing until wilted and free from moisture. Then sauté with squash. Blanch older, larger vegetables first, squeeze them dry, and sauté before adding to the squash.

Sautéed Cubed Squash

2 ½ lb squash
Salt
4 Tb butter
Freshly ground pepper

Wash, trim, and cube the squash. Toss with salt and let drain for 30 minutes. Pat dry. Heat the butter in a large frying pan and add the squash. Cook, stirring to coat with butter, for 5–6 minutes. The cooking time depends upon the size of the cubes. Season to taste with salt and pepper. (*Serves 4–6*)

- Sauté the cubes in butter or olive oil, adding garlic and hot pepper flakes if you wish. When the cubes are tender, stir in beaten eggs mixed with grated cheese, and continue stirring until the eggs begin to set.
- Combine sautéed squash with sautéed browned potato cubes and season generously with black pepper.
- Toss squash with *Persillade* (see *Appendix*).

Thinly Sliced Sautéed Squash

2–2 ½ lb squash
Salt
4 Tb butter
Freshly ground pepper
Chopped fresh herbs (optional)

Wash, dry, and trim the squash. Slice as thin as possible. Toss with salt and let drain for 30 minutes. Pat dry. Heat the butter and add the squash. Cook, tossing for 2–4 minutes, depending upon the amount in the pan. The slices should be tender but still retain their crunch. Toss with salt, pepper, and herbs (if you wish). (*Serves 4–6*)

- Combine with other vegetables, such as thinly sliced turnips, carrots, parsnips, kohlrabi, etc. Sauté the firmer-textured vegetables first until almost tender before adding the squash.
- Toss with paper-thin slices of peperoni. Eat as is, or fold into an omelet along with grated cheese.
- Julienne the slices and treat as above. Combine with julienned sweet red pepper.

Blanched Sautéed Squash Pieces

2 ½ lb squash
4 Tb butter
Salt and freshly ground pepper
Chopped fresh herbs
Lemon juice

Blanch whole squash in boiling water. The cooking time depends upon the squash size (see page 272). Place in cold water to stop the cooking action, drain, and pat dry. First cut the squash into strips and then into pieces. (I prefer 1–1 ½-inch diagonal or roll-cut pieces.) You can also cut squash into ½-inch slices, into chunks, or into logs. Patty pan squash is pretty sliced into disks. The cut is up to you.) Cook squash in butter until tender, 3–5 minutes. Large pieces may need to cook, covered, for a minute or two longer. Season with salt and pepper and sprinkle with chopped fresh herbs of your choice and lemon juice. (*Serves 4–6*)

- Roll-cut squash into 1-inch pieces. For each pound squash, heat 2 tablespoons peanut oil. Stir-fry squash for 1 minute, add salt, ½ teaspoon sugar, and a tablespoon of water. Cook 2–3 minutes longer.
- Prepare squash as above, but sauté only 2–3 minutes. Place in a buttered casserole, layer with grated cheese, and drizzle melted butter or oil onto each layer. Top with buttered bread crumbs and grated cheese. Bake in a preheated 400° oven until heated through. Place under the broiler until lightly browned. I like long, almost horizontal ½-inch slices for this preparation.
- Sauté the slices for 2 minutes, sprinkle with salt and pepper, and add 1 cup heavy cream. Cook slowly until the cream reduces and coats the squash. Vary the seasonings with herbs or spices.
- Undercook the squash and layer with 2 cups *Béchamel* or *Mornay Sauce* (see *Appendix*) in a baking dish. Top with grated cheese (optional) and bake in a preheated 400° oven for 15–20 minutes. Run under the broiler if you wish.

Sautéed Small Squash

Try with baby patty pan squash.

    Four 3–4-inch summer squash
    4–6 Tb butter
    Salt and freshly ground pepper
    Lemon juice

Wash and trim the squash. Dry and halve lengthwise (or across for patty-pan squash). Heat the butter and sauté the squash, cut side down, until lightly browned. Turn over, sprinkle with salt and pepper, and lower the heat. Cover the pan (add 1–2 tablespoons liquid if necessary), and cook until just tender, 5–10 minutes. Sprinkle with lemon juice before serving. (*Serves 4*)

- Substitute olive oil for butter, and add whole garlic cloves.
- Cook tiny 2–3-inch squash whole. Lightly sauté in butter, cover, and cook as above.

Stuffed Small Squash

    6 small straight-necked yellow or zucchini squash or
        8 small patty pan squash
    1 Tb butter
    3 Tb olive oil
    ½ lb sliced mushrooms
    ½ cup chopped onions
    1–2 tsp chopped garlic
    1½ cups peeled, seeded, and chopped tomatoes
    1 cup finely chopped walnuts
    ½ cup toasted pine nuts
    1 Tb chopped parsley
    1 Tb chopped fresh mint
    ½ tsp ground cardamom
    1 tsp oregano
    1 Tb lemon juice
    Salt and freshly ground pepper

Wash and trim the squash. Blanch in boiling salted water until tender, but still firmly shaped, approximately 5 minutes. Remove, cool in cold water, and drain. Halve lengthwise (or across for patty-pan squash) and scoop out the flesh, leaving just enough edge to hold the shells intact; set aside. Chop the excess flesh and put into a strainer to drain the excess water.

Heat the butter and 1 tablespoon of the oil, and lightly brown the mushrooms. Set aside. Cook the onions in 1 tablespoon of the oil until wilted and golden, add the garlic, and cook for 30 seconds. Add the drained squash flesh and the tomatoes. Cover the pan and cook for 2–3 minutes to release the juices, uncover, and cook rapidly to reduce the juices. Stir in the mushrooms, nuts, parsley, mint, cardamom, oregano, remaining 1 tablespoon oil, and lemon juice. Mix well and season with salt and pepper.

Spoon stuffing into squash shells and place in a greased baking pan. Film the bottom of the pan with water. Bake in a preheated 375° oven until the squash is tender. This will take 15–30 minutes, depending upon the thickness of the squash containers. (*Serves 6–8*)

- For a heartier stuffing see *Cindy Lydon's Nantucket Stuffed Squash.*
- See other ideas under *Eggplant*, such as *Eggplant Stuffed Vegetable Cases* (page 107) or *Eggplant Stuffed with Rice* (page 107).

Zucchini Stuffed with Corn and Cheese

Here is an easy corn and cheese stuffing for a light luncheon or a main-dish vegetable accompaniment.

    2 narrow 6–7-inch-long zucchini or yellow squash
    1 cup corn kernels
    1/2–2/3 cup ricotta cheese
    1–2 Tb chopped chives (optional)
    Salt and freshly ground black pepper
    3/4 cup grated Cheddar cheese

Blanch squash in boiling salted water for 5 minutes. Place under cold water and drain. Halve and scoop out the seeds, forming cavities. Coarsely purée the corn and ricotta cheese in a food processor or food mill. Add the chives (if you wish) and season with salt and pepper. Fill squash halves with the mixture, mounding slightly. Cover with grated cheese. Place in a buttered casserole and bake, covered, in a preheated 350° oven for 15 minutes. Uncover and bake 20–25 minutes or longer, until the squash is tender and the topping is browned. (*Serves 4*)

Cindy Lydon's Nantucket Stuffed Squash

This, and a salad, makes a delicious full-course meal.

    6 medium summer squash
    1 medium onion
    1/4 lb Muenster cheese
    1/2 lb linguica sausage
    3 Tb butter
    1 cup fresh bread crumbs
    2 Tb chopped parsley
    1 Tb chopped fresh tarragon
    1/2 cup sour cream
    Salt and freshly ground pepper

Prepare squash as in *Stuffed Summer Squash* (page 273). Scoop out flesh, chop, and put in strainer to drain. Chop onion. Cut cheese into 1/4-inch cubes. Remove skin from sausage and chop up meat. Sauté for 2–3 minutes to release fat; drain. Heat butter and sauté onion to wilt. Pat squash dry and sauté with onions to evaporate moisture and coat with butter, 4–5 minutes. Combine with sausage, crumbs, cheese, herbs, and sour cream. Season to taste. Fill the squash cases with the stuffing. Place in a greased baking dish and film with water. Bake

in a preheated 375° oven until the squash is tender and the filling heated through. This will take 15–30 minutes depending upon the thickness of the squash. (*Serves 6*)

Clockwise: stuffed yellow squash, stuffed zucchini, and stuffed patty pan.

Squash Fritters

I make squash fritters with both grated and mashed squash. Grated squash gives a lacier texture, while mashed squash has a more concentrated squash flavor. I have found very little difference between fritters made with unsalted squash and those made with salted squash: the wetness of the batter dictates how much flour you should add. I rather like incorporating all the natural vegetable water, but you certainly can make delicious fritters with salted and drained squash.

    Grated Squash Fritters
    2 eggs
    2 cups grated squash
    1/4 cup flour
    1 Tb melted butter
    Salt and freshly grated pepper
    3/4 tsp dried mint
    2 Tb finely crumbled feta cheese (or 1 Tb Parmesan)
    Oil

Beat eggs and combine with remaining ingredients except oil. Spoon 3–4 tablespoons mixture per fritter and fry in hot oil until browned and crisp on both sides. Drain and serve. (*Makes 6–8 medium fritters*)

- Add herbs or cheeses, grated onion, chives, or scallions. Season with lemon juice to taste.
- Make very tiny cocktail sizes, or 3-inch standard sizes as a vegetable accompaniment.
- Double or triple the recipe and fry up a grated squash frittata. (See *American Spinach Frittata*, page 265).
- If you salt and drain 4 cups grated squash (2 cups drained), the fritters will have more of a squash flavor and texture.

Mashed Squash Fritters
1 lb squash
1 egg
1 Tb melted butter
3 Tb flour
Salt and freshly ground pepper
Oil

Wash and trim the squash and blanch until tender. Drain. Chop, then mash, and drain again to remove excess moisture. Beat the egg and combine with the squash and remaining ingredients except oil. Heat the oil to 375°. Drop the batter into the oil, flattening slightly with the back of a spoon, and fry until brown and crisp all over. Drain before serving. (*Makes 6 medium fritters*)

Zucchini, Peppers, and Tomatoes

Here's a simple stir-fry which you can vary to your heart's content—grate the squash, or substitute other squash varieties and vegetables. This dish reheats well.

1 lb zucchini
Salt
2 Tb butter
1 Tb oil
1 cup sliced onions
1–2 cups sliced green peppers
1 1/2 cups peeled, seeded, and chopped tomatoes
1 tsp chopped fresh basil
1/2 tsp oregano
Freshly ground pepper
1/4 cup Parmesan cheese (optional)

Wash, trim, and slice the zucchini. Salt and let drain; pat dry. Heat the butter and oil and sauté the onions until wilted. Add the zucchini and peppers, and cook 2–3 minutes. Stir in the tomatoes, herbs, and salt and pepper to taste. Cook 4–5 minutes until the vegetables are tender. (If the tomatoes are extra juicy, cook over high heat to reduce the pan juices.) Stir in the Parmesan cheese if you like. Serve either hot or cold. (*Serves 4–6*)

- Omit the tomatoes and add sliced sweet red peppers.
- Cook in olive oil. Heat oil, add chopped garlic, sauté for 30 seconds, and then cook as above.
- Toss with crumbled feta cheese and sliced black olives.

Squash, Egg, and Cheese Casserole

Salt
4 cups sliced squash
2 Tb oil
2 Tb butter
Red pepper flakes
1 cup chopped onions
1 tsp minced garlic
2 eggs
1 1/2 cups grated Swiss cheese
1/2 cup crumbled feta cheese
1/4 cup chopped fresh parsley
1/4 cup chopped fresh dill
Lemon juice
Freshly ground pepper

Salt, drain, and pat the squash dry; set aside. Heat oil and butter in large sauté pan and sauté red pepper flakes for 2–3 minutes; remove from pan. Cook the onions until wilted and golden; add the garlic and cook for 30 seconds. Add the squash and sauté lightly. Beat the eggs with the cheeses and herbs. Combine with the cooked vegetables; season with lemon juice, salt, and pepper. Pour into a buttered 8 x 8-inch pan and bake in a preheated 350° oven for 25–30 minutes, or until set. (*Serves 6–8*)

- Use this mixture as a filling for a quiche. Bake in a partially baked 10-inch pie shell at 375° for 20 minutes, or until set.

Squash Stew

At our house, vegetable stews are never the same twice. I make up a stew depending on what is in the garden. When we have a squash glut, this stew helps the cause.

1 lb yellow squash
1 lb zucchini
1 lb patty pan squash
1 lb green beans
1/4 cup olive oil
2 cups sliced onions
2–3 tsp chopped garlic
1 tsp chopped hot peppers
2 cups peeled, seeded, and roughly
    chopped tomatoes
Salt and freshly ground pepper
2 cups freshly cut corn kernels

Wash and trim all the squash and cut into 1/2-inch chunks or slices. Wash the beans, trim, and snap into 1–1 1/2-inch lengths. Blanch the beans in boiling water until just tender, run under cool water, drain, and set aside. In a large heavy saucepan, heat the oil, add onions, and cook until wilted and golden. Add the garlic and sauté for 30 seconds; stir in the hot peppers and squash. Top with the tomatoes, and season to taste with salt and pepper. Reduce the heat, cover, and simmer 10–15 minutes or until the squash is tender. Uncover, add the beans and corn, and cook for 2–3 minutes until corn is just tender. Taste

and correct seasonings. (If you want a less liquid "stew," uncover earlier to let the juices reduce.) (*Serves 4–6*)

- Use your imagination. Add sweet peppers or other vegetables and sauté with the onions. If you are incorporating root vegetables such as potatoes and rutabaga, cut them into chunks and start cooking them before adding the softer-textured vegetables.
- Add the beans directly to the stew: however, a preliminary blanching retains their bright green color.
- Add fresh garden herbs.
- Don't be afraid to "beef" this up. At the last minute, stir in sautéed ham bits, leftover meats, chicken livers sautéed in butter, kidney beans, olives, or anchovies.

Two-Tone Summer Squash Loaf

This attractive loaf can be served either plain or topped with *Persillade* (see *Appendix*).

    1 lb zucchini
    1 lb yellow summer squash
    Salt
    1 bunch watercress
    4 Tb butter
    1/2 cup chopped shallots
    Freshly ground pepper
    2/3 cup heavy cream
    5 eggs
    1 cup grated cheese (a combination of Swiss, Ched-
        dar, or Parmesan)

Trim, wash, and dry the zucchini and yellow squash. Grate separately; salt and drain in separate bowls for 30 minutes. Wash the watercress and trim any heavy stems; chop. Once the squashes have drained, squeeze to remove excess moisture.

Combine the zucchini and watercress. In a sauté pan heat 2 tablespoons of the butter and cook half the shallots until wilted. Add the zucchini and watercress and sauté until heated through, 4–5 minutes. Season with salt and freshly ground pepper. Remove from pan and set aside.

Melt 2 tablespoons butter and cook the remaining shallots until wilted. Add the yellow squash, cook 4–5 minutes, season thoroughly, and set aside. Mix 1/3 cup of the cream into each squash mixture. Beat the eggs and add half of them to each bowl. Butter a 1 1/2-quart 9×5-inch loaf pan, and line with buttered waxed paper.

Spread half the zucchini mixture in the bottom of the pan and sprinkle with one-third of the cheese. Gently spread on half the yellow squash without disturbing the lower layer. Sprinkle on another third of the cheese. Repeat the layering once, ending with the yellow squash. Place the loaf pan into a larger baking dish and pour boiling water halfway up the side of the loaf pan. Bake in a preheated 375° oven for 15 minutes, lower the heat to 350°, and bake another 30 minutes or until the loaf is firm. Remove and let rest in the pan for 15–20 minutes before turning out onto a serving dish. (*Serves 8*)

Summer Squash Salads

Low-calorie summer squash makes a filling nibble and is a colorful addition to a crudités platter. I also toss sliced or julienned young raw squash in a salad. One of my favorite summer salads is completely green. I combine lettuces, cucumbers, zucchini, fresh green scallions or chives, and avocado, if it's available. Zucchini's crisp texture adds crunch as well as contributing to the gradations of green. Young squash doesn't need to be peeled, but to give a pretty edge, score the skins as you would cucumbers. *Aunt Pat's Summer Salad* (see *Cucumbers*) also utilizes summer squash.

Here are some of my other favorite salads:

- Finely slice young summer squash. Make a *Vinaigrette Sauce* (see *Appendix*), heat it in a sauté pan, add the sliced squash, and heat through. Cool and refrigerate before serving.
- Cook whole squash until barely tender. Remove, cool, pat dry, and slice into rounds or sticks. Sprinkle with a tasty olive oil and season with black pepper. Let stand at room temperature. Before serving, toss with fresh lemon juice and chopped fresh dill, mint, or basil.
- Toss blanched squash "logs" with peeled red and green pepper strips and dress with a mustard *Vinaigrette Sauce* (see *Appendix*).
- Sauté squash cubes and chopped onion in a garlic-flavored oil. Combine with cooked rice or a small-size pasta such as orzo. Add chopped fresh herbs and toss in olive oil, lemon juice, salt, pepper, and toasted pine nuts (optional). Cool before serving.

Zucchini and Brown Rice Soup

Brown rice adds some textural crunch to this hearty soup. For extra zing stir in a garlic and basil garnish, as in *Bean Soup with Pistou* (see *Beans*).

    1 lb zucchini
    1/2 lb spinach leaves
    6 cups chicken broth
    1/2 cup long-grain brown rice
    1 1/2 cups sliced onions
    3 Tb butter
    Salt and freshly ground pepper

Wash, trim, and grate the zucchini. Do not salt: the juices add flavor to the soup. Wash the spinach leaves, dry, and

Wash and trim the squash, and coarsely grate or chop. Heat the butter and cook the onions until wilted and lightly golden. Stir in the curry powder, and cook 30 seconds. Add the squash and stir until squash is coated with butter and wilted. Add 4 cups of broth. Bring the broth to a boil, reduce heat and cook gently, uncovered, until squash is tender. Purée in a blender. Add additional broth if you like a thinner consistency. Serve either hot or cold with a garnish of sour cream. (*Makes 2 quarts*)

- Omit the curry, substituting a bit of saffron for its beautiful color.
- Top with paper-thin slices of blanched yellow squash.
- Omit the curry, and substitute zucchini sautéed with chopped leeks.

Pasta with Zucchini

Top pasta with summer squash for a delicate vegetarian meal. Note the variations at end of recipe.

> 3 lb zucchini
> Salt
> 4 Tb butter or olive oil
> 1–2 tsp chopped garlic (optional)
> Freshly ground pepper
> 1 lb pasta, such as linguini, rigatoni, fettucini, etc.
> 3/4–1 cup grated Parmesan cheese

Wash, trim, and grate the zucchini. Salt and let drain for 30 minutes. Squeeze out the moisture. You should end up with 6 cups. In a sauté pan, heat the butter or oil and cook the garlic (if you like) for 30 seconds. Add the zucchini and cook until barely tender, stirring to coat with butter or oil. Season with salt and a generous amount of pepper.

In a large kettle cook the pasta *al dente*, drain, and toss with the sautéed zucchini, and half the grated cheese. Taste for seasonings, and serve with the remaining cheese. Add additional butter or oil if you like. (*Serves 4–6*)

- Use 6 cups chopped, julienned, or sliced zucchini. Salt and pat dry before proceeding. Combine the hot pasta with 1/2 pound grated mozzarella cheese, 1/2 cup grated Parmesan cheese, and squash. The cheese will melt into a creamy sauce.
- Use butter, not oil. Add 1 cup heavy cream to the sautéed squash; cook to thicken cream slightly. Add to pasta and cook, stirring, for 1–2 minutes so pasta is completely coated with cream. Season generously with black pepper.
- Add finely sliced prosciutto or ham strips.
- Combine the sautéed squash with your favorite tomato sauce.
- Julienne carrots and zucchini, sauté separately, and combine as a pasta topping. Or sauté julienned sweet red pepper with zucchini.
- Add sliced, sautéed mushrooms.
- Toss with chopped basil, parsley, mint, or other herbs.

cut into thin strips. Bring the broth to a boil, stir in the rice, lower heat, cover, and cook slowly until the rice is just tender, about 40 minutes. In a large sauté pan, cook onions in the butter until wilted and golden. Stir in zucchini and cook, stirring, for 4–5 minutes. There will be moisture left in the pan. Mix in the spinach, and cook, stirring, until barely wilted. Set aside. When the rice is cooked, stir in the zucchini mixture, heat through, and season with salt and pepper. The soup will have a beautiful green color and will be fairly thick. Thin with additional broth if you wish. (*Makes 2 quarts*)

- Add cooked chicken pieces.
- Substitute other greens such as Swiss chard for the spinach.
- Substitute a duck stock for the chicken stock. It gives a wonderful flavor.

Susan Mayer's Curried Summer Squash Soup

> 2 lb yellow squash
> 3 Tb butter
> 1 cup chopped onions
> 1 tsp curry powder
> 4–5 cups chicken broth
> Sour cream (optional)

Baked Zucchini and Linguini

Eat this excellent buffet or picnic dish either hot or cold. You can grate, chop, or slice the zucchini, but be sure to salt and drain it. The pasta, ricotta, and zucchini are mild-flavored foods—don't be afraid to zip up the seasonings.

> 6 Tb butter
> 1 cup chopped onions
> 2 tsp minced garlic
> 6 cups salted and drained zucchini
> Salt and freshly ground pepper
> 1 stick peperoni, approximately ½ lb
> 6 eggs
> 2 lb ricotta cheese
> 1 cup grated Romano or Parmesan cheese
> 1 lb linguini

Heat 4 tablespoons of the butter and cook the onions until wilted and golden. Add the garlic and cook for 30 seconds. Stir in the zucchini. Sauté until lightly coated with butter and almost tender. Season to taste with salt and pepper. Cool slightly. Thinly slice peperoni; set aside. Beat the eggs and combine thoroughly with the cheeses. Drop the linguini into a kettle of rapidly boiling salted water and cook until tender but still chewy (*al dente*).

While pasta is cooking, combine the cheese-egg mixture with the zucchini and peperoni. When the pasta is cooked, drain, and shake for a moment to remove excess moisture. Combine pasta and zucchini mixture. Season liberally and pour into a buttered 9½ x 14-inch pan. Dot with the remaining butter and bake in a preheated 350° oven for 45 minutes. (*Serves 8–10*)

- Substitute crumbled cooked sausage for the peperoni.

Zucchini, Tomato, and Cheese Pie

Here's a filling meal ideal for a hot summer day. Prebake the pie shell, sauté the zucchini and tomatoes ahead of time, and have nothing left to do but assemble the dish. Or you can omit the pie shell and bake in a buttered 9 x 12-inch dish.

> 10-inch pastry shell (recipe follows)
> 1½ lb zucchini
> Salt
> 3 medium-size ripe tomatoes
> 4 Tb butter
> 1 Tb oil
> 3 eggs, separated
> 2 cups grated Swiss cheese
> ½ cup feta cheese
> Freshly ground pepper
> 1 Tb chopped fresh basil or mint

Prepare and cook the pie shell; set aside to cool. Wash the zucchini, trim, and cut into ¼-inch slices if large; cut small zucchini lengthwise. Salt, drain, and pat dry. Meanwhile, peel the tomatoes, halve horizontally, and remove the seeds. Heat 2 tablespoons of the butter with the oil in a large sauté pan. Lightly brown the zucchini on both sides; drain on brown paper. Lightly brown the tomatoes until they soften slightly but do not become limp. Cool.

When you are ready to assemble the pie, beat the egg yolks, set aside. Place half the zucchini in the shell. Sprinkle with one-third of the grated Swiss cheese and half the feta cheese, dot with 1 tablespoon butter, and sprinkle with salt, pepper, and half the basil or mint. Beat the egg whites and fold into the yolks. Spread half of this mixture over cheeses. Slightly flatten the halved tomatoes, and arrange across the pie. Sprinkle with one-third of the Swiss cheese, half the feta cheese, and the remaining basil or mint. Top with the remaining zucchini slices, and season with salt and pepper. Spread with remaining egg mixture, top with the remaining Swiss cheese, and dot with remaining tablespoon of butter. Bake in a preheated 400° oven for 25–30 minutes or until the eggs are set. Cover the pastry edges with aluminum foil if they are getting too brown. (*Makes a 10-inch deep-dish pie*)

- Omit the eggs and proceed as above.

Pastry for Zucchini, Tomato, and Cheese Pie
10 Tb butter
1 ¾ cups flour
1 egg
Pinch of salt

Gradually mix the butter into the flour until the butter is broken up into pea-size bits. Beat the egg and add to mixture along with salt; mix until well combined. (This is quickly done in a food processor. When the dough balls on the processor blade, it is ready.) Wrap in waxed paper and refrigerate for 30 minutes. Roll out on a floured board. Place in a buttered 10-inch deep-dish pie plate, working with your fingers until it fits evenly. Prick dough with a fork, and cover with aluminum foil. Weight down. (I always use some clean gravel I keep in a container just for this purpose—you can also use dried beans or rice.) Bake in a preheated 400° oven for 20 minutes, or until the pastry is set and the bottom just about cooked through (it will bake further when the filling is added).

Zucchini Bread

Zucchini bread recipes abound. In this version, draining and squeezing the zucchini makes it less moist than most, and it is less sweet. Eat it with or without butter. The green flecks call to mind its zucchini origins.

> 1 lb zucchini
> Salt
> 2 3/4 cups flour
> 1 1/2 tsp baking powder
> 1 tsp baking soda
> 1/2 tsp cinnamon
> 3 eggs
> 1 cup sugar
> 1/2 cup vegetable oil
> Grated rind of one lemon
> 1 Tb lemon juice
> 1 tsp vanilla extract
> 1 cup chopped walnuts or pecans (optional)

Wash, trim, and coarsely grate the zucchini; salt, drain, and squeeze it dry. You should have 2 cups zucchini. Sift together the flour, baking powder, soda, cinnamon, and 1/2 teaspoon salt. Beat the eggs, sugar, and oil, and mix in the lemon rind, lemon juice, and vanilla. Beat in dry ingredients and stir in the zucchini. Add the nuts if you wish. Pour into a greased and floured 9×5-inch loaf pan, and bake in a preheated 350° oven for 50–60 minutes. (*Makes a 9 x 5-inch loaf*)

Lynn's Spicy Zucchini Bread

Here's a moist, dark, sweet zucchini bread.

> 3 cups flour
> 1 tsp baking powder
> 1 tsp baking soda
> 1 tsp salt
> 2 tsp cinnamon
> 1/2 tsp nutmeg
> 3 eggs
> 1 3/4 cups sugar
> 1 cup vegetable oil
> 1 1/2 tsp vanilla extract
> 2 cups lightly packed coarsely grated zucchini

> 1 cup raisins (optional)
> 3/4 cup nuts (optional)

Sift the dry ingredients together. Beat the eggs with the sugar, oil, and vanilla. Gradually beat in the dry ingredients. Stir in the zucchini, adding raisins and nuts if you like. Divide between 2 greased 9×5-inch loaf pans and bake in a preheated 350° oven for 50–60 minutes. (*Makes 2 loaves*)

Summer Squash Spice Cake

This cake ends up almost as dark as gingerbread. Don't bother to frost—just serve with applesauce or cream.

> 1 1/2 cups flour
> 1 tsp baking powder
> 1/2 tsp baking soda
> 1 1/2 tsp cinnamon
> 1/2 tsp nutmeg
> 1/4 tsp ground cloves
> 1/4 tsp ground ginger
> 1/2 tsp salt
> 2 eggs
> 1 packed cup dark-brown sugar
> 2/3 cup vegetable oil
> 2 tsp vanilla extract
> 1 1/2 cups grated summer squash

Sift together the dry ingredients. Beat the eggs, sugar, oil, and vanilla together. Beat in the dry ingredients. Stir in the grated squash. Pour into a greased 8 x 8-inch pan. Bake in a preheated 350° oven for approximately 45 minutes. (*Makes an 8×8-inch cake*)

Summer Squash Orange Cake

I have made this moist cake with both yellow and zucchini squashes—it makes no difference. You can frost it or sprinkle it with powdered sugar.

> 3 cups flour
> 3 tsp baking powder
> 1 tsp salt
> 1 tsp cinnamon
> 1 tsp nutmeg
> 1/4 tsp ground cloves
> 1 cup softened butter
> 1 3/4 packed cups dark-brown sugar
> 2 tsp grated orange rind
> 4 eggs
> 1/3 cup orange juice
> 1 1/2 cups grated squash

Sift the dry ingredients together. Cream the butter, sugar, and orange rind. Beat in the eggs. Slowly beat in the dry ingredients alternately with the orange juice. Stir in the squash. Pour into a greased and floured 10-inch tube pan and bake in a preheated 350° oven for 50–60 minutes. (*Makes a 10-inch tube cake*)

Evelyn Higginbotham's Zucchini Pickles

6–8 medium zucchini, 6 x 1½ inches
2 medium onions
¼ cup pickling or kosher salt
2 cups sugar
2 tsp mustard seed
½ tsp dry mustard
2 cups vinegar
1 tsp celery seed
½ tsp turmeric

Wash, trim, and slice the zucchini ⅜ inch thick. Peel and slice the onions ¼ inch thick. Layer in a glass or earthenware bowl, sprinkle with salt, and cover with cold water. Let stand for 2 hours. Drain, rinse the zucchini with fresh water, and drain again. Combine the remaining ingredients in a stainless steel or enamel pan. Bring to a boil, cook 2 minutes, then add the zucchini and onions. Immediately remove from the heat and let stand for 2 hours. Bring the mixture to a boil, cook for 5 minutes, and ladle into hot sterilized pint jars. Process in a boiling water bath for 5 minutes. (*Makes 4 pints*)

Easy Dilled Squash Spears

2 lb zucchini or yellow summer squash
6 Tb kosher salt
1 large sweet onion
2–3 cloves garlic
4 heads fresh dill, plus a bunch of leaves
1 cup white wine vinegar
2 Tb sugar
1 tsp celery seed
1 tsp mustard seeds

Wash and trim the squash. Cut into serving-size spears. Sprinkle with ¼ cup salt and cover with ice water. Let stand 2 hours. Drain, rinse, and drain once more. Slice the onion. Peel and slice the garlic. In a large bowl layer squash, onion slices, garlic, and dill. In an enameled or stainless steel saucepan, mix the vinegar, 1 cup water, 2 tablespoons salt, sugar, and celery and mustard seeds. Heat until the sugar and salt dissolve. Pour over the vegetables. Cover and refrigerate 2 days before using. (*Makes 2 quarts*)

Squash (Winter)

I am a hoarder. Even in the frenzy of spring cleaning, I find it nearly impossible to throw anything out. That must be the reason I get such pleasure contemplating Russ's hills of winter squash, for I know the time will come when I'll gather the squash in bushel baskets and head directly to the attic, which has the dry, cool conditions necessary for long-term storage. And what a pleasant feeling during the winter months to know that part of our summer garden awaits at the top of the stairs.

There are so many kinds of winter squash it's hard to believe they all belong to the same family, *Cucurbitaceae*. Squash are really edible gourds: winter and summer squash as well as pumpkins, both of which I've taken up in earlier sections, belong to the same family. Summer squash are harvested immature, while winter squash ripen on the vine, then are harvested in autumn and stored for winter use. Both groups include bush and vining types—although most winter squash are vining.

All winter squashes do not taste the same but have discernible flavor and textural characteristics. I'm partial to certain varieties, and I have friends who feel equally strongly about others. Try as many as you can and decide for yourself. I find a dry squash works up better in bread or cake recipes. For individual servings, what could look nicer than the dark green shells of Acorn or Buttercup squash? I swear by the flavor of Harris's Sweet Meat, while a friend is equally taken by Banana. Sweet Mama could win a popularity contest by name alone. Our all-time favorite for general use is Waltham Butternut, developed a few miles away at the University of Massachusetts' Waltham Field Station. Russ says it was bred to be disease and pest-resistant—especially to the squash vine borer, a pesky creature who ruins many a squash plant by tunneling between the bud and the stem. A true Waltham Butternut also will not crook, making it easier to peel; and being thin-skinned and meaty, it has more usable flesh per ounce—all in all, well worth cultivating.

Squash are tender plants which cannot be set out in the garden until all danger of frost is over. Seeds can be sown directly in the garden, but Russ prefers to get a head start on the crop by starting seeds indoors. About the third week of April or the first week of May, he plants two squash seeds in individual peat pots; he pinches off the weaker of the two when they're large enough to tell apart. (This planting in separate pots is important, as the plants resent root disturbance and otherwise would not transplant well.) Squash are heavy feeders, so he puts a bushel basket of well-rotted manure in hills placed 3 feet apart; this high amount of organic matter in each hill guarantees a good harvest. Each plant gets its own hill, and once established and watered regularly, the squash do well throughout the summer. Both at the Victory Garden and here at our home garden, squash are given

their own section of territory, as vines tend to trail off in all directions. (If your space is limited, select one of the new bush varieties recently introduced.) Fruits form in July, ripen in August, and are ready to harvest in September, anywhere from 90 to 110 days after they were planted. Winter squash, however, will not fully ripen unless nighttime temperatures have dropped, for sugars don't accumulate until night temperatures go down into the 50s. The scientists at the Waltham Field Station have found in blind taste tests that the squash ranking most flavorful are the ones with high sugar content. To develop squash with good sugar content hope for sunny days and cool nights. Gardeners in the South may have a difficult time raising sweet, flavorful squash because of this need for cool nights.

Squash blossom tempura and fritters are delicious. Make sure you gather only the male blossoms so as not to lose fruit. It's easy to tell the female and male blossoms apart. Look for a bulge at the base of the flower below the petals; this bulge will grow into a squash, and de-

notes a female blossom. The stem of the male blossom is thin and trim. Happily, there are far more male than female blossoms. Gather blossoms at midday—before they have closed up—leaving one inch of stem, and refrigerate in ice water until you're ready to cook. Before frying, pat blossoms dry, then coat with batter and deep-fry.

You don't have to worry about how large your winter squash are getting; quality stays the same regardless of size. There's no need to quickly can, freeze, or divide them among the neighbors, for, properly stored, squash will keep through to spring. Russ swears they improve with age. That may be only his opinion, but we dine off delicious squash "fresh" all winter long.

Harvesting couldn't be simpler, but do remember two things. First, wait to pick the squash until the skin has hardened; if it is still tender and soft, the squash is too young and will not be as flavorful or store as well. An easy test is to try to poke your fingernail through the flesh of the squash. If you have difficulty, the squash is ready to harvest. If you can easily prick the squash, it's still immature. (The wound will heal before it's time to pick the squash.) Don't, however, try this test at the supermarket. Second, leave the stems on the squash. Breaking off where the fruits and stems meet leaves an open "wound" which could allow rot to enter. When you're ready to cook, it's a simple matter to cut off the stems. Always harvest before a frost, which might cause chilling injuries.

Before storing, cure most winter squash by holding for 10–20 days at room temperature (about 70–80°). An exception is Acorn squash, which should not be cured because eating quality and storage life are damaged. Acorn squash also have a shorter storage life than most squash—they keep in good condition for 10–15 weeks rather than the usual 6 months.

Most winter squash varieties, as well as pumpkin, can be used interchangeably in the following recipes except for vegetable spaghetti squash, for which I'll give special directions.

For all-purpose cooking, I steam squash. For special recipes, or when the oven is already on, I bake them. Both methods are equally acceptable. I also occasionally sauté squash or fry it in deep fat. I rarely boil squash—it destroys the texture and flavor.

Marketing

At the market, it's often hard to buy whole squash, or sometimes to know what type of squash you're purchasing, since many markets cut large squash up into portions. If you ask, the produce manager should be able to identify the variety. Buy winter squash that's hard, heavy, and clean; avoid any that's cracked or has a soft or decayed spot.

Special Characteristics of Winter Squash

- *Acorn*: Don't purée; texture is best baked.
- *Buttercup*: Texture is very dry and smooth. Mild flavor.
- *Butternut*: Medium-sweet flavor, good texture, average moistness.
- *Hubbard*: Can be bland and watery.
- *Sweet Meat*: Dry, sweet, mealy texture.
- *Vegetable Spaghetti Squash*: Bland flavor; unique crunchy texture.

◇ Steamed Squash

I steam squash any time I need mashed or puréed squash or want to serve chunks of squash unadorned. Count on each pound of trimmed squash to equal 2 cups mashed squash.

Peel squash and cut into chunks. Boil ¾ inch water in steamer, put squash in colander or steam basket, and cover. The steaming time depends upon the size of the chunks: 1½–2-inch chunks will steam tender in 15–20 minutes.

◇ Boiled Squash

I do not recommend this method but it is occasionally convenient.

Peel squash and cut into chunks. Place in saucepan and barely cover with warm water. Cover, bring to a boil, reduce heat, and cook gently until tender. The cooking time depends on the size of the chunks: 1½-inch chunks will take approximately 5 minutes once the water has come to a boil.

Special Information

Yields

- 2½ pounds whole squash = 1½ pounds 10 ounces cut-up squash = 2¾–3 cups puréed squash
- 1 pound trimmed squash = approximately 2 cups cooked squash

Note: Due to the different sizes of squash and thickness of skins, each variety of squash will differ slightly in whole weight related to final trimmed weight. The above is an approximate guide.

Storage and Preserving

- Store squash at 50–55° in a dry spot with low humidity. (If stored below 50°, squash will suffer chilling injuries and start to deteriorate.) Don't put squashes in your basement—it's probably too moist and they will be more likely to rot; an attic or any other cool, dry spot is your best choice.
- Winter squash stores so well that there's no need to can or freeze it. However, cooked squash freezes nicely, and it's a convenience to have it ready to eat.

Hints

- Small chunks of squash are a good addition to soups and stews.
- Squash cooked with pot roast or a braised dish of any kind will thicken the sauce nicely when mashed.
- Raw squash is a delightful snack or addition to a crudités platter.
- Squash is low in sodium, so it's a good choice for restricted-salt diets.
- Use the flesh as well as the blossoms for *Squash Tempura* (see *Vegetable Tempura* in *Mixed Vegetables* for batter recipe). Just cut into thin, flat strips, dip in batter, and deep-fry.
- Substitute squash in *Duck with Turnip* (see page 332), for turnips. Add 4 allspice berries and a garlic clove to herb bouquet. Add ½ cup diced squash and a slice of ginger to the stock. Simmer as in the recipe, covered, for 45 minutes. Add 1½ pounds of squash, cut into 2-inch pieces, and cook, covered, another 45 minutes or until duck and squash are tender. Remove duck and squash pieces and keep warm. Degrease sauce, mash vegetables into it, and pour over duck and squash.
- Substitute disks of squash for eggplant in *Eggplant Parmesan* (see page 108). Use a 2½–3 pound peeled butternut squash. Cut across squash in ¼-inch slices,

Finishing Touches for Steamed or Boiled Squash

- Toss in melted butter, and season to taste.
- Mash or purée; add butter and seasonings to taste.
- Make a glaze. For 2 1/2 pounds squash, melt 3 tablespoons butter in a sauté pan large enough to hold the squash in one layer. Stir in 1 1/2 tablespoons sugar and add steamed squash chunks. Over low heat, turn squash in butter and sugar until completely glazed. Season with salt and pepper before serving.
- See *Steamed Squash with Ginger and Apple* (page 287).

◇ Baked Squash

Baking is a wonderful way to prepare squash as a final dish that you can serve just as it comes out of the oven. Unlike boiling, you really get the full flavor without the squash getting soggy.

Baked Whole Squash

Whole small squash go in the oven just as is—their skins protect the flesh. A 1 1/2-pound butternut squash will take approximately 45 minutes in a 350° oven, while a 2 1/2-pound butternut will take 1 1/4–1 1/2 hours (the bulbous end will unfortunately become very soft by the time the thick middle section is ready).

All good-size squash can be cleaned and baked whole, with or without stuffing. Cut an opening or lid in squash and scrape out seeds and stringy pulp. Brush with melted butter and season with salt and a bit of sugar if desired (see *Pumpkin* and *Giant Stuffed Banana Squash*). Cooking times vary, depending upon the size and the density of the squash. Hubbard squash takes less time

than banana squash because it is not as dense or thick-skinned. In the case of most large squash, count on at least an hour, and then start checking for tenderness by pricking with a fork.

Baked Squash Halves

Baking small halved squash is an easy and pretty way to prepare winter squash. I'll give you a basic preparation for Acorn squash—the most adaptable for baking. Buttercup's seed cavity is lopsided, so to get equal portions, halve lengthwise from stem to base. Thin-skinned butternut squash holds up poorly—one of its virtues, a small seed cavity, is a disadvantage for stuffing.

Halve Acorn squash either lengthwise or across the midsection, scooping out seeds and stringy portions, and cut a small slice off the bottom so the pieces sit securely. Brush the cut surfaces with melted butter, and sprinkle with salt. Arrange in a baking pan, cut sides down. Cover the bottom of the pan with water. Bake in a preheated 400° oven for 30 minutes.

Combine butter and brown sugar, honey, or maple or corn syrup. You will need approximately 1/3 cup melted butter and 1/4 cup sugar, honey, or syrup for every 2–2 1/4 pounds squash. Turn squash cut sides up and brush with butter/sugar mixture. Bake until tender, 15–30 minutes, basting occasionally with butter. Season with salt and pepper to taste.

- Sprinkle cheese in the cavities, omit sugar, and baste with the butter.

including half slices at bulbous end. Treat exactly like eggplant slices. If necessary refrigerate slices after they are coated so crumbs adhere well.

Microwave

- *Acorn Squash*: Two whole squash cut in half and covered will cook in 13 minutes. (Add no water.)
- *Hubbard Squash*: 2 pounds peeled squash cut into 1 1/2–2-inch chunks, placed on a glass pie plate, and covered will take 8 minutes to cook tender, but not soft.
- *Butternut*: A 2-pound squash cut in half (3 inches wide at center, 8 1/2 inches long), placed in a glass pie plate, and covered will cook in 12 minutes. (Uncover after 6 minutes and cook for 6 minutes longer.)
- *Spaghetti Squash*: A 3 1/2-pound whole spaghetti squash placed in oven will cook in 15 minutes.

Leftovers

- Freeze leftover squash—it's delicious reheated.
- Use small amounts added to yeast breads or pancake batters to give color and moisture.
- Use puréed in soups.

Baked Squash Chunks

When I'm baking squash chunks, I either bake plain with butter or cook with moisture. For 2½ pounds untrimmed squash, you will need approximately 3 tablespoons butter.

Butter-Baked Squash Chunks: Put butter in a baking pan and place in a preheated 400° oven just until melted. Trim squash, cut into 1½–2-inch chunks, and add to pan. Coat with butter, bake for 15 minutes, turn over, baste, and bake 10–15 minutes longer.

- Substitute pumpkin for squash.
- When squash is almost cooked, sprinkle 1½ teaspoons brown sugar over squash and butter. Mix and cook until glazed, 5–8 minutes.

Baked Squash Chunks—Moisture Method: This method prevents browning and is a good preliminary preparation for squash to be mashed or puréed.

Trim squash (or leave skin on) and cut into 1½–2½-inch chunks. Place in a baking pan and film the bottom of the pan with ¼ inch of water. Or bake in aluminum foil along with a bit of water. Cover and bake in a preheated 400° oven. Two and one-half pounds trimmed squash will cook in 15–25 minutes, depending upon the size of the chunks.

- Substitute pumpkin for squash.

Vegetable Spaghetti Squash

You may have seen this novelty squash in seed catalogs or at your grocery store. Spaghetti squash originated in Italy as a light green squash with dark green spots. Around the turn of the century, a Japanese outfit began experimenting with that squash and, after 70 years, came up with the winning vegetable we now call spaghetti squash. It has none of the characteristics of other winter squashes and must be treated differently. The name refers to the flesh, which, when cooked, forms loose spaghetti-like golden strands.

The squash itself is practically tasteless; it is the crunchy texture that makes it so appealing—to say nothing of the fact that it has virtually no calories. It is a low-calorie crisp-textured vehicle for sauces or seasonings. To make Russ's favorite version, toss cooked squash strands in butter, then fold in lots of grated cheese. I have served it this way at the restaurant as a first course: one evening, we had one party send back for three helpings! We also use a *White Clam Sauce Topping*.

Boiled Whole Spaghetti Squash

Heat up a big kettle of water, large enough to hold the whole squash. When water is boiling, drop in the vegetable spaghetti squash and cook for 20–30 minutes, depending upon its size. When a fork goes easily into the flesh, the squash is done. Remove from water, and let cool. (The whole squash can also be steamed, but it takes longer.) When cool enough to handle, split lengthwise down the middle of the squash, and remove the seeds and stringy portion.

Now comes the fun. With a fork, "comb" the squash flesh and the "spaghetti" will pull off in long strands. You'll end up with a bowl of vegetable spaghetti which can be refrigerated for later use or served right away. Sauté in butter or top with your favorite sauce. Steam to reheat if you are cutting down on fat.

Baked Spaghetti Squash

Prick squash with a long-tined fork so the skin won't burst while cooking. Bake in a preheated 350° oven 40 minutes to 1½ hours, depending upon the size, or until the flesh is tender. Treat as above.

White Clam Sauce Topping

As summer turns into fall and we do the last of our clamming and musseling, this is a favorite topping.

2–3 dozen topneck or littleneck clams
⅓ cup white wine
¼ cup olive oil
3–4 cloves garlic, finely minced
Freshly ground pepper
¼ cup chopped parsley
Salt (optional)

Scrub clams well, then steam in wine. Remove the flesh, discarding shells, then strain the broth and reserve. Heat oil and sauté garlic until cooked but not browned. Add clam broth to oil, grind in pepper (about ½ teaspoon), bring to a boil, lower heat, and simmer for 5 minutes. Add clams to sauce. Pour over hot spaghetti squash and toss with parsley. Season with additional salt and pepper if necessary. (*This will coat 6–8 cups of shredded squash*)

Steamed Squash with Ginger and Apple

As delicious as it is plain, squash also beautifully accepts herbs and essences. "Scenting" the steam water imbues the squash with flavoring fragrances, while reducing the water produces a subtle glaze to coat the squash. Use any combination of herbs or fruits you like: here is a favorite combination of mine.

2 ½ lb winter squash
1 apple
1 quarter-size slice fresh ginger
1 Tb butter

Trim squash and cut into 1½-inch chunks. Put ¾ inch water in steamer. Peel the apple, placing peels into water. Cut up apple coarsely and add to water along with ginger and butter. Bring water to boil, put squash in steamer basket, cover, and steam until tender, 15–20 minutes. Remove squash and strain liquid into a saucepan, pushing some of the pulp through the sieve. Boil steaming liquid until it is reduced to about ¾ cup syrup. Add squash chunks to syrup and reheat. (*Serves 4*)

Sautéed Grated Squash

2–2 ½ lb winter squash
1 clove garlic
4 Tb butter
1 tsp sugar
⅓ cup heavy cream (optional)
Salt and freshly ground pepper

Peel squash and cut into large chunks, then grate on largest side of grater or in a food processor. Mince garlic. Melt 3 tablespoons butter in a large sauté pan and sauté garlic for 1 minute without browning; add squash. Sprinkle on sugar, turn squash until coated. Cover, lower heat and cook for 5–8 minutes until softened but still retaining texture. Remove cover, turn up heat, and stir in remaining butter. Mix in cream (if you like) and heat together for 2–3 minutes; season to taste. (*Serves 4–6*)

Sautéed Squash Cubes

2–2 ½ lb winter squash
4 Tb butter
2 tsp sugar (optional)
Salt and freshly ground pepper

Peel squash and cut into ½-inch cubes. Melt 2 tablespoons butter in a sauté pan large enough to hold the squash cubes in one layer. Stir in sugar (if you like). Over medium-high heat, brown squash cubes on all sides, 8–10 minutes. Turn heat to lowest setting, add remaining butter if the squash seems dry, cover, and let gently cook until just tender, 5 minutes or less. Check to make sure squash cubes do not burn. Season with salt and pepper. (*Serves 4–6*)

Baked Mashed Squash

An absolute must at our house for Thanksgiving is baked mashed squash. Not only is it delicious, it is also easily made ahead of time. Allow extra baking time if it's been refrigerated.

2 ½–3 lb unpeeled winter squash
5 Tb butter
Salt and freshly ground pepper
Brown sugar (optional)
¼–⅓ cup chopped nuts (optional)

Peel squash and steam or bake until tender. Mash. You should have 1½–2 cups squash. Mix in 4 tablespoons butter and season to taste with salt and pepper. Place squash in a buttered 1-quart baking dish, dot with remaining butter, and cover with a sprinkling of brown sugar and nuts, if you wish. Bake in a preheated 350° oven for 30 minutes. (*Serves 4*)

- Spread 1 cup grated Swiss cheese or combination of cheeses over top. Sauté 2 tablespoons chopped onions in 3 tablespoons butter along with ½ cup fresh bread crumbs. Cover cheese and bake as above.
- Melt 2 tablespoons butter and sauté 1 large chopped apple until cooked through; season with cinnamon and sugar and spread over squash. Bake as above.
- Cover with sour cream, crumbled bacon bits, or fresh herbs such as dill.

Squash Pancakes

These pancakes are good for breakfast, lunch, supper, or as a vegetable course with dinner. Serve with maple syrup, honey, sour cream, or applesauce.

1 egg
1 cup mashed cooked winter squash
½ cup flour
1 ½–2 Tb sugar
¼ tsp salt
½ tsp baking powder
¼ tsp cinnamon
¼ tsp nutmeg
1 tsp melted butter
1 Tb milk

Beat egg and mix with squash. Sift together all dry ingredients and add to squash and egg. Stir in butter and milk. Mix well and ladle onto heated griddle or fry pan. Cook on one side until bubbles appear; turn and cook on other side. (*Makes 6–8 small pancakes*)

Gratin of Squash with Rutabaga

The French, who grow a squash similar to Hubbard, often combine it with garlic. The added flavor of a bit of rutabaga is a pleasant addition, should you have some in the garden. If you want to omit the rutabaga, add ½ pound additional squash. Note that the squash cooks down considerably.

    2 lb trimmed winter squash
    ½ lb trimmed rutabaga
    3–4 cloves garlic, or more to taste
    ⅓ cup chopped parsley
    ¼ cup finely crumbled fresh bread crumbs
    4 Tb flour
    1 tsp salt
    Freshly ground pepper
    ¼ cup olive oil

Chop squash and rutabaga into ½-inch cubes—easily done by first cutting into ½-inch rounds, then into ½-inch slices, then cubing. (If the rutabaga is old, blanch in boiling water for 5 minutes to remove its strong taste, drain, and pat dry.) Chop garlic and combine with parsley and bread crumbs. Toss squash and rutabaga cubes with flour and salt until lightly coated, then toss in crumb mixture. Grind in pepper to taste.

Brush 1½-quart ovenproof dish with oil. Put squash mixture in dish and press down lightly. Drizzle remaining oil over the mixture and bake in a preheated 325° oven for 2–2½ hours, or until the top has browned and crusted over. The top will be crunchy, with a soft interior that retains the cube shapes. (*Serves 4*)

- The last 30 minutes, sprinkle grated Parmesan cheese, or a combination of Parmesan and Swiss, on top.

Squash Pudding Ring

I have used squash in this timbale, but any root vegetable could be treated in the same manner. In fact, 3 cups of most vegetables could be substituted for the grated squash—just blanch and sauté them first. You can make in advance and refrigerate until you are ready to bake. Cooking in a ring mold makes a timbale that's attractive and easy to serve; fill the center and circle the sides with buttered sliced carrots. Serve with sour cream if you like.

    2–2½ lb winter squash
    3 Tb finely chopped onion
    3 Tb butter
    5 eggs
    ⅔ packed cup fresh bread crumbs
    ½ cup grated cheese, Swiss and Cheddar combined
    ¼ cup chopped parsley
    ¾ cup heavy cream
    3 Tb chopped fresh dill
    1 Tb sugar
    1 tsp salt
    Freshly ground pepper

Peel squash, cut into large pieces, and grate with large side of grater or in the food processor. You will end up with approximately 6 cups grated squash. Melt butter in

a large pan. Sauté onion for 1 minute, add squash, and turn in butter. Cover and cook slowly for 8–10 minutes. The squash will have cooked down to about 3 cups. If squash is very wet, remove cover, turn up heat, and cook until dried out, approximately 2 minutes. Stir constantly, and don't let burn. Let cool.

Beat eggs, and add squash and remaining ingredients. Stir to combine. Fill a buttered 1½-quart ring mold with mixture. Set mold in a baking pan and add hot water two-thirds up the sides of the mold. Bake in a preheated 325° oven for 35–45 minutes, or until a skewer stuck in the center comes out clean. Let rest for 10 minutes before unmolding. (*Serves 6–8*)

- Combine squash with grated parsnip.
- Use individual molds; cut baking time to 20–30 minutes.

Stuffed Acorn Squash

All sorts of stuffings work for squash. Try rice with a Moroccan touch of onions, currants, and pine nuts; or cube and sauté turnips, mix with sautéed peas, and fill the squash cups. Your favorite meat mixture, cooked and well seasoned and added in the last 15 minutes of cooking, would make a complete meal. Here are two easy-to-prepare fillings:

Acorn Squash with Apple Stuffing
    2 Acorn squash (about 1¼ lb each)
    2 Tb melted butter
    Salt
    Cinnamon
    ¼ cup raisins
    ¼ cup Madeira or port wine
    3 medium apples
    4 Tb butter
    ¼ cup brown sugar
    1 Tb lemon juice

Halve squashes and scoop out the seeds and stringy interiors; trim the undersides so the halves will sit flat. Brush cut surfaces with melted butter and sprinkle with salt and cinnamon. Place in a baking pan with cut sides down. Put ½ cup water in pan or enough to just cover the bottom of pan. Bake squash 30 minutes in a preheated 350° oven.

While squash is baking, soak raisins in wine to plump. Chop apples into ½-inch cubes—either peeled or unpeeled, as you like. In a small frying pan, melt butter and add apples. Cook for 3–5 minutes until slightly wilted; stir in sugar and lemon juice. When squash has cooked for 30 minutes, turn cut sides up. Drain raisins, add to apple mixture, then fill squash cavities. Cover and bake for 20–30 minutes more or until tender. (*Serves 4*)

- This fruit filling is particularly nice with ham or pork. Try pears, too.
- Remove cooked squash from the shell, purée, add some butter, cream, and seasonings, and refill squash. Sprinkle with buttered bread crumbs, reheat for 15 minutes, and run under broiler to brown.

Acorn Squash with Sour Cream
Sour cream melts and adds richness to the finished dish.

2 Acorn squash (about 1 1/4 lb each)
4 Tb butter
Salt
1/2 cup chopped scallions
1/2 cup finely chopped fennel or celery
2/3 cup sour cream
Freshly ground pepper
1/3 cup grated Swiss cheese (optional)

Cut squash in half and scoop out seeds and the stringy interior. Trim the underside so that the squash sits level. Melt 2 tablespoons of the butter. Brush the cut surfaces with melted butter, sprinkle with salt, and arrange cut sides down in baking pan. Put 1/2 cup water in pan or enough just to cover bottom of pan. Bake in a preheated 350° oven for 30 minutes.

Meanwhile, melt 2 tablespoons butter in a sauté pan and add scallions and fennel or celery. Cook lightly until just wilted and tender. Mix with sour cream; season with pepper. After squash has baked for 30 minutes, remove from oven and carefully scoop out as much flesh as possible, leaving the shells intact. Keep squash in chunky pieces rather than mashing, and combine with the sour cream mixture. Fill shells and bake for 20–25 minutes longer. Sprinkle with cheese if desired and run under the broiler to brown. (*Serves 4*)

Giant Stuffed Banana Squash for a Crowd

Recently, we had a reunion dinner of old friends, and Russ contributed the largest vegetable we had in the garden, a 2-foot-long, 20-pound banana squash! I stuffed it with rice, spinach, and cheese, making a glorious presentation to accompany the meat course (although a 20-pound squash does take a while to cook).

1 giant banana squash, up to 20 lb
1/2 lb butter, plus 3–6 Tb for dotting (optional)
Salt
Sugar
2–3 lb spinach
Freshly ground pepper
2 cups chopped onions
5 1/2 cups long-grain rice

1 cup heavy cream
3/4–1 cup finely grated Swiss cheese (optional)

Wash exterior of squash. Cut a lid—at least 4–5 inches wide—lengthwise, extending to within 5 inches of both ends. Clean out the interior of the squash, scraping away the seeds and stringy pulp. Melt 4 tablespoons of the butter and coat the inside. Sprinkle with salt and a bit of sugar. Put squash in a large baking pan; pour water 1/4 inch up the sides of the pan. Put squash lid on askew. Bake in a preheated 400° oven for 1 1/4 hours, adding more water as it evaporates.

Trim, wash, and blanch spinach. Drain, cool, and thinly slice. In a sauté pan, melt 1 tablespoon of the butter and, stirring constantly, cook spinach over high heat until moisture is evaporated. Add 2 tablespoons of the butter, and braise for 5–10 minutes. Season with salt and pepper; set aside. In the same pan, melt 2 tablespoons of the butter. Sauté the onions until softened, approximately 10 minutes; set aside. In a large saucepan, add rice, 11 cups of water, 6 tablespoons butter, and 2 tablespoons salt. Bring the water to a boil, stir once, cover, and simmer for 15–17 minutes or until the liquid is absorbed. Remove from heat; cover for 10 minutes. Put in a large bowl; stir in spinach and onions with a fork, not a spoon, so that you don't crush or bruise the rice. Season to taste.

With a fork, stir cream and cheese (if you like) into rice mixture. When squash has baked 1 1/4 hours, fill the cavity with rice mixture; dot with butter. Partially cover with lid and bake another 45 minutes to 1 1/2 hours or until the flesh is tender. (If the squash takes too long to cook, raise the oven temperature: it won't hurt the squash.) To serve, set on the table, cut the lid into chunks, and serve with rice filling. Scoop additional flesh from squash interior. (*Serves 20, at least*)

- Cook any large squash the same way. After 1 hour, begin checking for tenderness. Cooking times depend on the density of the flesh and its thickness. You can add the stuffing at the start of cooking (this may take a bit longer), at the halfway mark, or at the very end. The squash stays hot even when sitting.
- Use other vegetables, such as peas, squash cubes, or other julienned vegetables.
- Oysters poached in butter and chopped up in the stuffing give an indiscernibly subtle flavor to the stuffing.

Squash Stuffing
This dense stuffing is nice for game birds.

2 Tb butter
2/3 cup chopped celery
1/3 cup chopped onions
1 cup chopped apple
1 cup grated winter squash
1 Tb brown sugar
3/4 tsp salt
1 Tb poultry seasoning
3 cups homemade bread crumbs
1/2 cup chopped pecans (optional)

Melt butter and cook celery and onions until just wilted; add apple and squash, cover, and let cook over low heat. When wilted, stir in sugar, salt, poultry seasoning, bread crumbs, and nuts (if you like). Let cool before stuffing. (*Makes 6 cups*)

Two-Way Squash Slaw

After harvesting a Sweet Meat squash that was as orange and succulent as could be, I found that I much preferred to eat it raw rather than cooked.

> 2 lb untrimmed winter squash
> 1 cup raisins
> ^{2}/3 cup *Mayonnaise* (page 349)
> 1/2 tsp celery salt
> 1 1/2 tsp sugar
> 1 tsp wine vinegar
> 2–3 Tb heavy cream
> Salt and freshly ground pepper

Peel squash and cut into large chunks. Grate with the large side of a grater, or use a food processor. You should have 5–6 cups. Place in bowl and sprinkle in raisins, using more or less as desired. Mix together mayonnaise, celery salt, sugar, and vinegar; thin with heavy cream. Pour over squash and raisins and stir well. Season with salt and pepper to taste. (*Serves 4*)

- Use half as much squash and replace with 1 pound sliced cabbage. Vary dressing by replacing heavy cream with sour cream, or using half mayonnaise and half sour cream.

Squash Soup

This soup can be made without the chestnuts, but they add a rich and complex flavor, as well as being readily available in winter squash season.

> 1/2 lb raw chestnuts
> 2–2 1/2 lb Butternut squash

> 1 onion
> 1 carrot
> 1 stalk celery
> 2 Tb butter
> 5 cups chicken stock
> Salt
> 1/4 tsp ground ginger (optional)
> 1 1/2 cups light cream
> Freshly ground pepper

Peel chestnuts (see *Appendix*). Peel and seed squash and cut into 1/2-inch cubes. Chop onion, carrot, and celery, and add to butter melted in a 4-quart saucepan. Stew to wilt but not brown. Add chestnuts and squash and stir into vegetables. Add 4 cups chicken stock and 1/2 teaspoon salt. Bring to boil, cover, reduce heat, and cook for 30–40 minutes or until chestnuts and squash are tender. Stir in ginger if you like. Purée in a blender with remaining chicken stock. Add cream and season with salt and pepper to taste. Reheat and serve. (*Makes 8 cups*)

Squash and Meat Pie

This economical pie is equally good cold; and you can substitute leftover meat for ground beef.

> *Tart Pastry* (page 351)
>
> *Meat Layer*
> 3/4 lb ground beef
> 1 stalk celery
> 1 small onion
> 1/4 lb ham
> 2 Tb butter
> 1 egg
> 1/2 cup grated Swiss cheese
> 1/4 cup grated Parmesan cheese
> 1/4 cup chopped parsley
> 1 tsp thyme
> 1 1/2 tsp salt
> Freshly ground pepper

Topping

2 eggs
2 cups cooked mashed winter squash
1/2 cup cooked rice
2/3 cup cream
1 Tb melted butter
Salt and freshly ground pepper
1/4 cup grated Parmesan cheese

Make pastry for 10-inch pie pan and partially bake.

To make meat layer, brown ground beef, drain off fat, and put meat in mixing bowl. Chop celery and onion; cut ham into 1/4-inch pieces. Melt butter and sauté celery and onion until barely wilted, 3–5 minutes. Add ham and cook for 2 minutes. Stir into ground beef. Beat egg and mix with beef mixture along with cheeses, parsley, thyme, salt, and pepper. Taste and add more seasoning if necessary. Let cool.

For topping, beat eggs, then add squash, rice, cream, butter, salt, and pepper. Put cooled meat mixture in tart shell, pat down, then cover with squash topping up to sides of tart shell. Sprinkle with Parmesan cheese. Bake in a preheated 350° oven for 15 minutes, then turn heat to 325° and bake for 20–30 minutes longer or until crust is nicely browned and filling is heated. (*Serves 4–6*)

Sweet Squash Pudding

This is lovely warm or cold, served with whipped cream or ice cream. It sinks as it cools, but that doesn't affect its taste.

4 eggs
1/2 cup sugar
1/4 tsp salt
2 Tb melted butter
2 Tb light rum
1/2 tsp cinnamon
1/4 tsp nutmeg
1 1/2 cups puréed cooked winter squash
1 cup heavy cream

Beat eggs, sugar, and salt together until thick, then add butter, rum, spices, and squash. Whip cream until it forms soft peaks; fold into squash mixture. Pour mixture into a buttered 1 1/2-quart baking dish and set into a larger baking pan. Fill pan with hot water two-thirds of the way up the baking dish. Bake in a preheated 325° oven for 40–50 minutes or until a skewer inserted in the center comes out clean. (*Serves 4–6*)

Winter Squash Crème with Caramel

I have always loved crème caramel. Well made, it's a delightful way to end a meal. This version retains the custard's lightness but adds the rich flavor of squash for an unusual fall or winter dessert.

Caramel
1/2 cup sugar
1/4 cup water

Squash Crème (Custard)
1 1/2 cups mashed cooked winter squash (preferably Butternut)
3 whole eggs
2 egg yolks
2 Tb brown sugar
1/2 tsp salt
1/2 tsp ground ginger
1/2 tsp cinnamon
1 cup milk
1 cup heavy cream

Bring sugar and water to a boil, stirring to dissolve sugar. Boil, swirling the pan as the syrup cooks, until it turns a rich tea brown. This can take 10 minutes or so. When the syrup is ready, pour into a 1-quart casserole or individual molds. Revolve dish rapidly so that caramel runs over the bottom and slides as evenly as possible. It hardens almost immediately, so work quickly. Remember caramel is very hot—use potholders, and be extremely careful not to burn yourself. The mold is now ready for the squash crème.

Purée the mashed squash to the very finest texture possible, using a blender or putting it through a sieve. Beat eggs and egg yolks together, then beat into them the sugar, salt, spices, and squash. Bring the milk and cream to a boil and add in a stream, very slowly at first, to the egg-squash mixture, beating all the time. Pour the mixture into the caramel-lined mold or molds and place in a deep larger pan. Pour boiling water halfway up the filled mold and set in the middle of a preheated 325° oven. Bake for 50 minutes or until a skewer inserted in the center comes out clean. Remove mold from water bath and chill for at least 3 hours before serving. To unmold, run knife around the edge and dip bottom of mold in hot water to loosen custard. Unmold on a chilled serving plate. (*Serves 6*)

- This crème can be molded perfectly well without the caramel. You might want to increase the amount of sugar to compensate for the loss of the caramel sweetness.
- Make a pie out of the same crème. Prepare a 9-inch pie crust, partially bake (see *Appendix*), then add custard. Bake in a preheated 450° oven for 10 minutes, lower heat to 325°, and bake for 30 minutes or until a knife inserted in the center comes out clean.

Old-Fashioned Squash Pie

1 recipe *Tart Pastry* (page 351)
2/3 cup sugar
1/2 tsp salt
1 1/2 tsp cinnamon
1/2 tsp ground ginger
1/2 tsp nutmeg
1/4 tsp allspice
1/4 tsp ground cloves
2 eggs
1 1/2 cups puréed cooked winter squash
1 2/3 cups evaporated milk
Whipped cream

Make a 9-inch pie shell. Combine sugar, salt, and spices. Beat eggs, then stir in squash and milk. Add dry ingredients and mix well, until smooth. Pour into pie shell. Bake in a preheated 425° oven for 15 minutes, reduce heat to 350°, and bake for 30–35 minutes or until set. Cool. Serve with whipped cream. (*Makes a 9-inch pie*)

- Substitute puréed cooked pumpkin for squash.
- *Squash or Pumpkin Pie with Pecan Topping*: Substitute light cream for the evaporated milk; add 2 tablespoons cognac. Bake pie as above. Meanwhile heat together ¹/₂ cup brown sugar and 6 tablespoons butter to dissolve, stir in 1 cup chopped pecans and set aside. Ten minutes before pie is done, arrange nut mixture in a band around the top of the pie.

Squash Cookies

These quickly made cookies have a spicy squash flavor.

¹/₂ cup softened butter
³/₄ cup granulated sugar
³/₄ cup brown sugar
2 eggs
1 ¹/₂ cups mashed cooked winter squash
2 ¹/₂ cups flour
2 ¹/₂ tsp baking powder
1 tsp baking soda
¹/₂ tsp salt
1 tsp cinnamon
¹/₂ tsp nutmeg
¹/₄ tsp ground ginger
¹/₄ tsp allspice
1 cup raisins
1 ¹/₂ cups chopped pecans or walnuts

Cream butter and sugars until fluffy. Beat in eggs, then squash. Sift dry ingredients together and stir into squash mixture. Stir in raisins and nuts. Spoon onto greased baking pans and bake in a preheated 375° oven for 10–12 minutes. (*Makes 5–6 dozen cookies*)

Lynn Wilson's Squash Nut Bread

My neighbor Lynn is no stranger to fresh vegetable cookery. Here and following are her squash bread and cake recipes.

¹/₃ cup butter
1 ¹/₃ cups sugar
2 eggs
1 ¹/₃ cups mashed cooked winter squash
1³/₄ cups flour
1 tsp baking soda
¹/₄ tsp baking powder
¹/₂ tsp salt
1 tsp cinnamon
¹/₂ tsp nutmeg
¹/₂ tsp ground ginger
¹/₄ tsp ground cloves
¹/₂ cup chopped nuts

Cream together butter and sugar until light and fluffy. Beat in eggs, then squash. Sift together remaining ingredients, reserving nuts. Stir dry ingredients into squash mixture; add nuts. Butter a loaf pan and pour in the batter. Let rest for 15 minutes. Bake in a preheated 350° oven for 1 hour or until a skewer in the center comes out clean. Keep bread in pan for 10 minutes before turning out. (*Makes 1 loaf*)

Squash Cake

Try this oblong cake topped with a good vanilla frosting and chopped nuts.

4 eggs
1²/₃ cups sugar
1 cup vegetable oil
1³/₄ cups mashed cooked winter squash
2 cups flour
2 tsp baking powder
1 tsp baking soda
1 tsp salt
2 tsp cinnamon
¹/₂ tsp nutmeg

Beat eggs, add sugar, oil, and squash, and mix well. Sift together dry ingredients and thoroughly mix into squash mixture. Spread in a buttered 13 ¹/₂×8³/₄×1³/₄-inch pan and bake in a preheated 350° oven for 25–30 minutes. (*Serves 10–12*)

Squash Cornbread

I love cornbread but sometimes find it too dry. One day I added squash to my cornbread as an experiment. To my delight, the bread turned out moist with a pleasant aftertaste of squash.

³/₄ cup yellow corn meal
³/₄ cup flour
4 tsp baking powder
¹/₂ tsp cinnamon
¹/₄ tsp allspice
¹/₂ tsp salt

½ cup soft butter
¼ packed cup brown sugar
2 eggs
1½ tsp lemon juice
1 cup puréed cooked winter squash
¼ cup milk

Combine corn meal, flour, baking powder, spices, and salt. Cream butter, add sugar, and beat until light. Add eggs, lemon juice, squash, and milk. Beat together, then gradually add dry ingredients until well combined. Pour batter into a buttered medium-size loaf pan. Bake in a preheated 350° oven for 50 minutes or until a skewer inserted in the center comes out clean. Cool in pan for 10 minutes; remove and cool on rack. (*Makes 1 loaf*)

Squash Yeast Rolls

The squash color and taste will be most predominant if you use all white flour, but I like the nutty, rich flavor that the addition of some rye or whole wheat grain flour gives to these rolls.

2 packages active dry yeast
Pinch of granulated sugar
½ cup lukewarm water (110°–115°)
5⅓ cups white flour
1 cup rye or whole wheat flour
½ cup light brown sugar
1 tsp salt
1½ cups puréed cooked winter squash
¼ cup lukewarm milk
12 Tb softened butter

Sprinkle yeast and granulated sugar onto water in a small bowl. Stir and set in a warm, draft-free spot for 5–10 minutes, or until yeast bubbles and mixture doubles in volume.

Sift together 4⅓ cups white flour, the rye or wheat flour, light-brown sugar, and salt in large bowl. Make a well in center and pour in the yeast mixture. Add squash, milk, and 8 tablespoons of the softened butter. Stir together and beat well to combine all ingredients, beating until dough comes together in a soft ball. Place dough on a floured surface and knead, incorporating only as much of the remaining flour as you need, until the dough is no longer sticky. Continue to knead for 10 minutes, or until the dough is shiny and elastic. Butter a large bowl, add the dough, and let rise in a draft-free place until doubled in volume, 1–2 hours, depending on the warmth of the room. A longer, slower rise is best. Lightly butter 3 baking sheet pans.

Punch the dough down with your fist, and roll out on floured surface to a rectangle approximately 1 inch thick. Melt 4 tablespoons butter. With a biscuit cutter or glass, cut the dough into 2½-inch rounds. With the blunt edge of a knife, make a crease just off center, making sure not to cut through dough. Lightly brush with melted butter. Fold the smaller part of the round over the larger and press edges together. Arrange rolls about 1 inch apart on baking sheets and brush the tops with melted butter. Set the rolls in a draft-free place to rise for 15–20 minutes. Bake the rolls in the middle of a preheated 450° oven for 10–14 minutes, or until golden brown. (*Makes approximately 30 rolls*)

- To replace sugar with honey, use 6½ tablespoons honey and eliminate the milk.
- Another way to shape rolls is to cut long 1-inch strips in the rectangle, then cut strips into 4-inch lengths. Roll out each length, and make a knot. Children love to do this.

Sweet Potatoes

Sweet potatoes by any other name are not yams—regardless of what the labeling at the supermarket might be. True yams are starchy tropical vegetables rarely seen outside of Latin markets because they require 8–11 months of warm weather to reach maturity. The "yams" or "Louisiana yams" you see at the store are sweet potatoes. No one knows for sure where this custom of nicknaming sweet potatoes "yams" originated, but the practice is widespread and has led to much confusion.

In this country we raise about forty different kinds of sweet potatoes, only a few of which find their way to the table as fresh vegetables. Some are dried for starch or livestock feed, while other varieties are destined for the cannery. Sweet potatoes are divided into two types: "moist-fleshed" and "dry-fleshed," which refers to how they taste rather than to their water content. Varieties that convert most of their starches to sugar during cooking, becoming quite sweet and soft, are called "moist-fleshed" or yam varieties; those that convert less starch, and are therefore less sweet, are known as "dry-fleshed" types. The kind you choose to eat is most likely a matter of regional preference: southern cooks prefer moist-fleshed sweet potatoes, such as Porto Rico, while northern cooks favor the drier-fleshed Nemagold or Jersey varieties. Color is no indication of sweetness, for sweet varieties exist in a range of colors from white to purple.

Although sweet potatoes are customarily thought of as tubers, they're actually the roots of trailing vines belonging to the morning glory family. The roots contain latex, which is what causes the chalky aftertaste some people dislike. Some varieties have more latex than others. How much each contains is a genetic characteristic. Cut into a raw sweet potato and you'll see the latex immediately appear on the surface as milky white fluid

droplets. The latex also can oxidize, causing a change of color, which is not a problem when sweet potatoes are cooked—the reason so many recipes start with cooked, rather than raw, sweet potatoes. In any case, you'll have no problem if you immediately place peeled, raw sweet potatoes into water to prevent discoloration, or grate them directly into a wet mixture.

Sweet potatoes are a tropical crop needing both warm days and warm nights, average summer temperatures above 72°, and four to five frost-free months for best results. Varieties such as Centennial have been developed that mature faster, allowing even northern gardeners to harvest a sweet potato crop.

You can't just cut up the roots and plant them in the garden, because sweet potatoes grow from sprouts, or "slips," produced from the seed potatoes. Long, trailing sweet potato vines take up a lot of room in the garden. In the Victory Garden, where space is limited, we've grown sweet potatoes in soil-filled bushel baskets, placing one slip per basket. We've found that these potatoes produce rounder, meatier roots than those grown in the garden, and the baskets also can be moved to a warmer spot should frost threaten.

At home, we plant the slips in a sandy rich loam 18 inches apart in rows 3 feet apart. We're careful to side-dress with a low-nitrogen fertilizer with a 1-2-3 ratio. (Nitrogen-rich fertilizers give beautiful leaves, but small roots, and should be avoided.) We water sparingly, for sweet potatoes are drought-resistant plants and do better when they're not overwatered. The one time it's essential to water thoroughly is about two months after planting when the roots really start developing.

Harvesting time depends completely upon the variety of sweet potato grown. We plant Centennial, an early variety maturing in 120 days, a must for northern gardeners. Southern gardeners have a wider choice of long-season types taking 150–160 days to maturity. Hard frosts damage any roots close to the soil's surface, so before frost strikes, we harvest the potatoes, cutting away the trailing vines and digging the roots up carefully with a potato fork. Their thin skins bruise easily, so we handle them like eggs, gently putting them into a basket kept out of direct sunlight. (As little as 30 minutes' exposure to sunlight could result in sun scald.) Similar to winter squash, sweet potatoes should be cured, so we spread them out indoors in a humid spot with a temperature of 80°. Curing allows surface cuts to heal and skins to toughen before winter storage. After five to ten days, we place the roots for final storage in a humid, well-ventilated area with a temperature around 55°. I never refrigerate raw sweet potatoes because they would spoil right away, developing soft spots and hard cores, the result of chilling temperatures. However, after sweet potatoes have been cooked, it's a different story: they'll keep quite nicely in the refrigerator.

Sweet potatoes need only a good washing to be all set for cooking. I usually bake them, unpeeled, to get the best flavor. When I do peel them, I bake or steam rather than boil them, because boiling causes a loss of texture and flavor. I boil sweet potatoes only when they are cooked in a special liquid which then becomes part of the final dish.

One point to note: Beware of cookbooks that tell you to substitute sweet potatoes for Irish (regular) potatoes in recipes. That usually doesn't work. Sweet potatoes lack the starch content of even medium-starch varieties of potatoes. I once tried using sweet potatoes for potatoes in potatoes Anna and deep-fried potato baskets: the sweet potatoes didn't bind together. Potato gnocchi, those lovely Italian morsels made with whipped potatoes, came out unpleasantly heavy when I used sweet potatoes.

Also, as sweet potatoes are richly flavored and heavy in texture, a little goes a long way: when layering a casserole of sweet potato slices or filling peach halves with sweet potato purée, easy does it. Oddly enough, sweet potatoes' rich taste softens and becomes almost indiscernible in a pie or soufflé. The amount of sugar called for in a recipe really depends on what variety of potato you're using. However, you'll notice that my sweet potato recipes use far less than is customary. I find myself at odds with the vast majority of advice on sweet potatoes—so many recipes have reams of sugar, honey, molasses, corn syrup, and yet more sugar. Sweet potatoes are naturally sweet and don't need this excess sweetening. A light glaze or a subtle fruit sauce is sufficient; smother them with extra sugar, marshmallows, heavy glazes, or other concoctions and you'll ruin the flavor. Cook sweet potatoes unadorned and experiment with different spices and seasonings. It's amazing to see how well they combine with other vegetables as well.

Marketing

Look for unblemished, firm roots with no soft spots or bruises. Remember that types labeled yams or Louisiana yams are sweet, moist-fleshed varieties.

Common Sweet Potato Varieties

- *Centennial*: Orange skin; moist, orange flesh. Heavy yielder; stores well; good choice for northern gardeners.
- *Georgia Red*: Red skin; moist, light orange flesh. Good baker; stores well.
- *Jerseys*: Tan-red skin; dry, yellow-orange flesh. Good baker with mealy flesh; short storage life.
- *Nemagold*: Orange-tan skin; semimoist orange flesh. Short storage life.
- *Porto Rico*: Copper skin; moist salmon-orange flesh. Good choice for southern gardeners.

Special Information

Yields

- 3 sweet potatoes approximately 5 x 2 inches = 1 pound
- 1/2 pound sweet potatoes = 2 cups grated
- 1 pound sweet potatoes = 1–1 1/4 cups puréed

Storage and Preserving

- Do not store raw in the refrigerator, but keep in a humid, well-ventilated spot at temperatures averaging 55–58°.
- Cooked whole or puréed sweet potatoes keep 1 week in refrigerator.
- Cooked mashed sweet potatoes freeze well.

Hints

- Use in place of fresh mashed pumpkin in cake, bread, and cookie recipes.
- Always drop in water immediately after peeling to prevent discoloration.
- Sweet potatoes are very high in vitamin A and calories. A 3 1/2-ounce sweet potato baked in its skin has almost 150 calories.
- Combine whipped sweet potatoes with mashed rutabaga or turnips.
- Wrap in aluminum foil and grill over hot coals.
- Bake alongside roast meats. Peel potatoes and rub with butter to prevent darkening. Place next to roast for the last 40–50 minutes of cooking, turning in drippings to brown. Or, parboil for 10–15 minutes and bake for 30 minutes.

- *Deep-Fried Sweet Potato Chips*: Peel and thinly slice sweet potatoes, place in ice water for 1–2 hours, drain and dry thoroughly. Deep-fry, following the instructions for *Potato Chips* (see *Potatoes*).

Microwave

- Whole sweet potatoes, pricked to prevent bursting, will cook in 8 minutes.
- 1 pound chunks in 1 1/2-inch pieces, rubbed with melted butter and placed in a covered dish, will cook in 5 minutes.

Leftovers

- Make potato cakes by combining mashed cooked sweet potatoes with leftover mashed white potatoes; pat with flour and fry in butter.
- Use in biscuits or breads.

◇ Baked Sweet Potatoes

Whole Potatoes

Preheat oven to 400°. Wash sweet potatoes and bake with skins on. An 8-ounce sweet potato will cook in 40–50 minutes, depending on its thickness.

Potato Chunks

Peel 1½-inch chunks, brush with melted butter to prevent discoloration, and bake in a covered dish in a preheated 400° oven. Potatoes will cook in 20–30 minutes.

- Bake sweet potatoes as in *Baked Honeyed Rutabaga Disks* (see *Turnips & Rutabagas*).

◇ Steamed Sweet Potatoes

Boil 1½ inches water in a steamer, then add whole unpeeled sweet potatoes placed in a steam basket; steam until tender. An 8-ounce sweet potato cooks in 40–50 minutes, depending on its shape.

Peeled ½–1-inch cubes or strips will take 12–15 minutes.

◇ Boiled Sweet Potatoes

Bring salted water to boil and drop in whole unpeeled sweet potatoes. An 8-ounce sweet potato will cook in 35–45 minutes, depending on its shape.

Finishing Touches for Cooked Sweet Potatoes

- *Scooped-out Baked Sweet Potatoes*: Bake potatoes, cut them lengthwise, then scoop out the interior flesh, leaving just enough flesh to retain the shape of the skin. Mash flesh with butter and a bit of cream if desired and season to taste. Sprinkle with grated cheese (optional), stuff shells, dot with butter, and place in a buttered baking dish. Reheat in a 350° oven for 20–30 minutes.

- Sauté bacon slices until crisp, crumble, and set aside. Sauté mushroom slices in butter until lightly browned. Combine bacon and mushrooms with sweet potato flesh, add cream to taste, and season with salt and pepper. Return to shells, dot with butter, and bake as above.

- *Buttered Sweet Potatoes*: Peel cooked sweet potatoes and melt butter in a frying pan. Slice potatoes lengthwise into halves or fourths, and sauté in butter to lightly brown sides. Sprinkle with a bit of sugar to lightly glaze, if desired, and season with salt and pepper to taste.

- *Caramel Topping for Sweet Potatoes*: Cook sweet potatoes, peel, and keep warm. Make caramel syrup by boiling together ¾ cup sugar and 5 tablespoons water. Swirl pan (do not stir) until liquid is clear. When syrup reaches a medium caramel brown, dip pan in cool water to stop the cooking process. Stir caramel, and when it has cooled slightly, spoon it over the sweet potatoes in thick strands. This ½ cup topping is sufficient for 6 large sweet potatoes.

- *Grilled Sweet Potatoes*: Cut peeled cooked sweet potatoes in half, brush with melted butter or a combination of melted butter and honey, and place under the broiler until lightly browned.

- *Mashed Sweet Potatoes*: Peel and mash warm cooked sweet potatoes. These are delicious combined with butter or a bit of cream, salt, and pepper. Or spice with lemon or orange juice.

- *Gladys Gifford's Puréed Sweet Potatoes*: Purée 4 cups mashed sweet potatoes with 1½ cups homemade apple sauce. Season with grated orange rind, cinnamon, nutmeg, salt, and pepper. Reheat with lots of butter.

- *Baked Mashed Sweet Potatoes*: Peel and mash cooked sweet potatoes. Add melted butter and your choice of seasoning as desired such as grated orange or lemon peel, honey or spices. (You could also add sugar or light rum.) Put in a buttered baking dish and dot with butter. Bake in a preheated 350° oven for 30–40 minutes until cooked through. For a variation, cover with chopped nuts before baking.

- *Mashed Sweet Potatoes with Fruit*: Simmer cubed, peeled, and cored apples, pears, peaches, or apricots until soft with a small amount of water and butter. Drain and purée with cooked sweet potatoes to taste. Add butter and seasonings if desired.

- *Candied Sweet Potatoes; Syrup Method*: In a saucepan, combine ½ packed cup brown sugar, ¼ cup water, 3 tablespoons butter, and a dash of salt and cinnamon; simmer together 3–4 minutes. Cut peeled cooked sweet potatoes lengthwise into halves or quarters and put in a buttered baking dish, then pour syrup over them and bake in a preheated 400° oven for approximately 20 minutes, basting frequently. (This amount of syrup is sufficient for potatoes in an 8 x 8-inch pan.)
  Variation. Make the syrup with honey and add orange juice, lemon juice, lime juice, or light rum instead of water.

- *Candied Sweet Potatoes; Layering Method*: Layer cut cooked peeled sweet potatoes in a greased baking dish. Pour on ¼ cup water, a touch of lemon juice, and a sprinkle of ½ cup brown sugar or honey (more or less to taste). Dot with 3 tablespoons butter, and squeeze over about 1 tablespoon of lemon juice, or add chopped stem or candied ginger and some of its syrup. (Stem ginger can be found in many Oriental markets. It's ginger preserved in a sweet syrup that keeps it soft.) Bake in a preheated 400° oven for approximately 20 minutes, basting occasionally.

Sweet Potatoes in Sweet Sauce

I enjoy a lighter glaze than most on sweet potatoes. You can adjust the ratio of honey, sugar, and vinegar to suit your taste.

    3 Tb honey
    1 Tb vinegar
    1/3 tsp salt
    2 cups water
    1–1 1/2 lb sweet potatoes

Mix together honey, vinegar, salt, and water and bring to a boil. Peel and cut sweet potatoes into 1/3-inch slices. Drop directly into glazing liquid; bring to a boil and cook, covered, until tender, approximately 10 minutes. Remove from liquid and place on a heated platter. Reduce liquid to a light syrup and pour over sweet potatoes. (*Serves 4*)

- Cut into thicker slices, chunks, or 1/2-inch lengthwise strips.
- Add or substitute other seasonings, such as orange juice or beef or chicken stock, instead of the water-honey mixture.

Sweet Potato Pone

"Pone" recipes, abundant in the southern United States, are often associated with "cornpone," a bread or cake of corn meal. I've found almost as many versions of a puddinglike sweet potato pone, but for my taste, many are too sweet—so I devised this version with less sugar than customary (but I still find it's sweet enough to serve as a dessert with cream). Its traditional role is as a hot accompaniment to ham or pork.

    2 eggs
    1 cup milk
    1 lb sweet potatoes
    1/4 cup melted butter
    1/2 cup light corn syrup
    1/2 cup flour
    1/2 tsp cinnamon
    1/2 tsp nutmeg
    1/2 tsp salt

Mix eggs and milk together and grate peeled potatoes directly into the mixture; stir to coat. Blend in melted butter and corn syrup. Sift dry ingredients into sweet potato mixture and stir to combine well. Pour into a buttered 1 1/2-quart baking dish and bake in a preheated 325° oven for 2 hours. Stir once during the first hour. Serve either warm or cold.

Sweet Potato Waffles

This recipe makes light waffles; you can use the same batter for pancakes, but note that they will be fat and fluffy rather than thin and firm.

    1/4 cup butter
    1 1/2 cups flour
    3 tsp baking powder
    1 tsp salt
    1/4 tsp nutmeg
    3 eggs, separated
    1 cup milk
    1 cup mashed cooked sweet potatoes

Melt butter; set it aside to cool slightly. Sift dry ingredients together. Beat egg yolks, then combine with milk, sweet potatoes, and melted butter. Stir in dry ingredients. Beat egg whites until they form soft peaks. Fold into sweet potato mixture. Cook on a preheated waffle iron as instructed by manufacturer. (*Makes 4 waffles*)

Sweet Potato–Tomato Soup

This soup can be served hot or cold. The tomatoes cut the potatoes' sweetness without compromising their flavor.

    2 large ripe tomatoes
    1 carrot
    1 stalk celery
    2 Tb butter
    8 cups beef stock
    1 1/2 lb sweet potatoes
    Salt and freshly ground pepper
    Sour cream (optional)

Peel, seed, juice, and chop the tomatoes. Finely slice or chop carrot and celery. Melt butter in a 4-quart saucepan and cook carrot and celery until soft but not browned. Add tomatoes and stew until vegetable liquids are slightly evaporated; add stock. Peel and thinly slice sweet potatoes and mix together with vegetables and stock; bring to a boil, reduce heat, and gently cook until potatoes are very soft, 20–30 minutes. Purée in a food processor, or pass through a medium sieve. Season to taste and serve with sour cream on top if you like. (*Serves 6–8*)

• *Creamed Soup*: Chill soup and stir in ³/₄–1 cup heavy or sour cream just before serving.

Sweet Potato and Chicken with Fruit Sauce

This lightly fruited sauce is not cloyingly sweet, and it nicely complements both the sweet potato and the chicken.

Three 8-ounce sweet potatoes
2 frying chickens
3 quarter-size slices peeled fresh ginger
4 Tb butter
2 Tb oil
Salt and freshly ground pepper
³/₄ cup dry white wine
1 ¹/₂ cups chicken stock
3 oranges
¹/₄ cup sugar
2 Tb water
1 Tb cornstarch
¹/₄ cup orange juice
1 banana
1 cup fresh or canned pineapple chunks

Wash sweet potatoes. Cut up chickens, wash, and pat dry. (Save wing tips and necks for chicken stock.) Slice ginger into matchstick strips. Melt 2 tablespoons butter with oil in a large saucepan, and cook chicken on all sides to lightly brown. (It will probably be necessary to cook in two batches.) When all pieces are browned, remove chicken and pour off all fat from pan. Return chicken to pan, add half the ginger strips, and lightly salt and pepper the chicken. Pour on ¹/₂ cup wine and the chicken stock, cover, and simmer for 30–40 minutes or until chicken is tender.

While the chicken is cooking, bring 1 inch water to boil in a steamer and add the remaining ginger to the water. Place sweet potatoes in a steamer basket and steam for approximately 30 minutes until tender. Peel oranges and section flesh, discarding the white membrane. Combine sugar and water in a 2-quart saucepan over medium heat. Cook until syrup turns light brown, shaking pan occasionally. Dissolve cornstarch in ¹/₄ cup wine; set aside.

When chicken is cooked, drain off cooking liquid and remove fat from surface. (If the caramel syrup has cooled and hardened, reheat over low heat.) Add cooking juices and orange juice to syrup, stirring well, then stir in cornstarch mixture, cooking until lightly thickened. Peel and slice banana. In a sauté pan, melt 2 tablespoons butter and sauté oranges, pineapple, and banana for 1 minute, then mix into sauce. Taste and season with salt and pepper if necessary. Peel sweet potatoes and slice in half lengthwise, or in fourths if you prefer. Place the chicken in the center of a warm platter and arrange sweet potatoes around the chicken. Spoon fruit sauce over the chicken and potatoes. Pass extra sauce at the table. (*Serves 6–8*)

• Game birds, such as Cornish game hen or duck, work equally well.
• Experiment with other fruits, such as grapes, melon, or cherries.

Sweet Potato, Lamb, and Sausage Stew

The Eastern spices in this recipe cut the rich taste of sweet potatoes and provide a pleasant change of pace from traditional sugared, buttered sweet potatoes.

4–5 cups peeled and seeded ripe tomatoes
1 carrot
1 celery stalk
2 medium onions
6 Italian sausages
4 lb whole small lamb shanks (cut into 2-inch lengths if larger)
3 Tb oil
Salt and freshly ground pepper
¹/₂ tsp turmeric
¹/₂ tsp ground ginger
¹/₄ tsp cumin
¹/₄ cup beef stock or water
1–1 ¹/₂ lb sweet potatoes
¹/₄ cup chopped parsley

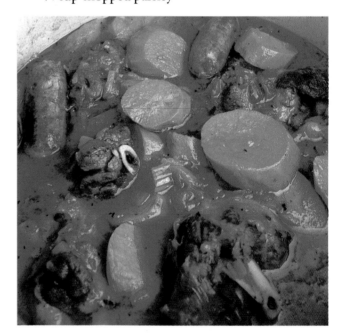

Chop tomatoes into ¹/₂-inch chunks (or use drained and seeded canned tomatoes). Set aside. Finely chop carrot and celery; combine. Chop onions and set aside. Prick sausages, cover with water in a saucepan, and bring to a boil. Lower heat and simmer for 10 minutes to release fat, then drain and pat dry.

Trim lamb of all fat. Heat oil in a large ovenproof casserole, brown lamb on all sides, and remove. In the same oil, lightly brown sausages on all sides. Remove sausages and drain fat from casserole, leaving just a film of oil. Add carrot and celery, sauté for 3–4 minutes, then add onions and cook for 3 minutes until wilted. Return lamb and sausages to casserole; sprinkle with 1 teaspoon salt. Cover, turn heat to low, and cook for 15 minutes. Uncover casserole and stir in pepper, turmeric, ginger, and cumin. Add chopped tomatoes and beef stock or water. Cover and cook over low heat for 1 hour, adding additional liquid as needed.

Meanwhile peel sweet potatoes and cut into 1/2-inch slices or 1/2-inch-wide lengthwise strips, dropping them into water until used so they won't discolor. Drain and add to the casserole. Continue cooking for 30 minutes or until the meat and potatoes are tender. If the juices are too thin, drain off and boil down until thickened. Pour back over meat and vegetables, and sprinkle with parsley. (*Serves 4–6*)

- Use beef chunks, cut into 1 1/2–2-inch pieces, with or without sausage.
- Add additional sliced carrots along with sweet potatoes, or garnish with blanched peas.

Sweet Potato Pudding

This dessert pudding is best served warm, but can also be chilled. Serve warm with sweet cream or chilled with whipped cream on the side.

5 Tb flour
2 Tb sugar
1/8 tsp salt
1/8 tsp nutmeg
1/3 cup raisins
1 cup milk
3 eggs
1 1/4 cups puréed cooked sweet potatoes
1 Tb melted butter
1/4 cup heavy cream
1–2 tsp lemon juice
1 tsp grated lemon peel (optional)

Sift together dry ingredients; set aside. Plump raisins in milk for 10 minutes and drain, reserving milk. Beat eggs, then beat in sweet potatoes, butter, milk, cream, lemon juice, and peel (if you like). Add dry ingredients and whisk together. Stir in raisins. Pour into a greased 6×9-inch baking pan. Set in a larger pan and pour in hot water to halfway up outer sides of the dish. Bake in a preheated 350° oven for 40–45 minutes. (*Serves 6–8*)

- Substitute winter squash or pumpkin for the sweet potato.
- To convert to a vegetable side dish, omit raisins and all but 1 teaspoon sugar.

Frozen Ginger–Sweet Potato Soufflé

Allow 4–5 hours in the freezer for the mixture to freeze slightly while still remaining creamy. If served after that point, the soufflé will taste fine, but the texture will have hardened and be more like ice cream.

6 eggs, separated
1/4 cup plus 1 Tb sugar
2 Tb water
1 1/2 cups mashed cooked sweet potatoes
1/4 tsp salt
1 tsp vanilla extract
1 Tb lemon juice
2 Tb rum
1 cup heavy cream
2 Tb finely chopped stem or candied ginger
Shaved chocolate

Prepare a 1 1/2-quart soufflé dish with a 2–3-inch aluminum foil or waxed paper collar. Beat egg yolks until thick and pale-colored. Stir together 1/4 cup sugar and 2 tablespoons water in a small saucepan and swirl pan until sugar is melted, 2–3 minutes. Then boil to a clear syrup stage, shaking pan as it cooks. Add very gradually to egg yolks, beating constantly. Add sweet potatoes, salt, vanilla, lemon juice, and rum. Whip cream and fold into mixture. Beat egg whites to soft-peak stage, sprinkle on remaining sugar, and continue beating until the mixture forms soft, glossy peaks. Stir a quarter of the egg whites into the sweet potato mixture to lighten it, then fold in remaining egg whites. Fold in ginger lightly and quickly. Pour into prepared soufflé dish and place in the freezer for 4–5 hours. When ready to serve, remove collar and decorate with shaved chocolate. (*Makes 1 1/2 quarts*)

Sweet Potato–Lime Chiffon Pie

4 eggs
1/4 cup melted butter
1/4 cup light brown sugar
2 cups mashed sweet potatoes
1/2 tsp salt
1/2 tsp cinnamon
1/4 tsp nutmeg
1/8 tsp cloves
2–3 Tb fresh lime juice
Grated rind of lime
1 cup light cream
1 Tb sugar
9-inch partially baked pie crust (page 351)

Preheat oven to 400°. Separate eggs and set aside. Cream butter and brown sugar until light. Beat in sweet pota-

toes and egg yolks, then add salt, spices, lime juice, rind, and cream. Beat egg whites, adding 1 tablespoon sugar when foamy, until they form soft glossy peaks. Stir in a quarter of whites to lighten sweet potato mixture, then quickly fold in the remaining egg whites. Turn into a partially baked pie crust. Bake for 10 minutes in a preheated 400° oven, reduce heat to 325° and bake for 45-40 minutes longer or until set. Serve cold. (*Makes a 9-inch pie*)

Sweet Potato Squares

One of my favorite apple cakes was the inspiration for this moist, easily prepared dessert.

> 1 cup flour
> 1 tsp baking soda
> ½ tsp salt
> ½ tsp nutmeg
> ½ tsp cinnamon
> 4 Tb butter
> 1 cup sugar
> 1 egg
> 1 large or 2 medium apples
> ½ lb sweet potato
> 1 tsp vanilla extract
> ½ cup chopped nuts

Sift together the flour, soda, salt, and spices and set aside. Cream together butter and sugar; beat in egg. Peel and grate apple and sweet potatoes and stir into the sugar mixture along with the vanilla. Add dry ingredients to sweet potato mixture and stir well. Stir in nuts. Pour into a greased 8-inch-square baking dish and bake in a preheated 350° oven for 35–40 minutes. Cool before cutting into squares. (*Makes 8-inch-square cake*)

Sweet Potato–Chocolate Nut Cake

The natural sweet potato orange color looks beautiful swirled together with chocolate, while the flavors complement each other. Sprinkle this cake with confectioners' sugar or drizzle it with the sugar glaze that follows recipe.

> 4 oz semisweet chocolate
> 1 tsp vanilla extract
> 3 cups flour
> 1½ cups sugar
> 2 tsp baking powder
> 2 tsp baking soda
> 2 tsp cinnamon
> ½ tsp ground ginger
> ¼ tsp ground cloves
> ¼ tsp nutmeg
> 1 tsp salt
> 2 cups mashed cooked sweet potatoes
> 1½ cups vegetable oil
> 4 eggs
> 1 cup chopped nuts

Butter and lightly flour a 10-inch tube pan. Place chocolate and vanilla in a small saucepan and set, covered, in a larger pan that you've just filled with boiling water.

Sift together all dry ingredients and set aside. In a large bowl, beat the sweet potatoes and oil together, then beat in the eggs one by one until well blended. Slowly add dry ingredients and mix well; stir in nuts. Put one-third of the mixture in another bowl and stir in the chocolate, which should be melted smooth by now. Alternate the batters in a tube pan, as you would with a marble cake. With a knife, cut through the two batters to slightly swirl together. Bake in a preheated 350° oven for 1–1¼ hours or until the sides have shrunk away from the pan, the top is springy, and tester comes out dry. Let cool 10 minutes and then remove from the pan and cool on a rack. (*Makes a 10-inch tube cake*)

Sugar Glaze
2–3 Tb boiling water
1½ cups confectioners' sugar

Beat water gradually into sugar until mixture has the consistency of a thick cream sauce; drizzle over cake.

Lynn's Sweet Potato–Bourbon Cake

This cake is lovely absolutely plain, but if you wish, sprinkle with confectioners' sugar.

> 3 cups cake flour
> 3 tsp baking powder
> 1 tsp salt
> 1 tsp cinnamon
> 1/2 tsp nutmeg
> 1/4 tsp ground cloves
> 1 1/2 cups salad oil
> 1 cup granulated sugar
> 1 cup brown sugar
> 5 eggs, separated
> 1/3 cup boiling water
> 2 Tb bourbon
> 1 cup chopped pecans
> 3/4 lb sweet potatoes
> 1/4 tsp cream of tartar
> 1/2 tsp salt

Grease a 10-inch tube pan. Sift together flour, baking powder, salt, cinnamon, nutmeg, and cloves. Set aside. Beat oil and sugars together until smooth. Beat egg yolks into mixture, add boiling water gradually, and beat for 2–3 minutes. Add dry ingredients to sugar mixture gradually, stirring well. Stir in bourbon and pecans.

Peel and grate sweet potatoes. (You should end up with 2 cups packed.) Stir into sugar mixture. Beat egg whites until they form soft peaks, adding the cream of tartar and salt when they are foamy. Stir one-quarter of the whites into the sweet potato mixture to lighten it, then fold in the remainder. Place in tube pan and bake approximately 1 hour in a preheated 350° oven. Cool in the pan for 15 minutes before unmolding. (*Makes a 10-inch tube cake*)

Sweet Potato Bread

Here's a quick way to use up leftover sweet potatoes.

> 2 cups flour
> 1 tsp baking soda
> 1/4 tsp baking powder
> 1/2 tsp salt
> 1 tsp cinnamon
> 1/2 tsp allspice
> 1/2 tsp ground ginger
> 2 eggs
> 1/2 cup oil
> 2/3 cup sugar
> 1 1/3 cups mashed cooked sweet potatoes
> 1/2 cup chopped nuts
> 1/2 cup raisins

Grease a 9 x 5-inch loaf pan. Sift together dry ingredients and set aside. Beat eggs; add oil, sugar, and sweet potatoes, beating after each addition. Add dry ingredients, stirring well. Stir in nuts and raisins and pour into the loaf pan, rapping the pan on the counter to settle the mixture. Bake in a preheated 350° oven for 50–60 minutes or until tester comes out dry. (*Makes a 9 x 5-inch loaf*)

Sweet Potato Biscuits

Sweet potatoes give a glorious golden color to these biscuits.

> 2 cups flour
> 4 tsp baking powder
> 1 tsp salt
> 1 tsp sugar
> 1/3 cup chilled shortening
> 3/4 cup mashed cooked sweet potatoes
> 1–2 Tb milk

Sift together dry ingredients. Cut in chilled shortening until it is broken into fine pinhead-size pieces. Beat in the sweet potatoes alternately with milk, using just enough milk to make the dough workable. (These steps can be quickly done in the food processor: put in the dry ingredients, add chilled shortening, turn machine on and off to break up the fat. Add the sweet potato, turn on the machine, and add the milk little by little until the dough balls up on the blade.) Place the dough on a lightly floured surface and, with the heel of your hand, quickly and lightly knead it until just pliable; pat or roll to 3/4-inch thickness. (The less you handle it, the tenderer the dough will be.) Cut into circles with a 2 1/4-inch round floured cutter. Transfer to an ungreased baking sheet. Bake for 12–15 minutes in a preheated 450° oven. (*Makes 10 biscuits*)

- *Sweet Potato Biscuit Crust:* Preheat oven to 400°. Heat meat pie mixture, chicken stew, etc., in an ovenproof 8–9-inch casserole. Pat or roll biscuit dough to 1/2-inch thickness and diameter of casserole top. Place on top of filling and press dough against the side of the casserole; brush with egg glaze. Bake for approximately 20 minutes or until raised and lightly browned.

Swiss Chard

A crop of Swiss chard is a bit like gaining two vegetables for the price of one, for this vegetable has absolutely no waste. Baby chard can be sautéed whole, and when it becomes larger, and cooking whole would result in overcooked leaves and undercooked ribs, you can cook them separately. The leaves can be cooked alone, combined with other vegetables, or substituted in recipes using other greens. The ribs, or stems, also can be cooked as is, or used as a cooked celery or asparagus substitute. In addition, the ribs possess a haunting beetlike aftertaste, which is not surprising because chard is a member of the beet family. (See for yourself: Try *Pickled Chard Ribs*.)

Seed companies list both white- and red-ribbed varieties, which taste the same, although the red is more ornamental. Although Swiss chard may be directly seeded into a garden, Russell sows seeds of Large White Rib or Fordhook indoors the first week of April to speed up the first harvest. The third week in May, he places seedlings 12 inches apart in one 10-foot garden row (more than long enough for our family). Swiss chard grows easily in average soil. Leaf miners usually show up the first week of June and can ruin the young tender leaves. Since there's no easy way to eliminate this pest, Russ simply removes spoiled leaves and waits for new growth.

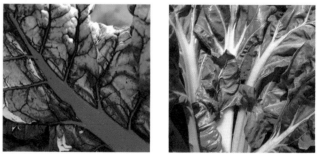

Leaf miners have definite life cycles, so generally if one "flush" of leaves is infested, the successive ones are not. In fact, some years leaf miners are no problem at all.

By mid-June, when the leaves reach 4–6 inches long, I start harvesting young ones for sautéing whole. I pick the larger 6–10-inch-long leaves throughout the summer and fall as needed, breaking off the outer (older) leaves at the base of the ribs so that the plants continue to grow, and separate the leaves from the ribs before cooking. Swiss chard will tolerate severe chilling temperatures, enabling us to enjoy fresh chard right through Thanksgiving.

This continual harvesting of chard means we usually avoid dealing with the huge sizes you see in the markets.

Sometimes, however, with such a large Swiss chard bed, the leaves do become oversize. That's fine, for the leaves and ribs still make delicious eating cooked separately.

Chard's high water content means it stores poorly, so I harvest chard as needed. Before cooking, I thoroughly wash it by dunking it up and down in a sinkful of luke-warm water and running it under the faucet.

How I decide to prepare chard completely depends upon its age. Chard with ribs less than ½ inch wide needs nothing more than a good wash in water. Once the ribs become ½–1 inch wide, I remove the leaves from the ribs and treat them separately. When the ribs are more than 1 inch wide, I not only cut off the leaves but also trim some of the heavy ribs that run up the back of the leaves. In addition, I peel large ribs like celery. Taking a knife, I

start at the end of the ribs, cut slightly into the flesh, and pull slowly down—the strings peel right off. You could also peel smaller ribs this way, but I think it's unnecessary.

My favorite way to cook Swiss chard is to sauté the whole baby leaves and ribs together. Larger leaves work well the same way as long as you slice them, then add gradually to the cooking pan.

Chard ribs tend to darken when they are cooked. Once I made the mistake of baking them raw, and they turned gray-black and unappetizing-looking. That's why I blanch ribs. If you insist upon a creamy white appearance, blanch ribs in a *Blanc* (see *Appendix*), exactly as you would Jerusalem artichokes and celeriac. If you don't mind a slight discoloration, just proceed without a blanc. It's up to you.

I both steam and blanch larger leaves, the method I use depending upon how large a quantity I'm cooking at a time. Blanching seems to be easier for large amounts, but when I'm cooking just for Russ and myself, I steam chard leaves. Both methods are equally good.

Marketing
Swiss chard is a prime example of a vegetable worth growing in order to get the very best quality. I have rarely seen chard that has stood up well to traveling and holding in the store. Out of season, it's almost impossible to find chard, and when you do locate it, it is usually not worth buying.

Special Information

Yields
- 1 pound Swiss chard = approximately ½ pound ribs and ½ pound leaves
- 1 pound whole chard = 5–6 packed cups leaves and 2½ cups ribs
- ½ pound chard leaves = 1–1½ packed cups cooked leaves
- ½ pound chard ribs = 2½ packed cups cooked ribs
- 1 pound whole chard = 3–4 servings
- 1 pound leaves = 2–3 servings
- 1 pound ribs = 2–3 servings

Storage and Preserving
- Refrigerated, unwashed, in a perforated plastic bag, chard will hold for 3–5 days.
- Once ribs or leaves are cooked, their shelf life in the refrigerator is minimal. The ribs become soft and unappetizing, and the leaves turn soggy and sour.
- Do not freeze chard ribs. They will be soggy.
- You can freeze chard leaves. However, remove all the ribs from the leaves or they will discolor. Blanch leaves for 2 minutes in boiling water, then immediately plunge into ice water for 2 minutes. Drain and package in freezer bags.

Hints
- Substitute chard leaves in most spinach recipes. You'll get a slightly "heartier" texture and taste. Or substitute spinach for chard.
- Substitute chard in the *Greens* recipes.
- Cook chard ribs as you would *Asparagus*. Serve with melted butter or sauce.
- Add raw sliced ribs or leaves to chowders and hearty soups. Add ribs 10 minutes before soup is done; add leaves 4–5 minutes before serving.
- String chard leaves if necessary.
- Sauté chard leaves along with other greens; or add to sautéed grated zucchini or yellow squash.
- Use both chard leaves and ribs in stir-fries. Add thinly sliced raw leaves directly to pan; blanch chard ribs until crisp-tender, cut into thin slices, then add to pan.
- Toss tender young leaves in a salad.

Microwave
I do not recommend microwaving either the leaves or the ribs.

Leftovers
- Use chopped cooked leaves and ribs in quiches, omelets, meat loaves, and stuffings.
- Add raw leftovers to stews and hearty soups.
- Purée leftover leaves with hot potatoes for a chard version of *Colcannon* (see *Kale*).
- Pickle leftover ribs. See *Dressings for Chard Ribs*.
- Add leftover cooked ribs to salads.
- See ideas under *Spinach*, *Greens*, and *Kale*.

Look for unblemished leaves with no trace of yellow. They should be fresh and crisp, not wilted and limp. The ribs should be a creamy white or mellow red color and firm to the touch. Swiss chard is usually sold whole, which means you have to take the very large outer leaves right down to the inner young ones. When chard is in season, look for loose leaves and choose the size you want. Stay away from the giant leaves and ribs—they're old and can be chewy.

◇ *Sautéed Swiss Chard*

For young Swiss chard only. Wash the chard; pat dry. Leave the chard whole, or slice it. In a sauté pan, heat equal quantities of oil and butter. Stir in chopped garlic (optional) and raw chard. Toss until coated with butter and oil. Cover pan, lower the heat, and cook for 3–4 minutes, stirring occasionally. Uncover pan, and raise heat to evaporate moisture. (Shake the pan so the chard doesn't stick.) Add more butter if necessary and season to taste. (For 4 cups leaves I would use 2–3 tablespoons butter and oil.)

Sliced or chopped older leaves work out fine cooked this way, but first stem them. The ribs can be sautéed if they are finely sliced across their width like celery. Blanch them first if you want to keep them white. You can sauté the sliced ribs first and when they are soft, add finely sliced leaves. Cook until both are perfectly tender.

◇ *Blanched Swiss Chard*

Blanch in a large pot of boiling salted water. Cut the ribs, regardless of their width, into 1–2-inch pieces. They will cook tender in 8 minutes once the water returns to the boil after the chard is added.

Depending upon their size and age, the leaves will cook in 2–4 minutes after the water returns to the boil.

To cook ribs and leaves together, first add the ribs and then add the leaves, adjusting times as above. Use a *Blanc* (see *Appendix*) if desired for ribs.

◇ *Steamed Swiss Chard*

Bring 1 inch of water to a boil in steamer pot or pot with colander in it. Ribs cut into 1–2-inch pieces will cook in 10–12 minutes. Leaves will cook in 4–6 minutes, depending upon their size and age.

Finishing Touches for Cooked Chard Leaves

Once leaves are blanched or steamed, you can prepare them the same ways as other greens (see *Greens*). It is essential to drain them, squeeze out the moisture thoroughly, and evaporate moisture further by cooking in butter and oil over heat. Add chopped onions, shallots, garlic, or other flavorings before you evaporate the moisture. Once the moisture is evaporated proceed as follows.

- *Sautéed in Butter*: For every 2 cups leaves, stir in 3 tablespoons butter. Cook slowly for 5–10 minutes, stirring until chard absorbs the butter. Season to taste and serve.
- *Creamed Chard*: For every 2 cups leaves, add 1 tablespoon flour to chard that has been sautéed in butter; stir for 2 minutes. Add 1 cup heavy cream; cook over low heat for 10–15 minutes or until the chard has absorbed the cream. Season to taste and serve.
- *Sautéed in Oil and Garlic*: In a sauté pan, heat olive oil and approximately 1 teaspoon chopped garlic. Add chard, stir to coat; heat through.
- *Chard Leaves in Mornay Sauce*: Make *Mornay Sauce* (see *Appendix*). Place 4–6 cups sautéed chard leaves, cut into 1–2-inch pieces, into a buttered casserole, add sauce, and top with buttered bread crumbs. Bake in a preheated 450° oven for 20–25 minutes or until the top has a light brown crust and the sides are bubbly.
- *Chard Leaves in Béchamel Sauce*: Make a *Béchamel Sauce* (see *Appendix*), add grated Parmesan cheese to the bread crumbs, and proceed as for *Chard Leaves in Mornay Sauce*.

Note: When you're making a sauced au gratin recipe or sautéed chard, you can combine the leaves and ribs after cooking them separately.

- *Swiss Chard with Oil and Lemon*: Cook both ribs and leaves. Drain well, squeeze gently to remove moisture, and coarsely chop. Sprinkle with salt and pepper and reheat in olive oil. Season with lemon juice to taste; serve with lemon wedges.

Finishing Touches for Cooked Chard Ribs

- *Sautéed*: Slice in thin diagonal slices across the rib and sauté in butter until tender.
- For every ½ pound drained blanched ribs, heat 3 tablespoons olive oil in a sauté pan. Cook 1–2 teaspoons chopped garlic until lightly browned. Add cut-up chard and sauté for 4–5 minutes, stirring con-

stantly. Season with salt, pepper, and chopped parsley (if desired).

- Heat 4–5 anchovies in oil, then mash anchovies until blended with oil. Add 3–4 tablespoons butter and the chard ribs. Cook as above.
- *Sautéed with Cream:* Simmer blanched ribs in 4 tablespoons butter for 4–5 minutes. Add ³/₄–1 cup heavy cream and briskly cook until cream is reduced and coats the chard. Season to taste.
- *Baked with Butter and Cheese:* Cut the blanched ribs into 1–2-inch pieces and place half into a buttered casserole. For every cup of ribs, pour over 1 tablespoon of melted butter, and sprinkle with grated cheese of your choice (Parmesan, combination of Parmesan and Swiss, Provolone, etc.). Sprinkle with herbs, salt, and pepper, and repeat layers, ending with cheese. Bake in a preheated 400° oven for 15–20 minutes.
- *Baked with Béchamel:* Make *Béchamel Sauce* (see *Appendix*). Place 3–4 cups drained blanched ribs, cut into 1–2-inch pieces, into a buttered casserole, add sauce, and top with a mixture of buttered bread crumbs and grated Parmesan cheese. Bake in a preheated 450° oven for 20–25 minutes or until the top has a light brown crust and the sides are bubbly.
- Make *Velouté Sauce* (see *Appendix*), and prepare as above. Add curry powder to the sauce.
- Make *Mornay Sauce* (see *Appendix*), omit the cheese in the topping, and prepare as above.

Dressings for Cooked Chard Ribs

- *Pickled Ribs:* It's amazing how similar pickled beets and pickled Swiss chard taste. Beet juice adds an attractive color, but water works just as well. Mix equal parts white vinegar and water or beet juice and add one-third to one-half the amount of sugar (for example, 1 cup vinegar, 1 cup water, ³/₄ cup sugar). Pour over cooked chard ribs; let stand for at least 30 minutes.
- *Ribs Vinaigrette:* Marinate warm ribs in a lemon-mustard *Vinaigrette Sauce* (see *Appendix*). Serve at room temperature.
- *Ribs à la Celeriac:* Mix cooked ribs with *Mustard–Sour Cream Dressing* (see *Celeriac*). Let stand 30 minutes; serve chilled.
- *Chard à la Asparagus:* Cut ribs into 4–5-inch pieces. Blanch as if they were asparagus, drain, and serve with a *Vinaigrette, White Butter,* or *Hollandaise Sauce* (see *Appendix*).

◇ *Stuffed Chard Leaves*

In a large pan or bowl, put large, perfect chard leaves from which you have trimmed the back ribs. Salt, pour boiling water over, cover, and steep for 5 minutes. Drain; pat dry. Fill with cooked stuffing, and roll the leaves around the stuffing, tucking in the leaf edges as you roll.

Place closely side by side on a bed of *Mirepoix* (see *Appendix*) in a saucepan. Pour broth to halfway up the side of the pan. Cover and cook gently for 15–20 minutes or until heated through. Remove leaves, reduce pan juices, then pour over chard. Or, cover chard with a hot tomato sauce. Or, sprinkle with cheese and run under the broiler. Make Greek dolma with Swiss chard, rather than grape leaves. Prepare leaves as above. See *Lettuce Leaf Dolmathis* for stuffing in *Salad Greens*.

Individual Swiss Chard Custards

½ lb Swiss chard leaves
1–2 fresh sorrel leaves (optional)
2 Tb butter
2 eggs
½ cup heavy cream
½ cup milk
1 tsp salt
Freshly ground pepper
Nutmeg

Cut off ribs on back sides of larger leaves. Fold each leaf and slice into ¼ x 2-inch diagonal slices. Slice sorrel (if using it), and add to chard. In a large sauté pan, toss chard and sorrel with butter, then lower heat. Cover pan and simmer for 3–4 minutes until wilted and tenderized. Uncover, turn up heat, and cook, stirring constantly, to evaporate moisture. Cool.

Beat together eggs, cream, milk, salt, pepper, and a dash of nutmeg. Butter four 6-ounce molds, and evenly distribute the chard and sorrel. Pour in the egg mixture, and stir each mold with a fork so that the chard and the custard are well mixed. Set molds in a baking dish and add boiling water halfway up. Bake in a preheated 350° oven for 25 minutes or until a knife inserted in the center of a custard tests clean. Remove molds from water bath. Let rest for a few minutes. Run a knife around the inside, and invert onto a serving platter. (*Serves 4*)

Chinese-Style Swiss Chard Soup

Here's a light, easy, and delicious soup that the dieters in our house appreciate. A good homemade broth is a distinct advantage.

> ¼ lb raw Swiss chard leaves
> 1 lb boned chicken breast·
> 1–1½ oz Chinese rice noodles
> 6–8 cups chicken broth
> 1 Tb soy sauce
> Black pepper
> 2–3 Tb chopped scallions
> Toasted chopped almonds (optional)

Diagonally slice chard into strips ½ inch wide by 2–3 inches long. Slice chicken paper-thin (easiest if the breast is partially frozen). In a large saucepan, layer chard, rice noodles, and chicken. Heat chicken broth to boiling, and pour it over the layers. Cook over medium heat for 3–4 minutes, then stir the broth. Add soy sauce and ladle into individual serving bowls. Sprinkle with pepper and scallions before serving, and pass toasted almonds if you wish. (*Makes 2 quarts*)

- Use a concentrated fish stock and thinly sliced fish rather than chicken.
- Omit noodles. Add homemade croutons just before serving.

Swiss Chard Soup

I like the texture and colors of this hearty soup. Purée and add cream, and you have a lovely beginning for a dinner party.

> 1 lb Swiss chard
> ½ cup sliced carrots
> 1 cup sliced celery
> 1 cup chopped leeks or onions
> 4 Tb butter
> ½ lb potatoes
> 5 cups chicken broth
> 2 tsp salt
> Freshly ground pepper

Wash chard; separate leaves and ribs. String ribs, if necessary, and thinly slice. Remove any thick ribs on the back of larger leaves, fold leaves in half, and slice into ½-inch pieces. In a large saucepan, stew chard ribs, carrots, celery, and leeks or onions in butter for 5 minutes until wilted.

Meanwhile, peel and chop potatoes; add to chard rib mixture along with broth and salt. Cover, bring to a boil, and simmer for 20 minutes or until the potatoes are tender. Mash some of the potatoes against the pan to thicken the broth. Stir in the chard leaves, and cook for 3–4 minutes or until the leaves are barely tender. Season with salt and pepper. (*Makes 6 cups*)

- *Cream of Chard Soup*: After the chard leaves have cooked for 2 minutes, cool soup slightly, then roughly purée in a processor or blender. Stir in ½ cup heavy cream, reheat, and season to taste. Serve with a spoonful of sour cream on top.

Layered Swiss Chard, Ham, and Cheese Custard

This is best chilled and cut in wedges, although it's also good hot or at room temperature. It can even be cubed and served as a cocktail nibble.

> 4–5 packed cups cooked Swiss chard leaves
> 1 cup chopped onions
> 1 Tb oil
> 4 Tb butter
> Salt and freshly ground pepper
> 1 lb thinly sliced ham
> ¼ lb Provolone cheese
> ¼ lb mozzarella cheese
> ¼ cup grated Parmesan cheese
> ½ cup ricotta or cottage cheese
> ½ cup cream
> 6 eggs
> 1¼ cups milk

Butter an 8–9-inch round baking dish 4–5 inches high, and place a buttered round of brown paper on the bottom of the dish. Squeeze moisture out of the chard; chop. In a sauté pan, cook the chopped onions until wilted in the oil and 2 tablespoons of the butter. Add chard, raise heat to high, and, stirring constantly, cook until moisture is evaporated. Season and set aside.

Cut the ham into 1-inch-wide strips, and cook until lightly browned in the remaining butter; set aside. Grate the Provolone and mozzarella cheeses and combine with Parmesan. Purée the ricotta or cottage cheese with the cream. Beat the eggs, then mix with cheeses and milk; season to taste.

Place one-third of the grated cheeses in the bottom of the baking dish. Drizzle some of the custard mixture on top. Place a third of the ham slices across the cheese, drizzling a little custard mixture in among them. Place a third of the Swiss chard on the ham; coat with custard. Repeat the layering twice, pouring custard on each layer. (The custard holds the layers together.) Top with waxed paper and foil. Place in a baking pan, pour boiling water halfway up the sides of the dish, and bake for 1 hour in a preheated 350° oven. Turn heat up to 400° and bake 30 minutes longer. Uncover for the last 10 minutes. Allow more time if you use a higher dish. When the custard sides have come away from the edges of the dish, and when the center tests dry, the custard is done. Place on a rack for 15–20 minutes before unmolding onto a serving platter. (*Serves 8–12*)

Note: If you omit the water bath, the bottom becomes brown, but the flavor stays the same.

- Use a combination of meats, such as ham, salami, or peperoni.
- Make a spectacular buffet dish by doubling the ingredients and making six layers.
- For thicker layers, repeat two rather than three times.

Swiss Chard Torta

Double recipe *Tart Pastry* (page 351)
3–4 packed cups cooked Swiss chard
3 Tb olive oil
1 cup chopped onions
2 tsp chopped garlic
Salt and freshly ground pepper
1 lb sausage (optional)
5 large eggs
1¼ cups ricotta cheese
½ cup Parmesan cheese
¼ tsp savory

Roll out ½ of the pie dough and bake in a 10-inch pie shell in a 425° oven for 10 minutes; set aside. Squeeze chard leaves and ribs; chop. Heat oil in a frying pan, and cook onions until wilted. Stir in garlic; cook for 1 minute. Add chard and cook over high heat, stirring constantly, to evaporate moisture; season with salt and pepper and set aside to cool.

Remove sausage from casing (if you are using it) and crumble. Cook the sausage for 10–15 minutes until lightly browned. Drain and combine with chard. Beat 4 of the eggs, combine with cheeses, and stir into chard. Add savory and more salt and pepper if necessary. Pour into the pie shell, cover with remaining pastry, make slits for steam, and paint pastry with a glaze of 1 egg beaten with 1 teaspoon water. Bake in a preheated 425° oven for 40 minutes. (*Serves 6–8*)

Striped Bass Stuffed with Swiss Chard

Striped bass and sea bass are particularly good, but you could also substitute red snapper or any firm white-fleshed fish. Use this filling to stuff breast of veal or lamb breast as well.

6 Tb butter
1 Tb oil
½ cup chopped shallots or minced onions
1 cup cooked Swiss chard leaves
¼ lb mushrooms
1½ cups fresh bread crumbs
½ tsp crushed fennel seed
1 Tb lemon juice
2 Tb heavy cream
Salt and freshly ground pepper
4–5-lb gutted and gilled whole striped bass
Fennel ribs and leaves (optional)
1–2 cups white wine
3 strips bacon (optional)

In 1 tablespoon of the butter and oil, sauté shallots or onions until wilted. Squeeze moisture from Swiss chard, finely chop, and cook over high heat until moisture is evaporated. Stir in 2 tablespoons of the butter; set aside. Finely chop mushrooms, squeeze in a towel to remove excess moisture, and sauté in 2 tablespoons of the butter until browned. Add to chard, along with shallots or onions, bread crumbs, fennel seed, lemon juice, cream, and salt and pepper to taste.

Wash and dry bass. Sprinkle cavity with salt and pepper, then stuff with chard mixture. Either sew fish together or use skewers and string. Strew the fennel (if you are using it) on the bottom of a buttered 12×15-inch pan. Pour in just enough wine to cover the pan bottom. Salt and pepper fish, then rub with melted butter or oil or place bacon strips across the top. Place over high heat until the wine simmers, then bake in a preheated 400° oven for 35–45 minutes, depending on thickness of fish, basting occasionally with the pan juices. When the flesh feels springy, the fish is done. Place fish on a heated platter, reduce pan juices, and pour over fish. (*Serves 4–6*)

Swiss Chard Ribs with Sea Trout

If you can't find sea trout, substitute any other thick white-fleshed fish fillets. Serve with sautéed chard leaves on the side.

5 cups cooked 1–2-inch Swiss chard ribs
Salt and freshly ground pepper
4 Tb melted butter
¾ cup grated Swiss and Parmesan cheeses
2 tsp mixed herbs, such as savory, oregano, and thyme
1½–2 lb sea trout fillets
1 Tb oil
2 Tb butter

Put half the chard into a medium-size buttered baking dish. Sprinkle with salt and pepper, drizzle with 2 tablespoons of the melted butter, and sprinkle with one-third of the cheese and herbs. Repeat layers. Cut the fish into 4 portions, rub with oil, and place on the chard. Season with salt and pepper, dot with butter, and sprinkle with the remaining herbs. Bake in a preheated 400° oven for 12–15 minutes or until the fish is springy (not soft), to your touch. Sprinkle with the remaining cheese, and run under the broiler to brown. (*Serves 4*)

- Substitute chicken breasts for the fish. Rub chicken with lemon and butter, and cover with waxed paper before cooking.

Swiss Chard and Pork Gayettes

Gayettes—a kind of sausage—are standard fare in the Provençal region of France. Traditionally, they're wrapped in caul fat, but bacon works well and is easier to find. Serve them cold for a picnic or hot accompanied by a dish of the chard stalks baked with cheese.

    2 cups cooked Swiss chard leaves
    1 large leaf sorrel (optional)
    1 cup chopped white portions of leeks or onions
    1 Tb oil
    2 Tb butter
    2 tsp minced garlic
    Salt and freshly ground pepper
    4 Tb beef consommé
    1 package unflavored gelatin
    1/2 lb chicken or pork liver
    2 lb ground pork, half lean and half fat
    1 Tb salt
    1/2 tsp coarsely ground black pepper

    1/4 tsp allspice
    1/4 tsp crushed bay leaf
    4 slices bacon

Squeeze chard, and chop with sorrel (if available). Stew the leeks or onions in the oil and butter until wilted, 5–10 minutes. Add garlic, cook for 30 seconds, mix in chard, and cook over high heat, stirring constantly, until moisture is evaporated. Season with salt and pepper; set aside. Heat consommé and dissolve gelatin in it; set aside. Finely chop or grind liver, add to pork along with all the spices, consommé, and chard; mix thoroughly. (Sauté a small amount, taste, and correct seasonings if necessary.)

Chill the mixture; then form into either 2–3-inch balls or thick patties. Place on a buttered baking pan. Cut bacon strips into 16 pieces and place one on each gayette. Bake in a preheated 375° oven for 35–45 minutes, turning once, if desired. (*Makes 16 gayettes*)

Tomatoes

Tomatoes are the most popular home-grown vegetable in America. In fact, Americans are so addicted to tomatoes that we even put up with those hard pink tennis balls shipped north each winter under the name of fresh tomatoes. I honestly think we all ought to treat tomatoes like asparagus and eat them fresh only in season. In our house, we never eat a tomato salad unless we've picked the tomatoes in our garden or greenhouse. In winter, the only time I buy market tomatoes is on a rare occasion when I want to augment the flavor and color of my home-canned tomatoes with some firm, hard (and I mean hard) texture.

Tomatoes come in basically three shapes: a standard round tomato; the fleshy plum tomato (especially good for canning and recipes calling for a lot of pulp); and the small very sweet, round cherry tomatoes—wonderful for a snack or as a garnish.

Old-fashioned varieties rarely grown commercially, such as plum or pear yellow tomatoes, are colorful addi-

tions to a tomato crop. In addition, every gardener knows the bonus of unripened tomatoes—cooking and preserving green tomatoes is an addictive and traditional way to use up the end of the harvest. I knew I was accepted as a future daughter-in-law when I was allowed to join the two-day processing of *Nana's Mustard Pickle*.

With literally dozens of tomato varieties in the seed catalogs, it's important to choose a variety that grows well in your climate. We've tried many types both at the Victory Garden and at home: it's not unusual for Russ to be testing ten varieties of tomatoes in the garden at any one time. We've had consistently good results with Gardener's Delight, a cherry tomato; Early Girl; the midseason Jet Star; the main crop hybrid Super Fantastic; the Italian plum tomato Roma; and one of the yellow plum or pear tomato varieties. Patio and Tiny Tim are good choices for containers.

If you have a greenhouse, look for a variety bred especially for greenhouse production with more fruit

and less vine. We grow three plants in our greenhouse all winter. While not on a par with the summer garden tomatoes, these greenhouse tomatoes are far superior to supermarket varieties; I have friends who come begging for them in the middle of January.

Russ sows seeds indoors in mid-April, about six weeks before setting outdoors. He'll quite frequently transplant the seedlings into 6–8-inch individual pots so that the roots have ample room to develop. This way, he's able to grow the plants to quite a good size before they go outside.

Once the danger of frost is over and the ground is warm, Russ transplants the tomatoes into a sunny spot with sweet soil. (Tomatoes do not do well in acidic soil, so check your soil's pH and work in limestone the previous fall if necessary.) He sets the plants 3 feet apart in cages made of 6-inch mesh concrete reinforcing wire. The cages support the tomatoes, the foliage protects the fruit from sun scald, and the tomatoes don't need to be pruned.

Tomatoes need a steady supply of moisture. Once the ground is really warm, Russ mulches the tomatoes with a 3–6-inch-deep pile of salt marsh hay. (If you're not near the coast, leaves or other mulching materials will do almost as well.) Mulching conserves moisture in the soil, which, in turn, helps guard against blossom-end rot.

By the end of July, I start to harvest tomatoes. I remove the fruit with a gentle twist, leaving the stem on the vine.

Special Information

Yields

- 2 large 3–3½-inch tomatoes = approximately 1 pound
- 3 medium 2–2½-inch tomatoes = approximately 1 pound
- 8–9 plum tomatoes = approximately 1 pound
- 24 cherry tomatoes = approximately 1 pound
- 1 pound tomatoes = approximately ¾ pound or 1½ cups peeled and seeded pulp

Storage and Preserving

Storing

- For daily use hold tomatoes at room temperatures between 55° and 80°. Do not refrigerate unless necessary. Temperatures below 55° slow down and prevent ripening, while temperatures above 80° cause tomatoes to spoil quickly. Refrigerate only extra-ripe tomatoes you want to keep from ripening any further. Store in the refrigerator and bring back to room temperature before serving. Peeled, seeded pulp will hold in the refrigerator for 2–3 days if covered well. Drain the "water" exuded by the tomatoes.
- If tomatoes need to ripen, I put them in my ripening bowl, which is simply a large plastic covered bowl with holes drilled in the top. The cover traps the tomatoes' natural ethylene gas and speeds up the ripening process; the air holes allow proper air and moisture circulation.
- For long-term storage, set tomatoes on a rack without touching. Tomatoes that have started to turn red can be held in a dark area with temperatures of 55–60°. The storage spot must be humid (85° is ideal) but not damp, or the tomatoes will rot.
- To ripen green tomatoes, store in a warmer spot with temperatures between 65° and 70°. The tomatoes can be stored in a cool place but will take longer to ripen. Under good conditions, you can hold tomatoes 4–6 weeks, which is surely enough time to can them!
- Some gardeners dig up the entire plant from the garden and hang it in a cool garage or outbuilding. This works only as long as the garage has the proper storage conditions and good air circulation.

Canning

- See *Canned Stewed Tomatoes*.
- While standard and plum tomatoes have plenty of pulp for canning, cherry tomatoes have a high ratio of seeds, juice, and skin to actual pulp—so don't bother trying to can cherry tomatoes. Eat them fresh.

Freezing

- Many of my friends simply put whole or peeled tomatoes into plastic bags in the freezer and use them for cooking during the winter. I don't care for the taste or texture of these nearly as well as home-canned or even store-bought canned tomatoes. However, tomato sauce freezes beautifully (see *Marinara Sauce* and *Fall Freezer Tomato Sauce*).

Hints

- Tomatoes' acidity reacts with certain metals (such as aluminum) and you end up with an off-taste. Cook in stainless steel, enamel, or some of the newer coated pans.

As much as tomatoes thrive in warm weather, after they're harvested they should not be left in hot places—such as a windowsill in the sun. Use ripe tomatoes immediately or hold them at room temperature. Do not refrigerate unless necessary. Cold temperatures below 55° can slow down and even prevent the ripening process. (You'll notice this in the garden when excessively cool nighttime temperatures slow down the ripening process and make the color blotchy, the flesh watery, and the skins tough.) If you have extra-ripe tomatoes you need to hold for a day or so, refrigerate them, but realize that the flavor will suffer. Bring back to room temperature before eating.

If tomatoes need to be ripened, keep them at room temperature out of the sunlight, or put into one of the new commercial large, plastic ripening containers with a slightly perforated domed top. This allows some exchange of air but traps the ethylene gases the tomatoes give off which helps them to ripen. Look for them under the name of "fruit ripeners."

Perhaps the most sublime way to eat tomatoes is in the garden, when they're still warm from the sun. I also like them sliced, sprinkled with kosher salt and fresh herbs, or peeled in an elegant salad.

Seeding and peeling tomatoes is almost mandatory when you want only the pulp to add to a recipe. The seeds toughen when cooked, while the stringy skin adds nothing. It may sound like a time-consuming task, but it's really easy. I have peeled and seeded two cases of tomatoes while chatting with an old friend—and that's a lot of tomatoes.

Peeling takes but a minute once you have brought a saucepan of water to a boil. Meanwhile, cut a cone shape to remove the stem core in each tomato. (Some cooks prefer to core tomatoes after removing them from water—I find no difference in the result.) Drop the tomatoes into the boiling water, and let them cook for 10

- Simone Beck neutralizes acidity in tomato sauces by stirring in ½ teaspoon instant coffee dissolved in ½ cup of the sauce for every 2 cups of sauce.
- If your fresh, peeled, and seeded tomatoes are less than flavorful, add canned sieved and drained plum tomatoes for color and flavor.
- Bake whole or half tomatoes in their skins to retain their shape.
- Make a *Tomato Mayonnaise* to accompany cold shellfish. Combine 1 cup homemade mayonnaise with 1 tablespoon heavy cream and 2 tablespoons tomato purée. Fold in ½ cup diced tomato pulp.
- For salads, slice raw tomatoes vertically: the inner pulp holds its shape better.
- Use cherry tomatoes as a garnish. Sautéed, they give color to hot meals; cold, they enhance all kinds of salads. For example, halve them, toss in *Vinaigrette Sauce* (see *Appendix*), and strew across a bean salad.
- Tomatoes and zucchini are an attractive combination (see *Zucchini, Tomato, and Cheese Pie* in *Summer Squash*). Make the dish just with tomatoes or omit the crust.
- When you are adding raw tomatoes to a dish to be cooked, drain them well so the tomatoes will not thin the sauce with their "water."
- Add layers of peeled, seeded, and drained sliced tomatoes to a macaroni and cheese bake.
- Layer 1 pound peeled, sliced, and drained green tomatoes with 1 pound sliced apples for a green tomato-apple pie.
- Raw chopped tomatoes mix well with other vegetables (see *Aunt Pat's Summer Salad* in *Cucumbers*).

- Mix with a fresh mint and lemon *Vinaigrette Sauce* (see *Appendix*).
- Russ likes honey and sliced tomatoes on his English muffins.
- Add broth to extra cold tomato sauce for a refreshing soup.
- Make a *Chilled Tomato Broth*: Thoroughly degrease 4 cups chicken or beef broth. Refrigerate the broth, lift off the solidified fat, and use paper towels to sop up the very last trace of fat. Combine broth, 2 cups puréed raw tomatoes, ½ cup tomato juice, and herbs to taste. Simmer for 10 minutes. Strain through cheesecloth, then season with lemon juice, salt, and pepper. Chill before serving.
- A bit of sugar or sweet carrots cooked along with tomatoes counteracts excessive acidity.
- Tomato fondue freezes well and can be added to soups, stews, and sauces.
- Make *Tomato Cream Sauce* (see page 317) to fancy up poached fish or chicken.
- Use tomatoes to top a deep-dish pizza (see *Broccoli Deep-Dish Pizza*).

Microwave
- 1 pound tomatoes placed in a covered dish will cook in 3–4 minutes.

Leftovers
- Freeze leftover tomato sauces.
- Add leftover peeled and seeded tomatoes to soups and stews or omelets.
- Tomato skins and aging tomatoes are fine additions to the stock pot.

seconds, long enough for ripe tomatoes. Firmer tomatoes or winter tomatoes will take 15–30 seconds. Remove from the water with a skimmer, and cool on a wire rack or under cold water. If you're using the tomatoes raw in a salad, plunge them into cold water to stop the cooking.

When the tomatoes become cool enough to handle, pull off the skin with a small paring knife. Every once in a

while you get a skin that sticks: just return the tomato to hot water until the skin loosens. Then, to seed, halve the tomatoes parallel to their stem ends and gently squeeze out the jellylike juice and seeds. Don't throw away the

juice: sieve and drink it. The flesh that's left is the "pulp" or "meat" of the tomato. You'll notice, if you refrigerate the pulp in a covered bowl, that the tomatoes will continue to exude water. Drain this off before using. When you want to seed whole tomatoes, remove a slice from the top and scoop out the jelly and seeds with a small spoon or with your fingers.

The only time I don't peel tomatoes for cooking is when I plan to stuff them, because the skin helps to hold their shape. But I do remove the seeds and juice, then lightly salt and drain the tomatoes upside down to remove excess moisture.

I could fill a book with just tomato recipes. The recipes I'm giving you here are all favorites—the ones we eat most often. Enjoy them and make up your own. Do try different combinations of herbs and tomatoes: basil and tomatoes are a natural combination, but lovage and sweet marjoram are almost as nice. Peeled fresh tomatoes, garnished with julienned basil leaves and dressed with a vinaigrette sauce, can make a whole summer meal.

Marketing

During the tomato season, you should be able to find beautiful ripe tomatoes at your local stores or farm stands. Look for good color and firm flesh. Beware of super-ripe tomatoes unless you want to use them for sauces: in that case, buy "seconds" unless they have mold spots that could affect their flavor. I do not recommend buying tomatoes out-of-season unless you live in an area that gets good ripe produce from warmer climates (such as Mexican-grown tomatoes). In my part of the country, most winter tomatoes are worthless unless you just need firm texture. Do not buy packaged tomatoes if you can't see the whole tomato. Use good canned tomatoes for cooking and wait for the right time of year to enjoy fresh tomatoes.

Tomato Terms and Techniques

Aside from peeling and seeding, there are some basic tomato preparations that pop up over and over in recipe books.

Tomato Concassées (from the French *concasser*—the coarse chopping of food with a knife)
This means simply peeled and seeded tomatoes that are roughly chopped in preparation for cooking. If you are using the tomato pulp raw, it is diced or sliced.

Tomato Fondue (sometimes called *Coulis*)
This is chopped or diced tomato pulp that has been cooked in butter to make a light sauce. For 3 cups chopped pulp, use 2 tablespoons butter. Heat the butter and sauté 2–3 tablespoons minced onion or shallot until just softened. Add some minced garlic if desired and then add tomatoes. Cook over medium-high heat for 4–5 minutes to evaporate the juices and thicken the sauce. Season with salt, pepper, and herbs to taste (such as basil, oregano, thyme, etc.). This is a simple, pretty, and tasty accompaniment for many dishes, such as timbales, poached chicken or fish, and even scrambled eggs.

Uncooked Tomato "Sauce" or Garnish

This is especially luscious when topping hot pasta (see *Cold Tomato Sauce for Pasta*), but tastes wonderful by itself or with other chopped vegetables arranged on a salad platter. Toss 3 cups of diced tomato pulp with 2–3 tablespoons minced onion or shallots, ½ teaspoon red wine vinegar. Season with salt and pepper. Marinate for 5–10 minutes and then drain well in a sieve. If incorporating into an arranged salad to be dressed later, leave as is. If using alone, with pasta or with spaghetti squash, season with chopped herbs and dress with 2–3 tablespoons olive oil. Make a smooth sauce by puréeing the tomato pulp, then add the remaining ingredients, beating in oil at the end. Use more oil if necessary.

Salsa Ranchera

Salsa is Spanish for "sauce." There are many versions, both raw and cooked, hot or mild, that come to us from Mexican cuisine. This is a simple country style. I like it raw but it can be cooked as well. Although you can make uncooked salsa ahead of time, it has a crisper texture made just before serving. Halve 1 pound tomatoes and remove the seeds and the juice. Finely chop the pulp, and combine with ½ cup finely chopped onion or scallions, 1 teaspoon minced garlic (optional), 1–2 tablespoons finely chopped hot peppers, ¼ cup chopped coriander leaves (or parsley), 1 teaspoon salt (and ¼ teaspoon dried coriander leaves if you used fresh parsley). Mix together and add lime juice to taste. The "heat" of the salsa depends on the type and amount of hot pepper you use. Try mixing salsa with grated cheese as a dip for doritos.

Hot Tomato Sauce (see also *Marinara Sauce*)

This is a light sauce that uses 3 cups chopped tomato pulp. Sauté ¾–1 cup minced onion in 2 tablespoons olive oil until wilted and golden. Stir in 1 teaspoon minced garlic, the tomato pulp, ½–1 teaspoon dried herbs (such as basil and oregano), and salt and pepper. Bring the mixture to a boil, reduce heat, and simmer, partially covered, for 30 minutes. If the tomatoes exude a lot of juice, boil down a bit longer to thicken. Use for pizza topping.

Tomato Purée

Prepare *Hot Tomato Sauce* (above), adding 3–4 strips of dried orange peel and a dash of sugar if desired. Cook until the mixture is a thick purée. Put through a food processor or a blender. Cook again if the purée is too liquid. Season with salt and pepper. This freezes well.

Cold Tomato Cream

Season 1 cup of chilled tomato purée with salt, pepper, and lemon juice. Fold in 1 cup whipped heavy cream. Use as a side dish with cold vegetable appetizers, such as *Crudités* (see *Mixed Vegetables*).

Raw Tomatoes

◇ Sliced Tomatoes

Aside from eating them still warm from the sun, the next best treatment for tender-skinned ripe tomatoes is to slice them and serve simply as below. If you slice down the tomato parallel to the stem rather than across, you will lose less of the jelly. Slice and prepare the tomatoes just before serving for best results.

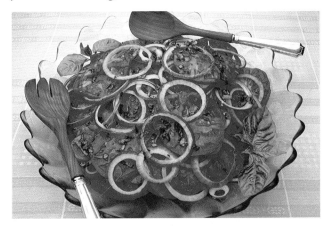

- Slice tomatoes and sprinkle with salt and herbs, then drizzle good-quality olive oil or *Vinaigrette Sauce* (see *Appendix*) over them.
- Slice and top with fresh basil cut into thin strips with scissors. Drizzle with olive oil or *Vinaigrette Sauce* (see *Appendix*). Add slices of hard-boiled egg if desired.
- Alternate tomato slices and thinly sliced mozzarella cheese. Top with basil or fresh oregano, and dress with olive oil.
- Alternate sliced tomatoes with thinly sliced sweet onion rings and top with chopped fresh herbs, salt, pepper, and good-quality olive oil.
- Make tea sandwiches: Slice tomatoes paper-thin and place on thinly sliced crustless bread buttered with sweet butter; add watercress, top with another slice of bread and cut into dainty shapes.

◇ Peeled Tomatoes

I do not peel tomatoes for serving sliced unless they have unusually thick skins, although all the sliced salads above are lovely with peeled tomatoes.

I find the big difference comes in serving raw wedges of tomatoes in an arranged salad, which is particularly attractive for a summer buffet or luncheon dish. Peel the tomatoes and cut them into wedges. Arrange on a platter. Just before serving, dress with a drizzle of good olive oil or *Vinaigrette Sauce* (see *Appendix*).

- *Lobster Salad*: Surround sliced cooked lobster meat with a circle of tomato wedges on edge or *Uncooked Tomato Sauce* and garnish with basil cut into thin strips or sliced cooked artichoke hearts. Serve with a good *Vinaigrette Sauce* (see *Appendix*) or, better yet, a homemade mayonnaise into which you have mixed the cooked red roe of the female lobsters.

- Make a fish, chicken, rice, pasta, or green bean salad. Heap the salad in the center of a serving platter and surround with a circle of peeled tomato wedges on edge. Garnish with watercress or baby spinach leaves. Drizzle oil or vinaigrette over the tomatoes and greens. Decorate the salad with black olives or toasted pine nuts.
- Cut tomatoes into wedges and dress with *Pesto Sauce* (see *Appendix*). Let stand 10 minutes.

◇ Stuffed Tomatoes

Cherry Tomatoes: Cherry or plum tomatoes can be stuffed if you have the patience. For an appetizer tray, try cherry tomatoes stuffed with herbed cheese, minced ham salad, smoked oysters, baby dilled shrimp, or try *Cherry Tomatoes with Smoked Fish Pâté*.

Standard Tomatoes: When regular-size tomatoes are stuffed with a cold filling, leave on the peel or, occasionally, for a softer texture, peel the tomatoes. Cut a slice off the top of the tomato and remove the seeds and pulp. Salt lightly and drain upside down on a rack. If you have large tomatoes, slice them in half and gently squeeze out the seeds and juice. Leave the pulp if desired, or remove it and chop it up for the stuffing (see *Tabbouleh with Tomatoes*). Very ripe, fresh garden tomatoes need only to be washed, cored, and then sliced down from the top into wedges without cutting through. The tomatoes fall open into a circle shape, excellent for stuffing with a salad.

Further Stuffing Suggestions
(Each stuffing fills 8 tomato shells)

Curried Chicken Salad
Combine 2 cups cut-up cooked chicken, 1 cup sliced celery, 1 cup chopped apple, and ½ cup plumped yellow raisins. Mix together 1 teaspoon curry (or more to taste), salt, pepper, and ¾–1 cup mayonnaise thinned with vinegar and a bit of cream. Add tomato pulp if desired. Mix with chicken mixture and stuff into tomato shells.

Chickpea Salad
Combine 3 cups cooked chickpeas with chopped tomato pulp, 6–8 chopped scallions, chopped red onion, and chopped parsley. Season with a *Vinaigrette Sauce* (see *Appendix*) and marinate for 3 hours. Stuff in tomato shells.

With Vegetable Stuffing
Leave pulp in the tomatoes. Cook 1 cup finely chopped onion in olive oil until wilted. Add 1 cup finely chopped zucchini and cook for 1 minute. Add chopped fresh basil, parsley, and grated cheese. Season with salt and pepper. Stuff tomatoes. Dot with butter and more grated cheese. Bake in a preheated 400° oven for 8–10 minutes. Serve at room temperature. Pour over a thin *Pesto Sauce* (see *Appendix*).

Fill tomatoes with coleslaw, potato salad, fish salad, dilled shrimp, cold shell bean salads, cucumber salad, egg salad, etc.

◇ Tomato Sandwich Ideas

There are hundreds of sandwich combinations using tomatoes. Be sure to use a firm textured, homemade style bread. Here are some of my favorites:

When I was growing up, my all-time favorite sandwich was a broiled tomato and cheese sandwich. Lightly toast a piece of bread. Top with a slice of cheese and tomato slices. Run under the broiler until the cheese melts and begins to bubble. Spread with a thin layer of mayonnaise.

Danish open-face sandwiches are another favorite: at a display in Tivoli Gardens in Copenhagen, I noticed how the Danes have perfected the art of keeping tomatoes from weeping and making the sandwich soggy. First, the breads were spread with a thin butter layer to prevent any juices from penetrating. All toppings— whether meat, fish, fowl, or vegetables—were curled or placed upright. For example, the meat was rolled, eggs overlapped, onions were placed on edge, etc. The tomatoes were thinly sliced, then a cut was made halfway through each slice, and the tomato ends were twisted in opposite directions and placed on top of the other ingredients. (You could also overlap the tomatoes.)

Danish Sandwiches
- Spread chicken liver pâté on bread. Sprinkle with crisp bacon or crumbled hard-boiled egg. Top with tomato twists.
- Roll roast beef into cornucopias and place on buttered bread. Tuck in watercress sprigs and top with tomato twists. Add a dab of horseradish cream.
- Spread bread with smoked fish or fish pâté. Arrange tomato and cucumber twists on top.

Cooked Tomatoes

I sauté, bake, broil, and grill tomatoes, do everything except steaming (and possibly you could consider the processing bath in canning a steam method).

◇ Sautéed Tomatoes

A perfectly delicious summer vegetable garnish is fresh cherry tomatoes sautéed in butter. I also slice larger tomatoes in half, then sauté them in butter just until heated through. Of course, sautéed green tomatoes are a traditional fall specialty.

Cherry Tomatoes: Thoroughly wash the tomatoes and remove the tiny caps. Drain them or pat dry. The skin of summer cherry tomatoes is so thin I find peeling unnecessary. Heat butter. Roll the tomatoes in butter for just a minute or two until heated through, then toss with chopped herbs, such as fresh dill, chives, or parsley.

Large Tomatoes: Halve the tomatoes and peel if the skins seem at all thick. Sauté tomatoes in butter, cut side down, for 1–2 minutes or until just lightly colored. Turn and sprinkle with minced onion, garlic, and/or chopped herbs. Drizzle with a touch of olive oil. Cover the pan, and cook only long enough to heat through. Season with salt and pepper to taste. Be careful to barely cook—the tomatoes fall apart readily.

Green Tomatoes: Wash green tomatoes and pat dry. Thickly slice. Dip into stone-ground corn meal, flour, or fine bread crumbs seasoned with salt and pepper. Shake off the excess coating. Sauté tomatoes until lightly browned in a butter-oil combination or in bacon fat. (You can also cook ripe tomatoes this way, as long as they are firm.)

◇ Broiled Tomatoes

Large Tomatoes: Wash and halve tomatoes. Arrange on an oiled baking pan. Sprinkle with salt and pepper, and dot with butter or drizzle with oil. Place the pan under the broiler and broil for 4–5 minutes or until the tomatoes are lightly colored and heated through.

- Top with buttered bread crumbs.
- Add grated cheese and dot with butter.
- Sprinkle with chopped fresh herbs before serving.

Whole Small Cherry or Plum Tomatoes: Wash and dry the tomatoes and cut a small slice on their stem ends. Roll in oil and set the tomatoes cut side down on an oiled pan. (This may be impossible for the plum tomatoes—just lay them on one side.) Broil 3–4-inches from the heat until the skin just begins to split. Season with salt, pepper, and chopped herbs.

◇ Grilled Tomatoes

Quarter regular tomatoes or use plum tomatoes whole. Thread on skewers, place on a hot grill, and cook, turning, just until the tomatoes are heated through. While it would seem that cherry tomatoes would grill successfully their small amount of pulp and high seed and juice content cause them to disintegrate rapidly.

◇ Baked Tomatoes

Bake tomatoes absolutely plain or jazz them up with toppings.

Plain Baked Tomatoes: Cut tomatoes in half horizontally and gently squeeze out the seeds. Place the tomatoes, cut sides up, in a buttered baking dish. Sprinkle the tops with minced onion and garlic (optional), or chopped fresh herbs. Season with salt and pepper and dot with butter. Bake in a preheated 400° oven for 8–15 minutes or until just heated through and the skins have begun to shrivel.

Baked Tomatoes with Toppings: Prepare tomatoes and spoon on topping, such as mushrooms sautéed with bread crumbs; season and heat as above. See *Baked Tomatoes with a Provençal-Style Crumb Topping* or make *Puréed Jerusalem Artichokes in Tomato Shells* (page 139).

Baked Whole Cherry or Plum Tomatoes: Wash tomatoes and remove the stems. Roll in oil or melted butter and bake in a buttered baking dish in a preheated 350° oven until the skins just begin to split.

◇ Baked Stuffed Tomatoes

Tomatoes make beautiful containers for presenting cooked foods. You can either retain the pulp, stuff the empty seed chambers, and top with the stuffing; or remove the interior pulp and incorporate it into the stuffing (or save for another use). Keep the skins on to help hold the tomatoes together.

Either halve the tomatoes parallel to the stems and remove the insides, making two cases, or slice off each top and remove the inside, making one large case. Salt the tomatoes lightly, and let the juices drain. Stuff tomatoes with cooked grated squashes, purées, or mixed vegetable dishes such as ratatouille—there is no end to the possible combinations that tomatoes can accommodate. Do not bake the tomatoes too long, or they will disintegrate. Stuff the tomatoes and bake in a preheated 400° oven for 8–15 minutes or until the stuffing is heated through. See *Tomatoes Filled with Lamb and Squash* or *Hot Tomatoes Stuffed with Rice*.

◇ *Stewed Tomatoes*

While I don't believe stewing tomatoes is the best way to prepare them, it is a fine method to use up those tomatoes that are so super-ripe that they can't hold their shape for anything else.

Plain stewed tomatoes are nothing fancier than tomatoes that have been skinned, seeded, and cooked until softened. Some cooks add a bit of water or broth to keep the tomatoes from sticking to the pan; others stew in butter, while others add nothing at all. The tomatoes usually need only to be cooked for 10 minutes. Season with any herbs you wish, sugar to taste, garlic and/or onions, and salt and pepper. To thicken the tomatoes, you can stir in bread cubes (the amount depends upon how thick you want the tomatoes to be).

A stewed tomato soup with just tomatoes and bread can be a pleasant, filling meal. Simply stew up the tomatoes with onions and garlic that have been cooked in olive oil. Add beef or chicken broth and lots of Italian or French bread cubes to obtain a thick soup. Season with salt, pepper, and fresh basil. A friend of mine also uses pilot crackers to thicken stewed tomatoes. They dissolve and almost form a tomato pudding.

◇ *Canned Tomatoes*

Stewed tomatoes, put up fresh from the garden, are the very best way to get flavorful cooking tomatoes throughout the winter. While commercially canned tomatoes can be quite good, nothing can compare to the homemade flavor. Many people insist that freezing tomatoes for winter cooking is easier than canning, but I don't find the flavor as good.

Methods for canning tomatoes have changed because today's tomato varieties have changed. Once, all tomatoes had a high acid content and could be safely placed in jars and then put in a water bath (the cold pack method). Nowadays, however, so many tomatoes have a lower acid content that the possibility of botulism does exist. Therefore, it is absolutely necessary to use the hot pack method for canning and advisable to add 1/2 teaspoon citric acid per quart of tomatoes to provide a safeguard against low-acid tomatoes.

To Can Tomatoes—Hot Pack Method

Allow approximately 3 pounds tomatoes per quart. Peel and seed the tomatoes. Plum tomatoes are particularly suited for canning, since they have a high ratio of pulp to seeds and juice. Some people prefer to leave the tomatoes whole and not seed them—skin the tomatoes in any case. Leave the tomatoes whole, halve, or quarter them. Measure the amount of tomatoes. For every quart tomatoes, add 1 teaspoon salt and 1/2 teaspoon citric acid (available at drugstores) if you don't know the acidity level of the tomatoes. Boil the tomatoes for 6 minutes in a large stainless steel or enamel saucepan. Then ladle directly into hot sterilized jars, filling up to 1/2 inch from the rim. Run a sterilized knife around the inside of the jar to release any air bubbles. Wipe the rims and seal. Place the jars in a deep canning pot filled halfway up with boiling water. Cover the jars 2 inches above their tops with boiling water, bring it again to a boil, cover, and cook at a rapid boil. Process quarts in the boiling water bath for 15 minutes; process pints 10 minutes. Remove from the water, complete the seals, and cool. Store in a cool dark place.

Canned Tomato Juice

While you have out all the equipment, why not make some homemade tomato juice as well?

Use very ripe tomatoes: wash, stem, and cut up the tomatoes into chunks. Make sure to remove any blemishes which could spoil the flavor of the juice. You will need approximately 2 quarts tomatoes for each quart of juice. Put the cut-up tomatoes into a stainless steel or enamel saucepan. Bring to a boil, and cook gently for 30 minutes or until the tomatoes are very soft and juicy. Put the mixture through a food mill or sieve to extract the skins and seeds. Let the tomatoes stand until the thicker juice settles and the "water" rises to the top. Ladle off the water. Add salt to taste and 1/2 teaspoon citric acid or 1 tablespoon lemon juice per quart of juice if the tomatoes are not high-acid tomatoes. You can add a bit of sugar to taste. Return the juice to a washed saucepan and bring it to a boil. Ladle into hot sterilized jars, filling to within 1 inch of their rims. Wipe the rims and seal. Process quarts in a hot water bath for 15 minutes; process pints 10 minutes.

- Add additional vegetables and spices to make a flavored juice or even a Bloody Mary mix. For each quart flavored tomato juice, add 1/4 cup each chopped onion, peppers, celery, carrots, and 1/4 teaspoon garlic (optional). For a spicy mix, add an additional 1/4 slice hot pepper, 2 teaspoons grated horseradish, 1/8 teaspoon coriander, basil, and mustard seed.

Note: Please consult a good canning book, such as Jean Anderson's *The Green Thumb Preserving Guide*, for additional tomato suggestions.

Baked Tomatoes with a Provençal-Style Crumb Topping

4 large ripe tomatoes
Salt
4 Tb butter or olive oil
1/2 cup finely chopped onions or shallots
1–2 tsp minced garlic (optional)
1 cup fresh bread crumbs
1/4 cup chopped fresh herbs (such as parsley, basil, thyme)
Freshly ground pepper

Halve the tomatoes and squeeze out the seeds. Lightly salt and drain upside down on a rack. Heat 2 tablespoons of the butter or oil in a sauté pan and lightly sauté the onions. Add the minced garlic (if using it) and the remaining butter or oil. Add the bread crumbs and sauté until lightly golden. Add the herbs, then season to taste with salt and pepper. Spoon the crumbs into the tomato halves and dot with butter or drizzle with oil. Place in a buttered baking dish and bake in a preheated 400° oven for 10–15 minutes or until the tomatoes are heated through and their skins are beginning to shrivel. Don't overcook or the tomatoes will collapse. Lightly brown under the broiler if you wish. (*Serves 4*)

- Add grated cheese to the bread crumbs.
- *With Onions and Peppers.* Bake as above, but fill the tomatoes with a mixture of 1/2 cup sautéed minced onions, 1 cup minced peppers, a touch of chili pepper, minced garlic (optional), and mushrooms (optional). Top with grated Monterey Jack cheese.

Scalloped Tomatoes

3 lb tomatoes
2 cups lightly packed fresh bread crumbs
8 Tb butter
1/2 cup minced onions or shallots
Chopped basil (optional)
Salt and freshly ground pepper

Peel and halve the tomatoes. Gently squeeze out the seeds. If the tomatoes are very large cut each half into 2 thick slices. Let drain while preparing the bread crumbs. Heat 7 tablespoons of the butter and sauté the onions or shallots until wilted; stir in the bread crumbs, coating with butter, and lightly cook. Add the basil (if you like), and season with salt and pepper. Place half the tomato slices in a buttered 8×8-inch baking dish. Top with half the crumb mixture. Repeat the layering and dot with remaining butter. Bake in a preheated 350° oven for 30 minutes. (*Serves 4–6*)

Hot Tomatoes Stuffed with Rice

This is a nice vegetable accompaniment. For smaller portions, halve tomatoes and make 8 servings.

4 tomatoes
Salt
3 Tb butter
1/2 cup chopped onions or scallions
1 tsp minced garlic
1 1/2 cups cooked rice
2 Tb chopped parsley
1 Tb chopped basil
1/2 cup grated Parmesan or Romano cheese
Freshly ground pepper

Remove the tops from the tomatoes, scoop out the seeds and pulp, salt lightly, turn upside down, and drain. Chop the pulp. Heat 2 tablespoons of the butter; cook the onions or scallions until wilted and golden. Add the tomato pulp and cook for 3–4 minutes until some of the moisture evaporates. Add garlic, cook for 30 seconds, then stir in the rice, parsley, basil, and cheese. Season well with salt and pepper. Stuff the tomatoes, dot with the remaining 1 tablespoon butter, and bake in a preheated 350° oven for 10–15 minutes or until just heated through. (*Serves 4*)

- Add sautéed mushrooms to filling.

- For a creamy consistency, add mozzarella cheese to taste.

Marinara Sauce

You can halve this recipe, but I like to make enough at one time to use for a crowd or for a few family dinners. Purists may object to the inclusion of tomato sauce. The marinara sauce is perfectly fine without it, but if you have some *Fall Freezer Tomato Sauce* on hand, it really does intensify the flavor.

1/4 cup olive oil
3 cups chopped onions
1 cup finely sliced carrots
1 Tb finely chopped garlic
8 cups peeled, seeded, and chopped tomatoes
2 cups tomato sauce (optional)
Salt and freshly ground pepper
2 Tb freshly chopped basil
1 Tb oregano
1/3–1/2 cup freshly grated Parmesan cheese (optional)
1/3 cup chopped parsley

Heat the oil and sauté the onions and carrots until golden. Add the garlic, tomatoes, and tomato sauce (if you wish) and simmer, partially covered, for 15 minutes. Process in a food processor or push through a sieve. Return to the pan and add 1–2 teaspoons salt, pepper to taste, basil, oregano, and cheese if desired. Simmer, partially covered, for 30 minutes. Stir in parsley and season once again. (*Makes about 10 cups*)

- *With Meatballs:* Simmer meatballs with the sauce for the last 30 minutes of cooking. To make thirty 1 1/2–2-inch meatballs, combine 1 pound each ground beef and pork and 1/2 cup each minced onion, chopped parsley, fresh bread crumbs, and grated Parmesan cheese. Add 2 beaten eggs, 1 teaspoon minced garlic, and salt and pepper to taste. Shape into meatballs and brown in oil before adding to *Marinara Sauce.*
- *With Sausages:* Prick sausages and blanch in water for 5 minutes to release excess fat. Brown in oil and add to *Marinara Sauce* during last 30 minutes of cooking.
- See *Marie's Manicotti.*
- Make a veal parmigiana. Sauté flattened, breaded veal cutlets until lightly browned. Place in baking dish, cover with *Marinara Sauce*, and top with mozzarella and parmesan cheese. Bake in a 350° oven for 30 minutes or until bubbly.

Tomato Cream Sauce

1 cup peeled and seeded *very ripe* (or canned) tomatoes
10 Tb chilled butter
1 Tb minced shallots
1/2 cup dry vermouth
1 cup heavy cream
Salt and freshly ground pepper
Lemon juice

Slice the tomatoes into lengthwise strips (prettier than chopped tomatoes). Heat 1 tablespoon of the butter in a sauté pan and cook shallots until wilted. Add tomatoes and sauté for 1–2 minutes. Add the vermouth and cook until liquids are reduced by half. Add the cream and cook until thickened and slightly reduced. Meanwhile, cut the remaining butter into small pieces, and over very low heat, gradually beat it, bit by bit, into the thickened sauce. Season with salt and pepper and lemon juice. (*Makes about 1½ cups*)

Note: Add additional butter to make more sauce.

- Replace tomatoes with mushrooms, sautéing to evaporate moisture and to lightly brown.

Cherry Tomatoes with Smoked Fish Pâté

40 cherry tomatoes
¼ lb smoked fish (smoked
    bluefish or smoked salmon bits)
2 Tb chopped shallots
2–3 Tb softened butter
1 lb. softened cream cheese
3 Tb finely minced parsley
2 Tbs lemon juice
Salt and freshly ground pepper
Heavy cream

Wash the tomatoes and cut off a thin slice on top. Scoop out insides with small spoon (leave the center pulpy ridge in if you prefer). Break up the smoked fish. If you are using a soft fish such as bluefish, break it with your fingers into bits and blend it. Firmer-textured smoked salmon bits will need to be ground or processed.

Combine fish with shallots, butter, cream cheese, and 2 tablespoons parsley. Season with lemon juice and salt and pepper. Thin, if desired, with heavy cream to a smooth consistency.

Fill each tomato shell and refrigerate until ready to serve. Sprinkle the tops with remaining chopped parsley. (*Makes about 2½ cups filling*)

Note: Depending on the type of fish, you may want to vary the amount of cream cheese and butter. For example, a very salty salmon may require more cheese and no salt. Judge by taste.

- Make the pâté from plain fish. Our favorite house giveaway hors d'oeuvre at the restaurant is bluefish pâté. Poach bluefish, cool, and use as above, doubling the amount of fish. Also double the onions and parsley.
- With smoked salmon, use chopped dill in combination with parsley. Garnish with dill.

Tabbouleh with Tomatoes

Tabbouleh, one of the most popular Mideastern appetizers or salads, uses soaked raw wheat and lots of fresh parsley and mint. The crisp romaine lettuce leaves are handy for scooping up the cold tabbouleh salad and provide crunch.

1 cup bulghur wheat
7 large ripe tomatoes
Salt
5 Tb lemon juice
1 cup finely chopped onions
⅓ cup finely chopped scallions
1½ cups chopped parsley
¼ cup chopped fresh mint or 2 Tb dried
½ cup olive oil
Freshly ground pepper
Whole small romaine lettuce leaves

Cover the bulghur wheat with cold water and let soak for 1 hour. Meanwhile, halve 4 tomatoes horizontally, and gently squeeze out the seeds and juice. Carefully scoop out the pulp. Sprinkle 6 of the shells with salt and drain upside down on a rack. Chop the remaining 2 shells along with the pulp. Toss the chopped pulp with 1 tablespoon of the lemon juice and salt. Set aside.

When the wheat has soaked, drain and squeeze dry in a towel. Fluff it up—the kernels should be dry. Add the onions, scallions, parsley, and mint. Combine the remaining lemon juice and oil, mix with the wheat mixture, and season to taste with salt and pepper. Let the mixture stand in a cold place for at least 1 hour. Drain the chopped tomatoes, toss with the wheat mixture, and evenly stuff the tomato shells. (Any extra stuffing can flow over the sides.) Place 1 stuffed shell on each plate. Cut each of the remaining 3 tomatoes into 6 wedges and garnish each plate with 3 tomato wedges, radiating them out like the spokes of a wheel; intersperse with romaine lettuce leaves. (*Serves 6*)

Gazpacho

I first made this version twenty years ago, and despite tastings of innumerable gazpachos, I find this simple formula the best. Tomatoes are the main ingredient, but without the bite of scallion and garlic, gazpacho would be drab indeed. It is essential to hand chop the vegetables! That texture is worth whatever time it may take. This soup may be easily doubled or tripled. Serve in *chilled* bowls.

4 large ripe tomatoes
2½ cucumbers
1 large green pepper

10–12 scallions
1–2 cloves garlic
Salt
¼ cup red wine vinegar
⅓ cup olive oil
3 cups tomato juice
1–1½ cups beef broth or water
Hot pepper sauce
Worcestershire sauce
Freshly ground pepper
Plain *Croutons* (page 348)

Peel, seed, and chop in ¼-inch dice the tomatoes, and 2 of the cucumbers. Wash and trim pepper and scallions and chop into ¼-inch dice. In a mortar, mash garlic and 1 teaspoon salt. Beat in the vinegar and oil. Combine this dressing with the chopped vegetables and stir in the tomato juice. Add broth or water, to the consistency you prefer. Season with a dash of hot pepper sauce, Worcestershire sauce, salt, and pepper. Chill. Slice ½ cucumber paper-thin. Serve gazpacho in chilled bowls topped with cucumber slices and croutons on the side. (*Serves 4–6*)

- Some people prefer a gazpacho with the traditional addition of bread crumbs. Add ½–1 cup soft fresh bread crumbs with the vinegar and oil.
- Mash in fresh herbs such as basil with the garlic.
- Serve soup with chopped vegetable garnishes, such as finely chopped cucumbers, red or green peppers, scallions, or celery.
- For a wonderful gazpacho salad, see *Julia Child and More Company*.

Fresh Tomato Soup

This is my favorite tomato soup. Absolutely ripe tomatoes are essential.

4 lb ripe tomatoes
3 Tb oil
2 cups chopped onions
1 cup chopped leeks
1 cup sliced carrots
1 clove garlic, chopped
½ tsp sugar
2 Tb flour
6 sprigs parsley
2 sprigs fresh lovage or a celery stalk with leaves
8 cups chicken broth
Salt and freshly ground pepper
Plain *Croutons* (page 348)

Peel, seed, and roughly chop tomatoes. You should have approximately 6 cups. In a large saucepan, heat oil and sauté the onions and leeks until wilted and golden. Add 2 cups of the tomatoes, the carrots, garlic, and sugar, and cook together, stirring, until the moisture has evaporated and the mixture is thick. The cooking time varies, from 10–25 minutes, depending upon the moisture of the tomatoes. Whisk in flour and cook for 2–3 minutes, stirring, to cook flour and make smooth. Tie together the parsley and lovage or celery and add to saucepan. Add remaining tomatoes, and 3 cups of the broth. Cook for 10–15 minutes to release the tomato juices and thicken slightly. Add the remaining broth; simmer for 20 minutes. Remove the parsley and lovage and lightly process soup in a food processor or put through a food mill. I like the soup to have some texture. Season with salt and pepper. Serve with croutons. (*Makes 2½–3 quarts*)

Three-in-One Velvety Tomato Soup

This soup can be served three ways: once the rice is cooked you can serve as is; purée for a smooth, thick soup, or add cream to make a creamy tomato soup.

3 lb ripe tomatoes
½–¾ cup chopped onions
½ cup chopped carrots (optional)
2 Tb butter
2 Tb oil
1 tsp chopped garlic
1 Tb tomato paste
1 bay leaf
½ tsp sugar (optional)
Salt
4 peppercorns
2 cups chicken or beef broth
2 Tb rice
½ cup cream (optional)

Wash tomatoes. Cut into slices or chunks; do not peel or core. Cook the onions and carrots (if you like) in the butter and oil until wilted. Add tomatoes, cover the pan, and cook for 5 minutes. Uncover, and add garlic, tomato paste, bay leaf, sugar (if desired), 1 teaspoon salt, and peppercorns. Boil slowly for 15 minutes, stirring occasionally. Put mixture through a food mill or sieve to remove the seeds and skins. Add the broth and rice. Bring to a boil, reduce heat, and simmer, covered, for 15–20 minutes or until the rice is tender. Taste for seasoning. You can serve as is or purée in a blender as described above. (*Makes 5–6 cups*)

If the tomatoes are not very juicy, add a bit more broth.

- Make this soup with half green and half red tomatoes.
- Garnish soup with peeled, seeded, and julienned tomato.
- Add flaked shellfish.

Straight Wharf Fish Soup

Here's the simple country fish soup I serve at the restaurant. Ripe tomatoes are essential.

2–3 Tb olive oil
2 cups thinly sliced sweet onions
1 cup thinly sliced white of leek
4 1/2 cups peeled, seeded, and rough-chopped ripe tomatoes
Herb bouquet:
    4 sprigs parsley
    1 peeled clove garlic
    1 tsp thyme
    1 bay leaf
    1/4 tsp fennel seed
3–4 strips dried orange peel
Saffron
2 qt *Fish Broth* (page 348)
Salt and freshly ground pepper
Hot pepper sauce (optional)
3 lb chunks of fish—cod, bass, scallops, cusk, etc.
Pernod (optional)
Plain *Croutons* (page 348)
Chopped parsley
Chopped basil
Rouille (page 180)

Heat the oil in a large saucepan and sauté onions and leeks until wilted and golden, approximately 10 minutes. Add the tomatoes, stir, cover, and cook for 5 minutes. Uncover the pan; add the herb bouquet, orange peel, a generous sprinkling of saffron threads, and the broth. Bring the broth to a boil, reduce heat, and simmer 30–40 minutes to intensify the flavors. Season with salt and pepper. Add a dash of hot pepper sauce if desired. Just before serving, cut fish into 1–2-inch pieces and add to soup. Cook for 5–8 minutes or until the fish is just cooked through. Add a splash of Pernod if desired. Serve with toasted bread rounds and sprinkle with chopped parsley and basil. Serve with *Rouille* to stir into soup. (*Makes 3–4 quarts*)

- Substitute half bottled clam juice and half water if you don't have fish broth.
- Sprinkle in hot pepper flakes along with tomatoes and onions.

Cold Tomato Sauce with Hot Pasta

Thoroughly ripe summer tomatoes are essential for this sauce. The tomatoes are uncooked and at room temperature.

3 cups diced tomato pulp
1/2 cup finely chopped sweet onions
1–2 tsp minced garlic
1/3 cup chopped basil
3 Tb chopped parsley
Wine vinegar (tarragon is nice)
Salt and freshly ground pepper
1 lb spaghetti
1/4 cup olive oil
Freshly grated Parmesan cheese

Mix tomato pulp with onions, garlic, and herbs. Toss with a teaspoon or so of vinegar and season with salt and pepper. Cook spaghetti until cooked through but still slightly chewy. Drain. Combine tomatoes and oil and toss with the pasta. Serve with cheese on the side. (*Serves 4*)

- For a smoother sauce, put all the sauce ingredients in a blender or food processor and blend to the desired consistency.
- Use different pastas, and add minced hot pepper if desired.
- Serve the sauce over hot spaghetti squash as well.
- Instead of Parmesan cheese, finely cube 1/2 pound mozzarella cheese. When cooked pasta is drained, toss with cheese so that the cheese melts. Then add the tomato mixture.

Marie's Manicotti

There's no need for a pasta machine with Marie Caratelli's manicotti; her crêpelike pasta is easily accomplished by hand and is just delicious. As with regular crêpes the batter is lighter when it "rests" for two hours after mixing.

1 1/2 cups sifted flour
8 eggs
1 cup liquid (1/2 cup milk, 1/2 cup water)
Salt
Oil
2 lb ricotta cheese
1 cup grated Romano or Parmesan cheese
1 cup grated mozzarella cheese
Freshly ground pepper
2–3 cups *Marinara Sauce* (page 317)

Beat the flour into 4 eggs in an electric mixer and beat in the liquid and salt, or blend together in an electric blender. You want a very smooth emulsion. (It may be necessary to strain.) Let sit for 2 hours in the refrigerator. Unlike regular crêpes, the pasta has no butter or oil in the batter so make sure you used a well-seasoned pan to cook them. Rub a small 6-inch frying pan (preferably non-stick) with oil. Heat the pan until it is just beginning to smoke. Pour slightly less than ¼ cup batter into the pan. Tilt the pan in all directions to evenly distribute the batter. Cook until just set and flip it over. Cook less than a minute on each side for you do not want it to brown. Slide the pasta out of the pan and continue with remaining batter. You should end up with 16–20 crêpes. Beat the remaining eggs and combine with ricotta cheese, ½ cup Romano and ½ cup of the mozzarella cheese. Season well with salt and pepper. Fill each "manicotti" with some of the cheese mixture and roll up. Butter a 13×9-inch baking dish. Spoon in a thin layer of marinara sauce. Place the rolled manicotti pieces on the sauce and cover with the remaining sauce, sprinkle remaining grated cheese on top. Cover and bake in a preheated 350° oven until bubbly, approximately 20–30 minutes. (*Serves 8*)

Chicken Breasts with Tomato à la Marengo

This recipe was first made for Napoleon at the battle of Marengo. Julia Child has a wonderful version of it in *From Julia Child's Kitchen*. In this dish, I combine some of the traditional ingredients in a simpler manner, but do retain the egg and crouton garnish (although you could omit it and decorate the platter with olives or toasted bread triangles).

4 whole chicken breasts
6 Tb butter
½ cup minced onions
2 tsp minced garlic
3 cups peeled, seeded, and chopped tomatoes
1 Tb freshly chopped tarragon or 1 tsp dried
¼ cup dry vermouth (optional)
Salt and freshly ground pepper
Flour
5 Tb oil
4–6 crustless bread triangles
12 large raw shrimp, peeled
⅓ cup olive oil
4–6 eggs
½ cup chopped parsley

Bone chicken breasts to get 8 pieces, or suprêmes; set aside. Heat 2 tablespoons of the butter and sauté the onions until wilted; stir in garlic, tomatoes, tarragon, vermouth (if desired), and salt and pepper to taste. Cover pan, cook for 5 minutes, uncover, and cook until mixture is thick and moisture is almost gone. Set aside.

Season chicken breasts with salt and pepper, coat with flour, and shake off excess. Heat 2 tablespoons of the butter and 1 tablespoon of the oil. Sauté the chicken for 1–2 minutes, turn the pieces, and sauté until browned and the flesh is springy to the touch. This will take only a few minutes: you want the chicken barely cooked through. Set aside. Clean out the sauté pan. Heat 2–3 tablespoons oil in sauté pan (just enough to coat the pan). Sauté the bread triangles until lightly browned on both sides. Drain on brown paper.

When you are ready to serve, gently reheat the chicken in the sauce. Heat 2 tablespoons of the butter and 1 tablespoon of the oil in a sauté pan. Sauté the shrimp until pink and cooked through, 1–2 minutes per side. Put on a warm plate. In a 4-inch saucepan, heat ⅓ cup olive oil. (What you are going to do is to poach-fry eggs in the oil. You could totally cover the eggs with oil, but this method works just as well.) When the oil is very hot but not smoking, cook the eggs one at a time. Break an egg into a shallow cup, and roll into the hot oil, tilting the pan to one side so that the egg is covered with oil. Should it not be covered completely, spoon over some oil. Let it rest for a minute, then turn it over with a spoon. Let the egg cook another minute or two and then drain on a plate lined with brown paper or paper toweling. Cook all the eggs. Arrange the chicken down the center of a warm platter and coat with the sauce. Top with a row of the sautéed shrimp. Place the bread triangles on both sides of the chicken and arrange an egg on each. Garnish with parsley sprinkled down the center. (*Serves 4–6*)

Gray Sole Duglère

Once the fish is poached, you have plenty of time to make the sauce—the fish is quite sturdy, despite its fragile appearance. The hollandaise sauce greatly enriches the sauce—but you can omit it and still have a delicious meal. You can use flounder or sole, but I especially like gray sole's firm texture.

2 lb gray sole fillets
Salt and freshly ground pepper
3 Tb minced shallots
½ cup dry white wine
1 cup *Fish Broth* (page 348)
2 ½ Tb butter
3 Tb flour
¾ cup light cream
2 cups peeled, seeded, and diced tomatoes
Lemon juice
⅓ cup *Hollandaise Sauce* (page 348)

Try to buy 8 4-ounce fillets of fish. Cut larger fillets in half lengthwise. Lightly score the darker side of the flesh and season with salt and pepper. Fold over each fillet, scored sides facing, to make a flat roll. Scatter the shallots in a buttered baking dish just large enough to hold the fish snugly. Top with fish and add wine and stock. Cover with a buttered piece of waxed paper. Poach in a preheated 400° oven for 6–10 minutes (the cooking time depends upon the thickness of the filets). The fish should be cooked through, but springy to the touch. Pour all the liquid into a small saucepan. Leave the waxed paper over the fish. Rapidly reduce the cooking juices to 1¼ cups Heat the butter in a medium saucepan and whisk in the flour. Cook 2–3 minutes, remove from heat, then whisk in the reduced cooking juices. Bring the sauce to a boil and cook until thickened, stirring, for 2 minutes. Also use any juices exuded by the fish. Whisk in cream and cook gently for 5–10 minutes. Stir in the tomatoes and heat together, seasoning with lemon juice, salt, and pepper. Remove from heat and fold in the hollandaise sauce. Either leave fish in the baking dish or arrange in 4 individual au gratin dishes. Spoon sauce over the fish and run directly under the broiler for 1–2 minutes to glaze the top. (*Serves 4*)

- Lighten the sauce by folding in a few spoonfuls of whipped cream.

Swordfish with Portugaise Sauce

2 lb swordfish
3 Tb olive oil
1 cup sliced scallions in ½-inch pieces
1 tsp chopped hot pepper or dash hot pepper sauce
2 tsp minced garlic
3 cups chopped tomato pulp
2 Tb capers
1 Tb red wine vinegar
Saffron
1 bay leaf
2 whole cloves
½ tsp Worcestershire sauce
Salt and freshly ground pepper
Flour
4 Tb butter
Lemon wedges

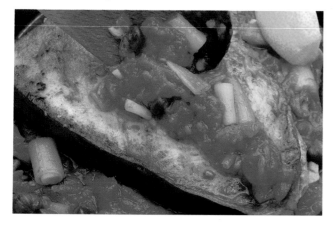

Ask the fishmonger to slice the swordfish into steaks no thicker than ½ inch each. You should have 4 slices of approximately 8 ounces each.

Heat the olive oil and sauté scallions until lightly browned. Add the hot pepper and garlic, cook for 30 seconds, then add tomatoes, capers, vinegar, a pinch of saffron, bay leaf, cloves, Worcestershire sauce, and salt and pepper to taste. Bring the sauce to a boil, lower the heat, cover and cook for 5 minutes, uncover and cook at a gentle roll for 30 minutes until the sauce is thickened. You will have approximately 2 cups. Remove the cloves and bay leaf and keep the sauce warm.

Dip the swordfish into flour, then shake off excess. Heat 2 tablespoons of the butter in a frying pan. When the butter is really hot, add half the swordfish and sauté until just cooked through and browned, 3–4 minutes per side. Repeat with remaining butter and remaining fish.

(The cooking time depends upon the thickness of the fish. Test with a sharp pointed knife: the flesh will be tender throughout, though resilient in the middle.) Place a few spoonfuls of sauce on individual warm plates and top with the fish. Top each slice with a spoonful of sauce and garnish with a lemon wedge. (*Serves 4*)

- *Cold Swordfish Portugaise*: Slice swordfish ¾-inch thick and then cut into 1½–2-inch pieces. Flour the fish and sauté until cooked through. Put in a baking dish and pour the sauce over fish. Let cool; serve cold as an appetizer.
- Substitute bluefish or mackerel for the swordfish.
- For thicker fish, such as monkfish, cook until barely stiffened on each side, then add cooked sauce, cover the pan, and gently braise the fish in sauce until done.

Tomatoes Filled with Lamb and Squash

4 large ripe tomatoes
Salt
½ cup chopped onions
4 Tb olive oil
1–2 tsp chopped garlic
1 lb ground lamb
½ cup chicken broth
1½–2 cups cubed, salted, and drained summer squash
1 cup bread crumbs
⅓ cup chopped mint and parsley
Freshly ground pepper
Grated cheese (optional)

Halve, seed, and remove the pulp from the tomatoes. Lightly salt the shells and drain. Chop the pulp. Sauté the onions in 2 tablesoons olive oil until wilted. Then add the garlic and ground lamb. Cook until the meat loses its red color; drain off the fat. Add the tomato pulp and chicken broth. Simmer, covered, for 20 minutes, then uncover the pan and simmer until the lamb is tender and the juices have evaporated. Drain. In remaining olive oil, sauté the summer squash until just tender. Combine with the lamb, bread crumbs, and herbs. Season to taste with salt and pepper. Stuff the tomato shells and drizzle with olive oil. Top with grated cheese. Bake in a preheated 400° oven for approximately 10 minutes. (*Serves 4*).

Ossobuco

This recipe uses veal shank, which is the bone and meat from the knee to the ankle. Ask for the hind portion, because it's meatier and less tendonous. Count on approximately 2 pounds shank per person.

8 lb veal shanks
Salt and freshly ground pepper
Flour
⅓ cup plus 2 Tb oil
2 Tb butter
1 cup finely sliced onions
½ cup finely sliced leeks (white portion)
½ cup finely sliced carrots

½ cup finely sliced celery
1 cup dry white wine
1 cup veal or beef broth
1 tsp basil
1 tsp thyme
Herb bouquet:
    4 parsley sprigs
    1 bay leaf
    2–3 pieces dried orange peel
    1 clove garlic, crushed
4 cups peeled, seeded, and chopped tomatoes
¼ cup orange juice (optional)
Gremolata:
    1 Tb grated lemon peel
    2 Tb chopped parsley
    1 tsp minced garlic

Ask the butcher to cut the shank into 2-inch pieces. Salt and pepper the veal and toss with flour; shake off excess.

Heat ⅓ cup of the oil in a large heavy sauté pan and brown the veal. In a large ovenproof casserole, heat 2 tablespoons oil with butter. Add the onions, leeks, carrots, and celery and cook until wilted and golden. Place the browned meat on the vegetables in one layer if possible. Pour the fat from the sauté pan and deglaze the pan with wine, scraping up brown bits sticking to the bottom. Add broth, basil, and thyme. Bring the broth to a boil; pour over the meat. Add the herb bouquet. Cover with tomatoes. The liquid should be approximately halfway up the sides of the meat (add more broth if necessary). Bring the liquids to a boil, cover the pan, and place in a preheated 350° oven. Immediately reduce the heat to 325° (or simmer on top of the stove). Cook for 1–1¼ hours or until the meat is tender.

Remove the meat to a warm platter. Skim fat from the cooking liquid, remove the herb bouquet, and add orange juice if you wish. Boil to thicken the sauce and intensify the flavor. You may strain out the vegetables, pressing down on them to remove the juices. I prefer to lightly mash the vegetables with a potato masher and leave them in the sauce. You will end up with approximately 3 cups sauce. Season with salt and pepper; keep warm. Mix together the gremolata of lemon peel, parsley, and garlic. Pour the sauce over the meat and sprinkle with gremolata garnish. (*Serves 4*)

- Often I will find a leg of veal on sale. I have the butcher saw the leg piece into chunks and proceed as above. The leg has more meat than the shank, so reduce the poundage.
- Remove the cooked meat from the casserole, and bake the meat in 500° oven for 4–5 minutes to glaze it.

Fall Freezer Tomato Sauce

6–7 lb tomatoes
4 Tb olive oil
2 cups finely chopped onions
½ cup chopped carrots
1½ cups finely chopped celery
1 cup finely chopped green peppers

2–3 tsp chopped garlic (optional)
½ cup beef broth
1 cup tomato paste
2 bay leaves
Salt and freshly ground pepper
¼ cup chopped fresh basil or 1 Tb dried
1 Tb freshly chopped thyme or 1½ tsp dried
1 tsp oregano

Peel, seed, and chop the tomatoes: you should end up with 9–10 cups. Heat oil, and sauté the onions and carrots until the onions are golden and wilted. Add celery and green peppers, cook for 2–3 minutes, add the garlic (if desired), and cook 30 seconds. Add beef broth, tomatoes, tomato paste, and crumbled bay leaves, and season with salt and pepper. Bring the broth to a boil, reduce heat, and simmer for 30 minutes. Add the herbs and simmer 5 minutes longer. Lightly process the sauce so it still has some texture (or blend it to a smooth sauce if you prefer). If you don't have a processor put the sauce through a food mill or mash it. Place the sauce in a bowl set in ice water so that it will cool quickly. When it falls to room temperature fill freezer containers, cover, and chill in refrigerator before freezing. (*Makes about 6 pints*)
Note: You can omit the tomato paste if you like. If so, simmer longer to concentrate the flavor.

Nana's Mustard Pickle

This is a Morash family tradition.

1 bunch celery
3 qt green tomatoes
3 qt onions
1 cauliflower
4–5 green peppers
Kosher salt
2 qt vinegar
5 Tb dry mustard
⅔ cup flour
¾ tsp turmeric
3–4 cups sugar
1 small hot red pepper
1 qt *Mixed Vegetable Pickles* (page 342)
    (optional)

Wash celery; remove leaves and strings if necessary. Cut into ½-inch slices. Wash, core, and slice the tomatoes. Peel and slice the onions. Wash the cauliflower, divide into small flowerets, and cut the fleshy part into small pieces. Wash and clean the peppers; cut into chunks. Make a brine of 1 cup salt for every 2 quarts water. Put the cut-up vegetables in a large stainless steel kettle and cover with brine. Let stand overnight. The following morning, heat to the boiling point.

Meanwhile, make the sauce by combining the vinegar, dry mustard, flour, turmeric, and sugar to taste. Mince the hot pepper. Bring the sauce to a boil; add the hot pepper and the mixed pickles, if you wish. Taste and adjust seasonings. Drain the boiling brine from the vegetables. Then combine the hot vegetables and the boiling sauce. Mix thoroughly and ladle into hot jars, leaving ¼-inch head space. Adjust caps and process for 10 minutes in a boiling-water bath. (*Makes 16–20 pints*)

Elsa Peretsman's Short-Term Pickled Green Tomatoes

This is a wonderful recipe for instant gratification with no work and no wait. My friend Elsa and I dislike pickled tomatoes that have become strong-flavored and soft, which happens when the tomatoes sit in the brine too long. To avoid this problem, pickle the tomatoes as you need them.

I let our end-of-the-harvest green tomatoes sit in a fairly cool place and pickle them as we run out, or steal some tomatoes at the height of the tomato season. You can place them in jars whole, but I like Elsa's slicing method—then you really can eat them the next day. Pickle any amount you want and store in old pickle jars, crocks, or whatever is handy. Just weight them down so the tomatoes stay under the brine.

Wash and thickly slice green tomatoes, or use whole green cherry tomatoes. Put in a container, and add 1 clove garlic and 1 teaspoon pickling spices for each quart of pickles. Measure water and bring to a boil. For each quart of water, add 3 tablespoons kosher salt and ½ cup white vinegar. Pour over the tomatoes and press down with a weight to keep the tomatoes under the brine. Leave at room temperature (refrigerating will slow down the pickling action). If you like crisp tomatoes, you can eat them the next day.

Piccalilli

1 qt green tomatoes
1 red pepper
1 green pepper
Kosher or pickling salt
2 cups chopped onions
2 cups vinegar
1 cup sugar (or more to taste)
1¾-oz box pickling spices

Wash, core, and chop the tomatoes. Wash, clean, and chop the peppers. Make a brine of ½ cup salt to 1 quart water and cover the chopped vegetables. Let sit overnight. Drain off the water. Heat the vinegar and sugar in an enameled or stainless steel saucepan until the sugar dissolves. Pour over the vegetables, bring to a boil, add the pickling spices tied in a cheesecloth bag, and boil gently for 30 minutes. Remove the pickling spices and ladle into hot jars leaving ¼-inch head room. Adjust caps and process 10 minutes in a boiling-water bath. (*Makes 4 pints*)

Turnips & Rutabagas

Why is it that people so often make a face when you mention turnips? I suspect it's because they remember only the strong-tasting boiled-to-death rutabagas that were forced on them as children. If they could only taste fresh garden varieties of turnips, carefully grown and properly cooked, I'm sure they'd change their minds.

Although turnips and rutabagas are frequently lumped together in one category, botanically they're quite different. Turnips, members of the mustard family, have been around since ancient times; rutabagas (or swede turnips) came along in the 1700s, originating in Scandinavia. Most turnips have white flesh and purple crowns, hairy leaves, a medium-grained texture, and rapid growth. They have a higher water content than rutabagas, so they don't store well.

Rutabagas, on the other hand, have a yellow-orange color, large fleshy leaves, and a smooth, dense texture; they mature over a long period of time and can be stored. Their large roots are high in vitamin A and are sweeter and stronger-flavored than turnips.

We grow turnips as a spring crop and rutabagas for the fall. (Gardeners with a longer growing season than ours could plant a second fall turnip crop.) Turnips grow easily as long as you meet their requirements of a rich, well-cultivated soil and continual moisture throughout the growing season. Should you neglect watering or let growth become checked at any point, you will harvest strongly flavored turnips with pithy, cardboardlike texture.

We've had good success with varieties such as Early Purple Top, Tokyo Cross and Sutton's Golden Perfection, a yellow turnip. Golden Perfection's lovely color and delicious taste make it a family favorite; in addition, we have found it to be the variety most resistant to the root maggot, an enemy to both turnips and rutabagas. As turnips are a cool-weather crop, our first sowing goes in at the same time as spinach and peas—usually in late March. Germination is almost 100 percent, so Russ sows seeds about 1 inch apart and thins only once. We begin to harvest the baby turnips about 50–60 days after sowing, at the point when they're most deliciously flavored. (I love these small turnips, gathered when they're an inch in diameter, to munch on raw or savor rolled in butter and gently simmered for a moment.) Turnips grown strictly

for greens should be harvested before the weather turns hot, because high temperatures cause greens to become bitter and inedible.

Harvesting is easy: as the roots grow partially out of the ground, we pull the tops aside periodically to check root size before pulling up. We never let turnips grow larger than golf balls, because their flesh becomes strong-flavored, woody, and pithy.

Because of their high water content, turnips tend to dehydrate rapidly. (I have seen a crisp turnip shrivel up after only a day at room temperature.) Ideally they should be stored in a cold, humid environment, although no matter how carefully you store turnips, they won't last long once out of the garden.

Around mid-July, we plant a crop of rutabagas, timed to mature in the cool weather of early fall. We've had good luck with the Purple Top and Marian varieties. Rutabagas, like turnips, need a fertile soil to produce a good crop. They also have a high germination rate, so we plant the seeds sparsely, eventually thinning the plants to 10 inches apart. Rutabagas need less water than turnips, but should be watered well in dry weather. Gardeners used to let rutabagas grow to giant sizes, but we now know that to ensure maximum sweetness and flavor, rutabagas should be harvested much younger. We dig up rutabagas any time after they're 3–4 inches in diameter, usually in mid-October to November. Although ruta-bagas will tolerate a light frost, they are damaged by a hard freeze; for, unlike parsnips, their flavor is not im-proved by frost.

There is no one correct way to treat turnips or ruta-bagas; the method I use depends on my recipe. Raw tur-nips are delicious eaten whole like radishes, or sliced into a salad, onto an appetizer platter, or as an addition to a stir-fry meal.

It's unnecessary to peel thin-skinned baby turnips be-fore cooking. But as turnips mature, their skins toughen and should be removed. Rutabagas' thick, tough skin is easier to remove with a knife than with a vegetable peeler: you'll lose a certain amount of flesh before you get down to the moist, crisp interior.

Perhaps my favorite preparation is to sauté, then braise, the vegetables. I use young white turnips whole or cut larger turnips and rutabagas into ovals. To make ovals, I pare the peeled turnips or rutabagas into 1½–2-inch lengths which are ¾ inch wide, then shape them into ovals. (Save the parings for soups, or grate into a salad.) I'll steam or boil turnips or rutabagas when a recipe requires preliminary cooking; in general, I prefer steaming, because the vegetables become less water-logged and retain a better flavor; however, boiling works almost as well. Baking is yet another good way to prepare these versatile vegetables (see *Baked Honeyed Rutabaga Disks*).

Consider how you're going to serve them, then select the most appropriate method of cooking. When turnips and rutabagas are interchangeable, I'll indicate the method I prefer, and the different cooking times in each recipe.

Marketing

Both turnips and rutabagas should be firm—any wrinkling is a sign they've lost moisture and will have a spongy texture. Pass by larger turnips—they are likely to be pithy or bitter—and select young ones, which are frequently sold in bunches with their greens. The greens should look fresh; don't throw out—save them for soups or greens. Rutabagas, most frequently sold trimmed, should feel heavy and look unblemished. They're usually waxed to prevent dehydration, a practice not necessary for the home gardener.

◇ *Glazed Turnip or Rutabaga Ovals*

Sautéing, then braising, small whole white turnips brings out their flavor. Forming ovals for larger turnips or for rutabagas takes a bit of time, but is well worth the effort, for they cook quickly and look beautiful.

2 lb turnips or rutabagas
3 Tb butter
1 tsp sugar
Salt and freshly ground pepper

Peel turnips or rutabagas. Use baby turnips whole; larger turnips or rutabagas should be pared into large oval shapes, 1½–2 inches long by ¾ inch wide. Melt butter in a sauté pan large enough to hold the turnips or rutabagas in one layer. Over medium high heat, roll them around in butter, then sprinkle on sugar. Turn to lightly brown sides, 5–8 minutes. Turn heat to low, cover, and let simmer, stirring occasionally. They will brown and glaze as they cook. Turnip ovals will take 5–8 minutes of covered cooking; rutabagas will take twice as long, depending on size. Season to taste with salt and pepper. (*Serves 6–8*)
- *Braised Turnip or Rutabaga Ovals*: Proceed as above, omitting sugar and adding ½ cup beef broth before

Special Information

Yields
- 1 pound trimmed turnips or rutabagas = 4 cups chopped
- = 4 cups grated
- = 2 cups mashed

Storage and Preserving
- Turnips deteriorate rapidly. Separate leaves from roots. Whole roots will hold no longer than 1 week in the refrigerator.
- Green turnip tops will keep 2–4 days in the refrigerator.
- Refrigerate rutabagas for 3–4 weeks.
- Rutabagas will keep in good condition for 2 months if stored unwashed at 35–40°. Store them in a well-mulched moistureproof container or tub in the ground, or hold them in dry sand, sawdust, or peat in the cellar.
- Freeze mashed or puréed turnips or rutabagas.

Hints
- If turnips are large or old, blanch in boiling water for 4–5 minutes to remove strong or bitter flavor.
- Make *Gratin of Squash with Rutabaga* (see *Winter Squash*).
- Julienne into matchstick pieces or slice paper-thin and add to stir-fry dishes or tempura.
- Eat raw turnips like radishes, or add to appetizer platters.
- Accompany roast meats with braised young turnips.
- Add turnip or rutabaga chunks or ovals to ragouts or stews. As they absorb meat juices or fats, their flavor becomes richer.
- Serve mashed rutabagas as a meat accompaniment, or put in soufflés or roulades.

- Purée to serve alone or use as a base for cream soup.
- Stuff a pork loin with chunks of rutabaga, apples, and prunes.
- Julienne rutabagas, broccoli stems, and carrots into matchstick pieces. Blanch the vegetables for 2 minutes and drain. Eat plain, coat with butter, or garnish a clear soup. Or blanch, drain, and sauté in butter for 2–3 minutes until wilted.
- Grate raw in salads.
- Make tiny ovals the size of green olives to garnish a clear soup.
- Make a salad. Slice young turnips, blanch in stock until barely tender (8–12 minutes), and toss in *Vinaigrette Sauce* (see *Appendix*).
- Substitute diced rutabagas for leeks in *Leek Tartlets* (see *Leeks*).

Microwave
- Rutabaga (2 pounds, trimmed), cut into ½-inch dice, placed on a covered glass pie plate, completely cooks in 12 minutes. The most flavorful method is to remove from oven after 8–10 minutes, let rest (rutabaga continues to cook), or sauté in butter. One pound whole white turnips (seven 1½-inch turnips) takes 4 minutes.

Leftovers
- Mashed rutabaga spiced up with sautéed onion, butter, and seasonings makes a flavorful topping for meat stews. Spread mixture over top of stew as mashed potatoes on shepherd's pie. Bake for 20–30 minutes in a 350° oven.

covering pan; the ovals will absorb the hearty meat flavor of the stock. When ovals are cooked through, remove cover and reduce broth quickly to glaze. Cooking time will be approximately the same as in basic recipe.

- *No-Butter Braised Turnip or Rutabaga Ovals*: Shape ovals and place in a sauté pan with ³/₄ cup beef stock or other liquid. Cover and braise for 10–12 minutes for turnips, 15–20 for rutabagas. Remove and reduce stock if desired to pour over the turnips when serving.

◇ Steamed Turnip or Rutabaga

Boil 1 inch water in steamer. Put rutabaga or turnip in basket or colander and steam as follows, remembering timing is approximate and depends on the age and size of the vegetables.

- *White turnip*: ¹/₂-inch cubes take 12–15 minutes. 1–1¹/₂-inch whole turnips take 20–25 minutes.
- *Rutabaga*: ¹/₂-inch cubes take 30–35 minutes.

◇ Boiled Turnip or Rutabaga

Bring a saucepan of water to a boil and drop in turnips or rutabagas; tender young vegetables will take less time.

- *White turnip*: ¹/₂-inch pieces take 5–8 minutes. 1–1¹/₂-inch whole turnips take 15–20 minutes.
- *Rutabaga*: ¹/₂-inch cubes take 20–25 minutes. 1–1¹/₂-inch whole ovals take 30 minutes.

Finishing Touches for Steamed or Boiled Turnip and Rutabaga

- *In Butter*: Prepare as above and roll in melted butter. Season with salt and pepper and decorate with fresh herbs. (A combination of cubed turnips and rutabaga is very pretty.)
- *In Cream Sauce*: Make a cream sauce with 2¹/₂ tablespoons butter and 3 tablespoons flour, 1¹/₂ cups cooking liquid, and ¹/₂ cup milk or light cream (or all milk). Season and fold cooked turnips or rutabagas into sauce and reheat. Add bread crumbs or cheese sauce if desired.
- *With Onions in Broth*: Steam or boil turnips or rutabagas to just barely tender. Cool and slice. Sauté sliced onions (¹/₂ cup per pound of turnips) in 1 tablespoon of butter until wilted. Lightly sprinkle onions with flour, cook together for 2 minutes, remove from heat, and stir in beef or chicken broth (¹/₄ cup per pound of turnips), return to heat, season, and fold in drained turnips. Cook together until just tender. Add more broth if needed.
- *Mashed Turnip or Rutabaga*: Mash or purée 2 pounds turnips or rutabagas with 2–3 tablespoons butter and 2–3 tablespoons heavy cream or sour cream if you wish. Season with salt and pepper. Combine with mashed potatoes if desired.

◇ Baked Turnips

Turnips bake beautifully; cooked alongside a roast, they absorb its juices and flavors. But don't hesitate to bake them by themselves.

Baked White Turnips

Leave small turnips whole (peel if you wish) or cut larger ones into 1¹/₂-inch chunks. Brush with melted butter or with a melted butter and oil combination. Bake in a preheated 350° oven for 30–45 minutes, depending on their size and age. The turnips are cooked when the flesh is just tender when pierced with a fork. Season to taste.

Baked Rutabagas

Peel and cut rutabagas into 1¹/₂-inch chunks. Brush with melted butter or with a melted butter and oil combination. Bake in a preheated 350° oven for 50–60 minutes, depending on their size and age.

◇ Julienned Rutabaga with Accompaniment

All sorts of gadgets—expensive French mandolines, food processors, and even dime store gadgets—will matchstick vegetables. Frankly, I much prefer to use my hands and a good, sharp knife.

Equal amounts of peeled broccoli stem
rutabagas
carrots

Julienne the broccoli stem into matchstick pieces, saving the flowerets to serve on their own. Julienne rutabagas and carrots and combine with broccoli.

Blanch Method

Blanching is the most practical preparation for a quick sauté or for adding vetegables to a clear soup or sauce. Bring a pot of water to a rapid boil, add a bit of salt, and drop in the julienned vegetables. Blanch for 1–2 minutes, remove, and drain. The vegetables are ready to eat as is, coated with butter, to glamorize a clear soup, or to garnish other dishes.

Sauté Method

Melt butter in a sauté pan and stir in the julienned vegetables. Cover and cook for 2–3 minutes to wilt.

Stir-Fry Method

For maximum crispness, rapidly stir-fry the raw julienned vegetables in peanut oil.

Baby Turnips and Greens

This is a recipe for gardeners, for its success depends upon freshly picked, young, sweet turnips and their greens.

16 small (1-inch) turnips with greens
5 Tb butter
Salt and freshly ground pepper

Cut leaves from turnips, trim, wash well, and dry. Cut large leaves into thin diagonal slices. Peel turnips, if desired, then melt 3 tablespoons butter in a sauté pan large enough to hold the turnips in one layer. Add turnips and sauté for 5–6 minutes until lightly browned all over. Lower heat, cover, and cook until tender but still crisp, 5–8 minutes; season to taste. The time depends on the size of the turnips, but watch carefully, for they may cook faster. Remove and keep warm. Melt remaining 2 tablespoons butter in pan, add greens, and stir to coat with butter and to wilt, 3–5 minutes. Season to taste and serve with turnips and greens arranged side by side or with turnips covering the greens. (*Serves 4*)

Baked Honeyed Rutabaga Disks

These rutabaga disks are sensational served alongside a large baked ham, with a heaping golden pile of glazed white turnip ovals at one end. Ham or no, these are good!

> 2 medium rutabagas (approximately 1 lb each)
> 4 Tb butter
> 1/4 cup honey

Slice a small piece off the end of each rutabaga so they will sit firmly on your counter surface. With a knife, remove the skins as if you were slicing down around a whole orange, ending up with peeled rutabaga balls. Now cut each ball across its width to make 4 large slices, approximately 1/2 inch thick. You should have 8 slices in all. Melt butter and brush some on a baking sheet. (Depending on the size of the disks, you may need two sheets.) Brush disks with butter, place on baking sheet, and bake in a preheated 400° oven 15 minutes; then turn and coat with honey. Bake another 15 minutes, turning disks once more and basting with butter and honey. You'll need to cook a few minutes longer if slices are uneven or thicker. (*Serves 4–6*)

- Steam the rutabaga for 20–30 minutes or until just tender. Melt butter and honey together and coat disks before serving—but you'll lose the browned glazing.

Grated White Turnips

Grated turnips can be added to salads raw, or sautéed as a vegetable dish. They hold a great deal of water, and lightly salting them removes excess moisture and improves the cooking process. Treat rutabaga in the same way—however, you don't need to salt.

> 2 lb turnips
> Salt
> 4 Tb butter
> Freshly ground pepper
> 3/4 cup heavy cream (optional)
> Herbs (optional)

Peel and grate turnips, then sprinkle with salt and set aside. After 30 minutes, squeeze the water out; you will have approximately 4 cups of turnips. Melt butter in a sauté pan and stir in turnips. Turn heat to low, cover, and simmer for 10 minutes. Uncover, turn heat to medium, season with salt and pepper, stir, add cream (if desired), and cook for another 1–2 minutes or until cream has heated through. Add some favorite herbs, such as marjoram or basil, if you wish. (*Serves 4*)

- Finely slice 1/2 cup leeks or onion and sauté in butter to wilt before adding turnip.

Dilled Gratin of Turnip and Carrot

A plain turnip gratin is delicious, but it's fun to experiment with various root vegetable combinations. This is a family favorite.

> 2 cups grated turnips
> Salt
> 7 Tb butter
> 3/4 cup fresh bread crumbs
> 2 cups grated carrot
> 1/2 tsp sugar
> 1 Tb chopped fresh dill
> Freshly ground pepper
> 3/4 cup heavy cream

Sprinkle the grated turnip with salt and set aside for 30 minutes. Meanwhile, melt 3 tablespoons butter, sauté bread crumbs, and set aside. Squeeze water from turnip; combine with grated carrot. Melt 4 tablespoons butter in a sauté pan and add turnip, carrot, and sugar. Turn heat to low, cover, and cook for 10 minutes, stirring occasionally. Uncover; stir in dill and salt and pepper to taste. Put turnip-carrot mixture in a buttered 1-quart ovenproof dish. Pour on cream and top with the buttered bread crumbs. Bake in a preheated 350° oven for 30 minutes or until brown and bubbly. (*Serves 4–6*)

- If you like, top with grated cheese.

Lynn Wilson's Rutabaga Pudding

During the nineteenth century, savory puddings were common. Try this one with a roast pork or ham or other main dish.

> 6 Tb butter
> 1 Tb grated onion
> 4 cups grated peeled rutabaga
> 3 eggs
> 3 oz cream cheese, softened
> 2 cups milk
> ¾ tsp salt
> Freshly ground pepper
> ¾ cup fresh bread crumbs

Melt 3 tablespoons butter in a large sauté pan and cook onion until lightly colored; add grated rutabaga. Stir to coat with butter and cook until wilted, 8–10 minutes. Meanwhile, beat eggs, add cream cheese, and beat together thoroughly. Heat milk, gradually add to egg mixture, then stir in the rutabaga mixture, salt, and pepper. Pour into a buttered 8 x 8-inch ovenproof dish. Melt remaining 3 tablespoons butter, sauté bread crumbs, and top the rutabaga with them. Bake for 30 minutes in a preheated 350° oven. (*Serves 4–6*)

Old-Fashioned Scalloped Turnips

The old-fashioned way of fixing scalloped potatoes is simply to layer with butter, flour, and milk. Here I've translated that method to turnips for an equally satisfying dish.

> 4 Tb butter
> ½ cup thinly sliced onions
> 4 cups peeled sliced turnips
> 2 Tb flour
> 1 tsp salt
> Freshly ground pepper
> 1 cup milk
> ½ cup light cream

Butter a 1-quart casserole. Melt 1 tablespoon butter and lightly sauté onions until just wilted. Layer a third of the sliced turnips in casserole, top with a third of the onion, sprinkle with 2 teaspoons flour and ⅓ teaspoon salt, and grind on some pepper; pat with 1 tablespoon butter. Repeat this layering twice. Mix milk and cream together and pour over turnips. Cover and bake in a preheated 350° oven for 30 minutes, then remove cover and bake for another 30–45 minutes, or until tender and bubbly. (*Serves 4*)

- *Turnips au Gratin*: Cover with ¾ cup grated cheese.

Rutabaga Roulade

A roulade is a flat soufflé, made with equal amounts of egg yolks and whites, baked in a jelly roll pan, spread with stuffing, and then rolled in the shape of a log. Almost any vegetable will adapt to this treatment. Serve this roulade plain, with *Mornay Sauce* (see *Appendix*), or with another sauce of your choice.

> 2–2½ lb rutabaga
> *Creamed Spinach* (page 262)
> 6 Tb butter
> 7½ Tb flour
> 1½ cups hot milk
> ½ tsp salt
> Freshly ground pepper
> 6 eggs
> ¼ tsp cream of tartar

Trim rutabaga; cut into quarters and into quarters again. Steam or boil until very tender and purée.

Meanwhile, prepare creamed spinach, chopping the spinach finely. Film with cream and set aside. Melt 2 tablespoons of the butter and brush on an 11×17-inch jelly roll pan; cover with a piece of waxed paper extending 2 inches over each end. Butter the waxed paper, dust with 2 tablespoons flour, shaking off any excess flour. Melt the remaining 4 tablespoons butter in a saucepan, blend in the remaining flour, and cook over medium heat for 2–3 minutes without browning. Remove from heat, pour in hot milk, and beat with whip until blended. Then, bring to a boil, stirring, and cook for 2 minutes. Stir in the rutabaga purée, salt, and pepper to taste.

Separate the eggs. Put rutabaga mixture in a large mixing bowl, add egg yolks one by one, and beat until thoroughly combined. Taste and correct seasoning, if necessary; set aside. Bring egg whites to room temperature, then beat at medium speed until foamy, add cream of tartar and a pinch of salt, and, gradually increasing speed to fast, beat until peaks are smooth and shiny. Stir one-quarter of the beaten whites into the turnip mixture to lighten it. Place the rest of the whites on top of the mixture and quickly fold them in. Spread the mixture evenly in the jelly roll pan and place on the middle shelf of a preheated 400° oven. Bake for 25 minutes or until the top feels slightly springy and has begun to shrink away from the sides of the pan. Remove roulade from oven, cover with a clean kitchen towel. Place a cookie sheet on top of towel. Turn pans so that cookie sheet is

on bottom, and let rest for 5 minutes. Lift the baking pan off the roulade. (A bit of the sides will come off; just trim.) Reheat the spinach and spread across the roulade to within 1 inch of the sides. Using the edge of the towel, lift and roll the roulade lengthwise as if you were making a jelly roll. Place a platter or board at the edge of the

towel and roll the roulade onto the platter. Serve immediately. (*Serves 4–6*)

• *Spinach Roulade*: Reverse the vegetables, making a spinach roulade with rutabaga filling. Substitute 2½ cups buttered chopped spinach for the puréed rutabaga. Use *Mashed Turnip Rutabaga* (page 327) for the filling.

Turnip Cases with Two Fillings

Hollowed-out white turnips create delicate vegetable cases for numerous fillings. I'll give you two recipes here. The first, turnips stuffed with golden mashed rutabaga, is a colorful distillation of these two root vegetables. The second, also a vegetable accompaniment, derives from Middle Eastern cooking, in which turnips play an important part. An essential tool is a melon baller.

Cases
6 turnips, 2–3-inches in diameter

Peel turnips, making a small flat surface on each bottom. Slice off one piece on top and, with a melon baller, hollow out a cavity, leaving only a ⅓–½-inch-thick shell. Reserve the pulp (to be used in filling). Boil turnips for approximately 5–8 minutes. Remove from water and drain, upside down, on a rack.

Filling 1
Reserved turnip pulp
Equal amount chopped rutabaga
2–3 Tb butter
2–3 Tb heavy cream
Salt and freshly ground pepper
⅓ cup chicken or beef broth

Steam turnip pulp and chopped rutabaga until tender, under 10 minutes. Add butter and purée, add cream; and season to taste. Stuff into hollowed-out turnips. Place into a buttered baking dish, pour in broth, and bake in a preheated 350° oven for 20–30 minutes or until heated through and tender. (*Serves 6*)

• Use either turnip or rutabaga. Season purée with ¼ teaspoon curry or cinnamon.
• Sprinkle cheese or bread crumbs on top.

Filling 2
¼ cup port wine
½ cup raisins
Half of reserved turnip pulp
1 small onion
5 Tb butter
½ tsp cumin
½ tsp salt
Freshly ground pepper
1 cup cooked rice
¼ cup pine nuts
1 Tb chopped parsley
⅓ cup chicken or beef broth

Heat port, pour over raisins, and let sit for 15 minutes. Chop turnip pulp and onion. Melt 4 tablespoons butter in sauté pan, add onions, and sauté until wilted. Add turnip and cook for 2 minutes or so until coated with butter. Stir in cumin, salt, and pepper, then add rice, raisins, and port. Cook together for 5–6 minutes, adjusting seasonings, if necessary. Mix in pine nuts and parsley. Fill turnip cases. Dot remaining butter on top, add broth, and bake covered in a preheated 350° oven for 30 minutes or until tender and heated through. (*Serves 6*)

Tart Turnip and Rutabaga Salad

Here is a grated raw salad with a Mideastern touch. Vary with other root vegetables, such as carrots, along with or replacing the rutabaga.

>   3/4 lb turnip
>   3/4 lb rutabaga
>   Salt
>   1/3 cup chopped scallions
>   1/2 cup chopped parsley
>   2 Tb chopped fresh mint or 1 1/2 tsp dried
>   1/3 cup lemon juice
>   1/2 cup combination olive and vegetable oil
>   Freshly ground pepper

Grate turnip and rutabaga. You should have about 4 cups packed. Sprinkle with salt and let sit for 30 minutes; squeeze moisture out. Mix turnip, rutabaga, scallions, parsley, and mint. Beat lemon juice and oils together and stir into turnip mixture; season with salt and pepper to taste. Marinate, refrigerated, for 1 hour before serving. (*Makes 5 cups*)

Spring Garden Soup

I like to gather some of the first vegetables of the year and make this soup to celebrate spring.

>   5–6 radishes
>   1 lb baby turnips
>   2 Tb butter
>   4–6 scallions
>   1 qt *Vegetable-Flavored Broth (Nage)* (page 352) or chicken broth
>   1 cup shelled peas
>   Salt and freshly ground pepper
>   Fresh herbs (optional)

Wash and slice radishes paper-thin and blanch in boiling water for 30 seconds; set aside. Peel and dice turnips. Melt butter in a 6-quart saucepan and slowly turn the turnips in the butter to wilt them slightly without browning. Chop scallions and cook with the turnips for 2–3 minutes. Bring vegetable broth to simmer and add to turnips and scallions, simmering until turnips are barely tender, 5–6 minutes. Drop peas in and cook for 1–2 minutes. Stir in blanched radish slices; season with salt and pepper and fresh herbs if desired. (*Serves 4–6*)
- Wash turnip greens, dry, and slice diagonally into thin strips; add to turnips with broth. If not using greens from turnips and radishes, save them for greens soup.

Turnip Soup

This is a light, delicate soup when made with young turnips and greens. You can also prepare it without greens at all, or substitute spinach or watercress in varying amounts.

>   1 1/2–2 lb young sweet turnips
>   Turnip greens plus additional spinach or watercress to equal 3 cups packed

>   5 Tb butter
>   Salt
>   1/2 tsp sugar
>   6 cups chicken stock (or chicken stock and water combined)
>   1/4 cup rice
>   Freshly ground pepper
>   Thyme
>   1 cup milk or light cream (optional)

Peel and slice turnips. Wash and trim turnip greens and spinach or watercress, dry, and chop. Melt 3 tablespoons butter in a sauté pan, add turnips, 1 teaspoon salt, and sugar, and cook gently over low heat to wilt without browning. Empty into a large saucepan and add chicken stock. Add rice; bring to a boil, reduce heat, and simmer 10–15 minutes or until turnips and rice are tender.

In the meantime, melt remaining 2 tablespoons butter in sauté pan. Add greens and sauté, stirring until wilted, 2–3 minutes; set aside, then add to turnips the last 5 minutes of cooking. Purée mixture. Season with salt, pepper, and thyme to taste. Thin with milk or cream if desired. (*Serves 6*)

Shinbone Soup with Turnip and Rutabaga

Turnips and rutabagas are a welcome addition to dozens of vegetable combinations. I augment my mother-in-law's "famous" shinbone soup with a large amount of turnips and rutabagas in the fall when we have an ample supply or use just one or the other. Remember to add the white turnips after rutabaga, as they take less time to cook. You can substitute beef broth and water for the shinbone soup broth, but this is so tasty—do try it.

>   2 lb meaty beef shinbones
>   2 Tb butter
>   2 Tb oil
>   2 tomatoes
>   1 small sliced onion
>   2 cups beef stock
>   Herb bouquet:
>   1 bay leaf
>   6 parsley sprigs
>   1 clove garlic
>   6 peppercorns
>   1 tsp thyme
>   1 celery stalk with leaves
>   1 Tb tomato paste
>   Salt
>   2 cups diced rutabaga
>   1 cup thinly sliced carrots
>   3/4 cup thinly sliced celery
>   1 cup finely sliced leeks
>   2 cups diced turnips
>   1/2 cup small pasta, such as ditatelli
>   Freshly ground pepper
>   Chopped parsley
>   Grated Parmesan cheese

Cut meat off shinbone in 1-inch chunks. In a large casserole, melt butter and oil; brown meat and bones. Cut tomatoes in half and squeeze out seeds. Add sliced onion to casserole and let lightly brown with meat. When meat is browned, drain fat from pan; add 2 quarts water and the beef stock. Bring to a boil and skim. Add the herb bouquet, celery stalk, tomatoes, tomato paste, and 1 teaspoon salt. Bring back to boil, reduce heat, and simmer partially covered for 1½–2 hours.

Strain the soup, setting the meat chunks aside. Press the juices from the vegetables, and discard them. Wash out the casserole or pot and return meat (which can be cut into smaller pieces) and broth. Reheat and add rutabaga, carrots, celery, and leeks. Partially cover and cook for 10 minutes, add turnips and pasta, and continue cooking until vegetables and pasta are tender, 15–20 minutes. Season to taste with salt and pepper and sprinkle with parsley. Pass Parmesan cheese separately. (*Makes 3 quarts*)

Irish Stew, Farmhouse Style

This full-bodied lamb stew with no need for browning is what I have always imagined a "country dish" to be. It improves with age, becoming even better the second day. Serve it with good country bread.

2–2½ lb lamb, shoulder or neck
1 lb potatoes
1½ lb white turnips
¾ lb leeks
1 clove garlic
1 bay leaf
Salt
Worcestershire sauce
Freshly ground pepper
Chopped parsley

Cut the lamb into 1½-inch chunks, trimming any fat or gristle. Peel and roughly chop potatoes and turnips. Wash and trim leeks, and finely slice the white and pale green parts. Put lamb in a large saucepan, cover with water, bring to a boil, then pour out water and rinse pan. (This helps to remove the scum.) Return lamb to pan; add potatoes, turnips, leeks, garlic, bay leaf, and 1 teaspoon salt. Cover with water, bring to a boil, reduce heat, and simmer 1–1½ hours or until meat is tender. With the back of a wooden spoon, mash the softened turnip and potato pieces against the side of the pot. Don't purée the stew or have it lumpy, but try for a thick mashed consistency. Stir in a teaspoon or more of Worcestershire sauce, grind in some pepper, and sprinkle with parsley. (*Serves 6*)

Braised Duck with Turnips

Duck with turnips is a delicious classic dish. I give the recipe for one duck; you could use two without changing the rest of the ingredients.

4–5-lb duck
3 onions
2 carrots
1 stalk celery
6 Tb butter
3 Tb oil
1–2 cups beef stock
Herb bouquet:
   6 sprigs parsley
   2 celery tops
   1 bay leaf
   ½ tsp thyme
½ cup white vermouth
1½ lb trimmed small turnips or turnip ovals
   (page 325)
Salt and freshly ground pepper

Wash duck and pat dry. Cut into 4 serving pieces, splitting down the back on both sides of the backbone and then again in half, separating the wing and leg portions. Remove wing ends at elbow and reserve, along with backbone and neck for stock. Cut off any extra skin and remove interior fat. Make a duck stock: Chop onions; set ⅔ aside. Chop carrots; set ½ aside. Chop celery. Melt 2 tablespoons butter and 1 tablespoon oil in a saucepan. Brown duck neck, backbone, gizzard, and wing ends along with ½ of the chopped carrot, celery, and ⅓ chopped onion. When lightly browned, pour off fat, add 1 cup beef stock and water to cover, simmer for 1 hour, then degrease and set aside. You should have 1 cup or more of stock.

Meanwhile, prick the skin of the duck, not going through to the meat. Heat 2 tablespoons oil in a heavy casserole and slowly brown the duck pieces for 20–30 minutes. The fat of a duck lies right under the skin, so sautéing it slowly will render a great deal of it out. Drain fat off as it accumulates. (I have rendered 1 cup and more on occasion.) When fat is rendered and pieces nicely browned, remove from casserole and wipe out. Melt 2 tablespoons butter in casserole and lightly brown remaining chopped onions and carrots, stirring. Place the browned duck on the carrots and onions and add herb bouquet, vermouth, and duck stock. (If duck stock is not enough, add beef stock to make 2 cups.) Cover and simmer 1–1 1/2 hours. Cooking time depends upon the age of the duck and whether it was fresh or frozen. Meanwhile, melt 2 tablespoons butter in a sauté pan and lightly brown the turnips. When the duck has cooked to just about tender, remove from casserole and strain all braising liquid, pressing down on the vegetables to extract juices. Remove fat and season braising liquid to taste. Return duck to casserole and surround with the browned turnips. Pour the braising liquid over turnips, thinning if necessary with stock, bring to a boil on top of the stove, cover, and return to oven for 12–15 minutes or until turnips and duck are tender. Serve duck surrounded with turnips. (*Serves 4*)

Chicken, Chickpeas, and Turnips

Paula Wolfert has written an excellent book on Moroccan food, *Couscous and Other Good Food from Morocco*. This recipe is a simple adaptation of one of her chicken kdra recipes. Once you taste it you will buy the book just to try more from the exotic world of Moroccan cookery.

  2 cups cooked chickpeas
  2 small (2 1/2-lb) fryer or broiler chickens
  3 Tb butter
  1 Tb oil
  2 onions
  5 cups chicken stock
  1/2 tsp white pepper
  1/4 tsp ground ginger
  1/8 tsp powdered saffron
  1/2 tsp turmeric
  1 1/2–2 lb small whole peeled turnips (if larger, cut into 1 1/2-inch chunks)
  2 cups chopped young turnip leaves and stems (or spinach or mustard greens)
  1/4 cup lemon juice
  Salt and freshly ground pepper
  Chopped parsley (optional)

Rinse chickpeas in water and rub lightly to remove their skins; drain and set aside. Cut chickens into quarters, removing wing tips and backbones; put them aside for stock. Melt butter and oil in a casserole and lightly brown chicken on all sides, cooking in 2 batches if necessary. Slice onions and stir into butter and oil to color. Then add the chickpeas, stock, pepper, ginger, saffron, and turmeric. Bring to a boil, reduce heat, cover, and simmer for 10 minutes. Add turnips and greens and simmer 20 minutes more.

Remove chicken and turnips to a covered warm dish. Boil sauce to reduce, mashing some of the chickpeas against the side of the pan to thicken the sauce: it may take 10–15 minutes to produce a nice thick sauce. Add lemon juice and salt and pepper to taste. Reheat chicken and turnips in the sauce. (The turnips take on the flavor of the chickpea sauce.) Garnish with parsley if desired. (*Serves 6–8*)

• Try using different legumes, such as kidney beans or lentils.

Rutabaga Pie

Root vegetables make wholesome yet delicate pies. I sweeten this pie with fresh fruit and just a bit of sugar and honey. Serve it with whipped cream or ice cream.

  3/4 lb rutabaga
  1 apple
  1 pear
  1 Tb honey
  1/2 tsp ground coriander
  1/4 tsp ground ginger
  1/2 tsp salt
  2 eggs
  2 Tb brown sugar
  1 cup light cream
  9-inch pie shell, partially baked (see *Tart Pastry*, page 351)

Peel rutabaga and cut into large slices or chunks. Peel apple and pear, reserving peels, cut in half, and remove cores. Put 1 inch water in steam pot and add peels to water. Put rutabaga in steam basket and steam for 15 minutes. Add apple and pear and steam for 15 minutes more or until rutabaga is soft. Remove rutabaga, apple, and pear and purée together, beating in honey, coriander, ginger, and salt. Beat eggs, add sugar, and beat thoroughly. Add rutabaga mixture, then cream, mixing well, and pour into the pie shell. Bake for 15 minutes in a preheated 400° oven, turn heat down to 350°, and bake another 25–30 minutes or until set. (*Makes a 9-inch pie*)

Zucchini

See *Squash (Summer)*, pages 269–282.

Mixed Vegetables

Crudités

Anyone with a vegetable garden owes it to his friends to treat them to freshly picked produce. I can't think of any finger food as appealing as newly harvested young vegetables, served with one or many dips (see following suggestions). Wash, peel, or string, and trim vegetables and arrange in a colorful pattern on a simple wooden tray. Incorporate slices of the more unusual vegetables such as fennel and Chinese cabbage in among the carrots and cauliflower.

Bagna Cauda

Keep this garlic-anchovy sauce warm over a low burner or in a chafing dish. The sauce can be either creamy or plain. Both versions are perfectly delicious—although I tend to lean toward the creamy version. Serve with homemade crusty bread.

With Cream
2 cups heavy cream
8 anchovy fillets
4 Tb butter
1–2 tsp minced garlic
Freshly ground pepper

Reduce the cream by gently boiling to half its volume, or approximately 1 cup; set aside. Rinse the anchovies in water, pat dry, and finely chop them. Melt the butter over a very low heat and stir in the garlic. You want to soften the garlic without browning until it is almost puréed, about 5 minutes. Stir in the anchovies, mash them into the butter and garlic, and continue to cook for 3–4 minutes. Gradually whisk in the cream, heat through, and season with pepper. Keep warm. (*Makes about 1 cup*)

Without Cream
8 Tb butter
1/2 cup olive oil
2 tsp minced garlic
10–12 anchovy fillets

Melt the butter and the oil together and, over low heat, stir in the garlic. Cook very slowly until garlic softens and is almost puréed without browning, about 5 minutes. Drain the anchovies and finely chop. Stir them into the oil and cook until dissolved in the sauce. (*Makes about 1 cup*)

Tarama Dip
A delicious dip made with carp roe (tarama). Purchase tarama in a jar and store it in the refrigerator. It keeps well.

3 slices fresh white bread
1/2 cup tarama
1–2 Tb chopped onions
Juice of 2 lemons
1–1 1/2 cups olive oil
Freshly ground pepper
Chopped parsley

Cut off the bread crusts. Moisten the bread slices with water, then squeeze dry. Place bread, tarama, onions, lemon juice, and 1/4 cup of the olive oil in a blender or food processor. Mix together; then, very gradually, add the remaining oil until sauce has a thick mayonnaise consistency. Season with pepper and more lemon juice if desired, and sprinkle with parsley. (*Makes about 2 cups*)

Joe Hyde's Russian Dressing
If you are serving more than one dip, you'll find this tangy cold dressing makes a beautiful contrast with the warm *Bagna Cauda*.

1 1/3 cups mayonnaise
1/4 cup finely chopped green peppers
1/4 cup finely chopped onions
2 Tb chili sauce
1 Tb red wine vinegar
Salt and freshly ground pepper

Mix all the ingredients and refrigerate. The sauce is best when allowed to marinate for 24 hours or longer. (*Makes 2 cups*)

My Mother's Roquefort Dip
8 oz softened cream cheese
1/2 cup sour cream
2 Tb chopped red onions
2–3 oz Roquefort or blue cheese
Salt and freshly ground pepper
1–2 tsp wine vinegar (optional)

Beat together the cream cheese and sour cream until smooth. Stir in the onions. Crumble in the cheese; stir lightly. You want to retain the texture of the crumbled cheese pieces. Season with salt, pepper, and vinegar if desired. (*Makes about 1 3/4 cups*)

Mixed Vegetables à la Grecque

A la Grecque Marinade
2 1/2 cups chicken stock or half stock and half water
1 cup dry white wine
1/2 cup olive oil
1/4 cup lemon juice
6 parsley sprigs
1 clove garlic, sliced
1/4 tsp thyme
8 peppercorns
1/2 tsp salt
1 celery stalk

Vegetables
Peeled broccoli flowerets
Tiny white peeled onions
Tiny white turnips
Tiny whole or sliced small summer squashes
Sliced peppers
Small whole snap beans
Small whole asparagus
Halved Brussels sprouts
Thin diagonal carrot slices or tiny whole baby carrots
Celery or fennel hearts
Scallions or small leeks
Peeled and scored strips of cucumbers
Cauliflower flowerets
Celery or fennel strips

Place all marinade ingredients in an enameled or stainless steel saucepan, cover, and simmer for 30 minutes. Strain out liquid and taste for seasoning. Use immediately, or refrigerate and reheat before covering vegetables.

When ready to cook the vegetables, bring the marinade to a boil and add vegetables one at a time; simmer or poach each vegetable until just barely tender. The vegetables will continue to cook as they marinate, so slightly undercook.

Each vegetable will cook in a different amount of time, depending upon its cut and texture. Small onions may take 15–20 minutes to cook, while squash slices will

be ready in 5 minutes or less. Watch the vegetables carefully and remove them to a shallow glass dish when they are cooked. After all the vegetables are cooked, pour over the marinade, cool, and then refrigerate, covered, for at least 4 hours. When serving, lift out of the marinade, season to taste, and garnish with lemon wedges. (*Makes 4 cups marinade*)

- For simple poached vegetables for a salad, cook the vegetables one at a time in chicken broth. Cool to room temperature and serve with *Mayonnaise* (see *Appendix*). Add tiny potatoes and beets to the list of possible vegetables—but cook beets last because they color the broth. Add a garlic clove to the broth for extra flavor.

Mixed Vegetable Antipasto

12–18 tiny white onions
1 small cauliflower
4 carrots
4 stalks celery
1 green pepper
1 red sweet pepper
1 1/2 cups wine vinegar
1/2 cup light olive oil
1/2 cup vegetable oil
2 Tb sugar
2 tsp salt
1 tsp oregano
Freshly ground pepper
1/2 cup or more pitted green or black olives

Peel the onions. Wash cauliflower, cut into small flowerets, and slice the remainder. Peel the carrots and cut into 1 1/2-inch logs or diagonal slices. Wash and string the celery and slice diagonally. Wash, trim, and cut the peppers into strips. In a saucepan, bring to a boil 1/2 cup water, the vinegar, oils, sugar, salt, oregano, and pepper to taste. Add the vegetables and olives. Cover the pan and cook for 3–4 minutes. Uncover, cool, and refrigerate for 24 hours. Drain before serving. (*Serves 6–8*)

Grilled Mixed Vegetables

How you cut the vegetables is arbitrary. When I marinate vegetables before skewering, I cut them into even-size chunks small enough to hold well on the skewers,

but when I do them straight on the grill, I usually cut them into halves or thick slices.

While I prefer to place vegetables directly on the grill so that they pick up that delicious lightly charred taste, another method is to wrap vegetables in aluminum foil and steam them in their own juices. This is particularly good for harder-textured vegetables which take longer to cook, such as potatoes or winter squashes.

It is really impossible to suggest accurate cooking times, since so much depends upon the cut and age of the vegetable and the heat of the fire (the most unpredictable factor).

When I'm cooking vegetables directly on the grill, I wait until the coals are ashen and place the rack about 6 inches from the heat. (The distance depends upon the intensity of the fire.) Sliced vegetables cook in the least amount of time. Baste with oil, or *Pat's Marinating Sauce for Both Meat and Vegetables* (page 337), or *Garlic Marinades* (page 179) to prevent them from drying out.

I always compose skewers using only one vegetable. Since they cook in slightly different times, I skewer all the onions together, the tomatoes together, mushrooms together, etc. That way, by placing the longer-cooking vegetables on the grill first, you can cook the vegetables evenly.

Aluminum-packaged vegetables take longer to cook. If you wish, for extra flavor before wrapping in foil, add herbs and seasonings to taste. Then, put the wrapped package on the grill. Beets, carrots, potatoes, winter squashes, etc., take 45 minutes or longer to cook, so allow plenty of time. Softer-textured wrapped vegetables, such as summer squash or eggplant, will be done in less time.

Here are some of the vegetables I grill:
- *Beets* (*In foil*): Dot small whole beets with butter, and wrap in foil.
- *Carrots* (*In foil*): Dot small whole or cut-up carrot slices with butter and wrap in foil.
- *Corn* (*In husks*): Pull down leaves without detaching, remove silk, and rewrap leaves up around kernels. Soak in water for 10 minutes to keep from burning. (If you have a very low fire and place corn far enough away from flame, you can grill without the soaking step.) Place on the grill, turning occasionally. (*In foil*): Remove the husks and silk, and brush with melted butter. Wrap in aluminum foil and roast on the grill. You can also place corn kernels in foil, dot with butter, and grill to hot.
- *Cucumbers* (*In foil*): Peel, score, and cut into chunks. Dot with butter, place in foil, and grill until heated through.
- *Eggplant* (*In foil*): Cut into chunks, dot with butter or toss with oil and herbs, and place in foil. (*On grill*): Halve lengthwise, and slash and salt flesh. Drain for 30 minutes. Pat dry, brush with oil, and place cut side down on the grill. Cook until golden brown; turn over. Continue to baste with oil or marinade until cooked barely tender. (*Sliced*): baste and turn them on the grill until browned and cooked through.

- *Fennel* (*In foil*): Slice fennel, dot with butter, and wrap in foil. (*On grill*): Halve lengthwise. Baste well with melted butter and oil and grill cut side down until browned. Turn, baste again, and cook until tender yet crunchy.
- *Jerusalem Artichokes* (*In foil*): Dot with pats of butter or roll in oil. Wrap in foil. (*On grill*): Rub with oil and turn often: watch carefully because the chokes become soft quickly.
- *Onions* (*In foil*): Put pats of butter on small white onions or sliced onions, wrap in foil. (*On grill*): Use large Spanish onions (perhaps my favorite grilled vegetable). Peel and halve horizontally. Brush with oil and place on the grill, cut side down. Let the onion become charred, turn, and baste again with oil. Cook until charred on the other side, keeping the onion in the hot area of grill. The cooking will take 15–20 minutes. Lightly scrape off the heavy char before serving. (*On skewers*): Marinate sweet onion chunks or baste with oil and place on skewers. Grill, turning until lightly charred on all sides.
- *Parsnips* (*In foil*): Cut into slices or chunks, dot with butter, and wrap in foil.
- *Peppers* (*In foil*): Slice or chunk, rub with oil, and wrap in foil. (Combining with sliced onions is nice.) (*On grill*): Grill whole, turning occasionally until charred on all sides; peel, skin, and cut into pieces; or halve pepper, brush with oil, and cook until lightly charred on both sides. (*On skewers*): Cut into chunks. Marinate or brush with oil and thread on skewers. Cook, turning, until cooked on all sides.
- *Potatoes* (*In foil*): Slice potatoes or use small new potatoes. Dot with butter and wrap in foil. Allow 60 minutes or longer for whole large potatoes, or bury in the coals.
- *Rutabagas and Turnips* (*In foil*): Use sliced rutabaga, sliced large or tiny small white turnips; dot with butter and wrap in foil.
- *Summer Squash* (*In foil*): Dot small whole or chunked large summer squash with butter and wrap in foil. (*On grill*): Halve summer squashes and baste with melted butter and oil. Place cut side down on the grill and cook until lightly browned. Then turn, baste, and cook until tender. (*Sliced*): Baste with oil or melted butter and grill on either side until tender. (*On skewers*): Chunk whole small squash, marinate, or baste with oil and thread on skewers. Grill, turning, until tender.
- *Tomatoes* (*In foil*): Dot whole cherry tomatoes with butter, wrap in foil, and cook until just heated through. (*On grill*): Halve large tomatoes, brush with oil, and grill, cut side down, until seared. Turn and baste with melted butter and herbs and dot with buttered bread crumbs and herbs if desired. Cook until hot and tender. (*On skewers*): Chunk tomatoes (plum tomatoes are a good choice), baste with oil or melted butter, and cook, turning, until just tender.
- *Winter Squash* (*In foil*): Cut into slices or chunks, dot with butter, and wrap in foil.

*Pat's Marinating Sauce for
Both Meat and Vegetables*
1/2 cup ketchup
1/2 cup water
2 Tb vegetable oil
2 Tb Worcestershire sauce
2 Tb cider vinegar
2 Tb sugar
1 tsp salt

Place all the ingredients in a saucepan and heat to boiling. Pour over meat. Cool slightly before pouring over vegetables. Marinate for 30 minutes or more. (*Makes about 1 1/2 cups*)

Vegetable Tempura

While tempura often includes fish and shellfish, my favorite is all vegetables. Young fresh vegetables cooked in a lacy crisp coating are really sensational. The choice of vegetables is almost limitless. The only point to remember in preparing is that the vegetables will be cooked in only a few minutes. Therefore prepare them all ahead: slice firm vegetables such as carrots, parsnips, and sweet potatoes very thin; string leafy vegetables such as spinach and chard leaves; use small vegetables like beans and sugar snap peas whole; peel vegetables with stringy skins such as asparagus and broccoli stems; break cauliflower or broccoli flowerets into small pieces.

Vegetables Suitable for Tempura
Thinly sliced eggplant
Thinly sliced zucchini or yellow squash
Thinly sliced patty pan squash rounds
Thinly sliced onion rounds (held together with a
    toothpick)
Thinly sliced peeled broccoli stalks
Thinly sliced winter squash or pumpkin
Flat carrot strips
Flat kohlrabi strips
White turnip rounds
Squash blossoms
Spinach or chard leaves
Parsley sprigs
Small whole green beans
Small whole sugar snap peas
Small broccoli or cauliflower flowerets

Cook tempura at the last minute. Once all the vegetables are prepared, set up the remaining ingredients when you are ready to cook and serve. The batter is very light and produces a crisp and lacy vegetable coating. The thickness of the coating depends upon the amount of ice water: for an extra-light coating, use more ice water; for a heavier coating, use less. Wait to make the batter until you are going to use it and mix just enough to combine the ingredients. It will be lumpy.

Batter for Tempura
2 eggs
2 cups ice water
2 cups sifted flour
Salt

Beat together the eggs and ice water. Add flour, salt to taste, and mix with a fork or chopsticks until barely combined. (*Makes approximately 3 ½ cups batter*)

Assembling and Cooking Tempura
Vegetable or peanut oil
Prepared vegetables
Flour
Batter (above)
Perforated spoon
Rack for draining
Chopsticks

I like to use a wok with an attached rack on which to drain the vegetables, so that the oil drips back into the wok. An electric wok is handy because the temperature light lets me know that the oil is at a consistent temperature. (An automatic deep-fry is even better.) If you do not own these tools, use any deep pan—just make sure the pan holds at least 2 inches of oil. Even heat is *essential* to proper deep-fat frying, and vegetables should be cooked at a lower temperature than fish or fowl: a good temperature range for batter-coated vegetables is 320°. Use a thermometer to keep track. Add only a few vegetables at a time so that the temperature of the oil doesn't drop.

Heat the oil to 350°. Meanwhile, check to make sure the vegetables are *very dry*. Dip into flour if you wish (which helps the batter adhere) and shake off excess. Dip into the batter and slide into hot oil. Cook 4–5 minutes or until the vegetables have a delicate, barely colored crust. Remove with a slotted spoon to the draining rack. Transfer to a warm platter to serve. The vegetables are traditionally served with a dipping sauce made from dashi, a Japanese seasoning made from dried bonito and dried kelp.

Dashi Dipping Sauce for Tempura
1 cup liquid dashi
¼ cup sweet rice wine
⅓ cup soy sauce
½ cup grated daikon radish or white turnip
1–2 tsp grated fresh ginger

Buy powdered dashi and mix with water until you have 1 cup liquid as directed on can. Heat together the dashi, rice wine, and soy sauce, then stir in grated daikon or turnip, and ginger.

Vegetable Terrine

Vegetable terrine is one of the more popular of the Nouvelle Cuisine preparations. Most recipes use a meat or fowl forcemeat to hold the blanched vegetables in suspension. I like this strictly vegetarian version, however. Use plain rice or try a flavored rice, such as *Easy Rice Pilaf* (see page 350).

Serve this terrine as a hot main course with *Sweet Pepper Sauce* (see page 206); as a vegetable accompaniment to meats, or as an unusual cold first course or picnic terrine, served with a *Tomato Fondue* (see page 312) or *Hot Pepper Sauce* (see page 206).

It's quite important to season each layer individually. If you're serving the terrine cold, slightly overseason it.

1 lb yellow summer squash
Salt
1 lb sweet red peppers
3 hard-boiled eggs
2 ½ cups cooked and cooled rice
3 Tb finely chopped fresh dill
1 Tb finely chopped parsley
5 Tb butter
2 Tb minced shallots or onions
Freshly ground pepper
2 cups finely julienned carrots
    Sugar (for older carrots)
2 cups finely chopped blanched broccoli
6 eggs
1 ⅓ cups milk or cream
¼ cup dried fine bread crumbs
1 cup grated Swiss cheese (optional)

Wash and trim the yellow squash, and grate on a large grater. Toss with 2 teaspoons salt and drain for 20–30 minutes.

Wash and halve the peppers. Remove the seeds and ribs and cut into large pieces. Then, grate with a hand grater or shred with the julienne blade of a food processor. Let drain in a sieve for 20 minutes.

Finely chop the eggs and combine with the rice and herbs. Heat ½ tablespoon of the butter and sauté the shallots until barely wilted. Stir them into the rice mixture, season with salt and pepper, and set aside.

Cook the carrots in 1½ tablespoons of the butter until softened but not browned, about 3–5 minutes. (Add a pinch of sugar for older carrots.) Season with salt and pepper, and set aside until slightly cooled.

Cook the broccoli in 1½ tablespoons of the butter until moisture evaporates. Season with salt and pepper and set aside to cool.

Squeeze the water out of the squash and peppers, and combine. Cook them in 1½ tablespoons butter to dry slightly. Season with salt and pepper and cool slightly. Beat together the eggs and cream and set aside.

Butter a 9×5×3-inch loaf pan. Line the bottom and the sides with cut pieces of waxed paper and butter the paper. Sprinkle the bottom of the loaf pan with half of the bread crumbs. Spread half of the rice mixture across the bottom of the dish. Sprinkle one quarter of the cheese (if you like) across the rice. Pour on enough egg-

cream mixture to barely cover. (With each vegetable layering, you will repeat the cheese and egg-cream steps.)

Spread on the carrots, sprinkle on cheese, then a little of the egg-cream mixture again. Spread on the broccoli, then the cheese and the egg-cream mixture. Spread on the squash-pepper mixture, then the cheese and the egg-cream mixture. Finally, spread on the remaining rice and the rest of the egg-cream mixture. Sprinkle with bread crumbs. Top with a buttered piece of waxed paper and cover with aluminum foil.

Place the loaf pan in a high-sided baking pan and pour boiling water halfway up the sides of the loaf pan.

Place in a preheated 350° oven and bake 1½ hours. The loaf should have pulled away from the sides of the pan and the egg-cream mixture should be thickened—you can test with a skewer. Remove the aluminum foil and let rest for 10–15 minutes. Then run a knife around the edge of the loaf pan. Remove the waxed paper on top of the vegetable terrine and invert it onto a plate. The terrine should easily separate from the sides of the pan. Pull off the remaining waxed paper. Slice in ¾-inch slices and serve as suggested above. (*Makes a 9×5-inch loaf*)

- Mix and match vegetables. Use grated sautéed cabbage, sautéed julienned leeks, fresh sweet peas, fennel, zucchini, and so on as long as you prepare each vegetable carefully and season before assembling.

- If you prefer not to use the rice, and egg and cream combination, try a mousse of chicken, ham, or veal and layer the vegetables in the mousse.

Pasta Primavera

Vegetables add a delightful crunch and beautiful colors to a pasta dish. Pasta primavera should be made with young vegetables that are blanched to a still crisp texture. Serve as an appetizer or main dish either hot or cold.

Hot Pasta Primavera
2 cups shelled peas
1½ cups broccoli, peeled and cut into small flowerets
2 cups diced yellow squash or zucchini
1 cup diced carrots
1 cup cherry tomatoes
3 Tb butter
1½ cups heavy cream
½–¾ cup freshly grated Parmesan cheese
1 lb thin pasta such as fettucini, linguini, or spaghetti
Salt and freshly ground pepper

Separately blanch peas, broccoli, squash, and carrots until barely tender. Drain and set aside. Sauté cherry toma-

toes for 1–2 minutes in 1 tablespoon butter; set aside. Heat cream, cheese, and remaining butter together; keep warm. Cook pasta in boiling salted water until just tender. Drain and place in large sauté pan. Add cream mixture and ³/₄ of the blanched vegetables. Cook for 1–2 minutes, tossing gently, to get nice and hot. Season with salt and pepper, turn out on a platter, and top with remaining blanched vegetables and cherry tomatoes. Serve with additional grated cheese. (*Serves 4–8*)

- Omit cream and cheese. Heat blanched vegetables quickly in ¹/₃ cup oil or butter. Pour over drained hot pasta, toss, and season. Add more oil if desired.
- Substitute vegetables such as beans or asparagus.

Pasta Primavera with Vinaigrette

2 cups shelled peas
2 cups broccoli flowerets
³/₄ lb yellow squash or zucchini
³/₄–1 cup *Vinaigrette Sauce* with garlic (page 352)
1 cup peeled, seeded, and diced tomatoes (optional)
1 cup peeled, seeded, and diced cucumbers
³/₄ lb thin pasta such as fettucini, linguini, or spaghetti
2 Tb light olive oil
Salt and freshly ground pepper
¹/₂ cup toasted pine nuts

Separately blanch peas and broccoli until tender. Drain well, refresh under cold water, and lightly toss in some vinaigrette; set aside. Blanch whole squash to just tender, cool and cut into ¹/₄-inch pieces. Toss with tomatoes, if you like, and cucumbers in vinaigrette; set aside.

Cook pasta in boiling salted water until just barely tender. Drain and run briefly under cold water. Drain thoroughly, place in a mixing bowl, and coat with olive oil. Add vegetables and gently toss all together, adding more vinaigrette if you like. Season with salt and pepper and garnish with pine nuts. (*Serves 4–8*)

- Add ¹/₂ cup chopped fresh basil, or a combination of basil with parsley, or other herbs.
- Substitute 1 cup mayonnaise diluted with 1–2 tablespoons vinegar for the *Vinaigrette Sauce* and mix in after adding the blanched vegetables to the pasta.
- Make an all-green primavera of asparagus, cucumber, peas, and zucchini squash.

Vegetable Packages

These are fun to make for a special occasion, and any number of vegetables can be presented this way.

Cut root vegetables such as carrots, parsnips, and turnips into "logs" approximately 3 × ¹/₄ inches. Blanch until just tender, cool, and set aside. Leave green snap beans whole; blanch, cool, and set aside. Peel and blanch asparagus and cut into equal lengths.

To make the "ribbons" for the bundles, take the longest green scallion tops you can find (some of our scallions grow 18 inches long). Blanch for 5–10 seconds, cool, and drain. Group each of the vegetables together, and place on top of a blanched scallion "ribbon." Tie the vegetables up with the scallion. When ready to serve, gently braise in clarified butter (so they won't brown) over low flame in a covered pan until the vegetables are just heated through. Season with salt and pepper to taste.

Mixed Vegetable Soups

A mixed vegetable soup is not only one of the simplest recipes to make; it is also one of the most satisfying. Vary the ingredients depending on what is in the garden, and serve the soup plain or with an array of embellishments such as meats, beans, rice, or cheese.

Techniques for cooking vegetable soups vary with the cook. You can "sweat" the vegetables in oil or butter and then add the liquid; or cook the vegetables directly in the liquid, and add the more tender or leafy vegetables toward the end of cooking. Some people cook the vegetables for an hour or more to meld all the flavors. I personally like to cook vegetable soup until the vegetables are tender but still retain texture. Even so, the softer vegetables you get in a leftover soup still taste good. Although some cooks use only water as the "broth" for vegetable soup, I prefer to use a good homemade stock, usually beef broth or more often a beef and chicken broth combination. I have vegetarian friends who always make their vegetable soups with a *Vegetable-Flavored Broth (Nage)*, (see *Appendix*).

Basic Vegetable Soup

Although I wilt the onions or leeks in butter, you can omit that step and simply add them to the broth. The length of cooking time depends largely on the size and cut of the vegetables.

> 2 Tb butter
> 2 cups chopped leeks (white portion) or onions or a combination of both
> 1 tsp minced garlic
> 2 cups peeled, seeded, and chopped tomatoes
> 1 cup finely sliced carrots
> 1 cup finely sliced celery
> 1 cup sliced turnips
> 8 cups half chicken and half beef broth
> 1 cup green beans cut into 1 1/2-inch pieces
> 1 1/2 cups diced zucchini or yellow squash
> 1 1/2 cups finely julienned Chinese cabbage
> 1/4 cup small pasta such as tubettini
> 1-2 Tb chopped fresh herbs (such as oregano, basil, or parsley)
> Salt and freshly ground pepper
> Grated cheese (optional)

Heat butter and cook the leeks or onions until wilted, 5-10 minutes. Add the garlic and cook for 30 seconds. Add tomatoes, carrots, celery, turnips, and broth. Bring the broth to a boil, reduce heat, and cook gently 5-8 minutes. Add the beans, squash, cabbage, and pasta; cook until tender, 8-10 minutes. Stir in the herbs and season with salt and pepper. Serve with grated cheese if desired. (*Makes 3 quarts*)

- Substitute rice or barley for the pasta, but add to broth before vegetables in order to cook tender.
- Make a *Minestrone*. Add chick peas, cannellini beans, or fresh shell beans.
- Substitute like mad. Use sliced or diced potatoes or parsnips for the turnips. Use julienned kale or spinach for the cabbage. Try kohlrabi for the squash. The only problem vegetable is beets because they will bleed in the soup.
- Add fresh peas or whole stringed sugar snap peas at the end of cooking.
- Add cooked meats, poultry, or shellfish.
- Make a shinbone or sparerib broth.(see *Shinbone Soup with Turnip or Rutabaga*, page 331)
- Add some minced prosciutto and sauté along with leeks for added flavor.
- Make a broth and add 3-4 types of finely julienned vegetables, such as peeled broccoli stems, carrots, peeled and seeded tomatoes, summer squash, etc. Use 1 1/2-2 cups vegetables for every quart of broth. Heat the vegetables in boiling broth for just a few minutes, depending upon the thickness of the cut.
- Grate vegetables and treat as above. Cook tubettini or orzo pasta with the vegetables until tender.
- Use a combination of julienned greens and cabbage and treat as above.

Mixed Vegetable Stew

I have other vegetable stews in this book, but this one includes everything but the kitchen sink. You can swap vegetables and change amounts with no problem. Serve hot, warm, or cold.

> Salt
> 4 cups eggplant in 1/2-inch cubes
> 2 cups zucchini in 1/2-inch cubes
> 2 cups yellow squash in 1/2-inch cubes
> 1/2 cup oil
> 1 cup sliced sweet red pepper
> 1 cup sliced green pepper
> 2 cups chopped onions
> 1 tsp minced garlic
> 2 cups cauliflower flowerets
> 1 cup sliced carrots
> 1 1/2 cups green beans
> 2 cups diced potatoes
> 1/2 cup sliced celery or celeriac
> 1 cup beef or chicken broth
> Chopped fresh herbs
> Freshly ground pepper

Salt the eggplant and squash, let drain for 30 minutes, and pat dry. Heat 1/4 cup of the oil in a large sauté pan. Sauté eggplant and squash in batches until lightly browned, adding additional oil as needed. Drain eggplant and squash; place in a large casserole. Lightly sauté peppers; add to the casserole. (Peeled peppers do not need to be sautéed.) Sauté the onions until wilted, stir in the garlic, cook for 30 seconds, and add to casserole. Stir in the remaining vegetables and the broth. Bring the broth to a boil, cover, and place in a preheated 350° oven. Cook for 30 minutes, uncover the pan, and cook, stirring occasionally, 30-40 minutes longer, until all the vegetables are tender and the juices have thickend. Add herbs, and season with salt and pepper to taste. (*Makes 10-12 cups*)

- Simmer, covered, on top of the stove if you prefer. Uncover near the end of the cooking time.
- Add rice to thicken the stew.
- Add curry and serve cold.
- Use small white onions, baby potatoes, turnips, etc.
- Add peas and/or corn at the end of the cooking time.
- Make Colache—a Mexican vegetable dish. Cut down on the amount of vegetables. Cook onions, garlic, lots of summer squash, string beans, hot peppers, tomatoes, and corn until tender. Once the onions are wilted, the cooking time will be about 15-20 minutes.

Mixed Vegetable Salads

I've been served canned peas, diced carrots, corn, and beans all bound together with an oily mayonnaise in the name of Vegetable Salad. There's no need for that, however, for the same vegetables fresh from the garden, blanched for a moment and dressed in a *Vinaigrette Sauce* (see *Appendix*), or a creamy homemade *Mayonnaise* (see *Appendix*), or a combination of the two, can be an absolutely heavenly mixture.

There is virtually no limit to the possible combinations. Sometimes I use just cooked vegetables—other times raw vegetables, and sometimes a combination of both. I like to keep the shapes of the vegetables similar, so one salad might feature julienned vegetables, another sliced vegetables, and so on. It's nice to present the vegetables in separate groups. You can serve them like that or toss them together at the table. Try special combination salads such as *Salade Niçoise* (see *Beans*); or the Brown Derby's Cobb Salad (see Julia Child's version in *Julia Child & More Company*); Russian salads with cooked vegetables combined with fish or meats; or a delicate julienne of vegetables combined with shellfish.

For a down-to-earth version try the following:

Basic Five Vegetable Salad

1 cup cooled, blanched green beans
1 cup peeled, seeded, and diced fresh tomatoes
1 Tb red wine vinegar
1 hard-boiled egg
2 Tb chopped parsley or fresh herbs
2 Tb heavy cream or sour cream
²/₃ cup *Vinaigrette Sauce* made with mustard (page 352)
Salt and freshly ground pepper
1 cup cooled, blanched cut corn kernels
1 cup cooled, blanched cubed summer squash
1 cup cooled, blanched lima beans
2 slices crumbled cooked bacon (optional)

Cut beans diagonally into ¹/₂-inch pieces. Toss tomatoes with vinegar and place in a strainer to drain their water. Finely chop the egg and combine with parsley. Add cream to the vinaigrette sauce and season. Toss each vegetable with 1 tablespoon of the vinaigrette sauce and season to taste.

On a round serving platter, arrange a mound of tomatoes in the center of the plate. Group the remaining vegetables in a cartwheel fashion around the tomatoes, with the green and yellow vegetables opposite each other. Top the tomatoes with the egg mixture and bacon (if desired). Drizzle on more of the vinaigrette sauce and serve. Toss together if desired. (*Serves 4*)

- Mix and match vegetables. Replace tomatoes with cooked beets or carrots or even raw cucumbers. Replace the lima beans with cooked peas or halved Brussels sprouts. Substitute cauliflower bits for the corn or use cooked turnip. Each vegetable salad can be a new creation!
- With a mouli grater or food processor, you can have a salad of finely shredded raw vegetables.

Julienne of Mixed Vegetables with Lobster
Here is a more elegant combination.

1 cup julienned carrot
1 cup julienned zucchini
1 cup julienned leeks
1 cup julienned celery
1 cup whole baby green snap beans
Vinaigrette Sauce made with tarragon or pear vinegar (page 352)
1 ¹/₂-lb lobster
Bibb lettuce

Cut the julienned vegetables into 1¹/₂–2-inch pieces. Blanch each vegetable separately for 10–15 seconds or until just barely tender. Cool, drain, and coat the vegetables with vinaigrette. Marinate for at least 30 minutes.

Meanwhile, steam the lobster for 15 minutes and remove the meat in as large chunks as possible. Place 2–3 lettuce leaves on each of 4 plates. Drain the vegetables and arrange in mounds on each plate. Slice the warm lobster claws and tail into ¹/₂-inch pieces; and arrange on top or to the side of the vegetables. Top with a bit of the vinaigrette. (*Serves 4*)

- If the lobster was female, sprinkle some of the cooked roe on top or mix the roe with mayonnaise and serve on the side.

Corn Relish

16–18 ears corn
2 tsp celery seed
2 tsp mustard seed
¹/₂ tsp turmeric
1 ¹/₂ qt white vinegar
¹/₂ qt water
¹/₄ cup salt
3 cups sugar
2 cups chopped onions
2 cups sliced cabbage
1 cup chopped green pepper
1 cup chopped sweet red pepper
¹/₄ cup chopped hot red pepper (optional)
1 cup chopped celery

Cut kernels from corn; you should have 10 cups kernels. In a large pan, bring to a boil the spices, vinegar, water, salt, and sugar; mix in vegetables. Lower heat and simmer for 30 minutes. Pack in sterilized jars, leaving ¹/₄-inch head room. Seal and process in a boiling water bath for 15 minutes. (*Makes 4 quarts*)

Mixed Vegetable Pickles

1 lb pickling onions (about 3 cups)
1 lb carrots
2 lb pickling cucumbers
1 small cauliflower
3–4 stalks celery
2 large red sweet peppers
Pickling salt
3 cups sugar
¹/₄ cup celery seeds
¹/₄ cup mustard seeds
2 tsp turmeric
1 tsp dried mustard
9 cups cider vinegar

Peel onions and carrots. Wash and trim remaining vegetables. Halve cucumbers lengthwise and then cut into 1-inch chunks. You will have approximately 7–8 cups. Cut cauliflower into small flowerets to make approximately 3 cups. Slice celery and carrots diagonally into ½-inch pieces. You will have 3 cups carrots and 2 cups celery. Cut peppers into 1-inch chunks to make 2 cups. Cover vegetables with a salt water brine made with ⅓ cup salt per quart of water. Refrigerate for 18–24 hours. The salt water will crisp the vegetables. Before pickling drain the vegetables, rinse well, and drain again. In a 6–8 quart saucepan combine remaining ingredients and bring to a boil. Boil for 3 minutes, add vegetables, return to boil, and cook for 2 minutes. Pack vegetables into hot jars and fill with brine, leaving ¼-inch head space. Adjust caps and process in a hot water bath for 15 minutes, following the jar manufacturer's directions. (*Makes 5 quarts*)

- For a lighter-colored mixed pickle use white vinegar and omit turmeric.
- Add, subtract, or substitute vegetables. Allow for 20 cups of prepared vegetables.

Vegetable Sherbet

While we think of a sherbet as a sweet dessert, traditionally a vegetable sherbet is served between courses as a refresher, or it could be a part of a summer luncheon.

Try a tomato ice first—it's one of my favorites—but don't stop there. While tomatoes can be puréed fresh, other vegetables such as pumpkin need to be cooked before puréeing. Add small amounts of flavoring to boost taste; for example, a dash of Pernod to fennel sherbet. If you are using liquor, however, add just a bit, for too much inhibits the freeze.

A good sherbet has a smooth, creamy texture achieved by making a simple sugar syrup with the correct density. Without getting too complicated, let me say that a sugar syrup with a 28° Baumé is what you're aiming for. Equal parts of 28° sugar syrup and vegetable purée will result in a mixture of 14–16° Baumé, just right for freezing.

How do you know when you have a 28° or 14° Baumé? Well, buy a hydrometer at any kitchen supply store. Place it in your syrup or final mixture, and it will give you the reading. If you don't want to bother with the instrument, estimate that a ratio of 5 cups water to 5½ cups sugar produces an approximate 28° Baumé.

Bring the water and sugar to a boil and boil 5 minutes until all the sugar is dissolved. Cool. Test mixture if you have a hydrometer, and add more sugar or water to get the right reading. This simple sugar syrup keeps in the refrigerator for months.

Make the vegetable purée as fine as possible: the best way to purée is to put the vegetables in a blender, purée, and strain. Then, purée once more and strain one last time. This double puréeing and straining gives you the finest possible texture. For 1 quart sherbet use:

1¾ cups sugar syrup at 28° Baumé
1¾ cups finely puréed vegetable
Lemon or lime juice
Salt (if necessary)

Combine equal amounts of sugar syrup and vegetable purée. (If the syrup is warm, cool the mixture in an ice bath.) The combined purée and sugar syrup should not be too thick, but liquid like the syrup. Freeze just a bit, taste, then add lemon or lime juice, or dissolved salt to taste. Place the mixture in an ice cream freezer container. Following the manufacturer's instructions, add ice and salt around the container and process for 20 minutes. When the sherbet is ready, it will have the consistency of thick ketchup and will just barely flow. Pack in container and place in freezer. (*Makes 1 quart*)

Appendix

Growing the Essential Herbs

Planting an herb garden is a bit like asking someone what they like to eat for dinner—it's a very personal choice. Our friend Jim Crockett helped us design our small herb garden.

The first step was to locate the best area for herbs on our grounds. "That's easy," Jim said. "The herb garden should be close to the kitchen door for accessibility; it should be near a window so you can catch the fragrances; and it should be in a sunny spot."

Fortunately, we had an ideal location on the south side of the house under my kitchen window, which was also sheltered from heavy winds.

Once we set the location, Jim laid out a simple design. I told him the herbs I enjoyed using, and he spaced them out in the garden. (I love the idea of having favorite perennial herbs such as chives, lovage, sorrel, rosemary, thyme, and tarragon appear year after year without a bit of fuss.)

Then we left space for annual herbs such as basil, and chervil, which we sow without fail each spring. There's even room left over for my whimseys: one year I plant savory, another year marjoram, and so on.

We grow dill and mint outside of the herb garden simply because of the space they require.

A great advantage of planting herbs is that while they do beautifully in a rich, well-drained soil, they produce nicely in a less fussed-over plot.

Here are the herbs we grow most frequently. You'll see how they are used throughout the book.

Basil

Basil is perhaps my favorite herb. Seed catalogs offer so many different kinds of basil it's hard to narrow down the choices. We grow three types: the large leaf Italian basil; the fine leaf basil (which is a more delicate-looking plant); and the ornamental basil, which not only has the familiar heady fragrance and flavor but also adds a rich burgundy color to the garden.

Most garden centers sell plants, but basil is easy to start from seeds. You can sow seeds and grow them under lights (or in a greenhouse), or sow the seeds directly into the garden in a sunny location.

When the seedlings are 2 inches high, we thin the plants to 12 inches apart, and pinch out the tips so the plants will be bushier. Continue the harvest by pinching out the tips. If you keep pinching, and don't let the flowers develop, you should have fresh basil until frost.

Basil does dry, but quickly loses flavor. The Italians layer basil in oil . . . the leaves darken but stay flavorful for months. The famous pesto uses cups of this delicious herb.

Chervil

Along with parsley and thyme, chervil is one of the classic French fines herbes. I find that its sweet, subtle taste fits somewhere between anise and parsley.

Chervil is tricky to grow. If you put it in too sunny a spot—or if the ground becomes too dry—it shrivels up quickly.

Because it transplants poorly, I sow seeds in their permanent location which has filtered sun—that is, shady part of the time—and well-drained soil. I thin seedlings 12–14 inches apart when they're 12 inches high.

I use a lot of chervil, so for a continuous supply, I sow seeds every two weeks until mid-July and make sure the plants don't set seeds. Chervil freezes adequately, but has little flavor when dried.

Chives

Try the garlic chives variety for the very best flavor. (See *Onions*)

Dill

We sow dill seeds directly in the vegetable garden because seedlings transplant poorly. Dill grows 2–4 feet tall, so we plant it out in the open garden where there's plenty of room.

I plant dill in full sun, in a spot with acid soil. I use a constant supply of dill leaves, so I sow seeds every three weeks until mid-July, and let some of the plants mature to produce seeds for pickling. Dill is particularly suited to fish dishes: in the restaurant we cure salmon with bunches and bunches of fresh dill. Dill's flavor also accents cucumber, both in fresh salads and in long-term storage pickles.

Lovage

We have had a perennial supply of lovage ever since we set it in the herb garden. Lovage is an unusual old-fashioned herb, much more popular years ago than now. It looks and tastes like celery.

Lovage seeds must be planted when they are ripe, so it is easier to start with plants. One plant is probably all you'll need, because eventually the lovage grows 5 feet tall and 2 feet wide. Be sure to plant it to one side of the garden. Each winter lovage dies back to the ground, but is the first perennial herb out of the ground come spring.

Lovage needs cold weather to complete its growth cycle—a plus for us northern gardeners. I freeze chopped lovage in ice cubes to add to winter soups. It dries poorly.

Mint

Mint practically multiplies overnight. Russ insists that the mint be placed in an out-of-the-way spot, far away from the regular garden. He prefers to plant it in containers. Mint grows equally nicely in partial shade or direct sunlight.

You can probably beg some mint from a gardening friend, but if you're buying plants, remember that you have more than one type of mint to choose from. Spearmint is the strongest, followed by peppermint—but you might also enjoy apple or orange mints, which are more subtle in flavor.

You can do little to hurt mints. They grow well in shade or sunlight. Just don't let them flower. Mint dries well. Cut the stems before the flowers open, dry in a dark well-ventilated spot, then crumble the leaves and store in an airtight jar.

Parsley

Parsley grows easily from seed, but is slow to germinate. You can soak the seeds for 24 hours before sowing, which sometimes speeds up the process. Water frequently during the germination period, which can take up to three weeks.

I first thin seedlings 6 inches apart, then 12 inches apart, because parsley grows poorly if crowded. As parsley is available year round in the markets, I see little point in either freezing or drying it.

Savory

In Germany, savory is commonly served with beans, and is referred to as the bean herb.

You can choose from winter and summer savories. We grow summer savory, which has a spicy, peppery flavor.

Savory is easy to start from seed in the garden. Just remember to give the plants plenty of room, thinning to 18 inches apart.

Savory dries well. Hung from the ceiling, it will give your house a warm country look.

Sorrel

I grow the perennial French sorrel, seeds of which can be obtained from any of the import seed companies. As a child I first noticed sorrel growing wild in the fields, and knew it as sour grass because of its biting, sharp lemon taste. Cultivated varieties still have the tart lemon taste, but are more refined in flavor.

Sow the seeds directly in the garden, in a permanent location, and thin the seedlings to 15 inches apart.

When the plants have formed several leaves, pick off the outer leaves. By concentrating growth in the center of the plant, it produces faster.

Whatever you do, don't let the seed stalks develop, or the plant loses flavor. I use loads of the leaves for sorrel sauces and soups throughout the summer. Again, plant to the rear or side of the garden because sorrel does get large. It can be preserved like basil in oil but it will darken.

Tarragon

While I'm washing dishes, I can look out the window at my French tarragon plants. French tarragon is the culinary variety: the Russian tarragon often listed in seed catalogs has a harsher, slightly unpleasant flavor.

Our tarragon plant is five or six years old, and we find one plant suffices for our family. Tarragon grows well in full sun as long as the soil is well drained and not too heavy. The plant is quite large, so we don't expect to grow anything too closely around it. Place them at least 2 feet apart or leave room for the spreading roots. Tarragon dries well (see drying instructions for *Mint*). Tarragon has a hint of anise and is slightly tart, but sweet. I use it in many recipes—its flavor scents stuffings, sauces, and poultry.

Thyme

English or French thyme is easily raised from seed, but be patient, for germination is very slow. For that reason, you might prefer to buy plants from an herb supplier.

Once a thyme plant is in place, it will last several years, but does become woody. It prefers light soil and a sunny location with good drainage. Every spring we cut it back to half its previous height to keep the stems tender and bushy. After three years, we take cuttings (or root the stems along the ground) and start anew. Thyme dries well (see *Mint*). Its strong, slightly pungent flavor is essential for a bouquet garni, but use in moderation, for it can overpower other tastes.

Basic Recipes
Batters

Beer Batter

This beer batter gives a nice, crisp result. It also gives a distinct beer aftertaste. If you wish, you can substitute ice water or milk for the beer.

> 1 cup flour
> ½ cup cornstarch
> 1 tsp salt
> 1½ cups chilled beer

Sift together the dry ingredients, then whisk in beer until smooth. Cover, and set in the refrigerator for 1 hour. Whisk again before using. (*Makes about 2 cups*)
- *Lemon Juice Batter*: Substitute 1 cup ice water and ½ cup lemon juice for beer.

Frying Batter

The beaten egg whites make this batter thinner, crispy, and light.

> 2 large eggs
> ½ tsp salt
> ¾ cup lukewarm water
> 1 Tb olive oil
> ¾ cup flour

Separate eggs. Beat together yolks, salt, water, and oil. Gradually sift in flour, beating constantly until you have a smooth consistency. Set aside for at least 1 hour, so that the flour particles can swell, guaranteeing a lighter batter. Just before using, beat egg whites to soft peaks and fold into batter. (*Makes 1½ cups*)

Béchamel Sauce

2 ½ Tb butter
3 Tb flour
2 cups heated milk
½ tsp salt
Freshly ground pepper

Melt butter, add flour, and whisk to remove lumps. Cook butter and flour slowly together for 2–3 minutes until flour is golden, but not browned. Remove pan from heat, add milk, and beat sauce vigorously to dissolve the flour and smooth the sauce. Bring to a boil, add salt, reduce heat to simmer, and cook slowly for at least 5 minutes to remove any floury taste. (Simmering longer will improve the flavor.) Thin with milk if too thick. Season with salt and pepper. (*Makes about 1 ½ cups*)

- *Velouté*: Use broth rather than milk, or half cooking liquid and half milk.
- Change the proportions of butter and flour to change the consistency of the sauce. Decreasing flour makes a thinner sauce, increasing it makes a thicker sauce.

Beurre Manié

This thickening agent is made of equal parts butter and flour. Mix the two together in a bowl (easiest with your fingers) and gradually whisk into the hot sauce, soup, or stew that needs thickening. Cook for a few minutes to desired thickness.

White Butter Sauce (Beurre Blanc)

The secret to success is *chilled* butter beaten over *very* low heat.

¼ cup white or red wine vinegar
¼ cup dry white wine or vermouth
3 Tb chopped shallots
¾ lb *chilled* butter
Salt and freshly ground pepper

Reduce vinegar, wine, and shallots until liquid just films the bottom of the pan (about 1–2 tablespoons liquid). Cut chilled butter into tablespoons; keep chilled. When liquid has reduced, turn heat very low. Whisking constantly, slowly add butter—piece by piece. With each addition, the sauce will become creamy and thick, and a light golden color. Season to taste with salt and pepper. Keep warm over water the same temperature as the sauce. (*Makes about 1 ½ cups*)

- If you prefer to omit the white wine or vermouth, add an additional ¼ cup vinegar, or make *Lemon Butter Sauce* below.
- For additional sauce, add more butter.
- To lighten sauce, add ¼– ⅓ cup heavy cream at end.
- *Lemon Butter Sauce*: Replace vinegar and wine with an equal amount of lemon juice; omit shallots. Prepare as above. After the sauce is prepared, stir in finely grated lemon zest if you wish.

Blanc

Some vegetables such as Jerusalem artichokes and celeriac darken when they are cut and exposed to air. Cooking in a blanc stops this process and helps preserve their natural color. Making a blanc is simple and well worth the effort.

¼ cup flour
1 qt water
2 Tb lemon juice
1 Tb butter or vegetable oil (optional)
1 tsp salt

Place flour in a saucepan and gradually whisk in water. Add lemon juice, butter or oil (if desired), and salt. (The butter or oil seals off the exposure of vegetables to air.) Boil for 2 minutes. That's all there is to it. (*Makes 1 quart*)

Caramel Syrup

¾ cup sugar
5 Tb water

Bring sugar and water to a boil in a small saucepan; remove from heat and swirl pan until the sugar has dissolved and the liquid is clear. Return pan to heat, bring to a boil again, and cook, swirling gently all the time. Do not stir. Watch syrup carefully as it starts to change color and remove from heat just as it reaches a lovely caramel color. Be careful—the syrup darkens quickly. (*Makes about ½ cup*)

Chestnuts

Peeling Whole Chestnuts
¾ pound chestnuts = ½ pound peeled chestnuts = 2 cups

With sharp paring knife, cut a cross into the flat side of the whole chestnut. Cut through the shell and into the flesh, piercing the inner skin. Drop the chestnuts into a large pot of boiling salted water; boil for 5–10 minutes. Drain, and keep in warm water while you peel. Insert a knife into the slit opening and peel away the shell and the brown inner skin. Most skin will peel off with the shell, but some may give you trouble. You may have to peel the skin off separately with the knife. If possible, keep the chestnuts whole.

Braised Chestnuts
This softens the chestnuts for serving with other vegetables, such as Brussels sprouts.

2 cups peeled chestnuts
1 cup chicken or beef broth
2 Tb butter

Bring all ingredients to a boil. Reduce heat, cover, and simmer for 20–30 minutes or until the chestnuts are tender but not falling apart or mushy. Now they are ready to combine with other ingredients. If they are to go in a stuffing that will cook a long time, braise for only 10–15 minutes.

Clarifying Butter

Clarifying butter removes any residues of milk particles left after churning. The milk is the part of the butter that burns when butter is overheated. A high percentage of milk in the butter causes a butter sauce to separate or fail to thicken.

Butters vary in the amount of milk they contain. Once you've clarified the butter (an easy process), you're certain of the quality of the butter with which you are working. Once clarified, the butter can be refrigerated for three or four weeks, or frozen.

Cut butter into chunks and place in a heavy saucepan. Melt over medium heat and gently boil, watching to make sure the butter doesn't boil over. The surface bubbles show the escape of the water from the milk. When the bubbles have just about subsided, the clarification is finished. There will be a milky crust on the bottom of the pan.

With a ladle, lift out only the absolutely clear liquid. You can strain it through cheesecloth if you wish. Store this clarified butter in a jar in the refrigerator. Although amounts vary, depending upon the quality of the butter, 1 pound butter should give you approximately 1 1/2 cups of clarified butter.

Clarifying Broth

2 qt broth
6 egg whites
Flavor ingredients, such as 1/4 cup each finely minced celery, carrot, onion, and herbs (optional)
1 cup wine (optional)

Make sure broth is fat-free. Beat egg whites and 1 cup broth together. Add flavorings and wine if you like. Heat remaining 7 cups broth to simmer, and whisk in the egg white mixture. Whisk slowly until mixture comes to a simmer. Move the saucepan to the burner side so that only one-third of it is resting on the burner. Do not stir again. Simmer for 5 minutes, then turn pot to expose second third to heat. After 5 minutes, rotate pot once more. The whites will have collected broth particles and formed a loose soft crust on the top of the pan. Under this crust, the broth will be sparkling clear. Ladle the broth and egg white crust into a strainer lined with 2 or 3 layers of washed cheesecloth. The clear liquid consommé passes through, leaving the residue of egg whites and broth particles behind.

Cream Cheese Frosting for Baked Goods

8 oz cream cheese
6 Tb soft sweet butter
1 tsp vanilla extract
2–2 1/2 cups confectioners' sugar

Combine the ingredients and beat until smooth and creamy. (*Makes 2 1/2–3 cups*)

Cream Salad Dressing

1 tsp Dijon mustard
1 tsp sugar
1 Tb wine vinegar
Salt and freshly ground pepper
3/4 cup heavy cream

Mix mustard and sugar together. Beat in vinegar and season with salt and pepper. Lightly whip heavy cream and fold into vinegar mixture. (*Makes 1 cup*)

Creamy Roquefort Dressing

I love to dress a salad with a good mustard vinaigrette sauce and then strew Roquefort cheese on top.

1/4 cup Roquefort cheese
1 Tb wine vinegar
1 Tb Dijon mustard
1/2 cup sour cream
2 Tb heavy cream
Salt and freshly ground pepper
Chopped chives (optional)

Mash the cheese with the vinegar and mustard. Beat in the sour and heavy creams. Season to taste with salt and pepper, and stir in chives if you like. (*Makes about 1 cup*)

Crème Fraîche

Crème fraîche is a thick cream with a very high butterfat content and a slightly nutty and acid, or fermented, flavor. Fresh cream that has not been pasteurized will thicken naturally and achieve the distinct tart flavor that is crème fraîche. However, pasteurization kills the lactic acid and ferments in cream that cause this action. Therefore our creams are sweet. In France, however, they return the ferments to the cream after pasteurization so the cream turns to crème fraîche.

This crème is a wonderful culinary aid. It has a body that will beautifully thicken sauces and soups. It can be boiled without fear of curdling. You can baste foods with it and run them under the broiler and the crème will not separate. And it is simply luscious served as a dip for raw vegetables or topping fresh fruit.

While crème fraîche is becoming available in American markets it is quite expensive. You can make a reasonable facsimile of crème fraîche by doctoring up sweet heavy cream. Three agents work: buttermilk, sour cream, and yogurt. Buttermilk creates the most acidic taste; yogurt the least. For every 2 cups heavy cream add 1 cup of the buttermilk, sour cream, or yogurt and stir well. Heat gently to a temperature of no more than 80°. Pour into a container, partially cover, and let sit for 6–8 hours or until the cream has thickened and tastes slightly acidic. (The time may be longer or shorter depending on room temperature.) The crème will keep up to two weeks in the refrigerator. When you need more you can use your crème fraîche as a "mother" or "starter." Use equal parts crème fraîche and heavy cream and proceed as above.

Note: There is now a powder available on the market sold

as a crème fraîche starter. It contains lactic bacteria, which will return the natural ferments to the cream. This is the nicest choice of all, available through Williams-Sonoma.

Creole Sauce à la Joe Hyde

This is a thick, mild, chili-like sauce that my friend Joe Hyde serves with sliced smoked tongue. When thinned with cooking juices or broth, it makes an unusual sauce for stuffed cabbage rolls, braised lettuces, onions, and other stuffed vegetables.

1/4 cup olive oil
3 cups finely sliced onions
3 cups finely sliced peppers
3 cups finely sliced mushrooms
3 Tb sugar
1 bay leaf
1 tsp allspice
1/4 cup wine vinegar
4 cups peeled, seeded, and chopped ripe tomatoes

In a saucepan, heat the oil and cook the onions, peppers, and mushrooms until wilted but not brown. Add the remaining ingredients and simmer for 2 hours, stirring occasionally. (*Makes about 4 cups*)

Croutons

Made from Toasted French Bread
Cut French bread rounds 3/4 inch thick. Dry out in a 350° oven for 10 minutes. Brush both sides with olive oil and rub with cut garlic. Return to the oven and bake another 10–15 minutes or until the bread is dried and lightly browned.
- When the bread has dried out, sprinkle grated cheese on one side and run under the broiler until lightly browned.
- Omit garlic.
- See also *Garlic Croutons* (following recipe).

Garlic
1 clove garlic
1/4 tsp salt
4 Tb olive oil
5–6 slices Italian or good homemade bread

Oven Method: Crush garlic with salt and mix in the oil. Remove crusts from bread. Brush bread on both sides with garlic-flavored oil. Cut into 1/2-inch pieces or larger if desired. Toast until dry in 350° oven.
Sauté Method: After oil and salt are mixed with garlic, strain into sauté pan. Heat over medium heat and toss in cubed bread. Sauté on both sides to light brown. For a milder garlic flavor, omit garlic mashed in oil. Simply heat plain olive oil in pan, toss in whole garlic clove, and cook in oil for a minute, then add bread cubes. Remove garlic when cubes are toasted.
- *Plain Croutons*: Omit garlic.

Fish Broth

Start with meaty fish frames. I prefer cod or haddock to fish such as bass and flounder because they seem to produce the purest broth. Remove the gills—they give an off-taste to the broth. Freeze as much as you like to have on hand for quick chowders or soups.

10 lb meaty fish frames (no gills, no guts)
4 large onions
5 stalks celery
1 tsp thyme
1 qt dry white wine (optional)

Place all the ingredients in a large stockpot; cover with water. Bring to a boil, skim to remove the scum, reduce heat, and simmer for 30 minutes. Strain. Season lightly if at all, for if you reduce the broth or add salty ingredients, such as clams, you should not overseason at this point. Reduce by boiling to intensify flavor if desired. (*Makes about 3 quarts*)

Hollandaise Sauce

Even experienced cooks shy away from hollandaise sauce, for it can be tricky—on occasion curdling or separating, or never thickening at all. Follow the directions below and you'll have no problems.
- The egg yolks and the butter must be the same temperature when they are combined.
- Don't rush. Quickly combining the ingredients can lead to failure: heat the egg yolks and add the butter slowly.
- Use good-quality butter. A butter with too high a water content can cause the hollandaise to separate.
Although hollandaise can be made by hand, it's much easier on the muscles when made in a blender or food processor. If you don't own either, substitute a good strong arm and balloon whisk.

1/2 lb butter
3 egg yolks
1 Tb water
Salt and freshly ground pepper
1–2 Tb lemon juice
Finely grated lemon zest (optional)

Melt butter and remove from heat; it should be warm but not boiling hot when added to the egg yolks. Put the egg yolks in a double boiler and add the water. Whisk together. Put over just simmering water and beat with a wire whisk until thickened. The thicker the egg yolks are at this point, the thicker your final sauce will be. If you want a light hollandaise to just coat a vegetable, let the eggs reach a light cream consistency. If you want a thick hollandaise, bring the eggs to a thicker texture. Melted butter will thicken the sauce slightly, but the basic consistency is formed with the eggs.

Once eggs have reached the thickness you want, remove them from the heat and, stirring with a rubber spatula, scrape them into a food processor or blender. Turn on the machine, and very slowly, drop by drop, add the warm melted butter. As the sauce thickens, increase the speed with which you add the butter. Do not incorporate the milky residue in the butter pan. Then, add salt and pepper and 1 tablespoon lemon juice, or more to taste, and the grated zest if you like. The sauce holds nicely over warm water. I put it in a double boiler with warm water held on the very lowest burner setting. (*Makes 1–1 1/2 cups*)

- If you're making by hand, just whisk the butter into the egg yolks with a wire whisk.
- You can also whisk in butter that has been softened to room temperature but not melted.
- If you've added the butter too quickly and the hollandaise has not thickened, or if the eggs separated, try this technique: In a clean mixing bowl, put 1 tablespoon of the hollandaise sauce and 1 tablespoon lemon juice. Beat together and then gradually beat all the sauce back in, a spoonful at a time, waiting until each addition thickens before adding the next.
- *Mousseline Sauce*: For every 1 1/2 cups *Hollandaise Sauce* beat 1/2 cup heavy cream. Fold into sauce just before serving to lighten texture.

Horseradish Sauce

1 cup heavy cream
2–3 Tb bottled horseradish or 1/2–3/4 cup freshly grated horseradish
1 tsp Dijon mustard (optional)

Whip cream until stiff and fold in horseradish. Add mustard if you like. Let stand for 15 minutes in the refrigerator to mingle flavors. (*Makes 1 1/2–2 cups*)

- Whip 1 1/2–2 cups sour cream until smooth and fold in horseradish as above, or combine equal amounts of whipped cream and sour cream before adding horseradish.

Mayonnaise

Homemade mayonnaise is so easy and delicious I wonder why we ever buy it. With a blender or food processor it is simplicity itself. Note, however, the difference in the ingredients between the hand method and the blender or food processor method. The inclusion of a whole egg in the blender version keeps the sauce from thickening too quickly. Use good oil. I prefer to use more vegetable and less olive oil for a lighter mayonnaise. Add the oil slowly at first so that the eggs will incorporate it—otherwise you will have a runny mess.

Blender or Processor Method
1 whole egg
3 egg yolks
1/2 tsp Dijon or dry mustard
1/2 tsp salt
1 Tb lemon juice or wine vinegar
1 1/2 cups vegetable oil
1/2 cup olive oil
Salt and freshly ground pepper
Extra lemon juice or wine vinegar (optional)

Whisk egg, egg yolks, mustard, salt, and lemon juice or vinegar together for 1 minute. Very slowly add oils, by droplets, until thickened. Once the mixture has thickened add the rest of the oil by tablespoons, making certain that each addition is incorporated before adding the next. Season with salt and pepper. Cover and refrigerate. If the mayonnaise becomes too thick, thin with drops of lemon juice or vinegar. (*Makes 2 cups*)

Hand Method
Use 4 egg yolks instead of 3 yolks and whole egg. Beat the egg yolks until pale and thick. Whisk in mustard, salt, and lemon juice or vinegar. Take 1/2 cup oil and very slowly, by droplets, add it steadily until the mixture has thickened into a heavy consistency. Once this has happened, you can add the remaining oil by tablespoons, making sure that each addition is incorporated before adding the next. Season to taste and refrigerate. (*Makes 2 cups*)

Mirepoix

A mirepoix is composed of equal amounts of finely chopped carrots, onions, and celery, often combined with ham and spices, which creates an aromatic addition to sauces or a base for braised dishes, or it can be used solely as a garnish.

Finely chopped celery
Finely chopped carrots
Finely chopped onions
Chopped ham cubes (optional)
Butter
Herbs such as chopped thyme, a bay leaf, or parsley
Salt

Combine the celery, carrots, onions, and ham, if you like, and sauté in butter. For each cup of combined vegetables, add 3–4 tablespoons ham. Cook in 2–3 tablespoons butter. Flavor with choice of herbs and add salt to taste. Simmer for 15–30 minutes until vegetables are softened, but not browned, stirring occasionally.

Mirepoix for Roasts
These same three vegetables add a great deal of flavor to the pan juices of a roast. Roughly chop equal amounts of celery, carrots, and onions. About 40 minutes before removing a roast from the oven, arrange the chopped vegetables around the roast. They will brown lightly as they cook. After removing the roast from the oven, simmer the pan juices on the stove, then strain the vegetables before serving.

Mornay Sauce

2 1/2 Tb butter
3 Tb flour
2 cups milk
1/2 cup combined grated Swiss and Parmesan cheeses

Melt butter in saucepan, add flour, and whisk to remove lumps. Cook slowly for 2–3 minutes, without browning. Off heat, add milk and stir well to remove lumps. Bring sauce to boil, reduce heat, and let simmer slowly at least 5 minutes, adding more milk if you want a thinner sauce. Stir in cheese and cook until cheese is melted and the sauce is smooth. (*Makes approximately 2 cups*)

Persillade

Persillade (from the French word for parsley) is a pretty garnish or a good addition to sautéed vegetables.

4 Tb butter (clarified if possible)
3–4 minced shallots
3/4 cup packed fresh bread crumbs
2 tsp minced garlic (optional)
1/4 cup chopped parsley
Salt and freshly ground pepper
Fresh herbs

Melt the butter, add the shallots, and stir for 1 minute. Add the crumbs and stir until a golden brown. Add the garlic if you like and stir 1 minute longer. Remove from the heat, toss with parsley, and season with salt and pepper. Add any herbs you like. (*Makes 3/4–1 cup*)

Pesto Sauce

Fresh basil and garlic are the essential ingredients in pesto—an absolutely delicious sauce reminiscent of the perfume of the Mediterranean countries. Use it to dress both hot and cold pasta. Count on at least 1 cup sauce for each pound of pasta. Dilute with 2 tablespoons of the cooking liquid before tossing with hot pasta. Pesto will keep when covered with olive oil and refrigerated or stored in a cold spot. Add the cheese just before using.

2 cloves garlic
1 tsp salt
3 cups packed basil leaves
2 Tb chopped parsley (optional)
2 Tb pine nuts
1/2 cup olive oil
1/2 cup finely grated fresh Parmesan cheese

Mortar Method

Peel and crush garlic and pound to a paste with the salt. Chop the basil leaves and parsley (if using it) and add to the mortar along with the pine nuts. Grind and crush until you have a paste. Gradually beat in the oil, beginning with a few drops at a time, to make a thick sauce, then stir in the cheese.

Blender Method

Put all the ingredients, except cheese, in a blender. Blend, pushing down with a rubber spatula until mixture is thoroughly puréed. Beat in the cheese. (*Makes about 1 cup*)

- For a different flavor, omit the pine nuts. Substitute 2 tablespoons chopped lemon rind or chopped anchovies.

Pickling Brine—All-Purpose

The concentration of vinegar to water here is higher than the open-crock brine I use for *Kosher Half-Sour Pickles* (see *Cucumbers*). This is a good brine for all kinds of high-acid vegetables. Crisp the vegetables in cold salt water for at least three hours. For each sterilized jar, put in the following:

1 clove unpeeled garlic, crushed
2 sprigs fresh dill
1/4 tsp dill seed
1 tsp pickling spices

Put in well-rinsed vegetables, whole, halved, quartered, or sliced. For every 2 cups water, add 2 cups vinegar and 1/4 cup pickling salt. Bring to a boil and pour over the vegetables, covering by 1/2 inch. Adjust caps and process in a boiling-water bath for 15 minutes.

Pierogi Dough

1 2/3 cups flour
1 tsp salt
2 eggs
5 Tb water
Filling (see *Sweet Cabbage Strudel*, page 47)
Melted butter

Combine flour and salt. Beat eggs with water; mix in flour. Knead until soft and pliable; let rest for 10 minutes. Roll out half the dough about 1/8 inch thick. Cut out 2 1/2-inch circles and place a heaping teaspoon of the filling on half of the circle. Fold over the other half and pinch the edges together, lightly wetting the edges to produce a seal. Poach the pierogis in simmering salted water for 5–6 minutes or until they float. Remove with a slotted spoon and dip into warm butter; place in a warm baking dish. Keep in a warm oven while you finish poaching all the pierogis. (*Makes 24 pierogis*)

Easy Rice Pilaf

4 Tb butter
1/2 cup thin pasta, such as vermicelli, broken into 1/2-inch pieces (optional)
1 cup rice
2 cups chicken stock (or combination of chicken stock and water)
Salt and freshly ground pepper

Heat butter; just before it begins to brown, add pasta if you wish. Stir until lightly browned. Stir in rice and sauté for a moment until lightly colored. Add liquid; stir once. Cover pan and bring to a boil. Reduce heat to a gentle boil. Cook until all the liquid is absorbed, 15–20 minutes. Add more butter if desired; season with salt and pepper. (*Makes 3-3 1/2 cups*)

Salsa Verde or Sharp Green Sauce

2 Tb finely chopped parsley
2 Tb finely chopped watercress
2 Tb finely chopped capers
4 anchovy fillets
1/2 tsp chopped garlic
2 Tb lemon juice
3/4 cups olive oil
Salt and freshly ground pepper

Combine parsley, watercress, and capers. Mash anchovies with garlic; add to herbs. Stir in lemon juice; gradually beat in oil. Season with salt and pepper. Add additional lemon juice for a very tart sauce. (*Makes about 1 cup*)

Skordalia

Here's a Greek version of the French aïoli, best made with rich, green Sicilian or Greek olive oil. It's delicious with fried eggplant, summer squashes, potatoes, vegetable fritters, or any kind of fried fish. You don't need to use the egg yolks, but they make the skordalia more like a mayonnaise.

5 cloves garlic
1/4 cup chopped almonds
2 slices bread
1/4 cup chopped parsley
Juice of 1/2 lemon
2 egg yolks (optional)
1/2 cup olive oil
Salt (optional)

Chop garlic and pulverize with the almonds. Remove bread crusts, soak bread in water for 1 second, and squeeze out the moisture. Beat the garlic, almonds, bread, parsley, lemon juice, and egg yolks (if you like), together by hand, in a mixer or food processor. Gradually beat in the oil to make a mayonnaise-like mixture. Season with salt if you wish. (*Makes about 1 cup*)

Tart Pastry

2 cups all-purpose or instant flour
3/4 tsp salt
12 Tb chilled butter
2 Tb chilled vegetable shortening
1/4–1/3 cup ice water

Mixer Method
Place flour and salt in bowl of electric mixer. Cut butter into small pieces and add to bowl along with shortening.

Turn beater on and off until butter and shortening have broken down to the size of peas. Quickly add the ice water, bit by bit, and stop the minute the dough begins to mass on the blade. Put dough on a lightly floured work surface and knead with the heel of your hand a few times to work the dough. Shape into a 5-inch circle and cover with waxed paper. Chill in the refrigerator for 2 hours before using.

Processor Method
Put flour and salt into bowl of food processor. Cut butter into small pieces and add to processor along with shortening. Turn processor on and process for 2–3 seconds to break butter into pea-size pieces. Add ice water little by little until dough forms a mass on blades. (This whole process takes about 15 seconds.) Put on a floured working surface and knead with heel of hand a few times to work dough and smooth it. Shape into a 5-inch circle, cover with wax paper and chill for 2 hours. (*Makes a 10-inch or 11-inch tart or 24 tartlets*)

To Bake Tart Partially
Roll out dough 3/16-inch thick and 2 inches larger than the buttered tart, pie, or tartlet pans that you are using. Fit into pan (or pans), pressing excess dough slightly down the inside to make the sides thicker. Fashion a decorative edge. Prick pastry with a fork. Refrigerate for 30 minutes. Butter aluminum foil slightly larger than the pan; place it buttered side down in the shell. Fill with dried beans or washed pebbles. Bake at 425° for 8 minutes. Remove shell from oven, take out beans and foil, straighten up pastry edges if they have sagged, prick the bottom of the dough again. Return to oven for 2–4 minutes to just faintly brown and set the dough. Let cool for 15 minutes.

To Bake Shell Completely
Bake as above. For final bake, leave in oven an additional 6–8 minutes or until nicely colored.

Shortcrust Pastry
This is a richer tasting pastry than the above.

2 cups flour
1 tsp salt
8 Tb chilled butter
6 Tb chilled lard
1/4–1/3 cup ice water

Follow directions for making *Tart Pastry* (preceding recipe), substituting lard for shortening. (*Makes a 10- or 11-inch tart or 24 tartlets*)

Toasted Sesame Seeds
Toasting brings out the nutlike flavor of sesame seeds. Spread seeds on a cookie sheet. Toast in a 350° oven for 15–20 minutes, stirring often.

Vegetable-Flavored Broth (Nage)

Use in recipes as an alternative to chicken or beef broth.

> 3–4 onions
> 4 carrots
> 1 clove garlic
> 2 leeks, white portions only (optional)
> 3–4 stalks celery
> Herb bouquet:
>> Bay leaf
>> 4–6 sprigs parsley
>> Thyme
>> 2 coriander seeds
>> 1 clove
> 1 sprig fresh tarragon or ½ tsp dried
> ¼ tsp cayenne pepper
> Salt and freshly ground pepper
> Pinch of saffron threads
> 2 qt water

Roughly chop onions; slice carrots. Combine with remaining ingredients in a large saucepan or soup pot; bring to a boil. Keep at a gentle boil for 30–40 minutes. Broth will reduce to approximately 1 quart. Strain broth and discard vegetables. (*Makes 1 quart*)

Vinaigrette Sauce

For a lighter version, use half vegetable oil and half olive oil.

> 1 clove garlic, chopped (optional)
> ¼ tsp salt
> 2 Tb wine vinegar
> ¼ tsp Dijon mustard (optional)
> 9 Tb olive oil
> Freshly ground pepper

Mash garlic (if you wish to use it) and salt together. Stir in vinegar and mustard (if you like). Gradually beat in oil. Grind on pepper. (*Makes ⅔ cup—enough for salad for 10–12*)

- Beat an egg white and whisk into vinaigrette. It will help hold the vinaigrette onto the vegetables.
- *Lemon Vinaigrette Sauce*: Replace wine vinegar with lemon juice.

Yogurt Herb Dressing

> 1 clove garlic
> 1 tsp salt
> 1 tsp Dijon mustard
> 1 Tb wine vinegar
> 2 Tb oil
> 1 cup yogurt
> 1 tsp chopped chervil
> 1 tsp chopped dill
> 1 tsp chopped parsley
> Freshly ground pepper

Mash together the garlic and salt. Beat in the mustard and vinegar, then beat in the oil and yogurt. Stir in the herbs. Season with pepper. (*Makes about 1¼ cups*)

A Selected List of Seed Suppliers

Here's a list of reputable seed suppliers; it is by no means complete, but includes some we have dealt with. Obviously there are omissions, but that does not mean that suppliers we have not included are less reputable than those listed.

Burpee Seeds
Warminster, Pennsylvania 18991: A full-color catalog offering flower and vegetable seeds, also perennials, trees, shrubs, and roses. A big catalog . . . good for many winter evenings in front of the fire.

DeGiorgi Company
1411 3rd Street, Council Bluffs, Iowa 51502: A selection of vegetable and flower seeds including many unusual varieties.

J. A. Demonchaux Company
827 North Kansas Avenue, Topeka, Kansas 66608: Owned by a Frenchman who immigrated to the United States and imports European seeds and gourmet products.

Epicure Seeds
Box 69, Avon, New York 14414: Features seeds from some of Europe's oldest seed houses, such as Hurst & Suttons in England; Vilmorin in France; seed houses in Holland, Denmark, Belgium, Italy, and Germany.

Gurney Seed and Nursery Company
Yankton, South Dakota 57079: Good variety of vegetable seeds, and they do stock yellow fingerling seed potatoes.

Joseph Harris Company
Moreton Farm, Rochester, New York 14624: Complete selection . . . we like their vegetables.

Herbst Brothers
1000 N. Main Street, Brewster, New York 10509: A professional catalog featuring seeds of vegetables, flowers, vines, shrubs, and trees. Detailed information and a home-garden vegetable planting guide.

Johnny's Selected Seeds
Albion, Maine 04910: This company is certified by the Maine Organic Farmers and Gardeners Assn. They claim that no other seed company in the U.S. has a growing season as short and cool as theirs. No fancy color in this catalog but lots of good, solid information about each variety of seed. Sensible people to deal with.

Park Seed Company
Greenwood, South Carolina 29647: A full-color catalog featuring vegetables, fruits, and flowers. There's a special feature on vegetables that are suited to growing in containers and small gardens.

Steele Plant Company
Gleason, Tennessee 38229: Supplier of sweet potato plants.

Stokes
737 Main Street, Box 548, Buffalo, New York 14240: Vegetables, flowers, and garden accessories. Good information, some canning and preserving items.

Vermont Bean Seed Company
Garden Lane, Bomoseen, Vermont 05732: Lots and lots of information. You'll enjoy this one.

Index

All photographs by Bill Schwob except as follows:

James Scherer, *v* (upper), *vi* (left), *vii* (upper), 2, 3, 5, 7, 8, 20, 21, 25, 35, 50, 52, 69, 83, 85 (lower right), 110, 135 (upper), 154, 162 (left), 168, 193, 194, 196, 200, 201 (left), 211, 260, 261, 262, 266, 267, 275, 302 (lower left)

Russell Morash, *v* (lower), 76, 135 (lower), 142 (lower), 143, 254, 283 (upper)

Gary Mottau (back cover)

Michael Lutch, *vi* (right)

Paul Souza, *viii*

Michael Warren (England), 115

Cloth cover illustrations: © 1982 by Robin Brickman

Set in Linoterm and VIP Galliard by Supershift Composing Room, Inc., New York, New York, and The Composing Room of New England, Boston, Massachusetts. Galliard, introduced in 1978 by Mergenthaler Linotype Company, was designed by Matthew Carter, based on the sixteenth-century drawings of Robert Granjon.

Separations by Toppan Printing Company, New York, New York

Printed and bound by Kingsport Press, Kingsport, Tennessee

Designed by Tom Sumida, WGBH Design, Boston, Massachusetts

Design Assistant, Abby Gladstone